ement

PEARSON
Education

We work with leading authors to develop the
strongest educational materials in business,
bringing cutting-edge thinking and best
learning practice to a global market.

Under a range of well-known imprints, including
Financial Times Prentice Hall, we craft high quality
print and electronic publications which help readers
to understand and apply their content, whether
studying or at work.

To find out more about the complete range of our
publishing, please visit us on the World Wide Web at:
www.pearsoned.co.uk

JOHN NAYLOR

Introduction to Operations Management

Second Edition

FINANCIAL TIMES

Prentice Hall

An imprint of **Pearson Education**

Harlow, England · London · New York · Reading, Massachusetts · San Francisco · Toronto · Don Mills, Ontario · Sydney
Tokyo · Singapore · Hong Kong · Seoul · Taipei · Cape Town · Madrid · Mexico City · Amsterdam · Munich · Paris · Milan

Pearson Education Limited
Edinburgh Gate
Harlow
Essex CM20 2JE
England

and Associated Companies throughout the world

Visit us on the World Wide Web at:
www.pearsoned.co.uk

First published as *Operations Management*
under the Financial Times Pitman Publishing imprint 1996
Second edition 2002

ISBN 0 273 65578 7

British Library Cataloguing-in-Publication Data
A catalogue record for this book is available from the British Library

10 9 8 7 6 5 4 3 2
08 07 06 05 04

Typeset in 9^1/$_2$/12pt Stone Serif by 35
Printed by Ashford Colour Press Ltd., Gosport

Contents

Part Two LOCATION AND LAYOUT

Preface to second edition

The value of this book comes from its comprehensive coverage of operations management for those coming to the subject for the first time. The treatment is rigorous, using mathematical models and concepts where they illustrate, aid understanding and support problem solving. It does not assume, however, a strong background in areas such as mathematics or finance. The focus is on management, facing the question of how best to plan and control processes to achieve objectives. There are many references to examples and case studies to open and close each chapter. Most of these are new, with the rest rewritten for this edition.

Other new features, found in each chapter, are the exercises placed throughout and the wide range of questions at the end. For the book as a whole, more than 150 diagrams illustrate and support explanations. The larger format chosen by the publisher for this second edition allows the diagrams to fit more comfortably on the page and thus integrate with the text.

In preparing this second edition, I have gained immensely from the comments and advice offered by colleagues and students. Among colleagues, Alastair Balchin and Alex Douglas suggested both improvements to the text and material for case studies. The contribution of students at Liverpool Business School, in interpreting my previous efforts and bringing in further ideas, has been immense. At Pearson, an editorial team guided by Anna Herbert has been a constant support.

Finally, I must acknowledge the debt I owe to my wife Maureen who took on her more than fair share of the domestic load while I struggled to meet tight deadlines. Once again, she made it happen.

John Naylor

PART ONE

Production and operations in context

CHAPTER 1

Scope of operations management

OBJECTIVES

When you have finished studying this chapter, you should be able to:

- Define operations management and distinguish it from the notion of operational-level management.
- Define management and explain how managers have to balance efficiency, effectiveness and equity in achieving their objectives.
- Compare goods and services and show how organisations produce varying bundles.
- Explain and illustrate the types of resource used in an operating system.
- Contrast the manufacturing and service transformation systems.
- Identify and illustrate the key decision areas for operations managers and relate them to time horizons.
- Use the value chain and organisation charts to show how the operations function fits within an organisation.
- Use mind maps and flow charts to summarise ideas about operations management.

OPENING CASE

Making music[1]

The Yamaha Corporation was founded in 1897, some ten years after Torakusu Yamaha built his first organ. It concentrated on making high-quality keyboard instruments for which it gained a worldwide reputation. From the 1950s, Yamaha expanded through improving its products, developing new product lines and entering new markets. Examples include: electronic organs; hi-fi products; archery and ski equipment; and the establishment of Yamaha de Mexico, S.A., the first overseas distribution company. The first motorcycles appeared in 1954, leading to the foundation of the Yamaha Motor Company, now a separate business. Building on a strong investment in acoustical research, the company launched wind instruments in 1965, followed by guitars and drums a year later. The policy of improvement and diversification continues to the present day with musical and audio products accounting for some three-quarters of the £3 billion sales.

When a customer buys a Yamaha clarinet, the sale may be from the retailer's stock. Some customers, with more musical experience, require special features incorporated by skilled workers to suit their personal needs. In either case,

▶

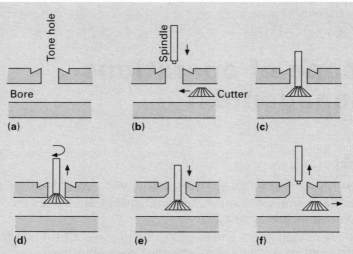

Figure 1.1 Undercutting the tone hole

buyers send messages to the company about the products they want. Naturally, Yamaha needs more information than this. It does not simply wait for orders to arrive. It studies the market to work out what people like and what features they value most highly. Furthermore, after the sale, the interaction continues. In what it hopes is a long-lasting relationship, the company learns more about the way the customer uses the clarinet while the latter benefits from after-sales service and may buy spares such as an extra mouthpiece.

Operations managers at Yamaha collect and analyse all this information to transform raw materials of best granadilla wood, brass and cork, into the clarinet models that customers want. They take an overview of the whole manufacturing chain with 15 plants in seven countries. Furthermore, they plan each process in detail to achieve a product with a correct pitch and beautiful sound. For instance, the undercutting of tone holes has a great impact on sound quality. Working inside the bore of the clarinet needs special cutters with separate spindles, sketched in Figure 1.1. In top of the range products, skilled staff finish these processes by hand.

1.1 Introduction

We started with a practical illustration of the issues faced by operations managers as they work on supplying products wanted by customers. We see a process of transforming inputs into outputs, this time on a global scale; this takes place in concert with other business functions such as marketing, design, development and finance. We see the way investment in product development, training and equipment is converted into profit. Focusing more closely, we see the detailed elements, such as hole cutting, that must be planned and co-ordinated if the grand effect is to be achieved. Control is exercised over inventories, costs, quality and many other dimensions. This snapshot of Yamaha shows how operations lie at the heart of all organisations.

1.1.1 Why study operations management?

A general answer to this question is that operations management is important, all pervasive and can be done well by competent people. This is because:

- The operations function is the core of the organisation and continuously manages the flow of resources through it. In many organisations, operations accounts for 80% of the employees and hence most of the added value.

- The output of the operations system is the bundle of goods and services consumed in society. An organisation that does not continuously satisfy the needs of customers fails.

- All organisations have an operations activity. The techniques and skills of operations management can be applied across a range of apparently diverse businesses, institutions, authorities and so on, whatever sector of the economy they occupy. This means that many skills learnt in one context can be transferred to another and, further, it is possible to learn directly applicable knowledge from sources such as this book.

- Operations management is management in that it offers the challenge, the complexity and the responsibility which are part of any managerial role. A good operations manager does not define the task as merely tinkering with techniques to run part of the business on a day-to-day basis. The role is larger than this, being also concerned with developing operating processes, products, locations and so on to meet the demands and pressures of the changing environment.

- In a broader sense, any nation depends heavily, for its international competitiveness, on the efficiency and effectiveness of the operations in its organisations. So much talk has been about getting the strategy right that the need to invest in, develop and manage competitive operating systems is often forgotten. It is in all our interests to have properly functioning operating systems, whether within manufacturing organisations or in the more public domain of services, whether from banking to buses or hairdressing to healthcare.

1.1.2 What is operations management?

Before moving on to discuss the position of operations management in the organisation, we can set out and explain the following definition:

> **Operations management is concerned with creating, operating and controlling a transformation system that takes inputs of a variety of resources and produces outputs of goods and services needed by customers.**

The definition contains key ideas that require further explanation. These concern operations management:

- as a management activity
- producing outputs of goods and services needed by customers
- using a variety of resources
- creating, operating and controlling a transformation system.

Throughout this chapter, we will investigate each of these points but, before moving on to them, we should look at two difficulties with terminology. First, some authors use the label *production/operations management* (abbreviated to POM) but, in this book, we shall use the more general *operations management*. Not only is our label easier to use but also it takes us away from ideas of the engineering aspects of manufacture connected with the POM term. As we shall see, most production systems furnish a mixture of goods and services and using the single term underlines this point. Second, the terms *operating* or *operational* are often used to describe a level in a managerial hierarchy or a phase of a planning cycle:

- Strategic planning is concerned with pursuit of long-term aims identified within the planning process. A typical time scale would be one to six years, or even longer.
- Intermediate (or administrative) planning may occur in large organisations and is concerned with the contributions of sub-units to the general plan. The time scale may be six months to three years.
- Operational planning is concerned with achieving specific tasks with known resources. This level plans for a maximum of a year down to weeks, days or even hours.

We should not allow the notion of the operational level to be confused with operations management. All the functions of the organisation, from personnel to purchasing, engineering to sales, can be seen to have this hierarchy of planning and decision making and we shall look at it again in Chapter 2. Operations management, by way of contrast, is concerned with transformation of inputs into outputs and has, as its concerns, decisions at all levels of the managerial hierarchy.

1.2 Operations as management activity

1.2.1 Operations management as management

Good management is the key to good organisational performance. A poorly managed taxi business uses unreliable vehicles, not-so-polite staff, arrives late for, or misses, pick-ups and handles its finances carelessly. It quickly earns a bad reputation. A well-managed business does not fail on any of these counts and prospers. The choice is the choice of the managers – it is possible to succeed or fail within the same general circumstances. What are the key features of the management process?

> **Management is the process of achieving organisational objectives within a changing environment by:**
>
> ■ **balancing efficiency, effectiveness and equity,**
> ■ **obtaining the most from limited resources, and**
> ■ **working with and through people.**

The next paragraphs amplify the parts of this definition.

Achieving organisational objectives . . .

An objective is a target to be striven for. Individuals and organisations are more successful if they have targets that are clear, challenging and achievable. The targets are means by which the individual can plan and co-ordinate work with others and how the leaders of an organisation communicate its overall aims in order to mobilise effort. For example, Yamaha will set targets for quality and output for the tone hole bevelling process. Such standards guide staff and are the basis of management decision making, whether it concerns equipment investment, staff training and selection or inspection rates.

. . . within a changing environment . . .

We shall see in Chapter 2 how the organisation cannot fix its objectives for all time. Continually changing environments impose new demands and problems, whether they concern shortage of raw materials, rising energy prices, new customer requirements or tougher competitive policies of rivals. Yamaha's competitors, such as Roland, also strive for advantage through improving their process capabilities. A key part of the management function is to maintain an awareness of such changes and prepare responses to them.

. . . balancing efficiency, effectiveness and equity . . .

Separating the three Es of the management balance is worthwhile because it enables us to understand something of the dilemma faced by managers in making decisions. Efficiency is a measure of *how well resources are transformed into outputs*. We are encouraged to compare things we buy in terms of their efficiency. Washing machine suppliers state the energy consumption per cycle; car manufacturers are required to state fuel consumption under standard test conditions; audio equipment manufacturers stress minimal distortion losses. In all these cases, efficiency is being assessed according to the use of a key input resource, be it energy or incoming sound.

But what if the washer does not wash very well, the car is too small or the hi-fi not powerful enough? The product, in other words, may not be capable of achieving its purpose. We have fallen into the trap of overemphasising efficiency at the expense of effectiveness. Effectiveness is *an assessment of how far a stated objective is achieved*; it is a measure of 'getting the job done'. It is stressed, for example, when managing a crisis. In the ultimate crisis, war, leaders aim for 'winning at all costs' and play down the question of how efficiently this is achieved. In the main, however, managers' overemphasis on effectiveness leads to a loss of efficiency in terms of wasted resources. Contrariwise, too much stress on efficiency may mean that the task is not done at all. The right balance is a management decision. To take a case of customer service, narrow considerations of efficiency would suggest that hotels and shops should not employ attendants when lifts are easy to operate. Yet, the well-known Galeries Lafayette department store in Paris has an attendant in every lift. It is an effective way of reassuring customers and offering guidance and assistance at the instant when they demand it.

Exercise 1.1	How else might a department store offer the reassurance given by a lift attendant?

Equity is the third of the three Es in the manager's mixture. It concerns the *distribution of outputs among customers* and is particularly important in public sector and not-for-profit organisations whose outputs are not traded in the conventional market place. The manager in the private business may have few qualms in restricting supplies only to those who will pay. Yet, the manager of the hospital or social work department has to ensure that all clients are treated fairly according to their needs, irrespective of how well off they are. Who gets to use the kidney machine; which village gets the bypass; which schools have to close: these are questions which not only include issues of efficiency and effectiveness but are also concerned with equity.

The best blend of the three Es is a choice to be reviewed regularly. Not only do different organisations tend to have distinct patterns, which help to give them their character, but also, as has been suggested, the mixtures will vary according to circumstances. A crisis may require resolution at all costs, while in calmer times the manager may be expected to achieve a defined output while operating as efficiently as possible. Equity brings further complexity. Organisations in the public service, joined by the increasing number of private businesses that accept their social responsibilities, face difficult questions of how to prioritise outputs among the many competing demands.

. . . obtaining the most from limited resources . . .

We can stress the limitation of resources available to managers as it takes us beyond basic questions of efficiency in the current operations. Managers have to recognise that resources have to be found and obtained, that they often have a limited life and, therefore, the processes and products of the organisation have to be adapted accordingly. Low energy consumption is not simply part of the efficiency equation for products and processes; it also concerns the search for new products and processes whose overall performance is even better. We shall return to identifying the resources used in operations management later in this chapter.

. . . working with and through people

Management is primarily a social process. We should recognise that, while much of operations management has been presented in terms of techniques for optimising the levels of stock or the flow of goods through a warehouse or machine shop, all such changes are both carried out and constrained by the people who work within those functions. An example, discussed in Chapter 16, is the quality improvement programme. Without the cooperation of all the staff involved, such initiatives are doomed to failure. Ambitious managers who do not work well with others find that, whatever good ideas and plans they create, they will be unsuccessful in implementing any change.

1.3 Producing outputs of goods and services needed by customers

1.3.1 Goods and services as products

Goods are manufactured. They are material, made, distributed, sold and then used by buyers at their will. Services are immaterial, transitory and consumed at the moment that they are produced. At first sight, the production of goods, which is manufacturing, appears to be quite different from the production of services. One can contrast the manufacture of furniture to having a haircut. Yet, although the scale, technology and location of these two examples are not the same, the two sectors can have much in common. Comparing furniture making with hairdressing, both producers will experience variations in demand and will have to vary capacity or make allowances for queuing; both will have made location decisions; both will have to set the production activity in the context of a business so as to manage and control it effectively.

Useful goods and services are the products. Operations managers use the term *product* to describe the outputs supplied to customers, whether they are physical objects or intangible services. Viewing all outputs in this general way is an important perspective because it enables us to seek out the similarities in operations as apparently diverse as oil refining, printing, shoe repair and banking.

1.3.2 A service economy?

It is often suggested that modern western capitalist societies are moving away from being based on manufacturing towards becoming service economies. Consumption patterns change and reflect rising incomes, education levels and interest in leisure of most of the population. This trend, however, is often seen as full of risk for future national prosperity. For instance, frequent references are made to the fall in the United Kingdom's manufacturing output during the past decades. Many advocate policies to 'rebuild the manufacturing base' and return the country to being a net exporter of manufactured goods, a state which had been maintained for almost 200 years. This type of argument creates two difficulties for study of production in its societal context: first, is there really a trend towards a service economy and, second, does it imply that the production of services is somewhat inferior to the production of goods?

To verify the existence of a trend towards a service economy is not easy. There are problems with both definitions and data. One common way of measuring industrial trends is to examine the nature of employment. A glance at the situations vacant columns suggests many more openings in the service sector than there used to be. Yet, do such changes mark real shifts in the nature of what is produced? Compare the jobs of machinist and lawyer where the difference between their roles may not be so great as appears at first.

An electrician can work on the production of goods for sale, for example, completing the wiring of a Yamaha Clavinova electric piano. Alternatively, the same person may work on maintenance of traffic signals or hotel lifts. The remoteness of these jobs from the direct production of material goods must surely place the electrician in the service sector.

The lawyer appears to produce a service and would clearly be doing so when representing a client in a dispute over, say, a family matter. The lawyer could, however, represent the interests of a manufacturer in protecting patent rights. Indeed, the lawyer could be a permanent employee of this manufacturer; leading pharmaceutical companies, such as Zeneca, employ lawyers specialising in such intellectual property. In such a case it could be argued that the lawyer is as closely concerned with the production of material goods as is the maintenance electrician.

We can see that the same role can be classified as delivering service (providing legal advice) or manufacturing (participating in the manufacture of equipment) depending on one's point of view. Drawing such distinctions has been made more difficult in recent years by the trend in many companies towards subcontracting, or *outsourcing*, functions which were previously performed in-house. For example, a factory which contracts its cleaning or security services to specialist companies transfers jobs, which would once have been counted as being in manufacturing, into the service sector. Yet, the same tasks may be carried out by the same people. Whether workers fall into one or the other category is, therefore, rather arbitrary.

Employment data

Even when the difficulties of categorisation are overcome, the data do not support the notion of a long-term, steady shift towards service employment. A simple model of the employment split sees the rising labour productivity of manufacturing leading to a static or declining labour force in that sector. Surplus labour is then taken up by the service sector, which is inherently more labour intensive and for which demand is rising. Yet, evidence from the past 100 years or so shows that many manufacturing industries have boomed and died. In 1841, 35.5% of the British population were employed in manufacturing, a figure that did not vary by more than three percentage points during the next 130 years. The last quarter of the 20th century seemed different. Table 1.1 uses data from more recent years to show the relatively rapid fall in employment in manufacturing. Beyond more subcontracting of functions, there were two other main trends during this period. First, there was a fall in manufacturing output resulting from lost international competitiveness; second, the output per employee continued to rise steadily; the many firms that did survive were those which invested and used their resources more efficiently and effectively.

The general rise in service employment hides many trends in different directions. In the 19th century, the increase in service employment was mainly a result of more women going into domestic service. This role has all but disappeared yet at one time it employed one-quarter of all women. Later, the domestic servant was

Table 1.1 People in employment, United Kingdom, last quarter[2] (000s)

	1980	1985	1990	1995	2000
All employment	23,691	22,675	24,050	23,452	25,380
Agriculture, hunting, forestry and fishing	426	361	313	283	315
Construction	1,350	1,155	1,238	917	1,150
Energy and water supply	754	571	418	242	187
Manufacturing	6,159	5,038	4,630	4,138	3,880
	26%	22%	19%	18%	15%
Total services	15,002	15,551	17,451	17,872	19,847
	63%	69%	73%	76%	78%
Distribution, hotels and restaurants	4,823	4,886	5,457	5,507	6,138
Transport, storage and communication	1,537	1,385	1,468	1,362	1,576
Banking, finance, insurance etc.	2,659	3,063	3,779	4,098	4,781
Public administration, education and health	5,060	5,246	5,720	5,832	6,086
Other services	923	971	1,027	1,077	1,267

partly replaced by the laundry and then the launderette. Yet even these services have largely come and gone and been replaced by a manufactured good, the washing machine. The domestic kitchen now contains more powerful machinery than many factories in the early stages of the Industrial Revolution; the washing machine uses up to four horsepower! For many domestic functions, self-service is the order of the day.

1.3.3 Goods superior to services?

My washing machine performs a function equivalent to the domestic servant or laundry. This is but one example of the interchangeability of many goods and services. Yet, there remains an attachment to the notion that it is better to manufacture than to deliver services. These are historical ideas, possibly related to the 19th-century notion of the inherent nobleness of work. Adam Smith, for one, classed the work of servants as 'barren and unproductive', seeing it as having no value:

> [It] consists in services which perish generally in the very instant of their performance, and does not fix or realise itself in any vendible commodity which can replace the value of their wages and maintenance. The labour, on the contrary, of artificers, manufacturers and merchants, naturally does fix and realise itself in some such commodity.[3]

Smith contrasted the work of merchants. For him, they were essential adjuncts to the manufacturing process and, therefore, valuable. The merchant of Smith's day could just as well be the financial adviser of today, a role that is much further removed from a manufacturing process. Yet, one could surely not sustain an argument for the superiority of one role over another.

1.3.4 The bundle of goods and services

It is evident, then, that the distinction between goods and services is not as clear as the original definitions suggest. Neither is it clear whether there is a single general trend towards service delivery in the post-industrial age. Furthermore, the notion that the production of goods is in some way superior to the production of services breaks down when distinctions between roles are attempted.

Many businesses both manufacture and supply service. Manufacturers primarily produce goods. For them, processes such as advice giving, delivery and installation are adjuncts to the manufacturing. Service producers such as taxi companies do no manufacturing. There are, however, many hybrids. To take a case in point: a newly completed washing machine stands in the warehouse at the Hotpoint factory. This is a manufactured good. Yet, as soon as the distributor places an order and the delivery process starts, service begins to be important. The value of the washing machine is enhanced by its despatch from Colwyn Bay to its destination. When displayed in the retail shop, the offer is a mixture or bundle of good and service. The machine has been manufactured, delivered and is about to be sold and delivered again complete with a guarantee of further service. If a fault develops, Hotpoint sends out a technician to perform a repair service, which may include the exchange of a manufactured component.

Exercise 1.2

Here is a list of some further purchases in which you may have been involved. Mark your estimate of the proportions of good and service in each transaction.

	100% goods				100% service
Car wash	☐	☐	☐	☐	☐
Dinner in restaurant	☐	☐	☐	☐	☐
Financial advice	☐	☐	☐	☐	☐
Food from discount retailer	☐	☐	☐	☐	☐
Gardening	☐	☐	☐	☐	☐
Hamburger, ready to eat	☐	☐	☐	☐	☐
Medical treatment	☐	☐	☐	☐	☐
House painting	☐	☐	☐	☐	☐
Self-service petrol	☐	☐	☐	☐	☐

Exercise 1.2 illustrates that most firms offer a mix of goods and services. Rather than making the sometimes arbitrary distinction, they plan to offer a 'bundle' of the two. By improving any aspect of this bundle, they strive to do better than their rivals in satisfying their customers' needs. Kotler and colleagues[4] show that managers think of products on three levels:

- The *core product* is what the customer is really buying. It refers to the fundamental benefits that count. A firm buys a safer lift truck; a consumer wants cleaner clothes; an instrumentalist seeks a sweeter sound from her instrument.

- The *actual product* is the set of features that provide the core benefits. Rival products offer different combinations of features, styling, quality, packaging and so on. For example, Yamaha clarinets offer a recognisable tone and have particular lever arrangements, colour, case design, reliability. Furthermore, they carry a well-known brand name shared with the famous motorcycles.

- The *enhanced product* comprises the set of extra benefits and services that give the product an edge in the market place. These may include delivery, installation, warranties and support. Yamaha offers customisation to profes-sional standard musicians, lifetime guarantees on its workmanship and has set up schools throughout the world where over 170,000 learn to play.

1.3.5 Integration of manufacture and service

Peters underlines the emerging recognition of the importance and integration of the service element. He goes beyond the data of Table 1.1 in saying: 'Would you believe that 96% of us ply service trades? . . . 79% of us work in the service sector . . . and of the 19% still employed in so-called manufacturing, 90% do ser-vice work (design, engineering, finance, marketing, distribution and so on).'[5] One of the reasons given for the recovery of competitiveness of the United States' economy in the mid-1990s is its edge in service productivity.

Many manufacturers are enhancing their service elements to increase customer satisfaction. Boeing developed a new generation of Delta-4 rockets that cut satel-lite launching costs by 25%. To find new customers, the company decided to offer not only the vehicle but a complete service package to put the satellite into the correct orbit.[6]

Exercise 1.3

In offering customisation of its products as well as other activities mentioned in the case, Yamaha is changing its goods–service mix. Suggest three areas where it might gain from this development and three problems that might arise.

1.3.6 Comparison of manufacturing and service provision

Although we have shown that the classification of firms into categories is rather arbitrary, thinking of manufacture and service does have a point. In identifying these *ideal types*,[7] however, we can discuss the likely characteristics that distin-guish them. Then, in studying a case of an actual firm, we can recognise the degree to which it produces goods or services and therefore identify the sort of policies and operations systems it will require to produce them. The balance of manufacturing and service in any firm is decided by its business strategy which is itself a response to the environment in which the firm operates and is deter-mined by the long-term goals.

Manufacturing and services: similarities

In many manufacturing organisations, there is a rigid separation between the production of goods and the associated activities of dealing with the customer. Marketing is often called a boundary-spanning function because, in one sense, it connects the organisation to the outside market yet, at the same time, provides a buffer between the uncertainty of that market place and the production system which can then operate more efficiently if undisturbed.

The same kind of separation can be advantageous in a service operation. Those activities that can be isolated from the interaction of the customer and the organisation are uncoupled and carried out either at another time or in another place. The number of staff engaged in direct dealing with customers is then reduced and the 'isolated' operations can be managed using similar methods to those used in manufacture.

Aircraft maintenance is carried out by specialists located at various bases throughout the world. Not only is it important for the airline to have a short downtime for maintenance but a predictable time is also needed. Major components such as engines are not, therefore, maintained in situ but are exchanged for replacements already serviced. The engines can then be taken apart and rebuilt under factory conditions after the aircraft has resumed flying.

Manufacturing and services: differences

Manufacture and service operations are most similar when much of the service operation can be isolated from the point of delivery. It follows, then, that differences will become most apparent when the service has to be wholly produced at the delivery point. Examples include entertainment, fast food and medical diagnosis. In the case of routine service such as that delivered in a hamburger bar or by a travel company, it is possible to reduce costs by standardisation of products and incorporation of rules to make operations and control straightforward. Nevertheless, such mass service operations are different from mass production. The emphasis is on customer care rather than technical skills in arranging flows of goods, although the latter can be very important. The most successful firms have discovered ways of getting staff to apply interactive skills routinely and repetitively when the customer is so directly involved in the process.

1.4 Using a variety of resources

1.4.1 Categories of resources

Our definition of operations management includes the use of resources not just because these are obviously needed, there being no such thing as a free lunch. The emphasis is placed on the resources because the operations function consumes such a variety and, in most organisations, such a large proportion of the total used by the organisation. They can be categorised as follows:

- *Material resources.* The raw materials and components that are consumed, or converted, by the system. Besides the material that is to be processed, the system will require energy and consumables such as processing tools and other variable items used in the process. Yamaha's factories consume sandpaper and polishing materials; hospitals consume bandages and blood.

- *Capital equipment.* The plant and property required to carry out the operations function. Buildings include depots, stores and factories while the plant ranges from machine tools to oil refineries, refrigerators to freight vehicles. Yamaha has its plant, sales offices, distribution centres and music schools throughout the world.

- *Labour.* The people who run the operations function. These range from machinists to wood finishers and cleaners to managers. Each has a vital role to play in the success of the function.

- *Information.* The intangible nature of information means it is often not seen as a management resource in the same way as the others listed previously. Leading companies realise, however, that knowledge is an important resource and take steps to gather, disseminate, apply and secure it. Many have introduced formal knowledge management processes and have begun to assess its value in annual reports.[8] Furthermore, for some organisations such as computer bureaux, market research companies, broadcasting organisations and universities, information is a critical raw material converted by the operating system into refined information as its key output.

1.5 Creating, operating and controlling the transformation system

The transformation system converts input resources into the appropriate bundle of product for the customer. The simplest system model of this process, Figure 1.2, shows the transformation process receiving inputs from suppliers and making them available as outputs to customers. While this is a very simple model (and you may easily pass over it with a glance) you should recognise that it is a basic building block of operations models developed in more detail throughout this book. It is a *process model* whose idea is to capture the way processes are connected by links along which pass flows of materials, information and so on. We shall extend the model here to show the different configurations of systems that occur when the roles of stock and the customer are taken into account.

1.5.1 Operations within the manufacturing and supply chain

First, we can look at the use of inventory as a buffer between the operating system and its suppliers and customers. As we shall see later, this is because of uncertainty in both supply and demand as well as because the flow rates through the different stages cannot easily be matched. Figures 1.3 to 1.6, drawn from Wild's rather more complex presentation,[9] show four arrangements for manufacturing, supply or isolated service chains, which result from whether and where

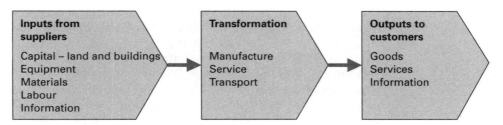

Figure 1.2 Operations as a transformation system

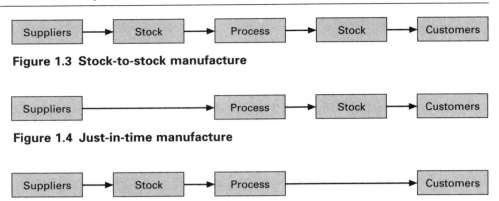

Figure 1.3 Stock-to-stock manufacture

Figure 1.4 Just-in-time manufacture

Figure 1.5 Direct to customer manufacture

inventories are placed. As the figures show, they may separate the transformation process from both suppliers and customers.

The first arrangement, Figure 1.3, can be called *stock-to-stock process*. It is very common. For manufacturing systems, it has the benefit of using inventories to isolate the internal processes from interruptions and variations in the patterns of supplier performance and customer requirements. It is repeated at other stages of the sometimes long supply chain from sources of raw materials through to the ultimate consumer. An example is a distributor transforming goods stored in bulk, say at an import depot, by moving them to local cash and carry warehouses where retailers can draw on them as needed. At Yamaha, manufacture and distribution are carried out within the company. Whatever the ownership, Figure 1.3 brings out the most obvious drawback of such a system: expensive stock has to be stored between each stage of the chain.

The remaining manufacturing examples follow from Figure 1.3 by eliminating one or both of the inventories. In *just-in-time manufacture* (Figure 1.4), the supplier and transformation process are closely matched and not separated by the buffer. Sometimes the firms decide that the input material is so perishable that it is worth tying the two stages together very closely. Canners and freezers of vegetables have for many years had plant whose packing capacity copes with the very seasonal flows of product from the fields and for the rest of the year remains idle. This ensures that the food is packed in the best condition. At the other end of the temperature scale, manufacturers have found it valuable to transport molten iron from plant to plant using special rail wagons. This avoids the costs of reheating but requires that the outputs of one plant be carefully balanced with the inputs of the other.

Ideas of saving inventory have gained ground in recent years through the introduction of just-in-time (JIT) supply systems to reduce the buffer stock sizes almost to zero. We shall look at this in more detail in Chapter 4, but can note here that JIT is not a simple solution. Management attention is shifted from stocks to maintaining carefully balanced supply chains.

Direct to customer processes (Figure 1.5) eliminates the stock holding after the transformation process. It can also represent JIT input for the next process in a chain. Generally, however, the design covers customers who have goods made to order and these are supplied when they are ready. Examples range from Pizza

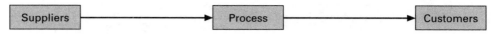

Figure 1.6 Zero stock manufacture

Express delivery service to Pronuptia, which specialises in the making of wedding dresses. Neither firm likes to carry finished stock. In the special finishing process at Yamaha, a skilled worker draws an unfinished clarinet from stock and transforms it according to the customer's wishes. Supply occurs as soon as the task is complete.

Zero stock manufacture (Figure 1.6) covers many engineering companies producing individual products. They aim not to carry inward stocks unless they are ordered under specific contracts. Further, they hand over the finished items when they are ready. Shipbuilders and civil engineers fall into this category. As with the two previous categories, zero stock processing can also occur in a chain of processes fully linked by JIT arrangements.

Electricity distribution is a rather special example of zero stock because of the perishable nature of both inputs and outputs. With no storage capacity, companies such as ScottishPower have continuously to match customer demand. This burden is in turn placed on the power generators who have some limited storage capacity. For the most part, they must use the flexibility of some power stations to match variations minute by minute.

1.5.2 Operations within service-orientated systems

Operations such as transport and personal service differ from these examples for two reasons. First, the customer is more closely involved in the process, providing inputs as well as receiving the outputs. Second, the outputs of the service transformation cannot be stocked. For example, if a freight train fails to pass through a bottleneck, such as a tunnel or busy junction, at the appointed time, this represents capacity lost by the system for ever. Similarly, it is no use the taxi arriving an hour after the time for which it was booked.

Seeing the customer as part of the transformation process and recognising the impracticability of storing service takes us on to three further models which are illustrated in Figures 1.7 to 1.9. The most general case of *flexible service*, shown in Figure 1.7, is very typical. It shows the service resources being always present and offering some spare capacity, known as slack. At the same time, the customer arrives and, in principle, joins a queue before being served. The process model shows the customer 'passing through' the transformation to benefit from its outputs.

We may suggest that the flexible service arrangement is illogical as there would not normally be spare service capacity and a queue at the same time. While this is true, the model represents the case where uncertainties cause continual imbalances between customer demands and the capability of satisfying them. Visit many a public house around 7 o'clock on a Saturday and you will see slack resources. Three hours later, you will be lucky if you are served immediately or can get a seat. Hospital accident departments are busy an hour or so after this as well as on Sundays after the morning football matches. The balance between

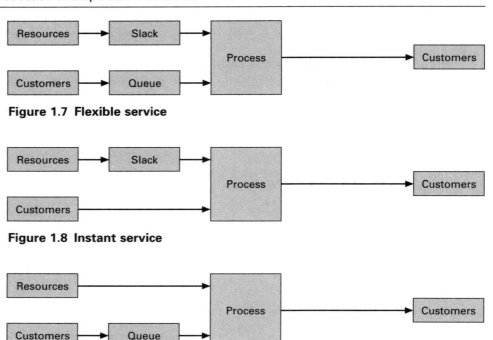

Figure 1.7 Flexible service

Figure 1.8 Instant service

Figure 1.9 Low-cost service

having queues at peak times and offering excess capacity at others is a critical problem for service operations managers that we shall look into in Chapter 12.

The Figure 1.8 configuration, *instant service*, shows the previous model without queues. It sets out to offer surplus capacity at all times. Examples range from the fast-service restaurant to the expensive private hospital, from the motel which advertises 'Rooms always available' to emergency services where crews sometimes experience long periods on stand-by. Again, management of the high costs of such service operations is a problem. Sometimes, the excess capacity, especially of labour, can be devoted to other functions, such as training, when it is not called on for service.

In Figure 1.9, *low-cost service* tips the efficiency–effectiveness balance towards the former. Even equity may be placed on one side if resources are very short. The dentist in the United Kingdom public service is mostly paid per task carried out. Therefore, the practice cannot maintain enough income unless its facilities are in full use throughout the working day. There are no slack resources. A queue of two or three weeks, with exceptions for emergency cases, enables efficiency to be maintained while recognising the possibility of some equitable treatment for those in greatest need.

Exercise 1.4

In the opening case to Chapter 15, we shall see how Swiss Federal Railways sees its operations management as producing train traffic. Another transport organisation would see itself as moving passengers and freight. How might you represent these different views?

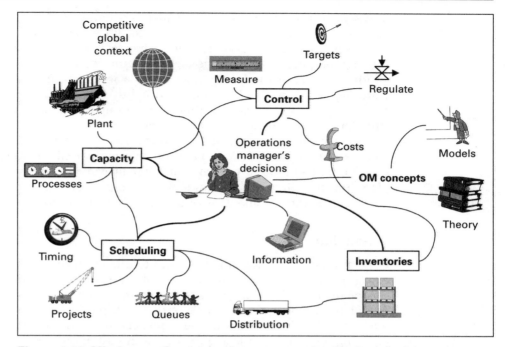

Figure 1.10 Mind map of an operations manager's principal decision areas

1.5.3 Issues within the transformation system

What are the decisions that the operations manager must make when setting up and running the transformation process? Four areas have particular significance. They are capacity management, scheduling, inventory management and control of all kinds. Figure 1.10 summarises the elements and their interrelationships in a mind map (see Box 1.1). It represents the way an operations manager may think about the OM field and the issues faced by the company. The integrated nature of operations is seen in the way that the elements are interlinked in the map.

Capacity

In the short term, the capacity of an operating system can only be changed within limits. For instance, the doctor, faced with an outbreak of an infectious

BOX 1.1 Mind mapping

Mind mapping is a valuable study skill. You can use maps to summarise ideas and explore their relationships. You can use words or sketches at will. Although some authors, such as Buzan,[10] have tried to define the style of the map with links radiating from the centre, others prefer a more informal, networked representation. The former is sometimes called a concept map while the latter, especially when many icons are used, is often called a 'rich picture'.

disease, can respond by working harder and longer and, perhaps, by delaying visits to non-urgent cases. Manufacturing facilities may rely on overtime working to increase capacity by about 20%. In each case, it is unwise to attempt to sustain the high output for long. In the medium term, the medical centre may take on another partner or the factory may set up a second shift. Each requires careful planning, a task not to be undertaken lightly. Capacity changes outside these ranges require even longer leadtimes, perhaps up to a decade in the case of construction and commissioning of brand new facilities.

Operations managers are not just concerned, then, with the short term. They have to be involved in choices about system capacity well into the future. It is here that the function interacts with strategic management, which is the long-range planning and policy accomplishment of the organisation. Strategic management incorporates learning about issues in the global and competitive environments.

Scheduling

Generally, activity scheduling has a shorter time horizon. While some industries engage in operations which themselves take several years to complete, civil engineers being a notable example, the state of mind remains very much the same. The plans are made to suit the agreed overall productive capacity and activity scheduling involves itself with the sequence, speed and timing of all the manufacturing and service tasks required to meet customers' needs. Within stock-to-stock manufacture, scheduling is very much an internal affair, working out the best ways of transforming the inward inventory into product ready for despatch to customers on demand. The other manufacturing models, by the same token, dispense with the buffers. They require an integration of scheduling systems of the linked organisations, which can increase the complexity of the task. For the service systems seen in Figures 1.7 to 1.9, scheduling is more responsive to customers' immediate and variable needs. The operations manager has to focus on questions of how much spare capacity to have in place as well as how to manage queues to best effect.

Inventory

We have seen that the importance of inventory management will vary according to how much stock is carried. Managers seek to balance the cost of carrying high stocks with the risk of non-service after a stockout.

Control

Finally, control is a key element of Figure 1.5. All operations activities need to be monitored and controlled so that they achieve their targets in terms of efficiency, effectiveness and, where appropriate, equity. At the same time, control can be expensive and intrusive for those engaged in the tasks. The manager, therefore, must understand how control can be exercised as well as how much is needed.

These four critical elements, plus two other issues displayed in Figure 1.10, capture the essence of operations management. They will dealt with in detail in later chapters, especially 4, 11, 12 and 14. We now continue to study how operations fits into the wider organisation.

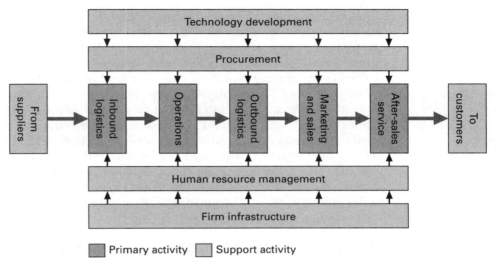

Figure 1.11 **The organisation's value chain**

1.6 The operations function within the whole organisation

1.6.1 The organisation's value chain

The value chain has become a well-known tool for setting out the key processes of the organisation as a whole. First proposed by Porter,[11] its essential features are activities, both internal and external, and integration. Through the nine generic activities, which the model identifies, the firm adds to the total value of its product. Note that, while taking the form of a process model, it does not describe the flows through any particular organisation. Instead, it represents the elements that Porter argued are present in all effective transformation systems. He divides business activities into those which directly operate upon the product or service eventually delivered, the so-called *primary* activities, and the other necessary functions, or *support* activities, which provide a framework to back up the main line. Figure 1.11 shows the primary activities set out as links in a chain. These are reinforced by the four *support* activities, explained as follows:

- *Procurement*. The obtaining of purchased inputs of all kinds.
- *Technology development*. Basic research and the design and development of both products and processes.
- *Human resource management*. Recruiting, training, developing and organising of personnel.
- *Firm infrastructure*. Managerial processes such as planning and control, quality management, obtaining and allocating funds, the work of the legal department and dealing with governments.

As presented here, the model is made up of the elements of the typical profit-making producer of a bundle of goods and services. The layout and labelling of the model can be adapted to suit organisations which carry out other significant primary activities, such as social work departments, or where key support is needed from different functions, such as a legal or international department.

The purpose of introducing the model here is to use it to illustrate how operations fits within a typical organisation. The function forms the working core of the organisation yet it should not be seen as embracing every part of it. Good organisation requires both the separation of functions and giving them clearly defined roles together with methods by which the functions are to be linked together. This is the nub of the classic study of Lawrence and Lorsch[12] who also showed that the degree of such differentiation and integration should be related to the setting in which the organisation was established.

1.6.2 Operations management and organisational structure

Firms have a choice about how to allocate tasks and fit them together. Figure 1.12 shows the scope of the operations management task in two businesses. First, the narrow ellipse shows the scope in a manufacturing firm. Of the primary activities, the operations manager is responsible for production and some aspects of stockholding. The manager is also heavily involved with support activities from product and process development to quality assurance. Primary activities

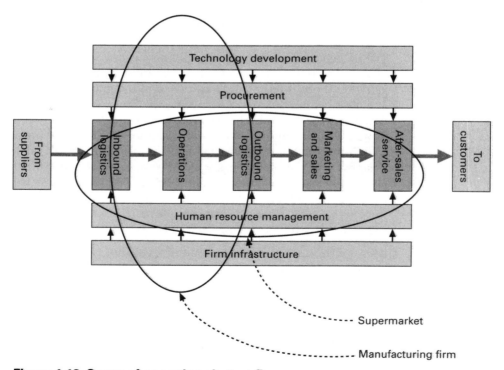

Figure 1.12 Scope of operations in two firms

of delivery, sales and marketing and after-sales service are handled by other departments.

The second firm is a supermarket retailer. Here, store operations from inbound logistics through to selling are more closely integrated at the operational level. Support activities are frequently head office functions carried out by specialists on behalf of all the stores within the group. The value chain model, therefore, identifies stores management as responsible for all primary activities, that is the flow of goods from the unloading of incoming transport through to consumer after-sales service.

1.6.3 Organisation structure

To examine how these choices work out in practice, we can compare the organisation structures of the two firms in Figure 1.12. In the manufacturing company, the attention of the operations function (here called production) is on converting stock to stock. Consequently, production is separated from suppliers and customers by the purchasing and sales departments whose role is to deal with the inputs and outputs. Figure 1.13 shows this typical arrangement. To manage continuous operations, the production director is responsible not only for the manufacturing facility but for other support functions with which it has to be integrated on a daily basis. These include:

- production planning, scheduling and control
- jig and tool design and manufacture
- maintenance of plant and equipment
- industrial engineering, which includes work measurement, method study and the management of any related payment scheme
- quality assurance.

In the supermarket firm, illustrated in Figure 1.14, the main operations activities are divided into two parts under the distribution director and the stores operations director. One involves the receipt and storage of supplies from manufacturers and their distribution to the stores; the other is store management itself. Other functions at head office include merchandising, which looks after relations with suppliers and studies the introduction of new lines. The stores managers,

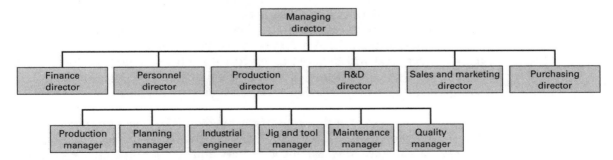

Figure 1.13 Production as the operations function in a manufacturing firm

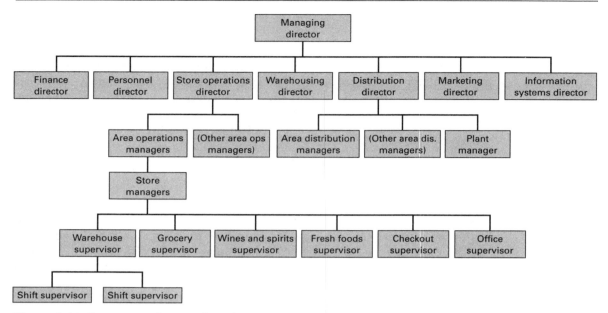

Figure 1.14 Structure of operations in a supermarket firm

reporting to area operations managers, manage the flow of goods in the stores from the moment they are received at the goods-inward bay until they are taken away by the customer. Figure 1.14 shows just some departments that may be established, depending on the size of the store. Others could be bakery, pharmacy, delicatessen, white goods, textiles and so on. At the local level, therefore, the store manager, as operations manager, is responsible for all stages of the firm's value chain as follows:

- inbound logistics, including unloading, unpacking and storing
- sales, including display, pricing and promotion
- outbound logistics from checkout operations to enabling customers to take purchases away conveniently
- in-store and after-sales customer service.

Comparing the responsibilities of the operations managers in the two cases, we can see several similarities and differences. The roles are similar in that they lie at the heart of the business and drive it along on a day-to-day basis. The roles differ in that the manufacturing operations are isolated from direct contact with customers and will be more involved with other functions in long-range questions such as product and process development. In the supermarket case, decisions about new products, new locations and so on are taken by specialists at head office.

It can be seen, then, that the scope of the operations manager's responsibilities varies from organisation to organisation and depends on issues such as the operating system structure, the size of the activity and the personal choice of those involved.

✔ Quick check-up

Can you:
☐ Define operations management.
☐ Explain the differences between efficiency, effectiveness and equity.
☐ Outline what is meant by the 'service economy'.
☐ Name four types of input resources.
☐ Sketch seven transformation system arrangements.
☐ Identify four key decision areas for the operations manager.
☐ Outline the value chain.
☐ Sketch typical organisation structures for a manufacturer and retailer.

❓ Questions

Chapter review

1.1 Why do organisations produce a bundle of goods and service?

1.2 Explain the different roles of the customer in the manufacturing and service transformation systems.

1.3 Why are operations managers in manufacturing and retail organisations responsible for different activities?

Application

1.4 For each of the core products listed in Exercise 1.1, give an example of the actual and augmented products.

1.5 From the opening case, *Making music*, sketch a mind map showing the important issues faced by a senior operations manager at Yamaha.

1.6 There are two transformations mentioned in the *Making music* case study, producing for stock and supplying to special order. What do you think are the management issues in the two examples?

Investigation

1.7 Yamaha is one of several companies that provide a virtual 'factory tour' on the Internet. Produce a flow diagram based on the Yamaha tour.[13]

CLOSING CASE

Operations management in a nursing home

Nursing homes are set up to satisfy the needs of those who require 24-hour nursing care. They are inspected and approved by local authorities but are owned and managed by a range of bodies including individuals, companies and charitable organisations.

The Newton Nursing Home has space for 40 patients in a three-storey building converted from a pair of large Victorian houses. It is part of a business with 25 similar establishments throughout north-west England. The local manager

▶

is the matron who is responsible for all operations at the home. Helped by qualified sisters who work shifts, the matron has to ensure that care to the required standard is available at all times. One-third of the patients stay in bed, only a handful of the others can walk unsupported. The operations managers, therefore, must ensure that each patient is looked after according to his or her needs. The care tasks include: providing and supervising personal care; preparing and serving meals; cleaning and washing; dealing with visiting medical practitioners; arranging visits to the hospital; providing ancillary services such as hairdressing and chiropody. Beyond these direct service responsibilities the managers deal with friends and relatives of the patients and arrange occasional events such as outings and informal concerts.

Staffing is a continual problem. There are standards, enforced by the licensing authority, for the minimum number of staff on the premises at any time. To cover the periods when permanent staff are unavailable, the managers maintain lists of carers looking for occasional employment. They also use agencies and sometimes fall back on persuading a member of staff to work an extra shift.

Patients pay for their accommodation and care, prices varying from £290 to £360 per week depending on the room. Most patients receive some support from the social security system; in some cases services are paid for entirely. Payments from public funds can be made directly to the company. For the rest, patients or their representatives are invoiced by head office and matron is responsible for chasing slow payers. The matron also looks after the day-to-day repairs of the building and equipment. To do this she employs a repair person who possesses skills from gardening to interior decorating.

Few patients recover. When a room becomes vacant, the matron arranges to have it redecorated and let as soon as possible. To this end, she maintains a waiting list of a few names and sometimes places an advertisement in the local paper.

Questions

1 Is Newton Nursing Home a 'pure service' business? What operating system structure exists at the home? What resources are converted into what outputs?

2 What, in terms of the three Es, are the operating system objectives?

3 Relate the principal operating decisions to the categories of Figures 1.3 to 1.9.

Notes and references

1. Yamaha Corporation (2000) *Annual Report 2001*. Hamamatsu, Yamaha Corporation; www.yamaha.co.jp/english/product/winds/index.htm; accessed 4 October 2001.
2. Office of National Statistics (2001) http://www.statistics.gov.uk/statbase/tsdataset.asp?vlnk=341; accessed 19 April.
3. Smith, A., *The Wealth of Nations* 1981 edition. London: Methuen.
4. Kotler, P., Armstrong, G., Saunders, J. and Wong, V. (1996) *Principles of Marketing: The European Edition*. London: Prentice Hall, p.14.
5. Peters, T. (1984) 'Hit and run strategy for hypercompetition', *The Independent on Sunday Business News*, 9 October, p.22.

6. Marsh, P. (2001) 'Learning how to make it a lot better: Industries have to get all their operations rights, not just the fabrication and assembly aspects', *Financial Times: Survey – Manufacturing Excellence*, 21 May.

7. The ideal type is not the same as a simple classification or an empirical model. In constructing such a description one is searching for the basic characteristics of a particular sort of organisation and not attempting to describe any actual situation.

8. KPMG (1998) *Knowledge Management Research Report*, www.kpmg.com/home.htm, accessed 20 May 2000; Skandia Insurance Company (1997) 'Customer relationships and growth in value', *Intellectual Capital: Supplement to 1996 Annual Report*, Stockholm: Skandia Insurance.

9. Wild, R. (1991) *Production and Operations Management*, 4th edition. London: Cassell, pp.7–11.

10. Buzan, T. (1995) *Use Your Head,* revised edition, London: BBC Books; Mind Tools Ltd *Improved note taking with mind maps*, www.mindtools.com, accessed 3 March 2001.

11. Porter, M.E. (1985) *Competitive Advantage*. New York: Free Press.

12. Lawrence, P.R. and Lorsch, J.W. (1967) *Organisation and Environment*, Homewood, IL: Irwin.

13. Yamaha Corporation (1999) http://www.yamaha.co.jp/edu/english/factory/cl/index.html; accessed 21 April 2001.

CHAPTER 2

Operations management in the organisational context

OBJECTIVES

When you have finished studying this chapter, you should be able to:

- Define a system, explain its key elements and give reasons for systems thinking in analysing operations.
- Distinguish between structural and process models of systems and organisations.
- Describe an organisation in terms of input–output models and classify flows between the elements in terms of input, output, planning and control.
- Explain the term market orientation and describe the key activities of the marketing function.
- Describe the marketing mix and the communications mix.
- Identify the main processes involved in design and development and discuss how and why these are being modified in modern organisations.
- Explain and illustrate the concept of manufacturability.
- Demonstrate the construction of budgets for operation and investment and show how these form links between finance and operations.
- Define and explain the significance of the break-even point to operations managers.
- Compare different financial methods of appraising investment proposals.

OPENING CASE ## Repairing wholes, not holes[1]

In 1945, Dr Edward Earle Shouldice opened his hospital in Toronto, Canada, with a nurse, secretary and cook. In one operating room, he repaired two hernias per day. Success of his method led to rising demand so he expanded by buying adjoining buildings and taking on more staff. In 1953, Shouldice bought the Thornhill country estate to establish a second hospital where all surgery now takes place. Now, in Thornhill's five operating theatres, 12 surgeons carry out 7,000 hernia operations annually. There are 170 employees, with an average length of service of 12.5 years.

Typical of the Canadian system, Shouldice Hospital is a not-for-profit institution licensed by the government. It achieves a remarkable success rate. Complications and infections occur in about 0.05% (1 in 2,000) of cases. Of the 270,000 operations since 1945, the overall recurrence rate is about 1%, compared with the reported North American average of some 10%. Some have attempted to copy the secret formula of the 'Shouldice Technique' yet the hospital denies that a secret exists. Visiting doctors are welcomed as observers but they frequently miss, or are unable to copy, the holistic approach to patient care. This goes beyond the surgeons' skills to having all aspects of patient service delivered to a high standard.

Patients have come from more than 80 countries. Shouldice does not support the trend towards low-cost day surgery treatment but keeps the patient in for about three days. They return to normal activity, on average, eight days after the operation. The Shouldice model of holistic healthcare is less about fixing holes in abdominal walls but more about treating the whole person, physical, psychological and spiritual. For instance: careful attention is paid to the diagnostic and reception processes to ensure that waiting times are short and stress is low; allocation of patients to surgeons is done in advance so that personal links can be made; meals are of high quality using fresh ingredients only; and, after the 45-minute operation, patients are encouraged to walk and exercise as quickly as possible.

The ability to improve standards continuously comes partly from patient follow-up. Anyone who has had surgery becomes a member of the alumni club. Each receives an annual letter asking about state of health; newsletters build and maintain contact; and all are invited to the January banquet in Toronto. This month is a little quieter than normal because many patients want to avoid travel for treatment during the cold weather. Therefore, during the few days either side of the event, surgeons meet and examine many of the 1,000 to 1,500 alumni who attend the dinner. The long-term relationship has two merits. First, the hospital can use its database to learn how to do even better. Nowadays, people who think they have a hernia can log on to www.shouldice.com and do their own diagnosis. Second, former patients are the best advertisements for further business. Referrals and word of mouth create most new custom while the focused efficiency of the service means that prices are some 60% of similar treatments elsewhere.

2.1 Introduction

The question of why the Shouldice Hernia Centre succeeds is asked of many organisations. The answer is never simple and we should be wary of the easy formula. After all, many visitors have tried to copy the methods of Dr Shouldice, with mixed success. Some have concentrated on the focus on clear goals and limited range of service; others suggest organisation; yet others identify the skills of the people and their leadership; a fourth group suggests innovative products and advanced process technologies. What is clear is that the reason lies in a complex mixture of these and other factors. The hospital was developed by a group that linked many ideas into a holistic approach to treatment. It then put it into practice and continually sought ways to improve.

Recognising the way the organisation works as a whole, therefore, helps us to understand how the best transformation systems work. In this chapter, we shall learn more about this holistic perspective by studying how operations management fits into the broader context. To start the process, we shall examine the nature of systems.

2.2 Systems thinking

In the last chapter, we used *process* models to investigate the flows that pass through a transformation system. We also presented some *structural* models, summarising the relationships among organisational parts. These give us a starting point for investigating systems.

2.2.1 Structure and process

Studying organisations can be confusing. On the one hand, we see elements which are almost unchanging while, on the other, we see activities that change all the time. We refer to the former as structural elements, and to the latter as processes:

- The term *structure* refers to the set of relatively unchanging elements within a system. In an operations system, they include buildings, facilities, vehicles or machinery, the basic organisation, information systems, work rules and trade union agreements. All of these change from time to time but it can be useful to treat them as fixed. For instance, during a study of the way a hernia patient is treated, it is valuable to take the hospital management structure, physical layout and service policies as fixed.

- The term *process* refers to those features of a system that change continually within the fixed structure. In operations, they include flows of goods and service, energy, new recruits, cash and information. Therefore, we can study the service offered to a sample of 100 patients over several months within a given structure. The structure provides the 'framework' for processes to be carried out.

2.2.2 Systems as wholes

When we observe something we call a *system*, we tend to speak of it as a whole and ascribe to the whole system attributes which we cannot find in any particular part of it. It is as though the system behaves in a way that is different from simply a sum of the behaviour of all its parts. While it is true that, if we knew enough about each element in detail, we could predict the behaviour of the system as a whole, in reality this is not usually possible because systems are characterised by complexity. The following are examples of systems: a shoal of fish, the electricity supply grid, FIAT, the Football Association, the insurance industry.

'But,' you may say, taking the first example, 'a shoal of fish is a system comprising a vast number of fish that are themselves systems!' That is indeed true. One could also add that the shoal is but one small element of all life in the ocean that is often itself referred to as an ecosystem. Moreover, the oceanic ecosystem is part of the earth system (Gaia), which is part of the solar system and so on. These are realistic responses. In fact, they refer to two further important features of the way we think about systems: recognition of the existence of a hierarchy and the notion of a boundary used to separate one system from another.

2.2.3 System definition

These ideas lead us to the definition of a system:

> **A system is a set of parts connected together in significant ways.**

Central to the idea of system, captured by this definition, are the significant connections or relationships among the components. It is as though the arrangement of these parts, and the way they work together, are at least as important as the parts themselves. Let us summarise these general features of systems before giving an example:

- *Holism*. This term is given to the notion that the whole of the system behaves in ways greater than the sum of its parts. We call the attributes displayed by the system as a whole *emergent properties*.

- *Hierarchy*. Each system consists of parts that are themselves systems. We may refer to these parts as *subsystems* when we recognise that they, too, can be subdivided. Does the fact that systems are composed of subsystems mean that we require an immensely complex and deep investigation each time we want to answer a question? The answer is no. We only need to probe as far as we need to. The notion of hierarchy makes us sensitive to the possibility of complexity. The depth of investigation, that is the degree of resolution of these systems, will depend on the relevance it has for our investigation.[2]

- *Boundary*. The boundary is the notional line separating the system from the elements outside it. For instance, in a business organisation, what it owns and whom it employs are usually easy to define. Contrariwise, what of the charity relying on volunteers? What about cooperating groups of organisations? The boundary in these cases is not easy to draw; yet thinking about it can help to clarify what managing them is all about.

- *Environment*. Elements outside the system interacting with it in meaningful ways make up the environment. When we recognise the importance of environments we refer to systems as *open systems*.

- *Significance*. The term *significant* in the definition is important. Just as a marine biologist can see meaning in fish forming shoals to enhance survival, an operations manager sees particular forms of production system as more likely to achieve the set goals. Others, such as employees or customers may perceive the system and its goals in quite different ways. These contrasting perceptions of operating systems, especially those brought in by customers of service systems, have to be considered by the effective manager.

2.2.4 Representing a system

Just as there are many perceptions, there are many ways of representing them. Despite their richness, two-dimensional diagrams can only display a limited part of the complexity present in real organisations. In selecting our diagrams, therefore, we must specialise depending on which feature we want to bring out. We

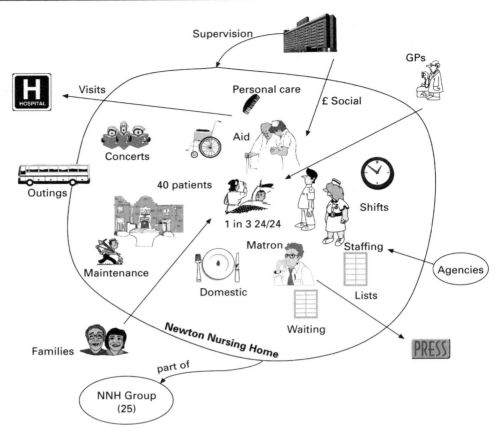

Figure 2.1 Rich picture of Newton Nursing Home

have already examined, in Chapter 1, representations of structure and process. Two more follow from the wish to represent systems.

Rich picture or situation summary

A rich picture captures our initial impressions of a situation *before* we have attempted to analyse it. This means we try to summarise, using icons, jottings and notes, the essence of the situation in a simple diagram. Rather than continually poring over a written description, the rich picture encourages us to think about the case as a whole, looking around for links among elements and insights into problems and questions that may arise. As we produce the picture, and continually reorganise it, these questions become clearer and we move towards thinking of the situation in systems terms.

Figure 2.1 summarises the Newton Nursing Home case from the end of Chapter 1. It picks out elements of structure (home, contents, staff, environment) and process (care, recruitment, payments, visits, outings) that are relevant to operations management at the home. In identifying the boundary of the organisation, it forms a basis for representing the home as a system.

Exercise 2.1

There are no established rules for drawing a rich picture. However, it is usual to capture the basic structural and process elements. Further, it should do these in summary form so that the whole appears in one diagram. Brief notes can be valuable. A good test of the effectiveness of your *situation summary* is that you can use it to speak about the case for a few minutes without further aids.

Using Figure 2.1 as a guide, sketch a rich picture for the Shouldice Hernia Centre. Then test your summary by explaining the case to a friend using only your picture as a guide.

Systems map

When doing the summary, we become aware of the important elements of the situation and the links among them. In doing this, we are beginning to think in systems terms. We have identified the boundary, some of the elements within the system and some of the important influences that arise outside it. A *systems map* is a means of representing these features more formally than in the rich picture. It is a structural model in that it concentrates on the more or less fixed elements of the system, seeing them as the framework within which processes take place.

Figure 2.2 shows Shouldice Hospital as a system. It represents the general features we see in many systems, although the selection and arrangement are unique to this case. The boundary separates components from environments.

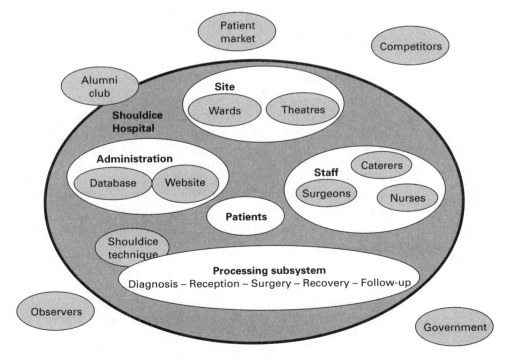

Figure 2.2 Systems map of Shouldice Hospital

Some components are themselves systems with components of their own. Examples of these *subsystems* are site, staff and administration. The processes for which Shouldice is renowned are represented by the processing subsystem. More detail could always be asked for, but this systems map is designed to be a simple representation of the main elements and their hierarchical relationship.

2.2.5 Justification for systems thinking

One objection to systems thinking may be made at this stage. It introduces a great deal of unnecessary complexity. Why be concerned with notions of boundary and hierarchy and this mysterious idea of emergent properties? The answer is that systems ideas help us to do several things: we can more easily picture and cope with the complexity of operating systems; we can recognise the different perspectives brought by different people in these complex situations; we can find features in common among such systems and thus transfer learning from one to another. We made this last point at the start of Chapter 1 as one of the reasons for studying operations management.

Complexity

Making a decision about a simple issue, such as which loaf of bread to buy, requires limited investigation. It costs little if the wrong decision is made. What if you are, instead, seeking to make a long-term deal over millions of buns for a restaurant chain? There are many issues to be explored, many variables to be taken into account. The problem needs a thorough investigation, recognising the complexity of interactions. Systems thinking assists in recognising and coping with the complexity.

Subjectivity

Different people will define systems, and therefore problems within them, in different ways. Although we may see this as an unfortunate hindrance to progress, we must recognise it as possible. In some situations, it may be possible to impose a particular point of view or discover a sustainable consensus. In others, the perspectives of different groups (managers, workers, customers) will be so different that the manager will have to cope by other means. They may have to bargain, trading off the needs of one group against those of another. Again, systems thinking can help, this time in coping with subjectivity.

Generality

Scholars have searched for a general systems theory that covers the behaviour of systems in all spheres of reality, for example biology, ecology, politics, economics and business. It seeks universal statements about organisation, complexity, control and so on.[3] Although the task has proved very difficult, valuable insights have been gained. It is useful to think of general notions, for instance the nature of control theory developed in engineering, when considering effective management of operations systems. Again, when we learn an approach to problem solving, such as developed in later chapters, we can recognise its general properties and apply it in many situations.

2.3 Operations within the organisational system

2.3.1 Process models

The organisation, as a system, is a set of parts connected together in ways that make the whole greater than these parts. The connections are set up by managers to achieve their plans. Furthermore, the organisation links with a complex environment with elements such as competitors, customers, suppliers, the government, the legal system, the labour market, trades unions, banks and so on. How these links are managed makes a difference to performance. We shall take up this process model of organisation and environment when we come to look at planning in Chapter 4.

Within the organisation, there are several subsystems interacting with each other and with the environment. There are almost as many ways of presenting the arrangement of these components as there are authors writing on the subject. For instance, the value chain model of a business organisation appeared in Chapter 1. This type of model, which presents the business as an input–output (I–O) system within an environment, is very common. Figure 2.3 is a more detailed process model of the functions of a manufacturing business.

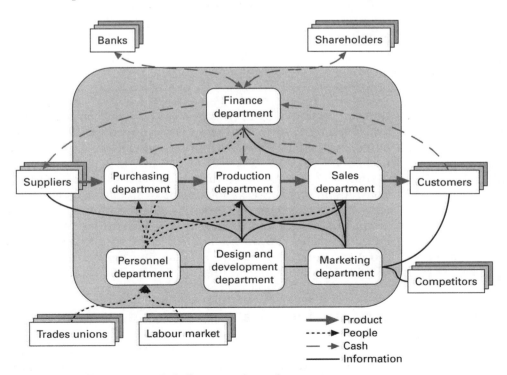

Figure 2.3 Process model of a manufacturing system

In Figure 2.3, the output of each stage of the value chain is the input of goods to the next stage. Thus, the subsystems of the business are themselves perceived as I–O (input–output) systems. By extension, each component of these subsystems can be analysed in the same way. For example the paint shop, part of the production system, takes in unpainted goods and sends out painted ones. This transformation is the contribution of the department to the total production system that takes in raw materials and transforms them into finished goods.

Figure 2.3 shows how the flow of goods passes from purchasing to production to sales and finally to customers. What of the other departments such as personnel? Are they less involved in the purpose of the business? No, these backup activities are important links in the chain because, for example, the production subsystem requires people who must be recruited, trained and managed. Indeed, from the point of view of the personnel manager, the personnel function is also an I–O system. Among other activities, it takes in recruits and provides competent staff to the other subsystems.

2.3.2 The roles of subsystems

Other subsystems in Figure 2.3 fulfil different roles. The finance function controls the flows of cash into, out of and around the business. Knowledge is managed and exchanged among the departments. It relates to operational issues, such as orders and immediate plans, or it supports other decision areas of management including planning and control, discussed in detail in Chapter 4.

A planning system looks ahead and decides what is to be done in the future. Production planning entails day-to-day scheduling; process and pre-production planning involves looking further ahead to make it possible for production to take place, for instance by the provision of special equipment; strategic planning for production has a time scale of several years and includes decisions about new processes, changes in capacity or location.

A control system includes, on a day-to-day basis, activities such as inspection, standard costing, progress monitoring and stock control. Looking further ahead, progress towards long-term plans is monitored. In all these cases, data are collected, compared with original plans and corrective, control action taken when necessary.

Thus, we can draw up an inventory, as in Table 2.1, which outlines the relationships among various components of the production system and other systems within the business. Table 2.1 demonstrates that the links between the production system and the rest of the business are many and complex. These links include the fundamental ones of inputs and outputs between stages of the process to the managerial links of planning and control. Chapter 4 develops the relationships between planning, operating and control.

2.3.3 Structural models

As we have seen, process models are not the only ways to represent operations systems. Structural models examine the relationships among the relatively fixed components. We have already seen a systems map showing the organisation with

Table 2.1 Links among business subsystems

Business subsystem	Link to operations subsystem	Relevant features
Purchasing	Input	Buying, quality assurance, vendor rating
Stock holding	Input Control Output	Raw materials Intermediate stocks Finished stocks
Distribution	Output	Finished stocks or immediate despatch
Sales	Planning	Orders matched to production plans
Marketing	Planning	Long-term product and process plans
Personnel and training	Input Planning	Staff required at once Staff and skills needed in the future
Finance	Control Input Planning	Costs of all inputs Working capital Budgets
Design and development	Input Planning	Manufacturing instructions Future products and processes

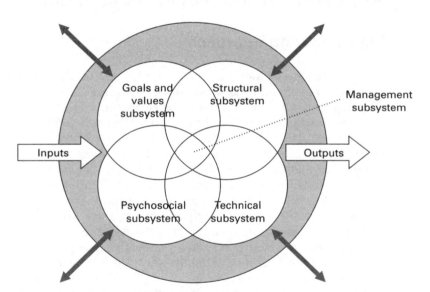

Figure 2.4 The organisation as a complex system

functions such as operating and marketing. Systems thinking, however, encourages us to take a wider view than this, recognising that the organisation consists of several linked subsystems of different types. The *socio-technical systems* view examines the organisation in terms of the intertwining of the technical system with the social system. Chapter 3 examines this in more detail. Kast and Rosenzweig[4] advanced a more general model, stressing that the organisation had several major subsystems, as shown in Figure 2.4.

The diagram shows that it is possible to look at the organisation in several ways. The traditional management approach was to emphasise the structural system and describe the organisation in terms of hierarchical charts such as those used in Chapter 1. The behavioural scientist focused on the psychosocial subsystem, concentrating on developing ideas about the behaviour of individuals and groups. The political scientist would start by looking at goals and values. The traditional production management specialist saw the organisation in terms of a collection of facilities to be optimised. The technical system was the centre and other factors were seen only in terms of constraints on choice. The modern view of organisations considers all the subsystems and the interactions between them. Not only does each subsystem have a two-way interaction with the environment but also the system *as a whole* works to convert inputs into outputs. For the operations manager, understanding interactions is important. An example is the relationship between the psychosocial and the technical subsystems, which is covered in Chapter 3. For the rest of this chapter, we shall return to the general input–output picture presented in Figure 2.3 to examine links between operations and three other functions in more detail.

2.4 Marketing and the operations function

2.4.1 The marketing approach

Of all the business functions, marketing is the one that most clearly links the organisation to the outside world. Indeed its prime focus is boundary spanning; it is concerned with relations with the customer.

The marketing approach to business involves a fundamental commitment to satisfying the needs of customers. It is both a set of beliefs (concerning market orientation) about the direction in which businesses should be facing and a set of processes that express the beliefs in practice. The commitment to satisfying customer needs has been interpreted differently throughout history. During the Industrial Revolution, firms produced goods and services in rapidly increasing volumes. Prices fell so dramatically and demand was so great that success in manufacturing stemmed from obtaining raw materials and using machinery to reduce costs and maximise output. James Watt's steam engine was four times more efficient than the ones it replaced. In 1813, there were about 2,000 power looms in the Lancashire cotton weaving industry; by 1820 some 14,000 and the 100,000 mark arrived in 1833. In these circumstances, it is not surprising that most companies focused their efforts on production to overcome the shortages hindering economic growth.

Rising competition among companies made them realise that something more would have to be done to encourage the customer to buy products, especially when there were so many to choose from. Firms began to consider what the customers wanted. They remained conditioned by the desire to produce in large volumes to keep costs and prices down. The early *production orientation* changed to a *sales orientation* in which the accent was on selling whatever the company had to offer. The tools of selling and promotion came into widespread use. These included advertising, personal persuasion and offering financial incentives and discounts. Yet even sales-orientated firms were not good at keeping up with rapidly changing customers' tastes. As these tastes shifted, the firms faced the struggle to keep costs below the prices that increasingly disenchanted customers were prepared to pay.

2.4.2 Market orientation

Market orientation begins with the customer. It recognises that customers buy to satisfy needs. This implies two broad stages of marketing activity – discovering and interpreting needs and then devising ways of satisfying them. Of course, customers' needs depend on what firms have to offer. Many firms, therefore, try to mould or create needs through various forms of persuasion. Overall, having a market orientation means that the firm sees itself as engaged in a continual exchange with its customers. Consider the early years of rivalry between Ford and General Motors in the United States:

Ford had defined customer needs for motoring in terms of basic transportation at the cheapest possible price. Starting from this definition, the astonishingly successful Model T was produced at low cost by the new manufacturing systems Ford had developed. In 1926, Ford's output was one million vehicles, twice that of GM. Nevertheless, in emerging as one of the first major companies with clear marketing orientation, GM reinterpreted the customer need to include the notion that customers also wanted to travel *in comfort*. New technology, that of being able to press sheet steel cheaply to make body panels, allowed GM to introduce a range of cars with enclosed bodies. By 1930, Ford's 2:1 lead had been reversed. The Model T became obsolete and GM has never relinquished its place as the world's leading manufacturer.

GM's exploitation of pressing technology made the difference. The new cars were more expensive than Ford's. They had to be made affordable, convenient and desirable. Instalment payments were introduced, as were trade-ins. A distribution and servicing network was formally established. There was the idea of a *model range* with different sizes and styles, with annual changes to keep the car up to date. GM was bringing together the *marketing mix* (see later) in offering a combination of *product, promotion, price and place* to satisfy the customer. It recognised that a customer wanted more than a manufactured good. Service was just as important.[5]

Not all companies adopt a market orientation. This may be because of blinkered management or because circumstances do not warrant it. Witness the following example of production orientation:

When asked about the competition between rail and road transport in his country, the General Manager of Pakistan National Railways replied: 'The question is not whether the roads are a problem for Pakistan railways. I am unable to cope with the load which is laid upon me. In the passenger sector, I am responsible for 50% of the traffic yet the demand is 20% more than that. In the freight sector, the figures are similar. I do not have the equipment to carry the demand. Road transport, therefore, is not a problem for me.'[6]

Throughout the interview, the manager frequently used the first person. In so doing, he presented himself as the embodiment of the railway company. Note also the way in which he showed his production orientation both by denying the significance of competition and in the choice of words he used to describe his problems.

Do you agree with the manager's belief that the best thing to do when faced with excessive demand is to concentrate on achieving the greatest output?

2.4.3 Marketing definition

The many aspects of marketing can be brought together in the following definition:

> **Marketing is the process of identifying, anticipating, influencing and supplying customer requirements efficiently and profitably.**

In the next sections, we shall examine each element in turn.

Identifying customer requirements

Market research includes finding out about markets, customers and their requirements. For example, the firm benefits from knowing the location of its customers and potential customers as well as other information such as their tastes, buying habits and consumption of competitors' goods and services. Market research information is used by both research and development and design functions to create successful products as well as by market planners to provide forecasts of demand.

Incorporating the 'voice' of the customer has become increasingly important in surviving in competitive environments. One method of involving customers in design which has gathered ground in recent years is quality function deployment.[7] QFD aims to relate the features valued by the customer to the factors to be considered in making a product work. Clearly different customers attach different values to product attributes. In designing a car, for example, attention may be focused on doors. Customers may recognise the value of those that are easy to open and close, those that provide extra side impact protection, those which carry features such as electric windows. The balance among these could be the subject of a survey.

Meanwhile, designers may explore different approaches to door design which offer the attributes identified among customers. QFD establishes specific measures for combinations of these engineering characteristics. Some will score highly on one dimension but not well on others. Electric windows may be valued for their convenience but the presence of the motor within the door increases its weight and makes it less easy to open and close. They also put up the costs of materials and assembly.

QFD then brings the preferred attributes and engineering characteristics together in a planning matrix to point the way towards optimal design selection. The method is covered in more detail in Chapter 17.

Anticipating customer requirements: the product life cycle

Anticipation is the province of market forecasting in which, by methods such as projection of historic trends, an organisation seeks to be ready for change.

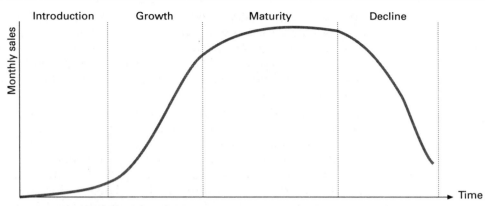

Figure 2.5 The product life cycle

Attention could be paid to annual growth rates or seasonal fluctuations in demand for current products or, with rather more difficulty, new products.

Marketers often use the *product life cycle* (PLC) for describing the way the fortunes of individual products change as time passes (Figure 2.5). Used in the right way, the PLC is a tool giving valuable insight into planning and strategy formulation, as we shall see in Chapter 4. It also aids communication among managers when discussing plans.

Many products go through a cycle, after their introduction to the market, of growth, stability and subsequent decline. The PLC is a representation of such a sequence. In our version, four phases can be identified, as in Figure 2.5. The PLC is a time series model representing the volume of sales after the product's introduction. What happens to a new product? In the initial stages, the business has to make potential customers aware of the product, explaining to them the way it is used and when or where it is to be supplied and establishing effective channels of distribution. Growth, therefore, is slow.

After this *introduction* phase, if successful, growth picks up. In the *growth* phase, the business begins to recoup its investment in development and the production system will be working at its planned capacity. Success, however, attracts competition and rivals will begin to take a share of the market. The business will need to continue its selling efforts to defend market share. Later, the sales rate begins to slow as the market enters its *maturity* phase. During this time several factors contribute to stabilisation of sales: it may be that most potential customers have bought the product and confine themselves to replacement purchases; customers may tire of whatever features the product has to offer; it may be that there is a gradual shift towards alternatives satisfying their needs in better ways. Finally, the product goes into *decline*. Competitors gradually drop out as sales fall and the residue of demand is shared among the remaining firms.

Limits of the PLC model

We shall see in Chapter 4 how operations policies should be deliberately changed to match stages of the life cycle. It is sufficient to note here that while the model gives a basic general view of market behaviour it has its weaknesses:

- The PLC is a generalised model that does not always apply. The sales of some basic products, such as domestic piped water, hardly change decade by decade and variations depend much more on weather and (to a lesser extent) price than any underlying trend towards water going out of fashion! Other products have a long history – Beecham's Powders, sold for more than 100 years, are 'Still going strong'.

- The life spans of products within industries may be changing. We have already looked at the example of General Motors' introduction of annual styling changes. Eventually, the customers began to see such relaunches as wasteful. Manufacturers increased the periods between model changes, especially as the costs of new model development rose rapidly. Recently, however, competition has intensified and new computer-aided design processes have cut the cost of model changes. The trend in the European automobile industry is once again towards shorter periods between new launches.

- The PLC is simply a *descriptive* model, that is a summary of the way many products turn out. This raises two points of caution. First, it is not a forecasting tool; the preceding paragraphs suggest two reasons for this. Second, it not be treated as *prescriptive*, that is being a statement of the way markets ought to behave. A marketing manager, then, should only use the PLC for thinking about the policy issues at various stages of a product's life.

2.4.4 Linking the PLC to operations and finance

To link the PLC to the operations and finance functions, we must take the time line back into the development phase. This is because spending starts well before sales begin; the development period can extend to several years. Products require cash investment, not only for product and process development but also for the initial marketing activity. Figure 2.6 presents both sales revenue and total cash flow throughout this extended period. At first, cash is spent on development costs with no balancing revenue. Recovery only begins after sales revenue comes in. When the cash line crosses the zero axis, the project has recovered all its

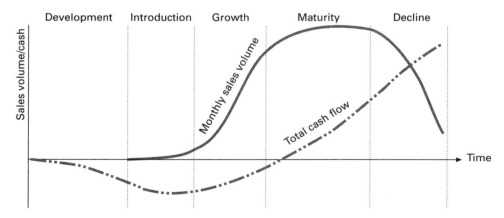

Figure 2.6 Cash flow during the PLC

initial expenditure. This is the *project break-even point*. For example, in new pharmaceutical products, break-even comes eight or more years from start-up. After this point, revenues exceed costs and the business begins to make a profit.

The operations manager must also be aware of the general form of the PLC, while avoiding using it on its own as a predictive tool. For instance, the rate of required output gradually builds up during the introduction phase. Then, during growth, the operations function must ensure output increases quickly. At maturity, extra capacity is no longer required and the operations manager must ensure that the capacity investment programme is slowed down.

Influencing customer requirements: the communications mix

Influencing customers is the third part of the marketing definition. To achieve this, marketers think in terms of the communications mix, as follows:

Advertising

This has many purposes depending on whether a product is well known or is being introduced for the first time. In the former case, the idea may be to persuade a customer to consume more and then repeat the purchase; in the latter, the advertisement may focus on product information and persuading someone to try it. Marketing managers have to choose the amount to spend on advertising, its pattern and intensity, the media to be used and the message to be conveyed. Plans in this area must be taken into account operating implications. Increased demand would be worthless without the ability to supply. Benefits may flow from timing advertising to boost demand during slack periods, especially where they coincide with a known pattern such as the seasons.

Public relations

PR usually refers to communications addressed to a wider audience than just customers and markets, for example, the safety assurances continually stressed by the nuclear industry. Yet, PR can affect sales by giving general support to the image of a supplier.

Promotion

Promotion is the range of activities and product features giving that last little 'push' in achieving a sale. In some goods, packaging may be an important feature of the product's image as well as contributing to its value in use. Luxurious wrappings aid image building. For services, the working environment has a significant influence on customers: consider how you compare different greengrocers' shops. Promotional campaigns may affect sales in the short term and, hence, the operations function.

Selling

Personal selling is a significant feature of influencing customers. This is especially true where the sale involves a complex bundle of goods and service. Good children's shoe shops, such as Clark's, measure feet as a matter of course; this involves selling and providing service simultaneously. This close relationship of selling and the service operations is something we shall return to in Chapter 3.

Supplying customer requirements

In order to supply products to customers organisations face two types of decision:

Channels of distribution

The range of available channels is very wide. They vary from the simplest 'direct to the consumer' through to involving several intermediate stages such as distributors or international agencies. The selection of channel will depend on the scale and location of the supplier and the number of final customers. For example, national newspapers seek to have as short a time as possible from printing to sales at a large number of outlets. New technology allows for printing at several locations using page settings distributed electronically. The distribution system from the print works relies on major contractors, such as TNT, to deliver to wholesalers who then break down the loads and distribute them locally. Distribution is, of course, the operation function of the transport companies. The pattern of the complete network emerges from a complex interaction of decisions among many companies.

Management of channels

Having selected broad patterns of distribution, managers are concerned with questions such as: detailed process design including warehouse layout and equipment as well as choices of vehicle sizes and routes; the levels of stock to keep within the distribution channel and how to combine it with the appropriate level of service. The service level decision lies at the interface of marketing and operations.

Balancing stocks and service in distribution channels

One way to regard the interface between operations and sales is to see the functions separated by the buffer of finished goods stock. This is the relationship in the upper part of Figure 2.7. The production system is isolated from variations in the market by the finished goods stock and the sales department is engaged in the boundary spanning between the firm and the market. The solid arrows suggest the flows of goods and the dotted arrows are orders passing from sales to the stock warehouse and from the stock warehouse to the production system.

The problem for operations managers here is that the only information received about customer demand is through the stock information. For sales, the problem is the lack of direct knowledge about operating performance or plans. Stock levels of finished goods can be optimised under this system, as shown in Chapter 15, but a much greater improvement is available if the two functions share information directly on both current activities and on forecasts and plans for the future. This extra communication link is shown in the lower half of Figure 2.7. Such integration allows the sales and marketing function to understand the consequences of demand changes for the bundle of goods and service and hence work with the operations function to satisfy them.

The marketing mix

The marketing mix was referred to briefly in the discussion of General Motors. It consists of the various factors for marketing managers to consider in successfully

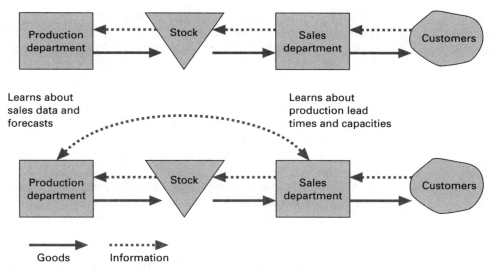

Figure 2.7 Using information to manage flows in distribution channel

carrying out their function. Each has interactions with and implications for operational decisions.

The marketing mix of any one company is a unique balance of four elements, the first two of which we have only looked at in passing. The mix is often called the *4 Ps*:

- *Product* – the bundle of goods and service which is offered to the customer.
- *Price* – sometimes the initial purchase price may be stressed but the costs of ownership, from running expenses to finance costs, are also often relevant.
- *Place* – the place at which the bundle is offered.
- *Promotion* – the publicity, advertising and final selling effort.

Exercise 2.3   Compare Shouldice Hospital's marketing mix with that of its competitors.

We have already discussed the last two of these items. We shall now, therefore, investigate product and price.

2.4.5 The product and the customer

Fundamentally, the enterprise exploits its chosen markets through matching its offering to market needs. The way this is to be achieved strongly effects the links between operations and marketing. Markets are composed of individual buyers, whether they act on their own behalf or buy for other organisations. Each demands a different bundle. To take a simple example, both my father and I like a certain brand of beer. Yet he wants to buy it in his club and I in mine. Reaching these two customers requires a variation in the marketing mix, this time on the place dimension.

How to respond to the individual needs of customers depends on many factors from competition to technology. To give each customer a unique service is expensive; to offer no variety leads to failure. Take the example of milk.

The approach of milk producers for many years was to support dairy farmers by minimising the costs of getting the product to the consumer. This meant that processing, from pasteurisation to bottling, was carried out at large plants before delivery. The need to deliver to the doorstep and collect empty bottles was another pressure for standardisation. The market was supplied with pints of full-cream milk. Advertising reinforced both the goodness of the product and its packaging – 'Drinka pinta milka day.' Variations in customer demand were largely ignored.

This policy is one of *market aggregation*, in which the widest possible range of customers is satisfied with offerings from a very limited product range. There is no attempt to match different offerings to identified groups. At the other end of the scale lies *customisation* in which each customer is supplied with a unique bundle. While possible for single contracts or expensive products such as individually designed houses or clothes, full customisation is not feasible for the average producer. In the middle lies *market segmentation* in which potential customers are separated into groups with common features such as needs, tastes, lifestyle and so on. The supplier then attempts to match product features to each different segment.

Market segmentation is a problem. Segments may be clearly defined or the boundaries may be unclear. *Product differentiation*, in either case, responds to the existence of segments by offering products with discernible, special features. These mark them out, both from others within the same range and from those of competitors. Clearly, the policy has a bearing on the operations system as differentiation implies extra costs. Further, the goods-plus-service bundle may be changed for each segment. There may be variations in quality, speed of service, time of service, design and so on. Branding, supported by image-building advertising, is a means of sustaining perceptions of differences in consumers' minds.

2.4.6 Price

Pricing has an indirect effect on the operations function in that changes in price usually have effects on demand and on the mix of products sold. The interaction between pricing and operational issues can be important in some service industries where demand fluctuations are difficult to cope with. Peak tariffs exist in many cases, from transport to telephones, holidays to haircuts. In such cases, the supplier is trying to optimise revenue by raising prices at the times when demand is excessive. There is some hope that some demand will be transferred to slack times.

Price is important in those markets that are sensitive to it. Generally, this occurs where product differentiation is low and customers have, or can obtain, enough information to compare one offering with another. Examples range from petrol, where filling stations are required to have prominent price displays, to standard package holidays. In each of these industries, however, suppliers attempt to raise perceptions of differentiation through branding and adding on extra items of service to the bundle.

In situations of price sensitivity, the operations manager may be encouraged to focus on reducing costs, thus enabling price to be cut further and market share increased. This is a wasteful policy in other situations.

2.5 Design, development and the operations function

2.5.1 Product and process design and development

Product design is another route along which the influence of the market reaches the operations system. We need to distinguish product design, which is the creation of a set of specifications for the product, from process design, which concerns how to create the product. In the supply of services, these two aspects are clearly related, as the process is part of the service offered. What is not so obvious is the intrinsic closeness of product and process design in manufacture. Not so long ago, designers would pass the product specification 'over the wall' to the process engineers who would then have the task of finding a way to make it. Modern ideas of parallel engineering and manufacturability recognise the waste that this can create. Disassembly, from nuclear plant to plastic vehicle parts, has also become a design issue in recent years.

Good design in business is about discovering what people want and taking steps to deliver it. Marketers know that satisfied customers tend to tell a few others; dissatisfied ones tell many more. The design process may not seem very costly in itself but it is a stage where up to 90% of the costs of supplying a product are decided. In other words, the design function has a very significant effect upon operations.

Design and development have so many features in common that many organisations do not separate them. Differences, if any, lie in the starting points of the process. Design starts from an expression of customer need, such as an architect being requested to design a health centre, a furniture designer working on a range of seats for a new airport lounge or a fashion designer creating some new clothes for the next season. Development, however, springs out of basic research where initial 'blue-sky' ideas are taken forward to practical application.

2.5.2 The design and development processes

Design and development decisions have much in common with other managerial decisions, including those in operations management. They can be set out in terms of a process, or methodology, which takes the decision making from an initial awareness of a question through to finished product. Stages of a typical development process are as follows.

1 Perceive opportunity or problem to be solved

Identification of opportunity or problem setting within which a solution is to be found. Sometimes an opportunity is quite clear ('I need a house built here'); other

BOX 2.1 **Filling the vacuum**

While James Dyson was vacuuming, he realised that the bag cleaner had stopped working. Imagining the bag to be full, he changed it but was disappointed that, after a short time, the cleaner again lost suction. Having seen large cyclone air cleaners in saw mills, he began thinking about applying the idea. He felt that, if he could make his idea work, there would be a strong demand. Stuck within the paradigm of blowing air through a filter of declining efficiency, the industry offered little choice.

After five years, Dyson cleaners had come to dominate the market. They had taken more than half of European sales, which themselves had grown substantially. By 2002 Dyson cleaners worth more than £2 billion had been sold.[8]

times there may be unease about a current problem situation ('Our products don't seem to be as good as those of our competitor'). A good example of the latter is given in Box 2.1. Dyson, already an inventor, was frustrated about the status quo and saw a way to make things better.

2 Develop working brief

The problem identification leads on to the brief or specification, which sets out what is required. For design carried out by a third party, there will be an agreement between the designer and client about what is required.

3 Generate and compare alternatives

Given time, a range of alternatives will be created and investigated. These may be candidates for the final product. This phase involves divergent thinking, with the aim of studying as many alternatives as practicable. Developers' experience and skill will be backed by basic research studies.

4 Select one or more ideas with potential

Proposals are gradually reduced in number by a process of selection, which may involve the client. Although they may have issued a detailed brief, clients often prefer to make choices from a limited range presented to them. This is true where outcomes are uncertain: they could be highly innovative or depend on taste and aesthetics. Selection should also consider the costs and capability of manufacturing.

5 Prototype and trial manufacture

The success of any design may not be apparent until a product has actually been produced. Prototypes have various purposes:

- They can be in the form of scale models to display in three dimensions the relationships between components and to make sure they all fit. In the design of a major power plant, for example, staff work with carefully constructed scale models to ensure that the work of different groups fits together well.

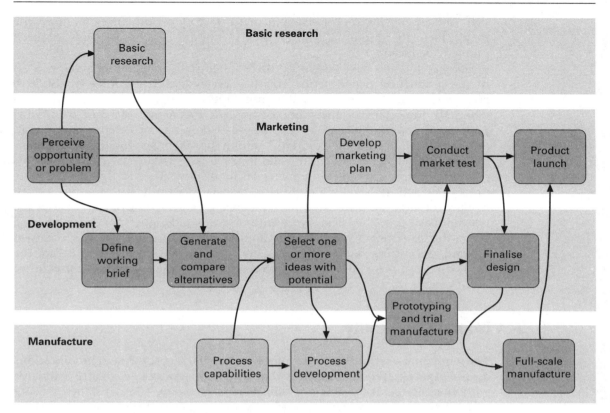

Figure 2.8 Links among business functions during product development

- They can be used to test performance before resources are invested in full-scale production. Aircraft are always tested in prototype form before production lines are equipped with expensive jigs and tools.

- They can test client or market reaction to include not only their aesthetic preferences but also questions of safety and reliability.

6 Finalise design and proceed to manufacture and product launch

The design brief may be satisfied once the completed design is handed over to the client. In other cases, the designer is required to supervise the implementation of the design (an architect supervises construction from the design point of view) or continue involvement with adaptations in the light of changing circumstances.

Figure 2.8 sets out these steps as a process model overlaid on a map of the four functions or departments involved. In addition to the steps listed above (emphasised in darker tint), the map includes elements such as basic research, marketing planning and so on. When looked at this way, we can see how the development process involves integration and linkage among departments at many points in its progress.

2.5.3 The design–production sequence

Although not shown in Figure 2.8, the design and development methodology is iterative. This means that it may be necessary to return to earlier stages in the light of later experience. For example, unsatisfactory performance of a prototype may lead to the immortal phrase, 'Back to the drawing board!' How are such problems reduced?

Many companies have developed their design staff from among qualified staff in the production departments. This has advantages in ensuring an intuitive acceptance among designers of the limitations of production processes. This is especially important in the jobbing shop. At the Alenia Marconi plant near Portsmouth, some 850 employees make a wide range of defence equipment, more than half of which is exported.[9] Among the 100 or so products, annual output ranges from 1,000 guided missiles to three large radar sets. To improve this complex, customised operation, managers broke down the variety into 132 basic processes. Each has a set of design tasks associated with it. For example, a team working on tank simulators has highly skilled people capable of carrying out the relevant basic processes. They work with one or two designers. At the end of one order, the team moves on to the next similar one. In this way, learning is carried forward, permitting higher efficiency and quicker delivery. Long gone are the days when completed designs were passed from the office with the instructions, 'Here you are. Make that!'

2.5.4 Manufacturability

The sequential relationship is one of the causes of the costly design modifications as, for example, production finds that it cannot produce to quality standards without a high rate of rejects. Stressing *manufacturability*,[10] the capability of being manufactured, is a key factor in finding a solution. Apart from technical analysis of production issues, however, the dominance of design should be reduced. Rather than design serving customers through the marketing function, it may be better to see design serving production that in turn serves marketing.

The problem is not confined to manufacturing. For example, in civil engineering, it has been argued[11] that attention to 'constructibility' and value engineering typically yields construction cost savings of 10 to 20 times the costs of the extra design input. In other cases, design difficulties lead to construction delays leading to late revenue streams. The Channel Tunnel project was delayed by changing specifications during the construction phase. Before operating licences were granted, the fire in King's Cross underground station led to the British and French governments changing the safety standards. Particularly affected was the design of passenger rolling stock. In November 1996, a serious fire in one of the tunnels meant its closure for months. This again led to changes in design standards, huge expenditure to modify shuttle wagons and a setback in the growth of business. Although 7 million people used the facility in 1997, this figure represented a fall in market share of some 2%.[12]

2.5.5 Improvements to design–production relationships

In contrast to the traditional design–production link, the production function can be seen as imposing a constraint upon what technologists and designers would wish to produce and marketers would wish to sell. In the production area,

BOX 2.2 **Manufacturability of milk cartons**

Cardboard milk cartons have advantages over other packaging methods yet these advantages would be forgotten by the consumer during the daily struggle between weak fingers and carton tops which never seem to tear. Suddenly the milk gushes out down your suit and you wonder how it is it that such a design failure ever reached the shelves.

In spite of the problem of opening, the cardboard carton has strong advantages over its rivals. Milk turns sour more quickly when exposed to light. The opacity of the cartons coupled with few questions over their disposability mean that they easily beat glass or plastic bottles for supermarket distribution. In addition, their rectangular form yields economy in transport and display. Cardboard is easier to print on than plastic or glass so there are better opportunities for the display of promotional messages and so on.

The problem of opening stems from the need to line the cardboard with thin polythene. The cardboard supports the polythene yet must tear easily enough, and bring the polythene with it, to form the spout. Some boxes work better than others do; those with the 'gable top' cause less difficulty than the 'bricks'. More than 40 billion of the former are used each year.

Manufacturers have tried various designs, including openers similar to those found on soft drinks cans. It has proved difficult to combine, within acceptable cost, ease of opening with reliability of seal in transit. Tetrapak, the market leader, has met customer resistance to covering the extra cost. Easycarton Limited, by way of contrast, has developed a polythene ring pull for the gable top that can be fitted at very low cost.[13]

with its usually clear cost structures, the tensions between customer quality perceptions and costs can be felt acutely. Yet, one of the functions of good design must be manufacturability. The example of the milk carton (see Box 2.2) shows the problems created by a market demand for an improved design that cannot be supplied using existing materials and processes.

DFMA (Design for manufacturability and assembly) is an example of parallel, or concurrent, design moving away from reliance on the traditional sequential approach. It focuses on improving both component manufacture and assembly through:

- simplifying designs
- reducing the number of components
- using standard components
- sharing components among several products
- speeding processes through new forms of fixing and finishing.

More generally, *parallel design* uses computer graphics to enable a range of experts from different departments to work together on design projects. The software allows proposed design changes to be evaluated very quickly and, by the time the design is complete, a manufacturing specification is already available, complete with schedules and costs. Not only is the total development time reduced but many expensive prototypes can be avoided.

Another modern development, *design for disassembly*, brings recycling issues into the original design. One problem with the use of plastics in cars, for example, is the range of applications within the car and the corresponding detailed variations in choice of materials. This can make recycling difficult. Studies are aiming at reducing this variety so that all the plastic material can be recycled. Other studies of assembly processes seek to avoid the use of glues and hidden screws to aid disassembly.

2.5.6 Assessing outcomes

The assessment of an innovation or design will be made according to company criteria. These usually include:

- *Innovation and engineering.* How valuable are the technical aspects of the new product? What contributions will they make to company success?
- *Manufacturability.* What are the operations implications of the new product? How much change is required? Is the product compatible with existing lines? Will manufacturing costs be made higher than the added value to be gained in the market place?
- *Marketing.* How does the new product gain competitive edge in the market place? Does it offer advantages that customers are willing to pay for?

Different firms will have different mixes of such questions. One product, which had high innovative and engineering content and was capable of being manufactured, is the Concorde supersonic aircraft. Its relative failure came from the unwillingness of customers to pay such premium prices for the added benefit of high-speed travel. Box 2.2 showed another example where production is possible but not at a price acceptable in the market place.

2.6 Finance and the operations function

As outlined in Table 2.1, the links between the finance function and operations consist of the provision of working capital and a contribution to both planning and control through the budgeting process. The eventual survival of all organisations, whatever their sector, depends on their *stewardship*, that is how well they have acquired, allocated and controlled the funds to which they are entitled. Cash is not only a necessary ingredient to many transactions in which the organisation is involved but it also forms a useful common denominator in evaluation of performance. In other words, the measuring stick has a single scale. For example, we shall see throughout this book how comparisons between different operations policies are based principally on their financial outcomes. Overemphasis on the financial measures, however, can lead to problems; we shall note the difference between a financial and strategic approach later in this chapter.

Central to the interaction between finance and operations is the budget. In the following sections, we shall illustrate the different types of budget, operating and capital, and their use within the organisation.

Table 2.2 Operating budget and outcomes for FFC

Farndon Forge Company
Operating budget for 2005

£000

	Budgeted	Actual	Variance	
			Favourable	Unfavourable
Sales income	1,300	1,380	80	
Raw materials	315	325		10
Direct labour costs	340	319	21	
Indirect labour	220	227		7
Equipment maintenance and consumables	70	90		20
Training	40	40		
Factory overhead	112	118		6
Total costs	1,097	1,119		22
Operating profit	203	261	58	

2.6.1 The operating budget

A budget is a formal projection of performance set out in financial terms. The operating budget covers a period of up to a year and is valuable to the manager because it not only incorporates the plan but it provides an objective measure against which outcomes can be assessed.

Budgets are prepared for operations activities according to whatever processes are involved. They may start from estimates of demand during the next period. In a simple case, such as the annual budget for Farndon Forge Company (see Table 2.2), the costs are broken down into categories representing those of various systems such as raw materials supplies, direct labour and so on. Following a hierarchy of systems, these costs can, in turn, be separated into further categories, for instance factory overhead can be divided into items covering heating and lighting, rates, maintenance and so on.

The other means of division useful for operational managers is to express the annual plan as a set of monthly, or even weekly, budgets. These enable the timing of control to be reasonably close to the activities and events being monitored.

Managers exercise control when comparing actual figures with the budget. They focus their attention on differences known as *budget variances*. Table 2.2 shows how the outcomes of FFC's year indicate both overspending and underspending, that is favourable and unfavourable variances. Sales revenue was higher than planned, but so were the costs. Possibly because of higher production levels, there were increases in most items. The exceptions were direct labour where there was a favourable variance which may have resulted from increased efficiency or lower than expected hourly payments. Further cost analysis, especially within the context of monthly budgets, would enable the reasons to be pinpointed more closely.

One of the weaknesses of the type of budget set out in Table 2.2 is that many of the variances arise because of changing output levels. This means they do not arise from the skill, or fault, of the operating managers. To overcome this problem, flexible budgets, based on standard costs, are often used. To understand the basis of flexible budgeting, we must first distinguish between direct and indirect costs.

2.6.2 Direct and indirect costs

Products to be supplied incur *direct* and *indirect* costs. In manufacturing, direct costs are those, such as item-by-item component purchase costs, which can be considered as being directly part of each item being manufactured. The labour used in assembly can also be measured and seen as a direct cost. Indirect costs, by the same token, cannot be attributed to each individual item of production; examples include heating, administration, training and auditing costs. These are often budgeted as *overheads*, although, for the purposes of working out total costs of each item, accountants in most companies derive methods to share out the overheads among all produced items.

Service organisations also have difficulties in establishing the cost base. A solicitor who charges a client £75 for a half-hour interview is not only recovering the cost of her own time but also having to charge for the firm's overheads, which include administration, premises, insurance and so on. In all these instances, there will also be an element of profit.

As sales increase, indirect costs remain unchanged while direct costs rise in proportion. It can be said that indirect costs are a function of time while direct costs are a function of volume. We can speak of rent, building maintenance, general lighting and training budgets in terms of pounds per year. For direct costs, we can think of costs of components per item and we can calculate the cost of direct labour or process energy from basic measurements.

2.6.3 The flexible budget

Standard costs separate the volume effect from the other factors making up the budget variance. For example, in the case shown in Table 2.3, the Farndon Forge

Table 2.3 Operating budget and outcomes for FFC using standard costs

Farndon Forge Company
Operating budget for 2005

£000

	Actual	Standard	Variance	
			Favourable	Unfavourable
Sales income	1,380			
Raw materials	325	334	9	
Direct labour costs	319	361	42	
Indirect labour	227			
Equipment maintenance and consumables	90	74		16
Training	40			
Factory overhead	118			
Total costs	1,119			
Operating profit	261			

Company will recognise that, for each pound of sales revenue, the budget allows for 315/1300 or £0.24 to be spent on raw materials. Therefore, if an item sells for £1,000, the standard cost of its material is £240.

The flexible budget adjusts for changes in volume by recalculating the budgeted direct costs. For example, if sales revenue at FFC were higher than the budget, assumed in this simple example to result from increased volume of sales, then the amount spent on raw materials would be expected to rise in proportion. In this case, the budgeted cost of raw materials is adjusted, in proportion to output, to £334,000. Table 2.3 outlines how the direct costs could be analysed. The only variances now presented are those arising from changes in the methods of operations management rather than from the change in the total volume of output.

Note how the variances now highlight the following:

- extra spent on maintaining equipment or supplying consumables such as grinding discs or welding rods
- better than expected use of direct labour
- lower than expected cost of materials.

The first two points in the list confirm, with different figures, the impression gained from the fixed budget comparison. The third, in contrast, tells a different story about raw materials. There were savings per unit of output, indicating that buying was more effective or there was less waste in the manufacturing process.

In this simple example, we have not adjusted indirect costs. There are methods of adjusting overhead allocations, but these are beyond our scope. Furthermore, we should note that the variances calculated in the two methods do not match. In the first case, we are measuring *total* variance, while in the second we are measuring *operating* variance.

2.6.4 Break-even analysis

Budgets are not simply tools for control after the event. As we shall see in Chapter 4, the budgeting procedure is part of the planning process, designed to ensure that profit is a forethought of active managers rather than an afterthought discovered after the books have been added up. The notion of dividing costs into *variable*, or direct, and *fixed*, or indirect, costs has an important application in break-even analysis. Often called *cost-volume-profit* analysis, the technique is used to look for the *break-even point* of output at which the firm makes neither a profit nor a loss. For sales below the break-even point, there is a loss; above break-even, a profit is made.

A graphical representation of costs and revenues at various output levels is shown in Figure 2.9. The firm is selling its products at £500 per unit. The break-even point corresponds to the intersection of the revenue and total cost lines, in this case at an output of 10,000 units worth £5 million. At outputs below the break-even point, total costs exceed revenues. Above break-even, revenues exceed costs. The shaded areas represent the loss or profit obtained.

Naturally, a firm will budget to operate above the break-even point. Changes in output, prices and revenues will affect the situation and can be plotted on

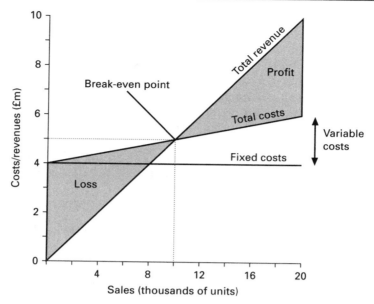

Figure 2.9 Break-even chart

charts. We shall not go into a detailed graphical analysis here. Clearly, if the firm is budgeted to operate close to the break-even point then small shifts may cause it to slip into loss. The *margin of safety* is a measure of how far the output is above the break-even point:

$$Margin\ of\ safety = \frac{Budgeted\ output - Break\text{-}even\ output}{Budgeted\ output} \times 100\%$$

The margin of safety is a measure of the risk faced by operations managers if costs or revenues were to change.

2.6.5 Patterns of fixed and variable costs

As part of their strategic planning process, organisations can choose between different patterns of fixed and variable costs to achieve the same outputs. For example, an investment in robots to replace labour on an assembly line changes that part of the work from a variable, direct labour, to a fixed cost.

Figure 2.10 shows a comparison between two possibilities for the business in Figure 2.9. For a budgeted output of, say, 15,000 units, both firms earn the same profit. The budgeted output is the point BO on the output scale in each case. The low fixed costs of Firm A mean that it operates with a high margin of safety (55%) and its profits are little affected by small changes in output. Firm B, however, operates closer to its break-even point (its margin of safety is 33%) and its profits are more sensitive to changes in volume of output. If its business is good, with sales above budgeted levels, then Firm B would do better than A since its profits

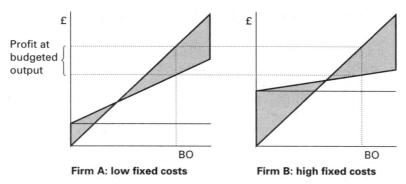

Figure 2.10 Break-even charts for firms with different cost structures

expand more quickly. Otherwise, B would do worse if sales were weak. Firm B is said to have higher *operational gearing* than Firm A.

With high fixed costs, newspaper managers experience continual pressure to maintain market share through promotions of all kinds.

Exercise 2.4

In 2001, Océ, the Dutch printing and copying equipment group, launched the first short-run newspaper production site. Its aim was to take a significant share of the $1 million daily sales of overseas business newspapers by opening between 30 and 50 sites worldwide. The first opened in London, followed by Copenhagen, New York, Johannesburg and Melbourne. The approach challenged the prevailing methods.

The first contract was with the Swiss national newspaper, *Neue Züricher Zeitung (NZZ)*, previously printed in Frankfurt and carried by lorry to London in about ten hours. Early morning readership was lost. By printing in London, the time to reach the reader fell to three hours, so a 1 am production could be read at breakfast. Further afield, deliveries of small batches of many titles are by air. This is how the *Financial Times* has a global circulation from its production sites in London and Frankfurt. Overseas readers pay premium prices for newspapers.

According to Océ, its innovation allows for profitable production from a run of 100, as opposed to the 5,000 required with traditional methods. Printing costs about $1.50 per copy, compared with the few cents by traditional lithography. Data are sent electronically to the $1.1 million Series 8000 printing machine. It can print 400 copies of a 48-page paper per hour and can change from one title to another in a few moments. The output has the look and feel of the conventional product.

When sold in its local market, a newspaper's sales revenue is about half the cover price. This is roughly matched by the advertising income. The rest of the customer's payment goes to distributors, with higher overseas prices reflecting almost the extra costs involved.

Identify which of the operating costs and revenues of a newspaper are fixed and variable. Use sketches of break-even charts to illustrate the effects of the innovation introduced by Océ.[14]

2.6.6 **Advantages and drawbacks of break-even analysis**

In common with other techniques discussed throughout this book, break-even analysis is not a universal solution. Its advantages are that it enables operations managers to understand the implications of different cost structures and perform analyses on them. The main drawback lies in the nature of the cost and revenue patterns themselves. Variable costs are not always linearly related to output as in the case of overtime payments for a few extra hours, shift premiums and changes in machine efficiency caused by running them away from their designed capacities. Similarly, fixed costs are often not truly fixed. Increased demand on a distribution system may require managers to rent or purchase extra warehousing space. In spite of these difficulties, the principle of identifying the behaviour of different costs remains a valid one. Operations managers, especially in those organisations with high fixed costs such as airlines, cinemas and car assembly plants, are very aware of the need to keep output well above the break-even point.

2.6.7 **The capital expenditure budget**

The capital expenditure budget is the result of decisions about the allocation of an organisation's capital resources. It is clear that many operational systems are based on huge amounts of invested capital and depend upon a continual stream of new investment if products and processes are to be kept up to date in terms of standards of efficiency and effectiveness. Examples of investments from the current business press include:

- The Post Office building a new £150 million international distribution centre near Heathrow Airport.
- Exxon annually spending £100 million with General Motors and Toyota to develop hydrogen and fuel cell technology.
- Gioma Grill buying 23 restaurants in the Netherlands and Switzerland for £15 million.
- Virgin trains' £600 million purchase of 53 tilting trains for the west coast route.

Since all involve new products and processes, they have considerable implications for the operations functions within the organisations.

The financial evaluation of a proposed investment should be made according to two broad criteria:

- Is the investment worth proceeding with?
- Is the investment the best of the alternatives which are presented to the company?

The first criterion requires a critical evaluation of the investment in terms of inputs and outputs during its life. The second, by way of contrast, compares the evaluation with all of the others on an agenda of possibilities. In circumstances where the amount of capital available to the organisation is limited, which is especially true in the public and voluntary sectors, there is a situation of capital rationing and projects may be selected according to rankings. Models of decision making under capital rationing are complex. We shall, in this chapter, concentrate on the framework for analysing individual investments and making simple comparisons.

2.6.8 Analysing investments: strategic and financial perspectives

The strategic perspective considers the relationship between the proposed use of funds and the objectives of the company and how they fit in with other developments in the long term. This broad approach is examined in Chapter 4.

The financial perspective considers the link between capital to be used, especially its cost, and the return to be made in terms of flows of funds and the risks associated with them. This perspective considers not only the question of whether an individual project is worth the investment it requires but it also takes into account whether the same funds can be better used on other schemes.

The two perspectives should be complementary, yet there is sometimes conflict. The strategic view may stress issues in the long-term development of the company and investment benefits which may not be easily measured in financial terms. The financial view, however, focuses on measurable values and possibly presents an over-rigid framework for comparison.

We can see the contrast between the two perspectives in the following example of a company setting up a joint venture in a foreign country:

The company, Elco, is considering a 50–50 joint venture with a foreign government to manufacture pharmaceutical products. Elco can make a broad estimate of the market size using data supplied by its partner. Its familiarity with the production technology enables it to estimate costs quite accurately. From this information, Elco can provide a broad picture of the likely financial return from the development. If this analysis shows a poor return, should Elco not go ahead? This is where the strategic perspective may conflict with the financial. There may be considerable benefits in the longer term which lie outside the basic financial analysis. They could include the opening up of further opportunities, the gaining of operating experience in a new territory or the restriction of the scope of rivals.

2.6.9 Financial comparisons

Methods of comparing proposed investments, when based on financial criteria, can be complex. Not only are the technical details of some of the techniques beyond the scope of this book, they are beyond the scope of many small and medium sized companies! We shall concern ourselves with an outline of four methods here. They are named after the measures they use, as follows:

- accounting rate of return (ARR)
- payback
- net present value (NPV)
- internal rate of return (IRR).

The simplest methods are ARR and payback, which are often used for quick calculations especially where the data can only be roughly estimated. NPV and IRR require analysis that is more careful and depend on at least some of the data being known with more confidence.

2.6.10 The accounting rate of return (ARR)

The most simple and unsophisticated approach to appraisal, the ARR method, is based on the following calculation:

$$ARR = \frac{Profit\ from\ investment}{Amount\ of\ investment} \times 100\%$$

As with all the methods, the ARR is compared with a target figure (say, 18%), which acts as a target level of return required. In addition, managers can compare proposals to rank them in order of the returns they offer.

Several difficulties with this formula lead to problems in applying the ARR. The most significant of these is the ignoring of the timing of the profits earned by the investment. Consider the two projects, A and B, in Table 2.4 Each requires an investment of £60,000; each produces the same profit; and, therefore, each produces the same ARR. *Profit after* depreciation means we assume that capital expenditure is fully depreciated as a charge against profits during the 5-year period covered by the table.

Clearly, each project earns the same total profit over the five years and it would seem that there would be little to choose between them. Yet, there is an important difference between the timing of the profits from the projects. Those from Project B come later and only exceed those from Project A in years 4 and 5.

Why would Project A be chosen? The answer lies in the time value associated with money. If it is possible to receive a given sum of money at two different future dates, then the earlier date will be preferred. Similarly, if one has to spend a given sum at a future date, a later date will be preferred. This brings out the weakness of the ARR measure. By treating all profits as being the same, irrespective of when they occur, the method ignores the time preferences of those involved in the decision.

Table 2.4 Profits from two projects, A and B

| | **Profit after depreciation** | |
| | | £000 |
Year	Project A	Project B
1	15	0
2	15	10
3	15	10
4	15	25
5	15	30
Total	75	75

Table 2.5 Profits from two projects, C and D

	Profit before depreciation	
		£000
Year	Project C	Project D
1	27	40
2	27	37
3	27	28
4	27	15
5	27	0
Total	135	120

2.6.11 The payback method

Investments in projects mean that money is 'tied up' in the projects until profits are earned to repay the investment. This is called the *opportunity cost* of the investment. Managers will recognise that early repayments of investments will enable them to re-use the money for others. The payback method recognises this argument. For example, consider Table 2.5, in which two projects, C and D, are set out. Each has an initial capital expenditure of £60,000 to purchase assets with a 5-year life.

Project C is the same as Project A in Table 2.4. However, in using the payback method, we table *profit before depreciation* as a measure of income. Each item in the profit column includes a contribution of £12,000 towards the original project cost. Taking cash flows is important, as we are as interested in the timing of all our income, including the repayment of capital.

Comparing the proposals, it can be seen that C (£135,000) earns more total cash returns than D (£120,000). In an ARR calculation, C would have a higher apparent return than D. Yet, would Project C always be chosen?

Suppose the management of the company sees a need for a quick payback on its investment. This may be because it is short of cash or it has a number of other competing projects in which it would invest were cash available. In such a case, Project D may be chosen. Overall, it reaches the target ARR and has the advantage of paying back the original investment more quickly. At the end of the second year, for instance, Project D will have paid back £77,000 whereas only £54,000 will have been returned by Project C.

We can formally compare the payback periods, that is the time it takes for the original cash outlay to come back. That of Project D is about $1^1/_2$ years, against $2^1/_4$ years for C. If we are worried about risk, we 'stick our necks out' for 27 months for C, yet only for 18 months for D. On this payback criterion, Project D will be selected.

2.6.12 Exclusivity and independence

Managers often find that projects such as C and D concern the same area of the business. For example, they could be alternative ways of changing the service delivery system to realise cost savings. Such pairs are said to be *operationally exclusive*, that is it would be impossible to carry out both projects. In other cases, they will be *operationally independent*. For example, one may be investment in new machinery and the other expenditure on opening up a market.

Although operationally independent, C and D may still be *financially exclusive* if they seek to use the same investment funds. If the organisation has access to plentiful financial resources, through bank loans for example, then this situation will not arise. Many, however, face *capital rationing* and have to choose between one project and the other. This brings out an advantage of the payback method: select the project with the shortest payback period, recycle the funds to the next shortest project and so on.

2.6.13 Discounted cash flow (DCF)

The ARR method concentrates on nominal returns on investments throughout the life of a project but ignores the timing of these returns. The payback method, by the same token, focuses its attention on the time it takes to recover the original expenditure but passes over the total profits during the life of the project.

The concept of discounted cash flow (DCF) goes some way to resolving these difficulties by recognising income over the life of a project while at the same time acknowledging the time value of money. DCF has two important features, cash flows and discounting.

Cash flows

Cash flows are used in the appraisals because they focus on liquidity of the enterprise, not its profitability. The timing of cash flows, for example those involved in buying land and plant at the start of a project, can be very different from the representation of these as depreciation charges in financial accounts.

The cash flows to be taken into account are all those future flows that arise because of the project. They include outgoings such as capital expenditure on the project and changes in income such as sales revenue. Changes in other costs, such as overheads, resulting from the project should also be considered but not those notional changes that arise solely from the methods of bookkeeping being used.

Discounting

Discounting assigns a higher value to cash flows that occur earlier. (See Box 2.3 to understand the principle.) Table 2.6 shows the present value of £1,000 at various times and discount rates. Using the 15% rate, £1,200 in eight years' time is worth £1200 × 0.327 = £392 now. This is less than £900 in 5 years (£447), illustrating the value we place on earlier money.

Combining cash flow and discounting, the concept of *discounted cash flow* (DCF) is used in the last two methods, net present value and internal rate of return.

BOX 2.3 **An explanation of discounting**

Imagine that you are taking part in the following hypothetical game.

You have been given £1,000. It is in a bank and is guaranteed to be yours in 1 year's time. How much is the money worth to you now? Would you take the host's offer of £990 now instead? It would be surprising if you would not. Would you accept £980 now? Probably yes. And so on . . . At the other end of the scale, you would not accept a rubber duck for the money. So the bank deposit is worth more than that.

Somewhere between £990 and the rubber duck, you come to an amount of cash that you think is worth exactly the same as the money in the bank. It may be £900. You have now discovered how to discount the value of future money to a present value. In assessing this discounted value, you have assessed what you could do with the money during the next 12 months and how much having it now is worth to you.

You are likely to get as many answers as there are individuals in the game. Each has a different way of valuing future cash flows, depending not only on the urgency of current needs but also on the size of the sums involved. For example, would you apply the same discounting ratio to £100 as to £1,000,000?

Within companies, DCF techniques are formalised so that standard discount rates are used. Table 2.6 illustrates the effect of discounting. It shows the present value of a sum of £1,000 were it made available at different times in the future. The discount rate of 15% is widely used, although some businesses look for 20% or even 25%.

Table 2.6 Present value of £1,000 at a range of discount rates

	Present value of £1,000		
Year	15% discount	20% discount	25% discount
0	1,000	1,000	1,000
1	870	833	800
2	756	694	640
3	658	579	512
4	572	482	410
5	497	402	328
6	432	335	262
7	376	279	210
8	327	233	168
9	284	194	134
10	247	162	107
15	123	65	35
20	61	26	12

Exercise 2.5

What is the most you would bet on one toss of a coin if the prize for the correct call were £1? Would you bet in the same proportion if the prize were £100; £10,000. Why?

What difference would it make if you knew there were to be ten tosses on which you could bet?

Table 2.7 NPV and IRR calculations

Cash flows from an 8-year project

£000

Year	Actual cash flow	Discounted at 15%	Discounted at 20%	Discounted at 25%
0	−800	−800	−800	−800
1	50	43	42	42
2	150	113	104	108
3	250	164	145	152
4	300	172	145	155
5	330	164	133	144
6	300	130	100	111
7	200	75	56	63
8	100	33	23	27
Total	880	94	−53	2

2.6.14 NPV and IRR methods

The net present value (NPV) is calculated by adding the discounted present values of all cash outflows and inflows using the company's target discount rate. If the NPV is positive, the project will yield a return on investment greater than the target rate and the project should be accepted. If it is negative, the project should be discarded.

Instead of the company deciding in advance on a discount rate, the IRR method calculates the discount rate implied by the project. The internal rate of return is the discount rate at which the NPV is zero. The example shown in Table 2.7 gives the main features of the process.

Table 2.7 presents the cash flows associated with an 8-year project. An investment of £800,000, spent entirely at the start, yields cash flows, which build up to year 5 and then decline to the end of the project's life in year 8. While the project yields a positive cash flow of £880,000 if the flows are not discounted, the application of discounting shows a different picture. The 15% discount rate plays down the value of the later cash inflows so the net present value of the project becomes £94,000. This is still a positive value but perhaps not large enough to justify going ahead. Errors in estimates may swallow up this figure.

The IRR calculation looks for the discount rate that yields a zero NPV. It proceeds as follows.

Starting without a defined target, take an initial guess of (say) 15% as the IRR and calculate its NPV. Repeat for other values until the NPV is near to zero. This is the best estimate of the IRR. In Table 2.7, the 15% discount rate yields a positive cash flow, while at 20% the flow is reversed to −53. This suggests a rate in between and the choice of 18% yields a NPV close to zero. The 18% is, therefore, the best estimate of the internal rate of return. Note that it would be unwise to calculate the IRR to fractional decimals. The accuracy of the forecasted data could rarely justify it.

Discount tables provide data for IRR calculations. Most leading spreadsheet packages enable NPV formulae to be inserted in worksheets. The tables in this chapter were produced using Microsoft Excel; NPV functions are available using *Insert/Function* or the f_x button.

2.6.15 Comparison of appraisal methods

Of the techniques demonstrated here, those based on the concept of discounting make the most sophisticated attempt to incorporate the time value of money into evaluation. Discounting builds in some allowances for uncertainty as well as recognition that individuals inherently prefer income now rather that in the future.

There are difficulties with the application of such sophisticated procedures. Their outcomes require both careful estimates of cash flows in an uncertain future and the selection of an appropriate discount rate. In response to uncertainty, sensitivity analysis helps to check whether possible changes in future cash flows have a great impact on the outcome of the calculation. Small and medium sized firms, however, do not use discounting methods but tend to rely on a combined view of the accounting rate of return and an estimate of the payback period.

BOX 2.4 Sensitivity analysis of EuroDisney investment

The Disneyland theme park near Paris was planned to open in 1992. While the Walt Disney Corporation invested most of the capital, external participation was invited through a share offering in France in 1989.

The prospectus accompanying the share sale showed a projected IRR of 13.3% for the first 25 years of operation. Clearly, this figure came from a combination of many estimates. The prospectus, however, went further than this. It was unusual in showing the outcomes of sensitivity analysis of these estimates. The company identified the main areas where it could not be confident in its forecasts and suggested low and high estimates of them. For each case, it calculated the effect on the IRR.

Parameter	Possible effect on IRR (%)
Attendances	12.7–13.8
Customer spending	12.3–14.1
Property income	13.0–13.5
Inflation	11.2–15.3
Interest	13.2–13.3
Residual value after 25 years	13.1–13.4

The data helped potential investors to reach their own conclusions about the risks involved in buying shares. They could see, for example, that the project's prospects were particularly sensitive to different inflation assumptions yet not at all sensitive to interest rates. Therefore, a prudent investor would include a view of inflation in determining whether or not to buy the shares.

This example also provides a warning about forecasting. In its early years, the park performed much worse than the forecasts had suggested. Although it was located within a day's drive of some 50 million people, the crowds were not attracted by the idea of a theme park in a cool climate. At the same time, falling fares on the Florida routes made Disneyworld a more attractive destination.

2.6.16 Sensitivity analysis

It is good management practice to test the outcomes of complex calculations by changing assumptions and studying their implications. The changed parameters may represent difficulties with estimating size of cash flows (uncertainty) or actual delays in the implementation of a project (risk). Delayed timing of incurred cash flows caused, for example, by unexpected difficulties during the start-up phase may seriously reduce the NPV of a project. Consider the case of EuroDisney shown in Box 2.4.

✔ Quick check-up

Can you:

☐ Define the terms:
 – system
 – holism
 – environment
 – boundary.
☐ Give an example of a structural and a process model.
☐ Illustrate types of market orientation.
☐ Define marketing.
☐ Sketch the product like cycle; summarise its limitations.
☐ Plot the flow of cash at different PLC stages.
☐ Name the elements of the marketing mix.
☐ Summarise the key stages of the development process.
☐ Give examples of manufacturability.
☐ Outline the principles of operating budgets and standard costs.
☐ Explain *break-even* point.
☐ Distinguish between:
 – ARR
 – payback
 – NPV
 – IRR

❓ Questions

Chapter review

2.1 Why have firms become market orientated? What does the concept mean for non-profit and public service organisations?

2.2 Explain the advantages and disadvantages of incorporating the discounting principle into investment appraisal.

2.3 What are standard costs and what benefits do they bring to budgeting in operations?

Application

2.4 What differences do you see in the market orientation of Shouldice Hospital and other medical services you know of?

2.5 Relate the experiences of Dr Shouldice in founding his hospital to issues in the design and development process.

Investigation

2.6 Produce a series of break-even charts to compare the production and supply of national newspapers. Note that there are occasional price wars and, in some promotions, copies are given away free.

2.7 Draw on a selection of case histories from the Design Council[15] to compare the origins and process of design innovation.

Improvements at IBM, Lexington

At the start of the 1980s the IBM typewriter plant at Lexington, Kentucky, faced problems of demand levelling off in a static market. There were 9 major competitors in 1979, growing to 30 by 1984 and 44 by 1986. Most were located in east Asia and competed on costs and quality.

In response, IBM invested $350 million during the period 1983–86 in order to become the lowest cost typewriter maker with its new product, the Quiet-Writer. The new line included keyboards and printers as well as related office machines.

As part of the new strategy, IBM streamlined the product line and improved productivity. For example, the keyboard of the QuietWriter was very similar to the one used on the IBM PC. They shared many components. Furthermore, the QuietWriter's printer became the letter-quality printer option for the PC.

Streamlining was not the only policy carried out during the three-year programme. About 300 robots and 200 minicomputers were installed. The number of parts suppliers was cut. Inspection was automated. Of the 700% improvement in productivity, however, about 200% came from automation and 500% from design for manufacturability. Cutting the number of parts and the number of suppliers was a decisive step towards streamlining the direct production activities and in removing much of the bureaucracy which had accumulated over the years.[16] The results of the new policy can be seen in the following figures.

Cost element	Before	After
Labour as % of cost	57%	23%
Material as % of cost	43%	77%
Direct labour per unit	7 hr	0.4 hr
Floor space (000 sq m)	400	200
Staff	7,500	2,000
Plant capacity per year	0.75 M	1.7 M
Different parts per unit	2,900	1,000
Average repairs per year	6	0
Number of suppliers	400	60
Time to produce product	?	2.5 hr

▶

Questions

1 Discuss the changes at IBM in terms of the linkages between operations and other functions of the business.

2 Using the figures presented in this chapter, show how graphical methods can be used to represent the themes set out in the case study.

Notes and references

1. Gummesson, E. (2001) 'Are you looking forward to your surgery?' *Managing Service Quality*, January 2001, pp.7–9; Shouldice Hernia Centre website http://www.shouldice.com, accessed 24 April 2001.
2. The systems message is expressed as follows:
   Little fleas have smaller fleas upon their backs to bite 'em,
   And smaller fleas have smaller fleas and so ad infinitum.
3. von Bertalanffy, Ludwig (1950) 'An outline of general systems theory', *The British Journal for the Philosophy of Science*, 1(2) Bertalanffy pioneered the search for GST. It is fair to say that the search for general principles has not been as successful as its pioneers may have wished.
4. Kast, F.E. and Rosenzweig, J.E. (1974) *Organisation and Management*, 2nd edition, Tokyo: McGraw-Hill Kogakusha, p.112.
5. Cannon, T. (1992) *Basic Marketing*, 3rd edition, London: Cassell, p.12.
6. Television interview conducted by Mark Tulley (1994) *Great Railway Journeys of the World*, BBC2, 17 February.
7. For more details, see Hauser, J.R. and Clausing, D. (1988) 'The house of quality', *Harvard Business Review*, 66(3) May–June, pp.63–73.
8. Dyson Appliances Ltd (2001), company website www.dyson.com, accessed April 2001; Design Council (2001) *Innovation Stories*, London: Design Council, www.designcouncil.org.uk/innovationstories/story_template.asp?prod_ID=603&search= accessed April 2001.
9. Marsh, P. (2001) 'How diversity can become a strength and a weakness', *Financial Times: Survey: Manufacturing Excellence*, 21 May.
10. Heidenreich, P. (1988) 'Designing for manufacturability', *Quality Progress*, May, pp.41–44.
11. McGeorge, J.F. (1988) 'Assuring quality in design engineering', *Journal of Management in Engineering*, 4(4), pp.350–62.
12. *Financial Times* (1996) 'Operator's shares dip while sea-going rivals gain', 20 November; AFX Europe (1998) 'Channel Tunnel 1997 business travel market share down vs 1996', 20 November.
13. Easycarton Limited (2001), company website http://www.easycarton.com/ accessed April 2001; Design Council (2001) *Innovation Stories: Easycarton Limited*, London: Design Council, www.designcouncil.org.uk/innovationstories/story_template.asp?prod_ID=5170&search= accessed April 2001.
14. Bickerton, I. (2001) 'Océ aims to revolutionise news printing', *Financial Times*, 24 May, p.17, www.oce.com/news/ accessed 29 May 2001.
15. You can access these at www.designcouncil.org.uk/innovationstories/
16. The description of IBM is based on Ernst, R.G. (1987) 'How to streamline operations', *The Journal of Business Strategy*, 8(2), pp.32–36.

CHAPTER 3

Technology and operations management

OBJECTIVES

When you have finished studying this chapter, you should be able to:

- Identify the main factors that influence the choice of operations processes.
- Show how customer involvement is the key difference between service provision and manufacture.
- Identify six service delivery patterns and explain why they are selected and changed.
- Identify the main features of the five basic systems of manufacture and isolated service.
- Outline hybrid systems, explaining why they are commonly found.
- Summarise the profiling approach to process selection.
- Sketch how the boundaries between production technologies are becoming blurred.
- Demonstrate the significance of Woodward's studies of socio-technical systems.

OPENING CASE

Flawless flooring from Amtico[1]

Maker of high-quality vinyl floorings, Amtico became an independent company in 1995 when its managers bought the business from Courtaulds for £49 million. Today its products lead the United Kingdom market, commanding a 30% price premium, and are in demand throughout the world. The 350 staff work on applications in both the luxury domestic sector and commercial sites where style must be combined with durability.

Having built its reputation over some 40 years, the company aims to be the most exciting flooring company in the world. Its extensive range, including vinyls that closely mimic natural materials, can be supplied in whatever combination a customer chooses. Patterns of sweeping curves or detailed mosaics are designed and cut using Amtico's CAD/CAM[2] technologies. Many customers visit the company's design studios across the world where, assisted by Amtico personnel, they create individual floors. The studios, which also act as regional headquarters, use CAD to finalise ideas and channel orders to the sales office. ▶

Amtico's policy of tailoring its products to customers' needs could only succeed if its manufacturing system copes with the variety of demand placed upon it. It makes its range of standard 300mm square tiles in batches according to anticipated demand. Then each order has to be cut precisely from these blanks, depending on the design. Service is very important in winning orders. Through reorganisation of production into cells, the lead time for these orders has fallen from three weeks to three days. Cells are groups of workers and machines that focus on a particular type of order. For instance, the 'Galaxy' cell offers quick turnaround for small floors for the residential market. It stands next to, and is controlled by, the sales office so that designers and producers work hand in hand.

3.1 Introduction

Amtico is one of many companies that have learned how to fulfil demand for individual products made from combinations of standard components. For this approach to work effectively at low cost, the *customisation* is delayed as long as possible in the supply chain. Therefore, most stages can work efficiently on large batches of standard components. Tailoring of goods or services to customers' different needs can occur in the distribution chain or at the output stage of the factory. Among the former, kitchen furniture is manufactured in standard units and fitted by installers who adapt them to the layout of the room. The customisation of cars, by the same token, with combinations of engines and trim, takes place within the assembly plant. In the case of Amtico, we see a combination of both. Staff work with customers in the studios to finalise product designs. Then, a special unit reporting to the sales office cuts the special tiles from standard blanks. We can envisage the plant as having a highly automated main production line mixing and forming tiles in batches of different patterns. The accent will be on streamlined efficiency. Then, finishing stages will handle the complexity of many varied customer orders, each being sorted and checked by hand.

Organisation of such operations proves very difficult for many businesses. The solution is to separate the process and organise them differently. Amtico places its main line within the production department but the Galaxy cell reports to sales. In this way, each unit specialises and can focus on the tasks it does best. But what makes the optimal organisation differ? The answer lies in the close relationship between process technology and organisation, the so-called *socio-technical* subsystem. We are not concerned here with the detailed analysis of the engineering aspects of each operation. Such studies lie in the domain of specialists, whether they are mining engineers, systems analysts, tailors or chefs. Our interests rest in the planning, organising and control of the processes as far as they form elements of the complete operations system. We shall start the chapter by outlining production systems and complete it by studying ways in which the technology affects the human organisation and vice versa.

3.2 Production system choices

3.2.1 Scale in manufacturing and service supply

The type of production used by a firm is decided by a variety of factors:

- Market demand in terms of quantity to be supplied, the places at which it is to be supplied, the range of different products required and the fluctuations in demand.
- Product design, including size, complexity and means of supply.
- Process technology for manufacture or service.
- Whatever system is already installed. While one may argue for an ideal match between the operations system and the items in the preceding list, the possibilities of change are limited and many organisations end with something of a mismatch. This issue can be investigated using *profiling*, shown later in the chapter.

The single most important variable effecting the organisation of production is scale. Large-scale production enables manufacturers to use plant dedicated to either one, or a limited range, of purposes. The production of large quantities enables plant and equipment designs to be tuned to achieve low costs for a given volume: this means they achieve *production economies of scale*. Examples of large-scale production are oil refining, paper making, bicycle assembly, newspaper printing and, among services, directory enquiries, banking and film processing.

Small-scale operations, often called *jobbing shops*, take business characterised by variety. While holding down costs remains important, such businesses achieve success by offering flexibility and producing a wide range of products to satisfy the needs of small and specialised sectors of the market. Examples of manufacturing jobbing are customised oil blending, printing of visiting cards, tailoring, bookbinding and, among services, medical treatment, bespoke training courses and television repairs.

3.2.2 Differences between service and manufacture

The key difference between service and manufacture lies in the degree of involvement of the customer directly in the service operation. As shown in Chapter 1, direct services are supplied in the presence of the customer, while isolated, or indirect, services are performed separately. The isolated service becomes more like manufacture and can be organised in a similar way.

Table 3.1 classifies operations according both to scale and to the degree of customer involvement. The basic focus is different. Direct services require that attention be paid both to interpersonal skills, that is an understanding of the needs of the customer in relation to the way the service is provided, and to some technical skills. Manufacturing and isolated service, in contrast, are not so concerned with personal interaction and depend more heavily on the technical skill in managing the production system. We shall look at each in turn, starting with services.

Table 3.1 Examples of scale in service and manufacturing operations

	Services direct to the customer emphasising interpersonal skills	Manufacturing or isolated service activities emphasising technical skills
Small scale	**Personal service:** legal advice, shoe repairs, gardening	**Jobbing:** building, *haute couture*, wedding cars
Large scale	**Mass service:** banking, buses, supermarkets	**Mass production:** car assembly, newspapers, pension management

3.3 Service system choices

3.3.1 Types of service process

We can think of service provision in terms of processes with distinct characteristics. Several authors[3] have identified four categories of services.

Professional service

Often regarded as the typical service operation, professional service describes those activities that are supplied in the presence of individual customers by trained personnel. Examples include doctors, counsellors, beauticians and individual music teachers.

Mass service

Pressed to reduce costs, mass services frequently try to replicate the supply of professional services on a large scale. They are carried out in the presence of groups or even crowds of customers. Examples include higher education, superstores and many aspects of broadcasting. Sometimes, however, service is best suited to the mass audience. The football match or rock concert are all the poorer without the crowd.

Service shop

The service shop is the means through which isolated service is made available to the customer. Each customer's needs are treated individually but the service takes place without the customer being present. Garages, some shoe repairers and estate agents operate in this mode.

Service factory

This is the service shop operating at large scale. The range of services available is standardised so that they can be offered, but not necessarily provided, by staff with limited specialised knowledge or skill. Much of the skilled supply activity of banks, post offices, large hotels and restaurants takes place away from the customer.

BOX 3.1 **Detailed attention to the process in large-scale service operations**

'The price has gone up again!'

A customer walks up to you in the shop, complaining that the price of a product is higher than it was last week. List the things you would say and do:

- *Listen to the complaint in a polite way.*
- *Offer to check the price.*
- *Explain the increase and suggest a cheaper alternative, if possible.*
- *Report to management if the customer has found an item cheaper elsewhere.*

3.3.2 Issues in service process design

The issues for managers vary according to the two dimensions of scale and customer involvement.

Scale issues

- *Small scale (professional service and service shop).* The labour intensity of these operations means that managers are continually concerned with overcoming the effects of labour cost increases while maintaining quality of service. The service may be offered at many small-scale outlets so there are problems of supervision and control. Because of the non-standard nature of the tasks to be carried out, staff must be flexible and be able to offer a variety of service on request.

- *Large scale (mass service and service factory).* Large-scale service operations seek efficiency increases through capital investment and reducing the reliance on labour. Managers have to face capital investment decisions concerning sites, buildings and equipment. Also, there is the challenge of establishing and maintaining the feeling of good-quality service through having appropriate physical surroundings and sufficient staff to offer personal contact when needed. Standardisation of the range of services offered reduces the reliance on individuals to cope with a large range of possibilities. In the main, they need not be as highly trained as in small-scale operations. However, the organisation relies on the staff being able to provide the limited service politely and quickly. This implies training and motivation aimed at high-quality, repetitive delivery. Successful large-scale organisations such as the major retailers pay great attention to the detailed steps of customer transactions and train their staff accordingly. Box 3.1 is taken from the staff training manual of Superdrug, the major retailer of household and personal care products.[4] The company stresses its commitment to offering high-quality goods at competitive prices.

Customer involvement issues

- *Direct service (professional service and mass service).* The focus is on the customer. Improved service quality flows from recruiting, developing and motivating staff. Questions of supervision and control also arise when the service is delivered in small outlets spread across different locations.

- *Isolated service (service shop and service factory).* Isolated service operations are managed, in the 'back room', in similar ways to manufacturing activities. Questions range from capital investment in new equipment to scheduling tasks and quality control. Customers access through designated 'gateways' and the emphasis in the service element is on effective and efficient gatekeeping. The gatekeeper must combine personal service skills with the ability to identify customer needs and arrange for the required service to be provided by others where necessary. With the large-scale service factory, the range of services is standardised and the gatekeeper offers whatever is appropriate out of the defined range.

3.3.3 Self-service

Beyond the two-dimensional classification just examined, *self-service* represents another means by which the provider seeks to control the costs of delivery. Compared with the direct service operations already discussed, the relative involvement of the customer in the service process is increased. Cost savings arise, in effect, from the 'employment' of the customer as provider of the service. Physical labour, as in carrying goods out of a supermarket, and decision making, such as selecting choices from a menu presented on a screen, are handed over. Self-service represents a step of *detachment* of the service provider from direct contact with the customer.

Detachment can be achieved in two ways:

- *Replacement of the human server.* Replacement of the service provider by capital equipment depends on recognition that costs can be reduced through automating some tasks carried out by humans. In large-scale service, dispensing machines and computers replace humans for routine processes from the sales of tickets and coffee to the supply and deposit of cash. The Internet is regularly used for automated processes from banking to travel booking. In small-scale service, the matching to individual needs requires equipment with more sophisticated programming based on expert systems technology. Proposals for medical diagnosis machines fall into this category. Such equipment needs to be interactive so that it responds to detailed information from the user.

- *Removal of barriers.* Many self-service facilities such as stores and restaurants depend on the removal of barriers traditionally separating the customer from the service. These barriers are both physical and psychological, that is customers must be enabled to access the facility and be willing to use it. Consequently, the skills required to provide the service have to be simplified and standardised with sufficient information given to enable the customer to cope. The layout of supermarkets is clearly designed to enable customers to reach the goods. At the same time there needs to be appropriate information, equipment and packaging to enable the transaction to take place.

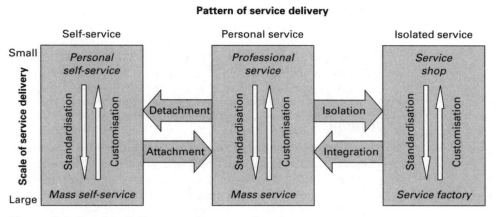

Figure 3.1 Service delivery: patterns and scale

3.3.4 Summary of service patterns

Figure 3.1 summarises the service delivery patterns just discussed along with the relationships among them. The three basic patterns are *self-service*, *personal service* and *isolated service*. Within each pattern, a shift from small to large scale means more than an increase in the volume of output. The search for cost reductions implies the standardisation of the service. In addition, there are the specialisation of roles and the deskilling of much of the process delivery. Trends in the opposite direction require customisation to match more closely the separate needs of each individual.

The other change directions suggested in Figure 3.1 are the switches between the patterns. Personal service becomes self-service through the process of detachment, again often as a means of maintaining quality while fighting against increases in price. Personal service becomes isolated service through the policy of isolation. The opposite policies of *attachment* and *integration* are also shown.

3.3.5 Examples of service patterns

We can illustrate the service patterns with three examples.

Car repairs

General car repairs were traditionally carried out in service shops providing an isolated service based on a diagnosis of the requirements of each customer's car. Rising costs and competition led to several changes in this industry. First, the suppliers and vehicle manufacturers identified standardised service packages which should be applied at intervals throughout the life of the car. The standardisation enables the garage to reduce its costs and improve the planning of its work. Second, specialists entered the repair business. Focusing their attention on the repair and service activities that are most frequently required, they reduced costs through scale economies. Tyre suppliers, for example, gain through intensive use of fitting and balancing equipment as well as, through bulk purchasing, reductions in input prices. They also benefit from using more specialist labour, which requires a narrower range of skills and therefore less training. Exhaust suppliers have gained similarly with companies such as Kwik-Fit also offering exchange of other items such as brakes. The specialists have transformed the industry from a series of service shops into a mixture or service shops and service factories.

Insurance

Direct selling of motor insurance has grown rapidly in recent years. Direct Line, a subsidiary of the Royal Bank of Scotland, provides insurance cover for one million motorists in 350,000 households. It claims that low premiums result from higher efficiency, close control of approved repairers and the absence of broker commissions. Conventional brokers respond, however, with accusations of 'cherry picking', which is building up a profile of low-risk customers. Guardian Direct only insures customers who have three years without claims and are over 21. Others only accept older customers; Royal Direct has a 30 minimum rule and Churchill 25.[5]

Exercise 3.1

Changes in service are occurring in many financial services. Retail banks face new competition offering services using different patterns. Use Figure 3.1 to show how the following competitors have gained advantages:

- *Upstarts* offer online and telephone banking and specialise in a few financial products: current and savings accounts; cheap mortgages; and straightforward insurance.

- *Specialists* select the most profitable business. Single product operators, such as MBNA offering credit cards, can be leaner and more competitive than traditional banks.

- *Financial cross-over operators*, such as insurance companies, use their rich experience, databases and technology to invade the banking sector.

- *Retailers turned bankers*, such as supermarkets, car manufacturers and other retailers now offer financial services beyond the traditional store credit cards or cheap loans for vehicles.[6]

We can see in these examples two trends:

- *Standardisation.* The offering of a defined range of standard services to a limited range of customers. This enables the service to be provided by operators trained in the use of computer screens. Decisions are made by algorithms based on customer information.

- *Detachment.* Rising awareness among customers of the products on offer, a readiness to take on the responsibility to shop around and the technology to access the information easily, in this case the telephone.

Travel tickets

Apart from the simplest ticket sold from mechanical dispensers, automatic sales of travel tickets have been held back by complexity. This results from multiple fare structures and the great variety of possible journeys that can be made over larger systems. Information system developments have changed all that. At main stations in France, for example, one can use machines to plan a journey to any station on the SNCF system and then buy an appropriate ticket. The compulsory seat reservations on the TGV trains can also be made in this way, minutes before departure. While payments can be in cash, most customers use bank cards. The Internet offers many opportunities for automated booking. The ticketless airline, easyJet, sells more than three-quarters of its seats through the Internet with the rest by telephone. The web is used for an even larger proportion of reservations for its associated company, easyRentacar.

Developments such as these result from online information systems. As well as storing and displaying information including times, routes, prices and seat availability, they can receive information from the customer to discover wishes, offer options and verify travel and credit status. In the introduction of simple dispensing machines, train ticket sales moved from mass service to mass self-service. The new systems, by incorporating much of the variety of services offered by SNCF and responding to the customers' needs, customise ticket sales and move towards personal self-service.

3.4 Manufacturing system choices

As with direct service systems, the choice of overall process design of manufacturing and isolated service operations is based on several variables. Again, the most important is scale but other factors, such as the size and homogeneity of the output have to be considered. The number of possible arrangements of equipment to produce given outputs is unlimited. In the following sections, however, we shall present the five main categories of manufacturing system.

3.4.1 Project

Project systems are used to manufacture goods that are difficult to move during assembly or after they have been completed. Reasons for immobility include scale and complexity of the output or of the tasks involved. Industries from civil and marine engineering to film making and research centres work on a project basis. While appearing dissimilar on the surface, these manufacturing tasks face many common challenges:

■ Different people and equipment are required to participate at different times. It is usual to bring these to the project location when they are needed. Consequently, there is a problem of scheduling the availability of such resources so that they are ready on time. Yet, they must not be wasted at other times.

■ Much project work involves the use of specialist staff and equipment, usually obtained through subcontracting. This again suggests an emphasis on accurate timing and co-ordination of the multiple roles involved.

■ The tasks involved in the project have to be sequenced within the total time allowed for completion. Frequently, many components of the final product are fabricated in stages and transported in parts to the assembly position. Their fabrication involves many skills and technologies. A power station needs coal-handling equipment, furnaces, boilers, turbines and generators, all of which require specialists in their supply. This variety underlines the need for planning, monitoring and control of progress.

■ The quality of the product depends on the skills and application of all those involved.

■ Since many projects are unique, planning takes place under much uncertainty. Managers have to be flexible in overcoming technical and operational problems as they arise. In contrast to other manufacturers, they work to a single goal, the completion of the project, which may be over a long period.

3.4.2 Jobbing

The jobbing shop is noted for its flexibility in being established to carry out a wide range of tasks. The products are supplied in small batches, even down to single items, as with the specialist car repairer mentioned earlier. The jobbing shop differs from the project operation in that its outputs are transportable. In engineering manufacture, many general machine shops, moulding plants and pattern makers work in this flexible way, making or repairing items to customer orders. Yet the jobbing shop is apparent in most manufacturing industries from printing to concrete moulding, electronic equipment to high fashion makers.

Since the patterns of demand for a jobbing shop are unpredictable and the size of any one order relatively small, the layout of the plant cannot be adapted to form product-related flow lines. It is conventional to group similar activities and staff together in departments such as casting, plating machining, painting and assembly. This enables the highly skilled staff to be used flexibly. There are often physical advantages, from ventilation to insulation, in keeping families of processes in one area.

As we shall see, the flow of materials through a jobbing shop is far from regular. The uninitiated will always feel a sense of chaos when entering such a plant. Good management is concerned with making plans that work under this uncertainty and then tracking all the work to ensure that it is completed on time and within budget. Managers must offer customers reliable delivery dates and know their costs in detail to ensure that profits are made.

Jobbing printers produce items from single-colour wedding invitations to full-colour promotional brochures for small and medium company clients. The smallest orders may be for 100 posters while the largest may be for thousands of mail shots. The printers compete by offering high-quality goods within the frequently near-impossible time scales demanded by the clients. The many combinations of printing machine designs and ink processes mean that most jobbing printers cannot offer the full range. However, they seek to satisfy all the needs of their regular customers. This is achieved by subcontracting specialised work to others in the district.

3.4.3 Batch

Batch processing is a step up from jobbing in terms of scale. While the two may overlap, there is no clear divide. Batch operations concentrate their attention on a more limited range of products produced in larger quantities than in the jobbing shop. Many batch companies organise their production stages through separate departments as with the jobbing shop. As we shall see, however, modern methods of production planning and control have led to significant changes in these arrangements. Examples include the creation of machining cells and an identification of critical bottlenecks.

Batch processing involves dividing the production activity into the tasks that must be carried out. Then a schedule is made which is designed to enable the batch to pass through each stage in the required sequence. The reduced product range means that complexity is less than in the jobbing shop, yet the setting out and achievement of the schedule remains a daunting task.

Batches are frequently derived from larger customer orders. For example, a contract to supply 20,000 garments over a period of a year may be divided into batches of a month's supply. In this way, the work load is spread out, stock levels are kept low and other garment contracts are fulfilled by the same processes. Other items made in batches include: moulded plastic car components; office furniture; castings and architectural masonry. In these cases, the size of any order does not justify the laying down of a dedicated production line.

3.4.4 Line

Line systems are established when demand for a product, or small range of similar products, is so great that it is worthwhile investing in a dedicated production line. The process is often called mass production.

The best-known example of line production is car assembly. Because of the demand for model variants, most assembly lines produce a small range of similar products rather than identical cars. The cars are similar enough to be handled on the same line and are specified to require mainly the same components. Variations in major items such as engine sizes and doors are managed by delivering these to the work stations in the sequence required. On General Motors' Astra lines, one sees what appears to be a random mix of vans and cars, saloons and hatchbacks and so on. When the paint shop feeds the main line directly, the common feature of the vehicles is colour; the paint process cannot be changed in the short interval between the vehicles arriving at the booths. Some manufacturers avoid this constraint by having a buffer stock of painted body shells between the paint shop and the assembly line. The latter then works in sequence of customer orders.

The line layout differs from the batch layout in the following respects:

- The line moves the product from each work station to the next. There is no build-up of items between the stages of production except those that are on the line. This means that all work stations must operate at the same rate. One problem for managers is to achieve *line balance*, that is to ensure that resources are deployed effectively among the work stations (see Chapter 8).

- Each work station fulfils only a small part of the complete task. From the employees' point of view, the resultant short cycle time and limited skill requirement mean that personal involvement in the work is severely limited. This problem is explored further in Chapter 5.

- The plant layout is dedicated to one product or a small family.
- The scheduling of production through the line is, in principle, much more simple than in batch production. By the same token, the line is much more sensitive to the absence of a key component so managers have to monitor supplies very carefully.

Line layouts may require expensive specialist equipment, as with the assembly of cars or electronic products or, in isolated service, mail sorting and despatching. Lines may also be created to improve the efficiency of labour-intensive work. Examples are packing hampers or large clerical tasks such as counting votes at a general election. In such cases, the lines created are only temporary yet they still incorporate the ideas of moving product and work specialisation.

3.4.5 Continuous

The four production systems described so far deliver so-called *integral* products (see Box 3.2). In contrast, continuous production systems produce high volumes of dimensional products. Continuous process plant is characterised by the way raw materials flow through it ceaselessly with very little build-up of stocks at any intermediate stage. As with other systems, it is possible to build flexibility into the plant design. Yet, variations in the product family are usually very small. Chemical plants producing soap, for example, can cope with different mixes of ingredients but remain dedicated to soap. Similarly, breweries will produce batches of different grades of beer.

We can see that continuous plant either runs with the same product all the time, as with electricity generation, or operates in large-batch mode. Its distinction from the other production processes comes from the dimensional nature of the product. High investment in specialised processing plant and automatic monitoring and control are usually required although some very specialised plant runs at small scale. Examples lie in pharmaceuticals where the small demand for some products is measured in kilograms per year.

It is often difficult to run a continuous process plant at an output other than the designed standard. Like mass production, the high fixed costs mean high operational gearing so that financial success is very sensitive to the volume of sales.

BOX 3.2 **Integral and dimensional products**

- *Integral products* can be counted. Thus a batch shop has an order for 1,000 stop valves; a computer assembly line produces 30 per hour; the local sandwich bar produces 300 filled rolls between 10 o'clock and lunch time.
- *Dimensional products* are measured by a dimension such as weight or volume. A quarry supplies 600 tonnes of stone per day; a brewery produces 100 million litres per year; a power station has an output of 1,200 megawatts of electricity.

3.4.6 Hybrid systems

We have presented the five production technologies as ideal types. This means we have identified their key features in order to recognise them and separate them from the rest. In practice, however, they rarely exist in their ideal forms. For instance, many firms combine two or more at different stages of the production process. The choice depends on the nature of the product and details of the manufacturing process. Some common examples are:

Batch → Line

In this frequently found arrangement, components are made in batches ready to be assembled on a line. The upstream batch processes may run much faster than the assembly process or they may be geographically distant from the assembly plant. In the latter case, the transport system requires the items to be produced in batches.

Many car components are made and delivered in small batches for line assembly. Instructions to make each car at Nissan's plant near Sunderland trigger signals to local component suppliers. Sommer Albert, 3 km away, produces 120 variations of carpet and trim. At the signal, a set of materials is picked, trimmed and packed in installation sequence. Small batches arrive at the track side just in time to be fitted.

Continuous → Line or Continuous → Batch

Raw materials, made in continuous plant, are finished and packed on dedicated lines or even in batches if the variety is great. Bulk aspirin manufacture is a continuous process while packing is line. This recognises the need for special plant to produce the raw material. Yet, pelleting and packing lines can be used for a range of products to be distributed and sold in the same form. Batch finishing occurs in oil refineries. Lubricating oil is normally packed on filling lines but some markets require special sizes or shapes of packaging. These are filled off-line in batches.

Jobbing → Project or Batch → Project

Project work is frequently made difficult by the need to work in unfamiliar and exposed conditions. Modern developments in construction have led to more items being pre-assembled in factories before delivery and erection on site. Reinforced concrete bridge beams are an example. The quality of materials and dimensional accuracy are improved if the beams are made in special plant. There they can be protected from the weather during the curing time. This switch in process technology has an influence on design since structures have to be made of transportable components rather than cast on-site from concrete in large moulds.

Amtico, described in the opening case, produces batches of tiles on a continuous plant. Changes between batches affect colour and surface finish. Downstream from this plant comes a mixture of process technologies. Batch production packs tiles for sale as standard products. Meanwhile, manufacturing cells cut and pack items to customer specifications, treating each order as a project.

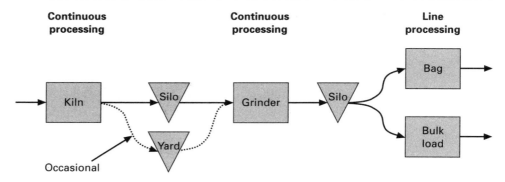

Figure 3.2 Schematic flow diagram of Castle Cement Works showing buffer stocks

The examples suggest two main reasons why hybrids are formed from two production processes. First, there is the nature of the product itself. Project and continuous processes are quite different from the others in this respect. The individual nature of the project and the dimensional form of the continuous product set them apart from jobbing, batch and line which, in principle, can produce the same product. The last three relate to the scale of production rather than its basic physical characteristics. Second, the different processes run at different optimal speeds so they tend to be separated by buffer stocks. These are stores of semi-finished goods in quantities which rise and fall with the production cycles. These buffer stocks separate the different sections of a hybrid plant.

The Castle Cement Works at Padeswood, Clwyd, North Wales is a continuous → line hybrid (see Figure 3.2). It manufactures Portland cement and related products from the limestone quarried nearby. The process involves heating a mixture of limestone, shale and sand to 1500°C in a rotating kiln. Output is in the form of glass-like clinker, which is then ground to cement dust in high-speed ball mills. Additives to modify the cement properties are put in during the grinding. Some cement is despatched in bulk tankers while most is passed to the packing line to fill the familiar 50-kilogram sacks. Although the grinding stage has a higher capacity than the kiln, the two are normally balanced so that the small intermediate silo carries just a few minutes' inventory. Again, the packing line has a higher capacity than is usually required so its feed silo is also small. Any section can be stopped for cleaning or maintenance. To avoid losing output when the grinding or packing are stopped, an open yard enables an overflow inventory of clinker from the kiln to be stacked for several days. The finished cement powder cannot, of course, be stored in this way.

3.4.7 System choice

Manufacturing managers have to choose among the range and mix of process technologies. This is an important decision since selection of an inappropriate system leads to high operating costs or a waste of capital investment. We have shown how project and continuous processes are clearly determined by the nature of the product. The choice of jobbing, batch and line, however, is dependent on scale and managers have to relate process choice to considerations of demand and product variety.

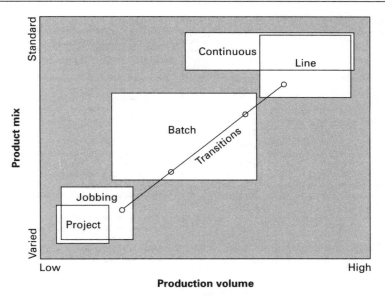

Figure 3.3 Scale, variety and choice of manufacturing systems

This question is illustrated in Figure 3.3. Line processing suits operations of high volume of standard products. At the other extreme, jobbing shops produce small quantities of a variety of items. Batch processing occurs somewhere between the two, the transitions between the stages, illustrated by the sloping line, depending on circumstances. Through decisions to seek larger orders, for example, jobbing shops move towards becoming batch processors and batch shops begin to lay down dedicated production lines. Within batch processing itself, managers can look to narrow the product range, reduce flexibility and increase the scale of output. In practice, there is little difference between a jobbing shop and a small batch operation. Similarly, the step from large batch to line processing can be imperceptible. Large steps rarely occur successfully as they require complete overhaul of the physical plant and operating systems.

Table 3.2 summarises the key factors in the choice of process in manufacturing and isolated service systems. As with the process descriptions, the processes are ideal types and the factors generalisations. The table is intended to set out the important differences among the processes. It can be seen that batch production is presented as something of an intermediate between the jobbing and line processes. Its position on the scales in the table, such as high to low, depends on the particular circumstances. There is never a single, correct set of choices of operating systems. The choice is a blend of issues from how a firm embraces competition through to the current process layout, which is itself an accumulation of many related decisions in the past.

3.4.8 Developments in production systems

We mentioned in Chapter 2 how Ford's line assembly revolutionised manufacturing and brought cheap vehicles to the mass market. Technical advance is often

Table 3.2 Product and process factors in the choice of process technology

		Chosen process technology				
		Project	Jobbing	Batch	Line	Continuous
Product factors	Product range	Diverse	Diverse	←——→	Standard	Standard
	Quantity produced	One	Small	←——→	Large	Very large
	Design	Unique	Customers' needs	←——→	Standard	Fixed
	Technology focus	Product	Product	←——→	Product/ process	Process
	Value offered	Skill, time, capability	Skill, time, capability	←——→	Low price	Low price, uniqueness
Process factors	Process changeable	Flexible	Flexible	←——→	Inflexible	Inflexible
	Capital	Low	Low	←——→	High	High
	Speed	Flexible, worker paced	Flexible, worker paced	←——→	Fixed, machine paced	Process paced
	Impact of breakdown	Low	Low	←——→	High	Very high
	Inventory in process	High and rising	High	←——→	Low	Very low
	Control of production	Supervision and simple records	Supervision and simple records	←——→	Machine paced	Automated
	Control of quality	External verification	Individual obligation	←——→	End of line checking	Built into process

seen in this light, the creation of systems for production on larger and larger scales. Yet, such developments do not mean that the older systems of production organisation become obsolete. Each has its own application. Jobbing will continue for as long as single items are required. Indeed, as we shall see in Chapter 4, as more markets become dominated by mass-produced items, the more likely there will be demand for individual, or customised, items.

Intolerance of the apparent chaos of jobbing and batch shops has a long history. Urwick, a writer of the classical school of management thought, argued: 'To allow the individual idiosyncrasies of a wide range of customers to drive administration away from the principles on which it can manufacture is suicidal.'[7] To such writers, standardisation and simplification were the keys to success. To Urwick, such truths were self-evident for we base our high standard of living on the ability to carry out many functions more efficiently than did our ancestors. At the same time, however, our rising wealth enables us to demand at least some goods and services which more closely match our idiosyncrasies. The growth of McDonald's has not made lunching at the Savoy any less desirable!

There is room, then, in markets for both individual and mass-produced goods. Therefore, we should not think that one production system is superior to another but that each must be used appropriately. Having selected a system that matches the needs of the environment, the challenge lies in running it well.

Table 3.3 Effective and ineffective profiles

		Chosen process technology			
		Jobbing	Batch	Line	
Product range	Diverse	♠	♦	♣	Standard
Quantity required	Small	♠♣	♦		Large
Process changes	Flexible	♠	♦	♣	Inflexible
Speed	Worker paced	♠	♦	♣	Machine paced
Inventory in process	High	♠♣	♦		Low
Control of quality	Individual	♠	♦	♣	Inspection

3.4.9 Profiling

Hill[8] developed a method of profiling to investigate the relationships between the different production processes, the rest of the business and its markets. Many companies fail to understand and incorporate these trade-offs. Furthermore, as market environments or business policies change, they fail to see how their internal processes become increasingly unmatched. A firm's new policy to reduce work in progress may cause its production managers to reduce batch sizes. This means an increase in the cost of machine idle time as more effort is put into changing them over from one product to another. A business can, of course, compete for the sort of business that looks for smaller quantities but the one in question may not be successful if it tries to win large orders with a small-batch mentality.

Table 3.3 illustrates the profiling process. It is simplified from Table 3.2 by removing project and continuous technologies and cutting the number of rows. The firm selects relevant characteristics of products and processes as shown in the left-hand column. The product and process characteristics are then positioned on the scale (jobbing to line) whose measures are set out in each row. Three product profiles are shown in the table. Two represent products displaying a consistent pattern while one does not:

Product ♠ represents the manufacture of *haute couture* clothing or the installation of fitted kitchens. Such products are demanded in ones or, at most, very small batches. The company accepts the role of workers in deciding output and quality and motivates and trains them accordingly. Expected levels of inventory in process are high. The firm is consistent in its process choices. In the fitted kitchen example, it will use components made in batches but each order is treated as an individual job. Indeed, in taking place on the customer's premises the service offered has many of the characteristics of a project.

Product ♦ is similarly well balanced, being a varied family of goods or services, such as printed cards or restaurant meals. In batch processing, the product range, process flexibility and inventory are smaller than in the jobbing shop. Production rates are partially determined by machines and quality will be controlled by end of production inspection combined with a reliance on the skills of individual workers.

Product ♣ in contrast, has an inconsistent profile. The supplier is using line production methods to produce small quantities of standard products. This yields the worst of both worlds; high inventories are set alongside high running costs as the production lines are stopped to switch from one product to another.

The profiling approach is intended to be illustrative and exploratory rather than definitive. Its value lies in the generation of insights and debate among operating managers as to the sorts of production systems they require.

3.4.10 Transitional process technologies

We have seen how the gap between jobbing and small batch production is not clear cut. Furthermore, there is little to choose between the layouts of some large batch and line producers. The distinctions have become even less clear with the developments of process innovations to bridge these gaps and gain corresponding benefits. We shall look at each transition in turn.

The jobbing–batch transition

The costs of setting up machines for different items has traditionally set the minimum limits to economical batch sizes. For smaller quantities, it is often cheaper to use simpler equipment.

Figure 3.4 shows how costs vary with volume in printing. Conventional presses apply one colour at each stage. Therefore, to produce four colours, a printer may pass the same material through the press four times, using different inks and plates on each occasion. Figure 3.4 shows the total cost of such a job. This comprises the set-up cost, S_1, and the variable cost, which is related to volume. A four-colour press enables the work to be printed in one pass. It has four stages linked in sequence with sophisticated paper-handling and control equipment. As expected, the set-up cost, S_4, is higher than S_1. The running cost per item, however, is much lower as only one pass is required. The cost line for the four-colour

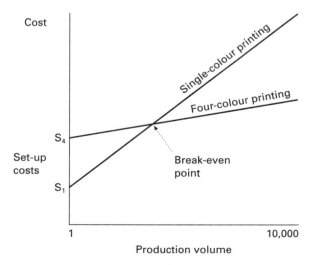

Figure 3.4 Printing costs for the same job on different presses

machine, therefore, climbs less steeply than the single-colour one. At volumes above the break-even point, the more sophisticated machine comes into its own. Break-even is typically several thousand copies.

Many companies have worked on reducing changeover times. At L'Oréal, the cosmetics company, engineers found out how to reduce the time for switching between hair colourants from 120 to 8 minutes. Batch sizes fell from 30,000 to 2,000, enabling greater flexibility and reduced stocks.

Developments using information technology to control machine tools have reduced the break-even points. Computer numerically controlled (CNC) machine tools and robots have reduced set-up times so much that some companies are able to run with batch sizes of one! A smart bicycle at distributors of National Bicycle measures customers' height, weight, leg length and so on. In a few minutes, these details reach the factory in Osaka where the computer issues instructions to tube-cutting and welding machines, paint robots and other processes. There are more than 10 million variations including the ability to paint the customer's name or other details on the frame. Prices are about 15% higher than for mass-produced models. Delivery could be measured in days but National Bicycle promises two weeks; research showed customers did not believe that customisation could be done more quickly.[9]

Machining centres are another development. They group machines together under the control of a computer. Robots and conveyors allow products and tools to be moved under software control. While these arrangements are hardly simple, their complexity is lower than mechanical transfer lines and the cost of switching from batch to batch is again reduced.

The batch–line transition

At the batch–line transition lie processes that have their roots in either process. *Group technology*, also known as *cell-based manufacturing*, identifies common characteristics among batched products so that they form a basic pattern with variations. There is more on this in Chapter 8. Based on this commonality, groups of machines are laid out to carry out the basic processes with ancillary machines to handle the variations on the way. The same mode of thinking has led to increasing the flexibility of assembly lines so that they can cope with a wider range of products while operating without interruption. The general principle is to keep materials flowing through the manufacturing process.

Figure 3.5 plots the transitional processes on a grid relating product variety and volume. At their appropriate mixes of volume and flexibility, these applications modify the scope of the basic processes. For example, group technology enables higher outputs from batch layouts without resort to laid down assembly lines. Flexible assembly lines allow for increased variety. Toshiba uses such a line at its Ome plant to link staff engaged in assembling computers. Switching occurs after batches as few as 20. Planning, engineering and the line are integrated through control systems. A screen at each work station displays drawings and work instructions. When the flow changes, so do the screens.

3.4.11 Organisational factors

So far, we have discussed process technologies with a focus on their technical features. Yet, as explained in Chapter 2, operations managers need to understand

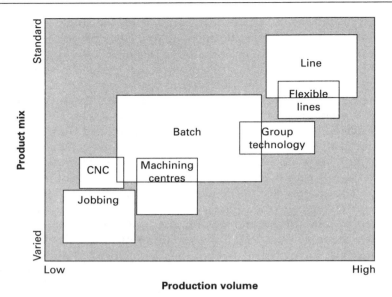

Figure 3.5 Transitional processes

Table 3.4 Selected data on firms with different production systems

	Jobbing	Line	Continuous
Mean number of levels in hierarchy	3	4	6
Percentage of costs allocated to wages and salaries	40	35	15
Mean span of control of first-line supervisors	22	49	13
Mean ratio of managers and supervisors to all staff	35	17	7

the close relationship between people and processes within the *socio-technical* subsystem. Among the first to relate process technology to human behaviour was Woodward[10] in her classic study. It led her towards a theory of production organisation.

In the study of 92 manufacturing firms in south Essex, England, during the 1960s, Woodward collected data on many aspects of production operations and management as well as measures of success. Data included, for example, the percentage of total costs allocated to payment to employees, the number of levels in the hierarchy and the span of control[11] of supervisors.

Woodward concluded that, according to similarities among key organisational variables, the different systems of production fell into three clusters of firms whose characteristics were broadly similar. These she called *unit and small batch*, *large batch and mass* and *process* systems. They correspond to the jobbing, line and continuous categories we have been using so far.

Table 3.4 summarises some of the many observations made. So far, we can see that she described the firms in one area of the country and fitted them into clusters according to similarities among their production systems. If this were the only output of the work, then it may never have been seen as particularly significant. She went further, however. In collecting data about the success of firms in the sample, Woodward investigated what features distinguished the better performing firms from the rest. In doing so, she was looking to see whether it was

Table 3.5 Spans of control in continuous process firms

	Number of people controlled					
	<10	11–20	21–30	31–40	Median	Number
All firms	6	12	5	2	13	25
More successful	1	5	—	—	—	6
Less successful	1	—	1	2	—	4

possible to make statements about the ways firms *ought* to be organised, that is to develop a *normative theory* of the organisation of production.

Woodward's data presentation is illustrated in Table 3.5. Here, we can see that the more successful process firms had spans of control close both to each other and to the median of the group as a whole. The less successful firms tended to be scattered. This tallied with Woodward's observations of other organisational factors. They showed the more successful firms being more similar to each other and closer to mean values. This result pointed the way to the normative theory:

> The figures relating to the span of control of the chief executive, the number of levels in the line of command, labour costs, and the various labour ratios showed a similar trend. The fact that organizational characteristics, technology, and success were linked together in this way suggested that not only was the system of production an important variable in the determination of organization structure, but also that one particular form of organization was most appropriate to each system of production. In unit [jobbing] production, for example, not only did short and relatively broadly based pyramids predominate, but they also appeared to ensure success. Process production, on the other hand, would seem to require the taller and more narrowly based pyramid.[12]

These conclusions leave us a long way from a general theory of production organisations. Woodward, in order to achieve rigour in her research, was taking a limited perspective. She took the production systems in each company as given and did not investigate, for example, whether each was appropriate to its market situation. Furthermore, there was no allowance made for the historical development of each company – structures often exist because they have always been that way. Despite these comments, however, the study did enlighten the debate about the implications of different types of production technology.

3.4.12 Supervisors and employees

One resemblance between jobbing and continuous production is that both employ a greater proportion of skilled workers than line production systems. In jobbing shops, the skilled workers are engaged directly in manufacture, doing it, so to speak, with their own hands. In continuous production systems, no worker is engaged in direct work upon the product. There are few workers and the skill required in such systems is directed at overall process control and plant maintenance. Again, these require highly competent workers. It is in line assembly that we find many more semi-skilled or unqualified employees engaged in specialised repetitive tasks requiring less general skill. Naturally, these tasks themselves can be automated and many firms have taken the investment route towards achieving lower costs.

Recognising the different mixtures of skills among shop floor workers in the three production systems, it may be surprising to encounter Woodward's conclusion on the spans of control at the first level. This was much larger (1:49) in line production than in jobbing (1:22) or continuous systems (1:13). The explanation lies in understanding the nature of the supervisory role. In jobbing and continuous production factories, the workforce is broken down into small groups. In this situation, the supervisor is expected to display leadership in problem solving related to tasks as well as maintaining links with other departments. These involve obtaining tools and materials, arranging for despatch and so on. The work groups, therefore, tend to include the supervisor and the consequent personal relationships are informal.

Line production is different. Detailed process planning has been carried out before the line is laid out. Repetitive jobs throw up few technical problems as the perceptual and conceptual skill elements typical of jobbing work have been removed. Workers are employed for their dexterity. Problems that do arise tend to be dealt with by specialist engineers. The supervisor is, therefore, less involved in the workers' tasks. Leadership concentrates on ensuring that assemblies are carried out at the predetermined line speed. Having allocated workers to the line, the supervisor maintains discipline, arranges work breaks and so on. The relationship is formal and, with the pace having been set by the machine, each supervisor can manage many more workers.

✔ Quick check-up

Can you:
☐ Name three factors influencing the selection of the operations process.
☐ Name the type of service closest to manufacturing.
☐ List six service delivery patterns.
☐ List five basic manufacturing technologies and name two dimensions that influence the choice among them.
☐ Place CNC and group technology correctly at the boundaries of these technologies.
☐ Outline the key features of Woodward's study for continuous process firms.

? Questions

Chapter review

3.1 Why is scale so important in the selection of operations processes?

3.2 Use examples to illustrate why a manufacturer may adopt a hybrid production process.

3.3 Discuss the significance of Woodward's studies in relation to process classification and the development of related theory.

Application

3.4 Suggest how Amtico might use profiling in the selection of its manufacturing systems.

3.5 Compare the operations process developed at Shouldice Hospital (Chapter 2) with that offered by a general practitioner. How do modern GPs cope with the variety of demands placed upon them?

Investigation

3.6 Use Figure 3.1 to compare a number of restaurants with which you are familiar. What clues might this analysis provide to a person establishing a new business?

CLOSING CASE

Meubles Grange[13]

Meubles Grange makes furniture in its factory in the Rhône valley some 40 km from Lyon, France. The styles, mainly in cherry wood, follow French traditions from about 1750 to 1900. They include Trianon, Louis Philippe and Consulat. Some are copies of particular pieces, such as the dressing table of Marie-Antoinette, Napoleon's travelling furniture and desks of Jules Verne and Hector Berlioz. With beds, wardrobes, mirrors, bookcases, sideboards, bureaux, tables and chairs, the number of designs shown in the catalogue is about 180, not counting size options for items from beds to shelves. This variety is increased by three colour shades and three levels of distressing, making nine possible finishes in all. The furniture is expensive; a medium-sized buffet sideboard retails at over £1,000. For a premium, Grange prides itself in meeting special customer requests for dimensions, colour finishes or interior fittings.

The range is updated annually with a new catalogue. Items selling fewer than about 100 per year are considered for replacement. The company has been broadening its range in two directions. First, there are complementary soft furnishings that enable Grange to offer a total look, *le savoir-vivre à la française*, to customers. Second, the company offers traditional designs in metal or rattan made by subcontractors in the Far East. These sell well in the spring whereas the timber products peak in the autumn. The company, founded by cabinet maker Joseph Grange in 1905, has grown to a £25 million turnover with some 400 employees. About 84% of output is exported, the most important markets being Germany, the United States and the United Kingdom although others, from Australia and Korea to the Netherlands and Canada, are also served. Sales are through distributors to specialist furniture stores who display room settings showing the company's products. In recent years, the company has opened its own boutiques in selected centres, such as in major French cities and Harrod's in London.

Deliveries are by road trailer in Europe, with each outlet receiving a delivery every two weeks. Traffic farther afield goes in containers. While the look of the furniture is traditional, Grange does not replicate old methods of manufacture. Rough sawn timber is dried in modern kilns. Furniture components, many of which are common across several lines, are made on high-quality wood machines. Assembly is aided by modern fixings and special jigs to ensure accuracy of fit. Finishing, in contrast, is done by hand. One craftsman works on all the items of a customer's order, applying the appropriate varnishes and waxes to give the required finish. The aim is to give a consistent high-quality finish

▶

across all items ordered by the customer. Grange is constantly searching to reduce the number of complaints from the present 0.3% of orders. Making to customers' orders means that the only stocks of finished goods, apart from goods in transit, are the metal and rattan lines.

Questions

1 What bundle of goods and service has Grange chosen to offer?

2 Identify the types of production system you would expect at Meubles Grange and how they relate to the markets the company serves.

Notes and references

1. New, C. and Wheatley, M. (1996) 'The Amtico Company', *Management Today*, November, pp.84–87.

2. Computer-aided design and computer-aided manufacture. Many companies gain advantages from these technologies and the way they combine them into a complete manufacturing process.

3. Schmenner, R.W. (1993) *Production/Operations Management*, New York: Macmillan, pp.18–22; Krajewski, Lee J. and Ritzman, Larry P. (1999) *Operations Management: Strategy and analysis*, 5th edition, Reading, MS: Addison-Wesley, p.105.

4. Superdrug (1993) *Success: Customer Care and Service Skills Programm*, unpublished company materials.

5. Hunter, T. (1994) 'Direct insurers picking low-risk cherries in a battle for the premium customers', *The Guardian*, 5 March, p.31.

6. Based on BBC News On-line (1998) *Business: The Economy: The account snatchers*, 16 November, http://news2.thdo.bbc.co.uk/hi/english/business/the_economy/newsid_214000/214989.stm, accessed 8 May 2001.

7. Urwick, L. (1943) *Elements of Administration*, London: Pitman.

8. Hill, T. (2000) *Operations Management: Strategic context and managerial analysis*, Basingstoke: Macmillan, pp.127–130.

9. Kotha, S. (1996) 'From mass production to mass customization: the case of the National Industrial Bicycle Company of Japan', *European Journal of Management*, 14(5), pp.442–450.

10. Woodward, J. (1971) *Industrial Organisation: Theory and practice*, London: Oxford University Press.

11. The span of control is the number of subordinates who are directly responsible to a manager or supervisor, that is occupying the next lower level in the hierarchy. Firms often try to even out responsibilities among staff at a particular level by taking span of control into account. Other factors, such as spatial dispersion or technical content, are also brought into play. Woodward's comparisons use averages for each firm.

12. Woodward, op.cit. pp.69–71.

13. Case study based on personal observation; see also http://www.grange.fr/indexgb.htm

CHAPTER 4

Planning and control

OBJECTIVES

When you have finished studying this chapter, you should be able to:

- Explain the key roles of planning and control in the management of organisations and their operations.

- Sketch the planning and control cycle and explain how planning and control relate to the strategic and operational levels of management.

- Identify types of uncertainty under which plans are made and how organisations respond.

- Define and explain the purpose of objectives; identify the features of good objectives; and discuss their limitations in practice.

- Demonstrate how a sequence of actions and decisions can be set out in a flow chart.

- Define strategic management and outline the features of its main stages: analysis, choice, implementation and control.

- Outline competitive and cooperative strategies and show their implications for operations management.

- Summarise the lessons of just-in-time and total quality management.

- Identify three control systems and show how they are applied in the operations context.

- Review some control problems in human activity systems.

OPENING CASE	**Milking the market?**[1]

In 2001, Robert Wiseman Dairies, based in Scotland, began processing milk at its new £35 million plant at Droitwich, Worcestershire. Until then, its Manchester dairy had been its most southerly plant. Designed to produce 350 Ml (million litres) each year, it had been running at 400 Ml. Droitwich was planned to take up the excess output as well as form a platform for increased sales further south. Moving some 90 Ml of output from Manchester would bring the new facility close to break-even, although its capacity is 200 Ml per annum.

The milk market is mature, so Wiseman must take business from rivals to make a return on its investment in Droitwich. Its main customers are the supermarkets – Asda, Morrison, Tesco and Safeway. With 25% over-capacity in the liquid milk market, analysts noted that Wiseman's expansion efforts could only put more downward pressure on margins, harming the profits of all dairy

▶

companies. For instance, industry leader Express Dairies blamed intense competition and surplus capacity when warning of falls in profits and dividend.

Meanwhile, United Milk, a group owned by farmers, announced it would build a £45 million dairy in Wiltshire; Dairy Crest said it would expand two plants into 'super dairies' while closing some older facilities.

4.1 Introduction

What is happening in the liquid milk industry? We see companies engaged in typical operations planning activities. They are deciding plant sizes and locations and when to withdraw out-of-date facilities. Clearly, they do not do this in isolation. The consumer market is declining and the distributors are expecting the processors to make price cuts that they can pass on to their customers. Some companies, such as Express and United Milk are heavily dependent on milk; for others, it forms just one of the 20,000 lines carried in the typical supermarket. Yet, milk is important in the price battlefield. Consumers know milk prices and are sensitive to changes; retailers know the way key prices act as markers in impressions of value for money.

We also see Wiseman and others ignoring the conventional message that states, 'No investment in a declining business.' Perhaps they can buck the trend and beat the rivals? Or perhaps each firm's particular strategic position causes it to take a different position? There are plans being laid and controls put in place, each crafted to achieve a firm's objectives. Planning selects the direction and points the organisation along the route; control ensures that the direction is maintained. These activities form the planning and control cycle shown in Figure 4.1. While in practice they form a continuous loop, we can think of the cycle initiated

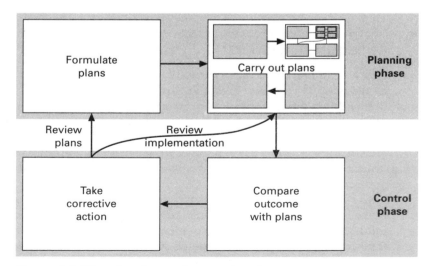

Figure 4.1 The planning and control cycle

by top management formulating strategic plans. These plans are carried out through their interpretation into more detailed intermediate and operating plans. Therefore, planning is arranged in a hierarchy. Within the *carry out plans* cell of Figure 4.1 there are other loops, and within those loops even smaller ones, and so on. It is a recursive picture, containing within the cell its own image.

The control function comes into play when the plans are set in motion. Through comparison of results with the plans, either in anticipation or in measurement after the event, corrective control action is taken. The control action can, if taken early enough, change the current implementation. Otherwise, gaps between results and plans should be considered in the next round of planning formulation. Thus, the cycle is completed through feedback control.

This chapter examines in detail the planning and control cycle. It explains how the operations function is involved with all planning levels, picking out the strategic level as particularly important. It then shows how various types of control can be used to ensure that objectives are achieved.

4.2 Planning

4.2.1 What is planning?

We are all planners, more than we might imagine. We plan meal menus, shopping trips, examination revision, holidays and careers. These plans, formal or informal as they may be, give shape and purpose to our lives and enable us to assemble resources and cooperate with others in their achievement. In the same way, business plans enable managers to gather their resources and impose their intentions upon the organisation. A plan in the business context is usually formal. We can define it as follows:

> **A plan is an explicit formalised statement of intention consisting of objectives and statements of actions needed to achieve them.**

Note that a plan is more than a statement of wishes. To be effective it must clarify what actions are required for its accomplishment. There is, however, a danger of overemphasis on formal plans if users become committed to them in spite of changing circumstances. The infamous 5-year plans of the soviet system illustrated how sticking closely to rigid plans could contribute to the ruin of economies. In the planning and control cycle, performance must be monitored and, if necessary, plans adjusted when circumstances change.

4.2.2 Planning under uncertainty

All plans are made in uncertain conditions. The uncertainty usually arises in the business environment. One purpose of the plan is to recognise uncertainty and make an effective response. There are three types of uncertainty:

■ *State uncertainty* refers to difficulties in predicting the future state of the environment. Operations managers continually face this problem. The return from investments in new facilities depends on future demand, which depends, in turn, on many factors. For example, the sales from a petrol station will be influenced by changes in road layouts or the success of a new estate agency depends on the unpredictable state of the housing market.

Sometimes, state uncertainty relates to timing. We may be very confident that something is going to happen but unsure about when. For example, in the opening case study, we may be confident that the demand for milk will continue its slow decline. Its slope, however, is variable, so it would be difficult to forecast when sales will be a quarter lower than they are today.

■ *Effect uncertainty* describes the unpredictable impact of environmental changes. Again, this problem affects operating managers. Organisations may be well aware of the changes yet remain uncertain of their impact. Examples include: the expansion of production facilities by a competitor may reduce one's own demand; a change in safety legislation which may affect operating costs of different companies in different ways; growing shortages of key raw materials may increase prices by an unknown amount; introduction of new taxes may reduce demand, again by an unknown amount.

■ *Response uncertainty* refers to the indeterminate consequences of a management decision. Some examples affecting operations managers are: the results of changing production processes or layouts may not be fully clear; the impact on quality of increasing production line speeds may be difficult to assess; market responses to product innovation are difficult to forecast; employee trade unions may respond unfavourably to plans for increased efficiency.

Exercise 4.1 Many organisations are involved in the milk supply industry. Identify four different organisations and give your own examples of the types of uncertainty they face.

We can often see all three types of uncertainty in the same situation. During the 1990s, British Airways was seeking to develop its routes in continental Europe. One objective was to obtain landing rights at Orly, the second airport of Paris. BA faced state uncertainty in not knowing whether the route licensing system was to be liberalised. The French government eventually agreed, at first without stating a date when operations could start. This uncertainty made marketing the new service difficult. When the routes did open to competition, BA could not know whether other airlines would try to operate them. This was effect uncertainty. Finally, BA recognised that at an existing French operator, Air Inter, would respond vigorously to its own entry to the Orly market. BA, therefore, faced response uncertainty that made estimating demand very difficult. BA opened its service in 1994.

Being able to respond to uncertainty is a mark of good operations management. We saw in Chapter 1 how internal operating structures with spare capacity or stocks of materials respond to short-term fluctuations in demand. We shall see later in this chapter how strategic management attempts to change relationships between the organisation and its environment to either influence it or reduce its effects. Forecasting can play its part also. Uncertainty would be eliminated if either:

- the organisation could forecast the environment with sufficient accuracy
- the organisation had sufficient influence over the environment to ensure that the planned for future actually happened.

Both cases are impossible in the long term. In the first, there is no known way of forecasting the future in the detail required. If forecasting were possible, the logic of such 'future models' would mean that all firms would have one. In such a world, each firm would have to include all other firms' models within its own. Planning would become a vast game, like a multiplayer chess match among grand masters.

The second case is an example of attempting to make the future come true. Some large organisations have succeeded for a while in using, say, monopoly power to control their environments. Yet, such success does not last long.

4.2.3 Forecasting

Forecasting, that is the making of predictions of future states or events, is not an exact science. The forecasts vary in their reliability and may vary from confident statements of conditions for the next few hours to little more than educated guesses covering five years or more. The process is, however, important to operations managers.

Table 4.1 shows how, for each type of uncertainty, a forecast could be useful in enabling managers to make effective plans to cope. In many businesses, the operations manager is not responsible for forecasting key variables such as demand and input prices and this may lead to conflict. Demand forecasting is the province of sales and marketing yet many an operations manager is aware of the optimism of sales people. The consequence is that operations managers are wary of establishing service capacity or building stocks according to forecasts that they 'know' are unlikely to turn out. This behaviour, in turn, causes sales to overestimate even more wildly and so on. Forecasting is one of the most important interactions between marketing and operations and needs to be managed more seriously than in this example. We shall see in Chapters 11 and 12 how forecasts are incorporated into operations decision making.

The type of forecast to be used depends not only on the time scale covered but also on the resources of time and effort that the organisation can devote to the

Table 4.1 Uncertainty and forecasts

Type of uncertainty	Appropriate forecast	Typical questions to be answered
State	Time series	What will be the sales of microwave cookers for the next three years?
Effect	Event outcome	What will be the effect on sales of our new product?
Response	Response	What will our competitors do after we lower our prices and increase our output?

process. In the small business, there are only resources for educated guesses, that is estimates illuminated by the awareness from being close to operations and customers. The large enterprise, by the same token, employs its own researchers and consulting groups so it gets an early warning of change in the environment. The time scale to be covered by the forecast relates to the planning process itself.

4.2.4 Levels of planning

As we saw in Figure 4.1, there are several levels of planning in an organisation. They are nested so that each level relates to the ones above and below. For discussion, we can divide them into three – strategic, intermediate and operational. In practice, however, there may be fewer or more and the boundaries between levels may not be as clear cut as suggested here.

4.2.5 Links among levels

The notional planning levels are shown in Table 4.2. We can note two points. First, the senior managers display a greater scope in the plans they are responsible for. They have to decide allocations of greater resources within broader constraints and must take a longer view of the impact of their decisions. Second, there are links both down and up the hierarchy of levels:

■ Using downward links, each level establishes broad parameters for the level below. These refer to objectives to be aimed for and the resources with which they should be achieved. Therefore, a means–ends chain is established in which each level provides the means to achieve the ends of the next higher layer. The milk processing company in Table 4.3 illustrates the point. The director of operations is responsible for the strategic plan to increase profits over three years. The intermediate and operations level managers, of whom only two are shown, have objectives and plans blended into this overall strategy. To the more senior managers, the lower level objectives are the means to achieve their own ends.

Table 4.2 Levels of planning

	Type of planning	*Managers involved*	*Typical time scale*
Strategic level	Achieving overall objectives by managing the long-term relationships between the organisation and its environment	Directors of operations and all other senior managers	One to ten years or more
Intermediate level	Allocating resources among sub-units and functions to give each a direction and to ensure coordination	Middle managers working both as a team and within their functions e.g. production, logistics and operations managers	Six months to two years
Operational level	Accomplishing closely defined tasks with available resources	Managers of operating units e.g. supervisors and first-line managers	From a few hours to one year

Table 4.3 The means–ends chain among objectives and plans in a milk processing business

Level	Managers involved	Typical objective
Strategic	Directors of operations	To increase annual operating margin to £700,000 within three years
		↑end ↓means
Intermediate	Manager of processing plant	To reduce operating costs by 5% by the end of the current financial year
		↑end ↓means
Operational	Despatch department supervisor	To reschedule staff rosters before 31 July so as to cut labour costs by 5% while maintaining output

■ Upward links, in a well-planned business, are found in the way that each level needs to consider the capacity and capability of the levels below in formulating plans. Otherwise, plans would be simply unrealistic. Good planning should involve a blend of leadership from the senior managers, top-down planning, with consultation over what is feasible with junior managers, bottom-up planning. This process may be informal, although in large organisations it will use formal methods such as management by objectives or the annual appraisal process.

Sometimes, vertical links may be unintended. For instance, changes in strategic plans may have unanticipated operational consequences. Indeed, many operations managers will count them among their greatest headaches. In the upward direction, operating decisions may have unintended strategic consequences, especially if the organisation is already prone to crisis. Difficulties with track and signalling maintenance led to several railway accidents in 2000. Repairs meant the closure of several routes for extended periods during the following winter, severely damaging the reputation of operating companies.[2]

4.2.6 Objectives

We have seen that a plan contains objectives and statements of the means to achieve them. Here we meet a difficulty for students because both managers and authors often use the terms aim, objective and goal interchangeably. When some emphasise differences among their own definitions they merely add to the confusion. We shall use the one term, objective, here:

> **An objective is a defined, measurable result to be achieved within a stated time.**

Objectives have a pivotal role in the planning process. Without them planning, which looks for statements of how objectives are to be achieved, cannot begin. Objectives have more value than this, however. Overall, they:

■ Provide managers with *clear targets* that they can work towards. Lacking organisational objectives, managers would tend to interpret situations in their own ways and would find it difficult to act in unison.

- Decide *priorities*. Among the objectives at any level of an organisation, the achievement of some will be more critical to success than others. It may be valuable to highlight these 'must do' objectives to separate them from others which may be desirable but could well be postponed if resources are not available.

- Build *commitment*. The process of objective setting involves encouraging all employees to commit themselves to the ends of the organisation. In so doing, clear objectives help in building commitment towards the combined ends.

- Serve as *measuring rods* to *underpin choices*. Many techniques of operations management presented later in this book start with selection of objectives. For example, operating schedules are dependent on the objectives given to those who have to set them out.

- Serve as *measuring rods* for *appraising performance*. Whether performance is measured for the allocation of the weekly production bonus or to assess promotion potential, the use of consistent standards helps in maintaining confidence in the appraisal scheme.

- Influence *motivation*. Beyond the inclusion of measurable standards within a formal appraisal scheme, clear and achievable objectives offer a sense of personal achievement.

4.2.7 Good objectives

From the definition given earlier, we can see that a good objective should be stated in quantitative terms – both measures of achievement and period. Furthermore, since objectives represent an agreement over means and ends among managers, they are normally written. The tests of a good objective should be threefold:

- Is the intended result clearly stated?
- Is it possible to measure whether the result has been achieved?
- Is the time scale made clear?

The examples given in Table 4.3 all satisfy these tests. They also bring out a further point that we shall meet again later, namely constraints. Take the example of the despatch department supervisor. This manager's objective is 'To reschedule staff hours before 31 July to reduce labour costs by 5% *while maintaining output.*' It would be easy for a line manager to cut total costs if output was also permitted to fall. However, the italicised part of the objective statement mentions a constraint upon cost cutting, emphasising that changes must take place within a framework of continuing activity. The framework defines the scope of decision making within which the objective has to be achieved. Objectives and constraints, then, usually go together. The constraints may be explicitly stated in a similar way to the objectives or implied by the conventions of the operations department.

| Exercise 4.2 | Other constraints will affect the objectives in Table 4.3. Suggest one further example for each of the levels. |

4.2.8 **Problems with objectives**

There are three problems with the formal, explicit setting of objectives, which should be mentioned here.

Change

However minor and trivial some may appear, all objectives form part of the carrying out of a general plan for the organisation. Relatively stable environments enable planning to be done with confidence while rapidly changing, or turbulent, environments pose great difficulties for the planner. No sooner is the plan made than it is out of date. Change outside a manager's control may make the pursuit of an objective either impossible or no longer relevant to success. Such situations need constant review and a much more flexible approach to the establishment and modification of plans and their objectives.

Conflict

As opposed to the single objectives given here as examples, managers are usually faced with multiple objectives which will almost certainly be in conflict. This is the managerial problem of 'keeping all balls in the air'. Almost anyone can juggle with one ball, focusing attention and energy on maintaining its movement. Having more than one makes the task more interesting yet less heed and fewer resources are then devoted to any one ball. For the manager, then, multiple objectives may mean that achieving one can be only done at the expense of another. Balancing efficiency and effectiveness, mentioned in Chapter 1, is a general statement of this difficulty.

Measurement

The achievement of some managerial tasks is very difficult to measure. Managers have to combine operational roles, such as ensuring short-term schedules are achieved, with other dimensions. These include building and creating work teams, developing subordinates and so on. The danger with having a mix of measurable and unmeasurable objectives is that managers will be tempted to focus their efforts on what can be measured in order to look good. There is also the problem of measurementship (defined later in this chapter) where employees deliberately set out to set low objectives so that they can appear good at the period end review.

Despite these problems, operations managers use objectives extensively in planning and controlling. Planning techniques have been developed by management scientists to add clarity and precision to the process. Their use stems from the desire to achieve clear objectives, through planning how they are to be achieved and monitoring the level of success so that control can be exercised. We shall be using examples of Gantt charts, networks, linear programmes and other methods later in the book. To illustrate the approach, however, we shall use a flow chart.

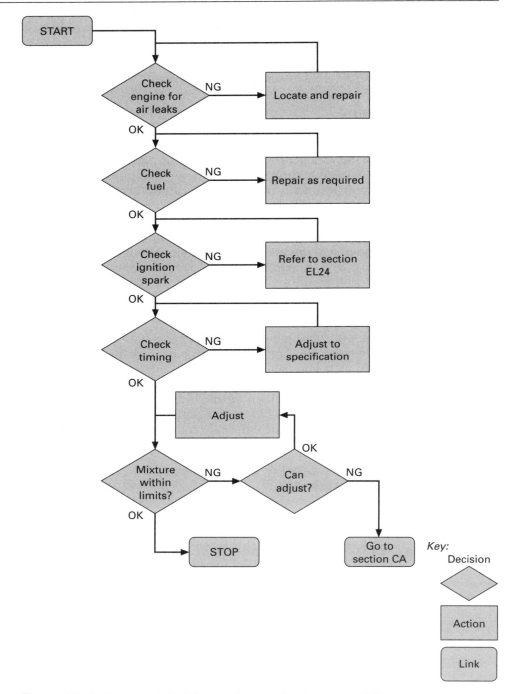

Figure 4.2 Actions and decisions when curing improper idling

4.2.9 **The flow chart**

Flow charts have many designs and applications. Generally, they set out sequences of events and decision points which, together, model action and decision sequences. All these are important in planning and we shall meet several versions in later chapters. Figure 4.2 lays out the sequence of actions and decisions in the case of overcoming what the authors call 'improper idling' of a petrol engine. The objective of the process is to return the system to good condition. Rather than be too concerned about the nature of the repair activities within the process, you should note how the model is built using a set of conventional symbols, indicated by the key.

Information specialists use this model, with some more symbols, as a basis for designing systems. While it is also useful for other managers, there are two limitations. First, there is no representation of time or cost within the diagram. It is useful for thinking about the sequence of events but less useful if one were allocating resources to them on an industrial scale. Second, operational processes quickly become too complex for representation in this way. We shall examine how to overcome these problems in later chapters.

4.3 Strategic management

In the long term, an organisation thrives if it can establish effective relationships with the many parts and elements of its environment. For most business organisations, this means that they have to find ways to compete successfully through obtaining resources and serving customers. Competition does not necessarily mean titanic struggles with rival companies. On the contrary, most organisations seek to limit the direct rivalry they face. They look for those parts of industries and markets within which they can protect themselves from larger and stronger competitors. Furthermore, many build their own defences through cooperation, an important and growing feature of the policies of many organisations. In the following sections, we shall examine strategic management as a process involving planning, control and reviewing policies in the context of both competition and cooperation.

4.3.1 **Strategic management defined**

Strategic management has developed from strategic planning which was concerned with how to plan for the use of the organisation's resources to pursue long-term objectives. This did not, however, concern itself with implementation or control. Accomplishment of plans was, somehow, left to people other than planners and control adjustments were only considered when the plans came round for review. Experience has shown that the best written plans frequently failed because of unanticipated problems and the basic resistance to change within many organisations.

The modern view, then, is that planning, implementation and control should be integrated into the complete process of strategic management. Ansoff gives the definition of strategic management as:

> **The positioning and relating of the organisation to its environment in a way which will assure its continued success and make it secure from surprises.**[3]

The implications of this definition and our discussion are that strategic management involves the following activities:

- Understanding the environment, including making forecasts about the way its various features are changing.
- Relating the organisation to key features of the environment with significant influence upon it. Depending on the organisation, these include suppliers, financiers, sources of labour, governments and so on.
- Deciding upon how the organisation will serve chosen sections of the environment through the supply of bundles of products.
- Obtaining and using resources so that the needs of the environment may be satisfied by the right balance of effectiveness, efficiency and equity.
- Monitoring, forecasting and controlling performance so that the plans made during the process can be achieved.

4.3.2 The strategic management process

As stated in the previous section, strategic management is planning, implementation and control. To look at the planning process in a little more detail we can divide it into stages of analysis and choice. Analysis is the process of deciding the general direction and goals of the organisation and understanding, in terms of the goals, both the environment and the internal strengths and weaknesses. Figure 4.3 is drawn from a study of IKEA, the global furniture retailer, about which more appears in Chapter 7.[4] The chart illustrates the way results can be presented as a SWOT profile, so called because of the four categories of strengths, weaknesses, opportunities and threats under which the internal and external appraisals are categorised.

The idea of a SWOT analysis is to focus managers' attention on the external and internal factors with the biggest impact in the long term. SWOTs are best drawn up by making a long list of items and then checking them to ensure they are significant. A checklist, such as in Figure 4.3, helps to generate ideas. By presenting the elements on a single page, links among them can be identified. Together, the items tell a 'strategic story'. The heavy lines in Figure 4.3 suggest that IKEA's low-cost, high-volume operations support its ability to satisfy growing demand and enter new national markets. They also help it resist competition, but at the expense of limited adaptation in some national markets.

Many tools and techniques are used during the appraisal process to interpret the fit between the organisation and its environment.[5] We have no space to detail them here. The general purpose, however, is to compare the expected future fit with the business objectives. A difference between the two, the so-called planning gap, means that corrective action is required. While it may be that the objectives are unrealistic and need modification, it will normally be the case that the firm must reconsider its activities and make plans to bridge the gap. This

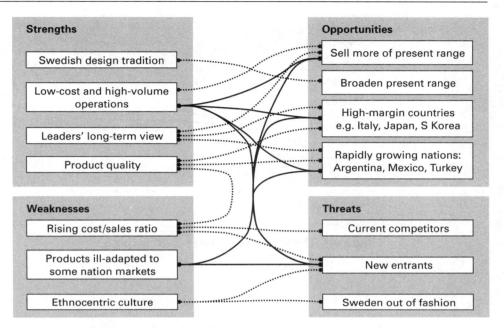

Figure 4.3 SWOT analysis for IKEA showing links among elements

could involve introducing new or updated products, entering new markets, improving customer service, investing in facilities and operational processes, financial restructuring and other possibilities that fundamentally change the nature of the organisation.

The identification of how best to bridge the planning gap forms the selection, or choice, stage of planning. The comparisons made in the appraisal would normally present the organisation with several possible means of closing the gap. The selection stage means looking at these in detail, comparing each for the benefits it brings and the related costs and risks. For example, the operations manager may recognise the opportunities in a new, emerging market for a firm's goods. This is known as market diversification. Having decided upon the main thrust of strategy, the managers will have to select a way of achieving it. The market could be supplied by export, manufacture by a local company under licence or by the firm itself establishing a new production facility within the target country. These choices will have to be analysed for their effects, especially on production and distribution.

Implementation forms the next step in the strategic management process. Good plans take into account four key factors that have strong influence on their success:

- Is the organisational structure appropriate to the plans being proposed?
- Is it possible to develop a coherent set of policies so that every member of the organisation understands the contribution each must make to the plan?
- Are people available with the appropriate training and experience?
- Are systems and processes in place both for carrying out the policies and for monitoring their outcomes?

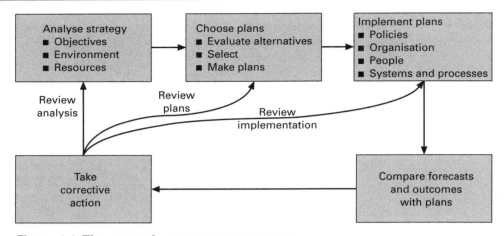

Figure 4.4 The strategic management process

The final element of strategic management is control. The relationship between this activity and the other parts of the process are illustrated in Figure 4.4. This has been developed from Figure 4.1 to emphasise the two steps in strategy formation, analysis and choice, and the different ways in which corrective action can be taken. Strategic control involves comparisons not only of current perform-ance with plans but also of forecasts of future performance. Corrective action can take place in the operational subsystem of the organisation, that is to change what and how things are currently done. Alternatively, two other forms of adjustment are shown in Figure 4.4. There can be adjustments to plans and, if it turns out that this does not bridge the planning gap, the company can review its strategic analysis. These actions are examples of feedforward, concurrent and feedback control, which are examined later in this chapter.

4.3.3 Strategy during the product life cycle

For many organisations, competitors are a critical part of the environment in which they operate. We saw in Chapter 2 how the idea of the product life cycle enables us to understand how the intensity of competition rises and falls with time. This has implications throughout the operations function as indicated in Table 4.4. The usefulness of the PLC idea varies from industry to industry. Some-times, experience shows that new products follow regular patterns. Examples range from pesticides, which may have a useful life of about seven years before they are superseded, to some toys that may only last a season if they are sold as tie-in merchandise connected with films or television series.

Industry analysts often apply the PLC model. Nevertheless, to base strategy solely on the assumed stage in the cycle would be foolish. In the opening case, Wiseman is increasing capacity in an industry that many think is in terminal decline. Yet, the managers take a different view. Perhaps they know their new plant will offer such cost savings that they can undercut many rivals. By the same token, competition may not mean head-on clashes that reduce prices as rapidly

Table 4.4 Competitive and operations strategies during the product life cycle

	Stage of product life cycle			
	Introduction	Growth	Maturity	Decline
Competitive strategy	Prepare for competition	Monitor competitors	Compete through improvements and updating	Compete on price
Basic operations	Build scale of operations: links with suppliers; production systems; distribution	Seek economies of scale throughout the whole operations system	Stop investing in extra capacity; focus on cutting costs in all areas; make low-cost improvements in product–service on continuous basis	Reduce scale of operations to match decline in demand

as theory might suggest. Indeed, there are many ways in which firms compete: operations managers offer quality, responsiveness, reliability, speed and service.

4.3.4 Generic competitive strategies

The best known model of competitive strategies is that developed by Porter.[6] As shown in Figure 4.5, Porter's model represents the combination of two strategic variables, competitive advantage and competitive scope:

- *Competitive advantage* is the sustainable strategic edge an organisation has in relation to its competitors. Improvements in performance, for example in reducing costs or increasing responsiveness of the operations function, enable the organisation to choose more ways to compete, that is to gain the edge.

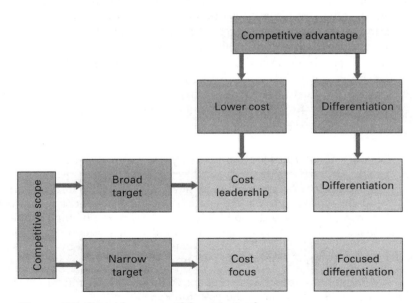

Figure 4.5 Generic competitive strategies

Well-chosen strategies gain ground more effectively. Porter argues that firms must choose between competing on low prices, and therefore low costs, or through differentiation. A firm that differentiates provides superior value, in terms of quality, service, extra features and so on, compared with the lower priced rivals. To be successful, enough customers must recognise the added value and be prepared to pay a premium price for it.

■ *Competitive scope* is the range or breadth over which the organisation chooses to compete. The range may be defined in terms such as the number of industries, countries, markets and products. To give two extreme examples: a very narrow scope may be a small dairy serving customers in one town with three grades of milk; a very broad scope is the many countries and markets served by a global corporation such as Unilever.

4.3.5 Four generic strategies

Porter's model encourages managers to think of their choice of combination of competitive advantage and scope which leads to one of the four generic strategies set out in Figure 4.5. The first two are built on broad competitive scope while the last two are narrow.

Cost leadership

Organisations pursuing this strategy aim to keep their total costs lower than those of their competitors. In most industries, this means operating at high volumes so that economies of scale are realised. Managers concentrate their attention on maintaining lower costs in relevant phases of their value chains. Large scale buying means low input prices. High volumes of throughput mean great efficiency in operations, distribution and marketing. The supermarket chain Asda, one of Wiseman's customers, stresses price as a key part of its competitive strategy. It offers keen prices every day, recognising the customer preference for this rather than a continually changing range of offers. It has led campaigns to overcome what it sees as price fixing in trade-marked goods, pharmaceuticals and fragrances, as in Box 4.1.[7]

Asda also illustrates the problem of newcomers entering the industry with even lower costs of operations. Competition from the LADs (limited assortment

BOX 4.1 Cost leadership strategies

In April 2001, Asda launched its new range cut-price designer sunglasses. The retailer, claiming to be largest non-food supermarket chain in the UK, said the sunglasses were ordered before the 7 April ruling by the European Court. This placed responsibility for deciding whether distribution restrictions were fair with national courts. The dispute had been triggered by Tesco's sales of Levi jeans imported from nations where distributors' prices were low.

Although the ruling was complex, Asda saw no reason why it should not source further items in the grey market.

discounters) intensified through the 1990s. The home-based chains, such as Kwik Save and Lo-Cost, were first augmented by firms from other EU countries such as Aldi (Germany), Netto (Denmark) and Ed (France). Then came warehouse clubs, including Costco, which claimed to shave another 10% off prices with their new form of trading. All the entrants threaten the established firms, especially those who pursue some aspect of the cost leadership strategy.

Differentiation

Only a few companies within an industry aim to compete using price as their most important weapon. Most differentiate by establishing in the customers' minds the idea of value for money. While Asda stresses price, Tesco offers variety, innovation and a high-quality image. Both Asda and Tesco have a broad competitive scope within the UK market. They are located in most regions and appeal to the large group of customers who seek the convenience of the large store with parking. Yet, Tesco, with its differentiation strategy, has been more successful than Asda. It has used advertising to establish its brand, widely recognised as being synonymous with quality; in its operations, it has striven for value for money in the mix of goods and services. Value for money must be stressed because a differentiator will not succeed if the extra prices it charges are greater than the extra value perceived by the customer.

Cost focus

The firm following the cost focus strategy seeks competitive advantage by supplying a narrowly defined market with an operations system designed to operate at low cost. The market is often defined by region or urban area. For example, free newspapers draw their revenue solely from advertising. They first competed with paid-for local newspapers by cutting costs of production, by dispensing with journalists and editorial staff. Yet, they quickly learned that they needed some news items among the advertising to encourage readers to turn the pages! Hence, they use column fillers and cheap syndicated articles on subjects such as travel, astrology and heraldry.

Nowadays, however, cost focus companies can become global. Ease of travel, lower trade barriers and, especially, the Internet, allow small manufacturing companies to deal internationally. These 'sliver' companies achieve economies of scale in manufacturing by subcontracting most processes and concentrating on design and marketing.[8]

Focused differentiation

In following a strategy of focused differentiation, the organisation delivers a superior product to a narrowly defined market segment. The segment could be geographical, although it could also be split by social group, gender, age and so on. The company operating the Newton Nursing Home (see Chapter 1) serves aged people in north-west England. It aims to offer a superior service to its customers by providing numerous little extras and comforts not provided by rivals. Through doing so it has established a reputation for good service and can charge a price some 10% above the market average.

Porter argues that organisations need to select a generic strategy and stick to it. Otherwise, there is a danger of being 'stuck in the middle', losing to threats from both cost leaders and differentiators. Others have found this to be false since it may be possible to arrange operations systems so that both cost leadership and differentiation are achieved simultaneously. Customisation is one aspect of this trend. Under this policy, the organisation supplies individually tailored outputs from production systems almost entirely based on mass production or mass service principles. Amtico, the opening case of Chapter 3, is a good example.

Exercise 4.3   Preferred generic strategies will vary throughout the product life cycle. Relate the four strategies to the stages set out in Table 4.4.

4.3.6 Strategic cooperation within the firm

So far, we have focused our attention on the competitive view of strategic management. Yet, many organisations have found that they can use their resources better if they cooperate. Indeed, one of the arguments for building up a diversified firm consisting of several related divisions is that advantage based on synergy can be gained. In sharing resources and functions such as finance, operations, marketing, distribution and so one, more can be gained than if they operated independently. Synergy is often called the 'two plus two equals five' effect.

To gain synergy, relationships among business units can exploit three types of connection, according to Porter.[9] First, the connections can be *tangible* in that the measurable extra costs of forging the link are exceeded by the benefits in terms of total cost savings or enhanced differentiation of products. The best activities to be considered for linking represent both a substantial proportion of costs and are sensitive to increases in scale or utilisation. Examples could be reaching a range of customers through a common distribution system or transferring process technologies to improve quality.

Intangible connections form the second group. Here business unit functions are similar in general terms such as facing the same type of buyer, making the same type of purchase or running the same type of manufacturing process. For instance, two units may be engaged in large-batch production and hence may share knowledge of the development of planning systems or materials handling technology. Costs and benefits of linking are, however, more difficult to measure than those in the tangible category.

Figure 4.6 illustrates both tangible and intangible connections. Two divisions of the same business are represented by their value chains (see Chapter 1). Here, tangible links could arise from sharing sales forces, distribution or technology. Intangible links lie in sharing ideas on manufacturing or in making common approaches to the government.

The third type of link arises from *competitor interrelationships*. Large corporations compete in many ways, often on a large scale. Taking a passive stance against a multifaceted competitor runs the risk of each business being 'picked off' in turn, as the opponent allocates promotional resources around its various units. An active protagonist should be prepared to match, indeed pre-empt, this sort of behaviour.

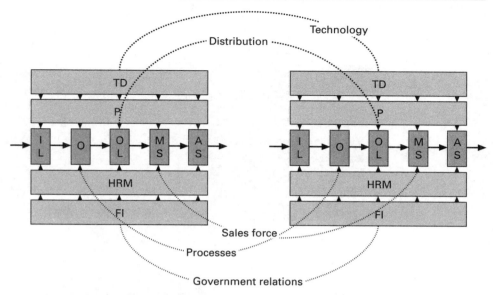

Figure 4.6 Links between businesses in a diversified firm

Despite the potential advantages of these links between divisions, many diversified firms do not cement such bonds effectively. Impediments may arise from human factors, such as different cultural and value systems, and technical reasons such as the way financial systems set up transfer prices which effect one unit less favourably than another. Head offices may be reluctant to intervene, as this would run counter to the spirit of operational decentralisation.

4.3.7 Strategic cooperation among firms

In the light of such difficulties, firms often look outside the group for coalition partners. Such ventures have been attempted for many years with varying degrees of success and there has been much discussion of alliances in the literature.[10] We shall illustrate three links with tangible benefits, namely resource pools, combination alliances and de-escalation alliances.[11]

Resource pools

These involve two or more organisations in putting relevant resources together. They do so to:

■ reduce duplication or redundancy

■ share or alleviate risk

■ combine efforts to compete with rivals

■ reach a scale threshold where they can become effective entrants to a market.

We can see such agreements linking key activities of the value chain. Figure 4.7 illustrates one possibility. Promoted by EU grants and agencies, sharing of

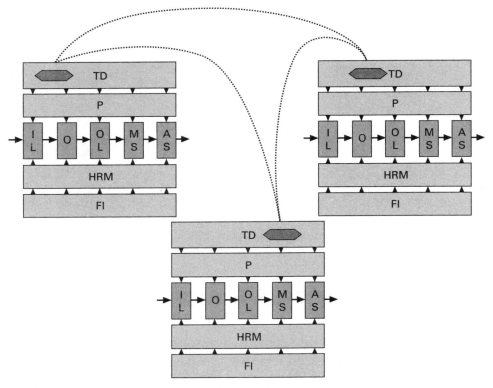

Figure 4.7 Firms accept EU grants to share aspects of technological development

technical development has become common in information technology, biotechnology and new materials.[12]

Combination alliances

These occur when partners combine or exchange complementary functions. For small and medium enterprises to engage in international business, alliances are a common route. Scottish whisky distillers Glenmorangie established joint ventures in India and China. In the former, bottling is carried out by the long-established Mohan Meakin distillery; in the latter, the partner also bottles, while Glenmorangie provides technological support. It advises on improving the quality and supply of local spirit. Figure 4.8 summarises a typical link.

The Glenmorangie links may be a step towards the widely practised partnership sourcing. Here, partners integrate primary activities to achieve just-in-time supplies and high-quality standards. Firms combining their outbound logistics with the downstream partner avoid the need for strength in sales and marketing and service (see Figure 4.9). Frequently, partners link their secondary activities, for example by having joint design activities for product modification or replacement. Effective partnership sourcing goes deeper than integrating stock control and quality monitoring. Just-in-time (JIT) is one approach to initiating and developing such strategic links. It is discussed later in this chapter.

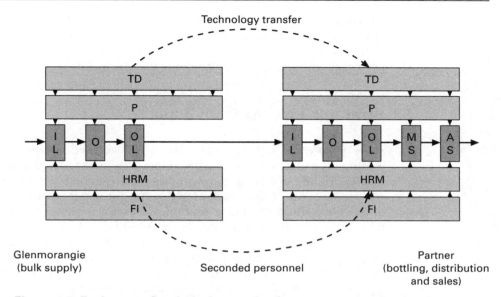

Figure 4.8 Exchange of technical expertise for access to local operations and markets

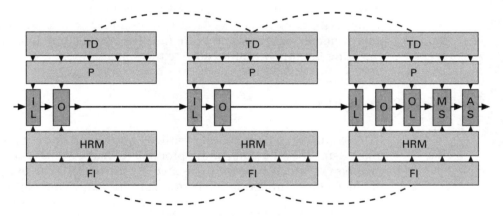

Figure 4.9 Partnership sourcing means close integration of activities

De-escalation alliances

De-escalation alliances are those in which members agree to reduce competition or attacks on each other. Each company can differentiate and focus its value activities, for example by providing complementary services. Timetabling cooperation between cross-channel ferry companies in the light of a new entrant to the business, Eurotunnel, is a case in point.

Besides the links already described, firms take part in alliances with less tangible benefits. These are less readily explained by the classification already examined. As Badaracco[13] pointed out, other issues come to the fore in these loose, tenuous arrangements. One is the transfer of embedded technical and managerial knowledge. 'How to make cars at the lowest cost in the world' is not knowledge possessed by an individual; neither is it written down. It is embedded within teams. Such transfer gradually occurs within any alliance and is the express purpose of many cooperative agreements in high technology.

4.3.8 Strategic lessons from Japan

Some Japanese companies have gradually achieved competitive advantage in leading manufacturing industries, especially automobiles and consumer electronics. There have been many studies seeking to explain this success. Reasons advanced vary from government policy and the social environment to the details of process planning and organisation. Common to these studies is a recognition that leading Japanese companies concentrate on eliminating waste and making continuous improvements. Tied in with these efforts are two general managerial philosophies, just-in-time and total quality management. These are called philosophies rather than techniques because a commitment to them is part of the way Japanese managers think that organisations ought to be managed.

Some westerners have mistakenly seen both JIT and TQM as means of setting up operations policies, as if they are techniques to be chosen when planning models suggest they are the best way forward. For Japanese firms, by way of contrast, both JIT and TQM are general approaches to producing improved results. Strategic thinking in Japan is as much grounded in incremental or continuous improvement (*kaizen*) as it is in formally setting out long-range plans and analysing new opportunities outside the organisation.

4.3.9 Just-in-time

JIT concentrates on eliminating waste by ensuring that only just enough of the input items for a manufacturing process are made available just in time and at the point at which they are to be used. At the operational level, JIT aims to cut the high stocks hindering the performance of many companies. In this sense it can be seen as a set of production management techniques designed to:

- improve purchasing procedures by linking suppliers more closely into the production schedules
- identify and eliminate bottlenecks
- ensure higher quality and hence eradicate scrap and rework
- cut machine and other process failures.

We shall be dealing with these issues at appropriate stages later in the book. At this point, however, we should recognise that JIT, successfully carried out, has deeper implications than are suggested by merely listing a set of techniques for use at the operational level. JIT is both a cause and a result of strategic change.

Improved performance of leading firms over the past few decades greatly affects the strategic environment of all business. The demands of customers have increased substantially, especially insofar as:

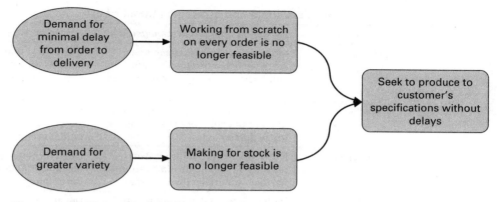

Figure 4.10 The manufacturing dilemma

- The volume and type of demand have become more variable. More models are on offer, product life cycles have become shorter and it is necessary to improve products more rapidly than ever.
- Delays in supply are no longer acceptable. Customers increasingly seek products closely matching their requirements but are not satisfied if this implies that each item is made from scratch with consequent long delays.
- Quality must be perfect yet the price must be as low as possible.

The strategic response to this emerging business environment is to create a manufacturing and distribution system which is capable of supplying a rising variety of products while being very flexible and offering very short delivery times. This dilemma facing many modern manufacturers is summarised in Figure 4.10. As we saw in Chapter 3, the production of long runs of products with little variety can be achieved through setting out production lines which convert raw materials to finished goods without the build-up on intermediate stocks of work-in-progress. Yet, most firms do not experience demand sufficiently large to justify this. They are committed to supply in limited batches. The basis of JIT in these firms is to achieve rapid rates of flow, as on the production line, through machines, which are, in effect, free standing.

JIT, then, looks to limit stocks and increase the speed of flow through all stages of the production system. Batch sizes are reduced to increase the speed of flow of items. For companies that fully take into account the JIT philosophy, the production system is seen as extending beyond their own boundaries to imply integration with both suppliers and customers.

The changes are sometimes cosmetic. In a recent conversation with a logistics manager of a component manufacturer, the author was told: 'Of course some customers pay lip service to the just-in-time philosophy. They use the idea as an excuse. They want us to deliver in smaller batches at no extra cost and because we are in a recession, we are forced to do so. But we still deliver into the receiving warehouse where the goods get stuck for days or weeks before being released on to the shop floor.'

Integration of manufacturers' and suppliers' systems to increase flow rates requires more effort than this. When set up with full commitment, JIT implies changes at all levels of management.

Table 4.5 Operational and strategic impact of JIT

Issue	Impact on operations management	Impact on strategic management
Flows	More speed; smaller batch sizes; more switches between orders; emphasis on cutting switching time	Changes in manufacturing layouts; integration with suppliers' and customers' flows; selection of single sources of supply
Stocks	Smaller input stocks delivered close to point of use; processed items move quickly	Stocks cut through whole system; smaller or no warehouses; small lot delivery systems
Flexibility	Need for changes in processes; responsive and flexible procedures; flexible, multiskilled work force	Need for total systems matching flexibility demanded; implications for training
Quality	High-quality goal at every stage; errors studied and learnt from	Developing total quality throughout the whole chain
Responsibility	The worker is the expert; local detailed operations control; each employee is responsible for quality	Recognising and instilling the philosophy of just-in-time

4.3.10 Implantation of JIT

For illustration, we can take just two of the planning levels suggested earlier in the chapter, strategic and operational. Using these as the categories, Table 4.5 summarises the impact that JIT philosophy has right through the organisation.

The increased flow speeds and greater flexibility of JIT are achieved, according to Japanese managers, by *jidoka*, making things visible. Eliminating inventory means that irregularities and delays in production, poor quality and uncertain planning are all exposed. The Japanese use the parable of a river. Figure 4.11 shows, at the top, the river flowing along slowly and, at the surface, smoothly. Yet, it does not flow at the same pace everywhere. Rocks, deep pools and other obstructions hinder the smooth flow and cause some water to, so to speak, lag behind. The water in the parable represents the flow of goods through the plant. The pools are the stocks and the rocks the barriers to smooth operations. These are problems of machine failure, poor quality, uncertain supplies and so on. To make the stream run faster, the obstacles must be removed. To accomplish this, the level in the river is gradually reduced so that the rocks become visible and can be taken away. In the plant, a policy of gradually reducing safety stocks and work in progress means that the imperfections become clear and action must be taken to correct them.

As it is not possible to have a river without water, some stocks are necessary for the process to work. This is not denied. Proponents of the JIT philosophy argue that manufacturing can be run with much less stock than is usually imagined. We shall return to the detailed means by which this can be achieved in Chapter 12.

JIT development implies the removal of hazards to the smooth flow of materials through the plant. A key hazard is quality and this takes us on to the second application of the Japanese ideas of waste elimination and continuous improvement – total quality.

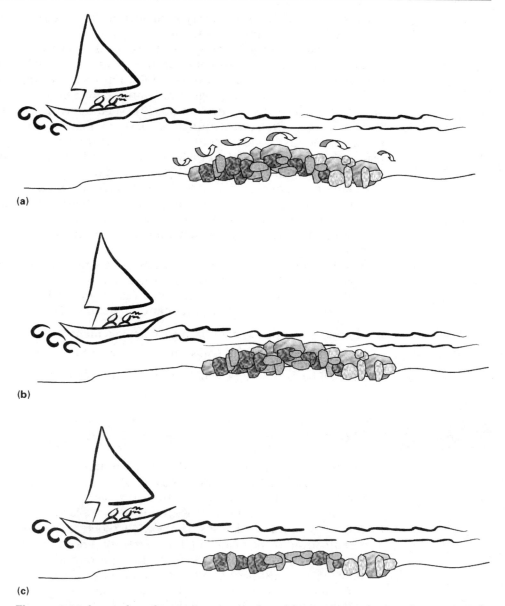

Figure 4.11 Lowering the water exposes problems that can then be removed

4.3.11 Total quality management

The gradual lowering of the water level exposes the hazards that account for why the water level is kept so high in the first place. In the same way, the factory tries to protect itself from diverse hazards, many of which can be seen as poor quality – defective components, breakdowns or maladjustments of machines and late delivery to the next stage. Continuous improvement relies on making these defects more visible so that every weakness in the system becomes noticed and ways are found of eliminating them.

Total quality management applies these ideas to every process in the whole organisation. Each department, section and individual must be seen as contributing to the quality of the organisation's output. Applications in manufacturing are obvious and programmes aiming for zero defects (ZD), no delays, and machine breakdowns are common. TQM goes further than this, recognising how employees in service functions have to make their contributions. For example, the first point of contact for many customers is the front gate of the plant or the reception desk of the hotel. The contribution of staff at these points is a key element in the customers' appreciation of the product they are supplied. Furthermore, many staff see neither the product nor the ultimate customer. Yet, if their work does have value, it is important to others in the organisation – their internal customers. Each link shows as a supplier–customer link with the effectiveness of the latter being strongly influenced by the quality of the work of the former.

TQM is, therefore, a system that needs to be embedded within the culture of an organisation. Teamwork, leadership and communication sustain TQM. Yet, it cannot work in a vacuum. Continuous improvement is impossible without a framework of analysis and measurement. Therefore, TQM also requires:

- a formally planned system of quality management
- measurement systems to collect performance information.

We shall be examining the details of these processes in Chapters 16 and 17.

4.4 Control

Robert Burns wrote, 'The best laid schemes o' mice and men gang aft a-gley.'[14] Possibly better known is Murphy's Law: 'If it is possible for something to go wrong, then it will.' Each of these statements may seem to be unduly pessimistic. They emphasise, however, that the outcomes of plans frequently deviate from intentions. This may be because of the hidden defects exposed in just-in-time. It also results from plans made under uncertainty. We should not simply set plans in motion and expect them to succeed. Systems out of control lead to spectacular disasters such as plant explosions or ship collisions. They may also lead to gradual, almost unnoticed, decline in performance so that, in the end, no one really knows why a business has failed.

The failure to control the system may have been temporary, as with the disaster, or permanent, as happens with gradual decline. In either case, we can see that we must not expect plans to succeed unless the planning and control cycle of Figure 4.1 is complete. In the following sections, we shall be looking more closely at types of control as they apply to strategy and operations.

4.4.1 The control process

We can define the general purpose of control as follows:

> **Control ensures that the plan is achieved in spite of obstacles, variations and uncertainties in both the organisation and its environment.**

To be effective, the control process must know the objectives and plans, be able to assess performance and then take the necessary actions to correct deviations between the measured performance and the plans. This is the classic control loop observed in many systems. Living systems frequently have built-in control mechanisms maintaining the delicate balance necessary for survival. The human body has thousands of them. For instance, the temperature of the brain must be maintained to within 0.1°C to allow effective functioning.

Organisations, of course, do not have natural controls. These must be designed and installed as part of each process. They can operate, however, in one way that natural systems usually cannot. They can forecast outcomes of current behaviour and take control action in anticipation of future deviations from the plan. Recognising this difference, we can discern three types of control, detailed in the following.

Feedback control

Feedback is a widely used term, suggesting that it is the most widely recognised form of control. Figure 4.12 shows the elements making up the control process. As we saw in Chapter 1, the transformation system converts inputs into outputs. This system could represent one day-to-day operational process, such as delivery, or the whole business working over a period of several years. The controller, a person or device such as a switch, is there to guide the transformation. It monitors the outputs to assess the performance of the system and compares its data with the goals set out in the plan. In the light of this comparison, control action follows. This can mean changes, either to the inputs or to the system itself, so that the progress towards the goals is restored.

In feedback control systems, managers use information about past activities to discover and learn from discrepancies and make changes to avoid them in the future. One of its problems is that corrections occur after the event, that is when

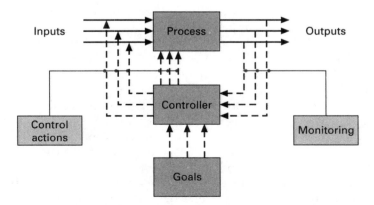

Figure 4.12 Feedback control monitors and acts after tasks are completed

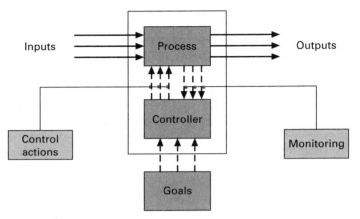

Figure 4.13 Concurrent control monitors and acts while tasks are in progress

errors have occurred and the costs or waste have already been created. For instance, budgetary control is based on reports of past events and, while delays can be reduced by use of shorter intervals between those reports, their usefulness is limited by their historic nature.

Concurrent control

Often called real-time control, concurrent control works as closely as possible with the present performance of the system. It means that the stages of monitoring, comparison and taking action are all rolled into one and the controller is brought very close to the system, as shown in Figure 4.13. Concurrent control is normal in work where the individual or team is responsible for performance. There will be a continual awareness of the need for efficiency, timeliness and quality and the group will continually check that such goals are being achieved.

End of line inspection is an example of feedback control where the errors are picked up on completion of the job. Using the notion of concurrent control, total quality management improves on the final inspection by building in quality monitoring at all stages of production, making every person responsible for the quality of their output as it happens.

It is argued that concurrent control is merely a variant of feedback control where the monitoring is carried out very quickly. To an extent, this is true. Nevertheless, there is an important difference in perspective. An analogy may be seen in a task such as cutting a hedge. Before starting the job, I find a stick whose length matches the height I want. Then I cut short sections of the hedge, keeping a line by eye and using the stick to check the height. I could examine these two monitoring processes as feedback mechanisms where control signals pass through my eyes, brain and muscle system. But this is the view of the biologist and not the gardener, who is not interested in such detail. Feedback control of the hedge height occurs when I stand back and judge whether the whole process was successful. If I then judge the hedge uneven or too high, I can repeat the task; if it is too low, I have to wait until the next year.

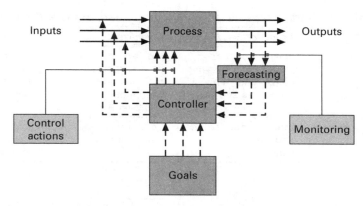

Figure 4.14 Feedforward control monitors, forecasts and acts in anticipation of deviations

Feedforward control

As the name implies, feedforward control involves the anticipation of problems and the taking of action before they arise. Conceptually, the data on current performance of the system are used to produce a forecast of its future state, as shown in Figure 4.14. Control action is based on this forecast. This implies the making of a plan within a plan. Yet the focus is not on planning, which is about where to go and how to get there. Feedforward control is about supporting the current plan to give it the greatest chance of success. Preventive maintenance, such as painting the outside of my house, is based on anticipation of the well-known consequences of not doing the work in time. This is a key point in feedforward control; the system needs to be sufficiently well understood to enable the forecasting stage to work successfully.

Because of the difficulties that managers have in understanding all the consequences of actions in a complex system, feedforward control is the most difficult to install and use. If, for example, a delivery driver is late because of heavy traffic, he may be able to warn the customer's logistics department. If the consequences of the delay were difficult to forecast, the control action would be unclear. In a JIT system, the flows of a whole plant may have to be suspended; in another case, a slight delay would be of little consequence, needing merely a simple resequencing. It is often difficult for managers to forecast the effects of such discrepancies and therefore pass on appropriate instructions.

4.4.2 Control in the operations system

We have given several examples of control in the preceding sections. None is, in principle, superior or more effective than the others. In modern organisations, all three types are used. Each has its own focus. Feedforward control helps in the avoidance of hazards and errors; concurrent control enables staff to identify and eliminate errors as they occur; and feedback control emphasises adjustment after the event so that the organisation learns not to repeat errors. To illustrate this combination, Table 4.6 shows how to use control in the management

Table 4.6 Control types in total quality management and stock control

	Feedback	*Concurrent*	*Feedforward*
TQM	Finished goods inspection; customer complaints; demand for repairs and spares	Monitoring of work in progress; preventive maintenance; continuous improvement	Monitoring quality of supplies and suppliers; investment in new equipment; skills training
Stock control	Monthly stock counts and checks on condition	Continuous monitoring	Inventory forecasts from sales forecasts and agreed production plans

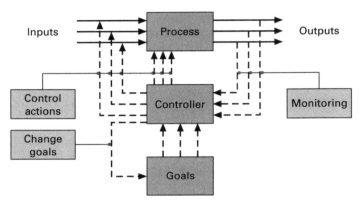

Figure 4.15 Feedback control with goal adjustment if they cannot be achieved

of both quality and stocks. The methods mentioned here appear again in later chapters.

Unachievable goals

Whatever the design, a problem arises if the control system cannot work. As suggested earlier, it may be that the process fails through momentary inattention. Or it may be that there have been years of neglect of maintenance and reinvestment. In such cases, the transformation process cannot achieve the required standards and to continue would only makes things worse. This takes us to our last variation of the control model, one that incorporates the possibility of changing the goals themselves. Figure 4.15 builds on Figure 4.12 by adding a feedback loop from the controller to the goals, suggesting that it may be necessary to change them in the light of circumstances.

This extra feedback loop is another way of looking at the levels of planning set out at the start of the chapter. At each level, goals can be changed either because they cannot be achieved or because their contribution to the next higher level is insufficient. In parallel with planning, therefore, there will be a hierarchy of interlinked control systems. These can be seen as follows:

■ *Strategic control.* Monitoring the performance of the organisation in relation to its environment and how well it is achieving its strategic plans. Taking strategic action.

- *Intermediate control.* Monitoring the performance of divisions or functions according to annual budgets and non-financial performance indicators such as meeting schedules, quality, safety and so on. Taking action in the short and medium term to correct deviations from plans, budgets and performance standards.

- *Operations control.* Monitoring performance of the operations function on a moment-by-moment or day-to-day basis in relation to production schedules. Taking immediate action to correct deviations from the detailed plans, for example by moving staff or changing schedules.

4.4.3 Control problems in the real organisation

The danger with presenting control as a series of diagrams with loops around which information flows is the suggestion that somehow the process is straightforward and automatic once it has been designed. The reality is some way from this. Control systems themselves are prone to difficulties and failure, not least because they exist within human activity systems. Therefore, beyond the technical problems of the design of control systems, we can note three further issues arising from the involvement of people: goal displacement, measurementship and budget games.

Goal displacement is the phenomenon of the means becoming the ends. Organisations, in striving to maintain efficiency, effectiveness and equity may become so bound up with rules that their members forget why they were set up in the first place. Bureaucratic paperwork becomes more important than human needs. We hear of cases (in America) of dying patients not receiving treatment until their insurance status is confirmed while in many countries the military type who sticks to procedures through everything is the butt of much derision.

Measurementship stems from the desire to appear good. It involves manipulating reports and the data that go to make them up. This goes right to the top of some organisations where various means of 'off-balance-sheet financing' enabled firms to present a sound impression to their shareholders while being as much in hock as ever. At lower levels, many directors are keen on seeing low finished goods stocks and take steps to stop the flow into finished goods warehouses in the days before the count is to be taken. This, of course, causes or increases the chaos elsewhere.

Budget games are played especially by those managers who perceive their bosses to have a punitive leadership style. For example, in project management, they seek a budget larger than necessary to protect themselves from later overruns. They then, naturally, have to find ways of spending the money, often in a hurry before the period end. Among the most common game tactics are asking for incremental increases on the previous year, asking for some items which will definitely be rejected while hoping to slip others through, only asking for a small funding for a new idea and talking up a crisis to put pressure on the boss.

4.4.4 Budgetary control

We will illustrate the practical application of control by reference to budgeting. Notwithstanding the difficulties mentioned in the previous section, all managers who are responsible for consuming resources should be given a budget. They should contain targets for revenue or, in the case of most operations, expenditures only for those areas for which the manager has responsibility.

The principles of budgeting have already been explained in Chapter 2. The process normally works on an annual cycle, sometimes with a one- or two-year extension that is itself updated every year. The idea of the extension is to combine relatively tight control of money with giving the manager scope to plan beyond the end of the immediate year. In many cases, there is scope to adjust budgets in the light of changing circumstances; indeed this is sometimes automatic as in the flexible budget. Allowances are made in advance for changed levels of activity occurring during the period. Hence, if demand for a product line were to rise in response to, say, unexpectedly good weather, then production output may have to rise. Naturally, the production budget would have to flex in relation to this change. The cost increases need not be in proportion to output. Extras may include shift or overtime payments, while savings may follow the use of plant more intensively than planned.

Exercise 4.4	Which costs at the Manchester plant, in the opening case, would be affected by running beyond the designed capacity?

Applying our ideas of planning and control, we can see that sound budgeting practice has the following features:

- Targets should be clear and agreed between managers and their superiors.
- The budgets should be integrated so that they are mutually consistent and contribute to the overall plan.
- Feedback should be clear, as early as possible and enable managers to identify differences between outcomes and the budget, the so-called *variances*.
- Where several managers are responsible for activities in a particular function, the process must recognise and sustain the communication and cooperation necessary.
- The budget reports should help in deciding upon control action.

✔ Quick check-up

Can you:

- ☐ Define: planning; objective; strategic management; control.
- ☐ Sketch the planning and control cycle and give examples of upward and downward links in planning.
- ☐ Name three types of uncertainty.
- ☐ List the threefold test of a good objective.
- ☐ Outline the strategic planning process, naming the four generic competitive strategies.

☐ Delineate three types of strategic alliance.

☐ Summarise JIT and TQM.

☐ List three types of control with examples from quality and inventory.

☐ Name three problems with control in organisations.

❓ Questions

Chapter review

4.1 Explain why the planning cycle includes means for correcting deviations from any plan.

4.2 To what extent is the position in the product life cycle a good indicator of the generic strategy that should be adopted?

4.3 Why is it argued in the chapter that JIT and TQM have strategic impact?

Application

4.4 Explain how policies pursued by Wiseman and other companies in the opening case study fit into the generic strategy framework.

4.5 For typical domestic tasks such as cooking or cleaning, explain how the control models yield insights into how they might be managed. What differences occur if the same tasks are operated in a business context?

Investigation

4.6 Through interviews and personal observation, investigate how any manager approaches planning and control. To what extent does this experience match the discussion of this chapter?

CLOSING CASE ## Jaeger[15]

Jaeger is famous for manufacturing and selling high-quality clothing. It is a vertically integrated company in that it manufactures and distributes through its own wholesale and retail outlets. More than 90% of its goods are made in the United Kingdom. There are 80 Jaeger ladies' shops in the UK with a similar number abroad. Jaeger sells its products through other outlets so the wholesale operations both at home and for export are as important as the retail. This is a successful business widely recognised for excellent design.

In common with other leading firms in the retail industry, Jaeger has moved away from having just two sales seasons each year, spring and autumn, towards a more continuous replenishment of the stores with new designs. According to the chairman, this means five seasons per year, there being two (early and late) for spring.

It takes 11 months from conception of a range to the delivery of the first batch to the shops. This represents the minimum time for everything to be done. Clearly, it is in the interests of the company to delay the start of this design process for as long as possible so that decisions can be based on

▶

Table 4.7 Planning steps ahead of a season

Time to the season	Actions, events
From 56–52 weeks	Initial colour direction Initial communications with fibre and fabric suppliers
At 50 weeks	. . .

knowledge of the latest trends. Colour is the starting point. For a spring range, the colours are decided between December and January and discussed with fibre and fabric suppliers. Mid-February is the deadline for the merchandise director to decide the direction of the range. From February to May cloth selection and ordering of sample lengths take place. From 1 April to the middle of June Jaeger goes through fabric modelling and sampling. Designing and modelling of garments runs from May to late June while fabric is being obtained for pattern cards and swatches. By 1 June the merchandise director and product managers review the design work. This gives one month for pilot and sample orders to be placed and filled. While these activities are progressing, the company buys cloth. Cloth has a long lead time so that 70% of purchase orders are committed by 10 May and the final purchase order is placed by 10 September, a date the manufacturers find quite late.

Sales are estimated and Jaeger's factories are expected to have production plans for the new range ready by 20 July. Delivery dates are agreed by the end of that month. This means that the sales department can begin to accept firm orders during August. Before any orders are received, however, Jaeger has itself to place firm garment requisitions on its own factories. It does this by 1 August. One-quarter of estimated sales are ordered on the first of each month until November.

1 August is also the decision date for the range information including prices. The samples, ordered in June, are delivered to the warehouse on 10 August and selling starts in earnest on the 20th.

Managers, right up to the chairman, receive weekly reports of progress against plans, reminding everyone of the decisions which are due and who has to make them.

Questions

1 Summarise the information in the case using a rich picture, accompanied by a chart or table of dates. Table 4.7 proposes a layout; otherwise, you might use a Gantt chart as in Chapter 12.

2 Identify the types of uncertainty faced by Jaeger, suggesting how they respond to them.

3 Give examples of the sort of planning described in the case study. From your general knowledge of retailing, what would comprise strategic planning at Jaeger?

4 Choose examples of three types of control and set them out using suitable diagrams.

Notes and references

1. Urry, M. (2001) 'Robert Wiseman dairy plans may yet turn sour', *Financial Times*, 24 April.
2. Adams, C. and Burt, T. (2000) 'Rail chaos to continue this week', *Financial Times*, 30 October, p.1; Jowit, J. (2001) 'Network disintegrates amid cycle of blame: Juliette Jowit analyses the divisions in the rail industry and says it is spiralling in a seemingly unbreakable deadlock', *Financial Times*, 4 May.
3. Ansoff, H.I. (1984) *Implanting Strategic Management*, Eaglewood Cliffs: Prentice Hall.
4. Naylor, J. (1999) *Management*, Harlow: Financial Times Prentice Hall, p.315.
5. For example, see Lynch, R. (2000) *Corporate Strategy*, 2nd edition, Harlow: Financial Times Prentice Hall; Johnson, G. and Scholes, K. (1999) *Exploring Corporate Strategy*, 5th edition, Hemel Hempstead: Prentice Hall Europe.
6. Porter, M.E. (1980) *Competitive Strategy*, New York: Free Press.
7. Tighe, C. (2001) 'Asda to use "grey market"', *Financial Times*, 12 April.
8. Marsh, P. (2001) 'Valve makers keep it in the cluster: Sliver companies', *Financial Times: Survey – Manufacturing Excellence*, 21 May.
9. Porter, M.E. (1985) *Competitive Advantage*, New York: Free Press, p.323.
10. See, for example: Doz, Y.L. and Hamel, G. (2001) 'Alliance advantage, the art of creating value through partnering', *Supply Chain Management*, 6(1), pp.48–51; Beverland, M. and Bretherton, P. (2001) 'The uncertain search for opportunities: determinants of strategic alliances', *Qualitative Market Research: an International Journal*, 4(2), pp.88–99; Bhatnagar, R. and Viswanathan, S. (2000) 'Re-engineering global supply chains: Alliances between manufacturing firms and global logistics services providers', *International Journal of Physical Distribution & Logistics Management*, 30(1), pp.13–34; Butler, C., Kenny, B. and Anchor, J. (2000) 'Strategic alliances in the European Defence industry', *European Business Review*, 12(6), pp.308–322; Mockler, R.J. (2001) 'Making decisions on enterprise-wide strategic alignment in multinational alliances', *Management Decision*, 39(2), pp.90–99; Song, Y., Maher, T.E., Nicholson, J.D. and Gurney, N.P. (2000) 'Strategic alliances in logistics outsourcing', *Asia Pacific Journal of Marketing & Logistics*, 12(4), pp.3–21.
11. Devlin, G. and Bleakley, M. (1988) 'Strategic alliances: guidelines for success', *Long Range Planning*, 21(5), pp.18–23.
12. Hagedoorn, J. and Shakenraad, J. (1990) *Leading Companies and the Structure of Strategic Alliances in Core Technologies*, discussion paper, MERIT, Limburg University, Maastricht.
13. Badaracco, J. (1991) *The Knowledge Link: How firms compete through strategic alliances*, Cambridge, MA: Harvard Business School Press.
14. *To a mouse*: '. . . often go wrong'.
15. Young, G. (1985) untitled seminar paper in McAlhone, B. (ed.) *Directors on design: The 1985 SIAD design management seminar*, London: The Design Council; Worth, G. (1997) 'What is a textile design consultant? Tradition, innovation and change', Second European Academy of Design Conference, Stockholm.

CHAPTER 5

Organising and staffing for operations

OBJECTIVES

When you have finished studying this chapter, you should be able to:

■ Explain the common features of organisations, interpret organisation charts and compare departmental, matrix and network structures.

■ Make clear the scope of human resource management as it supports operations.

■ Outline recruitment and appraisal processes; explain the difficulties with the unstructured interview and how they may be overcome.

■ Describe the main features of a good training programme.

■ Lay out the elements of the interpersonal communication process and how it may be improved; clarify why and how organisations can improve communications.

■ Review the key theories of motivation and show how they apply to management of the operations function; explain the advantages of good job design and participation.

■ Outline the range of rewards available from employment and relate these to various schemes of payment.

■ Summarise the importance of good leadership.

OPENING CASE

Abbott's structural dilemma[1]

Ranked 137th on Fortune's 2001 list of US companies, Illinois-based Abbott Laboratories has been in healthcare for more than a century. Some 40% of 2001 sales of $13 billion occurred outside the United States. Abbott's strategy is to grow while maintaining its reputation for consistent financial performance. The strategy has four elements – internal R&D, market expansion, external collaboration and acquisition. Commitment to the first two is shown by the spending of $2 billion on R&D, the primary driver of growth and recruiting the best researchers and salespeople. Collaboration and acquisition cover the full range of market research, licensing, manufacturing and entry to new business areas. In 2001, for example, Abbott formed a strategic alliance with Millennium Pharmaceuticals covering discovery, development and commercialisation in the field of obesity and diabetes. In another joint venture, formed in 1977 with Japan's Takeda Chemical Industries, sales exceeded £2.5 billion.

At the turn of the millennium, senior managers were wrestling with the problem of how to reconcile two alternative organisational models that had grown up. It was in the late 1960s that Abbott first split itself into three product-based divisions – pharmaceuticals, hospital products and nutritional preparations. Each operated as a self-contained business including R&D, manufacturing and marketing. A fourth division, Abbott International with 25% of group sales, handled all operations in 130 countries outside the United States. It was organised on geographic, as opposed to product, lines.

Parallel to the four divisions, however, a new business emerged. Formed in 1973 by bringing together several disparate activities, the diagnostics division has become a world leader with sales reaching $2.8 billion. Contrary to the other businesses, it is managed globally, using its own personnel and not working through Abbott International. Therefore, two approaches to running international business appear within the same company.

Abbott could live with this difference for another 25 years were it not for changes in the environment. These have stimulated an internal debate on the best way forward. The first change has been towards global product development in the healthcare industry. Intent on cutting launch costs and speeding the rate of market entry, companies look to co-ordinate trials of new drug formulations in all major markets. New technologies, such as the spin-offs from genome research, increase this pressure. The same is true of hospital products for which launching in the United States and subsequent trials abroad mean delays and expensive modifications. This trend, then, pushes companies towards having global product divisions.

The second change pulls companies in the opposite direction. Healthcare purchasers in the United States are consolidating their activities, either because of merger or through buying groups. Co-ordination is occurring across product ranges. This means that suppliers such as Abbott look towards building company-based relationships rather than focusing on selling each line independently. Abbott has to find a way of linking its divisions' marketing in its home market. One benefit is the possibility of synergy among products of different divisions. For instance, Abbott has an HIV diagnostic test, a nutritional product for AIDS sufferers and a drug, Norvir, which shows promise in reducing HIV to undetectable levels. To achieve such linkages, Abbott has created a separate marketing unit to build closer ties with key customers.

Should the home business become more like the international? Alternatively, should the international mirror the home one on a global scale? These questions are difficult for any company, perhaps more so for a successful one such as Abbott.

5.1 Introduction

Like many leaders, the directors of Abbott Laboratories look for the best way to organise their business. This is a continual question as circumstances and people change, and what is fresh in one era is outdated in the next. They also know that any changes they might introduce can be brought in neither quickly nor cheaply. Their company's size means inflexibility; and some within it will resist change. The motivation of members is important. The form of any organisation, then, is a blend of what is desirable and what is practicable. In this chapter, we shall study some basic forms of organisation and the behaviour of participants.

Clearly, operations are usually carried out by organisations, omnipresent features of modern life. Without the social cooperation implied by productive organisations, very little would be achieved. Yet how often does one hear the complaints, 'There's no organisation round here,' or, 'Why don't they get themselves organised?' The trouble in such cases lies not in the absence of organisation, since this is evidenced by the fact that some sort of activity is taking place. It stems from the poor *quality* of the organisation. Some are clearly more successful than others are. Their management requires the application of many skills from staffing to strategy making and communicating to controlling. These need to be co-ordinated. Study of organisations is, therefore, very important to the operations manager who is often responsible for many staff whose work has to be co-ordinated.

Many authors have defined organisations yet the well-known definition of Barnard[2] remains one of the simplest and clearest:

> **An organisation is a system of consciously co-ordinated activities or forces of two or more persons.**

We have encountered many features of this definition. For instance, the notion of system was developed in Chapter 2 and the suggestion of conscious choice among structural forms was brought out, both in the discussion of Chapter 1 and in the Abbott case at the beginning of this chapter. We shall develop themes from Barnard's definition in this chapter. In particular, we shall look at the use of structure to achieve co-ordination, the management of individuals and groups within the organisation and the application of communication and motivation to achieve the vital order without which little of value would happen.

5.2 Organisations

5.2.1 Common features of organisations

Barnard's definition implies the following features present in all organisations:

- *Common goals*. In our discussion of goals in Chapter 4, an underlying implication was that people within an organisation come together to achieve common ends. For productive organisations to function, this is clearly necessary and the goals, effectively communicated among members, act as a banner around which they can be expected to rally.

- *Specialisation*. Organisations achieve their success through specialisation of work. The total task is divided so that individuals can bring their skills to each part and, in total, achieve more than they could do separately. There are dangers in excessive specialisation, however. The organisation may lose the flexibility which comes from having individuals who can perform many tasks and the individual may lose motivation if the job is too repetitive and boring.

- *Conscious co-ordination.* While they may often appear 'like Topsy' to have 'growed', organisations are designed by those who are responsible for them. Co-ordination is the counterpart of specialisation. If the work is to be shared among individuals then the relationships among them have to be managed effectively. As we saw in Chapter 3 in the discussion of socio-technical systems, some patterns of organisation are better suited to different process technologies. This is, however, only one feature which needs to be considered.

- *Hierarchy.* The goals, specialisation and co-ordination of organisations imply a hierarchy of authority. Hierarchy means that some people are given the *authority* to direct and co-ordinate the work of others. Along with this authority goes the *accountability* for its use. The authority and accountability are defined and clarified through the *chain of command* which is itself often represented by the levels and links of the organisation chart. Therefore, for the organisation represented in Figure 1.13, the managing director has the authority to direct and co-ordinate the work of the other senior managers. In turn, the production director has authority with respect to others in the production department and so on. At the same time, each manager is responsible to the superior in the hierarchy, known as the *line manager.*

These features are the least required before an organisation can be said to exist. They do not, however, describe or define organisations in any detail. It all depends on how the features are implemented. Hierarchical relationships can sometimes be oppressive, eliminating initiative and denying creativity. In contrast, they can both be highly efficient and bring satisfaction to the people who are employed within them.

5.2.2 Organisation charts

Organisation charts display the official positions and formal lines of authority and responsibility. In showing the organisation's skeleton, they do present a basic structure but that is all. Just as a picture of the skeleton only partly describes a living creature, so the chart only partly represents the organisation. They are useful, however, in studying the lines of command and formal communication and the ways people are deployed.

Each organisation chart presents us with a description along two dimensions:

- *Vertical.* The hierarchy – the number of levels and the chain of command.

- *Horizontal.* Specialisation – the way tasks are divided between managers and departments and who is responsible for co-ordinating them at each level.

To clarify accountability, it is conventional to allocate each individual to a single line manager. In Figure 1.13, the production director's role as line manager of six subordinates is to ensure that work, which may have been done by one person in a much smaller firm, is effectively co-ordinated. Thus, as organisations grow, they can reap the benefits of specialisation of work yet have to pay the penalty of the extra effort required in co-ordinating that work. The challenge for organisational designers is to achieve the right balance between specialisation and co-ordination.

5.2.3 Departmental organisation structures

The vertical and horizontal dimensions of the organisation chart help us to distinguish between various organisational forms. These are all attempts by managers to solve the problem of specialisation of work while simultaneously achieving co-ordination between relevant employees. The organisation structure both *differentiates* and *integrates* at the same time. This is an important issue for the operations manager. From the operations perspective, the identification of the tasks required to take a product through each step of its value chain is one thing, whereas to allocate these differentiated tasks to staff and then to integrate their work is quite another. The most common way of achieving this is through departments. A department groups employees whose jobs are more or less related – the problem is that they can be related in various ways and each situation demands its own solution. We can identify four criteria for the creation of departments.

Function

Functional departments exist around the similarity of tasks performed, or technical skills required, by the people within them. They follow disciplines such as production, marketing, finance or personnel. Figure 1.13 is an example of a company creating functional departments at two levels. First, the whole business splits into production, personnel and so on. At the next level, the production department itself divides into sub-departments around the disciplines indicated.

The advantage of functional departments lies in the affinity which staff with similar skills feel with one another, thus making co-ordination straightforward. They appear frequently in small, growing organisations as each manager takes on assistants to cope with the increasing work load. Their disadvantages lie in the narrow outlook that may develop among departmental members whose concern with the specialism may outweigh broader considerations of the success of the company as a whole. Especially in the case of large functional departments, they emphasise differentiation at the expense of integration.

Hospitals often have functional departments, based around medical and paramedical specialities. This arrangement rightly encourages the professional development of staff within each discipline and the need for departmental heads to have specialised knowledge. By the same token, hospitals have a history of interdepartmental rivalry with professional interests being advanced at the expense of the system as a whole. Figure 5.1 shows the functional departments, known as clinical divisions or support directorates, within South Tees NHS Trust. The former can be said to be primary value chain activities, delivering services directly to clients while the latter are the support activities. Heads of the units shown in bold form the management group to oversee operations. Strategic direction is provided by the trust board, comprising the chief executive, medical director, heads of each support directorate and some non-executive members. The switch

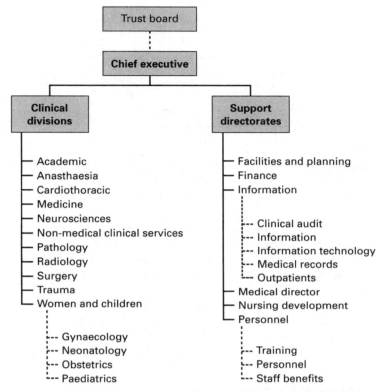

Figure 5.1 Organisation chart for South Tees Hospital Trust in 2001

to increased operational control of medical functions by general managers has created much tension in the health service.

Product

The unifying theme of the product department, often called division, is its output. Each division operates as if it is almost an autonomous business within the whole organisation. This type of organisation is valuable where:

- the size of each division is sufficient for it to be able to provide its own specialisms, such as accounting and personnel
- the work of each division is relatively independent so that their operations do not have to be closely co-ordinated.

Many large organisations are organised on this basis. Its advantage lies in the unification of effort towards the supply of a particular bundle of goods and services. Figure 5.2 shows the organisation structure created at the Vítkovice Works in Ostrava, in the Czech Republic, shortly after the revolution of 1989.[3] The reorganisation was to prepare for privatisation. Employing more than 20,000 people in total, the product divisions can be seen within each of the main sections of the business, namely basic iron and steel making and heavy engineering. Focus on products as the main factor in divisionalisation was not, however,

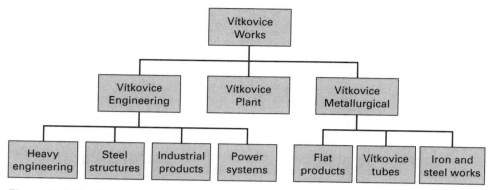

Figure 5.2 Organisation chart for the market economy: Vítkovice Company

complete. While the responsibility for operations within each division should be autonomous, the sales and marketing activities remained centralised as a unit. So much output was exported and the company was unwilling to introduce duplicated international sales functions to replace those handled through a single government agency.

Duplication through a proliferation of support functions is one of the difficulties of product divisions. Furthermore, there is danger that divisions forget they are part of a larger organisation. Then they fail to take opportunities to co-ordinate activities among themselves in order to face competition more effectively.

Geographic location

Geography is common basis for structural design, especially in large companies whose operations are widely dispersed. Service companies, from transport to retailing, can offer the same group of products to customers in many locations. They may then be best organised by region. British Airways has geographic divisions, such as BA Manchester; large bus operators such as Badgerline run services in different towns and cities in separate divisions usually keeping the names of previous companies; the electricity company ScottishPower organises its maintenance operations by district.

Differences between regions push managers towards organising geographically so that the business can respond more effectively to local conditions. International organisations face variations in cultural settings and economic conditions with strong influences on every aspect of marketing, employment, finance and so on. Oxfam's charitable work in central African countries, for example, has to take into account famine and the displacement of peoples from one country to another. In Brazil, however, work is among disadvantaged groups within a country whose economy is among the world's top ten.

Customer facing

The fourth basic structural form is based on the type of customer. This approach is useful when different customer groups demand different products or require them to be supplied in different ways. A business can compete more effectively against the targeting of one of its customer groups by a rival. The dilemma of

Abbott Laboratories concerned the extent to which it should focus its activities in the United States on one critical set of customers – the consolidating groups of hospitals. Many businesses divide their markets, and their product/service bundle, according to customers. For example, Dell separates its sales and service organisations between businesses and consumers. The former is further divided between small business, medium and large business and Internet service providers.[4] The company finds this is the best way to respond to the diverse needs of these groups.

Exercise 5.1	Apart from the customer example given here, what other design principles are seen in the Abbott Laboratories case?

We have presented each of the four bases for departments in its ideal form. In practice, organisations do not stick to the ideals; they adapt these principles according to circumstances. This point is shown in the South Tees Hospital Trust structure (see Figure 5.1). It has as a mixture of customer facing (most of the clinical divisions) and functional designs at the same horizontal level. Organisations, moreover, may use different criteria at each level in the hierarchy. The supermarket firm of Figure 1.14 starts with a functional division at board level, then has two levels divided geographically and finally has product departments within the store.

Each organisation structure is something of a compromise from the operations manager's point of view. If one principle is used to create and integrate departments or divisions, and some staff are brought more closely together in teams, this is at the expense of linkages which may have been created if another principle was used. For example, BT moved from a regional to a customer-facing structure. In urban areas where all types of customer appear in abundance, maintaining service levels to both was feasible. In remote rural areas, however, a community may have a few domestic subscribers and even fewer businesses. There it would be less sensible to provide separate installation teams for the two types of customer. BT judged that the focus on the customer, provided by the new organisation in areas of high competition, was the more important factor to be considered.

5.2.4 Matrix organisation structures

The problem of seeking to integrate organisations in several ways simultaneously has led some companies, especially large ones, to consider having dual lines of authority. Companies engaged in large project work in civil engineering or aerospace found that it was difficult to keep these projects going while operating within a traditional departmental structure. The emerging organisation, referred to under the general title of *matrix organisation*, originally involved staff reporting to both their functional departmental manager and, for the duration, to a manager designated for the particular project.

The organisation shown in Figure 5.3 illustrates how Vítkovice sets up change projects. These may mean the introduction of new products or processes, control systems and so on. The work is carried out by multifunctional teams led by project

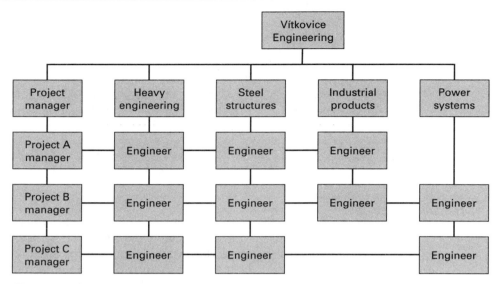

Figure 5.3 Matrix structure for projects: Vítkovice Company

managers. Team members, shown as engineers in the diagram, may work on a project full time or for part of their time. Their attachment to the team is temporary. For the rest of their responsibilities, they report to their line managers. The chart resembles a chessboard. In Figure 5.3, projects A and C span three departments while B requires the efforts of four to be integrated. Normal manufacturing operations continue unaffected.

In some multinational companies, matrix structures become permanent. Co-ordination is based on a least two dimensions. First, the work of operating and marketing managers in every country has to be co-ordinated along both product and geographic dimensions: the company wants to integrate the supply and demand for each product line on a world scale. Second, it wishes to co-ordinate different activities *within* each country from the point of view of finance and taxation, employment, training and so on.

A complex example of a matrix structure occurs in the 'major appliances' (or 'white goods') product division of Electrolux.[5] This widely dispersed organisation has about 500 business units. Each is a nationally based company with its own balance sheet and profit and loss account. The white goods division has some 43 factories in 15 countries grouped in three 'product areas', namely cold, hot and wet. Within the product areas, the national 'product divisions' have at most two factories each. Generally, the factories do not duplicate production so each is responsible for the supply of its lines for all markets where the item is sold. There are 135 marketing and sales companies in 40 countries, their work co-ordinated by one of the two international marketing co-ordinators.

Electrolux does not ignore variations between countries, as in many global firms. It sees the country managers as central in achieving high performance among the companies within each territory. They deal with national issues, such as relations with large retail customers and trades unions, and overseeing national salary structures. Figure 5.4 gives a simple summary of the structural relationships referred to here.

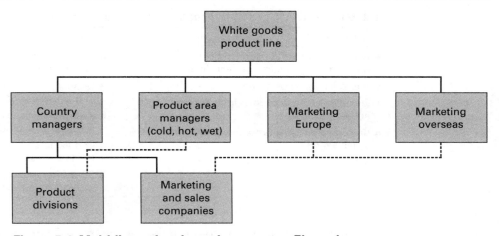

Figure 5.4 Multidimensional matrix structure: Electrolux

The arrangement of the white goods division at Electrolux is, therefore, designed to integrate both operational and strategy-making activity in three dimensions:

■ Country managers monitor performance of production and sales companies in their territories.

■ Product area managers are responsible for product design and development, deciding where each is to be made and planning output flows in liaison with the marketing groups.

■ Marketing managers control sales and marketing including the co-ordination of brands (such as Electrolux and Zanussi) and promotion across frontiers using satellites and other cross-border media.

The claimed advantages of the arrangement lie in good co-ordination and allocation of responsibility. These, however, are at the expense of internal tensions between the various managers and co-ordinators. Many questions and problems do not fall readily into the remit of one or the other type of manager. Direct contact should resolve these problems quickly.

This example of a permanent matrix design brings out both the advantages and disadvantages of such structures. These have been summarised in Table 5.1. Problems arise because a basic notion of each person in the organisation having a single supervisor is breached. This can lead at least to stressful ambiguity and, at worst, to destructive power struggles among managers. We should not forget, however, that such difficulties also frequently arise in the simpler departmental structures we discussed earlier. Structures alone do not create well-managed organisations. More than anything, success depends on the skills and willingness of the managers to interact within them in a positive way.

For some organisations, such as Electrolux, the matrix organisation is seen as the only way to co-ordinate large groups effectively. Others have found that the excessive complexity leads to such loss of efficiency that detailed co-ordination of operations by central managers is dispensed with. Texas Instruments, for example, gave up its matrix structure in the early 1980s in favour of a simpler structure to co-ordinate more independent business units. These units are

Table 5.1 Advantages and disadvantages of a matrix organisation structure

Advantages	Disadvantages
■ Integration of key functions: sales and marketing, production, project management	■ Conflict among managers over range of responsibilities
■ Improved information flow	■ Doubts over more information being at the expense of quality
■ Flexible response to changing markets and competition	■ Possible efficiency loss from extra managerial overhead
■ Co-ordination at appropriate levels in the organisation	■ Conflict to be referred to higher levels for resolution
■ Managers report directly to those responsible	■ Stress from having several bosses with potentially conflicting interests

expected to decide what co-ordination is necessary and make the relevant arrangements themselves. This takes us towards the *network* or *virtual* organisations, discussed in the next section.

5.2.5 New organisational trends

In many industries, the pace of change has been increasing. The problem of increasing complexity of traditional organisations has become more acute. They are seen as too inflexible, slow, uncreative and expensive. The search is for simpler structures with lower costs. Some important trends are as follows.

Fewer layers

Removing layers of middle management, leading to so-called *lean structures* can have a great impact on the number of managers and therefore costs. In the early 1990s, General Motors Europe reduced its layers from seven to six. Toyota, by way of contrast, has only seven for its whole organisation, the third largest car producer in the world. A few numbers illustrate the dramatic effect of reducing layers. With 100,000 employees and an average span of control for each supervisor of seven, the organisation requires $100,000/7 = 14,286$ first-line supervisors, and so on. The total of managers is, therefore:

$$14,286 + 2,041 + 292 + 42 + 6 + 1 = 16,668 \text{ managers in six levels.}$$

Were the span of control nine, there would be:

$$11,111 + 1,235 + 137 + 15 + 1 = 12,499 \text{ managers in five levels.}$$

This argument does not mean that hierarchies are unnecessary. Many are questioning old assumptions, however, in the light of changes in culture, management style and information systems.

Cross-functional teams

Delegation of responsibility to teams blending the work of different functions is another trend. Rather than the top-down co-ordination of the matrix structure, however, self-management is becoming more important. The teams for, say, quality improvement, may set their own patterns of work and focus attention on the issues they consider the most important. Their success depends on having access to more information as well as developing individual skills and mutual trust among members.

Reduction of scale and complexity

The division of large corporations into semi-autonomous units reduces the degree of complexity which the top managers have to cope with and hence enables their numbers to be cut. Co-ordination is achieved through strategic planning and budgeting but not through detailed operating management.

The reorganisation of the UK National Health Service was justified partly by a need to remove the heavy and complex central management. Co-ordinated planning was perceived as not delivering healthcare sufficiently responsive to the needs of the people. Individual operating units, from district hospitals to ambulance services are now established as independent units.

Network or virtual organisations

New forms of organisation extend the trend towards disaggregation – splitting the business into separate units linked by a small core. Many have always sub-contracted specialist functions, from advertising to auditing and recruitment to removals. The network organisation pursues this policy as much as possible, retaining only the core skills that provide the whole system with its strength. Bennetton, for example, makes and sells its clothes through a global network of contracted manufacturers, distributors and franchised retailers. Its strength lies in design and marketing. Privatisation of services in United Kingdom local authorities is another example.

Network organisations benefit from:

- sharing resources and risk
- matching complementary skills
- increasing actual, or perceived, size
- reaching new markets.[6]

Virtual organisations take the uncoupling even further. Made possible by high-quality communication systems, these allow teams to be formed and tasks performed anywhere.[7]

Like the cast for a film or play, the team is formed for a limited time and then disbanded. Members do not, however, have to perform in the same place. Advantages and disadvantages are summarised in Table 5.2.

Whether labelled network or virtual organisations, we see in these new forms the replacement of formal, hierarchical links by contracts. Bureaucracies, showing diseconomies of scale, are replaced by markets.[8] This change means the operations manager has to focus less on internal processes and more on managing the supply chain. This is the whole system of cooperating firms and individuals engaged in supply the customer with the final product. Chapter 12 has more on this developing theme.

Table 5.2 Gains and problems with virtual organisations

Advantages	Disadvantages
■ Productivity	■ Productivity may not overcome hurdles
■ Lower direct costs and overheads	■ Cost, rather than outcome, focus
■ Service speed and responsiveness	■ Organisation does not learn to do better
■ High level of expertise	■ Relying on existing expertise; little development
■ Flexibility to match customers' needs	■ May be difficult to communicate customers' needs in detail
■ Time zone constraints overcome	■ Constraints overcome at personal expense
■ Some staff prefer the lifestyle	■ Some staff hate the lifestyle

5.3 Human resource management

5.3.1 Scope of human resource management

We are all encouraged to participate in organisations, whether as member of voluntary groups, teams and clubs, participants in higher education or employees. Most work of economic significance takes place within organisational contexts. The relationship between the individual and the organisation is, therefore, very important – if constructive the collective effort can lead to excellent results, but if disharmonious, the relationship can be counterproductive. From the point of view of the organisation, the processes of bringing in an individual and achieving a harmonious relationship is the domain of personnel management. This has two aspects, providing and developing the staffing resource, now usually called *human resource management*, and leading, motivating and controlling staff within their assigned roles. The latter aspect is the responsibility of line managers although uniformity of treatment in terms of appraisal, remuneration and so on is achieved through having consistent personnel policies throughout the organisation.

Human resource management is concerned with ensuring that the appropriate number of skilled people is available at the right time to fill the roles required. A general model of this process appears in the flow diagram of Figure 5.5. Many techniques of operations management that we shall examine later in this book have equal applicability to the personnel management function. In other words, personnel management has its operational as well as administrative and strategic aspects. It manages the flows of people. We shall look in turn at each step given in Figure 5.5.

5.3.2 Human resource planning

Human resource planning starts from the total strategy of the organisation. Like planning in general, it means the development of an overall approach to satisfying future human resource needs. In most cases, recruitment and development of employees should be treated as investment. These expensive decisions are often difficult to reverse if errors are made. If hiring is carried out on an ad hoc basis,

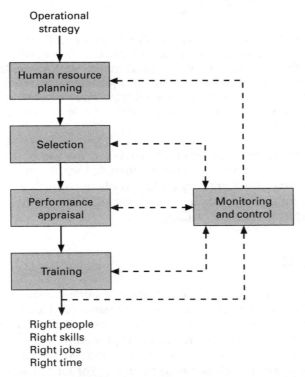

Figure 5.5 The human resource management process

continuity and development may be put at risk. Planning should involve not only an analysis of current human resources and needs but also take into account future changes in the business. Changes within the environment can quickly lead to a mismatch between the ideal and actual staffing levels. Consider the following examples.

Nuclear Electric

Nuclear Electric is responsible for the construction and operation of nuclear power stations. It awards contracts for station building to civil engineering companies but, during the construction phase, requires a continually changing mix of design, supervisory and commissioning engineers of its own. When a station is complete, the company needs operating engineers whose skills and experience differ from the others.

To maintain continuity of employment of the teams of engineers of the various disciplines, Nuclear Electric used to rely on a steady construction programme. When, in the late 1980s, it became clear that the government would not place any new orders, the company had to work out how to maintain sufficient staff to complete its current contracts. Furthermore, it had to develop a policy of what to do with its staff after the building ceased. In so doing, the company examined the skills, age and other details of its entire engineering staff. It offered severance terms to those it no longer could employ and retraining to others who could eventually become operating engineers. With the company being the major employer of nuclear experts in the country, it was not feasible to recruit new staff directly from the labour market.

Banking

During periods of recession, banks recruit few junior staff. This policy follows the need to control costs, reinforced by branch closures and service automation. This had unusual effects on staffing in branches. Junior staff normally start with mundane backroom tasks, eventually moving on to jobs requiring more experience. With a five-year gap in recruitment, and therefore no replacements, managers face the problem of motivating the maturing juniors while at the same time having the routine tasks carried out.

The outcome of the planning process is a detailed analysis of the staffing requirements for the organisation in the future. Included within the plan will be measures for filling any gaps. Large organisations blend recruiting and training to fill posts – recruiting can be internal or external and may, in either case, be followed by an appropriate amount of training.

5.3.3 Recruitment

Recruitment involves finding staff with the appropriate attributes to fill available jobs. A simplified version of the procedure is shown in Figure 5.6. Starting from an agreement over the availability of a job, together with its definition, the personnel manager would plan the recruitment process so that sufficient candidates of appropriate calibre come forward for selection. At the same time, decisions are made about how the choice is to be made. For all but temporary or casual

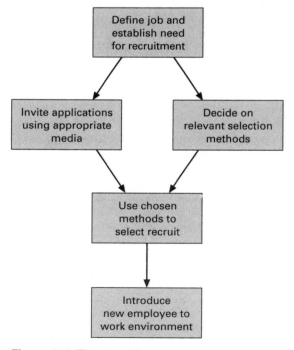

Figure 5.6 The recruitment process

Table 5.3 Schedule for a structured interview

Question category	Information looked for	Example of a supervisor's job in a jobbing machine shop
Situational	Handling the range of circumstances met with on the job	What would you do if you saw a long-serving employee using a grindstone without wearing goggles?
Job knowledge	Knowledge of practical, technical, legal etc. aspects of the job	Can you explain the differences between the various grades of aluminium used in . . . manufacture?
Job simulation	Carrying out critical aspects of the job	Demonstrate the instructions you would give if you were asked to arrange for . . . to be done
Personal requirements	Meeting the demands of the job in terms of hours, travel, location and so on	Are you willing to work nights if required to do so?

appointments, there is usually a series of screens which filter out less suitable prospects until a shortlist is presented to a group of managers for the final choice. The screens may include checks on qualifications, skills and experience, physical and psychological tests, work tests and so on.

It is important to note that, as in all aspects of employment, it is unlawful to discriminate against members of minority groups. Sometimes discrimination can occur unwittingly. For example, the methods of inviting applications may be biased against some groups. Many employers used to rely on word of mouth to spread the news that there were vacancies. The effect of such a policy is that the applicants would tend to represent the backgrounds of those already in employment and therefore not give equal opportunities to all.

Selection procedures must likewise be fair as well as effective. The interview is the most widely used technique in personnel management and is especially important in the selection process of most organisations. Operations managers are often involved in interviewing shortlists of candidates set up by the personnel department. It is important to guard as far as possible against the defects of the *unstructured interview*. This has no prepared schedule or format and involves no systematic scoring. While a strength of the interview is its flexibility, this feature can be a weakness too. Without structure, the interview is notoriously ineffective in selecting the best candidate. Many managers believe they are good interviewers and, lacking feedback on results, rely too much on the process itself. Unstructured interviews often stray into discussion of irrelevant and personal issues which, when meeting the preferences and prejudices of the interviewer, distort decisions. Legal challenges to these selection and promotion decisions have been mounted in recent years under equal opportunities legislation. Unstructured selection procedures have proved difficult to defend.

It is important, then, that all managers use the interview as effectively as possible. The *structured interview* is built around a series of job-related questions asked of all candidates. Table 5.3 shows four question categories often tested. The information could be sought at interview but that concerning job knowledge and ability could be gathered from practical tests or observation of behaviour in a simulated situation. Giving candidates full information about the job helps to clear up many potential misunderstandings over personal matters before the interview stage is reached. Yet, it is wise to invite candidates to discuss the fourth category, possibly by reference to previous experience.

The four items in Table 5.3 are not a complete list. For example, in the recruitment of young trainees, an organisation may be as concerned with potential as with current ability. Qualifications and school reports would be important and the interviewer may seek to probe learning ability rather than current technical skills.

Using a panel of interviewers can be expensive but helps in removing personal bias. Whether interviewers act alone or in a group, the schedule provides a formal basis for personnel records as well as being available later to show that the process was conducted equitably.

The difficulties of effective recruitment are highlighted by the case of trainee pilots in the RAF. The air force needs to maintain its planned ratio of pilots to aircraft. Pilots both fly and are officers; they must have appropriate physical skills and be leaders of others. Initial selection is based on tests and interviews to cover these two aspects. All those who pass the initial selection move on to various courses: initial officer training; basic flying and then streaming into one of three categories – fast jet, multi-engine or helicopter. The fast jet role is seen as the most demanding. These trainees move on to advanced training and then operational conversion. Each stage builds up the accumulated investment in the trainee, who can fail at any point. The cost of training a fast jet pilot is approximately £1.5 million. The problem for the RAF is to minimise wastage in training while maintaining a supply of pilots of the necessary quality.[9]

5.3.4 Performance appraisal

Performance appraisal means evaluating the performance of persons within their jobs in order to make reasoned personnel decisions. These decisions cover salary, giving general advice, development and training, promotion opportunities and human resource planning. While formal systems are gradually being extended to cover more managers and supervisors, they are little used for those employees for whom the relationship with the organisation is treated much more in terms of a temporary economic link. These include many shop floor workers, sales staff and so on. In such cases, performance is measured, where possible, in output terms and rewarded under a bonus scheme. With so many employees in this category, the operations manager has to be familiar with methods of direct payment by results and we shall look at this aspect in Chapter 6.

Within a formal appraisal system, there will be an appraisal interview. This raises many of the difficulties of fairness and consistency that were discussed in the previous section. The interview, then, should be set within a framework of planning and control to counter these problems. An effective and equitable appraisal system should contain:

- analysis of the range and number of jobs to be appraised and the organisational context in which the system is to be established
- clarification of and agreement over the purpose of the appraisal
- training of appraisers in the necessary skills
- a statement of the procedures to be followed and the outcomes expected
- regular review of the process to ensure improvement.

Three general orientations for appraisal have been noted – trait, outcome and behaviour.[10] Of these, the last is the least common yet is the most strongly recommended by experts:

- *Trait-orientated* appraisal is widely used yet, since it concentrates on personality traits, is one of the weakest and most susceptible to prejudice. Traits such as 'charm', 'ambition' or 'initiative' have been found irrelevant or inconsistently held in different job situations. They do not account for achievement of job outcomes.

- *Outcome-orientated* appraisal focuses on outcomes. Management by objectives (see Chapter 4) assesses how well employees meet previously agreed goals. Yet, since goals are individualised in this way, there is no consistent basis for comparing one person with another. Outcome-orientated approaches are, therefore, unsuitable for systems primarily designed to rank employees for merit pay or promotion.

- *Behaviour-orientated* appraisal highlights behaviour relevant to the job. In principle, this is the most effective, for behaviour is the root of success or failure. Discovering reliable dimensions is difficult and likely to be worthwhile only when there are many staff with similar roles.

Whatever system of performance appraisal is used, the manager should be aware of its limitations and its basic contradictions. For example, appraisal systems frequently seek to combine evaluation of an employee's performance with advising and agreeing upon routes to improving that performance. Each is a laudable purpose yet, in combination, they create problems. The manager is to be seen as both an evaluator, being prepared to note underperformance and, simultaneously, an advisor. In the latter role, the manager appears as supporter or trusted friend who can arrange to have development opportunities made available.

5.3.5 Training

Training is critical to good operations management. We can define training as:

> **The provision of guided experience to change employee behaviour, attitudes or opinions.**[11]

Implied within this definition is the notion that the changes are to be related to the job. Therefore, planning a training programme should start with a comparison of the attributes required to perform the job effectively and the attributes of the employee. This *training needs analysis* identifies gaps in the person's capabilities. In turn, the *training gaps* form the basis of a training plan.

The delivery of instruction is a personal service. In principle, each needs analysis establishes an individualised plan. Managers then face the problem of supplying the service to each employee within budget constraints. It is not surprising that a compromise is reached and employees are given standardised training courses in spite of their not needing every element of them. To some extent, training resources are wasted.

Table 5.4 Comparison of styles of training

	Advantages	Disadvantages
On-the-job training	■ Skills directly applicable ■ May not need special trainers ■ Trainee contributes to output ■ Cheap	■ May provide too narrow experience ■ Bad habits passed on ■ Trainee may impede efficiency
Off-the-job training	■ Suitable for tasks not currently carried out ■ Necessary where trainee's errors can be expensive or disastrous ■ Provides wider experience and practice in unusual situations ■ More readily controlled by professional trainers	■ Difficult to fit to current job and to match individuals' needs ■ May require expensive development and testing if to be successful ■ Expensive ■ Attending training centres often used as reward for good performance

Training takes place either within the workplace, *on-the-job training*, or away from it, *off-the-job training*. Each has its advantages and disadvantages as summarised in Table 5.4. Off-the-job training is often criticised because of the difficulty of transferring any learning directly back to the work situation. Unless the training is combined with other changes, the employee immediately unlearns whatever learning has been provided. A combination of both modes of training will ensure retention and optimise the new skills, which are transferred to the job. For this to happen the training should:

■ take place in circumstances similar to the job

■ enlarge the trainee's experience

■ offer a range of experience not normally met by the trainee

■ enable learning of underlying ideas rather than simple rote following of instructions

■ happen at a time when the trainee can appreciate and use the benefits of the programme.

For example, to train a clerk in the use of new software, off-the-job training may be advisable so that it can take place without interruption. There may be a series of modules teaching procedures and giving understanding of the reasons for them. As the programme advances, the trainee should have access to the software and begin to use it within the job situation. It is valuable to compare off-the-job training in simulators for airline pilots with on-the-job methods used for car drivers. For pilots, much can be done, and indeed has to be done, to prepare them before they take the controls of a real aircraft. In contrast, most people come to the driving school with a high awareness of the context of the task. The learner is rehearsing a set of skills to be combined and made intuitive before being able to drive successfully.

Training contrasts

There is a danger in job-based needs analysis. It can lead to very narrow training prescriptions if the behavioural approach brought out in a focused analysis is

Figure 5.7 Pouring tea for three people in a Japanese bank

overemphasised. For example, bank trainees expect their employers to teach them all the processes which working in a branch entails. These range from counting cash to checking customers' accounts and so on. Yet, the service function must go further than this. Service in banking involves being able to relate to customers at the personal level. Generally, western employers try to achieve this by using training to influence trainees' *attitudes*. For instance, they stress that the customer is always right and that it is better if staff are always pleasant. They may go so far as to suggest to staff things they may do in critical service situations, as with a complaint (see Box 3.2). Within the general frameworks set out, however, employees are encouraged to express their own personality in the way they give service. Banks rely on effective initial recruitment and gradual development to produce staff with appropriate interpersonal skills.

Compare this with the way service training can be given in Japan. Figure 5.7 is based on one of many sketches in the training manual of a Japanese bank.[12] The book features dozens of instructions of how to behave within the work environment. Greetings, addressing clients, colleagues and superiors and many other aspects of social behaviour are laid out in detail. The formal processes of social interaction are, of course, much more important in Japan than in most western countries. Therefore, employers stress behaviour in their training. This example illustrates how important it is to consider cultural differences when managing a service facility.

Safety training

Training is an important factor in ensuring that work is safe. The focus of responsibility has shifted over the years. For employers, there has been a shift from compliance with detailed regulations towards a more general duty to ensure safe premises, products and working practices. Each process must be studied for safety implications, with risk analysis being a regular practice. The process should be designed to be as safe as possible and workers should be trained accordingly. It has been found that conformance is best achieved if staff are encouraged to develop positive attitudes towards, and opinions about, safety.

5.4 Communicating, motivating and leading

While the personnel department provides a valuable support service in the functions described earlier, the ultimate responsibility in ensuring that the primary activities of the organisation are carried out lies with the line manager. This is, in our case, the operations manager. In the following sections, we shall study the role of the line manager in leading and motivating the staff, using communications skills to do so effectively.

5.4.1 The importance of good communications

To carry out their function, managers spend their time communicating. They are responsible for planning, controlling, development, decision making, problem solving and so on. Few of these activities can take place without sharing of information with others. Kreitner[13] presented the results of several studies, summarised as follows:

- Organisational and individual performance improves when there is effective communication.
- Managers spend most of their time communicating (typically 80% of the working day).
- Managers communicate primarily face to face (75%, compared with 10% by telephone).
- Managers in small organisations (fewer than 50 employees) rely heavily on horizontal communication, interacting with other specialists.
- Managers in large organisations (more than 500 employees) direct 58% of their communication vertically, to their superiors or subordinates.

Good communication is not only required between pairs of individuals working on the details of a task. It is required to gain cooperation of all members of the organisation in achieving the common goals. Within any organisation, we find two systems of communication: the formal system controlled by management and the informal system or *grapevine*. The latter is frequently very fast with news; it operates through a network of relationships based on family ties, club memberships, physical proximity or even chance meetings on the bus. The grapevine can be influential but can operate destructively. It must, however, be recognised that it will always exist. It is part of the organisation's culture.

Managers can respond to the tendency to rely on informal communications by:

- Having well-co-ordinated formal communications. This extends from giving clear information and instructions on issues that matter through to using corporate newsletters to tell staff about wider developments.
- Monitoring the grapevine as a means of eliciting general feelings over organisational issues.
- Taking steps to counter malicious rumours. (They may be tempted to do this by feeding information, or leaks, into the grapevine, but their lack of control may mean that the outcomes are negative.)

Two aspects of communications stand out from this discussion, the need for individual managers to be effective communicators and how organisations can design good communications systems. We shall examine these in turn.

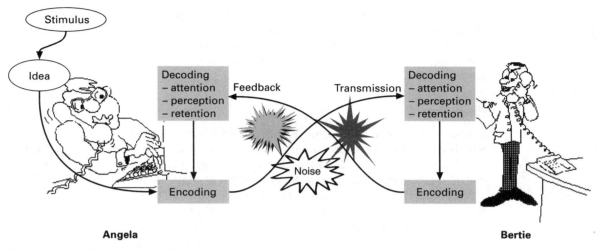

Figure 5.8 A flow model of interpersonal communication

5.4.2 Interpersonal communication

The process of communication can be defined as:

> **Transferring information and understanding from one person to another.**

There are two important features in this definition:

1. *The accent is on person-to-person flow.*
While it may appear that many situations involve large numbers of senders or receivers – the televised speech or the audience cheering the soloist at the end of the concert – each link is from individual to individual. This makes analysis very complex.

At the 1994 Eurovision Song Contest, the entry for Bosnia-Herzegovina received loud and long applause from the Irish audience. Did all think it was a good song? Was there sympathy for an oppressed nation? Was it a political gesture towards the then inactive European powers? Many probably had intentions beyond approving the performance.

2. *Communication is more than merely sending data.*
It is inevitable that the receiver interprets the information in some way. The purpose of good communication is to ensure that the recipient interprets the information in the *intended way*. Then common understanding will be achieved.

Recipients often interpret messages which the other party had no intention of sending. I bought some roofing timbers from a demolition site. Having sorted out the pile of material and agreed the price, I asked the seller if he would take a cheque. Hearing that he wanted cash, I walked 100 metres to the bank, put my tools on the counter, pulled out my cheque book and began to write. The teller, meanwhile, summoned assistance. She thought it was a hold-up. I had not realised how much soot was covering my face and clothes.

The process can be modelled using the stages set out in Figure 5.8. Here we see a telephone interaction between two people: Angela the sender and Bertie, the receiver. Angela has an idea she wants to send to Bertie. To do this, she translates the idea into a form that is both meaningful and can be transmitted as a message along a channel. Bertie then interprets the message into a meaningful form. He may acknowledge the message, for example through an 'Aha', to confirm receipt and suggest common understanding. This is feedback. The features of the process are as follows.

Encoding

Encoding involves the translation of internal ideas into a common language which the receiver can understand. In our case, this code or language is speech which uses not only a shared vocabulary but also pace, tone of voice and non-verbal sounds. In other circumstances gestures, pictures and so on are included.

Encoding is a skill. It should recognise the purpose of the message as well as the strengths and limitations of the medium being used. Telephones are good for sending simple messages but poor for complex technical data.

Medium

The medium both constrains the message and becomes part of it. Each medium has advantages and disadvantages. When the sender has a choice, the match between message purpose and medium should be considered. The capacity of a medium to carry information and facilitate understanding is called its *richness*. Face-to-face meetings are rich because there are many language cues, from words to gestures, feedback is immediate and the context is personally involving. Our telephone contact is less rich than this because some cues are eliminated and each participant has less awareness of the environment of the other. Very lean media are impersonal and have no immediate feedback. Most forms of printed text and web pages have little direct interaction.

Lean media are best used for routine messages such as production instructions or monthly budget reports. Rich media are better for non-routine situations in which, say, the manager seeks to persuade someone of a change of plan. A mismatch can be frustrating. There are too many boring meetings used by a boss to present detailed information (rich medium – routine information). Even worse is the use of memoranda to give people surprising or shocking personal information such as decisions over redundancy (lean medium – non-routine information).

Decoding

However well the message is composed, understanding depends on the receiver's decoding and perception. Successful decoding requires that both parties use the same coding system, that is they use the same language. Much military training is devoted to learning and using common codes that can be used successfully in situations of great stress. Organisations and professions develop their own codes, referred to as jargon. Perception of the sender's intention is also conditioned by what the receiver already knows both of the message and the purpose of the sender as well as the receiver's own psychological make-up.

Feedback

The communication process will be often incomplete without some feedback from the receiver. Again, referring to the military context, the sender seeks assurance of 'Message received and understood.' Feedback completes the loop, as in the ubiquitous control model. Responsibility for feedback rests on both parties – the sender to establish and monitor feedback links, the receiver to supply the feedback messages, to ask questions and to express any feelings of not having understood.

Noise

Noise is any interference with the transfer of understanding from one person to the other. This is not simply sound interference but covers a wide range of influences disturbing any stage. They include:

- *encoding* – unfamiliar language; poor literacy, numeracy, drawing or modelling skills; physical disabilities
- *message* – poor transmission technology; competing messages; interference of all kinds
- *decoding* – unfamiliar language; poor listening or reading skills; aural or visual disabilities
- *perception* – negative attitudes towards sender or message; unanticipated outside influences.

To overcome the effects of noise, managers have available two remedies. First, they should search for and remove sources of noise. Second, they can improve the quality of messages to make them as clear as possible. Often, messages contain a high degree of *redundancy*, which is information above the minimum required for encoding the sender's meaning. Natural languages are full of redundancy and good communicators deliberately include an appropriate amount of repetition to ensure that their messages get through. A maxim for a good oral presentation is, 'First tell them what you are going to say. Then say it. Then tell them what you have said.'

5.4.3 Organisational communication

Organisations work through communication. Given the problems reviewed in the preceding section, one may wonder how information can ever be transmitted through an organisation. Extra barriers to communication arise from organisational divisions, either between levels or between the specialists of different departments. Approaches to resolving these difficulties include:

- removing physical barriers between people through the choice of facility location and layout
- using training to help colleagues understand the language and attitudes of other specialists
- avoiding disputes over semantics which touch on personal beliefs while ensuring that the language in use does not demean others
- building an atmosphere of trust so that staff feel free to communicate.

This last point is one of the most intractable. Subordinates may feel unconfident in communicating with superiors, especially in settings such as formal meetings. These feelings impose constraints on the vital process of upward communication.

Upward communication

Leaders of large organisations need information from lower levels for two reasons. The first can be termed *intelligence*. People at the grassroots are frequently in close contact with customers, suppliers and, sometimes, competitors. They may observe operating problems, customer reactions or changes in the organisation's environment but not appreciate their significance. At the same time, others would recognise the significance if only they had the information! The problem is to ensure that the two aspects are brought together. The second reason for upward communication is to collect the ideas and understand the feelings of subordinates. With many at the base of the pyramid and few at the top, there is a problem. How can upward communication be achieved?

In the armed services, the problem of intelligence is addressed by having a separate department specialising in its collection. Among its many tasks, the role of military intelligence is to collect information from soldiers who have been on missions, debriefing them on what they have seen of the enemy's behaviour. By assembling this collective observation as soon as possible, officers may recognise the significance of what may otherwise seem a disparate pattern of events.

In non-military organisations, such an approach would normally be unacceptable and too expensive. Managers, though, do have several means of gathering and encouraging the upward flow. These are summarised in Box 5.1.

BOX 5.1 Encouraging upward communication

Information on employee attitudes

- *Regular formal surveys*. To gain commitment from those expected to complete questionnaires, managers should be committed to publishing their results and making changes.

- *Grievance procedures*. Usually confined to the problems of an individual, most large organisations have agreed formal processes for listening to and dealing with complaints.

- *Informal listening*. Management by wandering around (MBWA) was popularised at Hewlett-Packard by its founders. It means what it says: managers must spend time going round listening. Other managers use an open-door policy, which encourages any employee to bring forward a problem.

- *Exit interviews*. Often conducted by specialists in the personnel department, exit interviews are designed to find out why an employee is leaving. Results are compared in order to pick out trends.

Employee ideas and intelligence

- *Suggestion schemes*. Based on the notion that it is the people doing the job who often have the best ideas about it, these schemes are used by many employers with varying degrees of success to reward good technical ideas.

- *Working parties or task forces*. Cutting across levels and functions, work teams will break down barriers if there is sufficient confidence in the value of their outcomes. This approach has been used in quality circles (see Chapter 15).

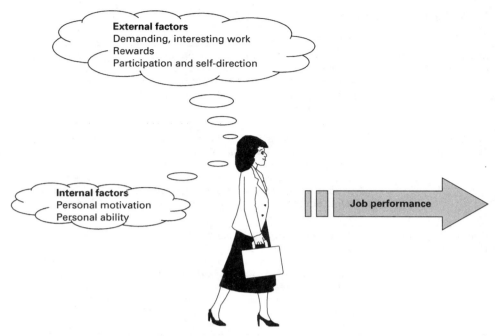

Figure 5.9 Motivation factors in job performance

5.4.4 Motivation

For the operations manager, who is usually responsible for the majority of staff in the organisation, motivation is important. We can define individual motivation as:

The internal processes which direct behaviour.

Managers try to understand these processes so that they can persuade employees to accept and follow the objectives of the team, department or organisation. Their desired outcome is job performance. This comes from a combination of factors, both internal and external to the employee. First, as set out in Figure 5.9, an individual brings to the job a blend of personal motivation and ability. Personal ability accumulates from experience and training, some of which can be provided by the employer. Second, external factors such as the design and context of the job must be recognised. The job may offer demanding and interesting activity; it may give the opportunity for participation in management; and it may offer rewards from cash to recognition and personal satisfaction. Various theories and practices of motivation lay emphasis on different combinations of these elements.

5.4.5 Theories of motivation

Table 5.5 summarises four of the most influential theories of motivation. Each takes a different approach to the issues and hence illuminates them in a different

Table 5.5 Some significant theories of motivation

Theory	Summary	Comment
Maslow's Hierarchy of Needs (1943)	Five levels of need arranged in hierarchy People not conscious of needs but all proceed along predictable route from bottom to top: physiological → safety → affection → esteem → self-actualisation	Widely known and influential mainly because simple, plausible and old! Maslow made original tentative proposal after studying mentally ill patients. Little supporting evidence from employment studies
Herzberg's Two Factor Theory (1950)	Motivation results from satisfaction Factors divided into dissatisfiers (supervision, conditions, pay, security and so on) and satisfiers (achievement, advancement, responsibility, recognition and work itself) Points out that dissatisfaction and satisfaction are not opposites	As well known and influential as Maslow's theory but less well understood Based on study of professional engineers and accountants but challenged by many others since Only weak evidence found elsewhere
Vroom's Expectancy Theory (1964)	Motivational strength depends on expectations of outcomes and rewards Increases if a person's perceptions of both outcomes of efforts and rewards from these outcomes increase Takes into account different people's assessments of circumstances and rewards and how these may change in time	Focuses on the individual's appraisal of the situation Supported by empirical evidence and in line with common sense Explains how motivation can quickly change with circumstances
Locke's Goal-Setting Theory (1984)	Stresses participation to achieve personal ownership of goals These motivate through pointing towards a target, encouraging effort in moving towards the target, promoting tenacity in the effort in spite of problems and enabling the creation of strategies and plans	General theory that clearly applies to those motivated by goals Research emphasises the value of feedback Basis of programmes such as MBO (see Chapter 4) and employee participation

light. Such is the complexity of the field that a universally applicable theory has not emerged.

Maslow's theory is perhaps the most widely known. Developed in a clinical, rather than employment, context, the theory has a weak empirical base. Its popularity stems from simplicity and surface plausibility. While a practising manager would be unwise to base policy on a slavish following of the hierarchy, the theory does point out that employees are unlikely to respond to appeals to presumed needs for self-actualisation if their basic pay and conditions are well below par.

Herzberg's contribution, again based on shaky evidence, was to focus on the psychology of work and pick out the difference between dissatisfiers and satisfiers. The former will demotivate workers. Above a satisfactory level, however, no amount of extra investment in their improvement will bring gains in motivation. Satisfiers, by the same token, are the true motivators. Managers should focus on these, having eliminated the dissatisfiers. The theory points to the inherent value of work itself and how gains can result from job enrichment. One problem is that later evidence suggests that some of the factors are treated differently by different people, especially pay. Some are motivated by incremental increases in income while others are not so influenced if pay is at a satisfactory level. For the former, it is a satisfier, whereas for the latter it is a dissatisfier.

The theories of both Maslow and Herzberg generalise about reward factors in a search for universal applicability. They are known as *content* theories – they focus on what motivates. In contrast, Vroom and Locke were among many who look to explain a *process*. More complex than the content theories, they identify a set of factors to explain behaviour. Expectancy theory says little about rewards and returns to a study of the individual. Whatever the rewards, each person will make a different evaluation of the combined probabilities of achieving performance from effort and reward from performance. For example, it has long been recognised that output-related rewards for workers on a long assembly line have little motivational effect because, for an individual, there is no link between effort and output. In taking the analysis to the personal level, the theory also recognises how motivation changes through time. Telling a subordinate that there is no chance of promotion may change that person's motivation for the worse; telling them, some time later, that there is a possibility may rekindle the wish to perform better. For the manager, the stress is on *understanding the meaning* of rewards to individuals and ensuring that they have a good chance of achieving them. Therefore, the links in the effort–performance–rewards chain must be clear to all.

Advocates of goal-setting theory attempt to bridge the gap between an individual's wants within the job and organisational objectives. This is achieved both by encouraging a shared ownership of the goals and by making feedback on performance available to all. The approach suggests that there should be both a high degree of participation in the goal-setting process and feedback systems for self-control to be exercised.

A study by Hackman and Oldham[14] questioned the causal link from satisfaction to motivation proposed by Maslow and Herzberg. They returned to the search for general factors within the job tasks that would lead to high motivation. They suggested that there are certain *core job characteristics* influencing both job satisfaction and job motivation. In other words, the last two elements are outputs of the job system. The three-step chain proposed by Hackman and Oldham is set out in Figure 5.10. The *results* of the job arise from *critical psychological states*, which are in turn caused by *core job characteristics*. Differences between individuals are recognised by suggesting that each link is influenced by mediating factors – personal knowledge and skill, desire for personal growth and satisfaction with the job context. Figure 5.10 shows the components of each step. These are returned to in the next section.

5.4.6 Job design

Job design refers to the identification and arrangement of tasks making up a job. It is clear that boring jobs carried out under adverse conditions are demotivating. At the same time, excessive challenge, variety and excitement can also be tiring and demotivating. In designing jobs, managers have to pay attention to the relationship between the demands that they make and capabilities and motivation of their employees. There are two basic approaches to the relationship – matching people to jobs and matching jobs to people.

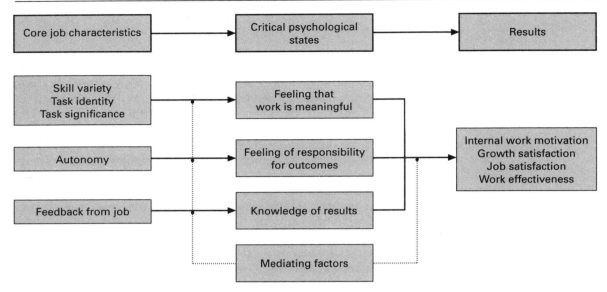

Figure 5.10 The motivation process theory of Hackman and Oldham

Matching people to jobs

The design of many jobs is often dominated by technology. Within the socio-technical system (see Chapter 2), a stronger technological element may arise from a combination of economic circumstances and the current state of knowledge. Competition forced manufacturers to create assembly lines to supply high volumes at low cost. Only more recently have they begun to devise ways of replacing workers by robots. In the service sector, many surveillance tasks are also dull yet require that the employee remains vigilant. Again they exist through necessity and because they have yet to be automated. People are expected to fit within these frameworks.

These jobs have negative consequences for motivation and, often, for health. What can managers do to relieve some of their negative consequences? There are three possibilities:

1 *Establishing clear expectations*
By making the nature of the job clear, managers can dampen unjustified expectations. It is far better to advertise 'The most boring job in the world' than to pretend that there are numerous possibilities of variety and job satisfaction.

2 *Job rotation*
Moving people from one task to another at intervals prevents stagnation and even relieves physical fatigue if the various tasks involve different working positions. A balance needs to be struck between the benefits of change and the disturbance caused by this change being seen as pointless. For instance, surveillance workers may experience mixed benefits from job rotation. Janitors at the Museum of Anatolian Cultures in Ankara change their positions at every break. In discussion, one told me, 'I'd rather stay in one place. In that way I would only have one boring job instead of four.'

3 *Earning relief*
Some employers report gains from *contingent time off*. In one example, a group were producing 160 units in an eight-hour day with a 10% reject rate. They agreed a new target of 200 per day plus three for every rejected unit. Within one week of the agreement, output rose to over 200 and defects fell to 1.5%. The average working time was 6.5 hours, after which the staff could go home. Notwithstanding the poor state of affairs that must have existed before this change, it is clear that the workers found the possibility of earning time off to be highly motivating. Yet, despite these reported successes, formal CTO agreements are rare.

Matching jobs to people

The limited possibilities of moulding people have led many firms to redress the balance between the two aspects of the socio-technical system. Here, the nature and boundaries of the job are considered alongside concern with the needs of employees. The aim is to achieve productivity and satisfaction for the people simultaneously. Two approaches are common:

1 *Job enlargement*
Some degree of involvement and variety can be created if several divided tasks are combined into a single job. This may sometimes be easy to achieve. Each of four clerical staff handling different stages of order processing takes over a quarter of the orders. In other cases, process design may have to be altered and more equipment made available. For example, on a line putting together electrical items, each worker would need to have all components available and be furnished with a complete set of tools and assembly jigs. These can, however, often be supplied at low cost.

Critics point out that combining a few boring tasks does not of itself make an interesting job. Yet, if the job cycle time is increased substantially by combining a dozen or more tasks, employees' feelings of frustration and boredom may recede.

2 *Job enrichment*
The accent on job enrichment is to redesign the job with the express intention of increasing its influence on motivation. In our discussion of process theories, we saw how Hackman and Oldham saw both motivation and satisfaction as outputs from the job. Hence, they could both be affected by job design. Their model is one approach to understanding the ways to enrich jobs. We can use it to look at some possibilities. In many cases, the core job characteristics can be changed:

- *Skill variety*. Requiring that a range of skills is used, for instance manual, planning, leading, communicating, calculating, monitoring and so on.
- *Task identity*. Enabling a person to complete a whole task with a meaningful outcome, for example, assembling a complete unit or handling all the requirements of a customer.
- *Task significance*. Designing the job to be important so that others depend on its successful completion. Encouraging staff to see others as customers of their work is one element in the development of a total quality approach.

- *Autonomy.* Allowing the individual discretion in how the job is paced, sequenced, checked and so on. This does not imply personal isolation for, as we shall see below, autonomy can be given to a group.

- *Feedback from job.* Providing the person with information on how effectively they are working.

The other theories of motivation will also enable us to understand issues concerning job redesign. For example, the models of Maslow or Herzberg underscore the fact that employees may not be interested in such changes if their basic needs, or dissatisfiers, are not supported. It should also be noted that some employees do not seek enriched jobs. There are two difficult questions here:

1 Could an employee prefer a job with very low skill requiring merely surface mental attention? There are stories, possibly apocryphal, of doctoral students working on General Motors' assembly lines to earn their keep. The job gave them eight hours a day to think about their theses.

2 Does enrichment increase managerial power? Some workers regard the process as a further example of management's manipulation. This is reinforced in those cases where managers retain the control of job design. In encouraging conformance to the new arrangements, those in charge may demonstrate that it is only they who can set the boundaries of control and responsibility. A more open approach, with consultation, increases uncertainty over outcomes yet may gain greater long-term commitment.

5.4.7 Motivation from participation

Participation means that managers give power to subordinates to take control of their work situation. Instead of managers carrying out the managerial tasks from goal setting, through planning and implementation, to control, they delegate some of these to lower levels. This is not new. Organisations would never work if every task were to be carried out at the top. The point about participative management is that it has to be a positive programme of change. It counters the tendency of many managers, through habit, fear or lack of confidence, to draw all decision making and control into themselves.

In general, coercive management styles do achieve *some* level of output. This is, however, at the expense of creating an alienated and instrumental workforce. Improvements to performance require more coercion, which continues the vicious circle of alienation. In many processes, managers can never supervise tasks closely enough to overcome the negative effects of dissatisfied staff. Box 5.2 quotes one of several acts of sabotage reported by Beynon.[15]

Exercise 5.2 How would you relate acts of sabotage to the theory of Hackman and Oldham?

Participation can spring from the creation of teams to share ownership of groups of tasks. This enables the core job characteristics of task significance and autonomy to be brought out. Two types of team are important to the operations manager.

BOX 5.2 **The wet deck at Ford, Halewood, 1970**

'In the paint shop the car, after an early coat of paint, passes through the wet deck where a team of men armed with electric sanders – "whirlies" – sand the body while it is being heavily sprayed with water . . .

'If there was a problem on the wet deck, a manning problem, speed-up, if the foreman had stepped out of line, they always had a comeback. They could sand the paint off the style lines – the fine edges of the body that gave it its distinctive shape. And nobody could know. The water streaming down, the whirlies flailing about, the lads on either side of the car, some of them moving off to change their soaking clothes. The foreman could stand over them and he couldn't spot it happening. Three hours later, the body shell would emerge with bare metal along the style lines. They knew it was happening.'

Quality circles

Improvements to quality often require changes cutting across traditional functional boundaries. They also benefit from the detailed knowledge held by staff currently engaged in the relevant tasks. Quality circles are usually made up of groups of volunteers who work together on projects they select as potentially fruitful. The circles can break up and reform as projects change. Success requires management encouragement and recognition. QCs are discussed in more detail in Chapter 16.

Job teams

In contrast to quality circles, meeting outside the immediate job context, these autonomous work groups are permanently engaged in the productive task. Many manufacturing plants and service facilities have changed over to such arrangements, the groups taking responsibility for decisions such as task allocation and rotation, quality, rest breaks, flow of materials, minor maintenance and cleanliness of the work area.

The introduction of teamwork presents two immediate problems. The first is the resistance of supervisors whose roles are changed, reduced in scope or eliminated altogether. The second is resistance from the workers themselves who may be suspicious of managerial motives, especially where relations have not been healthy. Teamwork demands higher commitment and ability on behalf of workers and change may be costly in terms of the extra training required.

5.4.8 Motivation from rewards

Expectancy theory stresses the importance of rewards and the probability of gaining them as essential ingredients in motivation. For the individual, they are the ultimate pay-offs for carrying out tasks at work. The work may be willingly done, with the rewards flowing accordingly, or carried out grudgingly as with the alienated workers of Ford's wet deck in Box 5.2. In that case, the workers took the pay for the job but also gained satisfaction from sabotage.

Table 5.6 Jahoda's classification of rewards from employment

Extrinsic rewards	Latent functions
■ Pay	■ Achievement
■ Employee benefits	■ Personal identity
■ Advancement at work	■ Regular activity
■ Recognition by managers, colleagues and wider society	■ Self-regard
	■ Self-fulfilment
■ Status	■ Satisfaction from work itself
■ Status symbols	■ Time structure to the day

Rewards can be divided into those supplied by others, *extrinsic rewards*, and those that are experienced within the person and hidden from the public domain. Jahoda termed these the *latent functions of employment*.[16] Employment brings a bundle of both types, as shown in Table 5.6. Some of the latent functions may not seem pleasant and are only noticed when a job is lost. 'It is not uncommon for unemployed people to report that, while they hated the sniping, nagging and gossip which went on when they had a job, when they lost it they missed it terribly.'[17]

Heading the list of extrinsic rewards is money. There are almost as many payment systems as there are employers but we can generalise, first, about principles and then about practical examples. How should payment systems be designed if they are to effectively motivate performance? Our review of motivation theory suggests the following points:

■ Staff should see links between both effort and performance, and performance and reward.

■ The distribution of rewards must be fair and be seen to be fair.

■ The rewards must appeal to each individual.

These principles are readily stated but most difficult to achieve in practice. Not all jobs have easily measured outputs, often performance is not related to the person's own effort, sometimes individuals can only gain at the expense of others. In many jobs, pay is only loosely related to achievement and, therefore, much reliance is placed on the extrinsic rewards other than pay coupled with the latent functions. Such are the employment arrangements for many doorkeepers and doctors, shop assistants and surgeons.

Formal pay schemes may include rewards tied to performance. Table 5.7 lists some common schemes, although there are many variations. Piecework, production bonuses and commission are the methods that tie effort, performance and pay most closely together. Modern production bonus schemes are often tied to time standards using formulae explained in the next chapter. The schemes do have such disadvantages that their use in business operations is declining. Technological developments sever the links between personal effort and outcomes and the schemes may encourage excessive striving after bonus, especially where it represents a large proportion of income. For example, insurance companies have been heavily criticised for relying on high commissions to motivate their salespeople. Customers rely on advice from these personnel because insurance,

Table 5.7 Incentive payment schemes

Pay scheme	Method	Advantages and disadvantages
Piece work	Payment per unit produced	Direct relationship with output, but has reputation for exploitation among outworkers; individual absorbs business risk in cyclical market
Production bonus	Payments related to output by formula	Clear relationship with output, but requires the establishment of time standards and can be complex to administer
Commission	Formula based on sales revenue	Clear relationship to sales personally achieved, but encourages competition between staff; can be seen as unfair by those not receiving the bonuses
Profit sharing	Formula based on end of period profits	Invites interest in company's performance, but profits not obviously related to personal effort
Share options	Free or discounted shares in company	Personal stake in long-term performance of company, but capital growth not obviously related to personal effort; resented by non-participants and increases problems if company suffers setbacks
Benefit sharing	Distribution of benefits from gains in productivity; can be difficult to calculate	Encourages individuals and teams to improve performance, but may create problems in other areas
Business incentives	Combine operating and financial, e.g. output, quality, service and return on investment; can be group or individual	Communicates priorities; builds business understanding; can relate to organisational, group or individual performance
Merit pay	Bonus for excellent performance	Applies to staff whose output not directly related to effort, but requires subjective assessment and therefore difficult to operate fairly
Pay based on skills	Bonuses for achieving and maintaining capabilities	Inspires staff to reach high standards and keep them up, but may be unnecessary and hence waste training resources
Fixed rate	Rate per hour or year	Simple and clear; hourly rates encourage attendance, but little incentive to produce more at work

especially pensions and life insurance, is something they rarely buy and little understand. This relationship has been exploited by unscrupulous staff selling unsuitable products.

In other schemes in the list, the proportion of personal income covered by variable pay rarely exceeds 10%. In a United States' sample, however, Abosch reported a rising trend. The proportion of variable pay in the total payroll rose from 4.2 to 7.8% in the eight years to 1998.[18] Growth was in the area of group business incentive awards, with schemes for individuals declining. The use of moderate sums of money assures formality of appraisal. The rewards given then mean more as statements of recognition than as radical changes to the receiver's standard of living. As a colleague stated, 'It's better than a slap on the back.'

Pay rates have functions beyond motivation within the job context. Labour economists add two more aspects – recruitment and binding. Clearly, pay needs to be high enough to attract applicants of the right quality. 'Pay peanuts, hire monkeys' is a well-known expression of this view. Then, after staff join, the level should retain the most productive people. Binding includes both cooperating with others in a team and being retained by the organisation in the long term.

5.4.9 Leadership

We have focused on motivation methods as the way to persuade people to accept and then follow the objectives of the organisation. There are, however, other important persuasive influences. Managers have formal power vested in them by their position in the organisation. In using this power, they can exercise formal leadership with respect to those in positions beneath them. Their power is limited by the power possessed by others. Workers, for example, can exercise economic power, particularly strong if they act collectively to resist managers' efforts.

Leadership is the process of persuading others to voluntarily accept the organisation's goals. When we say that an organisation has succeeded through 'good leadership', we probably mean that the people at the top, the leaders, are good managers. This means that they have succeeded as much by making good decisions about marketing, investment, technology and organisation structure as they have at influencing everyone to march in the same direction. Indeed, as Perrow[19] points out, the non-personal decisions appear to have more effect on performance than the methods used to lead people. Leadership, however, is important in getting that extra drop of commitment from others in the team.

Many theories of leadership have been advocated, the more modern ones rejecting universal models and emphasising the importance of situational factors. From these contingency theories, we shall pick out Fiedler's to illustrate the issues.[20] Fiedler showed that the climate of the group had a substantial impact upon whether a particular leadership style would be effective. The climate could be favourable, with good relations between a well-established leader and the group and with tasks relatively easily planned and controlled. An unfavourable climate refers to an unestablished leader not enjoying good personal relations with staff where tasks to be performed are unclear. Interacting with the climate are the leader's own basic motivations. According to Fiedler, leaders are either task orientated or relationship orientated. The former are more concerned with production, whereas the latter are more concerned with people. A simple best match between styles and climate was not found. Indeed, where the situation was either highly favourable or highly unfavourable, task-orientated managers did better. This can be explained as follows. In a favourable climate, the best leader is one who provides task direction, the group itself being able to sort out the interpersonal relations. In an unfavourable climate, close supervision of tasks is called for because any effort by the manager to counter the bad personal relations will be wasted. It is only in intermediate situations where a people-orientated leader will be of value in building group relations and resolving subordinates' concerns over tasks and rewards.

We must, therefore, look beyond the notion of motivation as applying a set of techniques to job design and reward. Encouraging commitment to the aims of the organisation requires managers to exercise a wide range of approaches including: participation in planning and controlling; appealing to reason; giving inspiration; politicking and bargaining; applying pressure; flattery; and appealing to the influence of third parties such as senior managers or outsiders.

✔ Quick check-up

Can you:

☐ Define organisation, training, communication, motivation, leadership.

☐ Name four common features of organisations.

☐ Identify functional, product, geographic and customer-facing structures.

☐ Explain temporary and permanent matrix structures.

☐ Explain why network structures are formed.

☐ List four main elements of HRM as a process.

☐ Name four question categories in a structured interview.

☐ Define training.

☐ Name the steps in the communication model.

☐ Define job rotation, enlargement and enrichment.

☐ Identify five incentive payment schemes.

❓ Questions

Chapter review

5.1 Why do organisation structures move away from hierarchies with departments?

5.2 Compare participation and rewards schemes with the theories of motivation summarised in the chapter.

5.3 What is training for? Personal development or filling holes in organisations?

Application

5.4 What is Abbott Laboratories' structural dilemma? How, based on this chapter, would you advise the company on its choices?

5.5 What organisation structure would you expect to see at Shouldice Hospital (Chapter 2)? Explain your reasoning.

Investigation

5.6 By taking a sample from local newspapers, summarise the frequency of different types of variable pay scheme. What conclusions can you draw from relating job types to scheme?

5.7 Compare the organisation structures found at a selection of NHS hospitals with the South Tees example given in the chapter.[21]

CLOSING CASE

Personal development on tap at Anglia Water[22]

Feelings of insecurity frequently reduce performance, but many employers find they cannot promise the long-term careers they once could. After privatisation, Anglia Water lost 900 jobs. Concerned with the effects if this problem, managers looked to move 'ownership' of careers to the individual, thus transforming insecurity into opportunity.

▶

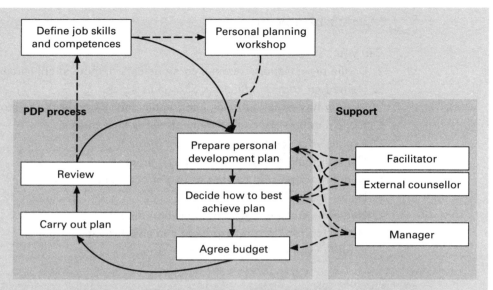

Figure 5.11 Personal development planning at Anglia Water

Each employee has a personal development plan. This provides a start for dialogue with the organisation. Anglia believes that encouraging all to think about personal development widens the pool of available talent to the company and aligns individual and corporate interests. For instance, many staff have experience gained in previous employment that the company had not sought to use. During the reorganisation, Anglia decided on a programme of counselling training to support those who were losing their jobs. It found enough people who were already practised counsellors. They now form a network to help any employee in difficulties.

Individuals now take responsibility for their training and development plans. They start by thinking about the qualifications, skills and experience they need for roles within the company. Then they identify their other skills which might be valuable in the business. Examples are languages, musical skills, travel experience, fitness and sport or do-it-yourself. Lastly, staff consider the roles they play in their families and communities, such as parent, volunteer, magistrate, preacher or school governor.

Employees, therefore, consider their whole lives, with their hopes, ambitions and expectations. They build and own a plan in this context. It will sustain them both within the company and beyond it.

Planning follows the steps set out in Figure 5.11. It starts with definition of skills and competences. The PDP workshop is a gathering of the work group to introduce the next stages. Meetings with managers over the next two months share the aims and expectations of the organisation and individuals. Another month later, each person discusses development with a company training facilitator: external careers advisers are also used. The draft plan is discussed with the facilitator, manager and, if different, the holder of the budget. Implementation is followed by reflection, review and updating.

The development activities are not confined to company training courses. Support is given to any training that benefits the business. Anglia defines benefit broadly, so that evening classes involving new learning are supported. The principle is for individuals to shed their dependence on the company to define their careers.

Questions

1 Use the theories of motivation outlined in the chapter to suggest reasons why the PDP policy at Anglia Water may, or may not, motivate staff.

2 How does the idea of transferring 'ownership' of careers contrast with the idea of human resource planning?

3 It has been said that such schemes do not reduce feelings of job insecurity. Comment.

Notes and references

1. Waters, R. (1995) 'Two's company – Abbott Laboratories, debating the best way to run an international business', *The Financial Times*, 7 July, p.17; Burnham, D.L. and Hodgson, T.R. (1997) *1996 Annual Report to Shareholders*, Abbott Park, IL: Abbott Laboratories Inc.; *2000 Annual* Report http://abbott.com/# accessed 30 May 2001; for a summary of the drug development process, see http://www.discoverabbott.com/timeline/timeline_chart.phtml

2. Barnard, C.I. (1938) *The Functions of the Executive*, Cambridge, MA: Harvard University Press, p.78.

3. Macák, F. (1991) 'Re-structuralization and privatization of the Vítkovice Works of Ostrava', *Vítkovice 91*, No. 4, December.

4. See www.dell.co.uk accessed 1 June 2001.

5. Lorenz, C. (1994) 'Management: How to bridge functional gaps', *The Financial Times*, 25 November, p.14.

6. Morgan, S.J. (1995) 'Virtual corporations offer real advantages', *Executive Issues*, 6(3), Summer, Aresty Institute, Wharton School, University of Pennsylvania.

7. Davidow, W. and Malone, M. (1993) *The Virtual Corporation*, New York: Harper Business.

8. Ouchi, W.G. (1979) 'Markets, bureaucracies and clans', *Administrative Science Quarterly*, 25(1), pp.833–49.

9. Moffat, J. (1992) 'Three case studies of operational research for the Royal Air Force', *Journal of the Operational Research Society*, 43(10), pp.955–60.

10. Mullins, L.J. (1996) *Management and Organisational Behaviour*, 4th edition, Harlow: Financial Times Prentice Hall, p.644.

11. Naylor, J. (1999) *Management*, Harlow: Financial Times Prentice Hall, p.498.

12. Hiroshima Sogo Bank (1994) *Watashitati no tekisuto [Our textbook]*, 32nd edition, Hiroshima Sogo Bank, Personnel Training Section, p.114.

13. Kreitner, R. (1998) *Management*, 4th edition, Boston: Houghton Mifflin, pp.352–3.

14. Hackman, J.R. and Oldham, G.R. (1980) *Work Redesign*, New York: Addison-Wesley.

15. Beynon, H. (1973) *Working for Ford*, Harmondsworth: Penguin, pp.140–1.

16. Jahoda, M. (1992) *Employment and Unemployment*, Cambridge: Cambridge University Press.

17. Naylor, J. and Senior, B. (1988) *Incompressible Unemployment*, Aldershot: Gower, p.26.

18. Abosch, K.S. (1998) 'Variable pay: Do we have the basics in place?' *Compensation and Benefits Review*, American Management Association, July/August, 30(4), pp.12–22.

19. Perrow, C. (1972) *Complex Organisations: A critical essay*, Glenview, IL: Scott, Foresman and Company, p.101.

20. Fiedler, F.E. (1967) *A Theory of Leadership Effectiveness*, New York: McGraw-Hill.

21. You can find these with a web search on 'hospital trust'.

22. Taylor, D. and Edge, D. (1997) 'Personal development plans: unlocking the future', *Career Development International*, 2(1), pp.21–3.

CHAPTER 6

Studying work

OBJECTIVES

When you have finished studying this chapter, you should be able to:

- Outline and illustrate the role of ergonomics in work design.
- Recognise differences in performance of humans and machines, illustrating problems of their interaction through displays and controls.
- Suggest reasons for vigilance decrement and variations of human performance over time and show their implications for management.
- Identify key issues in the design of the working environment for efficiency, health and safety.
- Summarise why and how accidents occur at work and how they can be prevented.
- Justify work study, identifying areas where it can be used advantageously.
- Explain the principles of *method study*; demonstrate the use of flow diagrams, process charts and multiple activity charts and sketch out how motion study is used for close analysis.
- Define *work measurement*, showing how industrial engineers can establish normal and standard times for jobs.
- Explain the value of productivity measures to the operations manager.
- Compare different methods of incentive payment for work performance and relate such systems to *job evaluation*.

| OPENING CASE | **Causes and consequences of pilot error**[1] |

On 20 October 1993, a Boeing 737 landed at night on Taxiway 2 at London Gatwick Airport. It had attempted to land on Runway 26R. This is the right hand of a pair of runways at Gatwick whose orientation is 260°, that is 10° south of west. Fortunately, the parallel Taxiway 2 was unoccupied at the time and the aircraft was taxied to the parking area where the passengers and crew disembarked normally.

The Air Accidents Investigation Branch investigates all such incidents within United Kingdom jurisdiction. Its report concluded:

1 Although the runway was clearly visible during the approach, the pilots had looked for and selected a pattern of lights to the right of it. They assumed that 26R was in fact 26L and thought that the designated runway must be to its right.

2 The crew had not briefed themselves on the lighting pattern they would see on Runway 26R once the change of runway had been confirmed.

▶

3 Misinterpreting the visual cues was aided by:
(a) Similarities among the nighttime views of Runways 26L and 26R and associated taxiways to the right. The latter were marked with green centre lighting.
(b) The use of 26R sometimes as a runway with edge lighting and sometimes as a taxiway with centre lighting.
(c) Setting the centreline lights of Taxiway 2 to a brilliance of 30% until the aircraft was about 2 miles from touchdown when they were reset to 10%. During the time the lights were at 30%, the chance of mistaking Taxiway 2 for the runway increased considerably.

Among the safety recommendations was an improvement to runway lighting to distinguish more clearly the runways from the taxiways. This was not the only time such a recommendation has been made. In January 1998, a Boeing 757 struck the ground to the right of Runway 26 when attempting to land at Puerto Plata, Dominican Republic. After the contact, the aircraft diverted to Santo Domingo, where it landed safely. It had minor damage to the tail.

During the flight, the cabin crew had dealt with a disruptive passenger. The commander wrote a report for the ground staff and, after allowing a flight deck visit by another passenger, had little time for briefing before commencing descent. There was no approach lighting at Puerto Plata, the only lights being at its threshold and edges. The standard landing procedure is to approach using instruments and descend below 600 feet only when visual contact is made. Having made two such approaches and not seen the runway until too late, the commander broke the operating instructions, which were to divert to another airfield. Another aircraft that had been circling had diverted, although two local ones had landed safely. Since about half of the contact with the tower was in Spanish, the crew did not develop a full picture of what was happening.

During the second approach, the commander could see the coast but not the runway. He observed that air to the right, over the sea, was clear and circled low to gain and keep sight of the runway. In the final turn, however, he caught his head set on the map holder, dislodging his spectacles. During the slight delay, the crew missed alignment with the runway centre line by 400 feet. Trying to correct this by banking sharply at low speed, the aircraft continued to lose height and hit the ground.

It was only after landing and partly disembarking the passengers that the crew found out which part of the 757 had hit the ground. A smell of leaking fuel was detected when the cabin doors were opened and it was then that the commander asked for fire cover.

6.1 Introduction

Investigation procedures mean that the tasks of cabin crews are very closely studied. In the incidents reported in the case study, we see pilot error. This results partly from people not following instructions. The 737 crew should have routinely checked the route manual to check the layout once they knew they would use an unfamiliar runway. The 757 commander, under commercial pressure to land at the planned destination, took a chance to attempt a visual approach. In both cases, weaknesses in runway lighting contributed to the incident. At Gatwick, it was possible to mistake one runway for another; at Puerto Plata, there was insufficient approach lighting below the descent path to initiate the visual contact. The work environment, already stressful, hindered effective performance.

These incidents highlight problems of organisation and motivation, covered in Chapter 5, and questions of detailed design of human–machine links. Defects in task design always run the risk of following the first of Murphy's laws: 'If something can go wrong, it will go wrong.'[2] Within the operating context, many complex processes must be planned and managed to achieve objectives. Many require human involvement. In some cases people do the physical work themselves, while in others their role may be that of controller of machinery in which skills of setting up, monitoring and maintenance are brought to the fore.

It is easy to slip into thinking of people as components of these operating systems and treat them as equivalent to, or even part of, machines whose performance can be predicted and can be expected to be consistent. Humans sometimes show inferior task performance compared with machines whereas, in other aspects, their performance is superior. The differences are important. Therefore, in this chapter we will look at the relationship between people and machines at work. This physical and psychological approach contrasts with the mainly social aspects considered in Chapter 5. As well as forming a basis for *work study*, it brings out issues in *health and safety*. This is an important area of great concern to all operations managers.

Whether we examine operations that involve people, machines or a combination of both, we need to search for the best ways of carrying out tasks, especially when these are done frequently. This is the role of *method study*, which analyses the sequencing and layout of tasks, sometimes in close detail to find the best ways of doing things. Since we must also bear in mind that organisations are engaged in economic activities, it is common to use some form of *work measurement* to both plan the resources required to carry out tasks and to control performance against established standards. This comparison produces various measures of *productivity* that can be used as the basis of bonus payments which form part of work motivation as discussed in Chapter 5.

6.2 Humans and machines

6.2.1 Ergonomics

We noted in Chapter 5 that job design refers to the identification and arrangement of tasks that together form a job. Then we went on to consider the sociopsychological effects of jobs and the how far the task or the person can be adapted to improve what otherwise would be difficult and tedious activities. In studying humans and machines together, however, we can move closer to the tasks they do. This is the realm of *ergonomics*, the study of human factors in work. Ergonomic studies focus on designing jobs to fit people and work environments

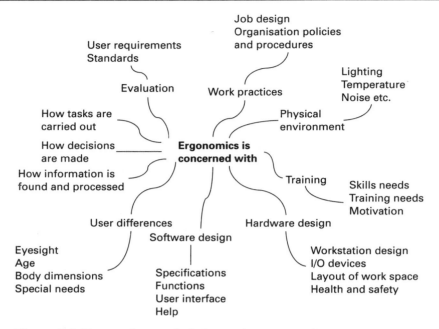

Figure 6.1 Human factors in information processing

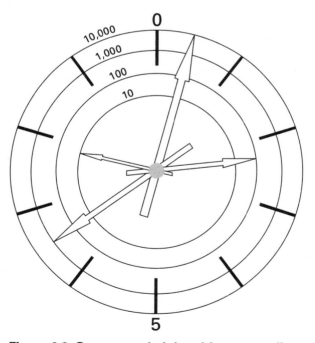

Figure 6.2 Guess your height: altimeter reading made difficult

BOX 6.1 **Ergonomics of the keyboard**

The dominant QWERTY typewriter keyboard was deliberately arranged to slow typists down. In the early mechanical typewriters, the levers tended to jam when efficient typists were working. Hence, the keys were placed in an inconvenient arrangement. For instance, many key sequences used in common words require consecutive use of the same finger or hand so the movements between key strokes slow down the speed.

In mechanical typewriters, the user has not only to expend effort in moving the levers but also has to perform other motions such as moving the paper carriage at the end of each line. Word processors have reduced the distance moved and effort expended in each key stroke and have curtailed the frequency of other movements. This change has resulted in an increase in carpal tunnel syndrome, a form of wrist injury caused by small repetitive movements using little effort.

Different keyboard layouts can improve typing speeds on modern equipment yet these may result in even more wrist problems. Other innovations include adjustable key spacing and the splitting of the board into two sections, each of which is contoured to fit the shape of the hand and allow each wrist to rest in a more natural position. The conventional keyboard demands a horizontal palm position which, if the upper arms are to hang vertically from the shoulders, means that the forearm is permanently twisted.

that are efficient and safe. Figure 6.1 is a mind map representing its scope in the context of an information-processing task. Questions for ergonomists include the layout of workplaces, human–machine communication and the quality of the working environment itself. We can use studies of typing, word processing and data input tasks to illustrate these questions.

The conventional keyboard is an example of poor ergonomic design, as shown in Box 6.1. In spite of attempts to overcome its deficiencies, continual data input risks carpal tunnel syndrome and tendonitis, two common forms of strain injury. These have long affected some manual workers such as chicken pluckers, meat cutters, postal workers and those on assembly lines.[3] Data from the Health and Safety Executive suggests that two-thirds of all United Kingdom workers have jobs involving a repetition of the same sequence. Among young workers, the proportion is 78%, with more than half having to work in awkward or tiring positions.[4]

Taking a broader view of the work system, ergonomists have also studied the design of workplace layouts, for instance the height and shape of benches, desks and chairs, to reduce the strain caused by staying in one place for long periods. Even wider solutions to physical stress could include job enlargement so that no individual spends excessive periods in one position carrying out a single task.

The design of displays and controls highlights problems of human–machine communication. Where information is difficult to collect, errors will almost certainly follow. Physical and cost constraints often lead to information being presented in less than ideal ways. At Gatwick airport, the visual cues from the runway lights were confusing. In another example from aviation, consider the design of an altimeter fitted to some aircraft in the Second World War (Figure 6.2). Space and simplicity of manufacture demanded that alternate pointers rotated

BOX 6.2 **Failings of digital watches**

Reading a traditional watch is an acquired skill. This skill enables us to judge angles on the dial and estimate the time to the nearest minute, an accuracy suited to most purposes. When wanting an idea of the time, a glance will suffice. Yet another advantage is the way we use angles on the face to estimate elapsed time, for example if a train is to leave at 20 minutes to the hour, a quick look will tell if we have to hurry. In contrast, reading a digital face requires the same degree of concentration whatever accuracy is required and estimates of elapsed times require computation.

When resetting the time on an analogue we develop a concept of gear train between knob and fingers. Turn one way for forwards and the other for back. The controls on the digital watch bear no relation to these ideas. For example, one cannot move the numbers backwards. What has happened is that what is good for the chip designer is not good for the user. All clocks and watches used to operate in more or less the same way; now one needs a book of instructions, a magnifying glass, fine fingers and about 20 minutes to change to summer time. When the alarm goes off during a funeral one is left pressing knobs at random while trying to pretend the sound is coming from somewhere else.

in opposite directions on the common dial. In the example, we can see that the aircraft is flying at something more than 3,000 feet but to be more precise than that requires some practice! It would be difficult to make consistently accurate readings in the difficult conditions of a cockpit, especially during engagement with the enemy.

These illustrations are of analogue displays, now often superseded by digital presentation. This area of information seems, however, to be particularly prone to technology-driven innovations that add complexity and without careful analysis of function. Take the example of the digital watch (Box 6.2). The digital watch promised high accuracy and reliability at very low cost. Yet, it is flawed. Packaged in many ways to incorporate radios, games, alarms and chimes, defects occur at the interface with users.

Controls are another area where ergonomists have studied difficulties. The conventional gate on the gearbox of a vehicle allows drivers to change without looking down. (For the same reason, displays in military aircraft present key information to the pilot without having to move the head.) Drivers are engaged in the general task of process control. In such cases, careful attention to the form and location of control levers can assist in promoting safe and accurate operations. This applies whether the process is driving a vehicle, a machine tool or a piece of domestic equipment. For instance, we are used to gas and water valves opening anti-clockwise whereas electric rheostats (such as volume controls on a radio) turn clockwise. What happens on one of those domestic cookers with both gas and electric rings? Errors in such cases are irritating rather than serious and can be prevented with both interlocks and warnings.

The control problem becomes more acute as machines and equipment become larger and more complex. This is illustrated by the task of preparing an oil well for production. This is the province of roughnecks, used to the dirt and danger.

BOX 6.3 **Ergonomic design to improve efficiency and reduce danger**

Completing an oil well is a complex and dangerous task. After drilling and lining with steel, a large volume of drilling waste must be removed. The machinery feeds a 3,000 metre reel of flexible steel tube down the hole using an injector head. Pumping nitrogen down this narrow tube blows out the mud. The traditional method involves four heavy vehicles worth $3 million. Operators and supervisor use radio links to communicate. They have to watch the injector closely. With the wrong tension, the tube can rush down the hole, possibly tearing the reel off the truck; if there is a sudden pressure rise underground, the tube can be blown upwards, spraying out acid and pressurised nitrogen.

Schlumberger, an oil and gas services company, launched a new unit in 1999. Costing $1.5 million, it rides on two trailer trucks and needs three operators. One person, housed in an air-conditioned booth, is in charge of it all, concentrating on the overall plan and not the individual elements. A special chair has integrated key pads and joysticks; information comes from a pair of flat screen displays. The speed of the new injector head is monitored by sensors with integrated controllers making corrections while alerting the operator.

Nevertheless, risks to men and machines must be reduced to the minimum possible. (See Box 6.3.)[5]

6.2.2 **Human abilities**

We have seen how weaknesses of ergonomic design can at best lead to loss of efficiency and, at worst, threaten safety. Links between humans and machines need to take into account their characteristics. Humans and machines are radically different, not different versions of the same sort of information processor. Table 6.1 illustrates some differences in human and machine capability when it comes to information handling. For instance, the limitations of humans as *data sensors* have many implications for the operations manager. The sensory organs are more responsive to some kinds of information than others: they will detect some dangerous gases but not others; they do not notice dangerous radiation; sensitivity to sound waves is limited to frequencies up to about 20 kHz, declines with age and can easily be impaired. In contrast, with training and experience, humans can discriminate among complex information such as assessing the quality of a beer. In spite of control automation, the brewer tastes the product at each stage before it is passed to the next.

Data processing by people is remarkably good in those areas for which the body has been 'designed', such as the processing of visual or aural signals to recognise a pattern, say a friend's face or voice. It is clear, however, that machines are better for computation and rapid storage and retrieval of large quantities of data. Machines are also being developed to pick out patterns from complex data. Statistical smoothing algorithms are a common example. Furthermore, machines generally score well on *scope and vigilance* criteria, whether it is the smoke detector or thickness gauge in a paper mill.

Table 6.1 Data-processing capabilities of humans and machines

	Data activity	Human capability	Machine capability
Data sensing	Infrequent events	Can appreciate unlikely or low-frequency events	Complexity limited by design
	Sensitivity	Good under right conditions; but limited range	Not so good; depends on design
	Noise	Can sort out signals from noise	Poor
	Other information	Able to collect incidental information	Depends on design
Data processing	Pattern recognition	Good	Limited; improving
	Reliability	Good but limited by conditions	Very high
	Computation	Poor	Unlimited
	Channel capacity	All have slow transmission rates	Unlimited
	Memory	Poor	Unlimited
Scope and vigilance	Monitoring physical phenomena	Limited range; low accuracy	Very high range and accuracy
	Time	Performance declines	No decline

Vigilance

Vigilance refers to the capability of a person to perform a task over a long period. Here, people experience the feeling that their efficiency deteriorates and that they have to increase their efforts to maintain their performance. This problem is important to operations managers and their staff. Tasks such as driving, machine control, data entry, surveillance and so on are all subject to this *vigilance decrement*.

Explanations of the decrement range from psychological to physiological. Some examples of the former are:

- *Arousal*. The level of arousal has an impact upon performance. In any task, there is an optimal level. If people are too active or too drowsy, they will not do so well. Since arousal itself varies with time then there will be deterioration in achievement.

- *Inhibition*. Resistance, or inhibition, builds up within the nervous system. This may result from an event having occurred very frequently, or not at all, during the vigilance period. In either case, the person may find it difficult to react to the next occurrence.

- *Filtering*. When carrying out difficult tasks or working in distractive environments, humans learn to filter out information irrelevant to their role. This may result in failure to detect rare signals or to appreciate their significance.

Whatever the explanation, and none is complete, it is clear that tiredness, over-activity, inhibition and inattention contribute to performance decline. Jobs that are affected must be designed carefully. Attention is needed not only to rest periods but also to the work environment. There should be sufficient stimulus to maintain arousal but not so much that excessive filtering takes place.

Biorhythms

Studies of the physiological factors in changing human performance over long periods have identified the so-called *biorhythms*, especially the *circadian rhythm*. This is the continuous daily cycle observed in measures such as body temperature and concentrations of chemical such as cortisone. For instance, young people with normal sleep patterns show oral temperatures varying from a low of 36.1° in the early morning, through 36.6° by 9, to a peak of 36.9° by mid-evening. Efficiency on continuous tasks is highest at peak body temperature. There are implications in these data for all work patterns, especially shift work. Where an employee works the same shift permanently, the circadian rhythm shifts after about a week to become entrained in the person's work cycle. Under rotating shifts, however, the rhythm retains the normal pattern.

Longer cycles in human performance have been detected. It has been suggested, for example, that pilots do not fly on certain days of the month. It is important, however, to keep the study of rhythms in perspective. While the physical measures may be well established, the resulting differences in performance may not be so clear and other social and psychological factors are likely to be much more important.

6.2.3 Work environment

The efficiency and safety of staff are affected by environmental factors, many of which are within the managers' control.

Lighting

Obviously, the level of illumination necessary for tasks involving detail, such as sewing or surgery, will be higher than for a warehouse where large objects are stored. In general, brighter lighting is required under the following conditions:

- *Fine work.* Working with small objects and tools, reading fine scales accurately.
- *Low colour or brightness contrast.* Including inspection or surveillance where special colour lighting can increase contrast.
- *High speed.* Care must be taken to avoid stroboscopic effects where moving objects can appear stationary.
- High standards of accuracy, surface finish and cleanliness are needed.
- Tasks are carried out over long periods.

Noise

Working areas always have some sound noise. High levels damage hearing; extended exposure to levels above 90 dB is regarded as dangerous. Depending on the nature of the sound, lower levels can be distracting. Table 6.2 illustrates some examples. Decibels are a logarithmic scale with zero defined as the quietest sound

Table 6.2 Many sounds are dangerous

Decibels	Power	Typical examples
30	10^3	Speech in studio
40	10^4	Suburbs at night
50	10^5	Average house
60	10^6	Quiet office
70	10^7	Near main road; train at 30m; vacuum cleaner at 3m
80	10^8	Inside box van at cruising speed; pneumatic drill at 20m
90	10^9	Ship's engine room; train at 6m; some loud discotheques
100	10^{10}	Near noisy industrial plant; operating pneumatic hammer
110	10^{11}	Very noisy plant; operating heavy riveting equipment
120	10^{12}	Deck of aircraft carrier at take-off

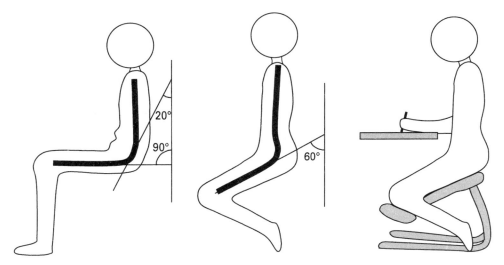

Figure 6.3 Sitting to maintain lumbar lordosis

that can be heard; the second column of the table gives the ratio of sound power compared with this notional minimum.

Physical demands

Mention has already been made of the design of workstations to minimise fatigue. We can illustrate this with seating design. Since many work in the sitting position, efforts have been made to improve chairs for offices and industrial use. When sitting on an ordinary office chair for example, most of the right angle between thighs and trunk is achieved by bending the hip joint. After 60° however, unless we are very supple, further flexing is resisted by tension in the hamstrings. The final 30°, therefore, is taken up by rotation of the pelvis. This in turn makes us lose the concave curve in the spine, the lordosis. This is normal in the standing position with the spine in natural alignment. In Figure 6.3, the first sketch shows how sitting on a flat chair loses the lordosis; the second shows how it can be preserved.

The effort of sitting up straight, then, comes from overcoming the hamstring tension when they are stretched beyond their relaxed length. The conventional design solution to this problem includes a sloping chair back, adjustable and shaped to the desired profile of the spine.[6] More radically, other designs have the seat sloping forward by about 15°.[7] To prevent sliding down the seat, however, the feet have to exert a backward force. This is will not work if the chair is on castors! Some designs incorporate a kneeler both to resolve this problem and to achieve the 30° slope. This is the *Balans* chair, shown in the third sketch.[8]

This example of chair design shows one of many issues facing the designer of tools and equipment. Humans developed tools as extensions to their own bodies, the direct contact and personal source of power ensuring human–machine integration. The modern machine tool, with its own separate power sources and indirect contact through programmes, is a much more complex problem. The information transfer between the two is the most significant design issue.

6.2.4 Health and safety at work

Many items discussed so far in this chapter have an impact on the health of staff and the safety of workplace operations. On both ethical and legal grounds, the safety of all people affected by an organisation's operations must be of major concern to the manager. In the countries of the European Union, national legislation has been supplemented by a series of EU directives aimed at harmonising standards and practices. Some of these directives are general while others, such as goods vehicle drivers' hours or standards for the shoring of trenches, are specific to certain industries and practices. Safety, in the way that it has an impact on costs, has economic implications. European governments are anxious to avoid the possibility of some countries becoming havens for cheap and unsafe industrial processes.

In the United Kingdom, the Health and Safety at Work Act 1974 provides the basic framework. In setting basic principles, it imposes the following duties on those involved:

- Every employer should ensure the health and safety at work of all employees.

- Every employer and self-employed person must conduct business in such a way as not to expose third parties to risks to their health and safety.

- Every employee at work must take reasonable care for his or her own safety and that of others and must cooperate with the employer on matters related to safety.

Standards are not fixed since the Act frequently uses the phrase 'as is reasonably practicable' to qualify its provisions. With innovation in safe procedures and new awareness of hazards, what may be acceptable and practicable in one era may be seen as hazardous and unacceptable in another. For example, since the Act was passed, more attention has been paid to the dangers of asbestos, radioactivity, noise, effluent, monitor radiation and passive smoking.

In giving expression to these general principles, legislation specifies the following duties for employers:

- To produce a statement of general safety policy and how it is to be implemented and to distribute it to all employees.

- Ensure that workplaces and their plant and processes are safe and do not have health risks.

- Ensure that all materials are transported, stored, handled and used in a safe manner.
- Provide safe means of entry, exit and escape from all premises and work areas.
- Instruct, supervise and train all employees in good health and safety practices in the work place.
- Consult with, according to published codes of practice, employees' representatives on all matters related to health and safety; set up safety committees if asked by the representatives.
- Ensure that persons who are not employed are given information on safety and hazards both in relation to their working within the premises and their use of equipment and materials.

To give force to its intentions, the Act defined for the first time several criminal offences that would arise from failure to discharge duties, breach of specific sections or non-compliance with the requirements of an inspector working under the Act. Personal responsibility for safety was thus imposed on the directors and senior managers of companies and other organisations.

6.2.5 Accidents

Both employers and employees do not want accidents to occur for they know that they can result in personal suffering as well as impose costs. Accidents do occur, because not only is there no such thing as a perfectly safe design but also because people tend to place themselves in positions where some risk is being taken. They intuitively trade off the risk of the accident against the cost of reducing that risk. As the risk becomes smaller, further reductions become prohibitively expensive or inconvenient. The risk assessment made by individuals can be very poor, however. For example, although the UK has among the safest roads in the world, measured by accidents per distance travelled, this is in spite of some common bad driving practices – jumping red lights, tailgating and driving too fast in fog. In the work place, specific regulations and policies are required to prevent practices such as using grindstones without wearing goggles, entering certain areas without protective clothing and smoking near hazardous chemicals. If these did not exist, some staff would take the chance, thinking, 'It could never happen to me.'

A labourer is carrying a small stack of half a dozen bricks. The top brick is loose and, as the person trips slightly on a plank, it falls. There could be several outcomes of this event.

BOX 6.4 Causes and consequences of accidents

- The employee may be unaware that the brick is loose and not notice its fall to the ground.
- Aware that the brick is loose, the worker moves out of the way when it falls.
- Whether aware of the looseness or not, the brick lands on the navvy's toes with painful consequences.
- Safety boots protect the toes when the brick falls.

Safety policies require an understanding of both events and their consequences. Take the example given in Box 6.4. One can see that the event of the brick falling arises from more than one cause. The brick is loose and the labourer trips. The outcomes of the event depend on yet further conditions. In the first case, the hazardous event occurs yet no one notices and it has no unfavourable effects. In the second case, the person knows of the hazardous practice but relies on personal vigilance to avoid any consequences. The third and fourth cases illustrate the need for safety equipment to eliminate negative effects of accidents.

We can define an accident as *an unplanned, unwanted and uncontrolled event in a process involving people, objects or substances*. Accidents may result in injury to people, damage to objects and equipment and loss of materials and production output. Much attention is directed towards major accidents, asking why they occurred. Usually, the answer is complex. Rasmussen pointed out that they do not result from a random coincidence of failures but by a 'systemic migration of organisational behaviour towards the boundaries of safe operation'. Accidents are the side-effect of decisions made by several actors in different places at different times. Usually, they are 'all doing their best to be effective locally'.[9]

Beyond the events that make headlines, many more incidents are hazardous. Yet, for one reason or another, they have no negative consequences. In industrial setting, these are equally worthy of investigation yet, generally, they go unreported. Riggs[10] quoted insurance company data to show that, for every 300 work accidents that result in no injury, there are 29 causing minor injuries and one resulting in major injury. This means that, for each major injury, there are 330 events whose recognition and investigation could lead to improved safety.

Multicausality is typical of accidents. There will be unsafe acts taking place in unsafe conditions. A complex combination of acts and conditions can lead to an accident. Unsafe acts stem from recklessness, anxiety, obduracy, distraction, ignorance and poor training, poor health and inability to learn. They take many forms including:

- operating without authorisation or training
- taking shortcuts
- overriding safety devices or rules
- not using the correct equipment
- not wearing appropriate clothing
- horseplay.

Unsafe conditions originate in the design, layout and condition of the workplace and its equipment. The following are some examples:

- Floors, paths and walkways, stairs and ladders that are uneven, slippery, cluttered or lack guard rails; inadequate side and overhead clearances; blind corners.
- Unsuitable or unreliable equipment for processing, handling and storage of materials.
- Unclear controls on plant and machinery and ambiguous warnings and alarms.
- Poor ventilation, high noise levels and light flashes that can cause distraction and loss of vigilance.

- Fire risks; processes that create unguarded flames and sparks; poor insulation; unnecessary presence of inflammable materials; inadequate means of fire fighting and escape.
- Poor equipment maintenance and housekeeping.

Exercise 6.1 Show how the incidents of pilot error in the opening case can be used to illustrate the discussion of accidents.

6.2.6 Safety policies and programmes

The Health and Safety at Work Act requires that a safety policy be published and that there should be programmes of instruction and training to ensure its accomplishment. Typical company safety policies reiterate the general principles of the

BOX 6.5 Safety programme in a despatch department

Safety in forklift operations

Policy statement

1 All staff are responsible for their own, each other's and outsiders' safety.
2 The departmental safety committee, with representatives from all sections, is charged with monitoring and improving safety standards.

Operations

1 The company will, when purchasing equipment, select only that which is known to have a good safety record. New equipment will not be used until staff are trained in its safe operation.
2 Equipment will be inspected, maintained and modified to keep it in safe running order and will never be used if it is unsafe.
3 New applicants will be tested for their ability to work safely. All staff will be fully trained in the use of equipment before they are expected to use it.

Reporting

1 All accidents resulting in personal injury must be recorded in the accident book.
2 All staff are requested to inform the safety representatives of potential hazards or incidents that do not cause injury. The representatives are to bring this information to the safety committee.

Investigation

1 The safety committee will consider all accident and hazard reports at its meetings and will arrange for investigation and analysis as required.
2 The safety committee may require that any procedure or method of working be immediately suspended. It may make recommendations to management on any matter related to health and safety in the workplace.

Improvement

The safety committee may nominate individuals for rewards under the company safety scheme where they have demonstrated improved working in their own jobs or have made suggestions that have been successfully applied in other departments.

Act, expressing them in the company context. They should identify where the senior management responsibility lies and how managers and staff should work together through recognised committees to identify and resolve problems.

A safety programme follows from the policy by applying it to each department or group of staff. It should set out how health and safety will be promoted, planned and controlled within the section. For example, Box 6.5 outlines a programme for forklift truck drivers in a despatch warehouse. Note that the safety problem is addressed through a process of continuous improvement. There is a legal requirement to record all accidents resulting in loss of work time but this department encourages the reporting of other hazards and incidents. These are the 'non-injury accidents' mentioned earlier. Improvements come from analysis of these events and a search for new ways of working which will reduce their frequency or their impact.

6.3 Work study

In addition to its application in the field of health and safety, the study of humans and their employment has great economic impact in the design and development of work systems. The purpose of work study is both to establish the best means of carrying out tasks and then to set standards for, and measure, the times which jobs take. While the two aspects of work study, method study and work measurement, are here discussed sequentially, it should be understood that they are closely connected. Practitioners, often called *work study engineers* or *industrial engineers*, use time data when analysing methods or, when collecting time data, always have an eye on the question of whether the optimal methods are being used.

Wage systems frequently include some form of output bonus, based on achievement of standards set by work study. Sound costing systems use data based on staff or machine timings. These are but two examples of the ways operational systems benefit from having a reliable and respected analysis of their methods and times. Such data can have significant impact both within operations and between it and other elements of the organisation's value chain. The following identifies some of these links:

- *Operations*. Better methods improve output, quality, wastage rates, reliability and safety. Standard times help the planning and control of plant and labour.
- *Inbound and outbound logistics*. Batch sizes, time and place of deliveries and packaging systems all interact with operational processes.
- *Sales and marketing*. Improved methods and reduced times lead to cost reductions and quality improvements. These in turn improve product competitiveness.
- *Service*. Improvements through better working methods, whether service is part of the sale or is after-sales.
- *Procurement*. Process improvements imply new or changed equipment but may lead to less use of raw materials.
- *Technology development*. Designs of products and processes are influenced by methods currently in use.

■ *Human resource management.* Consistent time standards lead to equity in pay systems. They also link output plans to personnel requirements.

■ *Firm infrastructure.* Organisation structures and information systems have implications for work methods; studies of working practices can lead to change.

Since work study involves an external investigation of what employees do with their time, the industrial engineer is commonly seen as posing something of a threat. If the study is successful, its result will be some change in the status quo, a change that some employees may not want. In the worst case, for example, a study ostensibly directed at method improvement, may discover widespread inefficiency and the carrying out of unnecessary tasks. The threat is a carryover from the early emphasis on time studies where the 'time and motion man' was seen as an instrument for employers to increase the speed of output by driving the workers harder.

The industrial engineer has to be sensitive to these issues and carry out the function diplomatically. In particular, the following are needed:

■ Communication with staff and managers on the purpose and methods of the investigation.

■ Recognising the contribution of every person.

■ Avoiding criticism of any person, or of their skills and practices.

■ Sharing the results of the study with those affected.

■ A professional approach, including quality of work and presentation, discretion with personal information, and fairness in assessment.

6.3.1 Method study

Method study, sometimes called methods analysis or process analysis, is concerned with the way a task is carried out, whether this be delivering a parcel or forging a piece of metal. The industrial engineer is not simply trying to drive down the cost of operations but may be asked to carry out an investigation because there are problems with product quality, service reliability, personnel safety and so on. The techniques used are applied to all types of organisational activity from shop floor manufacturing to information handling in the office.

Studies have three phases – data collection, analysis and synthesis and presentation of results. Data collection is aided by specially developed charts used to record events and can later be used to consider and compare alternatives. Analysis involves questioning every part of the current process as a basis for synthesising new patterns. The aim is to eliminate, consolidate or change the sequence of operations. To help with this critical process, industrial engineers use the investigatory 5W+H questions. These were used by Kipling when training to be a journalist (see Box 6.6):

■ Who does the task? Why? (Could another person be better or less costly?)

■ What is achieved? Why? (Does it need to be done in whole or in part?)

■ Where is the task performed? Why? (Could it be done better or more cheaply elsewhere?)

BOX 6.6 The 5W+H questions

> I keep six honest serving men (They taught me all I knew);
> Their names are What and Why and When and How and Where and Who.
>
> Rudyard Kipling, *The Elephant's Child*

- When is the task done? Why? (Could the task be done earlier or later or in a different part of the sequence?)
- How is the task carried out? Why? (Is there a better way?)

Charts enable the 5W+H questions to be investigated and alternatives, for example to sequences, readily compared. They are especially useful in method study because of the complex and multifaceted nature of the information. Not only do they help in investigation but also they help in communication of results. In presenting 'before and after' designs in diagrammatic form, the practitioner can make a convincing case for the necessity and practicability of change. We shall look at some examples to illustrate applications of method study.

6.3.2 Flow diagrams

Flow diagrams are often used to investigate the movement of objects or people around a workshop, office or other work space. They provide a means of examining processes that have a relatively long cycle and where the movements themselves form a large proportion of the time. On a diagram of the workplace, a line is drawn for each movement; the accumulation of lines shows the paths most commonly taken. The questioning process then concentrates on whether equipment could be moved to reduce the distance travelled, especially along the frequent paths. Other questions concern eliminating or combining of processes, as suggested by passing through the 5W+H sequence.

Figure 6.4 shows the way a flow diagram was set out during a study in a railway repair shop. In this unit, laid out in a crowded corner of a large workshop, an operator turns wheel sets in a lathe. This process restores worn wheel surfaces to true circularity and profile. In the original plan, the wheel sets ready for turning were placed on a track by an overhead travelling crane. The machinist pushed the wheels along the track to a small turntable set in the floor. This enabled them to be directed towards the lathe jaws. The wheels rolled into the lathe and, after adjustments by the operator, the lathe cut the profile. After unloading, the operator pushed them to the turntable and thence to the output track. Because of irregular flow patterns, any backlog of wheels had to be stored on the shop floor beside the lathe.

The operator's movements during the cycle of one wheel set are shown in Figure 6.5. Besides handling one set into and out of the lathe, the operator had to help the crane driver to place a reserve set in the input queue and move an extra set to the output. Furthermore, he had to push the output line along to make space for the next set coming from the lathe. The diagram reveals the major movements, however, as those between the loaded wheel set and the lathe controls and the turntable and its control box. The former resulted from the need of

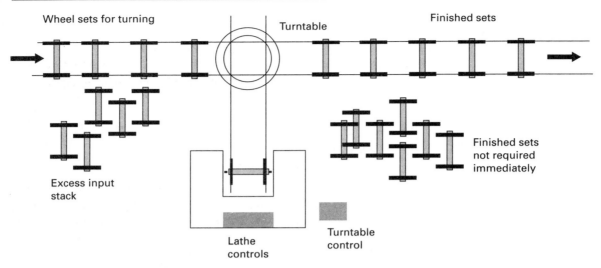

Figure 6.4 Layout of wheel-turning unit

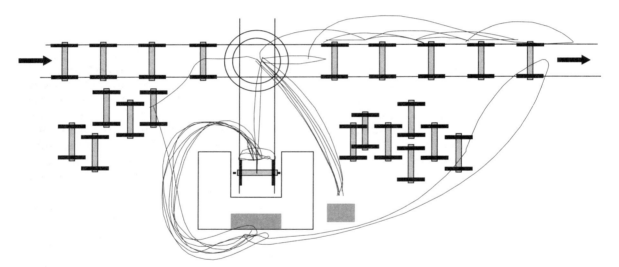

Figure 6.5 Operator movement during turning cycle

the operator to visually inspect the wheel surfaces before the cutting took place. To do so, he would advance the lathe one quarter rotation, move to check the exposed part of the rim and then repeat. Installing brighter lighting and windows in the machine guards allowed this inspection to occur from the control position with the machine turning slowly. This cut out most operator movement.

Movement to and from the control box arose because of its position away from the turntable for safety reasons. It was necessary to keep the floor free of fixed items like this. Again, however, some improvement followed, reinstalling the box close to the front of the lathe.

Many variants of flow diagram are used in projects from kitchen design to planning new roads. In one form, a pin is placed at each node; in the case of a kitchen these would be the sink, refrigerator, cooker, larder, table, door and so on. A thread, run from pin to pin, represents the travel of the person carrying out whatever task is being studied. This accounts for the diagrams often being called *string diagrams*. Computer modelling has largely replaced the string and pin technology. Possibilities of working in three dimensions, such as when studying traffic within a department store, or with more than one type of movement, such as people and goods, should also be noted.

Exercise 6.2 If you are able to observe, with permission, a regular task, such as serving in a shop or preparing a meal in a café or at home, try the following. On a floor plan, sketch what you expect to be the string diagram. Link nodes by lines whose thickness represents the number of movements. Then observe the process, recording movement on a fresh plan. Compare the two and comment.

String diagrams are part of a general family of proximity models. They are used in studying many operations problems from the layout shown here to the location of plants and distribution depots on an international scale. Representing movement and distance, further examples appear in Chapters 7 to 9.

6.3.3 Process charts

While flow charts focus on transport, process charts look at all the activities that go to make up a transformation. They separate activities into five categories, each with its own symbol as shown in Figure 6.6. This separation encourages the analyst to ask the 5W+H questions about the different types of activity. The operations symbol, O, records working directly on the product while the others, especially transport, delay and storage, can be combined or eliminated without loss. Charts are often printed with the symbols for convenience of use. They often contain columns to record distances travelled and times taken.

Figure 6.7 gives an example from a study of office work. It depicts the process for staff to order printing through the busy administrative office. The chart, which has had its headers removed for reasons of space, enables the analyst to quickly set out the steps of the process and record distance moved and time taken.

In this chart, there is space for comments that arise from the 5W+H questions. The case illustrates the way processes often develop for no apparent reason.

At one time, staff had been issued with three part-forms but, later, there was a shortage of supply. The office conserved its stocks by issuing single sheets to staff to be copied. During another budgetary crisis, the office supervisor was required to check

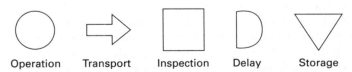

Operation   Transport   Inspection   Delay   Storage

Figure 6.6 Some symbols used in process charts

Print requests: current method

mtrs	secs	symbol	Operation description	Comments
	90	○⇒□D▽	Fill out printing request	Combine?
50+		○⇒□D▽	Take to clerk's in basket	
		○⇒□D▽	Await clerk's attention	
	30	○⇒□D▽	Copy details to three-part requisition	Eliminate?
	20	○⇒□D▽	Note details in progress book	Necessary?
30		○⇒□D▽	Take to supervisor's desk for authorisation	
		○⇒□D▽	Await supervisor's attention	
	10	○⇒□D▽	Supervisor checks and signs	Why?
30		○⇒□D▽	Pass to clerk's desk	
	20	○⇒□D▽	Add date and time to forms	Sequence?
	10	○⇒□D▽	Detach bottom two copies	
	10	○⇒□D▽	Place requisition in internal mail	
	10	○⇒□D▽	Send second copy to finance	
	40	○⇒□D▽	Third copy to file	File and book?
	15	○⇒□D▽	Note date and time in book	Sequence?
		○⇒□D▽		
		○⇒□D▽		
		○⇒□D▽		
		○⇒□D▽		

Figure 6.7 Process chart for print ordering

whether requests were necessary and if some could be delayed or cut in quantity. This problem had long since passed yet the supervisor continued to do nothing but initial a pile of forms every day.

6.3.4 Multiple activity charts

When the work to be studied includes two or more persons and machines, multiple activity charts are used to record how their tasks interacts. For example, one of the entities may be idle for considerable periods while the other carries out its tasks. A person may be employed to load, adjust and unload a machine, standing idle while the machine is operating. If these periods are sufficiently long, one person could manage more than one machine. In cotton spinning it has long been the practice to operate in this way, improvements to fibre quality, machine control and the working environment enabling one person to cover more and more spinning heads. The optimal number of heads is decided by comparing the costs of extra staff against the loss of output when threads break and heads are idle waiting for attention.

To illustrate the multiple activity chart, we can return to the wheel profiling example of Figures 6.4 and 6.5. To increase throughput, it was proposed that the machine operator be provided with an assistant. As the string diagram of Figure 6.5 showed, the operator's walking movements during loading and unloading seemed to waste valuable time. Figure 6.8 summarises, on the left, the activities of the operator and the machine during a typical 17-minute cycle. (For simplicity, extra

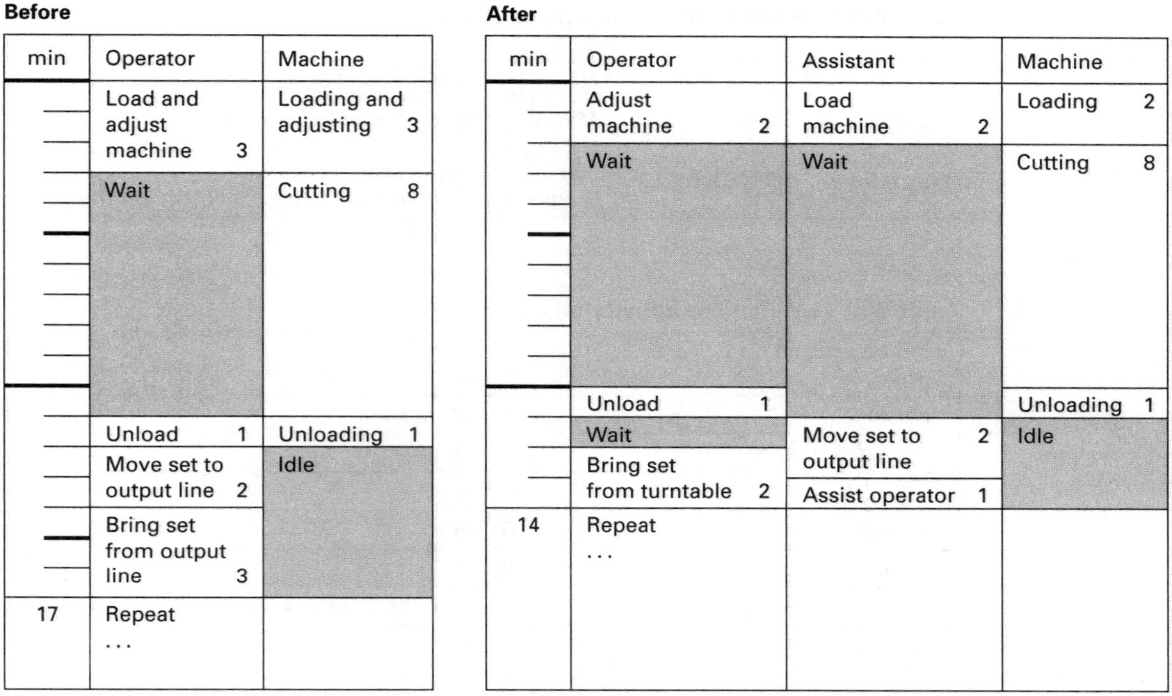

Before

min	Operator	Machine
	Load and adjust machine 3	Loading and adjusting 3
	Wait	Cutting 8
	Unload 1	Unloading 1
	Move set to output line 2	Idle
	Bring set from output line 3	
17	Repeat ...	

After

min	Operator	Assistant	Machine
	Adjust machine 2	Load machine 2	Loading 2
	Wait	Wait	Cutting 8
	Unload 1		Unloading 1
	Wait	Move set to output line 2	Idle
	Bring set from turntable 2	Assist operator 1	
14	Repeat ...		

Figure 6.8 Multiple activity chart for wheel-turning unit

movements made by the operator, such as housekeeping or working with the crane, are left out.) The chart is arranged in a standard form with a time scale running down the page and a column for each element in the investigation.

The right-hand side of Figure 6.8 shows the effect of introducing an assistant. There are two reasons for the reduced cycle time of 14 minutes. First, by working together, the crew can cut the loading and adjusting time. Second, each person can perform some tasks in parallel; one takes away a finished item while the other brings a new one forward. These two improvements are common.

The awkward layout of the loading and unloading paths in this case meant that the two operators could not move wheel sets during the machine cutting time. Therefore, the crew were idle for more than half the cycle. (Newer models of the lathe loaded and unloaded from different sides of the machine.) Despite this difficulty, management recognised that, when there was pressure to increase throughput, it was worth reducing the cycle time to 14 minutes and therefore increase output from some 26 to 32 sets per shift.

6.3.5 Motion study

Motion study refers to analysis in greater magnification than in the cases so far. Sometimes using high-speed cameras to record action, the studies examine operations that are frequently repeated and have cycle times of, say, two minutes or less. The detailed analysis is justified because shaving a few seconds here and there can produce significant cost savings. Motion charts are adaptations of

Table 6.3 Fundamental get and place motions

Symbol	Name	Movement
G	Get	Reaching for and taking hold of an object
P	Place	Moving an object to a target position
U	Use	Using an instrument or tool to achieve a purpose
A	Assemble	Joining two objects under control
H	Hold	Supporting with one hand while the other performs a task

Table 6.4 Two-handed activity chart

Left hand			Right hand
Starting position Operator seated at desk with stack of forms in front and four boxes for output to either side			
Take form from stack	G	H	Hold pen
Move to desk centre	P	H	
Open at page 2	G	H	
Check personal details complete	H	H	
	H	U	Tick any defects and initial
Open at page 3	G	H	
Check if Coverplan required	H	H	
	H	U	Initial if OK for Coverplan
Open at page 4	H	H	
Check if additional card required	H	H	
	H	U	Initial if details correct
Turn to page 1	G	H	
	H	U	Fill in routing details
Place in appropriate box	P	H	

multiple activity charts using either the same symbols or a set developed specially for this purpose, as in Table 6.3.

These *get and place* motions are used to record arm and hand movements, for example for staff working at a desk assembling equipment or doing office work. Study of motion in even smaller cycles, *microscopic analysis*, uses a further symbol set detailing hand and finger activity.

Table 6.4 shows an example of a get and place analysis of an administrative task. In opening and checking an application form, the person has to ensure that details have been completed correctly. In the light of the checks, the form is routed to other sections. The 5W+H questions can be asked of this process. For example, the pen is held in the right hand all the time while movement tasks are carried out by the left. Is it necessary to initial the form at every stage? Could we redesign the form so that pages do not have to be turned over and back? Are the in-stack and out-boxes positioned optimally? Apart from these questions of detail, it could also be asked whether the task is necessary at all. In other words, it is often worth investigating the wider system before becoming involved in analysing the components that it comprises.

6.3.6 Work measurement

Work measurement or time study is often thought of as carried out by the time and motion man armed with stopwatch and clipboard. It is widely practised in companies although much more in the West than in Japan. One survey found formal work measurement in some three-quarters of western firms and only one-quarter of Japanese.[11]

Work measurement is indeed one method that can be used for setting standards but it is only applicable to those jobs that can be observed: they must be current and regular so that the staff are familiar with what the task entails. In total, we can identify four ways to set time standards.

Historical data

For many employees and supervisors, experience will tell how long tasks are likely to take or how much they are likely to cost. The data may be available from time sheets or be embedded in custom and practice. The small jobbing builder, for instance, will often calculate a job cost by rule of thumb, working out the cost of materials and then adding the same again for labour. The disadvantages of historical data are threefold: there is no allowance for process change or method improvement; there is usually no record of whether the previous work was carried out at a slow or fast pace; in any case, these and any unusual factors become the subject of bargaining between the manager and staff. We should note, however, that historical data are cheap to obtain and are valuable when rough estimates of times are all that are needed.

Time studies

The most commonly used method, time studies use a stopwatch to measure activities. The observer will focus on tasks that make up the essence of the job and will ignore irregular elements and unnecessary movements that may result from abnormal conditions, inexperience of the worker or a deliberate ploy to extend the standard time. Time data rely on the experience of the industrial engineer to give a rating for the tempo at which work is being performed. See Section 6.3.7 for more details.

Synthetic times

Many processes are made up of common elements that occur repeatedly in the workplace. If a task can be analysed into these elements, and their normal times are already known, then they can be put together to estimate the normal time for the whole process. This approach has three advantages over the use of the stopwatch. First, the assessment can be made ahead of the task being done. Alternative approaches can be studied and the benefits of investment in more plant and equipment appraised. Second, the cost of setting the new time standards is much lower than making the necessary number of stopwatch observations. Third, the elemental times have been established and checked over many hundreds of observations thus avoiding disputes over their accuracy. Section 6.3.8 illustrates how the approach is used.

Work sampling

Rather than measure the duration of separate task cycles, work sampling is based on random observations of workers' activities during the whole period when they are engaged on the assigned tasks. Not only does the method enable the setting of time standards, but also it measures delays between cycles, whether these result from workers resting or are caused by interruptions in the flow of production. Details are outlined in Section 6.3.9.

6.3.7 Time studies

Although the stopwatch may be used to measure the time taken to complete an operation, this is just the first stage of establishing the standard time for the operation. The practitioner must make allowances for two factors, namely variations in the pace of different workers and the need to allow for rest.

Stopwatch times

The observer decides what tasks are going to be measured, whether it is an overall assessment of an operation taking several minutes or its individual elements that may only occupy seconds. Having taken sufficient observations, the observer calculates the *average cycle time*. The number of observations required depends on their variability and can only be strictly established after the observations have taken place. The statistical analysis of this variation need not concern us here, it is sufficient to note that between ten and 20 measures are adequate for operations lasting about five minutes.

Normal times

The normal time for an operation is the time that would be taken by an operator working at a normal pace with normal skill. (It is said to be equivalent to someone walking at three miles per hour – a task that could be sustained throughout the day given reasonable rest breaks.) The observer, while making the timings, must assess the worker's pace as a proportion of the norm. The rating is difficult. Although there are benchmarks and trainees have access to special films showing work carried out at different ratings, the assessment is subjective. In spite of these difficulties, the step is necessary to discover the normal time. This is found as follows:

Normal time = Average cycle time × Rating factor

Standard times

The final stage is to make an allowance for the fact that an employee cannot sustain the same tempo throughout the working day. There may be frequent interruptions in the work flow or many problems in the task requiring reference to instructions or the supervisor. There are also personal needs, including to wash and rest. The standard time is calculated as follows:

Standard time = Normal time × (1 + Allowance factor)

In a workshop with good conditions, the basic allowance for personal needs and rest will be a minimum of 5%, equivalent to some 24 minutes per 8-hour shift. Extra fatigue caused by working in awkward positions, the need to use physical force, bad light, high noise or poor environmental conditions is recognised by factors in the range 5 to 10%. Other elements that may be recognised are close mental attention, mental effort and monotony. These each have factors up to 5%. In heavy processing industries such as smelting, allowances for production workers will be around 35% while in machine shops, 15 to 20% is typical.

In one time study, the industrial engineer took 15 observations and found the average cycle time to be 3.5 minutes. The worker's pace was rated at 85% of normal. The job required some close attention and took place in a workshop where there was intermittent high noise. Each of these merited an allowance of 2% beyond the basic:

Average cycle time = 3.5 minutes
Normal time = 3.5 × 0.85 *or* 2.98 minutes
Standard time = 2.98 × (1 + 0.09 + 0.02 + 0.02) *or* 3.4 minutes

Time measurement seems, on the face of it, to be a sensible and rational approach to the question of establishing standards. Yet the sequence of steps needed to set the standards contains several pitfalls that we can summarise:

- Measurement cannot be done before the job starts and may be done while staff are still learning the job.
- Rating is a difficult task requiring trained specialists. Even so, Das et al.[12] have shown how operator bias and situational factors can combine to cause wide variations in assessments. Brisley and Fielder[13] demonstrated how, in a test, fewer than half the ratings were within 10% of their true value.
- The cycle time is based on observations that may vary widely and be subject to statistical error.
- Allowances may be controversial. Three issues arise: the same task may have a different standard time in different departments; an employee's work may be subject to frequent delays in the supply of components; fatigue is very difficult to assess.

No measurement system can eliminate all these pitfalls, especially the last that takes a subjective view of environment, delays and fatigue. Equitable standards are especially important where firms use them as a basis for incentive payments, as shown later in the chapter. Many organisations have arbitration procedures to resolve disputes in this area.

6.3.8 Synthetic times

Similar movements and tasks are repeated many times in any operational department. Therefore, the data from time studies can provide a base for estimating times for new operations that are commonly reorganised or developed from those carried out in the past. While the use of these synthetic times is both quicker and cheaper than relying on the stopwatch, there is a price to pay in terms of establishing the databank in the first place. Indeed, the cost for any firm to create a comprehensive database would be prohibitive.

Firms, then, can take two approaches. First, they can build up a database incrementally. This is valuable if the operations carried out do not vary much from year to year and the firm is satisfied with rough estimates. Painting and decorating businesses, for example, build up tables that give times per square or linear metre for applying different surface finishes to walls and ceilings. Other tables list correction factors to allow for: the quality of the surface being covered; the standard of finish required; the size and complexity of the surfaces; the height at which work is to be carried out; the working environment; and so on. Such data are vital to estimators and planners. In a situation where operations are much more regular and repetitive, greater attention to the quality of the data is needed and the industrial engineer will be concerned with measures of the micro-elements of work, as illustrated in Table 6.4. Fortunately, such data are commercially available.

Predetermined motion time standards (PMTS) have been established for the work elements, there being about 20 different basic motions. A scheme was originally developed by Frank and Lilian Gilbreth who coined the term *therblig* from their surname to label elements such as grasp, position, reach and assemble. The most commonly used system today is methods time measurement (MTM)[14] which has developed from work carried out and published in the 1940s.[15] The scope of the basic system of MTM is widespread and there are variants that have been developed for particular classes of operation such as small assembly or clerical work.

MTM-1, the basic system, is highly detailed and needs more than two hours to analyse one minute's worth of work. MTM-2 is higher level data in which the smaller elements are grouped into commonly used composite actions. For example:

Reach + Grasp + Move + Position + Release → Get

This simplification is at the expense of accuracy but has proved to be useful in analysing tasks with cycles greater than one minute or so. Even higher level data, MTM-X, have been developed to further speed up analysis. Such data can be set out on a small card and are handy for quick analyses by a trained person. Table 6.5 sets out the MTM-X basic actions with their corresponding times. Each unit is 0.00001 hr, which is 0.036 sec. Hence bending down is 1.04 seconds while rising is 1.15. The approximation in the data is evident in the way times for 'get' and 'put' are given just for near, far and variable distances whereas MTM-1 tables give data for the 'reach' movement for each 25mm of distance.

The repetitive tasks implied by the development of MTM systems are clear contenders for robot applications. Reasons are both economic, to save cost and ensure quality, and safety, to avoid the various forms of strain injury. The problem of planning assembly then shifts to making careful estimates of robot movement times to optimise their efficiency. RTM (robot time and motion) tables, mimicking MTM ones, have been created for this purpose.[16]

Table 6.5 Outline of MTM-X normal times

Work element	Distance		
	Near < 150mm	Far > 150mm	Variable distance
Get (easy)	8	16	13
Get (difficult)	17	25	20
Put (easy)	5	14	9
Put (difficult)	19	28	22

Regrasp	6
Handle weight	5
Apply pressure	14
Eye action	5
Step	18
Bend down	29
Arise from bend	32

6.3.9 Work sampling

Work sampling is a technique for analysing activities by observation but without the need for a stopwatch. It is useful for the investigation of certain types of question. For example, if several random observations are made of a machine during an 8-hour shift and on half these occasions the machine is not running, then it can be concluded that the machine utilisation was approximately 50%. Because the conclusion is based on sampling, it is subject to statistical variation and so will only be accurate within certain confidence limits. We will not look into the statistics here. We can note, however, that in the case given, 100 observations would be required to obtain an estimate that was accurate within 10% on more than 95% of occasions. The number of required observations increases when the observer is trying to classify activity into more categories, say working, changing tools, waiting for material and idle.

If work sampling is to be used to set time standards it should be recognised that it is an indirect method of obtaining cycle times. Observers do not have to use the stopwatch but they still have to assess the performance rating. When it comes to such detailed analysis, work sampling has little advantage over direct measurement.[17]

Work sampling can be used to evaluate other controls and allowances:

Allocation of wage costs at the research centre of British Gas is based on weekly time sheets. Employees may be engaged on several projects during a week so they are required to keep records of the hours they spend on each. This enables charges to be made to various client departments and is typical of cost analysis of such non-routine activities. Employees will typically fill the sheets in several days late and, naturally, will ensure that the total hours shown will match those given in their employment contracts! Work sampling is a way of checking the general accuracy of the time sheets.

In the Midas exhaust fitting centre, work sampling was used to evaluate the effect of operating a 'quick-fit' service on both labour and machine utilisation. The no-reservation operation gave advantages in the market place at the expense of having staff and lifts idle for some of the day. Idle time was difficult to evaluate because, as with the previous example, staff were reluctant to record that they were doing nothing! The study required 1,000 observations over 25 working days. Each, however, was simple to make and record.

6.3.10 Productivity

Productivity is of great interest to the operations manager and, of course, to all those who have a stake in the success of a country's organisations. Increases in productivity underpin increases in the standard of living. They represent improvements in the conversion of economic inputs, or resources, into outputs. Productivity is the measure of units produced compared with units used in their supply:

$$Productivity = \frac{Units\ produced}{Units\ of\ input\ used}$$

Note that productivity measures are not to be confined to assessment of labour efficiency. We also speak of the productivity of capital and other resources, although terms such as efficiency and yield are often used for these. The following examples are often seen:

- *Labour*:
  - Coal mining: tonnes per man shift
  - Car manufacture: vehicles per man shift
  - Transport: passenger km per employee
  - Retailing: sales per employee
  - Education: pupil–teacher ratio.
- *Capital*:
  - Agriculture: yield per hectare
  - Paper mill: output per machine hour
  - Transport: passengers per vehicle km
  - Hotels: room occupancy
  - Theatres: seat occupancy.
- *Other resources*:
  - Electricity generation: kWh per tonne of fuel
  - Stocks: inventory turnover.

While many measures appear precise, they are fraught with problems and can only be used as rules of thumb for rough comparisons. Comparisons are often made between productivity rates in key industries in different countries, for example car manufacture. Yet, to compare the numbers produced per shift is only valid if the cars are similar in work content and the manufacturers have the same degree of vertical integration. Even then, one should not draw the conclusion that higher outputs per shift are superior. Each manufacturer has to balance the mix of inputs according to circumstances. Where wages are high, it may be better to spend more on automation, when they are low, they may employ more labour.

This discussion illustrates both the advantages and disadvantages of using *single factor productivity measures*. On the one hand, single measures of the use of key resources are valuable as rules of thumb for operations managers. For instance, when I ran a finishing department, I knew the major constraint on output, or *bottleneck* (see Chapter 12). This was the spray painting line. Consequently, we kept a log of line throughput (measured in square metres per running hour) and a group met regularly to review problems.

The argument against single indices is that they encourage *measurementship*, the practice of managers to focus on one or a few factors at the expense of others. This can make their performance look good, at least in the short term. There may be too much emphasis on a few factors while managers lose sight of the overall reason for being in business. For example, in retailing, data on sales per metre of shelf or stock turnover can be improved if prices are drastically cut. Senior managers are particularly sensitive about the latter ratio as it is available to outside observers through the published accounts.

Multiple factor productivity measures address these problems by incorporating more outputs and inputs into the productivity equation:

$$Total\ productivity = \frac{Output}{Cost\ of\ capital,\ labour\ and\ purchased\ goods\ and\ sevices}$$

In the ultimate, this assembles all outputs and inputs into a single equation. This ratio gains because it provides a more rational basis for analysing change. It has two disadvantages: the breadth of its coverage means that it is unsuitable for use as a regular guide to the individual operations manager and it has now become a cost function, the inverse of cost per unit of output, commonly called *unit cost*.

Japanese managers are committed to productivity, which they tend to define in broad terms to include among the outputs quantity, quality and service. For each operation, broad assessments of productivity indices are made. The purpose of measurement is to find areas for improvement and ways to make the change. Detailed measurements are less common than in the West. Japan has about one-twentieth of the number of qualified accountants in the United Kingdom.[18]

The terms productivity and efficiency are often used interchangeably. Yet, there is a difference in that efficiency is often measured as a percentage while productivity is often assessed with different variables as we saw earlier. We shall see in the next section how wage systems often pay bonuses based on product-ivity. In this case, outputs (standard hours) and inputs (actual hours) use the same units and therefore labour efficiency and labour productivity are used to mean the same thing.

6.4 Payment systems

Work measurement almost inevitably leads on to the question of payments. Indeed, one main reason for the introduction of formal work measurement sys-tems is that employers seek to rationalise incentive payment systems that have grown up from bargains between supervisors and staff (see Box 6.7).

In Chapter 5 we discussed the question of whether wage incentives increase motivation. Whether they have a direct effect depends on the individual and on circumstances but it is important that, whatever system of payment is in

BOX 6.7 **The back of the book**

In my first job as a foreman, I had to authorise bonus payments for all the staff in the workshop. These payments, amounting to some 20% of earnings, were based on amounts to be paid for each job, such as overhauling a valve or brake cylinder or making and fitting a run of pipework. Each job had an agreed price. When a new job came into the shop, a new price was set by bargaining between one of the foremen and the respective chargehand. The job price incorporated the expected wage levels to be achieved at the time. Consequently, prices represented a mix of bargains made over a period of 20 years or more. The bonus for a job depended more on when its price was set than any other factor.

The foremen and chargehands used to connive at ameliorating the worst effects of this system. Documentation was slow and manual. In a good week, chargehands did not put in all the job tickets for bonus payments. Such action would have caused an investigation if the management became aware of high bonus levels. They kept a float of tickets 'in the back of the book' for the weeks when the job mix was not so favourable. Banking the float made bonus levels a little higher just before Christmas.

operation, it must be clearly understood and be seen to be fair. It is common, therefore, to base wage incentive plans on measured work because the standard hours form a rational basis for the payments. Measurement is, however, only the first step in the setting up of an effective payment scheme. The following need to be put into place:

- *A payment plan.* The plan should relate to management's objectives in terms of output. There should be consistency of treatment between individuals, groups and departments.

- *Scheme operations.* The scheme should be installed and maintained by personnel trained at assessing work. The measurement of actual work carried out should be through a good administrative system that calculates bonuses accurately. Special payments for non-standard work should be strictly limited.

- *Quality.* Checks should be made on quality to ensure that any increased output is not at the expense of slipshod work.

- *Agreement.* All aspects need to be agreed by those involved. In particular, there should be a process of resolving disputes and difficulties, possibly through arbitration.

6.4.1 Payment plans

There are many payment plans, each being adapted to suit local circumstances. They frequently compare productivity with a standard performance. Productivity is calculated as follows:

$$Productivity = \frac{Standard\ hours\ produced}{Actual\ hours\ taken}$$

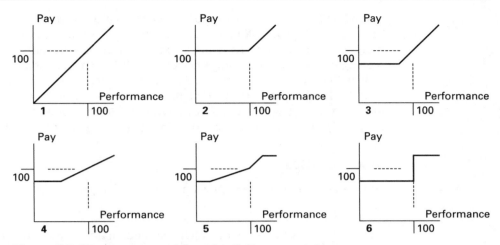

Figure 6.9 Some patterns of productivity payment

The standard performance of 100% is often used to trigger bonus payments. We shall review some of the main payment plans.

Piece rate

The most straightforward incentive plan is the piece rate system. Here, the only payment is for each unit of output. If based on measured work, each job has a standard time, usually measured in hours. A rate per hour is established for the period in question and an employee's earnings are simply:

Earnings = Payment rate per standard hour × Output in standard hours

Many types of contract labour, outworkers and casual workers are paid by this method. It enables the employer, for example a farmer employing fruit pickers, to know costs in advance and it can be highly motivating. Nevertheless, piece rates are not popular among many permanent employees whose earnings would be very sensitive to circumstances beyond their control. (See Figure 6.9, graph 1.)

Piece rate with guarantee

To overcome this risk of loss of earnings, the guarantee is brought in to set a minimum rate of pay for work below an agreed level, say standard performance as in graph 2. The effect of this is as follows. Below 100% performance, there is no bonus. Performance above 100% is paid as if it were piecework. Modifications of this approach relate to the level at which incentive payments come into play (see graph 3). The point of 3 is to include in the scheme those who perform at rates a little below standard. Those who work above standard are not affected.

Gain-sharing incentive

Gain sharing, or profit sharing, plans reward output over standard performance but at a bonus rate that is lower than the average rate per standard hour (see graph 4). The benefits of output above standard are shared with management. This reduced proportionality is one example of a *regressive* scheme that is designed to give some reward for extra output but prevents bonus levels from soaring out of control. If outputs were much higher than standard, a likely cause is defective work measurements. Sometimes, there is a *limit on bonus earnings*, setting a ceiling on the effect of such 'loose' times. In other cases, *staged incentive rates* may apply, with the rate of payment varying depending on performance. Graph 5 shows a scheme that combines two *progressive* steps with a ceiling.

Step incentive

Performance that reaches the standard, as in graph 6, generates the only bonus available.

The design of the payment system should match the circumstances. In some cases, where there is plenty of work, where standards are established and where employees decide the pace, simple systems with guarantees may be the most effective. Elsewhere, work may involve the interaction of many different staff and skills and it may be paramount to operate at an even, standard pace rather than encourage some to race ahead. In such cases, a single payment for standard performance will be more appropriate.

Organisations must also decide whether to tailor payment plans to individual performance or to assess output by work group or department. Again, the answer to this question depends on circumstances. Group incentives recognise that many staff must work in teams and they are generally less divisive than individual incentives. By the same token, the larger the group the less direct relationship there will be between the efforts of any person and his or her bonus, especially if the pace of activity is determined by machines. It may be, therefore, that where machine-paced work is carried out by groups, the notion of a productivity bonus should be dropped.

6.4.2 Job evaluation

The rate of pay for jobs in many organisations may be determined after systematic research by the personnel function. Otherwise, it may be the result of a long history of bargains and adjustments in response to the changing power of individuals and groups. Tradition has it that skilled workers are paid more than so-called semi-skilled and so on. Box 6.8 gives an example of a traditional system developed in railway manufacturing at Crewe up to the 1960s. The basic rates are nominal, being subject to multipliers to reach the totals of some £20 per week. We can notice: the high status afforded to the few patternmakers and toolmakers; the difference between the skilled and semi-skilled groups; and the low rate paid to sewing machinists, the only production grade occupied by women. Forty years ago, the battles over demarcation among trades and equal pay for women had hardly begun.

Job evaluation schemes attempt to rationalise the problems caused by haphazard pay systems. They build on the widely held notion that payments should be higher for more difficult and responsible jobs held by people who are more skilful and scarce. Both base rates in incentive payments schemes and fixed rates

BOX 6.8 Grades at Crewe Locomotive Works, 1960

Basic rate

83s.6d. Patternmaker; toolmaker

78s.6d. Blacksmith; brass fitter; boilermaker; coach body maker; coach finisher; electrician; fitter; french polisher; painter class I; plater; plumber; sheet metal worker; turner

75s.6d. Foundryman; machinist; pipe fitter; semi-skilled fitter; wagon builder; welder class I; wood machinist

72s.6d. Welder class II; wagon repairer

65s.0d. Crane driver; traverser operator

. . .

52s.0d. Labourer; sewing machinist

without bonuses are covered. A small job evaluation committee, with managers and staff representatives, is set up to identify and place all the roles covered by the scheme. The committee both creates the lists and arbitrates in any review.

Job ranking

The simplest method of evaluation is *job ranking*. It is based on the notions of ranking key jobs and interpolation. Taking first the general criterion of benefit to the company, the approach lists all jobs in rank order. Then, the pay rates for certain key jobs, spread out through the list, are decided by negotiation. This process may consider the rates paid elsewhere and is not part of the evaluation committee's function. Finally, the rates for the rest of the jobs are filled in between the key jobs.

Job classification

Job ranking is difficult in large organisations or where the committee is unfamiliar with the requirements for all the jobs. The *job classification* method improves on ranking by setting out a list of bands or classes into which all jobs are to be fitted. For guidance, each band is given a general description and examples are often included. The pay range for each band is then set by the pay review, an individual's earnings within the range being related to service or merit. This method is common in many branches of government and large commercial organisations. However, since the job fitting often means comparing chalk with cheese, fitting into bands becomes the subject of much dispute as employees seek to be regraded.

Point plan

To improve upon the problem of comparing different jobs, a *point plan* assigns points to agreed job-related attributes. In an industrial setting, the four factors of skill, responsibility, effort and working conditions may be assessed. In turn, these may be broken down into sub-factors. Each job is then scored and the resultant sum is the points value related to that job. Key jobs are selected as before for negotiation and the points values for the other jobs enable interpolation to be made on an agreed basis.

Job evaluation gains by bringing out into the open the basis for different payments for different jobs. Managers may rue the lack of flexibility that an ad hoc system permits. For example, the procedure is inflexible and may not enable the organisation to retain a very good employee who is offered a position at a higher salary elsewhere.

✔ Quick check-up

Can you:

- ☐ Define ergonomics; work accident; method study; work measurement; normal time; standard time; productivity job evaluation.
- ☐ Name three data activities where humans outperform machines and vice versa.
- ☐ List three causes of vigilance decrement.
- ☐ Summarise the main principles of the Health and Safety at Work Act.
- ☐ List five benefits, throughout the value chain, of reliable work measurement.
- ☐ Name the 5W+H questions.
- ☐ Sketch a string diagram and the axes of a process chart and multiple activity chart.
- ☐ Name four sources of time standards.
- ☐ Summarise four different variable payment plans related to output.

? Questions

Chapter review

6.1 What are the strengths and weaknesses of the main types of work measurement systems?

6.2 Compare string diagrams and process charts, outlining the benefits of each compared with the other.

Application

6.3 What personal, physical and environmental conditions inhibit top performance in a flight crew? Would bad weather tend to raise or lower accomplishment of duties?

6.4 How might you use work study methods in a small firm of office cleaners?

6.5 While the principle of job evaluation may be a rational, what difficulties may arise in its application in a complex setting such as a hospital?

Investigation

6.6 Interview people in work whose pay varies in some way according to performance. Ask for details of the methods used, the extent to which the bonus influences behaviour and whether the employee thinks the system is fair.

Change at Barr and Stroud[19]

Until 1987, when it was taken over by Pilkington, 96% of the work of Barr and Stroud was for defence. This long-established Glasgow engineering company was a world leader in thermal imaging equipment for tanks and submarine periscopes. With the collapse of defence contracts, profits fell in two years from a sound £8.6 million, on £85.3 million turnover, to a loss of £10 million.

Pilkington's new team found a bureaucratic and heavily over-manned business. There were nine management levels, seven graded canteens and four car parks with ranked distances from the factory. The new business strategy looked for a wider spread of international markets and productivity gains through computer-integrated manufacture (CIM). With the aid of consultants, a ten-year, four-stage programme of development was devised.

Initial results indicated dramatic change:

- profitability restored within 2 years
- inventories down by £15 million
- annual stock turnover up from 2.4 to 8.7
- sales/employee trebled to £79,000
- scheduled delivery up to 97%
- lead times halved to 7 months
- design changes halved
- backlog of orders down from 9,000 to 900.

The organisational change included the creation of teams around key processes. Job titles were cut from 200 to 30, banded into four broad grades each with a spread of jobs and salaries. Job titles abolished included departmental managers, turners, fitters, assemblers, senior and junior clerks and expediters. Many functions carried out in the personnel office became the responsibility of team leaders. The nine management layers became four.

The setting up of new multidisciplinary teams unearthed some supervisors and young engineers with high leadership potential while other managers found the change too great and left. Salaries were related as much to skills as to management responsibility so that some managers complained that subordinates were earning more than they were.

Phase 1 of the change included co-ordinating all manufacturing processes using a manufacturing resources planning (MRPII) system (see Chapters 12 and 15). The system improved communication and enabled layers of management to be removed. The inventory cut of £15 million financed a move to a new site. This change enabled many bad habits to be left behind. The three project phases to follow were: 'Right first time'; computerisation; and full CIM. Phases were planned like this because, according to the chief executive, the people acted as a constraint to change and could not take on the whole project at once.

Employee numbers fell from 2,500 in 1990 to 740 by 1993. There were 50 compulsory redundancies, the rest leaving by natural wastage. The four trade unions were involved from the start in both the jobs reductions and the design

▶

of the new pay structures. Skill-related pay is based on acquiring competences that must be relevant to business needs. A bonus scheme offered £50 to all if the budgeted profit was achieved. Better performance than that would increase the share in increments up to a maximum of £500. In the first year, the payment was £280. It rose to £500, leading managers to consider raising the maximum. Payment arrives just before the summer holidays.

Teamwork is important. Groups are expected to set monthly improvement targets focusing on quality. The company is now looking for a pay scheme that rewards cooperative effort by linking teams, instead of individuals, to business performance.

Questions

1 What are the advantages and disadvantages of the annual bonus?

2 Specialist workers at Barr and Stroud can, after the change, earn more than their line managers. What consequences might there be with this policy?

3 What comments and suggestions would you have for the company in its search for a pay scheme designed to reward quality and continuous improvement?

Notes and references

1. Air Accidents Investigation Branch (1999) *Report by the Dominican Republic Authorities into the accident to Boeing 757–200, G-WJAN at Puerto Plata Airfield, Dominican Republic on 1 January 1998*, Air Accident Report No 3/99, DETR; Air Accidents Investigation Branch (1994) *Boeing 737–2Y5A, 9H-ABA at London Gatwick Airport on 20 October 1993*, Aircraft Incident Report 3/94, DETR; see www.aaib.detr.gov.uk
2. The other two laws are, 'Some things that cannot go wrong will go wrong' and 'When things go wrong, they do so at the worst possible time.' There was no Murphy, the term is one of several used by engineers to refer to these important principles in contingency planning. See Naylor, J. (1999) *Management*, Harlow: Financial Times Prentice Hall, p.293.
3. Sambyall, A. and Kleiner, B.H. (2000) 'Development concerning repetitive strain injuries', *Management Research News*, 23(7/8), pp.71–3.
4. Hazards (2001) 'When work is a pain young workers face a terrible strain injuries risk', *Hazards and Workers' Health International Newsletter*, 73, 16 February; www.hazards.org/strainpain.htm accessed 2 June.
5. Brown, S.F. (1999) 'How great machines are born' *Fortune*, 139(4), 1 March, p.164
6. Pheasant, S. (1986) *Bodyspace: Anthropometry, Ergonomics and Design*, London: Taylor and Francis, p.162.
7. Mandal, Å.C. (1976) 'Work-chair with tilting seat', *Ergonomic*, 19(2), pp.157–64.
8. Best-known European manufacturers are the Norwegian companies Rybo and Stokke. See www.rybo.no/english/balans.htm and www.stokke-furniture.no/somet.html
9. Rasmussen, J. (2000) 'Human factors in a dynamic information society: where are we heading?' Triennial Congress of International Ergonomics Association, San Diego, August.
10. Riggs, J.L. (1987) *Production Systems: Planning, analysis and control*, 4th edition, New York: John Wiley & Sons, p.279.
11. Stainer, A. (1993) 'Competing on productivity – the Japanese way', *Management Services*, April, pp.12–17.

12. Das, B., Smith, D.R., Hennigan, J.K. and Yeager, R.J. (1993) 'Situational factors affecting performance – rating ability', *International Journal of Operations and Production Management*, 13(3), pp.49–56.
13. Brisley, C.L. and Fielder, W.F. (1982) 'Balancing cost and accuracy in setting up standards for work measurement', *Industrial Engineering*, 14(5), pp.82–9.
14. Data are published by MTM Association for Standards and Research, 16–01 Broadway, Fair Lawn, NJ 07410, USA.
15. Maynard, H.B., Stegmerten, G.J. and Schwad, J.L. (1944) *Methods-Time Measurement*, New York: McGraw-Hill.
16. Choi, C.K. and Ip, W.H. (1999) 'A comparison of MTM and RTM', *Work Study*, 48(2), pp.57–61.
17. Ho, C.-P. and Pape, E.-S. (2001) 'Continuous observation work sampling and its verification', *Work Study*, 50(1), pp.23–30.
18. Stainer, A., op. cit.
19. Based on Kennedy, C. (1994) 'Re-engineering: The human costs and benefits', *Long Range Planning*, 27(5), pp.64–72.

PART TWO

Location and layout

CHAPTER 7

Facility location

OBJECTIVES

When you have finished studying this chapter, you should be able to:

- Explain different location strategies followed by organisations.
- Describe the main factors to be considered in selecting locations.
- Outline and show the key elements that are required in a rational approach to selecting and choosing location.
- Describe in general terms the principles and processes involved in four techniques applied to the choice of location: factor rating, break-even analysis, the centre of gravity method and the transportation method.
- Identify the special issues in the siting of retail outlets.
- Analyse location decisions in practice.

OPENING CASE

IKEA's global flat packing[1]

In almost 50 years, Ingvar Kamprad has built IKEA into the world's leading furniture retailer. It operates 150 stores in 29 countries. The average size is 17,250 sq m. Each, when fully stocked, carries 10,000 separate lines. Allowing for colour and size variations, inventory can exceed 80,000 items. With 100 million copies, the catalogue is among the world's biggest print runs.

Kamprad's breakthrough was to encourage suppliers to use line production for flat-packed furniture coupled with self-service in huge stores. When the first IKEA store opened in Imhult in 1958, furnishing a flat could cost five times a new graduate's annual salary. From IKEA nowadays, the same furniture and fittings would cost less than half a year's pay.

International operations started with stores in Norway (1963) and Denmark (1963). Its largest current market is Germany (from 1974), followed by the United Kingdom (1987) and the United States (1985).

Although 10% comes from the Swedwood subsidiary, IKEA has around 1,700 closely monitored suppliers in 53 countries. Sweden (17%), China (9%), Poland (9%), Germany (7%) and Italy (7%) are the most important.

Expansion continues. In 2000, IKEA opened 25,000 sq m stores in San Francisco, Beijing, Shanghai and Moscow. Over 35,000 Muscovites turned up at its opening; Kamprad was there to greet them in his elementary Russian. The aim is to double sales worldwide in five years, with up to 70 new stores.

▶

In the United Kingdom, IKEA plans to spend almost £800 million over ten years to expand from ten to 30 outlets. An opening in Glasgow will be followed by Cardiff, Sheffield and Southampton in 2003. The stores will be supported by a new £40 million distribution centre in Peterborough.

Despite the popularity of the IKEA brand, store development frequently meets with opposition. IKEA's first forays in the United States met opposition from local retailers concerned about competition. Now local authorities are concerned with the impact on congestion and the environment. Yet they welcome the stores for their creation of several hundred jobs and up to $1 million of local sales taxes. Furthermore, they act as 'magnet' stores to enhance the prestige of shopping developments and often contribute to urban renewal. In the United States, IKEA uses agents to find potential sites and conduct the statutory environmental impact reports. In the San Francisco area, they found three eight-hectare sites close to major traffic flows, each capable of holding a 25,000 sq m store with 1,500 parking spaces. Further, they have identified a 180,000 sq m warehouse to serve the West Coast. Meanwhile, a traffic analysis in Chicago caused the planning department to reject an IKEA application for a site near a busy intersection. In Boston, IKEA has searched for 15 years for the right combination of space and location. Boston is attractive for its numbers of college graduates aged 20 to 50.

7.1 Introduction

One of the most critical strategic decisions made by an organisation is where to locate its facilities. IKEA demonstrates the full range of questions. First, at the strategic level, it is concerned with the pattern of global expansion. Which national markets should be targeted in which sequence and how many stores should be built in each? Where are supplies to come from? How should suppliers and outlets be linked into a chain – either directly or through distribution centres? Second, location decisions cascade down to details of sites. Retailers have to consider not only where the market is but also the availability of space and the acceptability of development when land is scarce.

Relocation decisions are most frequently made by small and medium enterprises faced with pressure to increase space, improve the scale and quality of their processes, reduce costs and so on. Many of these moves occur over short distances, maintaining continuity of managers and staff as well as proximity to local markets for purchases and sales. Larger facilities shift less frequently. Manufacturing plants employing more than 100 people relocate at the rate of 1% per annum compared with 3% for all establishments.[2] Put another way, the former move on average every 100 years!

More common than relocation, especially for large organisations, is the establishment of one or more new facilities. Firms, from energy companies to retail chains, reach out to new supplies and markets by locating near to resources or to customers. In some cases, the new facility will be unique in that its inputs come from clearly defined sources with its outputs supplied to an equally clear customer or group of customers. The location decision can then follow a search for the most economic place. In other cases, the firm will serve its customers from a network of points, each of which can supply, in principle, any of them. Now the pattern of supply is more complex and the choice of new locations more difficult as any new capacity will disturb the existing pattern. In its justification to local authorities, IKEA argued that its third store in the San Francisco Bay area would relieve road congestion around its others.

This decision area is one for which many optimisation models have been proposed, the model specification being influenced by factors including the number of sources and outlets. We shall be examining the application of some of the most important models in this chapter. While doing so, however, we should bear in mind that there are many qualitative factors in the choice that the more formal models do not capture. While the main points are outlined here, the models should be seen as pointers to the best choice rather than determinants of the outcome.

7.2 Location strategy

7.2.1 Location criteria

Whatever the type of establishment being set up, the best location involves the selection from among alternatives. The criterion for this selection comes itself from the total strategy of the organisation. For manufacturing plants, the best location may simply be the one where the total costs are minimised. Where the firm is service orientated, the customer is more closely engaged in the supply process and factors such as ease of access and speed of delivery come to the fore. We discussed, in Chapter 1, how many organisations in reality see themselves as producing a bundle of goods and services. In those cases, they have to combine ideas of cost, accessibility and speed of delivery into the assessment of location.

Product-based location

External and internal factors combine to influence facility location. Three basic strategies can be identified (see Box 7.1 for examples). Product-based location strategy is probably the most popular in large organisations. It reflects the product organisation structure (see Chapter 5) in which different operating divisions are each responsible for limited product ranges. A company, therefore, can have several semi-independent facilities in the same market area or even on adjacent sites. Their separation, however, enables each to adopt and utilise the appropriate process technology, work force and staff expertise, service level, style and image and so on. Factories or service facilities that are too large and attempt to supply a mixed range are often beset with problems of focus and control.

BOX 7.1 **Location strategy examples**

Product based

- Ford makes different model ranges at its plants, for example Jaguar at Coventry and Speke, Land Rover at Solihull.
- Kingfisher serves different markets through its retailing subsidiaries B&Q, Superdrug and Woolworth. These divisions create their own patterns of retail outlets and support warehouses to suit each product range.

Market based

- Cement manufacturer Castle serves the UK market from four plants whose location combines access to raw materials with proximity to four regions where demand is highest.
- New printing and data-transmission technologies have enabled national newspapers to print closer to their markets, permitting late news to be included and reducing distribution costs. Subcontractors are often used, boosting the fortunes of regional printing companies. The *Independent on Sunday* is printed in Derby, Northampton, Preston and Burgess Hill, near Brighton.

Vertically differentiated

- Coca-Cola produces its concentrate in one plant in order to protect both quality and the secrecy of its formulation. It sends this intermediate product from Atlanta to some 4,000 bottling plants throughout the world where water, sugar and carbon dioxide are added.
- Isolated service operations (see Chapter 3) are examples of vertical differentiation of location. Film-processing company Max Spielmann uses one Liverpool plant. Customers are dealt with at several dozen retail outlets throughout the region.

Market-based location

With a market-based location strategy, a business places facilities to serve market areas. It also reflects an organisation structure, this time one based on geographic divisions. Markets are the basic reasons for the location of retail outlets and distribution centres. Additionally, spatial considerations can justify plant locations where transport costs are high and other cost elements such as tariff barriers are important. Market-based location allows quick response to customer requirements.

Vertically differentiated location

A vertically differentiated location strategy means that different stages of the supply process are in different places. Some industries have vertically integrated firms who combine several stages of the manufacturing cycle. Rather than locate the whole operation on one site, location decisions are made for each stage. They have different economic characteristics and these influence the number and location of facilities. For instance, scale considerations may lead to a choice of just one plant at some stage, whereas, for the next stage, several plants located close to customers may be preferred.

Exercise 7.1

The Search and Rescue Service of the Royal Air Force has six flights of Sea King helicopters based as shown in Figure 7.1. In addition, the Royal Navy has two bases and the Coastguard four. Managed from the Air Rescue Coordination Centre at Kinloss, the combined service covers the sea from the Faeroe Islands to the English Channel. The RAF also has a mountain rescue service offering assistance to all in difficulties on high ground. How would you account for the location of these bases?

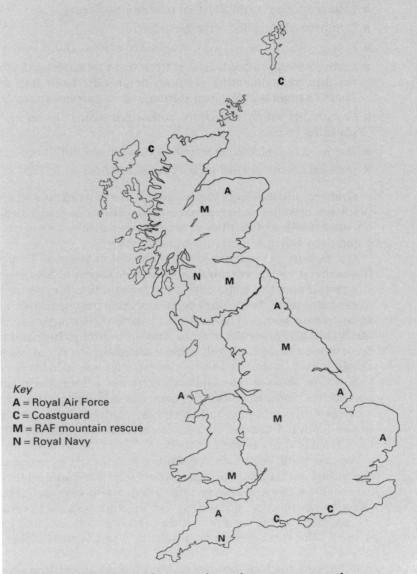

Key
A = Royal Air Force
C = Coastguard
M = RAF mountain rescue
N = Royal Navy

Figure 7.1 Locations of mountain and sea rescue services

Push and pull

It is useful to distinguish between *push* and *pull* factors in the location decision. Push factors stem from dissatisfaction with existing arrangements and cause the organisation to consider alternatives. Recognising and formulating the decision problem forms the first step in the decision process. The push factors include:

- A current site that is awkward, slow and expensive. This could include identifying the costs borne by customers if they have to visit.
- Labour shortages or industrial relations problems.
- Competitors' location strategies.
- Rising costs of site-related factors such as rents and property taxes.
- Changes in space needs related to shifts in total demand, changes in the product mix, new operating methods or pressure from staff for better facilities. These changes may create a shortage of, or surplus, space.
- Constraints set by regulatory authorities related to safety, effluent, noise or planning issues.
- The need to realise capital tied up in land and buildings.
- Unusual events or risks such as flood and fire.

Kirkham, Richbell and Watts confirm these items in a discussion of selecting plant for closure. Managers gave their reasons as small size, limited range of on-site activities, difficulties of access or expansion, labour problems, old capital equipment and remoteness from head office.[3]

The pull factors come later in the decision process. They represent a set of forces that draw the organisation to one area and site or another. As explained in Chapters 2 and 4, the strategy of the organisation is expressed at lower levels as a set of objectives. In location decisions, there may be conflicting objectives, such as cost versus service. These must be balanced. The factors to be studied, and the method of achieving the balance, vary from firm to firm and from time to time. Sometimes, the decision will be dominated by one factor, such as the search for skilled labour or the need to be close to a known market. On other occasions, a firm will be short of time and only carry out a limited evaluation of one or two alternatives. Some organisations carry out detailed location and site evaluations, whereas others will rely on judgement with very little quantitative assessment. Ingvar Kamprad decided on a hunch to open an IKEA store in Moscow, against the advice of other board members.

We can think of the choice among pull factors as made in two steps. First, depending on its size, an organisation selects a trading bloc, nation or region in which to create a new facility. Then it will examine detailed issues of site selection. In practice, these steps run together because the number of sites that are available, *or the number that the organisation is able and prepared to evaluate*, is small. The managers often search for a satisfactory, rather than an optimal, solution.

When constructing facilities to form part of an existing supply network, such as the telephone or electricity grids, sites very close to existing nodes are strongly favoured. Hence, Dungeness in England and Chinon in France have a series of nuclear power plants sharing resources.

A replacement electric power station was needed at Peel, Isle of Man. To be commissioned by 1995, the favoured site was next to the existing facility. Since this was near to houses, permission for its construction was given under stringent design conditions. This included the remarkably low noise level of 39 dB at 100 metres. (See Table 6.2 for examples of noise levels.)

7.2.2 Factors in location selection

The general criterion for location is to optimise economic benefit to the firm. This simply stated aim hides the complex nature of both benefits and costs. For example, it is not easy to assess the impact on profits of faster delivery times or easier access for customers. This is a common problem. Decisions combine many factors both quantitative and qualitative. It is useful to break the general criterion down into its constituent elements, some of which can be measured financially, others of which are the subject of judgement.

The factors to be considered are:

■ *Economic policies of governments at the supranational, national, regional and local levels*. Governments and organisations each have their own agendas when it comes to location policy. In contrast to the firm seeking to maximise its own economic benefit, governments look for benefits to their economies as a whole. Within the EU, governments support firms setting up in the weaker regions through a series of grants and tax incentives. Competition policy within the EU prevents governments from subsidising businesses unfairly but allows them give this limited support to help alleviate the effects of decline. Local governments and other agencies provide land, services and premises at low cost.

■ *International risks*. There are many risks associated with development. These are compounded by the financial risks of moving abroad, especially exchange rates and interest rates. Furthermore, for global companies, there are the political risks linked to operating in countries with unstable regimes or whose tax policies and currency controls shift frequently.

■ *Raw materials and energy sources*. Access to raw materials, components or supplies of energy is important, yielding cost advantages when these elements are expensive to transport or are perishable. This explains the siting of canning factories near to pea fields, iron works close to ore fields or ports and aluminium smelters near to electric power stations.

■ *Location of markets*. The reasons quoted for raw materials sources also apply to markets for goods. Transport costs of heavy, awkward or very bulky materials limit the range that can be supplied from one source. With self-service and personal service, clearly they must be offered close to the customer. How close depends on the service. Regular trips to the supermarket will be less than three miles for most customers in urban areas. some people, however, are prepared to travel the length of the country to attend an occasional concert or study at an attractive university.

■ *Transport links*. Quick and safe transport is needed at reasonable cost. While large organisations can afford to develop their own transport infrastructure at, say, ports, most have to rely on the communications networks provided by national governments.

■ *Climate and quality of life.* Climatic considerations used to influence the siting of certain processes, such as cotton spinning. Modern air conditioning means that climate now has less direct impact. It is now among the factors to be bundled into the general notion of quality of life. Firms are aware that, to attract and retain good staff, the local quality of life can be important. This is especially true of more mobile employees such as managers and engineers. Population drift to the sunbelts in the United States and southern France are an indication of many individuals' preferences for sunnier climes.

■ *Labour supply and training opportunities.* While some staff are recruited on a national or international level, cost considerations usually mean that most are drawn from local labour markets. The lack of availability of a potential work force, educated to appropriate levels will be a factor in rejecting some possibilities. Training schools and colleges will also aid the new company in building up its expertise. Cheap labour is not always the best, as the productivity of healthy and educated workers tends to be higher than for those without such advantages.

■ *Competitors and allies.* We have already noted that location is a strategic decision that will have an impact on the interaction with other organisations. A business may open a new facility on competitive grounds, to forestall the expansion of a major rival. An organisation whose work is interdependent with another will find it beneficial to operate close by.

■ *Availability of sites.* Sites with planning permissions and connections to utilities are in restricted supply in some areas. National and local governments use such controls and developments to influence industrial location. Prepared factory, distribution and office premises enable the new location to be developed quickly without the cost, delay and risk of individual development.

Government policies and changes in technology have changed the patterns of office location away from traditional sites in business districts close to urban centres. The city still has its attractions but congestion and high rents have led to the setting up of alternatives. These include peripheral office and business parks, sites close to airports or, nearer to the city centre, urban rehabilitation schemes. *Docklands* in London, *La Défense* in Paris, *EUR* in Rome and *City-Nord* in Hamburg are all examples of planned office centres designed in response to the demand for commercial premises.

It is worth noting that in the list of factors there is no generally dominant location factor that applies to business overall. When examining particular industries, however, different factors come to the fore. Karakaya and Canel studied location choices among firms in New York and New England. Their list, covering five industries, was headed by the availability of skilled labour, transport facilities and government regulation and taxation. Business consultants were particular influenced by access to airports, while retailers were concerned with land prices, construction costs and *low-cost* labour.[4]

In international business, car assemblers, component suppliers and electronics companies are concerned with trading bloc import tariffs and quotas. This has

BOX 7.2 **Some examples of inward investment to the United Kingdom**

- Alveo, a subsidiary of Sekisui Chemical Co. of Osaka, is among Europe's leading suppliers of polymer foams. More than half of the output from its Merthyr Tydfil plant is exported, mostly to the rest of Europe. Reasons for choice of location were English language; community of Japanese companies; and positive attitudes towards industry.

- United States-based Bibby Sterilin is one of the world's leading manufacturers of glassware for laboratories. It has 65% of the UK market and supplies products across the world. Good communications and the United Kingdom's location within the global service network are very important.

- Call centre management company TeleTech, based in Denver, Colorado, built its main European base in Glasgow to house more than 500 staff. The UK has the largest demand for call centres in Europe. Glasgow is one of Europe's major service centres.

- Sony's first British plant was built in Bridgend, South Wales, in 1973. Now it employs 4,500 people in the region to make 10,000 television sets daily as well as other devices. There is also one of the most active research and development groups within the Sony Corporation. Over 85% of Sony's Welsh production is for export. Further investment is justified by access to European markets, a supply of educated staff and a hospitable climate.

led to many deciding to establish manufacturing facilities in the European Union and the United States. Given a decision to move to Europe, the United Kingdom government's regional selective assistance has played a large part in persuading large foreign firms to set up in the country. Other frequently cited factors favouring the country are technical and financial expertise, reputation for innovation and the English language. With 1% of global population, the UK receives 8% of inward investment flows.

Local factors then come into play. The willingness of Welsh local authorities to support government grants with non-financial benefits such as the provision of special language classes is typical of the reasons for some companies setting up in the principality. Box 7.2 shows some recent examples of investments.[5] They all benefited from government assistance.

It should be noted that global corporations have great freedom in deciding where to locate, access to resources or markets being very important. These issues are brought out in Box 7.3, which is based on a survey of foreign firms' views of London compared with other European centres.[6] It is an attractive city for the financial sector, despite being among the world's most expensive. When firms are more closely tied to regional or national sources of supply or markets, government tax reductions and other inducements tend to have only marginal effects.[7] All types of firm frequently quote the availability of suitable labour.

BOX 7.3 Why financial sector and related firms set up in London

- Size and depth of financial markets make it vital for financial sector firms to be in London. Professional firms (consultancy, advertising, insurance, law) appear in proportion to the financial sector. A London location is not vital for manufacturing firms.
- Access to markets such as insurance, shipping and energy and the concentration of customers are further attractions.
- The availability of staff with appropriate skills is highly rated.
- Communications, law, language and jurisdiction contribute to the selection decision but to a lesser extent.
- London's social and entertainment values are important.
- Access to governments and international financial institutions is not significant in the decision.
- Second only to Tokyo, costs are high but not a deterrent to financial institutions.
- Lease contracts with upward-only rent reviews are not popular.
- Local transport is poor.

7.3 Evaluating alternative locations

In the next sections, we shall examine some main methods that have been proposed for comparing locations. The computations become more complex with each method. This should not suggest that the methods become in any way more reliable. It is just that different location questions make us use different approaches. Therefore, before we examine the methods, we should examine the general way in which questions are posed and responses obtained.

7.3.1 Optimising decisions

Location decisions are typical of many found in operations management; one is asked to find a best answer to a question. Here, the question may be framed in several ways. For example: 'Where should we build this distribution centre?' or, 'How many plants would we need to best serve this market and where should they be?' or, 'Which of our existing outlets should serve which customers?'

To discover the optimal answer to these questions, the following are required:

- *Clear statement of the objective sought.* This must be unambiguous so there is no room for having several objectives (for example speed, quality and cost) which are in conflict and have to be traded off, one against the other.
- *Recognition of constraints.* These may be drawn from the list given earlier in the chapter or be other business constraints. An example of the former would be, 'The facility must be within 2 km of a deep water port,' while the latter

would be represented by, 'The total spent on the project must not exceed £5 million.'

- *Recognition that the output,* or objective, *is dependent* on a combination of known inputs. This is the so-called *objective function* that can be expressed in general terms as:

$$Objective = Function\ of\ (Input_1, Input_2, Input_3, \ldots)$$

Or, simply:

$$O = f(I_1, I_2, I_3, \ldots)$$

Saying 'function of' means that we acknowledge that there is a relationship between the stated factors but may not have figured out what it is. For example, expressing all the factors in cost terms, we could say that the cost of operating at a site is a function of land and building costs, transport costs, labour costs and so on.

- There needs to be an efficient technique for discovering the optimal solution for the objective function within the stated constraints. As we shall see, this is straightforward when only a few possibilities are to be investigated. Then it is a question of calculating the value of the objective function for each site and making a choice. In contrast, when the number of options is greater, some kind of formal search or optimisation method makes the problem solution much more efficient.

Optimisation techniques have been developed for many common problems in operations management. Some, such as the critical path method and linear programming are widely used and we shall be reviewing their application in later chapters. Others are elegant processes of mathematical interest that may never have had much practical application or have been superseded by computer based search methods. In a third category worthy of note are problems for which only partial solutions have been found. The 'travelling representative problem' is not a location problem as such but it is a famous example of this category.

The travelling representative problem can be stated very succinctly. Given that the 'rep' wants to visit several places, what is the shortest, or quickest, route? (See Figure 7.2.) With three places, there are just six routes; with ten, there are 3,628,800; and with 100, the number would be 10^{156}! Search methods reaching optimal solutions have been proposed,[8] but there is yet no known method of homing in on the optimum other than by using computer power to try most combinations. While appearing to become unreal with large numbers, the travelling representative problem does come up frequently in business. In transport departments, for instance, dispatchers may plan lorry tours with 30 or 40 drops so that goods are stowed in reverse sequence of their unloading.

With respect to location choices, the four methods we shall look into are: factor rating, break-even analysis, the centre of gravity method and the transportation model.

7.3.2 Factor rating

The factor rating method is a general means to introduce objectivity to the process of comparing many factors in a decision. We are examining it here in the

Figure 7.2 Rep's tour. But is it optimal?

context of location choice but it can be used for many other cases. These may be where costs are hard to evaluate and there are several intangible factors such as quality of life, work force education and so on.

The simplest form of factor rating starts with a list of factors included in the decision. Managers are then asked to rate each alternative, either using a simple opinion scale (poor, satisfactory, good, very good, excellent) or by assigning a numerical value. Before debating the various sites, the decision makers then review each other's ratings.

Table 7.1 gives an example of a telephone-based service company faced with choices about its enquiries service. It needs to update its present facility in London (alternative A); or it could move the service to one of three other locations, these being available because of spare capacity in the leased trunk network.

Table 7.1 Factor scoring for a location decision

Factor	Alternative sites			
	A	B	C	D
Installation costs (£ million)	7	10	12	16
Changing in running costs (£ million)	0	−1	−1	−2
Room for expansion	1	3	3	3
Technical simplicity	4	3	2	1
Availability of work force	1	3	2	4
Acceptability of accent	3	2	4	2

Capital and running costs are expressed in millions of pounds, the latter being represented as savings in space and labour costs compared with the current operation. Other factors considered important are scored on a scale from 1 (disadvantageous) to 5 (advantageous). One important consideration is the ready availability of staff with accents close to standard English.

Study of the approach shown in Table 7.1 will show that it is little more than the setting out of an agenda. The factors chosen are merely listed and the decision makers are not faced with having to state, in advance, which factors are more important than others. In the case shown, the company may be very short of capital. In such a case, immediate expenditure will be the key factor and the option with the lowest installation cost will be favoured. The organisation may, however, be stressing the need to improve service levels and staff education and accent may come more to the fore.

To attempt greater objectivity and satisfy the requirement to develop an objective function as just described, managers must apply weighting to the decision factors.

The steps in the weighted factor rating process are as follows:

1 Agree a list of relevant factors. These could be drawn from a broader list such as the one given in this chapter.

2 Assign a weight to each selected factor that expresses the relative importance of that factor to the organisation.

3 Ask each person involved in the decision to assign a rating to each location for each factor. The rating is to a number on an agreed scale, say 0 to 5, 0 to 10 or 0 to 100.

4 Multiply each rating by the factor weight and add the results to produce a score for each location.

5 Make a recommendation based on the scores.

The recommended location will then be the one whose score is highest. In Table 7.2, the company is using a rating scale of 0 to 5. The weights add up to 100 so the maximum score for a location would be 500. Clearly, location D has the highest weighted total, closely followed by C. A sensible recommendation may be that both D and C are acceptable, adding that the differences between the two hinge on the availability and acceptability of staff. This point could be further discussed before a final decision is made.

Table 7.2 Weighted factor scoring

Factor	Alternative sites				Weights %	Weighted scores			
	A	B	C	D		A	B	C	D
Installation costs	2	3	4	5	15	30	45	60	75
Changing in running costs	2	3	3	4	15	30	45	45	60
Room for expansion	1	3	3	3	10	10	30	30	30
Technical simplicity	4	3	2	1	10	40	30	20	10
Availability of work force	1	3	2	4	25	25	75	50	100
Acceptability of accent	3	2	4	2	25	75	50	100	50
					100	210	275	305	325

7.3.3 Break-even analysis

We have already come across break-even analysis in Chapter 2, in our study of fixed and variable costs. A similar approach applies to location choices if good cost estimates are available and the decision is going to be made mainly on cost grounds. The steps in location break-even analysis are as follows:

1 Identify the costs for each location and figure out whether they are fixed or variable.

2 Produce a graph showing how costs vary with volume for each proposed site.

3 Make a recommendation based on the results.

Plant location

Location of a single plant will illustrate the approach.

In the Pilbara region of north-west Australia lie many large mineral deposits, especially iron. The largest iron deposit lies some 800 km inland. The climate of the region is very harsh, the land is desert and very few people lived there before the mining started. Several contractors mine and export the iron ore to markets mainly in Japan.

The basic processes involved in iron production from the Pilbara ore are mining, sintering and smelting. Huge trains, each carrying 10,000 tonnes, bring material down from the mines to the port for loading into bulk carriers for shipment. Mining clearly has a fixed location and smelting takes place in large, sophisticated plant in Japan. It needs 171 tonnes of ore, 109 tonnes of coking coal and 32 tonnes of limestone for every 100 tonnes of pig iron. The question is, where to locate the intermediate sintering process. Sintering is one of several possible beneficiating processes that can enrich the iron content, dumping the waste. Sintering requires coal. In this case, the choice is to be made on the grounds of costs, almost unhindered by space considerations because there is so much available. Three locations are possible: the mine, the port and in Japan.

First, sintering at an early stage would reduce transport costs because only enriched ore would be moved from the mine. Clearly, coal would be needed in moderate quantities at the mine, but empty trains run there anyway. However, to sinter at the mine would also involve the transport of other materials, plant and employees to that remote site, making the sintering process itself more expensive. Second, to set up at the port would be cheaper than at the mine and several mines could be served simultaneously, thus creating scale economies. The ore-carrying costs would be higher and waste would have to be dumped. Third, to sinter in Japan would be

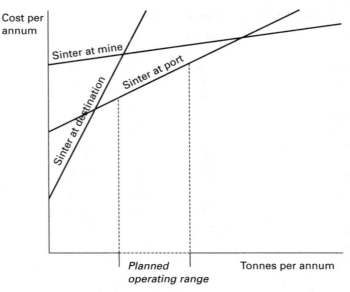

Figure 7.3 Break-even chart for sinter plant location

cheaper than in the Pilbara because of lower input costs and possible further economies of scale. Yet, the bulk carriers would be carrying more waste to that country.

Figure 7.3 presents the break-even chart for the Pilbara example. A recommendation would be based on the conclusion that to sinter at the port is the cheapest option for the planned mine output. To do this first stage of refining at the mine would only gain if volumes were much higher and to sinter in Japan is only preferred for small outputs.

7.3.4 Centre of gravity method

We shall study the centre of gravity method as the first of two techniques to use formal methods to search for the optimal value of the objective function. This method is applied to a special type of problem: What is the optimal location for a warehouse that is to serve several stores?

The framing of this question allows the problem to seen as one where the search is for the minimum transport cost. If the costs per unit of distance moved are uniform (for example, all despatches go by road), then the cost of supplying each store can be represented by loads and distance. The objective function, to be minimised, is:

$$Transport\ cost = f(loads,\ distances)$$

We can use tonne–kilometres to represent costs. The total cost is the sum of the individual tonne–km. That is:

$$Transport\ cost = loads_1 \times distance_1 + loads_2 \times distance_2 + loads_3 \times distance_3 + \ldots$$

The terms $loads_1$ and $distance_1$ represent, respectively, the number of loads carried and the distance from the warehouse to store number 1. The lowest value for

Table 7.3 Distribution centre location

Town	Tonnes (q_i) in 100s	x_i	y_i	$q_i x_i$	$q_i y_i$
Angoulème	34	13.3	12.4	452.20	421.60
Besançon	46	28.2	18.6	1,297.20	855.60
Caen	60	12.2	25.5	732.00	1,530.00
Lille	391	20.5	30.9	8,015.50	12,081.90
Limoges	35	16.2	13.1	567.00	458.50
Lyon	515	25.5	13.0	13,132.50	6,695.00
Meaux	1,025	20.0	24.3	20,500.00	24,907.50
Moulins	36	21.5	15.8	774.00	568.80
Nancy	233	28.3	24.0	6,593.90	5,592.00
Rennes	77	8.9	21.7	685.30	1,670.90
Toulouse	85	16.7	4.8	1,419.50	408.00
Tours	52	14.7	18.8	764.40	977.60
Totals	2,589			54,933.50	56,167.40
Centre of gravity at		21.22	21.69		

transport cost occurs when the warehouse is located at the so-called *centre of gravity* of the stores. Its location can be found from the following equations:

$$x_c = \frac{\sum q_i x_i}{\sum q_i} \text{ and } y_c = \frac{\sum q_i y_i}{\sum q_i}$$

x_c and y_c are the co-ordinates of the centre of gravity; x_i and y_i are the co-ordinates of location i; q_i represents the number of loads to be delivered to location i.

The co-ordinates can be measured using any units or grid. (This is not, of course, a real centre of gravity in the physical sense. The term is used, nevertheless, because the formulae are the same as those used in basic physics.)

The method, then, consists of the following steps:

1 Determine the depots to be supplied and the quantities they require according to a measure that is directly related to costs, for example tonnes, number of containers or volumes of liquid.

2 Using consistent units, tabulate the geographical co-ordinates of each site. The co-ordinates could be units on a map or actual distances.

3 Calculate and total the quantity x distance products, that is $q_i x_i$ and $q_i y_i$.

4 Calculate the co-ordinates of the centre of gravity by dividing the above by the total quantities.

5 Make a recommendation near these co-ordinates.

Baglin et al.[9] showed how to use the method for a single main distribution centre for products to be supplied to existing depots throughout France. Table 7.3 shows the basic data and calculations. The x and y co-ordinates represent east and north co-ordinates on a map.

The calculation proposes the optimal distribution centre somewhat to the east of Orléans. Based on this analysis the recommendation would be to search for a suitable site in that area.

Weaknesses of the model

The centre of gravity model as set out here has several weaknesses: it assumes that costs are linearly related to load and distance; 'crow-flies' distances are used, making no allowance for mountainous terrain or road tolls; there is no allowance made for regulatory constraints such as drivers' hours; finally, it assumes that the supplies originate at the distribution centre. In this last case, if the centre is to be supplied from a plant or plants at other locations, then its optimal co-ordinates will be found by including those sources in the centre of gravity calculation. More advanced versions of the gravity model are designed to overcome some of the other weaknesses.

7.3.5 The transportation method

In common with the centre of gravity method, the transportation method uses a formal algorithm to search efficiently for an optimal value of the objective function. Now, the question to be addressed is the best pattern of shipments from several sources of supply to several destinations of demand. We will start with the basic model. Here we are looking for the best way to *interconnect* an existing arrangement of facilities rather than find the optimal location for a new one. Let us represent the flow from source i to destination j by the term *flow*$_{ij}$, and the cost per unit transported along the same link to be *cost*$_{ij}$. Furthermore, let us assume that the cost per unit transported along a link does not vary with the flow. The objective function is:

$$Transport\ cost = \sum flow_{ij} \times cost_{ij} \text{ for all values of } i \text{ and } j$$

There are several methods of finding the optimal value for this equation. We shall use the *stepping-stone method*. This is typical of a family of linear programming techniques that moves from an initial estimate to the optimal solution in a series of stages. The sequence is as follows:

1 Determine quantities that each source supplies and each destination demands.

2 Identify the costs associated with the carriage of one unit between each source and each destination.

3 By working systematically through the data in a table, work out an *initial feasible solution*. At this stage, this is not a search for an optimal solution but for one where every source supplies and every destination is supplied to its capacity requirement.

4 Use the stepping-stone routine to move progressively towards the optimal solution.

5 Make a recommendation based on the resultant flows.

The procedure

To illustrate, let us assume that a supplier of special stone to the building industry has three quarries in Derbyshire, Cleveland and Cumbria. There are four depots, at Kilmarnock, Manchester, Bristol and Leeds. The capacities in tonnes per week, and the link costs, have been established and set out in Table 7.4.

Table 7.4 Capacities and costs of stone transport

to from	Kilmarnock	Manchester	Leeds	Bristol	Quarry production
Derbyshire	528	260	258	320	900
Cleveland	558	488	292	614	170
Cumbria	400	332	132	556	900
Depot demand	1,000	1,400	700	400	Total 3,500

Table 7.5 Initial allocation

to from	Kilmarnock	Manchester	Leeds	Bristol	Quarry production
Derbyshire	528 **900**	260	258	320	900
Cleveland	558 **100**	488 **1,400**	292 **200**	614	170
Cumbria	400	332	132 **500**	556 **400**	900
Depot Production	1,000	1,400	700	400	Total 3,500

The values in the clear cells are the costs of each link in pence per tonne and those in the shaded cells are the capacities. In this example, we have chosen the case where the total production capacity, at 3,500 tonnes, equals the demand.

An initial feasible solution can be found by the *north-west corner* method. This involves starting at the top-left cell and filling each in turn up to the production capacity of the row or the demand of the column. The Derbyshire–Kilmarnock cell thus has 900 tonnes per week, leaving zero for the other links in the first row. There will be 100 tonnes from Cleveland to Kilmarnock, and so on. Going down and across in steps, we produce Table 7.5.

The total weekly transport cost of this allocation is £15,610. To find a reduced cost solution, consider each empty cell in turn. For the unoccupied cell, calculate the effect on total costs if one tonne were carried along its route. The extra tonne will mean a change in flows on other links. Taking the Derbyshire–Bristol link as an example, the routine is as follows:

Table 7.6 First step in optimisation

to *from*	Kilmarnock	Manchester	Leeds	Bristol	*Quarry production*
Derbyshire	≺≺≺≺ ⋎	≺≺≺≺≺≺	≺≺≺≺≺≺	≺≺≺≺ ⋏	900
Cleveland	⋎ ≻≻≻≻	≻≻≻≻≻≻	≻≻≻≻	⋏ ⋏	170
Cumbria			⋎ ≻≻≻≻	⋏ ≻≻≻≻	900
Depot demand	1,000	1,400	700	400	Total 3,500

Table 7.7 Results of first step

to *from*	Kilmarnock	Manchester	Leeds	Bristol	*Quarry production*
Derbyshire	528 **900–1**	260	258	320 +1	900
Cleveland	558 **100+1**	488 **1,400**	292 **200–1**	614	170
Cumbria	400	332	132 **500+1**	556 **400–1**	900
Depot demand	1,000	1,400	700	400	Total 3,500

1 Trace a closed loop from the empty cell back to the original cell. Right-angled turns are only allowed at occupied cells. The only possible closed loop turning at occupied cells is shown in Table 7.6.

2 Since we are exploring the possibility of moving a tonne along the Derbyshire–Bristol link, place a +1 in that cell. Then pass round the route inserting –1 and +1 at alternate angles of the loop. A review of the rows and columns will show that these changes are needed to keep their totals constant. Table 7.7 shows the effect.

The change in weekly costs for the 1 tonne would then be: +320 – 528 + 558 – 292 + 132 – 556, which is a reduction of 366 pence. This is the *improvement index* for the cell.

3 Go on to calculate an improvement index for each empty cell. The improvement indices are shown as italicised figures in Table 7.8.

Table 7.8 Table with improvement indices

to from	Kilmarnock	Manchester	Leeds	Bristol	Quarry production
Derbyshire	528	260 −198	258 −4	320 −366	900
Cleveland	558	488	292	614 −102	170
Cumbria	400 −2	332 +4	132	556	900
Depot demand	1,000	1,400	700	400	Total 3,500

Table 7.9 Improved solution

to from	Kilmarnock	Manchester	Leeds	Bristol	Quarry production
Derbyshire	528 **700**	260	258	320 **200**	900
Cleveland	558 **300**	488 **1,400**	292	614	170
Cumbria	400	332	132 **700**	556 **200**	900
Depot demand	1,000	1,400	700	400	Total 3,500

4 Select the link with the largest negative value of the index. The greatest cost improvement comes from switching as much tonnage as possible on to the link. This is done by adding and subtracting tonnes round the relevant closed loop, making sure that no tonnage value becomes negative. Here, 200 tonnes are switched to Derbyshire–Bristol as this then empties the Cleveland–Leeds cell. The effect of this move is shown in Table 7.9.

5 Repeat stages 1 to 4. After several iterations, the result in Table 7.10 appears.

At this stage, no empty cell shows a negative improvement index. In other words, further shifts of tonnage cannot improve the objective function and we have found the optimal solution. The flows now represent the minimum total cost of £13,160 per week.

Many variants and improvements in this procedure result in a quicker optimisation of the objective function. However, most such linear programming problems

Table 7.10 Optimal solution

from \ to	Kilmarnock		Manchester		Leeds		Bristol		Quarry production
Derbyshire		528		260		258		320	900
	+198		500		+196		400		
Cleveland		558		488		292		614	170
	800		900			+2		+66	
Cumbria		400		332		132		556	900
	200			+2	700			+166	
Depot demand		1,000		1,400		700		400	Total 3,500

BOX 7.4 Early applications of the transportation method

From the 1950s, the National Coal Board carried out transportation studies. The calculations required desktop calculators and much effort; a 60 colliery to 60 customer problem took three days to solve! The Central Electricity Generating Board conducted similar studies at around the same period. Efficient movement from pit to power station was the focus. A regional model with 135 mines and 32 stations needed 71 iterations even though the most efficient procedures were used.

Such problems were ready made for the expanding computing facilities. By the late 1960s BP was one of the largest computer users in the country. Most of its usage was devoted to optimisation problems, concerned with forecasting, marketing, supply and so on.

lend themselves to solution by computer. See Box 7.4 for some early applications.[10] The purpose of this demonstration is, therefore, less to do with teaching details of the method and more with developing an understanding of the principles behind it.

The transportation method will extend to situations where the total capacities of sources and destinations are different. This is advantageous because, in practice, it would be rare for the whole system to be in balance. For example, a supermarket chain expanding into a new part of the country may first service its new outlets from existing distribution centres. Then, when the time is right, a new centre may be constructed in the new region. This itself would be built to cope with the planned growth in the number of shops. The company will draw up a shortlist of potential sites for the new centre and, for each, use a transportation algorithm to look for optimal supply patterns. The transportation method is thus changed from being a means of optimising flows in an existing system to being part of a facility location decision.

Other methods

Many variants of the transportation problem have been proposed, depending on the configuration of sources and outlets. For instance, de la Fuente and Lozano (1997) point out that sometimes clustering towns into zones to be served by individual warehouses is more important than siting the warehouses themselves. They propose a cluster analysis method to resolve the problem.[11]

7.3.6 Number of sources and destinations

So far, we have examined optimisation questions that have been narrowly defined and are capable of solution by standard methods. A much broader question is the definition of the number of depots with their siting. This is a complex question even if we limit it to a consideration of costs. Five cost relationships can now be brought into the objective function:

- *Links from factory to depots.* With a few depots, the supply costs will remain low since the company can take full advantage of full lorry or container loads. However, as the number of depots increases, each outlet will have to be supplied with part-loads and the costs per unit will rise.

- *Links from depots to customers.* With more outlets, the average length of these links will fall, thus gradually reducing the cost of this transport.

- *Depot stocks.* The total stocks held in many outlets will be greater than that held in a central facility. This is because each has to carry a safety stock as a buffer against random variations in demand. Theoretically, for the same level of service, the stock required increases in proportion to the square root of the number of depots; a doubling of outlets means a stock increase of 41%.

- *Storage and handling costs.* These costs increase because of the rise in stock levels just described. Furthermore, as the number of depots increases, each handles fewer orders and becomes less efficient.

- *Administration costs.* With decentralised order processing and an increase in the number of information links required, the administration cost per unit of throughput increases with the number of outlets.

We cannot generalise about the effects on the total distribution costs of these contradictory factors. Figure 7.4 represents them graphically. The first five graphs in the figure correspond to the costs identified in the list. (Note that the vertical scales in each will vary.) The sixth graph suggests a possible form of the total cost curve. There will be a range of numbers of depots that will result in operating costs close to the minimum. Companies considering how many centres they require and where they should be located will use such an approach to get close to the ideal number.

Similar considerations inform decisions on the number and location of health centres and hospitals. Depending on the degree of specialisation, a hospital serves a district of variable size. Current thinking sees general hospitals as serving populations of around 400,000. With larger catchment areas, travel distances for patients and visitors become too far. Otherwise, serving smaller populations means that the range of medical and support services expected in a general hospital can only be provided inefficiently.

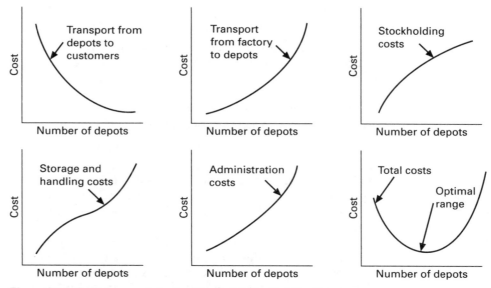

Figure 7.4 Costs associated with multiple distribution centres

7.4 **Retail location**

The selection of sites for retail outlets, whether they be shops, garages, pubs or restaurants, presents us with a set of considerations that are not normally of concern when locating factories or distribution centres. Retailers require visits from customers. This simple statement points to many *micro* issues in site selection of no interest to the factory or warehouse operator. The sales performance of sites even a few metres apart can differ substantially. As with other location decisions, many analytical models have been put forward, including those using data from geographic information systems. Hernández and Bennison conclude that these are being used more widely as the cost of computing falls. Many retailers do not fully integrate them into their decision processes, as political and cultural factors remain important.[12]

Bowlby and others[13] describe the ideal decision sequence for retail location as gradually narrowing the search from area to identified premises:

■ *Geographical area.* Choice of area may be based on identified area demand or may be part of a broader strategy such as aiming for full national coverage. For instance, Brewers Fayre is a chain of over 200 pubs with informal dining areas serving both individuals and families. Its location policy is to achieve national coverage using sites in the countryside or on the edges of towns. Each location has standard features such as parking and other facilities while preserving the character of the inn.

■ *Site identification.* The search for sites that fit broad selection criteria, such as nearness to markets, will generate a shortlist. In most areas, the number of viable sites is limited. Land values, existing developments and planning controls often cut the choices to a handful. These questions have concerned IKEA in its site selections in congested areas, such as San Francisco Bay.

■ *Micro issues.* Detailed examination of a site will cover many issues that contribute to potential performance. For location comparison, there are league tables published by estate agents such as DTZ Debenham Thorpe. These identify the sites which traders report to be the most successful. Some 300 locations are compared, retailers being asked to identify and rank those they find to be most successful. Measures include turnover and profitability.

A drawback of the league table approach is that it measures past performance and neither directly assesses the potential of a new site nor evaluates different retailing strategies. Starting from such a database, therefore, the major chains use sophisticated mapping models to compare different locations. The approach includes the use of *analogues* and *trade area mapping* underpinned by long experience.

Using the analogue procedure, the firm will assess features of the location that it expects to have influence upon store performance. It will compare these assessments with data from existing stores, using their grouped experience as a model for the new site. With many outlets, correlational studies become possible. Trade area mapping is a more extensive analysis based on the notion of catchment areas. It addresses the question of demand in relation to distance from the store and the location of competitors. Maps, based on electoral wards, give the population distribution according to distance. Furthermore, they give an analysis of income groups and family types. This information will then suggest likely demand, possibly through the analogue procedure. Geographical distance is not necessarily the determining factor. The perception of accessibility is as much a factor of travel time and general feelings of convenience. Large shopping centres, such as the Metrocentre at Gateshead, Sheffield's Meadowhall and the Trafford Centre near Manchester, have overlapping catchment areas. While they are up to 200 km apart, they lie on connecting motorway routes, the M1/M62.

Firms without formal databases may use checklists and, possibly, factor rating as described above. Four major decision factors in site evaluation are population, competition, accessibility and cost:

1 *Population*
The size and structure of the population in the assumed catchment area are recognised as having a strong influence on demand. Laura Ashley has a policy of opening stores in country towns such as Bath, Chester, Salisbury and Tunbridge Wells; Netto, the discount food retailer, entered the UK market by taking up sites within, or very close to, low-income residential areas in northern England; a newsagent will study the local estates.

2 *Competition*
Competition is a mixed blessing in retailing. Where outlets compete directly with similar product ranges, prices are likely to fall and the operator with the higher costs will suffer. On the other hand, customers are drawn to places where there are sufficient shops to render meaningful the idea of 'going shopping'. The significant role of anchor or magnet stores is noted in Chapter 9. In a shopping centre, however, not only are there shops but also supporting services from banks and building societies to bars and bistros. A store that depends for trade on

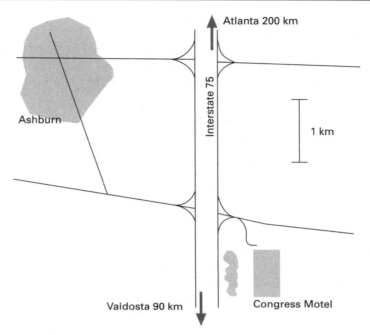

Figure 7.5 The Congress Motel site

comparative shopping is best located among others. There is indirect competition between related ranges of goods but within a much greater market. A remarkable example is the town of Hay on Wye, which is the world's largest centre for the sale of second-hand books.

3 *Accessibility*

Accessibility concerns customers, staff and suppliers. While customers are the prime consideration, inward and outward transport of goods has become an increasing problem in restricted town centres. Analysis of pedestrian flows (through *pavement counts*) and how they relate to nodes such as car parks and public transport termini is important, especially to those outlets that depend on passing trade. Confectioners do well near bus stops and it is said that there is always a flower shop at a Dutch railway station. Passing trade also applies to vehicular traffic; sites on different sides of roads or junctions can affect demand for petrol or places for rest and refreshment.

Robinson's case study of the Brown's lodging business[14] illustrates the importance of site position. The Congress Motel incorporated a campsite and trailer park next to the main interstate highway in south Georgia (see Figure 7.5). It had an attractive setting alongside its own lake in full view of the I-75 close to an exit ramp. The I-75 is used by people driving between the northern states and Florida during the holiday season.

A serious drawback of the site was that, while it lay in full view of the highway, it would be seen by southbound travellers *only after they had passed the intersection*. This group would be the more likely to be looking for somewhere to stay in the Ashburn district. As Calvin Brown put it, 'This location is just too short a distance from Florida. A northbound traveller can leave from anywhere across the middle of the state of Florida and pass this area in one day.' Picking up the southbound trade would also have generated repeat business at the end of the holiday. The Browns were further frustrated by the proposed new planning controls restricting roadside advertising. This would have meant the removal of the signs they had placed by the southbound carriageway ahead of the junction.

4 *Cost*
Rent and business rates dominate site operating costs in urban centres. For superstore sites, the development cost may have to include land values of around £5 million per hectare, the store needing between 2 and 3 ha depending on the size of its car park. Typically, costs of demolition and removal of contamination may double this figure. Large car parks may be necessary at peak periods but careful design is required if they are not to give an impression of a failed business at off-peak times.

7.4.1 Planning controls

Retail development takes place within a complex system of planning controls. Local authorities are the first assessors of planning applications. They work within the town and country planning acts and a set of planning policy guidance instructions. Some, usually large, developments are *called in* by the Secretary of State for the Environment. This usually occurs when it is judged that the development has implications beyond the remit of the individual local authority. The argument over the harm inflicted on high streets by edge-of-town developments is a case in point (see Box 7.5).[15] The likelihood of permission being granted for a site is a key consideration for developers. Authorities cannot use competition with existing businesses as a ground for refusal except in as far as a new centre may be shown to damage the general viability of existing ones.

Jones and Pal have traced the development of out-of-town service centres to match the trend in shopping.[16] Examples include cinemas, restaurants and football stadia. In 1997, Derby County moved to Pride Park and Bolton Wanderers to the Reebok Stadium; both locations are out of the centre and close to motorways. Local authorities have been instructed to favour central locations more strongly. For service sites, the first preference should be for the centre, then edge-of-centre and then district centres. Only if these places are not suitable should permission be given for out-of-town location.

Common grounds for refusal of permission may, in fact, hide underlying fears over competition. The reasons most commonly cited are changes of land use, effects on traffic and the wider impact. *Land use* restrictions on developments include building on open land, especially in the green belt found around many urban areas. The need to consider *traffic flows* springs from the experience of many early out-of-town developments where it was found that the road network was unable to cope. In many modern cases, developers offer, or are expected, to pay for road improvements if permission for land development is to be given. In 1994, GMI offered £400,000 for this purpose to back its application to Chester City Council to build an indoor tennis, squash and swimming centre on industrial land.[18] The *impact* on individual existing businesses cannot be used in judging an application. However, proposals for developments or change of use of premises can be refused on the grounds of impact on the local neighbourhood.

BOX 7.5 **The politics of retail planning**

At the end of 1994 there were four large out-of-town regional shopping centres in England. These were Metrocentre at Gateshead, Meadowhall at Sheffield, Merry Hill at Dudley and Lakeside at Thurrock. Not only had these sites come to dominate in terms of numbers of shoppers but also they were also highly profitable. On the Saturday before Christmas 1994 some 437,000 people visited these centres and 335,000 went on the Sunday.

The growth of out-of-town retail parks had been rapid. Throughout the latter half of the 1980s space was being added at the rate of $1/2$ million square metres per year. This meant that, by 1994, they accounted for one-quarter of all shopping space and some 27% of turnover. Profit was higher than for equivalent high-street stores because of lower costs of premises and operations. The effect of the growth on town centres began to be noticed, no more so than in Dudley but also in Newcastle and Sheffield. Pressure mounted on the government to exercise some restraint.

The secretary of state issued updated versions of various planning policy guidance notes. PPG 6, reissued in mid-1993, focused on protection of existing towns. It indicated that developments would not be allowed if they could be shown to harm nearby centres. PPG 13, of March 1994, drew on the commitment to reduce carbon dioxide emissions by casting doubt on schemes that would increase the use of the car.

Since many projects already had planning consent, it took time for the impact of the new policies to be seen on the ground. In the mid-1990s England received two new regional shopping centres, at Cribbs Causeway near Bristol and Bluewater Park near Dartford. Another opened at Brayhead in Glasgow. Yet, in 2001, the planning minister announced: 'For the first time since the early 1980s, new shopping floor space in major town centre schemes exceeded new floor space in out-of-town shopping centres and retail warehouse parks.'[17]

Nuisance from noise, for instance, may be a reason in cases as different as night clubs, pleasure parks and kennels.

The general impact of planning controls is mixed. Local authorities often face strong objections from groups in areas where development is proposed and, therefore, seek grounds for refusal. Given that these grounds are limited, especially in shopping development, councils recognise both the dangers of refusal, and the costs to their budgets, if the applicants go on to appeal and win. Consequently, they reach an accommodation, hedging permission with conditions such as the provision of open space and restrictions on hours of operation, deliveries and types of goods sold.

✔ Quick check-up

Can you:

☐ Name three basic location strategies.

☐ List five push and five pull factors.

☐ Define *objective function*.

☐ Name four formal methods of selecting a location.

☐ State the objective function of two of these.

☐ Name three key factors in choosing a retail site.

❓ Questions

Chapter review

7.1 Summarise, with examples, why a global service company may choose a particular location.

7.2 Explain why the location of goods and service organisations may be influenced by different factors.

7.3 Compare the principles underlying two of the four location selection techniques explained in this chapter.

Application

7.4 What factors do you think are most important in IKEA's location strategy?

7.5 What criteria would apply to the siting of general and specialist hospitals?

Investigation

7.6 Study a recent application for new development by a company in your area. Assess the reasons offered by the company in favour of the site and what steps it proposes to mitigate any adverse effects. Compare these with the views expressed by the local authority and any objectors. You should find this information in local newspapers or on the Internet.

7.7 Call centres employed about 2% of the United Kingdom work force in 2001. Investigate the reasons proposed for their location.

CLOSING CASE   Car assembly plants

In common with many other industries, the growth of vehicle manufacturing in any country concentrated in a few areas. It followed metal working, which had built up around sources of materials by the time the car industry was born. Building on this, there were advantages in the close communications between the vehicle assemblers and the vast network of suppliers that sustained them. Hence were established FIAT in Turin, General Motors in Detroit, Toyota in the Aichi prefecture near Tokyo and Rover and Jaguar in the West Midlands of England.

Perhaps the earliest large-scale plant planned in a wholly new location was that of Volkswagen at Wolfsburg where construction began in 1938. The site was by the Mittelland canal, close to autobahns and railways. Wolfsburg was, however, deliberately chosen to avoid disturbing existing industrial complexes and busy traffic flows. Workers were to be housed in a new town of about 100,000 people for which room had to be allowed. As it happened, the new town was not built immediately. After production restarted and expanded after the war, there was considerable commuting. For instance, in 1953, 3,000 employees (14%) were travelling daily the 80km from Hannover. Further expansion plans could not be accommodated at Wolfsburg so, from the mid-1950s the company expanded elsewhere, first at Hannover and then in other places in north-west Germany.

During the 1950s and 1960s, many governments became concerned about the location of their own motor industries. Through persuasion and financial incentives, they encouraged manufacturers to locate new facilities in regions of high unemployment. Thus, the car industry became an instrument of economic policy. In Britain, Ford and General Motors set up successfully on Merseyside, yet Rootes had a disastrous experience when it moved to Linwood in Scotland. In Italy, FIAT was persuaded to build a new plant south of Naples for the Alfa-Sud. Labour problems at Alfa-Sud included high absenteeism during the harvest season!

The 1970s saw a rise in international competition for government incentives. Ford, for example, discussed the location for a new plant for the Fiesta with several governments, including Austria, Britain and France, before deciding to move to Valencia in Spain.

Gradually, the motor industry has globalised. For the producer, it is no longer a question of where in a country a plant should be located but where in each trading bloc. The barriers to trade in goods among EU countries had virtually disappeared by 1991. The North American Free Trade Agreement also had the effect of creating a bloc. Plant location, especially of Japanese companies concerned about being excluded from these blocs by tariffs and quotas, has become a matter of politics and persuasion on an international scale. In the UK, there have been several developments by the well-known assemblers. Nissan is at Sunderland, Toyota at Derby and Deeside and Honda at Swindon. In their train have followed many component manufacturers setting up offices and plant.

Local, just-in-time sourcing, has become more important. A dozen JIT suppliers support the BMW Mini plant in Oxford, accounting for some 45% of the car's components. Almost half of the top 100 suppliers are in the UK. For the rest, the supply chain links companies in many countries. The circles in Figure 7.6 locate them, with diameters corresponding to the number of companies within each nation. Engines, from the Tritec plant in Brazil, spend six weeks at sea.[19]

Questions

1 Compare VW's location strategy of 1938 with that which it follows today. What elements have changed?

2 How has government policy towards vehicle plant location shifted over the years? How do manufacturers respond in their location decisions?

3 Competition is pushing manufacturers towards offering customised products while simultaneously improving the speed of delivery. What implications do these trends have for the location of plants and the design of distribution systems?

Figure 7.6 The international supply chain for the BMW Mini

Notes and references

1. Heller R. (2000) 'The billionaire next door', *Forbes*, 8 July; George, N. (2001) 'One furniture store fits all', *Financial Times*, 8 February; Voyle, S. (2001) 'Ikea stores for two more cities', *Financial Times*, 4 May; Materna, J. (2000) 'Ikea shops for third Bay Area location', *San Francisco Business Times*, 15 December; Goodison, D.L. (1999) 'Ikea group homes in on Somerville location', *Boston Business Journal*, 30 June.

2. Data for the United States from Schmenner, R.W. (1993) *Production/Operations Management*, New York: Macmillan, p.440.

3. Kirkham, J.D., Richbell, S.M. and Watts, H.D. (1998) 'Downsizing and facility location: plant closures in multiplant manufacturing firms', *Management Decision*, 36(3), pp.189–97.

4. Karakaya, F. and Canel, C. (1998) 'Underlying dimensions of business location decisions', *Industrial Management and Data Systems*, 98(7), pp.321–9.

5. Invest UK is the government's inward investment agency www.invest.uk.com; accessed 20 May 2001.

6. Society of Property Researchers (1992) *London as a Business Location*, SPR, c/o RICS Research Officer, 12 Great George Street, London SW1P 3AD, pp.1–2.

7. For example, see Artikis, G.P. (1992) 'Financial factors in plant location decisions', *International Journal of Operations and Production Management*, 13(8), pp.58–71.

8. Amin, S., Fernandez-Villacanas, J.-L. and Cochrane, P. (1994) 'A natural solution to the travelling salesman problem', *British Telecommunications Engineering*, 13(2), pp.117–22.

9. Baglin, G., Bruel, O., Garreau, A. and Greif, M. (1990) 'Management Industriel et Logistique Paris', *Economica*, p.369.

10. Ranyard, J.C. (1988) 'A history of OR and computing', *Journal of the Operational Research Society*, 39(12), pp.1073–86.

11. de la Fuente, D. and Lozano, J. (1997) 'Determining warehouse number and location in Spain by cluster analysis', *International Journal of Physical Distribution and Logistics Management*, 28(1), pp.68–79.

12. Hernández, T. and Bennison, D. (2000) 'The art and science of retail location decisions', *International Journal of Retail and Distribution Management*, 28(8), pp.357–67.

13. Bowlby, S., Breheny, M. and Foot, D. (1984) 'Store location: problems and methods 1', *Retail and Distribution Management*, 12(5), pp.31–3.

14. Robinson, R.B. (1982) 'Congress Motel and Brown's Overnite Trailer Park', case study in Pearce, J.A. and Robinson, R.B. (1985) *Strategic Management*, 2nd edition, Homewood, IL: Irwin, pp.939–68.

15. Cowe, R. (1994) 'The high street fights back', *The Guardian*, 24 December, p.32. Location rankings are drawn from the DTZ Debenham Thorpe survey mentioned earlier in the chapter.

16. Jones, P. and Pal, J. (1998) 'Retail services ride the wave', *International Journal of Retail and Distribution Management*, 26(9), pp.374–6.

17. Department of the Environment, Transport and the Regions, *News Release* 183, 28 March 2001.

18. Body, C. (1994) 'Tennis centre is back on', *The Chester Chronicle*, 2 December, p.7.

19. Information on BMW suppliers based on 'The Pacesetters', *Automobil-Produktion* special edition, *The New Mini*, Landsberg, July 2001, pp.42–5; 'The Brazilian power pack', pp.36–7.

CHAPTER 8

Facility layout: manufacture and isolated service

OBJECTIVES

When you have finished studying this chapter, you should be able to:

- Describe and explain different production system layouts, both ideal types and hybrids.

- Compare *process* and *product* layout design.

- Suggest the main advantages and disadvantages of fixed-position production.

- Illustrate the use of diagrams and models in the improvement of jobbing shop layouts.

- Discuss the advantages of *group technology* and show how its application could be investigated.

- Explain why *line balancing* is needed on production lines and summarise how this is achieved.

- Show how component reliability and line balancing are considered in continuous plant design.

- Suggest ways to consider human factors when planning layouts.

OPENING CASE

Heavy metal

Harvey Metal Products[1] converts plates and sections into finished assemblies for a wide range of industrial customers in the area around Wilkes-Barre, Pennsylvania. Its main processes are cutting, forming, welding and assembly. The shears will slice up to 9mm mild steel, while a 4 kilowatt laser cutter handles plate up to $3,000 \times 1,500 \times 19$mm. Lighter shears are used for gauges down to 2mm or so. Forming means bending cut plate into shapes for jobs as varied as special trailer chassis, transformer frames, building components and machine parts. Numerically controlled turret presses have a range of tool heads to notch angles and punch holes in sequence.

HMP has a spacious building, completed in 1994. Its 5,000 square metres have room for expansion. Inside, machines are laid out in groups, as shown in Figure 8.1. The heavy shears, presses and forming machines occupy a large area in the centre of the building. The laser cutter stands apart because of the need for fume extraction. Welding is carried out when jobs are assembled, next to the despatch bay.

▶

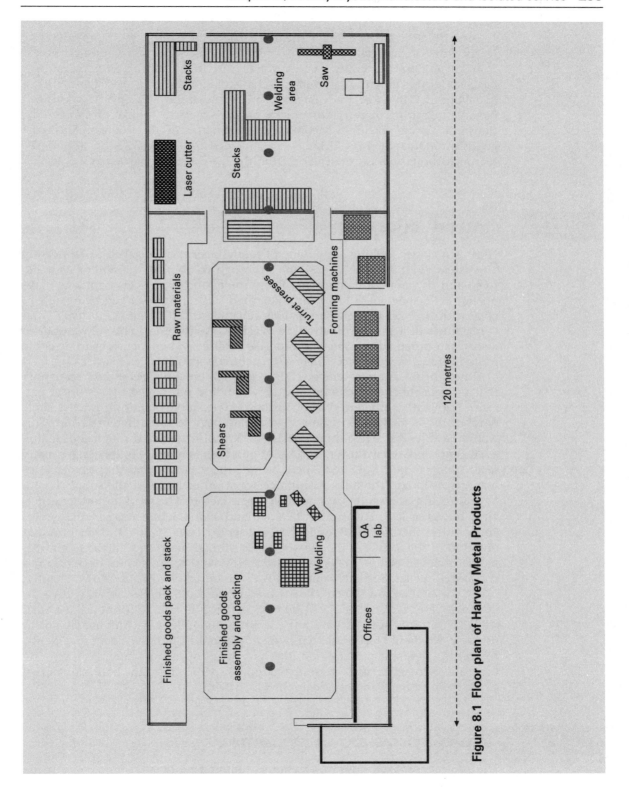

Figure 8.1 Floor plan of Harvey Metal Products

Apart from locating welding close to despatch, the plant layout does not represent flow of materials through a predetermined sequence. Contracts vary from cutting and punching a batch of flat plate to fabricating, in light-gauge, complex three-dimensional ducting elements for heating and ventilation installations. Therefore, movement of materials around the plant is unpredictable, requiring three forklift trucks. Supervisors have to take care to avoid the space among machines becoming clogged with work-in-progress. Finished goods are despatched on either a curtain-sided or a flatbed truck, although many customers collect their items from the five-vehicle loading bay.

8.1 Introduction

HMP is a classic jobbing shop. One of many businesses engaged in fabricating and assembly, it satisfies its customers through combining the skill of its workforce and its range of equipment. The number and type of its contracts make operations management unpredictable, often frustratingly so. Yet, being able to cope with the variety is the company's advantage. The layout is *functional*, that is machines of a similar function are placed close together. This allows staff to assist each other, share tools and other accessories and enables jobs to be easily routed through sections to whichever machine is available.

Although the arrangement at HMP may look obvious, we should remember that it was deliberately chosen in a new building unfettered by historical patterns. Had HMP a different type of business, for example building a smaller range of fabrications for fewer customers, we would have seen a different layout. This would have represented a more consistent flow of materials through the facility.

The appropriate layout for each set of processes is unique. In its design, many factors have to be considered. These include the scale of operations, the technology involved and the links with processes at other stages of the supply chain. Layouts could be classified according to these factors. The most important difference, however, lies between, on the one hand, manufacture and isolated service and, on the other, personal service and self-service (see Chapter 3). The dominant question in the former is the flow of goods through processes. In the latter, it is management of people's experiences as they flow through service resources and encounter queues. Since this question is a substantial one, it has its own chapter.

In Chapter 3 we saw how to classify manufacture and isolated service provision into five basic systems: project, jobbing, batch, line and continuous. We shall study layouts for these systems in the sections that follow. In studying layouts in this way, we should recognise that modern plants are often hybrid arrangements, combining different principles at different stages of manufacture. Furthermore, there are approaches, such as group technology, which lie at the boundary of two of the basic systems and can be applied in either.

8.2 Project production systems

The project, or fixed-position, layout is required when the item being made remains stationary. The staff, materials and equipment are brought to the work area when they are needed. We see that industries from civil and marine engineering to film making and research centres use such layouts. This is because of the uniqueness, complexity or weight and size of the items they produce. Civil engineering contractors are engaged in the supply of both unique products, such as roads and bridges, and those that they produce in batches, such as houses.

Difficulties that arise in fixed-position layouts include:

- Severe limitations of space for safe working and material storage.

- The flow of materials to their installed position is difficult to plan and implement.

- The number of staff required and the rate of use of materials varies so services from accommodation to transport are difficult to plan.

- Hazardous processes are troublesome to isolate.

- Many projects involve working out of doors or at remote sites, thus imposing extra costs and risks of delay.

- Supervision and inspection are difficult.

These difficulties can be alleviated by carrying out as much work as possible away from the assembly position or site. In heavy engineering, such as the manufacture of oil rigs, the policy is to make subassemblies indoors and bring them to the site only when needed. This approach is limited only by constraints in the transport system. House building in the UK has moved towards off-site assembly, notable developments being the use of pre-assembled roof trusses and ready-glazed windows. Gradual developments such as these have been successful both in reducing costs and time and in improving quality. The building industry is, however, used to a slow rate of innovation and to making minor adjustments to components as they are fixed. The system building movement of the 1960s illustrates the difficulties of a switch to off-site assembly without proper control of manufacture and supervision of installation (see Box 8.1).

BOX 8.1 **Failure of system building**

System-built flats were erected in many towns and cities during the 1960s. The low cost and rapid construction were attractive to local authorities pressed by housing shortages and budget constraints. After some ten years, however, investigations began to show that many of the structures were seriously defective.

The flats were built from room-sized concrete panels reinforced and insulated during factory manufacture. Built-in rubber seals were intended to make them watertight. Problems of dimensional accuracy in manufacture and careless assembly on site meant that gaps between panels were not watertight. Rain penetration led to dampness in the flats, the growth of black mould and rusting of steel reinforcing bars. Ill-fitting windows or poor ventilation and insulation often made these problems worse.

In the poor working conditions, often many metres in the air, it was difficult for inspectors to spot errors before they had been covered with wet cement or concrete, action that only made the resultant problems worse.

Most system-built flats have been demolished.

8.3 Jobbing production

In the jobbing factory, work is carried out either on single items or small batches, each of which is under a different contract. In principle, the type and sequence of tasks are unlimited but the sensible jobbing company will specialise in some way. Like others experts, it restricts the acceptance of orders to work within its capacity or uses subcontractors when the work is beyond its capability. The nature of the specialisation may be as follows:

■ *By facilities*. The jobber may have facilities such as printing machinery, lathes or saws that means that certain classes of work can be taken on. The specialisation allows the jobber to offer competitive prices. Harvey Metal specialises in medium fabrication and it is efficient in this area.

■ *By knowledge of customers or markets*. The jobber may be willing to carry out work connected with a particular product area or customer. The business is targeted at a set of consumers rather than a set of needs. Most of Harvey Metal's customers are within 50 miles of the plant.

Exercise 8.1

Among those engaged in servicing motor cars, identify two examples of each type of specialisation. Further, do you know of any garages that do not specialise in this way?

For layout decisions, jobbing shops usually have little obvious work sequence. Since the orders received are very unpredictable and the sequence of operations required to fulfil them equally so, there is usually no linkage of machinery into a production line. There is likely to be a range of general purpose machines and equipment with a demand for space for the storage of partly finished work around them. Some processes will be carried out in separate rooms or buildings because they require special conditions such as a clean atmosphere or quiet. Examples of these are painting, electronic assembly and testing.

This grouping of related machines and tasks into departments is called a *process-based* or *functional* layout. It gives high flexibility but at the cost of close control of flow by supervisors or production controllers. They arrange for orders to pass between the groups, or departments, as required. Because of uncertain loads in any department, jobbing shops tend to fill with part-finished orders. This makes them appear cluttered and increases the capital tied up in work-in-progress.

8.3.1 Functional layout design

Optimisation of the functional layout in a jobbing shop is a decision made under uncertainty about the pattern of future orders. Given this uncertainty, most organisations will be content with an approach that creates a sensible layout. This will consider cost estimates and an assessment of departments that need to be adjacent for technical reasons.

The cost approach examines the material flows among departments. This is broadly similar to the transportation models of the previous chapter. Yet here we

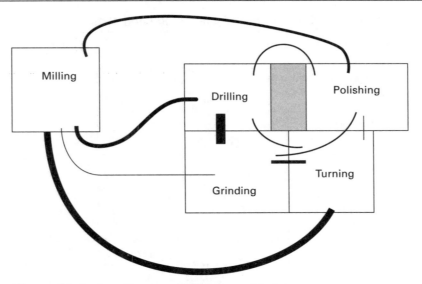

Figure 8.2 String diagram: jobbing machinist

are concerned with flows of materials at different stages of their manufacture, each involving different unit handling costs. We can use n_{ij} to represent the number of loads that pass between the pair of departments i and j and c_{ij} for the cost of moving one of these loads. The latter takes into account the distance as well as the handling difficulty of the material. There are d departments. The objective function here is then:

$$Total\ cost = \sum_{i=1}^{d}\sum_{j=1}^{d} n_{ij}\ c_{ij}$$

A practical approach to this problem is to compare layouts by trial and error. The method is as follows:

1 Produce a matrix that shows all the flows between the departments.
2 Take a proposed layout and, for each flow, calculate the cost of moving one load.
3 Calculate the total movement cost.
4 Repeat with adjusted layouts until reaching the optimum.
5 Make a recommendation based on this outcome.

We will show the first steps of this process here. There is no general optimising algorithm so, in principle, all possibilities have to be tried. However, many companies will only be considering a few possible layouts or a minor modification to an existing arrangement. The number of possibilities to be searched, therefore, will be small. Otherwise, computer software is available. The Computer Relationship Layout Planning (CORELAP) package is an example.

Figure 8.2 shows the departmental layout at a jobbing machinist. Apart from installation costs, there are no constraints on the position of any department,

Table 8.1 Movements and costs in jobbing shop

Two-way flows . . .	Turning		Grinding		Drilling		Polishing	
Milling	128		24		70		44	
		4		3		3		4
Turning			55		30		12	
				1		2		1
Grinding					92		32	
						1		2
Drilling							30	
								2
Total costs £	512		127		362		312	

their positions having been laid out in the two buildings by historical accident. The string diagram suggests that the milling department is badly placed and this can be investigated by further analysis.

Table 8.1 presents, in the upper left corners of the cells, the number of pallets moved among the departments in a typical week. In the lower right corners are figures giving estimated costs for each type of pallet movement. The total cost for this arrangement is £1,313, the cost of maintaining a forklift truck for this purpose. Were the company able to consider a rearrangement, the movement costs could be reduced. The costs would only be saved *if the idle time for the fork truck could be put to a useful alternative purpose*. In practice, it is difficult both to have such a facility on standby and to require it to perform other functions.

The cost approach is only useful if the focus is on the costs of one type of linkage, say material flows. Furthermore, it depends on the quality of the data for both the number of movements and the amount spent per movement. Where such information is not available, it may be better to rely on a qualitative approach. A *relationship chart* can be used to set out opinions of how close one department needs to be to another. Figure 8.3 shows, in outline, the relationship chart for a telephone-based credit control office. Each cell in the grid expresses how far the planners think the relevant staff or activity areas should be separated. For instance, a few pairings, centred on the receptionist, are seen as absolutely necessary. These are links with the office entrance and the fax and coffee machines. This would be because the receptionist receives the occasional visitor and would offer the person coffee while taking incoming calls and distributing fax messages. In addition, it is thought desirable for the senior managers not to be close to the entrance. Note that a full version of the grid would have many more cells. One should also recognise that office layouts can be as much about the representation of status as the desire to pursue efficiency.

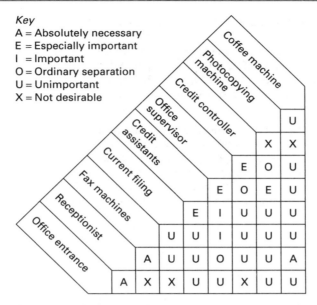

Figure 8.3 Relationship chart: credit control office

Exercise 8.2

Use the relationship chart in Figure 8.3 to design a layout for the branch office of an insurance broker. Instead of 'credit assistants', there are five sales assistants doing much of their work on the telephone. A partner manages the office.

Customers visit occasionally, although there are rarely more than two present. The company has leased about 100 square metres on the first floor. It prefers an informal layout, with space both to receive customers and relax during breaks. There is a very small kitchen and toilets are on the second floor.

8.4   Batch production

As we saw in Chapter 3, batch processing is a step up from jobbing in terms of scale. Batch firms concentrate their attention on a more limited range of products produced in larger quantities than in the jobbing shop. The process-based layout is still used in such operations. With increasing volumes of orders, it becomes economical to dedicate a family of machines and a team of specialists to use the *product-based* layout. This is often called the production line. Batch firms are often torn between the flexibility offered by the process system and the efficiency that comes from specialised lines. The balance between the two can shift as changes occur in the business environment. IBM found this to its cost (see Box 8.2).[2] An intermediate position can be achieved with group technology, discussed in 8.4.1. Section 8.5 covers production lines themselves.

> **BOX 8.2 Removal of robots at IBM, Greenock**
>
> In 1986 IBM at Greenock spent £6 million setting up a robotic assembly line for PC monitors. Yet, by 1993, the company had decided to dispense with the robots and increase the line manning. Before 1993 some 25 assembly staff, with their robots, produced 550 monitors per shift. Afterwards, 50 assembly workers made 700.
>
> IBM gives the reasons for the change as the rapid pace of technological development and the different safety standards that had been imposed in different countries. Both factors caused the product variety to increase and the line was not flexible enough to cope. To alter the product on the line, it had to be shut down and all the tools and holding mechanisms had to be changed. Now, the only remaining robots pack the finished items into cartons for shipment.

8.4.1 Group technology

Chapter 3 referred to how batch firms can achieve some of the benefits of line production through *group technology*, also called *cellular manufacturing*. The typical process layout is transformed into a product layout not for the whole production system but for subsystems or cells. These are devoted to the manufacture of families of similar products. In other words, rather than examine the scale of individual orders, none of which would be large enough to justify the setting up of a line, these orders are clustered according to predetermined criteria. These may refer to items with:

- similar size requiring similar processes, although not always in the same sequence
- special features that require the use of a particular process.

Group technology cells are then established depending on which criterion has been used. In the former case, the cell may consist of machines that are the same as those used throughout the factory, the mix depending on the product family. In the latter case, the cell may consist of the key machine or process, supported by others as necessary. We can see that the arrangement involves several mini-layouts each of which specialises in a subset of the whole product range. Skinner[3] used the term *focused factory* for this arrangement. It stresses the advantages of focus and simplicity in gaining efficiency.

Group technology recognises the value of involving skilled craftsmen in decisions concerning work flow, sequencing and so on rather than restrict them to controlling the machines themselves. Machine operation often requires skilled attention at the set-up stage then the machine can run with occasional checking until another job needs to be set up. Moreover, it is very difficult to avoid some machine idle time in a jobbing shop so to have one person per machine can waste labour costs.

Kumar and Hadjinicola[4] showed how cellular manufacturing (CM) was introduced to Champion Irrigation Products. The firm specialised in the manufacture of bronze irrigation products, in particular sprinkler nozzles. End users included

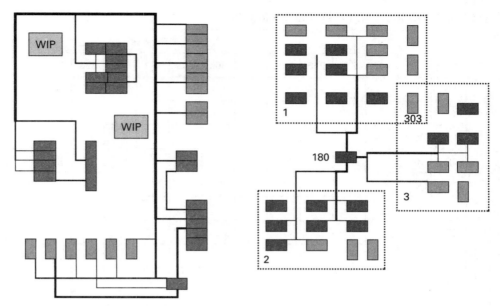

Figure 8.4 Change to cellular manufacture

golf courses as well as the domestic market, reached through do-it-yourself stores. CIP had been facing problems of highly seasonal demand and the lack of capacity to satisfy the peak. It sought to simplify and improve the production process. Sixteen products, representing some 70% of sales, had been selected for study. For these products, string diagrams were produced to show the routes that they took to pass through the factory. The left-hand half of Figure 8.4 is a sketch of the original layout. The machines are shown as shaded boxes and the connecting lines, by their thickness, indicate the main flows. The overall impression gained was of long and tortuous sequences through the machines.

For reasons of space, the following explanation has been simplified from the original study. The machining required by each product was identified and recorded. These data appear in Table 8.2. The rows in the table represent each product, the columns the machines. An 'X' entry in a cell indicates that the product required the corresponding machine for its manufacture. At first sight there does not seem to be much of a pattern. Yet, changing the sequence of rows and columns using a grouping algorithm changes this view. Product families emerge as similar items come together.

Table 8.3 shows the arrangement after the application of the algorithm. A moment's review will confirm that the matrices carry the same information in different order. We can see that the products and machines fall into three distinct families along the matrix diagonal. They are highlighted for emphasis.

The table also shows one of the problems of implementation. Products do not always fall neatly into families and some, such as 12, 15, 17, 18, 23 and 25, overlap into other groups. Furthermore, all products needed to pass through machine 180, shown in the first column.

Installation of cells at CIP was subject to several constraints. Size prevented some machines from being shifted; others required the removal of large amounts

Table 8.2 Products and their machining, CIP

		Machine codes														
		180	202	208	216	217	219	300	303	311	322	323	325	404	409	410	416
Product	12	X			X	X		X			X		X		X	X	
	13	X					X		X			X					
	14	X					X		X			X					X
	15	X		X	X	X		X			X		X			X	
	17	X	X	X				X		X				X			
	18	X	X	X					X	X						X	
	19	X				X		X			X		X				
	20	X	X	X						X				X			
	21	X		X						X				X			
	21a	X							X						X		X
	22	X							X			X			X		X
	23	X	X	X					X					X			
	24	X			X	X							X			X	
	25	X	X	X					X	X				X			
	26	X	X	X						X				X			
	26a	X					X		X						X		X

of waste. Furthermore, reorganisation had to be planned carefully to minimise disruption. The right-hand part of Figure 8.4 sketches how the machines were divided into the proposed cells. Machine 180 was moved to a more central position in the plant and 303 could be shared between Cells 1 and 3. Installation proceeded in small stages.

CIP reported benefits as follows:

- work-in-progress reduced by 70%
- production planning and control simplified
- separate code numbers for intermediate components eliminated
- improved quality: defect rate cut by 75%
- increased productivity
- greater flexibility and quicker response to demand.

Group technology will work best when there is a clear separation of products into families. Furthermore, given the costs involved, the reorganisation necessary to achieve a cell structure will only be justified if the company can rely on having a regular product mix.

Table 8.3 Product–machining list after sorting

		Machine codes															
		180	219	303	323	409	416	216	217	300	322	325	410	202	208	311	404
Product	13	X	X	X	X												
	14	X	X	X	X		X										
	21a	X		X		X	X										
	22	X		X	X	X	X										
	26a	X	X	X		X	X										
	12	X				X		X	X	X	X	X	X				
	15	X						X	X	X	X	X	X		X		
	19	X							X	X	X	X					
	24	X						X	X			X	X				
	17	X							X					X	X	X	X
	18	X		X									X	X	X	X	
	20	X												X	X	X	X
	21	X													X	X	X
	23	X		X										X	X		X
	25	X		X										X	X	X	X
	26	X												X	X	X	X

Cells for machining work, or combinations of machines and hand assembly, will work best if they are set out so that staff can work in close proximity. In this way, informal communication can do much to smooth the flow of work as well as increase job satisfaction. It may be possible, in theory, to simulate group technology without moving the equipment. Staff would have to move frequently and the implied complexity of the communication and control systems will rule out this option.

8.4.2 Flexible manufacturing systems

Cell-based manufacture does not rule out the possibility of automation. Indeed, at higher throughput volumes, there remains the option of investing in robots and transfer lines to help or replace the human element. An automated cell dealing with a variety of manufacturing tasks is called a *flexible manufacturing system*.

Flexible manufacturing systems, FMS, are generally found in high-volume batch production. In effect, they apply microelectronic control and computer technology to automate group technology. Transfer lines connect a family of machines.

In contrast to the traditional mass production line where all items pass through the same processes along a conveyor, the FMS takes up the cell idea in being able to pass any component through the set of machines in any number of ways. FMS has been made possible by the following developments:

- software to optimise production sequences and control the machine family
- robots to load equipment from the conveyors on to the machines
- multifunctional machines with modular tools and jigs fitted using a cartridge system.

The falling price of electronic components has gradually brought down the cost of FMS equipment. This in turn has reduced the break-even volume of output for which it is worthwhile making the investment. Furthermore, the design of machine tools themselves has developed so that single machines perform an increased variety of functions. The trend in flexible manufacturing is to set up cells with one or two robots handling products and tools for a single machine.

8.5 Line production

In line, or mass, production the manufacturer produces standardised designs in large volumes. These volumes are sufficiently high and stable to justify the equipment investment. The ideal type of line production system produces just one item. In practice, however, many lines can cope with a narrow range of similar products. They have highly specialised machine tools and other equipment connected by conveyors. In principle, each machine in the system operates at the same rate so that buffer stocks are not required between stages.

Mass production owes its efficiency to a combination of mechanisation and specialisation. The assembly line is both the symbol and the outstanding achievement of industrial engineering.

Ford's first moving car assembly lines, for the Model T, had work carried out while the product was fixed to the line and moving with it (see Box 8.3). Compared with previous methods, it was successful for the following reasons:

- The skill required was reduced. Jobs were divided into elements each requiring a small cycle time, sometimes as low as 30 seconds. This reduced the training time for workers.
- It stimulated the improvement of work methods that became integrated with the line design and the associated equipment specifications. Work stations

BOX 8.3 The inventor of the assembly line

Henry Ford is usually acknowledged as having been the first to introduce the modern line, although one of his engineers, Charles Sorensen, put it into effect. In 1913 Ford's magneto assembly line reduced the labour content per item from 20 minutes to 5. Sales of the Model T tripled to 248,000 in that year. By 1914 a vehicle line had reduced assembly time from 12.5 to 1.5 man hours and Ford had half of the US automobile market.[5]

BOX 8.4 Examples of line production

- The most popular canned vegetables are baked beans. Demand is so high that manufacturers such as Heinz are able to run canning lines dedicated solely to this product. They can other vegetables and soups in large batches and stop the lines for cleaning between runs.

- Carbonated drinks plants operate with large batch production. Bottlers, owned by the drinks companies or bottling under licence, mix syrup, water and gas in their process. Each line handles most flavours. Can and bottle design is standard and interchangeable. It is only with very large plants located close to major markets that there are lines dedicated to one product, often one of the colas.

could be designed to be highly efficient. For example, the four or five nuts on a car wheel could be tightened to the correct torque simultaneously using an electric or pneumatic spanner.

- The system cut the stock of work-in-progress. Feeder lines, acting as tributaries to the main line, were timed to deliver items at the rate required and therefore avoid excessive stocks.

In another line arrangement, production takes place at static work positions and the line conveys items from one station to another. Small variations in output between stations can be accommodated by fluctuations in buffer stocks either on the conveyors or at temporary storage points. The packaging of kit toys is an example of this type of work.

Most line production plant is of hybrid form in that it can produce a limited number of products with common characteristics. The plant is then involved in *large batch* production, switching from time to time from one product type to another as in the examples of Box 8.4.

At the planning stage, line production can be seen as either machine or labour paced. In the former, used for the fabrication of standardised components, the string of machines is designed so that they all work at the same rate. In the latter, characterised by assembly operations, the operating speed must be related to the tasks given to the staff running the line. When this is done, the times needed by each individual to complete the cycle are made as equal as possible. This is based on assigning groups of tasks among individuals to achieve both efficient use of their labour and equity among them. These *line balancing* processes are important in managing product-focused production systems.

8.5.1 Line balancing

In theory, each stage of the production line is designed to operate at the same rate. In practice, things may not be that simple, especially where the line is used for several products and the processes themselves are subject to gradual development. It is usually not possible to operate at 100% efficiency. The following worked example of a single line illustrates the difficulties.

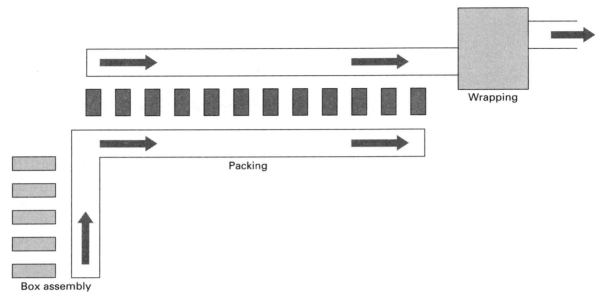

Figure 8.5 Model kit packing line

Balancing a simple line

A model kit packing line has three separate stages. It starts with operators assembling the boxes from cardboard outers and polystyrene filling pieces. The normal time for this operation is 0.2 minutes. The packers place each box on a conveyor that runs along behind a series of benches occupied by the packers. A packer picks a box from the conveyor and fills it with the appropriate mix of parts from trays located within reach on the bench. Normal time for filling is 0.45 minutes after which the box is returned to another conveyor. This feeds the last process, an automated wrapping machine that covers each box with cellophane with a cycle time of 0.04 minutes. Figure 8.5 shows the layout.

Questions for the production manager are:

■ What is the maximum output of the line?

■ What manning is needed?

■ What is the labour efficiency at this output?

The wrapping machine, processing one box every 0.04 minutes, determines the maximum output of the line. This is 1/0.04 items per minute; 25 per minute; or 1,500 per hour.

An assembler can make up a unit every 0.20 minutes. For the assembly section to achieve the 0.04-minute cycle time, the number of staff would be 0.2/0.04, which is 5. Similarly, the number of packers required would be 0.45/0.04, which is 11.25, or 12. Hence, the line requires 17 people in all.

The labour efficiency of this arrangement can be calculated from the ratio of output to input, each measured in minutes of work. Since the line output is 25 per minute, the standard labour content of such output is 25 × (0.2 + 0.45)

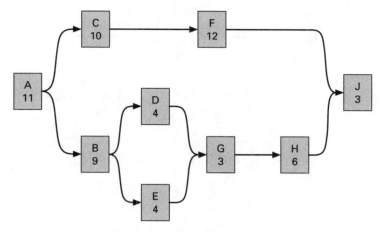

Figure 8.6 Precedence diagram for assembly tasks

minutes. With 17 staff, the input per minute of operation is 17 minutes. Line efficiency is then:

$$\frac{25(0.2 + 0.45)}{17} = 96\%$$

Such a performance would be high for any production line, 85% being a good figure where complexity is great. Note that the normal times given here only measure short-term performance and the industrial engineer would have to build in allowances for rest and breaks. A further difficulty lies in the errors made in the original measurements and the variations in performance between individuals. Fine-tuning of lines is often done by experimentation and the intervention of supervisors where bottlenecks occur.

The packing example is simple because the three steps take place in a defined sequence. On many assembly lines, some of the tasks can take place simultaneously and the balancing problem includes the allocation of these among the various staff. The following example shows how this is done.

Balancing interrelated assembly operations

Let us say that the assembly of an item consists of nine tasks. An initial study shows how these tasks can be set out in a *precedence diagram* (Figure 8.6). Each cell in the figure contains a number giving the time in minutes taken for the task; the arrows indicate the sequence in which the assembly must take place. This is a network using *activity-on-node* notation, a topic dealt with more fully in Chapter 14. The diagram means, for example, activity A must precede both B and C; C precedes F; and so on. Further, C can occur at the same time as B, D, E and so on. Note that the precedence diagram does not relate directly to shop floor layout, conveyors, machines or whatever.

If only one of these assemblies is required, it can be carried out by one person and the time would be simply a sum of the task times, which is 62 minutes. If more products are required at a faster rate than one every 62 minutes, then more

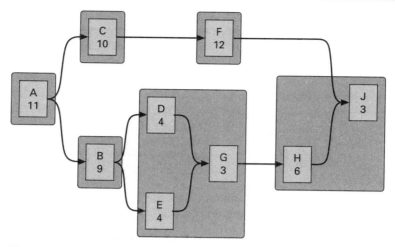

Figure 8.7 Precedence diagram showing one solution to balancing problem

staff are required. We shall assume that layout constraints mean that it is not possible to double up on any of the tasks.

Suppose demand means that an output of five units per hour is needed. How can the tasks be most effectively grouped? The method has three steps:

1 Calculate the *cycle time* implied by the demanded production rate. This is found from the relationship:

$$Cycle\ time = 1/Production\ rate$$

Here the cycle time is 1/5 hr or 12 min.

2 Calculate the minimum number of staff or work stations needed. This is:

$$Number\ of\ work\ stations = \frac{Total\ task\ time}{Cycle\ time}$$

Here, the minimum number of work stations is 62/12, that is 6.

3 Allocate the tasks among work stations, ensuring that each station has minimal idle time. This is the core of line balancing. In our example, the solution can easily be found by inspection and the tasks fall readily into the groupings shown in Figure 8.7.

In the proposal for a 12-minute cycle time, stations B and H/J are idle for 3 minutes, C is idle for 2 minutes per cycle while A and D/E/G would lose 1 minute. The efficiency of the operation is given by:

$$Efficiency = \frac{Total\ task\ time}{Number\ of\ work\ stations \times Cycle\ time}$$

In this case, the figure is 62/(6 × 12) or 86%.

The optimal arrangement of the work stations varies according the output demanded. Further, although optimal arrangements are made, the efficiency of the line varies with the demand. Table 8.4 shows the different numbers of

Table 8.4 Stations and efficiencies for different planned cycle times

Production rate per hour	2	3	4	5
Number of work stations	3	4	5	6
Efficiency	69%	78%	83%	86%

stations required, together with their corresponding efficiencies, for various production rates.

In Figure 8.7, we can see that station F is fully loaded whereas others are idle for up to one-quarter of the time. This has two implications. First, a good supervisor will be careful to share out the work, possibly, through job rotation, defined in Chapter 5. Not only will this aid motivation but it will provide opportunities for rest breaks. These are needed since the data being used are normal times, not standard times (see Chapter 6). The second implication is that station F is the *bottleneck* that decides the maximum speed of the whole assembly operation. As we shall see in Chapter 12, bottlenecks require careful attention and control if output is not to suffer.

The graphical approach, as shown in Figures 8.6 and 8.7, is adequate for small line-balancing tasks. There are algorithms that enable solutions to be found by hand. For long lines with many stages, programmes enable grouping of tasks to be optimised. This means that managers can continually adapt the grouping to consider staffing available, output required and any technical problems that may arise.

8.6 Continuous production

The ideal process plant runs continuously, producing an even flow of product to match market demands. While there are many plants that approach this level of continuity, most are shut down at regular intervals to maintain or replace worn components. Whether the plant can be kept going during such changes is a matter of design and, frequently, safety. Too many accidents to chemical plants take place during periods when repairs are being carried out.

Continuous process manufacturing is carried out for heavy chemicals, oils, polymers, paper, glass, beer, cement and some foods. The plant used is characterised by large-scale and high capital costs. Changes to capacity are often only available in large increments so that close attention needs to be paid to market demand before investments are made. For instance, in brewing for the mass market, increments of about 100 million litres per year are required if the plant is to maintain economies of scale.

Plant layout is usually decided by the nature of the product being produced. Machines are designed to have, theoretically, the same capacity and to allow the product to flow straight through the plant without stopping. Such would be the case in an oil refinery where there is little room to store intermediate products.

As with the case of mass production lines, the theoretical balancing of all the components of a process production plant is often not achieved. We shall examine two important issues related to this, reliability and capacity balancing.

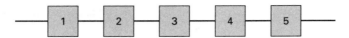

Figure 8.8 Series reliability structure

8.6.1 Reliability

The operation of a straight line process plant requires that all its components are operating at once. Figure 8.8 sets out the components of a process plant in the so-called *series reliability* structure. Clearly, failure of any piece of equipment in the line means that the whole has to stop.

For most pieces of equipment, it is possible to estimate the reliability, usually expressed as the probability of running for a given period. This could be the time between annual shutdowns. Let us express the reliability of the components as R_1, R_2 etc. We can then find the reliability of the whole plant surviving from one shutdown to the next by combining these probabilities as follows:

$$R_{plant} = (Item_1 \text{ survives}) \text{ and } (Item_2 \text{ survives}) \text{ and } \ldots$$

That is:

$$R_{plant} = R_1 \times R_2 \times R_3 \times R_4 \ldots$$

In the case of five stages, four of which have a reliability of 98% (one breakdown in 50 years) and the fifth having a reliability of 90% (one breakdown in 10 years) the reliability is:

$$R_{plant} = 0.98 \times 0.98 \times 0.98 \times 0.98 \times 0.90$$

This is 0.83, or 83%. The greater the number of components, the more the plant reliability will reduce. What could managers do about this problem? The most obvious step would be to improve the component with lowest reliability. For example, if the lowest were increased to 95%, the reliability of the chain would rise to 88%. Let us say, however, that it is not possible to achieve improvements in the individual components; they are the best we can buy at the moment. What then? The solution is to duplicate the weakest ones to incorporate a parallel reliability structure. In such an arrangement, the failure of one component does not mean that others will fail too. Such arrangements are not prone to sudden failure but deteriorate gradually. These structures are very common. For example, it would be extremely foolish to wire all the bulbs in Blackpool illuminations in a series structure!

Figure 8.9 sets out the same process plant as in Figure 8.7. Now the weakest (say, no. 3) component is backed up by several others in a parallel reliability structure at that stage.

For the parallel stage only, let us express the reliability of the components as R_a, R_b etc. We find the reliability of the stage surviving from one shutdown to the next by combining these probabilities as follows:

$$R_{stage} = (Item_a \text{ survives}) \text{ or } (Item_b \text{ survives}) \text{ or } \ldots$$

Expressed another way, if F represents probability of failure,

$$F_{stage} = (Item_a \text{ fails}) \text{ and } (Item_b \text{ fails}) \text{ and } \ldots$$

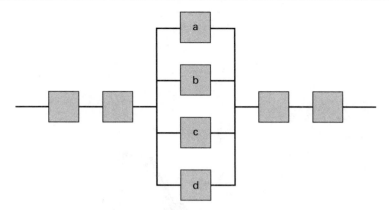

Figure 8.9 Parallel reliability structure

That is,

$$F_{stage} = F_a \times F_b \times F_c \times F_d \ldots$$

Since R and F are connected by the equation, R = (1 − F):

$$1 - R_{stage} = (1 - R_a) \times (1 - R_b) \times \ldots$$

$$R_{stage} = 1 - ((1 - R_a) \times (1 - R_b) \times \ldots$$

This means the more components in a stage, the greater its reliability. For example, in the case of duplicating a weak component, whose reliability is 90%, with another of the same capacity and reliability, the stage reliability is given by:

$$R_{stage} = 1 - ((1 - 0.9) \times (1 - 0.9)) = 0.99$$

Duplication increases the reliability from 90% to 99%. Adding a third component raises it again to 99.9%.

The reliability of plant can be increased by providing parallel structures at points where the equipment is unacceptably unreliable or when the provision of standby capacity has a low enough cost. Such decisions depend on achieving the right investment balance between the value of increased plant reliability and the cost of providing the spare capacity. Parallel reliability is built into the designs of many process plants; the cost of a standby motor or pump being far less than the consequences for the whole system of an avoidable shutdown. Safety is also a critical criterion in many cases.

We can think of the transmission networks of the gas, water, electricity and telephone companies as very large, and widely distributed, process plants. Their purpose is to maintain interconnection, either from sources to consumers or, in telephones, between any pair of users. They incorporate much duplication, known as *redundancy*, in routes and equipment. This is partly the result of historical development but also, in creating these distribution grids, there has been a deliberate policy of building parallel reliability structures. In 1994, Thames Water completed its ring main for supplies in London. The ring allows any section to be closed without interrupting supplies. The National Electricity Grid and the National Gas Transmission System are further, more complex examples. Figure 8.10 shows a schematic map of the gas grid.[6] It clearly shows parallel links

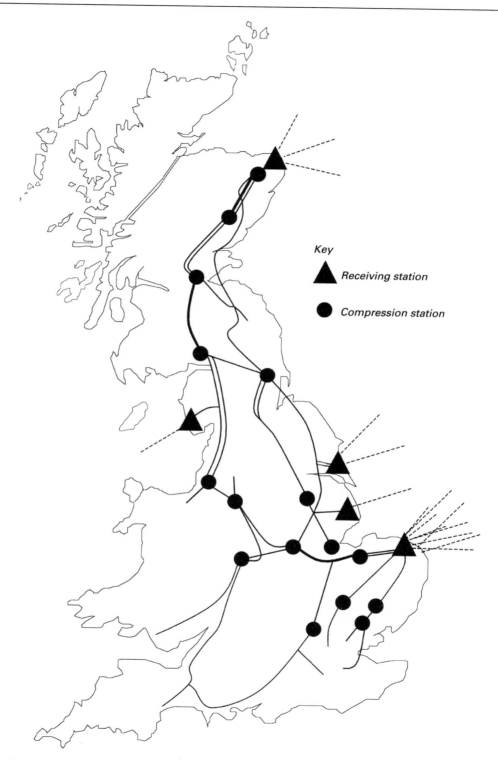

Figure 8.10 Sketch of National Gas Transmission System

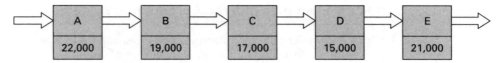

Figure 8.11 Five-stage plant with unbalanced component capacities

on many primary routes. Grids have their own problems of line balancing to ensure the most efficient distribution of energy.

8.6.2 Capacity balancing in process plants

Although a process plant may be designed with balanced stages, in reality the capacity of each is not fixed in the longer term. Continuous development of components and experience of operation means that operators find ways to increase potential output of the stage. Like a convoy, however, the plant only operates at the speed of the slowest. Managers will focus their attention on this bottleneck if they want to increase output. Yet, in the decision to increase stage capacity the question arises by how much to increase the capacity.

Consider a plant made up of five stages whose capacities, in units per hour, are as labelled in Figure 8.11. Here, component D, with the lowest capacity, would be the target for attention. To what level should its capacity be increased? Clearly, any size above C would be wasted in the immediate future. Yet, limiting investment in this way would ignore possible developments in C itself. Prudent management may, therefore, consider adding more capacity to D to take this into account. Improvements must be part of a plan that considers the development possibilities of each stage of the process and incorporates likely market demand.

8.7 Hybrid layouts

We have noted that many manufacturing plants do not follow the basic typology set out at the start of this chapter. Many combine two or more of the five basic systems – project, jobbing, batch, line and continuous – into hybrid layouts. It is important that these differences are recognised, for the processes of planning, control will have to adapt to each system. Some examples of hybrids are shown in Box 8.5.

Schmenner points out that common hybrids, namely *batch flow–line flow* and *batch flow–continuous* systems have the typical characteristic of imbalance between the two sections.[7] Significant blocks of time are needed in the batch system to set up machines to work on different components. This makes it impossible to match continuously the intermittent output of the batch process with the need for continuous input to the next stage. Pressure can be brought to bear to increase batch sizes but, as we shall see, this only increases total stocks and makes the difficulty worse. It is not possible to achieve a balance hour by hour in these

> **BOX 8.5 Examples of hybrid production systems**
>
> - A pharmaceutical manufacturer produces aspirin in a process plant. Batches are then packaged in bottles and packets of various sizes.
> - A maker of sinks and other bathroom fittings uses vitreous china. A process plant blends raw materials; items are moulded in both small and large batches; glazing and firing are mass production; lastly, the assembly of special lines is done on a jobbing basis.
> - A film processor develops film in a process plant and prints it in batches.
> - In the iron industry, casting used to be done as batch production. Recent years have, however, seen the growth of integrated steel works. This followed the invention of continuous casting. Downstream activities such as coating or galvanising are also continuous production but the cutting is done in batches to suit demand.

hybrid systems. It is normal to separate them by a *decoupling* stock or *buffer*. The continuous system feeds off the buffer, which is replenished intermittently by the upstream batch processes. Many food-processing companies prepare ingredients in batches and then mix and pack continuously. Therefore, managers must not only manage each part of these systems but they must also pay attention to their interface.

8.7.1 Human factors in layout design

In Chapter 5, we noted the importance of job rotation and job teams in motivation. A good work layout will consider these motivational aspects as well as other factors such as flexibility and control. Taking the traditional example of the assembly line, a straight line design is often chosen. It suits the ideal case of balanced work stations and well-controlled staff sticking to their separate tasks along the way. Yet, we know that the balanced line is unusual. The linear arrangement, therefore, may separate workers by such distances that any flexibility to be gained from sharing tasks is not available.

The traditional linear arrangement, as in example A of Figure 8.12, makes it difficult for the workers to form a coherent working group. A U-shaped layout, as in B and C may help in the development of communication. This can help in smoothing of the flow on the line and problems being anticipated before they occur. Plan B allows easy observation and eye contact at the expense of increasing the distances between staff, if they cannot cross the conveyor. Plan C, by way of contrast, has workers facing away from each other when at their work stations. Their proximity will make line balancing easier.

The advantages of U-shaped layouts should also be recognised in noisy working environments. These should, of course, never be regarded as good conditions, and staff should be provided with good ear protection. Where noise reduction is not feasible, non-verbal communication becomes more important in running the line. The ability of workers to see each other contributes both to efficiency and to safe working.

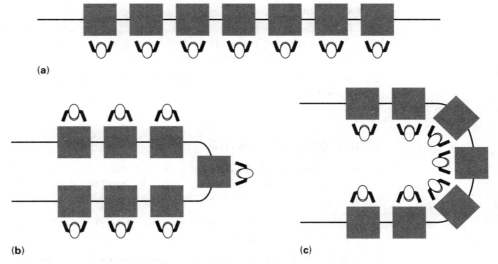

Figure 8.12 Two U-shaped layouts compared with a linear plan

✔ Quick check-up

Can you:

☐ List five problems found in fixed position layouts.

☐ Distinguish functional and product layouts.

☐ Summarise relationship models for layout design.

☐ Outline how to establish cellular manufacture.

☐ Explain the process of balancing line and process plants.

☐ Compare series and parallel reliability structures.

❓ Questions

Chapter review

8.1 Sum up the application of string diagrams in layout planning. What are their advantages and disadvantages?

8.2 The chapter proposes several advantages of the production line layout. Suggest and explain corresponding disadvantages.

8.3 Explain the concepts of series and parallel reliability structures by using several examples of each from the human body.

Application

8.4 'Had HMP a different type of business, for example building a smaller range of fabrications for fewer customers, we would have seen a different layout.' What factors would you consider in developing such a layout at HMP?

8.5 Explain how the principles of group technology might be applied in a busy home-delivery pizza business.

Investigation

8.6 Investigate changes to the model kit packing line as follows: a) An improvement in the wrapping machine increases its speed by 15%; b) Staff shortages mean that only 12 people are available for work.

8.7 Reconsider Table 8.4 if an extra job K, following J and requiring 9 minutes, is added to the process.

CLOSING CASE

Warehousing operations[8]

Warehousing is an isolated service whose planning focus is on operating efficiency. Group technology principles can be used to take advantage of similarities among key elements. There are criteria for doing this:

1 Products with a high chance of being 'picked' simultaneously. These could be stacked in the same area.

2 Products with a high chance of being loaded to the same group of vehicles. These could be picked simultaneously.

3 Matching individuals or teams of staff to product groups. This would cut the number of staff trips into the warehouse.

4 Dedicating bays on board vehicles to products.

A 4,000 square metre beer distribution warehouse held 55 product lines. The following day's deliveries were loaded each night on to 60 delivery lorries. Of these, 34 had 12 bays, 10 had 16 and 16 had 18 bays. Loading was carried out by eight forklift drivers, working in four pairs. High-volume products, loaded on pallets, were brought as needed from the warehouse and loaded straight into the lorry bays. Some stocks of low-volume items were kept in the loading area where the staff could select the required number of cases for their vehicles.

The potential GT improvements as listed were investigated:

1 The forklift trucks could not handle more than one pallet at a time, although heavier ones could do so. Consequently, the idea of simultaneous picking did not apply. Further, grouping similar products in the same area cuts across the need to change the stock balance in response to promotions and rotate it to keep it fresh.

2 Simultaneous picking for several vehicles was ruled out for the reasons given in 1. The bottleneck in operations was forklift trucking.

3 It was possible to dedicate staff to groups of product lines. This policy was already in operation informally. One loader concentrated on high-volume lines while the other looked after the low-volume stock kept in the loading bay itself.

4 Dedicating vehicle bays to products was the most promising approach for efficiency improvement. Loading instructions showed goods by bay and these varied each day. Some customers had to have their loads placed in identified positions because of access difficulties in, say, narrow alleys. Apart from this, bays could have the same products each day, as opposed to the current haphazard allocation. The low-volume stocks could then be stacked close to their dedicated bays and loading teams would spend less time sorting pallets that had been put in the wrong ones.

Questions

1 How would a cluster analysis be used to study any of the four proposed operating policies?

2 Simultaneous picking was not favoured here. In what sort of warehouse might this policy be advantageous?

3 Suggest other operational activities that might be improved by using GT principles.

Notes and references

1. Harvey Metal Products, 22 Ruddle Street, Wilkes-Barre, PA; www.hmpfab.com
2. Hallahan, S. (1994) 'All hands to the production lines', *The Times*, 29 July, p.15.
3. Skinner, W. (1974) 'The focused factory', *Harvard Business Review*, 52(3), May–June, pp.113–21.
4. Kumar, K.R. and Hadjinicola, G.C. (1993) 'Cellular manufacturing at Champion Irrigation Products', *International Journal of Operations and Production Management*, 13(8), pp.53–61.
5. Collier, P. and Horowitz, D. (1999) *Henry Ford (1863–1947): Loving the line*, San Francisco: Encounter Books.
6. Based on maps in the annual reports of British Gas.
7. Schmenner, R.W. (1993) *Production/Operations Management*, 5th edition, New York: Macmillan, pp.6–7.
8. Shafer, S.M. and Ernst, R. (1993) 'Applying group technology principles to warehouse operations', *International Journal of Purchasing and Materials Management*, 29(2), pp.38–42.

CHAPTER 9

Facility layout: personal and self-service

OBJECTIVES

When you have finished studying this chapter, you should be able to:

- Suggest some responses to the imbalance between demand and supply in services.
- Describe the basic elements of a queuing system; show how statistical distributions can model their behaviour.
- Set out the characteristics of some common queue structures, identifying appropriate applications.
- Explain the purpose simulation and outline its advantages and disadvantages.
- Demonstrate the Monte Carlo method applied to simulate queues.
- Explain why the acceptability of queue length varies from case to case.
- Outline the role of operations planning to avoid waiting.
- Demonstrate how an awareness of customer perceptions can lead to improvements in the waiting process.
- Clarify the key service issues in store and shopping centre layouts.

OPENING CASE

Supermarket rejuvenation[1]

Associated Supermarkets has a 1,100 square metre branch in 137th Street, Jamaica, New York State. Its layout, shown in Figure 9.1, had been gradually adapted over several years as the company introduced new lines to respond to market demand. As a result, customers were presented with a video department on a raised platform as they walked in through the narrow door. Frozen food was in the first aisle. Therefore, if customers followed the store sequence, their purchases thawed while they shopped.

Managers sought to improve the store by creating a wider, more welcoming entrance. Costs and technical constraints meant that it was easier to move both entrance and exit than to change internal layout radically. After the change, customers come across floral, produce, delicatessen and customer service departments as they enter the first aisle. Frozen food and ice cream come last in the traffic sequence. (See Figure 9.2 for the arrangement after the change.)

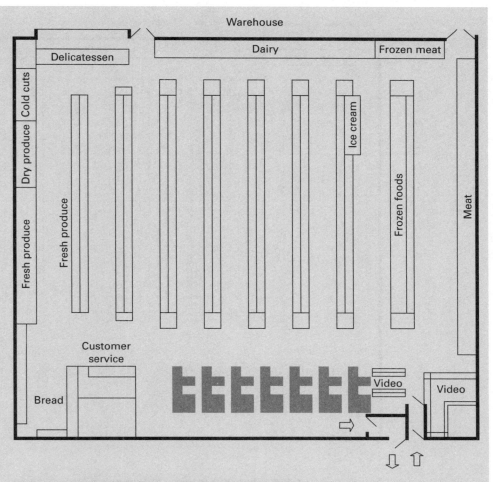

Figure 9.1 Supermarket layout before the change

The concept of traffic flow through a store is important to managers. Most customers will move straight ahead through the flowers and fresh produce departments. New island fixtures break up the flow and encourage them to browse, to try either new lines or promotions. By the time they have moved through this area, customers will be relaxed and moving at a speed where they can comfortably peruse the rest of the aisles.

Except in the smallest self-service unit, it is unusual to have a single route through the whole store. Associated encourages customers to call in to hire a video or pick up processed photographs without passing the food displays. Yet, it wants even these people to enjoy the attractive entrance, noticing displays of special offers as they pass.

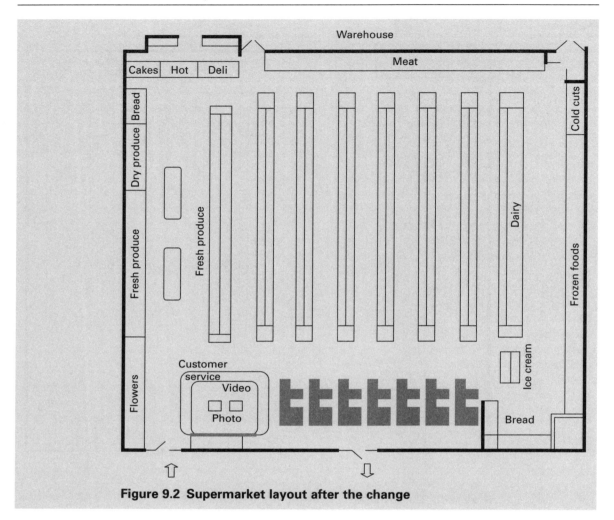

Figure 9.2 Supermarket layout after the change

Introduction

Customer presence in both personal and self-service businesses has important implications for layout design. Like others in the industry, Associated Supermarkets recognises that the store must be attractive and convenient for customers. Yet design goes further than looking clean and smart. Through combining and sequencing various physical elements, including sight, sounds, textures and smells, a store can tell a story to its customers. Depending on its target market, the story may imply low prices (high stacks on cheap fixtures), variety (sections for foods from different nations), concern about health or the environment (prominence of organic and low-calorie sections) or exceptional quality (spacious displays each designed to show contents in the best way). Good layout is an important element of sales promotion.

In the opening case, we see how a business must adapt its layout as circumstances change. Changing shopping habits, the desire to stock higher margin non-food items and demands for more convenience foods, such as hot meals, cause managers constantly to rethink their offer. They face constraints, too. For instance, the structure of the building, investment in plant and installation and the position of mains services all confront the designer. The moderate floor area, of 1,100 square metres (the average of Safeway's 480 United Kingdom stores is 3,100 square metres) means that only a few non-food lines can be carried if the shop is to maintain its full range of groceries. The focus on flowers, videos and photo processing reflects perceived opportunities in the local market.

Exercise 9.1	Beyond those mentioned already, what other constraints would surround the layout decision?

Self-service units promise quick, trouble-free shopping at times to suit the customer. Although firms have worked on the problem, supermarket shopping still terminates in an element of personal service. Moreover, that means a queue. It is a problem common to all service with unpredictable demand. Its importance means we start the chapter with its analysis before returning to the question of store layout.

Queues are not wholly outside the control of the organisation. From an understanding of how queues form and are sustained, the manager can both limit their extension beyond acceptable lengths and influence the perceptions of those who are in the line. How a service provider manages queues influences customers' attitudes of the service experience. A clear, active and fair approach to queue management is a key element of good service.

9.2 Balancing demand and capacity

It is rare for a service system to achieve the ideal of equilibrium between demand and capacity. At times when the system is out of balance, there is either a queue or over-capacity at the service points. Before investigating how to cope with these, we should note that, typically, there is scope for influencing either the demand or the capacity. The following are possible actions:

- *Demand*:
  - Segment the demand and restrict access to the facility at busy times to certain categories of customer.
  - Charge different prices at busy and slack periods.
  - Use other promotional incentives to encourage off-peak demand.
  - Have a reservation system, either continuously or at peak periods.

- *Capacity*:
  - Provide flexible capacity: employ extra staff at peak periods; ensure that staff are multi-skilled.
  - Adapt the service that is offered, switching, as demand varies, between standardised and customised service as shown in Figure 3.1.

- Switch between self-service and personal service, the processes of attachment and detachment of Figure 3.1.
- Share capacity with other organisations.
- Automate some operations to reduce service times.

Many service organisations follow one or more of these policies. For instance, many restaurants use differential pricing between lunch and evening and week-day and weekend; promotional offers may run from Mondays to Thursdays; they may offer a fixed-price quick-service lunch menu and a fuller one at dinner; reservations may be advised on weekend evenings; staff are employed according to anticipated demand.

In carrying out the balancing policies, managers must recognise constraints that exist both in the market and in their operating system. These include:

- The complexities of introducing and managing differential pricing structures. These have to be communicated to customers before they can influence behaviour and may not, therefore, have much effect on infrequent users.

- The risk of cheapening the service in the eyes of full-price customers.

- Significant deterioration in service quality.

- Limits to the flexibility that can be built into the service design.

- Perceptions of unfairness if some customers are treated differently from others.

How far the policies work is influenced by the traditions of each industry. Customers expect restaurants to vary their policy at different times, although perhaps not at The Ritz. The convention of higher fares on commuter trains is well established. Yet, higher prices for some long-distance tickets on 'Fridays, certain Saturdays in July and August, and 23rd December' are not well understood and cause frustration for some travellers. Complex charging structures for telephone calls are also not well understood and have little effect on those who do not pay the bills themselves.

9.2.1 The queuing problem

While some smoothing of demand and capacity can occur, an imbalance is inevitable in personal and self-service systems. Variability results in queues. Given this difficulty, the basic question is to reconcile the following objectives:

- to provide a service capacity that keeps waiting lines down to a tolerable length while not inducing excessive costs

- to limit the risk of creating dissatisfaction among customers, or even a loss of their business if excessive service times lead to their 'voting with their feet'.

Performance against these objectives can be assessed as follows. First, operations managers accept that there needs to some spare capacity at the service points. In other words, the service capacity utilisation will be less than 100%. Second, the effectiveness of managing queues can be assessed by counting their average length or measuring waiting time. Either figure gives an estimate of the likely customer responses.

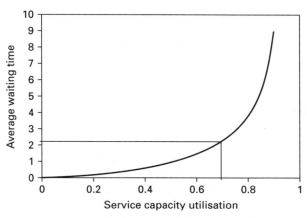

Figure 9.3 Queuing time and capacity utilisation

$$Service\ capacity\ utilisation = \frac{Service\ time\ demanded}{Service\ time\ made\ available}$$

This means of appraising responses will be imprecise because, as we shall see later in this chapter, managers have many ways to influence customers' perceptions of the queuing experience and therefore their attitudes towards it.

Exercise 9.2	Official measures of queue length in the National Health Service were changed in 2000 from counting the number of patients on the waiting list to estimating the average waiting time. This was presented by managers as a more realistic measure. Do you agree?

In summary, the following detailed measures of a queuing system's performance are readily obtained and used for assessment:

■ *Assessing the queue*:
 – Average time spent, either in the queue or in the system (including being served).
 – Average number of customers in the queue or in the system.
 – The probability that the number in the queue (or the system) will exceed a defined level or threshold.

■ *Assessing efficiency*:
 – Service capacity utilisation, as defined in the above equation.
 – The probability that a service station will be idle.

The relationship between queuing time and service capacity utilisation is not linear. Figure 9.3 shows how the gradient increases as utilisation approaches 100%. Clearly, increasing the service capacity reduces its utilisation. To take the case of supermarket checkouts, when utilisation is low, supervisors may close some desks with little effect on the average waiting time for customers. When utilisation is higher, however, attempts to further increase efficiency by this method will lead to proportionately greater increases in queuing time. A balance is needed between efficiency and queue length. Firms, therefore, set a performance threshold, as in Figure 9.3. The supervisors then adjust their capacity, and therefore checkout utilisation, in order to keep waiting times just below the threshold.

9.3 Modelling queues

Before investigating how managers can cope with queues in a positive way, we need to develop a deeper understanding of why and how they form and operate. After all, Figure 9.3 merely sketches the link between queuing and capacity. We will investigate some models of common situations in later sections. First, we must grasp the three basic elements of a queue system – the pattern of arrivals, the queue discipline and the service process.

9.3.1 Pattern of arrivals

There are two main factors to be considered when studying the pattern of arrivals at a service point – the size of the population from which the arrivals come and the time distribution of the arrivals themselves.

Source population

Most queuing models consider that the arrivals are *drawn from an infinite population*. The implication of this assumption is that the arrival of one customer for service does not affect the chances of the arrival of another. Demand, therefore, follows a consistent pattern. Although this pattern may be random, we assume it is governed by constant parameters. The arrival of customers at booking offices, calls to the fire service, approaches of vehicles to bottlenecks on the road and returns of faulty consumer goods for service are all assumed to have these characteristics.

Where service demands are *drawn from a finite population*, things get a little more complicated. Here, one demand for service will have an impact on the likelihood of another arising because the number of items not being serviced is reduced. The example of a vehicle service workshop will clarify the difference. A car arriving at a Kwikfit service centre will have negligible impact on the pattern of future demand at that or any other centre. It is, in effect, drawn from an infinite population. In contrast, if the maintenance shop is set up to service a limited number of special vehicles, such as aircraft or railway locomotives, the arrival of one machine for urgent repair in itself reduces the likelihood of another arriving. The existence of the finite population is, therefore, important in the establishment of service policies. This question frequently arises in plant maintenance. Consequently, detailed discussion is left until Chapter 10.

Distribution of arrivals

It has been found that the random pattern of arrivals at service facilities matches closely the *Poisson distribution*. This probability distribution describes the probability, P_x, of x events occurring within a period of length t. The relationship is:

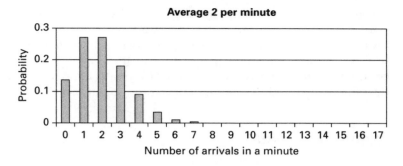

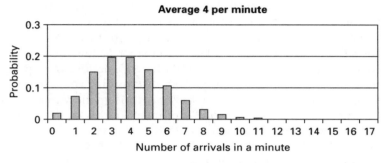

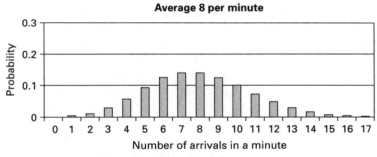

Figure 9.4 Examples of Poisson distribution

$$P_x = \frac{e^{-\lambda t}(\lambda t)^x}{x!}$$

The symbol λ represents the average arrival rate. This means the average number of arrivals that occur in time t is λt. The symbol $x!$ stands for factorial x, being the multiple of $x \times (x - 1) \times (x - 2) \times (x - 3) \times \ldots \ldots \times 1$. ($\lambda$ is pronounced *lamda*.)

Figure 9.4 shows Poisson distributions for three values of λt. We can see that, when the average arrival rate is two customers per minute, the probability of exactly two customers arriving in a given minute is 0.27, which is 27%. Further, the number of arrivals is spread across values from zero to nine or more, although the probability of high numbers arriving is very small. For instance, in some 13% of the intervals no one will arrive, whereas fewer than 1% of the minutes will see seven come. Even smaller chances apply to values higher than seven. Figure 9.4 also shows the distribution for two other average arrival rates. Similar patterns occur, although the spread is greater. The Poisson distribution, then, models the variability of the pattern of incoming demand. Note that, in the examples of Figure 9.4, the numbers of customers can only take integer values, hence the bar chart design.

Arrivals at a service point are not always distributed according to approximations of the Poisson formula. It is necessary to compare observations before this assumption is confirmed. Many cases do conform, however, and the simplicity of the formula's outcomes (if not its construction) helps its use in modelling common forms of queue. Simple statistical points are that the mean value of the distribution is λ and the standard deviation, the measure of spread, is $\sqrt{\lambda}$.

9.3.2 Queue discipline

Queue discipline refers to behaviour on arrival. Most models assume that customers are patient. They wait in queues until they are served; they do not switch from line to line; they do not decline to join if the file is too long; they do not back out after joining. We know that in real life such behaviour does occur. Indeed, it is possible to observe and model deviations from patient behaviour but this will only add complexity to our discussions. For instance, the likelihood of backing out will be affected by how easy it is, by how important the service is to the customer, by the individual's estimate of the wait and by his or her perception of the waiting experience itself. It is almost impossible to renege from a line of vehicles in a one-way street but much easier to pull out of a queue for a ride at a funfair or waiting for someone to answer the telephone.

Another possible response is for some people to cheat. We are used to FIFO, which is *first-in-first-out*, as the basic rule. Queue jumping is more common in some cultures than in others and, even within one country, more common at some times and places than at others. Compare, for example, your local newsagent's or bank with the frenzied atmosphere of the theatre bar during the interval. In the former, short queues and the fact that you are known support conventions of politeness; the latter, in contrast, is more like warfare among strangers. These circumstances are difficult to model usefully. Hence, our discussion of queue models assumes, for simplicity, a discipline where all customers line up according to the same rules. Figure 9.5 illustrates some common situations:

- The first is the simple system. There is one line to one server; all service is given in a single phase. Typical examples are book returns at the library, stored telephone calls to a single-manned enquiry desk and vehicles at a toll booth.

- The second line is less common. Specialist servers perform functions in sequence. Waiting twice makes such arrangements unpopular. Figure 9.5 could illustrate a queue of vehicles at a frontier where passports are checked by security officials and goods by customs. Banks in Italy often have separate cashier desks at which customers have to queue a second time. Sometimes this specialisation is found in hospitals where diagnosis is carried out in stages. A variant is at a blood donor centre where the first station screens out unsuitable candidates.

- The third arrangement shown in Figure 9.5 is the single line to multiple channels. This is commonly found in post offices but is also used in telephone queuing and entries to large car parks.

Other arrangements can be studied as variations on these themes. For example, the multiple lines in supermarkets can be understood as a set of single-line to

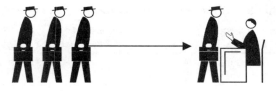

Single queue, single servers

Single queue, staged servers

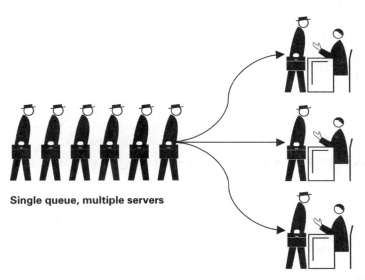

Single queue, multiple servers

Figure 9.5 Some common arrangements with a single queue

single-channel systems. This is if customers follow the queue disciplines set out earlier and do not leap from queue to queue!

9.4 Modelling the service process

It can be seen that there are many possible queue arrangements and as many models to go with them. Rather than go into excessive detail, we will examine in this section three that are commonly encountered. They are listed with their main characteristics in Table 9.1.

Table 9.1 Simple queuing systems with variations

Name of system	Number of service channels	Service time distribution	Example
Single queue, single server	1	Exponential	Simple purchase or customer enquiry
Single queue, multiple servers	>1	Exponential	Bank; telephone help line
Single queue, single server, fixed service time	1	Fixed	Photograph booth; fairground ride

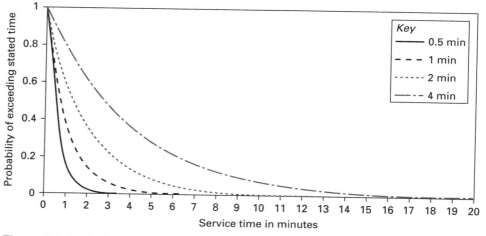

Figure 9.6 Probability of service exceeding stated time

Referring to Table 9.1, we will take the simple case first and then consider two changes to that case – increasing the number of channels and fixing the service time. The first two models allow for the cases where the service given to each customer is not constant. It is decided more by the customer's requirements than by the process or equipment used to supply the service. The statistical distribution that approximates closely to this type of service pattern is the *negative exponential* distribution. This allows for the observation that much service only takes a very short time and the probability of very long times is low. As with the Poisson distribution, the negative exponential is fully defined by its mean value μ, here the average number served per unit of time. (μ is pronounced *mew*.)

The curves in Figure 9.6 are distributions with different μ values. They show the probability that service will take longer than the number of minutes shown on the horizontal axis. Clearly, the family of curves all start where the probability = 1; all service lasts longer than zero time. We can interpret the graphs as follows. In the case with a mean service time of 4 minutes, the probability of the time exceeding 4 minutes is 0.36 or 36%. Further, some 28% of the customers require more than 5 minutes. Therefore, the number requiring service of between 4 and 5 minutes is 8%.

As with patterns of arrival times, one must take care with fitting curves to observed data. We have noted that some services, being machine paced or timetabled, have fixed durations. Even in personal service, however, patterns do not always match the exponential distribution. Hair cutting is one example; a normal distribution may represent such distributions better.

Considering all the assumptions we have made, we can now present results for the three systems being studied. These are as follows.

9.4.1 Single queue, single server

This is a special case of the more general one of multiple servers given next. It appears first for simplicity:

$$\text{Probability, } P_0, \text{ of zero customers in the system} = 1 - \frac{\lambda}{\mu}$$

$$\text{Average number of customers in the system} = \frac{\lambda}{\mu - \lambda}$$

$$\text{Average number of customers in the queue} = \frac{\lambda^2}{\mu(\mu - \lambda)}$$

$$\text{Average time spent in the system} = \frac{1}{\mu - \lambda}$$

$$\text{Average time spent in the queue} = \frac{\lambda}{\mu(\mu - \lambda)}$$

$$\text{System utilisation} = \frac{\lambda}{\mu}; \text{ proportion of idle time} = 1 - \frac{\lambda}{\mu}$$

9.4.2 Single queue, multiple servers

$$\text{Probability, } P_0, \text{ of zero customers in the system} = \frac{1}{\left(\sum_{x=0}^{N-1} \frac{1}{x!}\left(\frac{\lambda}{\mu}\right)^x\right) + \frac{1}{N!}\left(\frac{\lambda}{\mu}\right)^N \frac{N\mu}{N\mu - \lambda}}$$

$$\text{Average number of customers in the system} = \frac{\lambda\mu\left(\frac{\lambda}{\mu}\right)^N}{(N-1)!(N\mu - \lambda)^2}P_0 + \frac{\lambda}{\mu}$$

$$\text{Average time spent in the system} = \frac{\mu\left(\frac{\lambda}{\mu}\right)^N}{(N-1)!(N\mu - \lambda)^2}P_0 + \frac{1}{\mu}$$

$$\text{System utilisation} = \frac{\lambda}{N\mu}; \text{ proportion of idle time} = 1 - \frac{\lambda}{N\mu}$$

9.4.3 Single queue, single server, fixed service time

The results for this arrangement have a similar form to the case of variable server times. The difference is that queuing length and times are halved, reflecting the stabilising effect of the fixed service times:

$$\textit{Probability, } P_0, \textit{ of zero customers in the system} = 1 - \frac{\lambda}{\mu}$$

$$\textit{Average number of customers in the system} = \frac{\lambda^2}{2\mu(\mu - \lambda)} + \frac{\lambda}{\mu}$$

$$\textit{Average number of customers in the queue} = \frac{\lambda^2}{2\mu(\mu - \lambda)}$$

$$\textit{Average time spent in the system} = \frac{\lambda}{2\mu(\mu - \lambda)} + \frac{1}{\mu}$$

$$\textit{Average time spent in the queue} = \frac{\lambda}{2\mu(\mu - \lambda)}$$

$$\textit{System utilisation} = \frac{\lambda}{\mu} \textit{; proportion of idle time} = 1 - \frac{\lambda}{\mu}$$

These results illustrate three points we can learn about queues:

- Congestion at a service point begins to become a problem even when the system utilisation, λ/μ, is much less than 100%. The single queue to two service channels, shown in Figure 9.7, illustrates the problem. Here, the capacity of the two channels is 80 customers per hour. We can see that, when the arrival rate is 60, implying a utilisation of 75%, the *average* queue length is two persons. For an arrival rate of 70, the queue stretches to five.

- Modelling can show potential improvements that flow from changing queue structures. Figure 9.7 enables us to compare a single line to two servers with two independent systems. The two arrangements have the same nominal capacity, $2 \times 40 = 80$ customers per hour. To model the separate lines, we assume that customers arrive at each at random and do not switch from one to another. This would often be a rather artificial assumption but applies where there is no communication between the queues. Sometimes customers enter buildings such as theatres or stadia through different doors; telephone queues may have this structure.

  Figure 9.7 shows the potential improvements from combining two queues into a single line. With the same service capacity, the queue length is roughly halved. Combining lines while keeping the number of service points constant always increases the system performance.

- Fixed-time service systems perform better than variable ones. The equations allow a simple comparison to be made. They show that, for a given service standard, defined by λ and μ, both the number of customers in the queue and the time spent waiting are halved. This takes us back to the original problem of service provision – *the intrinsic variability of service creates efficiency problems.*

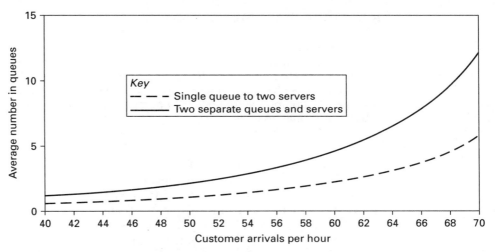

Figure 9.7 Separate and single queues compared

Many queuing situations have characteristics similar to the cases we have illustrated here. Theoretical models have been developed to cover many of them. In practice, however, managers are less concerned with the details of theoretical differences and more with taking practical steps to improve their operations. Therefore, they need some understanding of queue behaviour and some means of testing alternative approaches. These aims can be achieved through simulation.

9.5 Simulation models

As an alternative to mathematical modelling, simulation avoids some theoretical pitfalls. For example, the assumptions of Poisson distributions for arrival times and negative exponential distributions for service times need to be checked before the results obtained earlier can be used with confidence. Simulation can approach each situation more directly.

A simulation model duplicates the relevant features of a real system. Since the important features are dynamic, the model is constructed to represent the way they change through time. Simulation refers to the process of operating the model and, by observing its behaviour, drawing conclusions about the performance of the real system.

Models for simulation range across the full spread of model types: iconic, analogue and symbolic.

Iconic

Iconic models represent the key properties by duplicating them directly within the model itself. There is often a change in scale so that, in a (say) one-tenth scale model of an aircraft, each dimension is replicated in this proportion. This shows one immediate difficulty for such modelling in that not all properties scale down

BOX 9.1 JIT simulation at 'Engines'

Simulation was used to introduce JIT to the work force at a company producing vehicle components. Managers used cardboard boxes and spacers to demonstrate the working of a production line. They were able to show the differences between push and pull production control systems. The demonstration proved to be 'a very persuasive tool for introducing employees to the principal benefits of JIT'.

in the same proportion. The flying characteristics of the model aircraft are affected by the fact that the mass depends on the cube of the linear scale and the lift from the wings is proportionate to their surface area, which is their linear dimension squared. This means that even the most accurate scale model of an aircraft could not fly in the same way as the original.

Beyond their widespread use in engineering design and architecture, iconic models show their value in full size mock-ups of plant and equipment. These are used to test designs and to train operators before 'letting them loose' on the real thing. Examples include flight simulators, driving simulators and full-scale control rooms operating dummy nuclear power plants.

Analogue

In analogue models, system properties are represented by different, yet equivalent, properties in the model. For instance, the flow of goods through a distribution system may be compared to the flow of water through a system of channels and sluices, the latter representing bottlenecks at which delays occur. Study of such an analogue model *may* give insight into critical issues in the system itself. Analogue models are sometimes used for training, especially of people who are not used to thinking in abstract terms. Box 9.1 shows an example given by Kinnie and Staughton.[2] JIT, or just-in-time, is covered in Chapter 12.

Role plays, case studies and related exercises are often seen as analogue models to be used in management training. Both interviewers and interviewees, for example, are coached by means of such methods. While being of some value in bringing out issues for both parties, they often turn out to be inadequate preparation for the 'real thing'. This difficulty arises because the real interview and its analogue model diverge in critical ways. Clearly, for the interviewee, the level of stress will be significantly different.

Symbolic

Symbolic models are more abstract than analogue ones. While being sometimes more difficult to understand at first, this class of model can be immensely useful to the manager in understanding and solving problems. Algebraic models, such as the ones used throughout this book, have wide application. Other symbolic models use plain numbers, geometry or further notational forms such as logical symbols and pictograms. Graphs are also important although it can be argued that the fact that distances on the graphs correspond to real-life values places them in the analogue category.

9.5.1 Use of simulation models

Whatever the type of model, it will have one or more uses. First, and most straightforward, is *description*. Here we mean that, through mimicking relevant elements either of a system's structure or of its processes, we can describe the system itself. For example: an architect's drawing describes a structure; a map shows a route; a production plan sets out a series of required tasks; and a profit and loss account represents the performance of a business. Second, the model enables us to *understand and explain* features of the system. Through investigation of the models form and dynamic behaviour, we can identify and explain key relationships. Not all models allow this to happen. My son's 1/132 scale model of a Klingon battle cruiser tells me little about space travel, hyperspace or how the *Enterprise* always wins. By the same token, leave an experienced accountant with your cash flow account for an hour and you will be presented with a series of questions and comments on the health of your business.

In each of these purposes, description and understanding, the emphasis is on communication. This takes us to the third function of models, *control*. Understanding through the model leads to the notion of predicting system behaviour by use of the model and therefore taking control of it. This is the essence of *feedforward control* as discussed in Chapter 4. Finally, given that the controller has an objective, we see that the model can be used for *optimisation*. It can be available for use when the manager needs assistance with a decision or the model can be placed in permanent control of part or all the operations. This is *real-time process control* and can be seen in many process manufacturing plants, automatic pilots and computer-managed traffic signals.

9.5.2 Assessing simulation models

Table 9.2 summarises the pros and cons of using simulation models. Because they are often set out in a more intuitive way than the abstract mathematical models just described, many people find them easier to use and understand, at least in their simple forms. Their greatest disadvantage lies in the fact that each model is unique and, therefore, needs to be independently tested before it can be used for its intended purposes. Computer packages, many with associated graphical outputs, simplify the simulation of hundreds of system cycles, although the internal

Table 9.2 Assessing simulation models

Advantages	Disadvantages
■ Relatively straightforward to understand	■ Can be expensive and time consuming
■ Useful where there is no alternative model	■ Each model is unique; results from one simulation cannot be generalised
■ Valuable where distributions of events, such as the pattern of customer arrivals, do not match standard formulae	■ Avoiding standard distribution patterns may increase the effort involved in the modelling process
■ Often reveals the complex and interactive nature of system components as the simulation is taken through time	■ Models do not produce answers directly; optimal solutions must be found by trial and error

Table 9.3 Assignment of random digits to occurrences

Customers arriving within minute	Frequency (number of observations)	Probability of event (%)	Cumulative probability (%)	Random number interval
0	10	2	2	00 to 01
1	35	7	9	02 to 08
2	75	15	24	09 to 23
3	95	19	43	24 to 42
4	100	20	63	43 to 62
5	85	17	80	63 to 79
6	55	11	91	80 to 90
7	30	6	97	91 to 96
8	15	3	100	97 to 99
	500	100		

modelling logic of the package becomes more mysterious to the average user. In the next sections, we shall 'walk through' a queue simulation to explain the elements from which large models are built. First, however, we shall examine how the Monte Carlo method is used to simulate chance events.

The Monte Carlo method

The strength of many simulation models lies in the fact that they can incorporate chance events into their behaviour. This is the key to the approach. Once a simulated stream of activities has been generated, it is often a simple task to set out their sequence in a multiple activity chart of the type shown in Chapter 6.

The Monte Carlo method is so called because much of the thinking about probabilistic events was developed through study of games of chance played in the casino. We shall set out the procedure in five steps.

1 Generate a probability distribution

This is often done by observing behaviour, such as collecting data on customer serving times. It can, however, also be done by theoretical analysis. The chance of drawing a named card from a fair pack can be found by counting the pack and is 1 in 52. This probability can be confirmed, roughly, by drawing many times. The chance of matching six balls from 49 in the National Lottery, however, is $49!/43! \times 6!$; this comes to 1 in 13,983,816. This figure cannot be confirmed easily by experiment.

The normal method in practice involves collecting data on actual behaviour. For customer arrival times at a busy service office, we could do so during typical periods over several weeks. We should choose these periods at random while avoiding unusual patterns. These occur at the start and end of the day or during holidays. The first two columns of Table 9.3 show the results of such a collection. The second column shows the frequency of minute intervals when the stated number of customers arrived. The third column represents the data converted to a probability distribution. Each observation is divided by the total (500) and then expressed as a percentage.

2 Build a cumulative frequency distribution

The cumulative probability distribution is readily worked out. The value of each entry in column 4 is found by adding its probability to the cumulative value

Table 9.4 Random digits

19	38	64	30	57	95	62	53	88	85
53	47	37	41	02	86	86	55	29	72
81	31	94	51	67	74	51	39	19	85
96	42	70	53	52	10	33	67	87	74
49	53	55	36	19	55	31	24	94	18
50	75	40	93	12	16	21	35	53	36
83	91	33	97	59	16	33	61	94	67
35	08	78	37	71	64	40	77	68	69
82	08	18	27	52	90	67	58	53	23
92	90	44	62	93	03	93	25	88	63

that appears in the cell above. In a spreadsheet, the formula for D8 would be +D7+C8.

3 Assign groups of random numbers

A random number contains digits chosen at random. There are, for example 100 two digit random numbers from 00 to 99, each of which has an equally likely chance of occurrence. Thus, if we wanted to simulate an event that occurred 1% of the time, we could assign to the event the digits 00. Indeed, any other digits would do equally well. Then, running through lists of random numbers, we could simulate the occurrence every time our chosen digits came up.

Using ranges of random digits, we can cope with frequencies greater than 1%. For instance, 19% of the occasions are when three customers arrive. To simulate this possibility, all we have to do is allocate a range of 19 digits to this event. The process of building cumulative probabilities enables us to do this conveniently. Column 5 of Table 9.3 flows on from column 4. It can be seen that the range of digits allocated to each occurrence corresponds to its probability and that all the random digits from 00 to 99 have been used.

Note: In our example, the percentages in the third and fourth columns are integers. If we are interested in probabilities to an accuracy finer than 1%, they can be calibrated out of 1,000 or more and the random numbers can be chosen with three or more digits. This, however, is rare for a business problem.

We should also note that some authorities present the range of digits starting at 1 and finishing at 0, that is from 01 to 00 when two-digit values at used. This does not affect the outcome but the ranges should be checked to ensure that they work as intended.

4 Generate random numbers

Random numbers are often presented in lists as in Table 9.4. The layout in columns of two digits is designed for easy reading rather than to suggest that the digits come in pairs. Numbers, of any length, can be read in any direction. It is wise, of course, to choose the reading rule before looking at the page in order to avoid the possibility of unconscious selection. Tables can cover many pages. This enables many experiments to be carried out using independent streams of simulated data.

Exercise 9.3 Use Table 9.4 to write a random sum of money less than £10,000.00. Note how you did so.

Table 9.5 Assigning values in a simulation

Random numbers	19	38	64	30	57	95	62	53	88	85
Simulated number of customers	2	3	5	3	4	7	4	4	6	6

Leading spreadsheet programs incorporate a random number function. In Microsoft Excel®, for instance, the function RAND() returns a random value from 0 to .99999999. The two digit entries of Table 9.4 use the formula =INT(100*RAND()) in each cell. It multiplies the RAND() value by 100. Then, the INT function removes the part after the decimal point.

5 Simulate values of the variable

By taking each random number in turn, a list of values of the variable being simulated can be figured out. The numbers are fitted into column 5 of Table 9.3 and the type of event can be read in column 1. Therefore, '19' stands for two customers arriving and '38' stands for three. Table 9.5 shows simulated arrivals in a period of 10 minutes using the first row of digits of Table 9.4. Continuing this way for a long sequence is tedious. Fortunately, spreadsheets include a LOOKUP function to automate the procedure.

The values in the second row of Table 9.5 are random arrival rates. With such a short list, it is difficult to draw any conclusions. In the long run, however, the list would contain values corresponding in frequency to the original observations. This is the output of the Monte Carlo method. A simulation is not a prediction. We can think of it as representing how the customers *might* arrive on one day if our original assumptions about randomness and our observations are valid.

9.5.3 Simulating a queue

We can use Monte Carlo data for arrival rates and service times to simulate a queue. This can best be set out on a multiple activity chart, following the conventions introduced in Chapter 6. We shall illustrate the case of a single line to 15 vehicle service points. They are, for instance, being checked at a border crossing. A multiple activity chart records the behaviour of each element of the queuing system as time progresses. In Table 9.6, the time scale in minutes runs down the page; it appears in the first column. The second column gives the number of customers arriving in each minute, generated by simulation. The third column records the queue, if any. Then, each service point has a column to record whether it is idle (blank) or serving a customer. The asterisks at the top of the diagram are included because we assume some stations are busy from unidentified customers who arrived before the trial started.

The progress of the vehicles can be traced through the facility. When each moves to a service line, we generate the time needed from another look-up table. Therefore, the model requires simulations for both arrivals and service times. The relevant tables are not shown here but would be similar to Table 9.3.

The simulation could continue for several hours. While Table 9.6 shows individual progress, it is not usual to track each customer. If run on appropriate

Table 9.6 Simulation of single queue to 15 servers

Time	Arrivals	Number in queue	1	2	3	4	5	6	7	8	9	10	11	12	13	14	15
									Service point								
1	0		*	*	*	*	*	*	*	*	*	*					
2	2		*	*	*	*	*	*	☺	☺							
3	6		*	*	*	*	☺	☺			☺	☺	☺	☺			
4	5		*	*	☺	☺									☺	☺	☺
5	2		*	☺					☺			▓					
6	4	☺	☺									☺		☺			
7	3		☺				☺						☺		☺		
8	5	☺ ☺							☺	☺				☺			
9	6	☺ ☺ ☺ ☺				☺					☺	☺		☺			
10	4	☺ ☺ ☺ ☺					☺	☺					☺				☺
11	6	☺ ☺ ☺ ☺ ☺ ☺ ☺	☺					☺									
12	3	☺ ☺ ☺ ☺ ☺		☺			☺		☺	☺	☺				☺		
13	5	☺ ☺ ☺ ☺ ☺			☺	☺		☺		☺			☺				
14	etc.																
15																	
16																	
17																	

software, there will be a print of queue length and station idle time during the simulated period with summary statistics. The experiment can then be repeated with different management policies. These could, for example, be to increase the number of service points always open or to add to the basic number when the queue reaches a defined length.

9.6 Managing queues

We have seen that queues occur in many service situations. They consist not only of customers standing in line but also the following:

- *Waiting for service to arrive.* This could be in a restaurant, by the side of the road waiting for a breakdown van or lying in bed having called the doctor.

- *Waiting for an item to be serviced.* The item could be a tool or a piece of household equipment.

- *Waiting in an electronic queue.* These lines do not require that the customer be physically present but they can, nevertheless, be frustrating. Examples are waiting at the computer terminal and for telephones to be answered.

- *Waiting one's turn over a long period.* Long-term queuing may be for entering hospital, admission to a golf club or buying a Morgan car. The frustration felt by the person waiting depends largely on the desirability of the result.

We have also examined how it is possible to model the behaviour of queues, either to produce measures of mean lengths and times or to simulate their dynamic behaviour. Yet, none of this is of direct interest to the operations manager unless it can be turned to positive effect and lead to an understanding of *how queues can be managed.* Given the inevitability of waiting occasionally, the successful organisation will be one that can show its customers that it is aware of, and responding to, the situation in a positive way.

9.6.1 Acceptable queue lengths

The acceptable length of a queue depends on many factors that vary from individual to individual and from case to case:

- *The significance of the wait.* Some people have more time than others; they are prepared to wait for some services more than for others, possibly because these services are more important or there are few alternatives. It is accepted that there is to be some waiting time for a free hospital bed in non-urgent cases, although there is little consensus over how long this interval ought to be!

- *Perception of queue length.* Customers perceive the length of a line in different ways. For instance, there is the difficulty of comparing a short but slow-moving line with a longer one that is moving more quickly. Queue structures can, therefore, have an impact on customer response. Another issue is the sense of urgency felt by the customer. Lining up for a railway ticket well ahead of departure will be a more comfortable experience than if the train is about to leave.

BOX 9.2 **Competing over waiting lines**

> **If** there's ever more than one other customer in front of you at the checkout we'll aim to open another until all our tills are open.
>
> **TESCO Every little helps**

- *Information.* Besides the time lost in the line, another customer anxiety is uncertainty. Some organisations relieve this problem by informing customers of the likely period of the wait. For this policy to be successful, customers need to be confident that the estimated delays are accurate and that there is a commitment by the organisation to keep to them. Theme parks offering free rides, such as Alton Towers and Disneyland, incorporate signs in the queuing areas with such information.

- *Competition.* Standards may be set by competitive forces in industries where service quality can be defined as including the time spent waiting. Many airlines are installing fast or automated check-ins available to premium-price passengers as part of their strategies to gain in this important market sector. In supermarkets, the lengths of delay at some crowded competitors lay behind Tesco's advertising campaign of late 1994[3], an example of which appears in Box 9.2.

- *Priorities.* Competitive forces may be one of many factors that encourage organisations to discriminate among customers and replace the common first-come-first-served rule. Alternative priority criteria include:
  - *Urgency.* Medical services in an out-patients' clinic are given according to arrival times with emergencies being treated immediately.
  - *Consequences.* Emergency services will normally be sent to answer any call but, in case of overload, they are allocated according to the potential consequences of the fire or other crisis.
  - *Special customers.* Those who place large orders or who buy premium services, such as first-class tickets.

With our study of structures, these points suggest three approaches that may be taken to improve service operations: queue avoidance; queue differentiation and changing the experience of queuing.

9.6.2 Queue avoidance

A sensible alternative to the pressure and problems resulting from queuing is to avoid them through some form of reservation system. This will aim to regulate demand for service, either to cut it altogether or to shift it to times that are more favourable. One policy is to use price premiums at peak times but, as we have seen, this tends to be a relative blunt weapon. Other approaches have been adopted in various industries; in some, it is commonplace while in others it is not expected. Reservations are, for example, normal for international flights.

Passengers expect to have to book in advance for international flights yet the practice of selling 'open' tickets, under which a customer may not show and incur no

BOX 9.3 UCI's integrated information system

The UK subsidiary of United Cinemas International operates 37 cinemas throughout the country. In its Manchester headquarters, it has installed a computer answering system designed to answer 95% of calls in under 20 seconds. Customers make up to 23,000 calls per day using a range of Freephone numbers, each of which enables the computer to recognise from which cinema catchment the call originates.

When answering, the operator's screen shows the programme of the caller's local UCI together with prices and availability. After booking, all details are transmitted to the customer's cinema where tickets and receipts are prepared for collection. The facility is staffed for almost 100 hours per week. At other times, a touch-tone telephone can be used to make reservations.

Sales rose by about 6% in the year after installing the system. Since the cinemas were connected to the network in stages, it was possible to separate the effects of the better service from the impact of the films being shown.

Details of ticket sales and catering receipts are fed into databases. Cognos software processes it automatically to support managers. UCI also uses Swallow customer relationship management software to record all enquiries, concerns and complaints. These data are analysed to produce reports and spot trends.

penalty, works against filling all seats. To cope with this uncertainty, airlines offer a range of tickets at different prices. Open tickets are expensive. The cheaper, APEX tickets are only valid for identified flights. Holders of standby tickets have to queue!

One problem with reservation systems is that they can replace one type of waiting with another – lining up to make a reservation. This happened to cinemas as credit card booking systems replaced the need to stand in line to get to a popular film. UCI found that up to 60% of sales at some south-east cinemas were made by telephone. While busy centres had four operators, many calls were abandoned due to engaged tones or the long wait. In response to this problem, UCI has invested in a centralised reservation system that, in effect, has become a single line to multiple servers covering all its cinemas. Further details are in Box 9.3.[4]

A further difficulty for some customers is that a reservation system may increase the time spent waiting for service. A person with an urgent need may prefer to queue straight away rather than enter a slower queue or make an appointment for later. The former applies to people who have forgotten to renew their passports. For the latter, doctors operate dual systems as does the admissions system to higher education in Germany.

Admission to Fachhochschulen (technical university colleges) in north-west Germany is made on the following basis. Candidates apply after having passed the Abitur, the school leaving certificate giving entry to higher education. In any year, half of the places are offered to those in a list ranked by grade gained in the Abitur. The other half of the places goes to those with lower grades who have been waiting longer.

In some industries, it is possible, through the integrated management of flows and timetables, to avoid delays. This approach is used in large-scale transport facilities such as airports and the Channel Tunnel.

Airport landings are restricted by 4 km separation distances on the downward glide path towards the runway. Aircraft are kept apart to avoid the risk from one flying in the turbulent wake of another. Conventionally, those airports that operated near to full capacity required aircraft to queue, at 'stacks', until a path was available. Nowadays, the flow control system in use throughout much of Europe has done much to avoid this irritating and wasteful practice. Using short-term forecasting models, controllers make detailed landing plans several hours in advance. Flights do not leave their points of origin until they are, in effect, cleared to land. In flight, the plans can be continuously updated and the aircraft speed adjusted accordingly.

The Channel Tunnel has a capacity of 12 trains per hour in each direction. The headway of 5 minutes is the minimum allowed for safety reasons. Like a runway, if a slot is lost, it represents capacity lost for ever. The late arrival of an express train would mean loss of business unless it could be replaced by another train from a queue, for example a freight train or *Le Shuttle* car transporter service. Therefore, it is in the interests of the tunnel company to expect some of its traffic to queue in case a planned train is late.

Both facilities operate most efficiently if the separation distances are fixed and planes or trains move through at a constant rhythm. Planes are instructed to approach runways, and trains pass through the tunnel, at the same speed as all the others.

The policies for queue avoidance laid out in this section remain constrained by the need to maintain capacity that exceeds demand. While many businesses view excess capacity as wasteful, others will compete through promising that it will always be available. McDonald's and other quick-service restaurants, for instance, have high capacity, simple technology and flexible staffing that enable them to offer their service effectively under a wide range of demand conditions. The success of the investment in this approach to service is represented by the corresponding business growth.

9.6.3 Queue differentiation

As we have seen, the most common form of queue is the one that operates on a first-come-first-served basis. This system is generally operated and accepted in single server facilities in shops, banks and so on. When the operator provides several servers, complications arise, particularly where the layout and atmosphere of the serving area conflicts with the need for orderly lines to form. The theatre bar has already been mentioned as a case in point. Several arrangements are possible for multiple servers:

■ *Multiple queues to full-range servers.* This is the typical standard supermarket checkout or the arrangement found in many banks. Servers are not specialised so that customers choose queues they think are going to move quickly. Where the variability of service time among customers is high, customer frustration can become acute as queues move at different speeds. The problem is exacerbated for those with few purchases. Customers may switch lines.

■ *Multiple lines to specialised servers.* One common way of separating lines is to have some servers dedicated to particular transactions such as selling stamps in the post office or dealing with those with a few purchases, or paying cash, in the supermarket. This reduces the anxiety caused by multiple queues where service variability is high. A disadvantage is that some customers may see other lines empty while they are still waiting. Furthermore, excessive specialisation of the servers would mean that some customers have to wait in more than one queue to have their needs attended to. This is the experience of out-patients in some hospitals who, requiring several tests and examinations, have to move from queue to queue for several hours.

- *Single lines to multiple servers.* Perceived by many to be the fairest method, customers are served in order of arrival. This arrangement has been introduced into many banks and applies in telephone systems. Where volume of demand is high, the queue can appear to be very long, although it can move quickly. The arrangement requires that the waiting area can be set out in a convenient manner to maintain the queue organisation and that the servers are all able to provide the full service. As a variant, banks and others combine this scheme for most business with specialist counters for transactions such as share dealing and currency exchange.

Exercise 9.4 Why do most supermarkets not use the single line to multiple server system? What arrangements are you aware of and what are their benefits?

9.6.4 Changing the experience of queuing

As with all service business, excellence will only be achieved if the perspective of the customer is fully considered in planning what is on offer. This clearly includes the customers' perceptions of having to wait for service.

Both Maister[5] and Davies and Heineke[6] propose sets of hypotheses concerning personal queuing which draw together the discussion from the last sections. They are combined in Box 9.4. Note how the items higher in the list are more under the provider's control than those lower down. Customers' attitudes and value systems cannot be immediately changed by the firm and it will succeed by learning as much as it can about them before tailoring its service to suit. Chapter 16 takes up this important theme of quality.

Using the ideas in Box 9.4 as a basis, managers should consider the following actions:

- *Reducing the anxiety* that comes from uncertainty. Informing customers of the likely length of wait both enables them to plan what to do meanwhile and gives the impression that the managers care about their circumstances.

- *Influence the perception* of queuing time by distracting customers. Distractions include drinks in a restaurant, Mickey at Disneyland, videos in the post office, coffee at the garage and ensuring that parallel parts of the service are not too fast (see Box 9.5).[7] There is also the well-known story of the up-market New York hotel where customers complained of having to wait for the lifts. Grumbles became fewer when full-length mirrors were installed on each landing.

- *Identify stressful elements of the environment* and take steps to relieve these. Problems include room temperature and noise. The latter may, of course, be caused by the queue itself!

BOX 9.4 **Hypotheses concerning the perception of waiting**

Under firm's control

1 Queuing before the process feels longer than waiting during it.

2 Uncertainty makes queuing seem longer.

3 Unexplained queuing seems longer than explained queuing.

4 Unfair queuing seems longer than when lines are seen to be fair.

5 Uncomfortable waits seem longer than comfortable ones.

6 Idle time feels longer than occupied time.

7 Anxiety makes queuing seem longer.

8 The more valuable the service, the longer the customer will be prepared to queue.

9 Queuing alone seems longer than queuing in a group.

10 A customer's current attitude leads to a particular perception of the wait.

11 Customers' value systems lead to different perceptions of waiting.

Under customers' control

BOX 9.5 **Walking as a distraction**

The baggage reclaim hall at Dallas–Fort Worth airport is close to the gate area. Passengers have a short walk to collect their luggage but usually arrive first. At Los Angeles, they have to walk much further and arrive after the luggage. Dallas passengers grumble more about luggage delays.

- *Make the queuing time part of the service* by taking orders, handing out registration forms or briefing customers about what to expect.

- Use numbered tickets to *maintain the principle of first-come-first-served* while allowing people to leave the queue. For instance, this happens at the delicatessen counter within supermarkets.

Whatever the queue structure and management policies chosen by an enterprise, it is essential to show to clients that the operation is *under control*, for there is nothing more disheartening for the anxious customer than to feel that events are following their own course.

9.7 Service facility layouts

In this chapter, we have concentrated our attention on the waiting line. While this is a critical issue in the design of service layouts, we must not forget that the customer is present in other aspects of the service operation. Retail stores and shopping centres use design to create shopping environments that are both efficient and stimulate demand through their presentation.

BOX 9.6 **Issues in in-store bakery design: Safeway**

'We aim to foster a clear customer awareness of quality. . . .

'In-store bakeries, seen as one of the fresh food specialist areas in a store, must personify this expectation by the selection of range and the way we display our products. Expectations are just as high regarding the surroundings and fittings in which products are displayed. Atmosphere and interest are highly valued and a well-designed attractive department layout will provide a favourable background to product and service. . . .

'The department [is] defined with a distinct character by bringing all of the elements together, pre-pack sections, service counter, bread rack and self-selection chilled cake cabinet, all linked by a strong livery and unique fittings. . . . Strategically placed promotional units are an integral part of the department, creating extra volume sales. . . .

'Customer expectation in terms of service hygiene quality and choice is rising all the time, so we must never become complacent. A quality bakery department serves as a point of difference.'

9.7.1 **Store layout**

Retail managers have developed, through years of experience, many ploys to promote sales. For example, it is expected that goods presented at eye level are more likely to sell, as are goods displayed towards the ends of rows of shelves. The row end is a particularly strong promotional position. Less well known are the following observations: if there are no restrictions, customers tend to turn right when entering a shop; they take 20 paces to slow to browsing speed; in supermarket aisles they will push trolleys towards the right and scan shelves from left to right.[8] These rules of thumb are reinforced by research studies using direct observation of customer behaviour and analysis of sales mixes drawn from scanning checkouts.

Drawing on such data, leading chains plan their layouts centrally. They allocate some 50% of shelf space to own-label goods, perhaps 40% to the leading proprietary brand and 10% to other brands that may well have some local following. The last can be important in some categories or when makers of new lines are trying to build a following. Fair trade products, such as Café Direct, achieve higher sales in cities with well-educated populations. Sainsbury found particularly strong performance for this coffee in its Edinburgh Morningside store.

Store design is a critical component of company image and influences shoppers' perceptions of value. Compare the small cramped aisles of the discounter with the spacious layouts of the leading, quality-orientated superstores. Each attracts customers through messages concerning its price-quality image. Dividing a large store into sections, each with its own ambience created by scale, colour and, perhaps, smell is an extension of the overall design philosophy. Box 9.6[9] shows how a Safeway bakery department is created with its own identity to support the company's image of high-quality goods sold at reasonable prices.

9.7.2 Varying store layouts

As supermarkets diversify into non-food items, they have to rethink how they present the new lines to customers. Following introductions of products from clothes to pharmaceuticals comes the entry of services from film processing to dry cleaning. While the last of these has often been introduced in a separate shop, other new lines have often been merchandised (laid out and displayed) in similar ways to food. Yet, other arrangements are often more successful.

Three store layouts are commonly found in large retailers:

■ *Grid*. Exemplified by the Associated Supermarket case study before the change, the grid uses long racks arranged in a repetitive pattern. Standardised fixtures are cheap, easy to maintain and maximise the use of space. Consistent design allows regular customers to find what they want easily while all can be steered to walk round the whole store. Weaknesses include monotony and the feeling among customers of being rushed, cutting the time for browsing.

In one variant of the grid, *the racetrack*, the movement pattern is restricted to one or a few routes. The furniture display section in an IKEA store is a typical example. Customers follow a twisting path through all departments, giving an impression of a rich and varied stock holding within a rectangular building.

Exercise 9.5   Why would IKEA, in particular, choose this form of store layout?

■ *Free flow*. By arranging fixtures in less regular patterns, the free flow layout encourages an unstructured movement in a less formal atmosphere. Slower walking by customers stimulates browsing, an essential element in discretionary shopping. Floor space is not used so intensively and, for regular food shoppers, the arrangement can be frustrating. Many among these, however, shop with neither list nor clear idea of what they are about to buy.

■ *Boutique*. Moving further from the standardisation of the large superstore, the boutique layout comes from dividing the area into speciality shops distinguished by changes in ambience. Sometimes, these are managed by franchisees (as in Debenham's) and are referred to as 'shop-within-shop'. Whatever the ownership, the changes in design allow for closer matching to target customers' needs.

Clearly, the layouts are not mutually exclusive. We saw in the opening case how Associated Supermarkets introduced an element of free flow to its produce department. Hart and Davies[10] investigated the relative advantages of different layouts for non-food products from the point of view of customers. They found that, for clothes and entertainment, boutiques were the best display location and aisles in the grid were the worst. Explanations ranged from the ambience of browsing through to the benefits of added security for high-priced items. Preferences among other non-food lines were different. For household goods, stationery and health and beauty items, for example, customers preferred different fixtures and flooring away from the food, but within the main store. Having separate shops for these items was a less favoured option.

9.7.3 Shopping centre layout

Designers of shopping centres have to not only consider safe and comfortable conditions but also seek to persuade leading companies to take space within the development. Indeed, developments are often not started until such agreements are in place. Another aim is to achieve a mix of stores so that customers can be confident of having their needs satisfied 'under one roof'. This may appear to limit competition among the outlets but most are subject to indirect competition from other retailers as each pursues some diversification of its range. For the smaller operator, the negative effects of competition can be outweighed by the benefits from the 'pull' of the so-called anchor stores.[11] There is even positive interaction among sales of the major retailers. Sainsbury does well in areas where Marks & Spencer has high sales. The Metro Centre at Gateshead was developed with Carrefour, House of Fraser and Marks & Spencer among the main anchors. The Trafford Centre near Manchester incorporates many major names; Selfridges chose this location to make its first move outside London.

Not only do store designers have to consider the presentation of goods to customers to achieve sales, they should also pay attention to the needs for deliveries, storage, space for staff and security of staff, stock, cash and fittings.

✔ Quick check-up

Can you:
- ☐ Name four actions to manage service demand and five to adjust capacity.
- ☐ Define service capacity utilisation.
- ☐ Suggest three means of measuring queues.
- ☐ State the mean values of Poisson and negative exponential distributions.
- ☐ Name three common queue structures.
- ☐ List three basic models useful in operations management.
- ☐ Give five factors influencing perception of queue length.
- ☐ Name five ways managers can change the experience of queuing.
- ☐ Outline the pros and cons of three retail store layouts.

? Questions

Chapter review

9.1 Sketch the Poisson and exponential distributions, summarising their main properties, and give examples of how they are used in queue models.

9.2 Explain why many service positions cannot operate at full utilisation.

9.3 Compare the times spent within the three systems listed in Table 9.1 if 30 customers arrive every hour and the expected service capacity is 20 per hour for each of two servers.

Application

9.4 Outline how you would model queues at the checkout of a busy supermarket when there are lines with different rules; what data would you need and how would you collect them?

9.5 Having bought a loaf on one day, a customer returns for another on just 15% of the following days. Further, if the customer has not called on one day, there is an 80% chance of buying on the next. Through simulation, estimate the number of loaves sold to this person each month.

9.6 What are the implications of the material in this chapter for the design of services in facilities not mentioned? Examples could include airport lounges, doctors' surgeries or bus stops.

9.7 Why are the layouts of retail stores changing?

Investigation

9.8 If you can observe the behaviour of people joining a queuing system, check to see what decision rules they appear to follow. If they have a choice, how do they select a line? What makes them turn away?

9.9 Drivers entering car parks provided by large cinemas or retail outlets appear to follow one of two search strategies. They drive to the facility entrance and begin their search from that point or they head for a space as soon as they judge they have found a suitable one. Investigate whether this list is complete; then study the implications of these behaviours for the design of parking areas.

CLOSING CASE

Francis Thomas[12]

Francis Thomas is a family business selling fruit, vegetables and a few cut flowers from small premises in Town Hall Square, Chester. It was set up close by its present address in 1947 and has moved twice since. During the 1950s, the family had, for a time, two shops in the street and, in 1959, opened a branch in a suburb. The focus in town was on fruit (70%) while the suburban shop, in a poor area, sold mostly vegetables. The latter business was sold in 1962. The shop is now one of two the family owns, another suburban branch having been taken over in the early 1990s. There is also a substantial delivery business, accounting for some 25% of turnover, serving hotels and restaurants throughout the city. This shares the city shop premises. Competition comes from about six greengrocery stalls in the market hall, about 100 metres away, and several other shops within 200 metres. Thomas' prices are lower than those of competitors and up to 30% below those of the Tesco supermarket (about 200 metres away).

In 1994, Thomas' was unusual in being among the few food shops in which customers were still served with most of the items they wanted. Apart from the market stalls, all of the other greengrocers in the city centre were self-service.

Figure 9.8 shows the layout of the shop until 1995. There was always bustle. Because of the delivery business, staff were continually carrying goods through the shop, to and from a van parked outside. Until about 1990, customers used to wait until they estimated it was their turn. Then Mr Thomas introduced a makeshift barrier of steel posts and string to regulate the flow.

▶

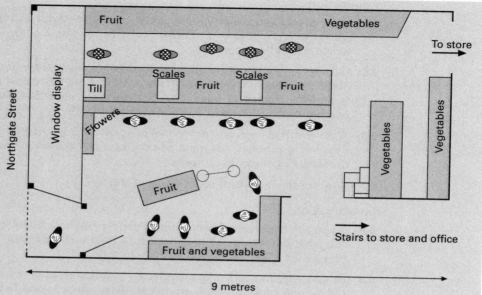

Figure 9.8 Francis Thomas: before 1995

The barrier was made permanent so that customers queued between it and a stack of empty boxes that usually stood against the adjacent wall. Then Mr Thomas fitted shelves on the same wall. These displayed some pre-packed fruit and vegetables that the customers could select while waiting. The shelves reduced the space in the shop so that about five customers could queue inside, two in the doorway and the rest in the street.

The shop assistants used weighing equipment that automatically produced an itemised bill for each customer. They then paid at the till on the way out. Flowers were displayed by the till and sold separately because they attracted VAT. Customers wanting to buy flowers only could bypass the main queue. At busy times up to six assistants served customers along the counter and the movement was considerable. When it was quieter, the assistants made up orders for delivery, refilled the shelves and did other shop work.

The year 1994 saw another change. The Thomases had found that the self-service experiment made it easier to display and sell a greater variety of fruit, including exotic varieties which customers were reluctant to ask for. The itemised sales records enabled them to track this change. At the same time, they were aware of the labour intensity of their current operation, accepted that there was a trend towards self-service and felt a switch would give a faster service to most customers.

The shop closed for a week in November to be rearranged as shown in Figure 9.9. The place was redecorated and fitted out with new lighting, simple racks and shelves designed to carry fruit boxes. Over the next few months, the decision proved itself in higher turnover and margins. The mix of customers changed towards more of both younger and older people. The former had been brought up to expect self-service while older folk liked the opportunity to shop

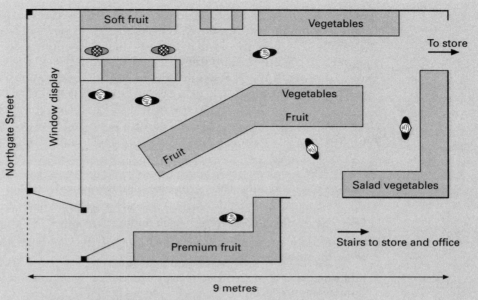

Figure 9.9 Francis Thomas: 1995 on

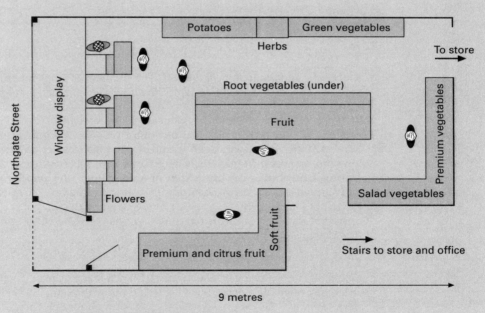

Figure 9.10 Francis Thomas: 2000 on

regularly for small quantities. The proportion of those whom Mark Thomas described as 'middle-aged fuddy duddies' fell.

Although the change of late 1994 had been successful, the Thomases had felt uncertain about its effects and had not invested in a complete refurbishment.

Furthermore, they had worried about the pending rent review. By 2000, therefore, the shop and fittings were very shabby. With new confidence, however, the family commissioned a craftsman to make a complete set of units while they relined the interior surfaces. The new design reflected the rising interest in exotic, short-season and named varieties of fruit. For an array of up to dozen apple boxes, for example, the new central fixture was higher than before, allowing for two layers of display on the fruit side. Root vegetables were ingeniously shown behind, below the top shelf of fruit. Shelves for other fruits and a rack for herbs also represented improvements. A sketch appears in Figure 9.10.

Questions

1 What methods did the Thomases use to manage the queue?

2 What happens to queue management when a shop changes to self-service? Does the relative importance of each approach change?

3 What criteria do greengrocers use to arrange the goods in their shops? How important is each of these?

4 From the case study, and your own experience, what are the trends in greengrocery shopping?

Notes and references

1. DY Design, 2 Broadlawn Avenue, Kings Point, NY 11024; www.dydesign.com/ accessed 20 June 2001.
2. Kinnie, N. and Staughton, R. (1994) 'The problem of implementing manufacturing strategy', in Storey, J. (ed.) *New Wave Manufacturing Strategies*, London: Paul Chapman, p.54.
3. Tesco plc (1994) media and handbill campaign, November.
4. Morton, N. (1994) 'Cinemas dial box-office hit', *The Independent on Sunday Business News*, 17 July, p.8; www.cognos.com/company/success/uci_uk.html and www.swallow.com/uk/pdfs/pr/toptier/UCICinemas.pdf both accessed 1 June 2001.
5. Maister, D.H. (1985) 'The psychology of waiting lines', in Czeipel, J.H., Solomon, M.R. and Surprenant, C.F. (eds) *The Service Encounter*, Lexington: D.C. Heath.
6. Davies, M.M. and Heineke, J. (1994) 'Understanding the roles of the customer and the operation for better queue management', *International Journal of Operations and Production Management*, 14(5), pp.24–31.
7. Render, B. and Heizer, J. (1994) *Principles of Operations Management*, Boston: Allyn and Bacon, p.356.
8. Mestel, R. (1998) 'Avarice', *New Scientist* 2127, 28 March; Ungar, L. (1999) 'Supermarket aisles may resemble a maze, but they're laid out with plenty of food for thought', *The News Journal*, 23 June; www.seattletimes.nwsource.com/news/lifestyles/html98/altshop_19990623.html accessed 20 June 2001.
9. Jenkins, R. (1993) 'The evolution process of the in-store bakery', *Paper No.379, Proceedings of British Society of Baking*, 76th Conference, October.
10. Hart, C. and Davies, M. (1996) 'The location and merchandising of non-food in supermarkets', *International Journal of Retail and Distribution Management*, 24(3), pp.17–25.
11. Anderson, P.M. (1985) 'Association of shopping centre anchors with performance of a non-anchor specialty chain's stores', *Journal of Retailing*, 61(2), pp.61–74.
12. I am grateful for the help given by the Thomas family in producing this case study.

CHAPTER 10

Maintenance

OBJECTIVES

When you have finished studying this chapter, you should be able to:

- Summarise terotechnology.
- Describe the patterns of failure which occur and explain the roles of FMEA and fault tree analysis in their investigation.
- Show how reliability is defined and how it changes through time; use the bath tub curve to illustrate.
- Identify different maintenance policies and suggest situations in which they may be applicable; give examples of preventive and predictive maintenance.
- Describe the main advantages of TPM in raising the availability of equipment.
- List and briefly compare repair and replacement policies.
- Explain key issues in managing the maintenance department.
- Demonstrate the contribution of the concept of maintainability to the analysis of costs-in-use.
- Outline how maintenance becomes a business and the disadvantages this may entail.

OPENING CASE

Getting to the root of a problem[1]

At an Eli Lilly pharmaceuticals plant in Indiana, an empty materials basket was being lifted from a 15-metre high storage tank. The cable holding the basket snapped without warning and the basket fell, striking the side of the tank as it did so. The tank was not ruptured and no one was hurt. Under pressure to resume work, many companies would repair the cable as quickly as possible and not investigate why the cable snapped.

At this plant, the practice is to investigate all such incidents thoroughly. Yet, the staff working around the scene had noticed nothing, apart from the breaking cable. Jeffrey Brown followed a systematic method to search for an explanation. Root cause failure analysis is based on studying five Ps. Like a good detective, Brown collected all the *parts*, including those not affected that may be related to the event. The *position* of each item of equipment at the moment of failure was recorded: this enabled him to recreate the incident. The *paper* trail meant studying the operating manual for the hoist, current inspection reports and a job risk analysis. Interviewing all operators and maintenance technicians covered the *people* aspect of the method.

▶

The last step was to evaluate the *paradigms*. These are the unchallenged assumptions, surrounding the hoist design, installation and operation. In this design, if the hoist were wound up too high, the pulley block would strike emergency switches. These would reverse the motor direction and prevent the block contacting the cable drum. The switches had never failed and everyone assumed they were not the cause of the problem. Working to challenge this paradigm, Brown examined both block and drum and found marks suggesting the two had come into contact.

Further investigation of the hoist motor showed that, if it jammed, it would produce an especially high torque strong enough to break the cable. Brown found that when the switches operated, the motor continued to turn for a moment before reversing. The reversal was not quick enough to stop the jamming. Consequently, the clearance between the pulley block and cable drum was increased to allow time for the switches to activate. Maintenance and inspection procedures were also modified.

10.1 Introduction

Often regarded as the poor brother by other functions of the business, maintenance is seen as imposing a cost that really ought to be avoided. Equipment failures or shutdowns are readily put forward as reasons why an order could not be completed or a delivery made. Yet, the perfectly reliable item of equipment has yet to be devised and, in any case, most items wear out in use. Maintenance is an essential part of the operations function and the question is not how it can be avoided but to work out and carry out effective maintenance policies that contribute to added value. Clearly, the issues go beyond sustaining output. As the opening case shows, operating equipment and practices must be safe. The good practice at Eli Lilly recognised the value of investigating all minor incidents as part of learning how to prevent major accidents. We saw in Chapter 6 how big failures are often the outcome of a series of unreported or neglected little ones.

Maintenance is mainly concerned with the physical assets of the business. Such is the growing recognition of its importance that a special branch of technology, *terotechnology*, has emerged. Its definition, following BS 3811, appears in Box 10.1.[2] It is a broad, co-ordinated approach to optimisation of costs throughout the life of an asset. Indeed, the interest goes beyond this life for, with information feedback, there is the intention to incorporate experience into the next generation of equipment. It goes looking at repair costs, for good maintenance can also prevent failure as well as offering a route to higher outputs, productivity and quality.

We can examine the maintenance question from three interrelated points of view. First, the aspect that will take up most of the chapter is terotechnology itself, the control of costs-in-use throughout the life of a physical asset. Second, since these physical assets are supplied before they are used, there is the issue of maintainability, the incorporation of best practice into design and construction so that the user is satisfied. Third, there is the way that maintenance itself

BOX 10.1 **Terotechnology defined**

A combination of management, financial, engineering, building and other practices applied to physical assets in pursuit of economic life cycle costs.

Its practice is concerned with the specification and design for reliability and maintainability of plant, machinery, equipment, buildings and structures, with their installation, commissioning, operation, maintenance, modification and replacement and with feedback of information on design, performance and costs.

becomes a business. This ranges from the small neighbourhood car repairer to specialist contractors with turnovers worth many hundreds of millions of pounds. For them, maintenance is not a tiresome burden but a major opportunity in the service sector.

The maintenance activity is concerned with preventing or responding to failure. Therefore, before we go on to compare maintenance policies we need to consider why and how assets fail. These events have consequences that can vary from a complete plant shutdown to a gradual loss of efficiency or quality of output.

10.2 Patterns of failure

We expect equipment to be reliable. To achieve this end, it should incorporate proven designs and be assembled from high-quality components using methods that have been tried and tested. Further, in cases where critical components have an uncertain, limited life, these should be duplicated following the parallel reliability ideas of Chapter 8. Finally, equipment should fail safely and, preferably, slowly.

Yet, as mentioned earlier, no item can be 100% reliable even if the amount spent on its manufacture is unlimited. In practice, capital budget restraints mean that equipment is likely to fail at some point. For a start, it is useful to distinguish differences in the scope and the rate of onset of failure. Table 10.1 gives a summary that is extended as follows.

Scope

■ *Total failure.* The asset is no longer able to perform its function. This is common in many simple machines from hair dryers to vacuum cleaners; the

Table 10.1 Modes of failure and their rates of onset: domestic vacuum cleaner

		Rates of onset	
		Gradual	*Sudden*
Failure scope	*Total*	Wear out of motor bearings	Control switch malfunction
	Partial	Fraying of beater brush bristles	Cracked handle

absence of redundancy in the design and a failure of a key component means that they will not work. Although such basic equipment fails in this way, many aspects have parallel reliability. For instance, *double insulation* means that the electrical safety function of the design does not fail.

- *Partial failure*. The asset continues to perform its function but less effectively than expected. A vacuum cleaner will function with worn beater brushes but not so well as when they are new. They can be replaced. The redundancy built into large plant, systems and networks ensures that partial failure is the common pattern. Under partial failure it may be possible to maintain a service to customers, yet sometimes at higher cost or lower quality. Transport companies reduce frequency or speed, for example.

Rates of onset

- *Gradual failure*. The deterioration in use of many items takes place in small increments. We can monitor these change, often very readily. The worn bearings will make the motor noisy; we can examine the brushes periodically. Tracking component condition is a key element in the maintenance of large plant and systems.

- *Sudden failure*. While in principle such failures may be predictable, it is not practicable to anticipate them in practice. Rather than regularly dismantle a vacuum cleaner for inspection, one would prefer to take the risk of being without it for a few days if it suddenly fails. The same is not true for facilities that are more important, where the consequences of failure are more serious. Therefore, they have regular inspection. Examples include vehicle braking systems as well as major components in many industrial plants and structures.

Exercise 10.1 Where would you place the incident at Eli Lilly into Table 10.1? Given the possible catastrophe following this sort of failure, what changes can you suggest?

As we saw in these examples, failures may result from wear in components or from damage. The latter may be the result of unrecognised weakness in the original design or assembly or from misuse. In the business setting, the sensitivity of much equipment to failure from misuse means that it is important to involve everyone in the checking, reporting and maintenance of the equipment that they use. This is a feature of total productive maintenance (TPM), discussed later in the chapter.

Many physical assets are indeed complex systems with many components. They can fail in many ways and these events can have different consequences. A component failure may result in one of the following conditions:

- *Fail-safe*. The equipment or system is shut down or run to a safe state, preferably in an orderly manner. This is the case when electrical systems fail and trip circuit breakers. Railway signals switch to red if there is a communication failure and train brakes are applied if key system components are damaged.

- *Fail-soft*. The equipment functions partially. Automatic controls may have failed so that continued operation is dependent on human intervention.

Passenger aircraft have multiple engines so they should be able to remain airborne if one is shut down.

■ *Fail-run.* Under fail-run conditions, equipment continues to operate almost normally. While sounding dangerous at first sight, fail-run is the desirable mode in systems where the consequences of a shutdown can themselves be dangerous or inconvenient. Water supply is an example. A burst pipe does not cause a complete shutdown.

These three results can exist in the same plant, depending on the equipment. Because of their complexity and the critical nature of many assets, a formal study of failure is a first step in the creation of a maintenance plan for the different sections. Such studies are known as failure mode and effect analysis (FMEA).

10.2.1 Failure mode and effect analysis

In complex systems where failures may result in safety risks or financial losses, FMEA is used at all stages of the life of equipment from design through operations and improvements. It addresses the question: What could the consequences be for the system because of a failure of a component? This is a detailed approach that starts from a definition of a system, its components and how they work. Each is then studied to see the ways in which it can fail. A gas valve, for example, can fail in both the fully closed and fully open positions as well as many between. Electrical wiring can suffer breakage and loss of current flow or insulation failure and leakage to earth. These are all failures but the modes differ.

Looking more closely, for each *failure mode* there may be more than one *failure mechanism*. For example, the gas valve stuck in the closed position may be the result of damage to any part of the control mechanism as well as seizure of the valve components themselves. By studying such possibilities in details, specialists build to a better understanding of the risk of each failure mode occurring.

Having studied the ways in which components fail and assessed the expected frequencies of these events, FMEA goes on to examine *failure effects*. In some designs with little redundancy, one malfunction will lead to system failure. In others, however, the outcome will require deeper investigation since the effect of one component going down will depend upon the state of others. The fault tree helps with this analysis.

The last step in the analysis forms the lead-in to maintenance planning. It identifies means by which failures can be detected, either in advance or in sufficient time after occurrence to relieve the failure effects noted previously. Maintenance planning begins by noting corrective action, either to be taken at the time of a fault or to reduce the frequency of breakdowns. In conducting FMEA, engineers use standard forms along the lines of Table 10.2.

Quantification of the FMEA approach is widely adopted. Safety engineers work on risk assessment of complex systems such as oil platforms and compare different designs and operating procedures using quantitative measures. These data are needed not only by operators but also by regulators and insurance assessors. Muhlemann *et al.*[3] propose an extension to FMEA which they call failure mode, effect and criticality analysis. Their *criticality index* is a product of rating indices given for probability of occurrence, severity of failure and difficulty of detection.

Table 10.2 FMEA: illustration of space heating boiler controls

Item	Failure mode	Failure mechanism	Failure effect	Failure detection	Corrective/ preventive action
Space thermostat – T101	Fail closed	Breaker points welded Springs failed Insulation damage in capacitor	Space overheats – waste of energy	Discomfort of occupants	Manual override until replacement
	Fail open	Connections open circuit Thermometer worn out	Space not heated	Discomfort of occupants	Immediate repair
Boiler thermostat – T102	Fail closed	Breaker points jammed Capacitor insulation	Boiler fails to cut out	Alarm – A41	Duplicate thermostat with indicator Immediate manual shutdown
	Fail open	Connections open circuit Thermometer worn out	Boiler does not cut in	Discomfort of occupants	Immediate repair
Alarm – A41	Fails to operate	Faulty installation Disturbed during maintenance Wiring failure	Failure of T102 and gas valve not detected	Unlikely during service	Regular testing and shutdown if fault detected

They would add columns to Table 10.2 to include assessments and index calculations. Harris and Ramsey[4] show how London Underground Ltd estimates the impact of failures of different parts of its system using a generalised cost equation common in public transport modelling. The social cost, from the passengers' point of view comprises a combination of price and time spent. Each element of time is weighted with a different constant. The equation has the form:

$$\textit{Generalised cost} = \textit{Fare} + b_1 \times \textit{Access time} + b_2 \times \textit{Waiting time} + b_3 \times \textit{Running time}$$

To this value can be added changes in operating revenue and cost because of diversions and so on.

While quantification has the advantage of setting out an agenda of issues and giving estimates of the impact of different events, there is a danger of placing too much reliance on the total scores. These depend largely on the choice of weighting factors applied to the equation components. For example, in the social cost case it is assumed that passengers regard increased travel time in a negative light and would assign notional costs to this time. Further, it is supposed that different values are placed on each minute depending on whether it is spent actually on the move, reaching a stop or waiting for the service. Since, for example, I read on the train but not when standing in the underground, time spent in transit is less of a loss to me than time spent waiting. Similar difficulties apply to all factor-weighted models, such as those covering location decisions in Chapter 8.

10.2.2 **Fault trees**

Studies of component breakdown would be incomplete without consideration of the interaction among them in the development of a failure. For instance, while it is difficult to forecast and prevent the occasional puncture in a car tyre, its impact can be lessened by carrying a spare. Strictly, one should also say that the following are required:

A spare wheel AND ((tools AND strength AND skill to use them) OR (roadside assistance))

Failure effects, then, are conditional on combinations of circumstances. Representing all but the simplest relationships in a formula such as the last is very complicated. A fault tree makes it much easier. Figure 10.1 is based on the mains supply to a hospital.[5] It models the causes of the undesired event, known as the top event: *No power on the 415V line*. In this case, it is represented by an *and gate 415VLIN*. The *and* indicates that the failure will occur if both the grid *and* the generator fail.

Generator failure is represented by an *or* gate, meaning that just one of the lower events is enough. The switch to disconnect the main supply may not work; *or* another switch may not cut in the generator, *or* the latter may not deliver power. Eventually, we reach root causes at the boundary of our study. Applying data on the frequency of failure of all the elements in the model allows the engineer to answer the following questions:

1 How safe are the operations?

2 Where are the weaknesses in the system?

3 How often will the system fail?

4 If it fails, for how long will it be out of service?

Exercise 10.2   Sketch a fault tree for the hoist in the opening case study.

10.2.3 **Reliability through time**

In Chapter 8, we defined reliability as a measure of the probability that an item survives a given time. We can express this as:

$$R_t = \frac{Number\ surviving\ until\ time\ t}{Number\ existing\ at\ time\ t = 0}$$

Failure is the complement of this measure, expressed as:

$$F_t = \frac{Number\ failing\ before\ time\ t}{Number\ existing\ at\ time\ t = 0}; \text{ so that } F_t = 1 - R_t$$

Existing equipment

In studying failures of existing equipment, we are less interested in the overall expected failure rate from the start of the equipment's life and more in what is likely to happen in the future. This parallels the recognition that, on average, a

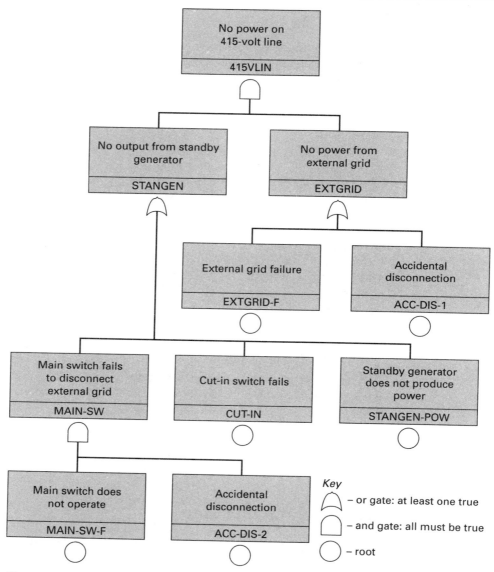

Figure 10.1 Fault tree for generator failure

person aged 50 is expected to live to a greater age than one aged 10. This is because the adult has already survived the risks and hazards associated with the intervening 40 years. As a practical measure of *current* failure risk, then, the *failure rate* is calculated as:

$$f_t = \frac{Number\ failing\ per\ unit\ time\ at\ time\ t}{Number\ existing\ at\ time\ t}$$

Here, reliability and failure rates have been expressed as ratios; for single items of equipment, they can be represented as probabilities. For instance, the failure rate is simply the probability of failure in unit time.

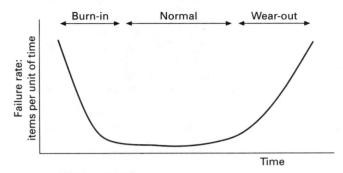

Figure 10.2 Bath tub curve

Risks of breakdown

Lastly, risks of breakdown are sometimes expressed in terms of the *mean time between failures* (MTBF). This helps the maintenance manager in planning how much attention needs to be given to each item. This is the reciprocal of the failure rate, so that:

$$MTBF_t = \frac{1}{f_t}$$

If we measure the failure rate in hazards per day, then the MTBF is the number of days between hazards. From its distinctive shape, a graph of a typical breakdown rate is known as the *bath tub curve* (see Figure 10.2). It shows three distinct phases:

- *Burn-in or infant phase.* Manufacturing, assembly, transport or installation defects become apparent early in the life of a product. Commissioning work on new installations concentrates on eliminating defects quickly. Vehicles have a running-in period and short service intervals during their infancy. Producers of items such as electronic equipment run them on test benches for a few hours to ensure that the burn-in phase has passed.

- *Normal or adult phase.* After the initial burn-in, the failure probability remains low as the equipment works through its designed life. If it is properly maintained at regular intervals, and not misused, the MTBF can be a high, and constant, figure.

- *Wear-out or aged phase.* The equipment moves towards the end of its designed life. Rejuvenation by replacing key items is possible but often expensive. The failure risk increases as one or another component reaches the end of its life.

While the three bath tub phases are seen in the lives of many items from simple machines to buildings, some have small or nonexistent burn-in and wear-out periods.

Car manufacturers used to stipulate speed maxima during the early life of their products to allow engines to run in. Many drivers ignored such restraints, especially as the consequences did not show up until much later in the engine's life. Most manufacturers now produce engines to such fine limits that running-in is unnecessary. Early-life service costs are lower.

Electronic components often show a high initial failure rate followed by a very long normal life with very few malfunctions. When servicing such systems, replacing electronic components runs the risk of moving back into the burn-in phase. Domestic electronic equipment usually breaks down through the loss of electro-mechanical ancillary items such as switches, tape transport mechanisms and sliding resistors. The solid-state components become obsolete before failure.

Having examined relevant properties of components and systems, we can apply our knowledge to investigate maintenance policies.

10.3 Maintenance policies

In the business organisation, maintenance supports the operating function by responding to demands to keep facilities in working order. The increasing trend towards lean production, operating just-in-time with very low buffer stocks at all stages, means that the unplanned shutdown of many assets can have significant effects. The asset may be a vehicle, ship, plant, small machine or personal computer. Maintenance underpins operational efficiency.

Maintenance policy, therefore, should be integrated with operational policy. Gits[6] expresses the closeness of this relationship by means of the diagram shown in Figure 10.3. There is an immediate feedback loop between the two activities. Demand for maintenance is one of the outputs of the operations transformation system. Therefore, choosing the maintenance capacity is part of the strategic decision about operating capacity. The maintenance function is thus part of the whole operations team. For instance, when the RAF supplies the United Nations with a fleet of helicopters for peace keeping, each requires 13 people to keep it operating; the maintenance staff cannot be considered as an afterthought to the supply of the helicopters and flying crew.

Maintenance supplies the operations system with its planned capacity. This statement suggests two main areas for policy making:

- *Reducing the failure frequency.* This can be achieved through ensuring correct installation of suitable equipment, preventive maintenance and replacement of items as they move into their wear-out phase.

- *Reducing the impact of failures.* To relieve the effect of operations of a component being out of service, approaches will include the provision of parallel

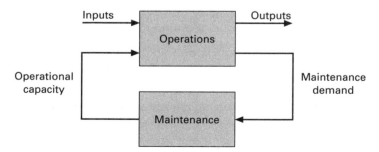

Figure 10.3 Operations and maintenance

capacity at key points and organising the maintenance activity to minimise repair times for critical items.

The criterion for choice should be the effect on the value offered by the operations function. We will return to this question of optimisation in Section 10.3.2 but first we should look at the different types of maintenance that are practised.

10.3.1 Types of maintenance

While a simple business may approach its maintenance in an unplanned way, it is unlikely to avoid problems once it begins to use buildings, vehicles and equipment of any substance. Maintenance policies can be grouped into two broad categories:[7]

- *Run to breakdown.* This may be the rational course in cases where failure is unpredictable, its consequences are minor and equipment is readily replaced. Within such an unplanned policy, there are two ways to respond. *Emergency* action is called for if there is a breakdown with potentially serious effects. It means immediate intervention. *Corrective* action, however, may be delayed. It involves routine work to be done within the near future; yet, there is no urgent operational demand.

- *Preventive.* This work is done on a planned basis. The service intervals are determined by experience, by manufacturers or, in the case of equipment such as aircraft or power stations, by external authorities. Preventive maintenance forestalls failure and reverses the gradual degradation caused by wear in equipment components. Continuous painting of the Forth Bridge is a famous example of structural preventive maintenance intended to stave off high repair costs in the future. For fixed plant, experience shows the value of regular shut downs for inspection. Vehicles have to be tested at least once a year with maintenance conditional on the results. *Diagnostic* or *predictive* maintenance is an alternative approach to prevention. It is based not on predetermined service intervals but on the condition of the equipment. Hence, an important part of the maintenance function is monitoring and inspection. This is vital for items expensive to replace.

It is also useful to distinguish when maintenance is carried out in the operations cycle. In many cases, *running maintenance* is done while assets are performing their functions. In others, *shutdown maintenance* is necessary for safety or other practical reasons. Finally, three levels of action can be distinguished. The first is *servicing*, the replacement of components consumed during use. Examples are printer cartridges, engine oil, air and fuel filters and lamps of all kinds. *Repair* action is the restoration of assets to an acceptable standard by repairing or renewing worn or damaged components. Changing worn or stiff bearings or seals in gearboxes are instances of repair. *Overhaul* refers to the comprehensive inspection and repair of assets to bring them up to the acceptable standard. It includes a detailed search for signs of wear that would not be noticed when the item is in service.

The relationships among the different categories introduced here are summarised in Figure 10.4. It is based on a Department of Industry model given by

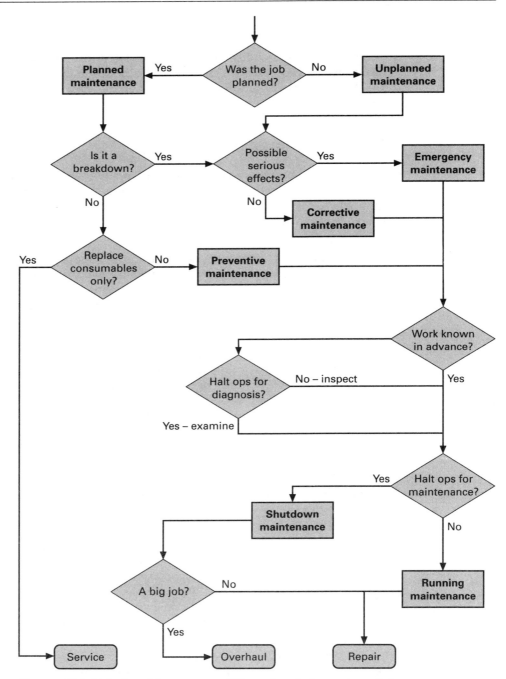

Figure 10.4 Relationships among different maintenance policies

Hill.[8] The model distinguishes between planned and unplanned policies yet recognises that breakdowns occur even though planned maintenance is in place. Preventive maintenance in the diagram includes the diagnostic approach mentioned earlier. The two are similar in intention but the latter is based on active monitoring of equipment and using the results as the basis of the planned actions.

An operations facility may combine the policies set out earlier. Items used intermittently, not critical and readily repaired can be attended to in an unplanned way. In contrast, when items are critical and repairs are expensive, planned maintenance is called for. There must be sufficient knowledge of failure modes and their corresponding rates as in the bath tub curve to support preventive maintenance. Thus, if the variation in expected life of an asset were low, a simple policy of disposal just before the life has expired would be effective.

10.3.2 Preventive maintenance

Introducing a preventive maintenance programme can be difficult. Since the policy aims to cut the number of events that are the traditional bread and butter or repair shops, there is the danger that, with few breakdowns, the repair function begins to be seen as an expensive luxury. Much preventive work, especially inspection, can appear to have no output. It is also difficult to get users to accept that inspection and service intervals cannot be extended. This is compounded by pressure from operations: 'If it ain't broke, don't fix it.'

A valuable test of the usefulness of preventive maintenance is to examine how it influences the total costs associated with the operations-maintenance subsystem of the business. These costs have three components:

- Costs associated with the preventive or predictive maintenance itself. These clearly increase as the effort devoted to prevention expands.

- Costs of emergency and corrective maintenance. These will fall under a planned maintenance programme but in a non-linear way. Since it will be applied to the easiest items first, a little preventive maintenance will bring the greatest benefits.

- Costs associated with lost output. Again, these will fall as more planned maintenance is introduced. Not only will the repair downtime be cut but also much will take place at off-peak periods to minimise disruption.

Figure 10.5 sketches the pattern of these costs to show that there may be an optimal mix of breakdown and planned maintenance where total costs are minimised. Some assets are best treated in one way while others are treated the opposite. In principle, each asset's maintenance requirements should be assessed. Various algorithms have been suggested for the decision. Osborne and Taj[9] propose a procedure, shown in Figure 10.6, for use with machines in high-volume operations. We can see that the algorithm establishes key points of interaction, namely periodic need, shutdown, time savings and range of components. The authors are particularly concerned with the integration of maintenance into manufacturing schedules and with the coupling of components that need repair or replacement. Thus, if a machine is taken out of service for the repair of one component, it can be worth giving attention to other parts although they have

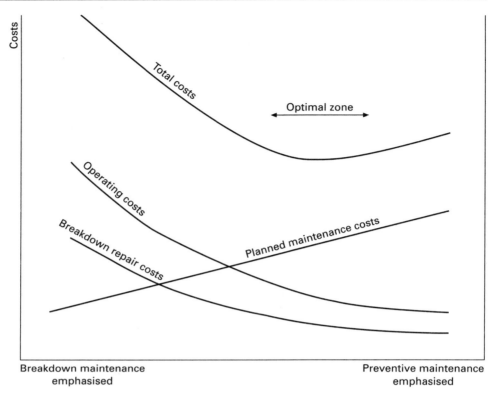

Figure 10.5 Cost variations depending on maintenance policy

not reached the end of their useful lives. Osborne and Taj report examples of poor practice:[10]

> While machinery was down for scheduled PM, the workers did not replace many of the inexpensive components that may reach failure in just a short time. When a component had yet to reach its prescribed useful life, it was left in the machine even when a component adjacent to it was replaced. Components costing just a few cents were preserved in the machine, sometimes costing hundreds of dollars in lost production in replacing them later.

The comparison is between the value remaining within the partly used component and the cost of having to stop the machine again to repair it in the future. A practical example is in car servicing. When a worn clutch plate is replaced, it is normal to replace the clutch release bearing irrespective of its condition. The item is cheap compared with the cost of having to strip down the car for further work in the future. Such ideas point the way towards practical benefits from planned maintenance. Similar ideas arise in many other operational settings.

10.3.3 Preventive maintenance in practice

Preventive maintenance, in its basic form, is founded on statistical analysis of an asset and its component parts. These data are obtainable from several sources.

For each repair need of the
machine (or system) . . .

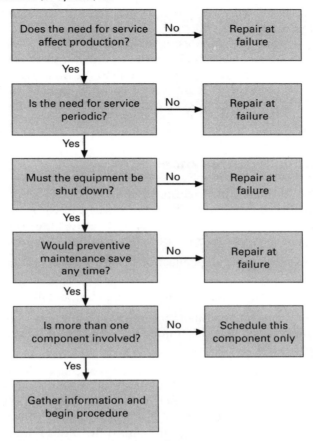

Figure 10.6 Algorithm for breakdown – preventive choice

Initially, they are available from equipment suppliers who propose, in the light
of their own experience, values of MTBF for major components. Preventive maintenance is suited to parts that follow the bath tub curve into the wear-out phase.
In other words, they experience mechanical wear or fatigue correlated with use.
As an operator develops experience in the use of assets in the local circumstances,
maintenance plans can build on internal databases. In this way, operators of
fleets of vehicles, such as buses, refine manufacturers' recommendations according to experience. Furthermore, in some industries, manufacturers are involved
with customers throughout the life of a product. This happens in aviation. Since
safety is such an important requirement, regulators require aircraft manufacturers
and users to share maintenance records. Patterns of common faults can then be
discovered.

Maintenance intervals are based on use or time. For many machines, deterioration is dependent on use, often measured in number of times used, running
hours or kilometres travelled. It is common to fit critical items of equipment with
meters or recorders to collect the data. In other cases, deterioration follows the

elapse of time. For instance, building and grounds maintenance follow the calendar intervals. Frequently the two policies are combined: installations such as railway tracks, cable ways, pipelines and roads deteriorate both through weight of use and weathering.

Preventive maintenance using estimates of MTBF is valuable to the smaller business that is unable to build up the record base of the large user. Replacement on a conservative basis may be preferable to the high costs associated with breakdown. For the heavy user, by way of contrast, unnecessarily early replacement will result in excessive costs. Predictive maintenance comes to the fore in these cases.

10.3.4 **Predictive maintenance**

Predictive, or diagnostic, maintenance is important where there is uncertainty over time between failures. This can be where there is no known expected life or where there is significant uncertainty over this life. Then it is better to use a diagnostic policy. The keys to predictive maintenance are:

- the possibility of regular collection of information on defined properties of the system
- effective linking of this information to potential failures.

Data for diagnostic maintenance need to be low cost, compared with the value of the components being examined and the cost of breakdown. They are available from several sources:

- *Inspection.* Regular checks carried out by operators or maintenance staff. Preferably, these checks are made without interrupting operations, either while in service or at normal breaks such as tool changing, end of trip turnarounds and so on. The length and detail of tests vary from the single hammer blow of the wheel tapper walking along the train to the ultrasonic weld tests (scanning of joints) of the nuclear inspectorate. Good equipment design includes ease of access for inspection.

- *Performance monitoring.* As we will see in Chapter 15, statistical control systems monitor process outputs and highlight variations in quality. Trends in product properties can reveal needs for equipment servicing or overhaul.

- *Built-in diagnostic systems.* Many items of equipment have built-in diagnostic devices. Depending on their level of sophistication, these indicate either simple warnings or full details of the state of internal components. The ignition or oil pressure warning lights in popular cars are examples of the former while we see the latter in the more complex engine systems of Formula 1 racers. Their on-board computers pass data on many parameters to the pits. These data are valuable during development testing but are also useful during a race in planning pit stops.

- *Indirect diagnosis.* There have been many developments in the field of indirect diagnosis in recent years. They are analogous to diagnostic practice in medicine where doctors use equipment from stethoscopes to scanners to assess patients' state of health. Two examples, which are both non-intrusive and provide good predictions at low cost, are given in Box 10.2.

BOX 10.2 **Examples of non-intrusive diagnosis**

Motor current signature analysis

Detailed analysis of the current taken by electric motors shows small changes in the waveform through time. It is as though each motor develops its personal 'signature' which it imposes on the basic alternating current. These changes can be associated with bearing wear and other variations in operating conditions. MCSA has been applied in nuclear plant where motors for items such as cooling fans can be difficult to reach.[11]

Lubricating oil diagnosis

Up to 80% of machine failures can be blamed on insufficient or excess lubrication or using the wrong type. A survey of 300 UK manufacturers showed how predictive maintenance was the most effective of the techniques used to maintain availability of machinery.

Texchek was set up by Texaco to run its oil diagnostic service. In one case, a manufacturer decided to recycle the cutting fluids used in its machine tools. The surface quality of the products deteriorated and Texchek pinned the responsibility on unfiltered contaminants.

Lubricating oil contains a history of wear. Applications include engines and gearboxes in trucks and buses, paper mills, mining, power stations and construction plant. Not only is the user interested in when to change lubricating oil – basing this on condition rather than on a predetermined period – but details of the content can provide information on plant condition.

Customers send regular samples to the Texchek laboratory at Stoke-on-Trent. Automated lines carry out tests for:

- *Metal content.* Minute particles of worn metal from bearings accumulate in the oil. Their formulations are compared with known bearing materials to establish their source.
- *Carbon content.* The build-up of soot in the oil originates as it burns on the sides of valves, pistons and cylinders and leaks past sealing rings.
- *Water content.* Water should not be present in lubricating oil. Small quantities may leak from cooling systems.
- *Fuel.* Fuel should not be present. It may indicate leakage or incomplete combustion in one section of the engine.
- *Viscosity.* The 'thickness' of the oil is a measure of its effectiveness and monitoring this property will indicate when the lubricant is reaching the end of its useful life.

Each set of test results is compared with trends and reported to clients. Any unanticipated change, indicating the imminent onset of failure, generates an urgent communication.[12]

Many examples of maintenance involve combinations of preventive and predictive approaches, the latter using a variety of data sources. Table 10.3 shows an extract from the schedule for a family car. Since the average user cannot diagnose engine oil quality, planned maintenance recommends a change of oil and filter every 10,000km. This interval is shortened for harsher, dusty conditions. Other items require an inspection at regular intervals and replacement if necessary.

Table 10.3 Extract from maintenance schedule for typical passenger car

Number of kilometres (in thousands)	1	10	20	30	40	50
Check torque of cylinder head bolts, exhaust and carburettor nuts, manifolds	x					
Adjust valve clearances	x		x		x	
Check drive belts for wear, fraying etc.	x		x		x	
Change engine oil[a]		x	x	x	x	x
Change engine oil filter[a]		x	x	x	x	x
Replace fuel filter					x	
Distributor points – check	x		x		x	
Distributor points – replace		x		x		x
Check brake linings, drums, etc. for wear[b]			x		x	

Notes

(a) Change oil and filter every 5,000km if: driving mainly short distances; city driving; driving in dusty conditions

(b) When driving in salty or other corrosive conditions, check every 10,000km or 6 months, whichever comes earlier

Note also the first service after 1,000km. This is to diagnose faults during running-in, that is during the burn-in phase.

The philosophy of integrating maintenance more closely with the productive process also applies to prevention. For instance, many parts of steam locomotives used to be given running attention by the driver. He took charge of tasks from replenishing supplies of oil to feeling the state of bearings. Only very few locomotives were fitted with any electrical device at all so there was a tradition of a close monitoring relationship between the operator and the machine. The coming of electric machinery running at high speed severed such links in many industries and the operators lost their commitment to maintenance. This became a specialised, technical activity somewhat remote from the operators. Osborne and Taj argue that there has been an overemphasis on seeing planned maintenance as an exercise in data gathering and implementation:

> The dynamic nature of all maintenance, and the large number of machines that must have maintenance programmed, necessitates that the majority of scheduling for PM be done by those close to the actual work. Supervisors, foremen and skilled trades leaders will do much of the day-to-day scheduling of preventive maintenance. Only a decision making process that can be used and interpreted by these people can have any real chance of being applied in the typical workplace.[13]

While these concerns are expressed here in terms of the hierarchy of those who should be involved, they do represent a return to recognising the operator–machine link. The emergence of total productive maintenance has revived interest in this link.

10.3.5 Total productive maintenance

TPM is an approach involving all employees from the shop floor to top managers. It is based on the notion of teamwork. Those who carry out operations are encouraged to control quality, change tools and do some equipment maintenance. In many cases, operator awareness is an excellent form of diagnosis and can lead to successful early intervention. Operators are aware of minor faults, unsuitable operating conditions, defective procedures and lapses in the regular attention required by preventive maintenance schedules.

According to Nakajima, TPM surfaced in Japan during the 1970s.[14] The notion of preventive maintenance had arrived from the west in the 1950s, followed by productive maintenance in the 1960s. TPM took these ideas and adapted them to the Japanese industrial situation. This unique working environment included a strong emphasis on cooperation with employees unconcerned with job categories. Consequently, when the idea of all employees participating in the development of maintenance policies and practice was put forward, it was readily accepted. At Toyota Motor Corporation, TPM developed alongside new production and quality systems. The company saw that none would be effective without the others.

At Land Rover, introduction of TPM was marred in its early implementation by two factors. First was the rapid introduction on too many machines, including several that were not critical to the production process. Second, operators were not involved in the choice of what to do. The company overcame these problems when it placed responsibility for its implementation within production (supported by maintenance) and integrated TPM within the quality strategy. The practice spread to other plants within the group with the accent on continuous improvement through incremental change.[15]

A TPM programme builds incrementally. Successful installations have been in those companies who are already carrying out basic preventive maintenance and trying to integrate it more closely with the production system. TPM aims to achieve zero breakdowns and zero defects through integration with other approaches to operations excellence, namely total quality management, quality circles, continuous improvement and just-in-time.[16] The programme starts with common sense switches of responsibility, for example for routine maintenance tasks that do not require much skill or training. These encompass cleaning, lubrication, inspection and minor adjustments. Unfortunately, even some limited applications have led to regressive steps, including:

- converting skilled maintenance staff into routine machine operators
- shifting line authority for maintenance crews to production managers
- pushing TPM as a means to reduce the apparent overhead of the maintenance department
- applying TPM principally to reduce maintenance costs.[17]

Taking the short-term perspective embodied in these points, the effect of TPM is to transfer a few tasks that seem costly when carried out by skilled workers into the hands of cheaper workers. Without training and further development, the advantages of having an experienced eye regularly look over equipment are lost. Maggard and Rhyne,[18] however, give a more favourable view when explaining how TPM was successfully put in place at Tennessee Eastman (see Box 10.3).

TPM problems

TPM, then, is preventive maintenance in which all employees participate. Operators are responsible for routine adjustments and repairs. It does work, however, without changes in attitudes towards responsibility. TPM tries to break

BOX 10.3 TPM at Tennessee Eastman Kodak

The need

The process plant produces a wide range of polymers on a scattered, 1,800 ha site. Maintenance, carried out by 1,200 personnel, was seen to be operating satisfactorily overall with formal procedures in place. Yet, as the plant implemented its total quality management programme, it was clear at shop floor level that maintenance support was not as good as it should have been. For instance, formal requests for work to be done often had to pass through many hands and organisational levels to gain approval. At a minimum, they involved an operator, supervisors for both production and maintenance and the skilled mechanic who actually performed the task. In addition, machine operators felt little sense of ownership of the equipment and the repair staff little sense of urgency to cut repair times.

Studies

It was found that 40% of conventional maintenance work could be done, with minimal training, by another employee. A further 40% required extra training, yet still not up to the competence level of the skilled mechanics. Therefore, a large element of task responsibility could pass from mechanics to operators. The company saw that TPM should be more than this. Each group should be trained in the other's activities. The operators can do much more maintenance, sufficient for them to assume 'ownership' of the equipment. Further, the mechanics can be trained in operations to help with prevention and make repairs easier.

Planning

The change to TPM was a major project with a leader, steering group, organisation, office and so on. Managers and team leaders received training in the principles. Selection of work areas followed 'opportunity audits' to assess current operations and maintenance according to: improvement potential; readiness for change; interest among the staff in a new approach; and whether visible success would have effects elsewhere. Goals and rewards were established. The former covered scope, costs, extension of TPM and detailed measures such as machine availability. Recognition events for successful work groups ranged from lunches and celebrations to managers giving written and oral praise and even washing employees' cars.

Results

After four years, there were 120 functioning TPM teams with over 85% of the 5,000 staff participating. Productivity rose, the annual benefits being estimated at $8 million. Failures of critical equipment fell, sometimes dramatically. In one year, a rise in availability of 1%–2% was attributed to TPM. Several serious failure incidents were avoided by timely operator intervention. Management estimated a pay-back period of six months for the project investment.

down traditional rivalry between maintenance crews and operators in which each attempts to protect its narrow interests. From a study of four companies in north-west England, Cooke identified entrenched departmental barriers and shop floor resistance as critical problems. In all cases, the use of skilled maintenance workers on simple tasks was inefficient. Lack of senior management support, through both tolerating resistance and providing little financial support for change, was a common theme.[19]

10.3.6 Repair and replacement

Whatever maintenance policy is adopted, the question of repair or replacement of components eventually arises. It is best to replace low-cost items whenever it is convenient to do so. For more expensive items, the question is more difficult. This is because of difficulties of estimating the remaining life of an asset after repair together with further costs in use. These costs should be compared with the cost of replacement by new equipment combined with associated operating costs and changes in productivity and quality.

Some items are replaced regularly. When a business has to maintain a group of such items in working order, it faces several choices:

- replace items when they fail
- replace failed items at predetermined intervals
- replace all items at predetermined intervals
- replace failed items when they fail and all items at predetermined intervals.

While at first sight some of these alternatives may be rejected, their selection depends on the operating situation. Factors include:

- *The bath tub curve for the items.* Many electronic components have an indefinite normal life after relatively high failure during burn-in. Replacement of items before they develop faults would only increase the average failure rate. Fixed interval replacement is preferable when the variation in expected life is small.
- *Costs of the replacement activity.* Difficulties of access mean that special equipment has to be used and processes interrupted. Thus, the cost of replacing a group of items hardly differs from the cost of replacing one. Light bulbs on a tall mast or along the centre of a motorway are cases in point.
- *Tolerance of failure.* Often a component is critical to an operational process and needs to be attended to immediately. In other cases, action could be delayed until a convenient break or until a defined proportion of items are out of service. Blackpool Illuminations is a fail-soft system in which odd failed lamps are not attended to.
- *Item costs.* As already indicated, items whose value is low compared with maintenance and associated lost output costs should be replaced more frequently.

10.3.7 The maintenance function

Since the function should be a cost-effective supplier of operations productivity, maintenance is a *flexible service* operation, as in Figure 1.7. Applying Figure 3.1 suggests that maintenance delivers *professional service*; it is an individualised service delivered in the presence of the customer, the operations department. In emergencies, it should offer the *instant* service of Figure 1.8. Like all stand-by resources, managers face internal inefficiencies caused by excess capacity. This can be filled by non-essential maintenance work.

Figure 3.1 and the earlier discussion point towards improving the efficiency of the department. Among possibilities are:

- *Isolation.* Separating maintenance service activity from operations turns activities into *isolated service.* This can be done through *unitisation* in which large components or subsystems of equipment can be quickly exchanged with service replacements. The faulty units are then taken away for overhaul. This policy works with many electronic components such as telephone exchange equipment, aircraft engines and motor vehicle tyres. Gains arise when the cost of obtaining and carrying spare components is lower than the lost output when repairs take place on the job.

  As we have seen, isolation is also achievable through planning. Planned maintenance enables servicing at off-peak times or when equipment is not in use.

- *Standardisation.* Standardisation, of both equipment and repair procedures, enables scale advantages to be obtained. Among other benefits are ease of training and development of staff together with limitation of the range of spares and special equipment that needs to be carried. Replacing a whole group of items after a specified interval is an example of standardised activity.

- *Detachment.* The discussion of TPM has picked out the possibility of operators doing routine maintenance on a self-service basis.

Such policies can be included in maintenance planning. While retaining the capability of responding to any sort of urgent repair request, good planning should ensure a significant proportion of non-urgent work. In this way, the department maintains a satisfactory level of internal efficiency.

Subcontracting

Subcontracting is an option taken up increasingly. Subcontractors will be favoured when some of the following factors apply:

- a need for specialist equipment
- a need for special technical knowledge
- regulations or policies require external supervision or certification
- internal costs are too high
- a special service is required at irregular intervals.

Exercise 10.3

Many firms use subcontractors for at least some of their maintenance work. Examples range from telephones to toilets and lifts to landscape gardening. Assess how far these items match the list we have just examined.

By the same token, many prefer to keep regular service operations in-house. This helps with co-ordination, especially within a TPM context. When a business buys new equipment, it will commonly rely on the suppliers' service engineers, especially during the warranty period. Then it will develop its own skills through courses, documentation and on-the-job coaching.

10.3.8 Modelling the maintenance function

As suggested in the previous section, general models of service activities are also applicable to maintenance. Techniques include Monte Carlo simulation to compare, for example, different patterns of resource deployment, the use of subcontractors, the number of spare items of equipment required and so on. The service element also suggests that queues are important.

The queuing models presented in Chapter 9 used assumptions that arrivals for service were drawn from an infinite population. Maintenance situations commonly do not satisfy this criterion. The number of machines, ships, cranes or computers is limited. The arrival rate is now *dependent* on the length of the queue. To take an extreme case, if all of Britain's four nuclear submarines were at their Faslane base simultaneously, then the arrival rate would fall to zero!

Calculating queue lengths and waiting times in such situations is beyond our scope; data appear in tables.[20] Figure 10.7, however, gives an example of an operator with five machines. The choice is whether to have one or two repair teams available to service them. The graph relates the average number of machines available for operations to the *service factor*. This is a measure of the amount of service each machine needs:

$$\text{Service factor} = \frac{\text{Mean service time}}{\text{Mean service time} + \text{Mean running time between service}}$$

It can be seen that, where machines have a high interval between maintenance (a low service factor), little improvement in availability comes from the extra service team. However, the data for higher service factors show a widening performance gap.

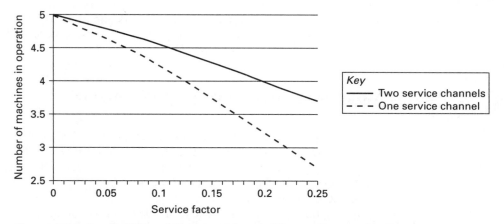

Figure 10.7 Availability of five machines with varying service factors

BOX 10.4 **Aircraft battle damage repairs**

In peacetime, aircraft are repaired to very high standards before being returned to operations. In war, however, the standards are not the same: the aircraft are repaired only to achieve the next mission.

Having defined the tasks and standards, the computer simulation takes aircraft and teams through the processes related to each sortie. These are pre-flight inspection, take-off, transit to and from the target, post-flight inspection, repair of battle damage and other faults. The relationship between aircraft and BDRs is one of a single queue to multiple servers. The post-flight inspection places at the head of the queue those aircraft needing the shortest service.

The results establish the optimal number of BDRs per base. Having more teams increases the number of sorties that could be generated, but each extra team brings a declining advantage. Further work is done on dispersed landing grounds, such as used for the Harrier GR3. This means dispersal of the servers, the BDRs. The problem became one of multiple queues to multiple servers.

The combination of computer simulation and queuing theory has been applied to the planning and development of maintenance systems. Moffat[21] reported a study of the maintenance of aircraft in war conditions (see Box 10.4).

Modern wars have taught that the ability to repair returned aircraft after a mission makes an important contribution to winning. With little recent practical experience, the RAF uses detailed computer models to represent engagements and simulate the sort of damage that might be sustained. This in turn produces data on repairs possible in the field. Since they are highly unpredictable, battle damage repair (BDR) teams are trained to deal with the wide variety of problems.

Exercise 10.4 Compare the availability among five operational helicopters if there are one or two BDR teams. The mean service time is one hour and the flying time four hours. How many teams would be needed if the flying time were nine hours?

10.3.9 Monitoring maintenance performance

For many organisations, the cost of maintenance is a significant fraction of total costs. Control is needed to ensure that the department adds value to the business through delivering productive and reliable assets. Performance ratios are convenient ways of assessing performance and comparing it with benchmarks. These can be drawn from industry standards or the experience of other divisions within a group. We shall use the example of a bus operator, studying accounting ratios, operating ratios and then performance within the maintenance garage itself.

Accounting ratios

One simple assessment is to relate maintenance costs to total costs or to sales revenue. Further analysis examines four components:

$$\frac{Labour\ costs}{Revenue}; \frac{Materials\ costs}{Revenue}; \frac{Overhead\ costs}{Revenue}; \frac{Subcontract\ costs}{Revenue}$$

Operating ratios

These evaluate the efficiency and effectiveness of the department compared with its objectives. From the point of view of minimising breakdowns, the MTBF (mean time between failures) gives a good indication of the *quality* of the work. Since in-service failures hinder good relations with customers, measuring the response times for such incidents is also important.

Availability ratios assess the contribution to capital productivity through having the fleet available for running. For instance:

$$Availability = \frac{Time\ vehicle\ available\ for\ use}{Time\ vehicle\ available\ for\ use + Time\ awaiting\ and\ undergoing\ maintenance}$$

This ratio has to be used with care. Having buses available at midnight does not contribute to covering the evening peak.

With fuel costs running at some 10% of the total, managers should take note of consumption of fuel and other factors. Industry practice compares these and other measures to vehicle movement:

$$\frac{Fuel\ consumption}{Vehicle\text{–}km}; \frac{Consumables}{Vehicle\text{–}km}; \frac{Maintenance\ costs}{Vehicle\text{–}km}$$

These data give a picture of departmental performance and also, when looked at in detail, of each vehicle in the fleet.

Departmental ratios

Finally, this set of ratios looks inside the garage to assess planning and organisation. Speed of service is important. Measuring the length of the queue in days or weeks assesses any backlog of vehicle repairs. Planned maintenance backlog is measured by:

$$\frac{Number\ of\ PM\ tasks\ outstanding}{PM\ tasks\ carried\ out\ per\ week}; or\ \frac{Hours\ of\ PM\ work\ outstanding}{Hours\ of\ PM\ planned\ per\ week}$$

Having most service tasks related to standard hours yields productivity measures (see Chapter 6):

$$Labour\ productivity = \frac{Standard\ hours\ of\ maintenance\ work\ carried\ out}{Actual\ hours\ worked}$$

An allowance has to be included in such a formula to allow for unscheduled and emergency work. It is common, however, to have standard times for planned maintenance. This is another advantage of PM systems.

10.3.10 **Maintainability**

There may be a tendency, both here and in many published articles, to regard maintenance as a reactive activity. This means it must look after whatever assets have been obtained. A longer term improvement is possible if maintenance is integrated into selecting and obtaining these assets. Maintainability, being the *capability of being maintained*, should be considered within the procurement process. This is rather like the discerning shopper looking at garment labels and rejecting those with a label stating 'dry clean only'.

When faced with the choice of obtaining an extra asset, or replacing a current one, the organisation compares total costs throughout the asset's life. The maintenance components include all the items set out in Figure 10.4. Briefly, these are:

- *Servicing.* Costs of consumable items such as lubricants, filters and items that wear quickly; whether fitting means interrupting operations; if interruptions are needed, the service time; whether the work requires special skill or equipment.

- *Preventive maintenance.* Ease of inspection; whether it is possible while the equipment is in use; arrangements for monitoring of performance and direct or indirect diagnosis.

- *Emergency or corrective maintenance.* Fault tolerance of the asset; access; time and skill required to repair; frequency of overhauls; MTBF.

Good estimates of these data are difficult to obtain. Even when equipment is in use, accounting information tends to be unreliable. Problems arise from:

- allocating fixed and semi-variable costs to a single asset and establishing which change through time
- disaggregating grouped data
- filling in gaps in records
- allocating operational losses from downtime
- converting costs spread over several years to present values.[22]

A further difficulty is that older machines are often 'relegated' to less arduous duties with the younger ones having to take more of the strain. Some of the operating costs of these younger machines should be counted as unreliability costs of the older group.

The unreliable cost data, therefore, should not be the sole basis for decisions. Yet, a business should aim to establish costs-in-use as part of its asset acquisition procedures.

Flint and Donoghue[23] reported on emerging questions of maintainability in the aircraft industry. Advances in commercial aircraft materials and systems are rapid. Operators cite the examples in Box 10.5 as cases of technology for technology's sake. Other authors point to maintenance being a significant portion of running cost in information technology[24] and road haulage[25] and these should be considered in procurement and operations.

BOX 10.5 Technology for technology's sake?

Composite structures

Such structures yield weight savings, increased malleability and lower corrosion. They are, however, more expensive. Further, a lack of standardisation in the materials means higher maintenance and recycling costs.

Advanced electronics and avionics

New control systems mean better and safer performance. Designers, however, are led by the technology. Higher prices and greater sophistication do not yield parallel gains in reliability.

10.3.11 The maintenance business

Subcontracting of maintenance is increasingly adopted by organisations. Needs for specialist facilities and knowledge and the ability to carry a range of spare parts are clearly examples of benefits of scale that could flow to a service provider doing business with many customers. We have noted how many service businesses focus on a limited range of activity from tyre depots to telephone answering services. Many domestic services gain from their specialist focus. Franchise agreements often protect them from direct competition. Examples are: Hotpoint's service centres; Dynorod's drain cleaning; and wood preservation offered by Rentokil.

Users of subcontract maintenance services also benefit from the speed and flexibility that may be difficult for an organisation to provide internally. For instance, oil production platforms require many different types of attention during the annual shutdown, such work being unwanted at other times. In effect, the production workers take a break to make way for teams of subcontractors during this period.

Ultimately, subcontractors gain because they offer their services at low cost. This may be because their customers have high internal labour rates or high overheads. Both partly explain why many local authorities have passed many functions from highways and grounds maintenance to computer servicing to private sector contractors.

British Airways is both a user of subcontract maintenance services and has been developing its own business as a supplier in this field[26] (see Box 10.6). The advantage to BA is that, with increased scale, there are possibilities of greater efficiencies in the use of all resources. These include the specialist equipment and supply of spares dedicated to each aircraft type. The danger is that the outside maintenance work may become an end in itself. The engineering department, recognising that it wins orders based on price, speed and flexibility, may be tempted to lower the priority given to internal work. Having been set financial performance targets, it would develop its own business strategy to ensure that a continuous supply of work was available. This illustrates a possible conflict between the function contributing to one value chain and its becoming a complete value chain in itself.

The author worked in a heavy engineering company where this happened. External business was taken on to smooth out demand between internal rebuilding

BOX 10.6 **BA as a subcontractor**

Maintenance is a critically important function for any airline. Governments normally closely regulate standards. British Airways was the first European airline to receive joint airworthiness requirement approval. The 19 nations in the JAR agreement agree to accept joint standards without resort to their own legislation.

The JAR approval gave BA competitive advantage in being able to offer its services to other airlines. After certification, it quadrupled its revenue from these sources to some £140 million. This was out of a total budget for the engineering department of £550 million. Most of the maintenance activity of BA is carried out at Heathrow and Gatwick airports. The company is, however, developing new facilities at Cardiff and Llantrisant where costs are lower.

Subcontractors are widely used in BA's operations. For example, FLS Aerospace Engineering at Stansted has a five-year contract to refurbish most of BA's 747 fleet. FLS has facilities for overhaul, anti-corrosion treatment and coating of this aircraft. It also does modification and overhaul work for major US airlines at Stansted and Manchester.

projects. Eventually, the works was so busy with a major refurbishment programme for a third-party customer that a large internal job was placed with a subcontractor overseas.

✔ Quick check-up

Can you:
- ☐ Summarise terotechnology.
- ☐ Relate failure scope to rate of onset.
- ☐ Discern fail-safe, fail-soft and fail-run.
- ☐ State the relationship between reliability and failure rates and MTBF.
- ☐ List seven categories of maintenance.
- ☐ Give four sources of predictive maintenance data.
- ☐ List five reasons for subcontracting maintenance services.
- ☐ Define maintainability and relate it to equipment purchase decisions.

❓ Questions

Chapter review

10.1 Explain the importance of the bath tub curve in developing maintenance policies.

10.2 Under what conditions is run-to-breakdown a sensible maintenance policy?

10.3 Why may TPM be resisted and how can managers overcome this resistance?

10.4 Compare the advantages and disadvantages of subcontracting maintenance activities.

Application

10.5 Use the human hand to illustrate the modes of failure in Table 10.1.

10.6 Outline a FMEA on a piece of equipment you own, such as a bicycle, multi-blade pen knife or electric kettle.

10.7 Suggest and justify a range of performance indicators for a business engaged to maintain a city-wide system of traffic signals.

Investigation

10.8 Compare the maintenance instructions issued with various items of commercial or domestic equipment. Examples can include cameras, cars, copiers, cookers and so on. Identify the recommendations given, fitting them into the policies explained in the chapter.

CLOSING CASE

Maintenance of fire-fighting vehicles[27]

The Greater Manchester Fire Brigade has more than 300 items of mobile equipment. To improve maintenance activity, managers studied some ten years' records of a sample group of equipment. They divided each vehicle type into a systems hierarchy. Typically, there were about seven subsystems per vehicle, each having eight components. This made 56 components in all. The maintenance data covered dates, times and costs for each component group with information on the type of failure that had occurred.

Failure analysis identified the components most subject to fault and the impact of these faults on system performance. Measures included: frequency of failure, mean time between failures (MTBF) and downtime. Failure rates were also matched to equipment age to figure out the lengths of useful lives. By eliminating the wear-out phase of the bath tub curve, it was possible to improve reliability and availability while reducing costs. The analysis showed the highest failure rate in the first year of operation.

Cost analysis examined planned and unplanned repairs. There were three aims: to find subsystems and components with the highest costs; to compare planned and unplanned maintenance; and to compare costs of internal, as opposed to subcontract, work.

Figure 10.8 shows a plot of faults occurring among 12 Dennis RS131 fire engines during their first six years of service. It shows a typical Pareto frequency distribution, at both subsystem and component levels. The results, combined with cost analysis, led to further investigation of causes.

The failures in the electrical subsystem, ancillary equipment and cab body were ascribed to corrosion. The high volume of water being carried and used caused this both in construction materials and among terminals, connections and switches. Water leaks were a problem and the electrical systems lacked a sufficiently high standard of waterproofing. The semi-automatic gearbox, also used on other fire engines in the fleet, appeared inadequate. First, the vehicles and their loads, including special equipment and 2 tonnes of water, were very heavy. Second, the driving practices included many rapid accelerations and decelerations.

Data on the maintenance of Vauxhall Chevette vans showed high repair costs for the cab and body, electrical equipment and the suspension system.

▶

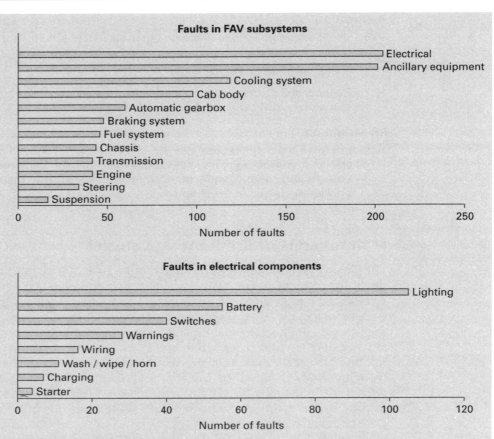

Figure 10.8 Fault analysis: Dennis RS131 fire appliance

These arose from the use of these general purpose vehicles by large numbers of different personnel.

There were two trailers used as mobile headquarters. These presented high costs among ancillary equipment, electrical subsystem, body work and brakes. The equipment repair costs were due to technical complexity, possibly enhanced by the two vehicles being over 11 years old.

Questions

1 Use a fault tree approach to explore the faults, including malfunctioning of a vehicle gearbox en route, that may combine to prevent the fire service achieving its normal standard.

2 What is the significance of the Pareto analysis?

3 From what you know of the way the fire service is organised and the special problems it faces, what issues would arise from a proposed move towards TPM?

4 What implications in terotechnology does this study have for the fire appliance manufacturers?

Notes and references

1. Brown, J.S. and Storey, K. (2000) *Eli Lilly Incident Profile – finding the root cause*, Hopewell, VA: Reliability Center; www.reliability.com/article27.htm accessed 5 December 2000.
2. British Standards Institute (1984) BS 3811, *Glossary of Maintenance Terms in Terotechnology*, London: BSI.
3. Muhlemann, A.P., Oakland, J.S. and Lockyer, K.G. (1992) *Production and Operations Management*, London: Pitman, p.116–7.
4. Harris, N.G. and Ramsey, J.B.H. (1994) 'Assessing the effects of railway infrastructure failure', *Journal of the Operational Research Society*, 45(6), June, pp.635–40.
5. Relcon (2001) *Example of methods for safety, reliability and availability analysis – fault Tree*, Stockholm: Relcon AB; Relcon produces Risk Spectrum software to aid modelling, http://www.riskspectrum.com/docs/methods_ft.htm accessed 20 June 2001.
6. Gits, C.W. (1994) 'Structuring maintenance control systems', *International Journal of Operations and Production Management*, 14(7), pp.5–17.
7. There is no generally accepted categorisation. Some authors use more than two. See, for example: Paz, N.M. (1993) 'Maintenance scheduling: issues, results and research needs', *International Journal of Production and Operations Management*, 14(8), pp.47–69. Different groupings are used by Gits, C.W. (1994) 'Structuring maintenance control systems', *International Journal of Operations and Production Management*, 14(7), pp.5–17; another set is given by Hill, T. (2000) *Operations Management: Strategic context and managerial analysis*, Basingstoke: Macmillan, p.448.
8. Hill, T. (1991) *Production and Operations Management: Text and cases*, Hemel Hempstead: Prentice Hall, p.422.
9. Osborne, D. and Taj, S. (1992) 'Preventive maintenance in a multiple shift and high volume manufacturing operation', *International Journal of Operations and Production Management*, 13(10), pp.76–83.
10. op.cit. p.77.
11. Gradin, L.P., Cartwright, W.B. and Nissen, M. (1994) 'Test method improves bearing wear assessment at Calvert Cliffs', *Power Engineering*, 98(6), June, pp.32–3; information on oil diagnosis from company sources.
12. Salter, P. (2001) 'Condition monitoring adds value to business', *Lubricants World*, 11(3), p.24.
13. Osborne and Taj, op.cit. p.77.
14. Nakajima, S., quoted in Teresko, J. (1992) 'Time bomb or profit centre?' *Industry Week*, 241(5), 2 March, pp.52–7.
15. Bohoris, G.A., Vamvalis, C., Tracey, W. and Ignatiadou, K. (1995) 'TPM implementation in Land Rover with assistance of a CMMS', *Journal of Quality in Maintenance Engineering*, 1(4); Holder, R. (1996) 'Major profits for Rover and LMP as TPM proves itself', *Works Management*, August, pp.16–17.
16. Al-Hassan, K., Chan, J.F. and Young, A. (2000) 'The role of total productive maintenance in business excellence', *Total Quality Management*, 11(4–6), pp.S596–S601. For JIT, see Chapter 12; for TQM and quality circles see Chapter 15.
17. Windle, W.W. (1993) 'TPM: More alphabet soup or a useful plant improvement concept?' *Plant Engineering*, 47(2), 4 February, pp.62–3.
18. Maggard, W.N. and Rhyne, D.R. (1992) 'Total productive maintenance: A timely integration of production and maintenance', *Production and Inventory Management Journal*, 33(4), pp.6–10.
19. Cooke, F.L. (2000) 'Implementing TPM in plant maintenance: Some organisational barriers', *International Journal of Quality and Reliability Management*, 17(9), pp.1003–16.

20. Peck, L.G. and Hazelwood, R.N. (1958) *Finite Queuing Tables*, New York: John Wiley.
21. Moffat, J. (1992) 'Three case studies of operational research for the Royal Air Force', *Journal of the Operational Research Society*, 43(10), October, pp.955–60.
22. Walker, J. (1994) 'Graphical analysis for machine replacement', *International Journal of Production and Operations Management*, 14(10), pp.54–63.
23. Flint, P. and Donoghue, J.A. (1992) 'The hidden cost of high tech', *Air Transport World*, 29(7), July, pp.22–34.
24. Corbitt, T. (1993) 'The computing iceberg', *Accountancy*, 111(1198), June, pp.67–8.
25. McKinnon, A.C., Stirling, I. and Kirkhope, J. (1993) 'Improving the fuel efficiency of road freight operations', *International Journal of Physical Distribution and Logistics Management*, 23(9), pp.3–11.
26. Shifrin, C.A. (1993) 'BA sees explosive growth in third-party maintenance', *Aviation Week and Space Technology*, 138(20), 17 May, pp.44–5; Reed A. (1994) 'Fishing an "overtrawled puddle"', *Air Transport World*, 31(3), March, pp.91–2.
27. Based on: Keller, A.Z., J.-Fendi Al-Saadi, S. and Leckie, L. (1992) 'Reliability assessment of fire-fighting vehicles and equipment', *International Journal of Quality and Reliability Management*, 9(2), pp.42–51.

PART THREE

Operations planning and control

CHAPTER 11

Capacity management

OBJECTIVES

When you have finished studying this chapter, you should be able to:

- Clarify designed, effective and achieved capacity and show how they are measured.
- Show how different work flow layouts influence capacity.
- Relate the problem of capacity planning to organisation strategy.
- Explain the role of forecasting in responding to uncertainty.
- Outline different forecasting procedures, relating them to time horizons.
- Demonstrate the application of time series and causal forecasting models in anticipating demand.
- Differentiate between financial and strategic views on capacity investment choices.
- Account for learning effects in capacity planning.
- Explain aggregate planning and compare policies of chasing demand and output levelling.

OPENING CASE

Keeping up with uncertain demand[1]

On 15 December 1999, electricity demand in England and Wales exceeded 50,000 MW for the first time. The previous record had stood for almost three years, yet, within a week, the new peak was passed. On 20 December, demand reached 50,587 MW. Both peaks occurred for the half-hour from 5 o'clock. No supply problems occurred on either occasion.

Since the restructuring and privatisation of 1990, uncertainty has posed a great challenge to companies in the industry. None has been more affected than National Grid plc, which links almost all power stations to points where power is taken both by the regional electricity companies and by some large customers. National Grid also operates interconnectors to exchange current with France and Scotland. Its policy has been to optimise the network utilisation and improve its reliability while simplifying its complexity. The last aim makes it easier to manage and maintain. National Grid invested about £2.6 billion in the system during the 1990s.

Electricity generation needs to cover consumer demand, losses in transmission and the power needed to run the stations. Demand forecasts focus on the winter peak, which is more than twice the summer peak load. Figure 11.1 shows the actual peak demand with a corrected demand, adjusted for variations in weather conditions and some operational factors. The mild winters of 1992/3 and 1994/5 show up clearly. The forecast made in 2000 extrapolated

▶

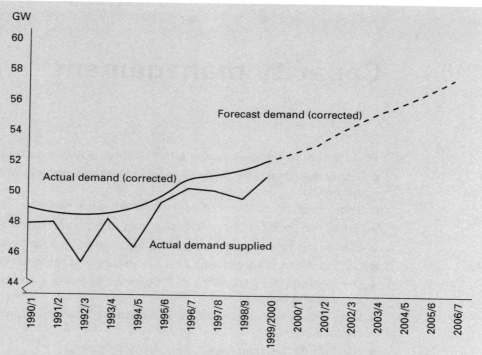

Figure 11.1 Demand for electricity at the winter peak for England and Wales

the corrected line, taking into account known information on customers' intentions. The growth rate was forecast to average 1.4%, yielding a peak of 57.4 GW during the winter of 2006/7. The degree of uncertainty is shown by variations in this forecast between 0.9% and 1.6% over recent years.

Since National Grid runs a transmission service, it has to anticipate generation as well as demand. The location of stations is as important as their size. Throughout the winter season, total generation capacity is adequate to meet peak loads. At low demand levels, the most efficient power stations are used. As consumption rises, more stations come into service. The pattern of distribution changes every few minutes as this happens. The complexity of these changes has increased since the establishment of a market in which generators sell and distributors buy. Looking several years ahead, National Grid expects new stations to come on stream and older ones to shut down. This leads to permanent changes in the flows around the network.

While the total generating capacity in the south is adequate, the fact that many stations have low efficiency means they run only at peaks. Power transfer from the north, especially the north-east, is increasing. This is consumed in the Midlands and the south. Since new stations are being commissioned along the south coast, however, this area, with the south-west, has a decreasing import requirement. Imports to central London, however, continue to grow. Local flows are difficult to predict so National Grid has to build flexible capacity. Equipment, such as transformers and switchgear are designed to be dismantled and used elsewhere.

11.1 Introduction

Capacity management is about matching the size of a facility to the demands placed on it. The Electricity Act, under which National Grid operates, requires it to maintain secure supply to the distribution companies at all times. The issues can be examined from short-, medium- and long-term points of view. In the short term, balancing is tactical. Controllers, supported by automatic systems, make minute-by-minute adjustments to the grid to transfer power with the minimum of losses and lowest risk of failure. In the medium term, the managers improve and adapt the current equipment to optimise performance; they arrange for the isolation of sections for maintenance at off-peak periods; they have contingency plans to maintain the current if there is a sudden failure, possibly caused by storms. In the long term, all capacity is variable. The shape and scale of the network is gradually adapted in response to rising demand in the south and the construction of new stations.

Choosing capacity is one of the riskiest decisions an organisation has to face. The business relies on its ability to forecast and then adapt itself over a period of years. For many, the behaviour of competitors is very important, but they can only estimate what rivals will do. National Grid has a monopoly, yet its forecasts of future demand are prone to error. Constructing new carrying capacity in anticipation of demand that does not materialise means wasted resources. The balance between fulfilling its mission to supply, while making a profit for investors, is difficult to find.

In this chapter, we shall look at the long-, medium- and short-term aspects of capacity decisions. Before we do so, however, we must consider important questions of definition, measurement and general process structure.

11.2 What is capacity?

11.2.1 Definitions

In everyday speech, we use the term *capacity* in several ways. Perhaps the most common is the way it refers to *storage* that held in a container, building or other space. Examples include: the 50-litre capacity of a family car's fuel tank; the 38,500 seating capacity at Arsenal's Highbury stadium; the 40 gigabyte storage of my hard disk. In another use, the word describes *capability*, as in: 'She has a tremendous capacity for hard work'; the boxer who has a 'tremendous capacity for soaking up punishment'; or my nephew who has an 'enormous capacity' for strawberry ice cream. Finally, capacity describes *flow rates* along chains or through operating processes. For instance: the road has a capacity of 3,000 vehicles per hour; the canning line can pack 10,000 litres per shift; the National Grid can distribute 55 GW of power.

In operations management, capacity is used both to describe stocks and flows. To avoid the confusion that this may cause, it is important to attach units of measure to any values under discussion. Stocks are measurable and can either be counted as numerical quantities or expressed in units of measurement such as litres, tonnes, square metres and so on. Flows relate to the production or supply of items over time and should always be expressed in terms of the movement of stocks per interval. Thus, we have the tap delivering 8 litres per minute; the Renault line producing 17 R25s per hour; the polyethylene plant running at 200,000 tonnes per year.

Operations managers are primarily interested in flows as they represent the transformation of inputs into outputs sold in the market place. Indeed, as we have seen, stocks are increasingly scrutinised for the way they add dead weight to the business. They occupy space and their cost acts as a drag on profitability. Just-in-time management focuses on optimising flow rates through manufacturing facilities to achieve this stock reduction.

Flows can, however, quickly transform themselves into stocks. In service settings, they become the queues discussed in Chapter 9. Like the stocks of work in progress, queues must be accommodated. Allowing the lines outside a night club to congest the pavement may be acceptable, but what happens at an airport? It may have a peak outward flow capacity of 10,000 passengers per hour. Yet, a problem, such as an accident or fault in the traffic control system, may delay flights by, say, half an hour. This places an immediate demand on terminal facilities. The queue may not seem very long in time but the lounges must cope with a backlog of 5,000 passengers who would otherwise be on their way.

Normally, therefore, the capacity of an operating system is expressed in terms of throughput per period. Good management will recognise, however, how the system must be capable of holding stocks or queues at intermediate points. Warehouses, storage yards, lounges and waiting rooms must have the stocking capacity to cope with flow variations.

11.2.2 Capacity measurement

Where a process is producing a standard product, it is easy to state its capacity as number of units per period. When products develop some variety, however, difficulties arise. Many firms respond by expressing the work content in standard units. Typically, in a jobbing or small batch business, the capacity of any operation can be expressed in terms of standard hours per week. If all jobs have time estimates then output is planned according to weekly available hours.

In service operations, variety becomes more of a problem, particularly in personal service. What, for instance, is the capacity of a waiter-service restaurant? Many use the number of seats as the capacity measure. Yet, we can see that the work cell is the table. Let us say that, in this restaurant, a table is occupied whatever the number of diners, from one to four. A working average may be three and, on this basis, a waiter may handle eight tables. With each meal taking an hour, the capacity of the section is 24 meals per hour. If, by chance, all tables were filled with four customers, could the system cope? It all depends on whether the waiter can serve the meals. Furthermore, can the kitchen produce the dishes at this rate?

Exercise 11.1

Apart from table occupancy, what other variations arise in the restaurant? Identify the possible changes in demand for a 32-table facility. What capacity would you suggest for the kitchen and how would you manage if demand were higher than this?

11.2.3 Capacity below maximum

A further problem in assessing capacity arises from the fact that facilities do not run full out all the time. We can distinguish among designed, effective and achieved capacity:

- *Designed capacity*. Otherwise known as *theoretical capacity*, this is the maximum achievable under ideal conditions. To maintain such momentum usually requires such an effort that, in almost all cases, facilities operate at a lower tempo. For instance, allowances are needed for breaks, planned maintenance, tool changing and so on. Changeover problems become more important when the product variety is higher.

- *Effective capacity*. This is the proportion of designed capacity that the organisation achieves given its plans for product mix, maintenance, shift patterns and so on. Otherwise known as *utilisation*, this proportion is a key factor in operational success. While never being able to operate at 100% of designed capacity, organisations that manage to increase utilisation to a few per cent higher than their rivals will have lower costs and, therefore, be more profitable. The 1994 liberalisation of shopping hours in England and Wales meant that many shops could increase their utilisation. This was particularly true of large self-service stores for whom fixed costs account for a greater proportion of the total operating cost. Sunday shopping and later opening hours thus brought them relative advantage.

- *Achieved capacity*. Effective capacity is reduced by inefficiency. This can arise from many sources from the lack of skill of operators or weak organisation through to the use of poor materials, tools and equipment. External factors range from weather to congestion and poor organisation of suppliers and subcontractors. Either these items are under management control or management can take steps to limit their influence. Commonly, the output is less than effective capacity; operating speed may be lower than planned or the *process yield* is cut by a proportion of poor quality product.

  Achieved capacity, known otherwise as *net output*, focuses on the *yield*. Managers will have targets to maintain or increase the yield and therefore increase achieved capacity. It is wise, nevertheless, for schedulers to base their plans on whatever net output the facility is currently achieving. The measures stated here are linked by the following equation:

$$Achieved\ capacity = Designed\ capacity \times Utilisation \times Yield$$

Throughout the construction period of the Channel Tunnel there was argument over its effective capacity. Eurotunnel, the owners, claimed that it would eventually be able to handle 20 trains per hour in each direction. This view was challenged partly on the grounds of tunnel and terminal design but also because of the service mix. The freight trains, travelling more slowly, would hold back the high-speed passenger trains. Critics quoted figures as low as ten for the effective capacity. By 2001, there were 360 trains and shuttles per day, which is an average of 7.5 per hour in each direction.[2]

In many industries, especially during recessions, demand is less than the total effective capacity and it is that, rather than internal factors, which acts as the constraint. The European automotive industry has displayed overcapacity for many years. For instance, in fiscal year 2000, the Honda plant at Swindon produced 74,500 cars, achieving 60% capacity utilisation. In the same year, Toyota produced 176,000 cars at Burnaston, reaching 78% utilisation. Both companies posted losses for the year. Although each planned to increase both capacity and output, they were concerned that the high value of sterling would restrict demand in export markets.[3]

Exercise 11.2   Honda increased the designed capacity of its plant to 180,000. For this, and Eurotunnel, identify some factors that may cause utilisation and yield to each fall below 100%.

11.2.4 Capacity and work flow layout

In finding out how different processes contribute to deciding total system capacity, we must consider how they are connected, if at all. There are three possible arrangements:

- *Processes in parallel.* The capacities of independent, parallel processes can be added to assess total system capacity. This is most clearly seen when two facilities are separated geographically. Very simply, two gas production platforms, each producing 100,000 cubic metres per day, supply a total of 200,000 cu m per day. Even in such simple additions, care must be taken to ensure that the facilities do not use the same resource or share a common distribution system, either of which could set a lower limit.

- *Processes in series.* The capacity of a system with a set of processes arranged in series is equal to the rate of the slowest. This is the *bottleneck* whose output decides the output of the whole system. We shall look at the significance of bottlenecks in the philosophy of optimised production technology in Chapter 12.

  Highways have bottlenecks. Whatever the length and state of a motorway, its capacity between two consecutive junctions is limited to the worst lane restriction. This is the world of the *contraflow* and the *tailback*. In contrast, the capacity of an urban road system is most affected by the design and operation of the junctions themselves. Links between junctions have little effect on network capacity provided they can take more vehicles than the intersections that they connect, which is usually the case. It is worth improving these roads but only to make them easier or safer, not to increase network capacity. This realisation, together with developments in control technology, has awakened interest in the use of city-wide traffic light systems and other methods of regulating traffic behaviour at junctions.

- *Joint processes.* Often, the production of an output requires the supply of many inputs that, while not being delivered from the same source in series, are nevertheless interrelated. The system capacity is again equal to the lowest among the elements. One example is in the restaurant where different resources are combined in the supply of the meal service. There is a series of processes from kitchen preparation, through waiter delivery to eating at the table. Yet these take place in parallel with the supply and maintenance of the seating capacity, clearing up and so on.

In manufacturing, two lines may produce components that only come together at the last, final assembly stage. The system cannot produce at a rate that exceeds the lower of the two supply lines and that decides its total capacity.

The question of system capacity arose in the context of line and process production in Chapter 8. A production system with a bottleneck and much spare capacity was out of balance. While irregularities of demand and operations make its achievement difficult, it is one aim of capacity management to ensure that processes run in close balance. Irregularity is especially apparent in jobbing shops.

11.3 Forecasting long-term capacity needs

The relationship between capacity and demand in the long term is summarised in Figure 11.2. It shows that product and market policies are intertwined. Demand for the products of an organisation are assessed by means of a forecast, first of the industry sales and then of the expected market share. In the light of this long-range view, the firm develops it product and marketing policies designed to satisfy the forecast demand. In turn, these strategic decisions will influence the demand through feedback loops. Frequently, this will be shown by changes in market share as the organisation offers enhanced products and promotes them more effectively. At the same time, the business has to decide whether to satisfy some or all demand itself or to use subcontractors.

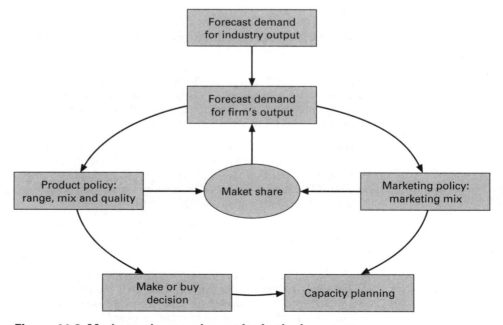

Figure 11.2 Markets, share and capacity in the long term

This last option is frequently seen as a tactical measure where companies need extra capacity in the short term. This is common and many firms offer very flexible capacity in order to act as subcontractors in this way. Longer term relationships are needed in cases where the contractor has to invest in space, plant, tooling, vehicles, training and so on. Such long-term links are often seen as a form of *strategic alliance*.

11.3.1 Uncertainty

As Figure 11.1 shows, a key element in the long-term capacity management process is the forecast. This is but one of the steps that are susceptible to the types of uncertainty set out in Chapter 4. We can illustrate this by reference to airport planning.

Box 11.1 gives a snapshot of the debate over runway planning in south-east England.[4] In the report, we can identify references to state, effect and response uncertainty:

■ *State uncertainty.* The key driver of the decision-making process is the demand forecast. If one ignores short-term fluctuations caused by fuel shortages or war, one can note that the underlying growth in air travel throughout the world has followed an exponential pattern. Passenger numbers have doubled every ten years. This corresponds to a cumulative 7% year-on-year increase. Whether demand in the south-east of the United Kingdom will continue to grow at this same rate is the problem. The equations below show that, if the actual rate fell to 6% each year until 2015, the forecast 170 million passengers would in error by some 18 million. Since the planning range is so long, the forecast is sensitive

---

BOX 11.1 Uncertainties in runway capacity planning

'The government will announce this week . . . that it is to wait until 2019, when a ban on a second runway at Gatwick expires, before expanding runway capacity in the south-east . . . [This change] will revive worries that inadequate capacity could end the dominance of London as the European hub for intercontinental flights.

'A 1993 report from a Ministry of Transport working group . . . forecasts a continuation of the 7% growth rate . . . the number of passengers using airports in the south-east would rise from the present 75 million to 170 million by 2015. [The report proposed] a further runway at Heathrow or Gatwick by 2010 or, if this were not provided, at Stansted by 2015.

'The Government will announce instead that better use should be made of existing runways. There is under-used capacity at Luton and particularly at Stansted which . . . could handle four times as many passengers . . .

'Redhill could be used for the large number of smaller aircraft that now use its big neighbour, Gatwick. At the moment, half the flights at Gatwick generate only one-fifth of the passengers. Transferring them to Redhill would increase its capacity by 10.5 million passengers a year.'

to small changes in the growth rate assumption. Compare $75 \times 1.07^{12} = 169$ with $75 \times 1.06^{12} = 151$.

- *Effect uncertainty.* The variable being forecast is passenger demand in south-east England. Yet, the capacity being planned is runways. The relationship between the two is not constant. Box 11.1 mentions some means by which existing runway capacity can be increased. These are changing the mix of aircraft and the operating procedures. Beyond this are developments in technology including aircraft design. For example, larger aircraft use runways more efficiently and quieter aircraft may be able to make more night movements. Therefore, we have uncertainty in the effect of changes in passenger demand on runway capacity needs.

- *Response uncertainty.* The third difficulty concerns responses to whatever decisions are made for capacity provision. For example, if the government directs British Airports to develop Stansted, what will be the reactions of airlines? Will they accept the extra costs of transferring connecting passengers and baggage among three airports or the competitive disadvantages of operating from a base further from the metropolis? Some may decide to move their 'hubs' for either passenger or freight business to other United Kingdom or European centres. Paris and Luxembourg, for instance, are both investing heavily in freight-handling facilities.[5]

The example used here is unusual in the length of the period the forecast is covering. Yet, as we shall see in the closing case of this chapter, to build a new runway at an existing airport can take at least ten years. Two management actions can alleviate some of the uncertainty. First, while in the end there may be a need for a significant investment in a single new facility, much can be done to incrementally improve existing assets to make them work harder and be more flexible. Adding terminals at airports increases capacity in large increments so that, for some time after opening, they tend to be underutilised. The 1986 opening of Terminal 4 at Heathrow raised capacity to about 38 million passengers per annum. A further increase of 4 million was achieved by refurbishment of Terminal 3 and more efficient use of the remaining terminals. Second, when an investment decision is eventually made, operations and marketing managers need to team up and run it to make it work. In other words, they commit their organisations to making the forecasts come true.

11.3.2 Forecasting demand

The passenger demand forecast just illustrated is but one of several approaches to prediction that are used. We should remember that the purpose of forecasting is to reduce uncertainty. It is used in many fields from the broad areas of economics, international relations and technology to the more specific ones of demand for the products of an individual firm. The former are not usually the province of the operations manager although an awareness of trends should be part of the development of operations strategy. The manager is more involved in demand and capacity. As we noted in Chapters 2 and 4, planning requires a forecasting method. Otherwise, the organisation must choose to adapt as events unfold.

Table 11.1 Time horizons in the electricity network, examples and responsibilities

Time horizon	Years	Issues requiring forecasts	Responsibility
Long term	2 to 10 or more	New long-distance transmission lines; switching centres and control systems	Led by senior managers
Medium term	1 to 3	Replacing switchgear, transformers; recruiting and training sufficient staff; reviewing major maintenance programme	Middle managers
Short term	0.0001 to 1	Job allocation, planning daily peak loading and routing	Junior managers and system controllers

Forecasts are usually made with *time horizons* in mind. This term relates to the limit of the period covered by the forecasts. In the opening case, the electricity demand forecast, with a horizon some seven years ahead, contrasts with the controller managing the connection of a station after its annual shutdown. Table 11.1 gives examples of three types of forecast, divided arbitrarily into long, medium and short term. The boundaries overlap. We can see, for example, that capital projects falling into the long-term band contain many elements planned and executed within shorter cycles. The purpose of the description is to show that longer-term forecasts involve broader issues. Because of their scale, and the uncertainty in the environment, more senior managers tend to be involved.

Medium- and short-term forecasts focus on narrower issues, often down to estimating the behaviour of one variable. This could be sales, the price of fuel or the congestion on a particular route. The accent is on producing firm, numerical values. Long-term forecasts incorporate many more factors and tend to include much qualitative data. Yet, how are these forecasts to be made? Methods fall into two categories, qualitative and quantitative.

Qualitative forecasting

These techniques attempt to gather experience, intuition and value systems of experts and leaders to reach a description of the long-term future. We can outline some here:

Delphi method

Named after the mystical Greek oracle, the Delphi method is a series of surveys of expert opinion. A panel, about ten in number not necessarily gathered in one place, are asked to speculate on questions about their field in ten or more years' time. If there is a lack of a consensus after this first stage, the organisers circulate all responses to all members of the panel. A second round of opinion gathering follows. Organisers expect some narrowing of differences and members begin to understand others' points of view. Rounds continue as necessary until the panel achieves consensus.

Questions asked may be, for example, 'What do you think the average size of intercontinental passenger aircraft will be in 2015?' or 'What changes will there be in steel production methods before the middle of the next decade?' While

Delphi methods often gather expert opinion on such topics, they can be used by groups of managers working on general forecasts of the business environment. There is support from background data, statistical trends and so on. This family of techniques is called jury methods.

Sales force survey

In the short term, sales data can be extrapolated to forecast demand. Using the opinion and contacts of the salespeople themselves, however, can considerably enrich this approach. They spend much time with customers, hear about developments and gain a feel for the actions of competitors. Sales force surveys, using unstructured interviews or focus groups, gather this qualitative information.

Customer survey

Many customer surveys attempt to gather accurate, quantitative data by customer research. They ask about or, better, observe actual behaviour. Hence the question, 'How often do you eat pub meals each month?' More future-orientated information comes from asking about future spending plans; this is gained either by surveys or through consumer panels that meet to discuss ideas and assess product proposals. Since customers are being asked to speculate, the results from these studies should be used with care in making firm forecasts.

Quantitative forecasting

There are many numerical techniques to gather data and model relationships among the variables under study. They lie in two categories, which we shall briefly summarise before looking at them in detail.

Time series model

A time series model is based on the simple assumption that the future depends on the past. For instance, combining recent data on newspaper sales gives us a good idea of what demand for the next three months. The methods are most effective if there is no major upheaval in the industry sector being covered. In the case of newspapers, if things remain more or less as they are, the best forecast of future sales in probably one based on recent trends. On the other hand, the outbreak of a price war disturbs patterns so much that trends are no longer followed.

Causal model

Causal models try to discover underlying relationships to explain behaviour of the variables under investigation. As with all good modelling, however, the assumed relationships need rigorous testing to avoid mistakes. Leaver and Al-Zubaidi[6] showed that sales of do-it-yourself goods during the 1980s grew during the boom in the housing market. This led many to conclude that sales were closely related to house moves. Yet, when the housing market slumped after 1988, DIY sales continued their strong growth. The study showed that conventional wisdom overestimated the significance of house moves. A combination of house prices, levels of owner occupation, car ownership and floor space in the stores gave a more reliable forecast of sales. Car ownership not only meant that people were spending more on accessories, but also they had better access to the new large-scale stores.

11.3.3 **Time series forecasting**

A time series is simply a list of values each of which is labelled with the time of its occurrence. We shall outline how time series forecasts are made from this stream of historical data. The first task is to decompose the series into its elements. Data streams are often affected by factors, such as seasonal variations, that hide the underlying trends. The idea is to separate trends and variations and study each separately. The second task is to forecast these elements.

Decomposition, therefore, means splitting the historical data into their components, each of which can be forecast. Typically, they number four:

■ *Trend*. The trend, often called the *underlying trend*, is the basic change in the data as time advances. It is contained in statements such as, 'Electricity consumption is rising at 1.4% per year.'

■ *Seasonality*. This not only refers to quarterly or annual changes such as represented by the *Christmas rush*, the *spring collection* or even *new potatoes*, but also to patterns that repeat hourly, daily, weekly and so on. Some of these are readily observed, the rush hour and the weekend being obvious examples. Others are internal to the organisation such as the weekly, four-weekly or monthly cash flows of wages and salaries and quarterly or annual variations in workload of the accounting office as it prepares financial statements.

■ *Cycles*. Occurring over periods of several years, cycles are important in those industries used to peaks and troughs. They are, in principle, similar to seasonal factors but, since they are notoriously difficult to forecast both in variation and in time, they are often treated separately. They are, however, important in sales and capacity planning.

■ *Random variations*. Changes that cannot be explained and captured in these three categories are treated as resulting from random events. Since they are random, they cannot be included in a forecast. A causal model may help in understanding them but will not support forecasting. We saw in Figure 11.1 how mild winters cause falls in electricity demand. Knowing this relationship cannot assist forecasting and planning for the next seven years.

Figure 11.3 shows how these components make up sales of a consumer product over several years. Clearly there is an annual cycle with consistent peaks and troughs. The actual sales line has the 'jagged' random component and, allowing for this, we can see the cycle combined with a steadily rising trend. Any long-term cycle, such an industry cycle, or the product life cycle, may not show up during the three-year time scale.

The decomposed demand formula is the assembly of the components just described. There are two forms, the multiplicative and the additive. In the more common multiplicative equation, the components are multiplied:

$$Sales = Trend \times Seasonal\ factor \times Cyclical\ factor$$

The additive equation looks like this:

$$Sales = Trend + Seasonal\ value + Cyclical\ value$$

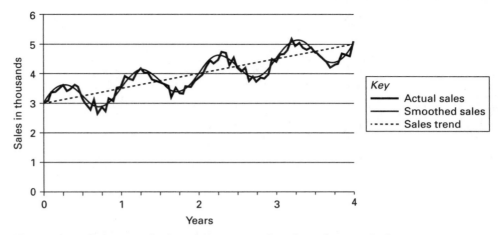

Figure 11.3 Sales graph showing seasonal and random variations

Since seasonal and cyclical values are assumed to be regular and random variations cannot be controlled, the forecasting stage of the time series approach is essentially one of moving the trend line forwards. Various methods are used:

■ *Simple approach*. Extending the trend line, often by sketching on the graph, can make a quick approximation. For short-term trends, it is quick and efficient.

■ *Moving averages*. Moving averages base immediate forecasts on the averages of previous periods. For example, where little trend is expected, an average of the past six months' sales will give a guide to future monthly sales as it will cut out the random variations. If a trend is expected, recent sales can be given more emphasis by given them greater weight in the formula. This is the technique of *weighted moving averages*.

Moving averages are easy to use and work well in stable conditions. They are good at smoothing out the random fluctuations. Yet, if the time over which averaging is made too long, they become less sensitive to underlying change. Indeed, they are poor at picking out trends. Since they are averages, they will, of course, always make a forecast within the range of the past data.

Exponential smoothing

Exponential smoothing places little reliance on averaging a stream of past data. Instead, it corrects the previous period's forecast according to the error in that forecast. A basic formula is:

Forecast = Previous forecast + $\alpha \times$ (Previous actual sales – Previous forecast)

The term α is the smoothing constant taking a value from 0 to 1.

The new forecast is the one made for the previous period adjusted by the error in that forecast. Since the forecast depends on previous forecasts, which in turn depend on the ones before them, exponential smoothing does take into account previous data in its projections. The amount of adjustment depends on the value chosen for the constant. If α is close to 0, the forecast changes little; if α

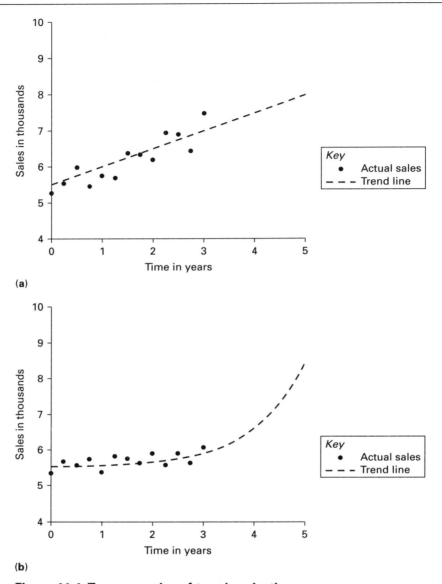

(a)

(b)

Figure 11.4 Two examples of trend projection

approaches 1, the forecast matches the most recent sales. More realistically, if α is set at 0.5, only the last three periods have much effect on the forecast. However, if α = 0.1, the effect of recent demand is downgraded and about 20 data values are smoothed out.

Trend analysis

In contrast to the extrapolation methods mentioned earlier, trend analysis works on the trend line by trying to fit a mathematical equation to it. Then future values can be forecast using the equation. The skill lies in choosing a line most likely to represent the behaviour being forecast. Figure 11.4 shows two examples, the linear trend and exponential growth. The former is simple and applies when no other model is thought better; the latter is applicable to cases of explosive growth where, say, sales double every several years. Having chosen the general form of the line, the regression analysis technique establishes the closest fit to the past data.

11.3.4 A practical example: electricity generation

We saw in the opening case how companies in the electricity industry place great emphasis on forecasting. The product cannot be stored directly. Operators use a mixture of quantitative and qualitative techniques to predict demand.

The most efficient stations operate almost continuously to produce the so-called base load. They do not run at full power, since the turbines and generators are most efficient at about 70% of maximum. There is, therefore, a spare capacity known as the *spinning reserve*. The machines are running at the correct speed and their power output can be increased in fractions of a second.

As demand increases during cold weather, older, less efficient stations are started up. The maximum demand of some 50 GW occurs at about 5.30 on a winter's evening. Short peaks usually relate to the breaks between popular television programmes. They are handled by the spinning reserve, quick-start gas turbine systems and pumped storage hydroelectricity. Such demand surges can be 10% or more. To anticipate these changes, operators use data from sources as varied as the meteorological office and *Radio Times*.

Figure 11.5 shows the time series of demand through two summer evenings during the 1990s. The typical summer time base load of about 29,500 MW shows some remarkable variations. Both events were important football matches between England and Germany. During the 1990 World Cup semi-final, the increasingly unpredictable surges occurred at half time (1,600 MW), full time (1,600), the end of extra time (300) and the end of the penalty shoot-out (2,800).[7]

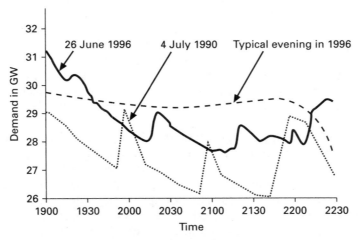

Figure 11.5 Electricity demand in England and Wales, 26 June 1996 and 4 July 1990

The last leap was equivalent to the output of a very large power station, some 9% of the load. Starting half an hour later, the 1996 European Championship match was also decided on penalties. The surges closely matched the pattern of six years earlier but were about half of the height. Known in the industry as 'television pick-ups' they arise mainly from consumers switching on electric kettles.

As we saw in the opening case, medium- and long-term forecasting are also critically important to the success of the electricity generators and distributors. National Grid combines its own time series extrapolations with the forecasts of its customers, the regional electricity companies. The RECs combine time series and causal methods. Among these, MANWEB[8] found that during the 20 years to 1990, sales changed as follows: an average annual increase of 1.5% to industrial customers; sales to commercial units increased by 4.1% per annum; domestic consumption remained stable. A time series extrapolation of each sector was a first attempt at future forecasting. However, the company had experienced a 15% fall of sales to industrial customers in 1980–81 when there was a significant recession. It also recognises the effect of the weather and the relative prices of other energy sources in those markets where there is competition. The identification of these links in the market sectors meant that causal forecasting, using time series extrapolations of underlying variables, gave a clearer picture of the future.

Exercise 11.3   Can you suggest any reason why the pick-ups were smaller in 1996? Furthermore, what might happen if there were another such match today?

11.3.5 Causal forecasting

Beyond trend analysis, regression analysis is also used in causal forecasting. Here, instead of using time as the independent variable, other factors are considered. In the simplest case, there is assumed to be just one independent (or input) variable and the relationship is assumed to be linear. This relationship is similar to the first graph of Figure 11.4.

The form of the regression equation is $\hat{y} = a + (b \times x)$, where $\hat{y}$ is the variable being forecast, x is the independent variable and a and b are constants. Regression methods allow a line to be fitted to an observed set of data and an estimate made of how well the line matches this known information.

An extension of this basic approach enables a model to be built with several independent variables x_1, x_2, x_3 and so on. This has the form: $\hat{y} = a + (b_1 \times x_1) + (b_2 \times x_2) + (b_3 \times x_3) + \ldots$.

Known as multiple regression, this is a powerful technique. It enables the analyst to explore interconnections between large numbers of variables within a system. We should note, however, that it needs to be used with care and still requires the independent variables to be predicted if it is to be used as a forecasting technique. Box 11.2 gives an example of how the method can produce usable results.[9] It was shown how Dettol sales could be related to four variables, two of which managers could control and the other two they could forecast. Managers were then able to insert their own pricing and advertising plans, as well as time series forecasts for the other variables, in order to estimate future sales.

BOX 11.2 **Factors affecting sales of Dettol**

The study sought to identify the main factors affecting the sales of Dettol, the leading domestic disinfectant and antiseptic. Managers found sales to have statistically significant relationships with:

- real personal disposable income (purchases tended to fall when consumers had relatively less money)
- the seasons (sales of all disinfectants and antiseptics are higher in the warmer months)
- price (adjusted for inflation)
- the weight of advertising.

With the first two factors outside the company's scope, the effects of price and advertising were of greatest interest. The study not only identified these factors but also measured their effect. Price elasticity was estimated at −0.44 and advertising elasticity at 0.19. These data, coupled with cost figures, enabled the company to show that rises in price and advertising expenditure were profitable.

11.4 Changing capacity

11.4.1 Capacity strategy

In Chapter 2, we saw how an organisation uses modelling techniques such as break-even analysis to assess the relative advantages of different mixes of fixed and variable costs. Further, the various methods of evaluating investments were reviewed. Typically, investments that take some years to complete and bring benefits are analysed using discounting methods.

While these methods are widely used and are to be recommended for an initial appraisal, they fall down on two counts. First, there are technical weaknesses in the accounting processes themselves. They include: difficulties in establishing values for risk, discount rates, inflation estimates and so on; over-optimistic appraisal of the benefits of new projects compared with maintaining the status quo; problems of coping with benefits that may flow a long time in the future; and underestimation of the costs of change, including organisational disruption. Second, there is the increasing recognition by managers that long-term benefits to the organisation flow not from a narrow concentration on financial return but on developing competitive advantage. Therefore, changes, such as increased flexibility, broadening the range of products on offer and improving quality and service, may be difficult to evaluate in financial terms. Yet, they may be crucial to long-range success.

Render and Heizer[10] recommended five strategic considerations to enhance analysis of investments in operations. They are:

- Investments should be part of a co-ordinated strategic plan. Rather than be considered in isolation, they should work together to win and retain customers.

- Investments should yield competitive advantage through, for example, flexibility, speed of delivery or service, quality, reliability and so on.
- Investments should consider product life cycles.
- The analysis should consider a variety of operating factors. Changes may affect scrap, rework, space requirements, inventory, maintenance and training needs.
- The analysis should be subjected to sensitivity tests on the key strategic variables.

Stadium capacity

The football industry illustrates many of these questions. Following the Hillsborough tragedy and the subsequent Taylor report, huge investments created all-seater stadia. The eventual cost of several hundred millions was borne by an industry losing about £10 million per year. In their conversion, most grounds had to cut capacity. More often than not, this occurred by default rather than through a concerted plan. How should an individual club decide the size of its stadium?

Design changes increased the difficulty of forecasting both short-term and long-term demand. Dobson and Goddard[11] showed that different influences affect demand for standing and seating places in mixed stadia. Standing fans responded to team form, significance of the game and geographical distance whereas seated customers were most influenced by historical record. In the switch to seating, the question was whether those who used to stand would behave as before or become more like their seated counterparts.

A narrow financial appraisal may base ground capacity investment on current attendances. At a construction cost of approximately £1,000 per seat and known ticket prices, it may be possible to assess the rate of return for each extra block or row of accommodation. Yet, for small clubs, this policy would create a poor image, display a lack of ambition and give no flexibility in holding the occasional big game (see Box 11.3). The Football League sets a minimum of 6,000. Large

BOX 11.3 **How big to build a stadium?**

Chester City FC opened its new 6,000-seater stadium during the 1993–4 season. The club was leading the Third Division and heading for Division Two. Yet, within weeks of the opening there were problems of unanticipated demand. The *Chester Chronicle* (8 April 1994) reported:

'Chester City have been savaged by their own fans and supporters from Preston following last Saturday's Third Division promotion clash at Deva Stadium. An estimated 300 Preston fans were locked out of the ground and, despite several appeals for them to leave, dozens forced their way in 25 minutes after the kick-off.'

A letter in the *Lancashire Evening Post* (2 April 1994) said: 'What a pathetic capacity for a League football club. Chester should be stripped of their League status.'

One year later, the team's form had slumped. By 2000, Chester had been relegated from the Football League. Average gates were 1,000.

clubs, moreover, always hope to increase attendances, stage internationals and other events and need an impressive stadium to attract the crowd. Few, such as Manchester United and Tottenham Hotspur, are public limited companies and build returns to shareholders into their decisions. To fathom the choices of the rest, one must enter the boardrooms to understand the motivation of club owners.

11.4.2 Learning to increase capacity

Many facilities, such as the football stadia we have just looked at, have fixed capacity. In other cases, where the capacity means flow through a complex set of processes, utilisation and yield tend to improve as processes are repeated. One simple explanation of the productivity improvement is that people do better with practice. As individuals, they gradually find ways to avoid interruptions, skip unnecessary movement, set up a machine more quickly and so on. Well-trained staff can switch from one job to another and apply their experience to the new task. This occurs quite quickly and is known as the short-term learning curve.

A further development lies in the way organisations learn. Not only does carrying out the tasks improve with practice but all departments and functions find ways of improving their performance, linking themselves together and creating a more efficient value chain. Therefore, output rises and costs fall. This is the long-term effect.

Learning curves are of negative exponential form as shown in the first sketch in Figure 11.6. A straight line reveals the exponential relationship when the plot is made on logarithmic scales. (See the second sketch graph of Figure 11.6.)

Many cases of rising productivity have been demonstrated, at least over short periods. The slope of the learning curve is often expressed in terms of the fall in costs following each doubling of output gradients, known as *learning rates*, lie in the range from 70 to 85%. This means that the standard hours required for the twentieth task are between 0.7 or 0.85 of those for the tenth. The fortieth requires a similar proportion of the ones used in the twentieth and so on. More formally, if we measure the hours for an item number n, then we can estimate them for item m from the formula:

$$\frac{\text{Standard hours for item } m}{\text{Standard hours for item } n} = \left(\frac{m}{n}\right)^{b}$$

The constant b is the slope of the logarithmic learning curve. We can see the effect of doubling output by setting the ratio $m/n = 2$. The cost reduction is then simply 2^b. This is the learning rate and Table 11.2 provides some values.

The exponential nature of the decline should be noted. It is always prudent to ignore times for the first few items since there may be many irregularities in the way the tasks are carried out. Afterwards, the tenth, twentieth, fortieth and so on will show reductions. As the intervals between outputs doubling increase, the curve represents the inevitable slowing down in learning.

Short-term learning is readily observed and easily measured. The long-term curve is controversial. Henderson argued that it hardly matters why it happens. It is a rule of thumb whose characteristic pattern is observable. 'That is all the experience curve says. Everything beyond this is an inference, a hypothesis, a

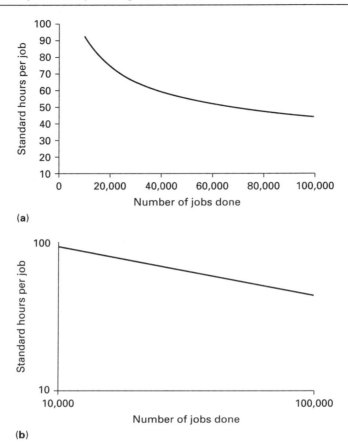

(a)

(b)

Figure 11.6 The learning curve

Table 11.2 Learning rates

Learning rate expressed as %	Slope of log curve, b
90	−0.152
85	−0.234
80	−0.322
75	−0.415
70	−0.515

corollary, or a theory. . . . The cost characteristics of experience curves can be observed in all elements of cost.'[12] Data supporting the existence of the long-term effect are hard to come by. Cost changes may originate elsewhere in the system, for instance from the way capital is depreciated. There are also difficulties with accounting comparisons over several years.

Effect on capacity

While care must be taken to not assume too much in relation to learning curves, there are several implications for the operations manager:

- Utilisation and yield will increase from both short-term and long-term learning. This means that achieved capacity will rise after a resource is introduced and staff learn how to obtain the best from it.

- Budgets for output rates and costs, such as labour, may incorporate expected productivity rises. Some firms involved in long production assembly runs, such as Texas Instruments, allow for these changes in their initial pricing. Alternatively, in assessing the amount to pay in a cost-plus contract for 250 special vehicles, the Ministry of Defence assesses productivity after (say) 20 items have been made, perhaps repeats the exercise after another 20 and then negotiates price improvements for the next batches.

- As some tasks are speeded up, scheduling assumptions will change.

- Improving performance will create strategic opportunities.

- Increasing the gradient of the learning curve may be possible. For example, training, continuous improvement programmes and encouraging minor innovations may all play their part.

11.4.3 Adjusting capacity in the medium term

We have seen in our discussion that there is no sharp distinction between the different time horizons for planning. As Table 11.1 shows, medium term suggests a period of six months to three years. Here we are referring to the possibility of making some changes to flexible parameters within a defined plant capacity. It is often known as *aggregate planning*. This is distinguished by making provision for operations over the medium term without changing the fixed capacity or getting down to the scheduling details of each order. It may be possible, for example, to change the number of weekly operating hours of a facility by increasing the number of staff. This usually requires a build-up and training of staff over several months.

Aggregate planning approaches diverge in different operating systems. They depend on whether stocks or queues (or both) can be used to smooth out variations in the match between demand and capacity.

Service systems

We noted the possibilities in Chapter 9. In summary, these are:

- flexibility of staffing through both multi-skilled and extra people
- switching between standardised and customised service
- changing service design, for example by switching between self-service and personal service
- sharing capacity with other organisations including subcontractors
- automation.

A further approach is to delay detailed planning as long as possible. Coach operators use this method to cope with changing demand at peak holidays. Urqhart is one of many companies operating New Year breaks. It books space in a variety of resort hotels a year in advance. In October, it outlines driver and coach schedules to ensure it has enough transport capacity. Breaks are sold either to specific hotels, named resorts or, at a further discount, as 'mystery tours'. Details of the route of each coach, with pick-up points, are confirmed just after Christmas as last-minute bookings come in.

Exercise 11.4 What is the advantage of the mystery tour? What other industries use a similar approach to maintaining flexibility?

Process and mass production

Many process plants operate at their technical limits, constrained by the performance of the slowest link in the chain. It is not usually possible to increase output of such plants through using additional personnel. In the longer term, managers may consider improvements to the slowest link through line balancing (explained in Chapter 8). In the medium term there may be opportunities based on replacing or bypassing the link. This would become urgent if there is a steady rise in demand.

The output of the fibreboard mill at Queensferry, North Wales, was limited by its capacity to grind timber chips into the main board ingredient, wood fibres. The grinding machines were expensive and had a long delivery time. A short-term improvement, arranged at four weeks notice, came from buying wood pulp from a firm that did not compete in the same market. This supplemented the flow after the grinding stage. Although the bought pulp was more expensive than the in-house variety, it increased the yield of whole plant and thus improved profits.

The net output of product is the key variable of concern to process plant managers. We noted earlier in the chapter that the net output of a process plant is given by:

$$Achieved\ capacity = Designed\ capacity \times Utilisation \times Yield$$

The medium-term management of process plant will concern itself with maintaining plant utilisation and reducing the amount of trim and waste. Yield is also an issue in other manufacturing systems. An item rejected for a defect found close to the finishing stage represents the loss of a unit of production capacity that can never be recovered. Avoiding such failures is an important benefit of aiming for zero defects in manufacture.

Mass production is similar to process production when it comes to considering these factors. Beyond these, however, many mass production lines have variable speed depending on the amount of personnel allocated to them. They can readily reduce their capacity provided the surplus staff can be redeployed elsewhere.

Jobbing and batch production

Jobbing and batch production have complex capacity-matching problems. As will be shown in Chapter 12, there is so much interference between products waiting for processing that scheduling a jobbing shop to anything approaching 100% capacity is impossible. The idea of an achievable, fixed capacity does not apply. It is found from experience. This does not mean that nothing can be done about utilisation. That is a key feature of MRP systems. Further, optimised production technology defines capacity not according to all the processes in the jobbing shop but just of those that act as bottlenecks.

Managers have, therefore, many opportunities to vary the capacity of these manufacturing facilities. If they are to do so efficiently, however, they need the backup of good data and good modelling techniques, from rules of thumb to computer-based MRP systems. Staff flexibility is an important feature of the successful implementation of approaches such as just-in-time systems. They depend on the ability to allocate resources to wherever processing delays are likely to occur. These questions are addressed again in Chapters 12 and 13.

11.4.4 Limits to chasing aggregate demand

Attempts to continually adjust capacity to match current and anticipated sales, known as *chasing demand*, are constrained by the inability to adjust capacity quickly. In some industries, the use of casual labour and other temporary resources is well established and a necessary part of operations. In other cases, however, employees are more highly trained and well organised; attempts to have total flexibility in their employment would fail.

Exercise 11.5   What other factors may limit the ability to chase demand?

Maintaining steady output is considered by many organisations to be good management. Therefore, they prefer to uncouple demand and throughput rates. The policy of *levelling output* looks attractive. The capacity is not changed in the short term and the facility can focus its efforts on being as efficient as possible. Japanese firms such as Nissan and Toyota believe that stable employment and consistent shop floor work lead to more experienced staff, easier supervision and better quality. Furthermore, the costs of change are eliminated and overtime working does not become habitual. Levelling output, however, requires either demand management or stocks and queues to separate the market and operating systems.

Level output policies are common in service industries. Passenger transport organisations have to plan their timetables months in advance and can only respond to random variations in customer flow by tolerating queues and congestion. Shops and personal service outlets have fixed opening hours. Mail order companies accept variations in order backlogs according to random demand changes.

Many organisations plan a mixed system with no shifts in capacity in response to short-term demand changes but occasional adjustments in the medium term. In this way, the operating core of the organisation is only changed to match established trends in the time series data rather than respond to its every 'blip' or seasonal fluctuation.

Figure 11.7 illustrates the policies of chasing demand and levelling output. It uses again the example of Figure 11.3, after removing the random effects. The

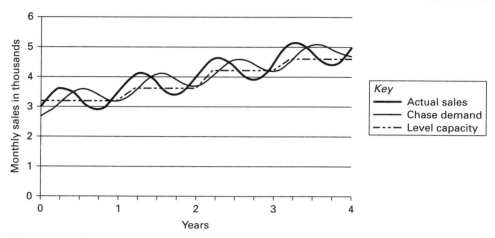

Figure 11.7 Approaches to smoothing capacity through aggregate planning

manufacturer attempts to satisfy demand that is steadily rising with seasonal variations. The chase demand approach adjusts capacity based on firm orders and short-term forecasts. The level demand policy makes annual adjustments according to the trend only. Differences between demand and production are absorbed by stock. The area lying between the actual sales line and the relevant production line represents stock changes. If the demand line is higher, stock is falling and vice versa. It can be seen that even the chase demand policy does not avoid the need for buffer stocks. Such variations and imperfections in whatever matching method is chosen mean that manufacturers follow a mixed policy. They combine capacity adjustments with both order backlogs (queues) and finished goods inventory.

The aggregate planning process creates a broad schedule for operations managers. As we can see in Figure 11.8, it bridges the gap between strategy and the short-term scheduling, such as MRP, which we will study in Chapter 12. For instance, at a cable manufacturer such as Pirelli, the aggregate plan covers a period of about a year. It is expressed in terms of tonnes of cable to be produced by each plant. Without being able to identify any order or product in detail, the plan helps to integrate the business. The personnel department ensures that enough staff are available, purchasing will place orders for those raw materials with long leadtimes, and accounting will prepare the cash budgets. Similar patterns occur in many firms: the seaside quick-service restaurant estimates demand a few weeks ahead; the mail order company plans the resources it needs to back up a new advertising campaign; and National Grid plans its maintenance to match the seasons.

✔ Quick check-up

Can you:
☐ Define designed, effective and achieved capacity.
☐ Distinguish state, effect and timing uncertainty.

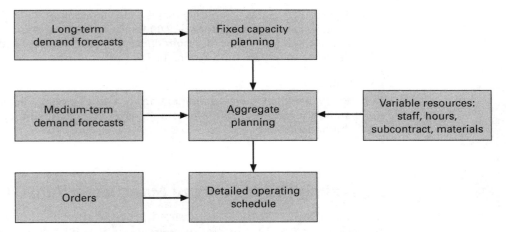

Figure 11.8 Aggregate planning as the link between capacity planning and detailed scheduling

☐ List three qualitative forecasting methods.

☐ Name two quantitative forecasting methods.

☐ Identify the four components of a typical time series in business.

☐ Suggest three reasons for the existence of learning curves.

☐ Summarise *chasing demand*.

❓ Questions

Chapter review

11.1 Compare the benefits and drawbacks of using qualitative forecasting methods.

11.2 Use the following monthly sales data to demonstrate the effect of the α constant in exponential forecasting:

36.1	36.6	44.6	44.3
35.7	38.2	47.2	44.3
32.4	42.5	48.0	43.1
35.8	42.5	45.7	39.4
37.5	43.9	43.7	40.0

The forecast for the first value was 35.9. Choose values for α of 0.1, 0.2 and 0.5.

11.3 Using examples, explain which sorts of operations are likely to increase their capacity through learning in the long term and which are unlikely to do so.

11.4 Why are the financial and strategic perspectives on capacity investment different? Discuss how they might be reconciled.

Application

11.5 Explain the advantages and disadvantages of using an exponentially smoothed time series to make the demand forecast shown in Figure 11.1.

11.6 Figure 11.7 shows monthly sales and production data for a company. Assuming an opening stock of 2,000 units, produce a graph or table showing the rise and fall of stock for both *chase demand* and *level capacity* strategies. Estimate your data from Figure 11.7.

Investigation

11.7 Study a recent policy statement from a government department or other authority. Identify the forecasts it uses and comment on the choice of methods used.[13]

| CLOSING CASE | # Expanding the capacity of Manchester Airport[14] |

Manchester Airport is the third busiest in the UK after Heathrow and Gatwick. In 1992 it handled 11.7 million passengers (mppa). By 2000, the number had grown to18.6 mppa and it was expected to handle 30 and 40 mppa in 2005 and 2015 respectively. Some 100 airlines offer 170 charter and scheduled services from the airport. Until 2001 it had one 3,048 metre runway served by three passenger terminals and a separate world freight terminal. Other airfield activities include maintenance and support such as fuelling.

Manchester Airport plc is a company established in 1986. Its shareholders are the ten local authorities of Greater Manchester with Manchester City Council holding the majority stake. The company has a licence to operate its airport from the Civil Aviation Authority. The CAA ensures fair access to all aircraft, allows for distribution of landing slots among airlines and sets hourly runway capacities consistent with safe working. Airlines' response to congestion and the unavailability of slots can be to increase the size of aircraft or to move their business elsewhere.

The primary purpose of an airport is to act as a node connecting air routes with each other and with those on the ground. While about 60% of passengers landing at London Heathrow leave by air, almost all transfers at Manchester are to ground transport. Passengers and freight pass through stages whose capacity must match demand and be balanced if the airport resources are to be used efficiently. The airport system can be seen as having three key subsystems: the runways, the terminals, where the interchange occurs, and the local ground network.

Runways

By the early 1990s Manchester had developed its single runway to achieve a 'best in class' performance of 42 air transport movements (ATMs) per hour. This output was required neither at all times of the day nor all year. Peak daily movement occurs from 0700 to 1000 and 1600 to 1930. Summer demand, especially for charter movements, is higher than in the winter. Furthermore, any runway is closed from time to time. Planned closure for maintenance occurs usually at night. Unplanned closure, happening at any time, results in a complete shutdown of the airport.

Announcing plans for a second runway in 1991, the company forecast that demand would rise to 22 mppa by 2000, implying a shortage of capacity on the single strip. Based on 100 passengers per flight, ATMs were calculated to be 220,000 in 2000 and 300,000 in 2005. The latter figure implied a peak capacity of at least 60 per hour, yielding an annual utilisation of 57%. The forecast 8% compound growth during the 1990s turned out to be 6% in practice, delaying the need for a second runway by about a year.

Terminals

Of the three terminals, the most recent is T2, whose first phase opened in 1993. Planned extensions and improvements to both T1 and T2 would take total capacity to around 30 mppa. T3, once a section of T1, handles British Airways services and the 16% of passengers on domestic routes not requiring passport and customs controls.

Ground transport

Road vehicle movements generated by the airport were, in 1991, about 52,000 during the effective 16-hour day. The projected growth would increase this to 124,000 by 2005. About 80% of the road vehicles use the M56 motorway. The airport expansion would increase the total traffic on this road by 13%. During the 1990s, both M56 and the connecting ring road to the M60 were widened and a new link to the M6 was being planned.

Planners have a target of 25% of all ground journeys to be by public transport by 2005. Some 100 trains per day run north into the city and south through Crewe. In 2000, the government approved the £289 million extension of the Metrolink tramway from the city.

Associated with terminal development is the Ground Transport Interchange, begun in 2000. Extending the current railway station facilities, this will be the first facility in the country to integrate transport connections and check-in facilities. All phases of passenger movement will be faster and more convenient, supporting the target in terms of capacity and quality. Since the node will contain railway, tramway, coach and bus stations, as well as a car and taxi drop-off area, it will generate traffic among people not taking flights but using the Interchange as a ground hub.

The second runway

The second runway proposal attracted widespread support and protest, coming to a head during the public enquiry of 1995. Objectors cited unnecessary environmental damage and the need to use capacity elsewhere, especially at Liverpool. The extension covered part of the small, picturesque Bollin Valley and require the demolition or removal of several historic farm buildings. To the south-east lies the village of Styal with its important heritage of the early industrial era (see Figure 11.9).

In its planning application, the airport company tried to anticipate and respond to many of the objections. It considered impact on the physical environment in terms of noise, air and water quality, landscape, wildlife and so on. Although a different orientation would limit the impact on some sensitive sites, safety requirements meant that the new runway would have to parallel the old. In response to the special nature of the Styal area, however, it was built

▶

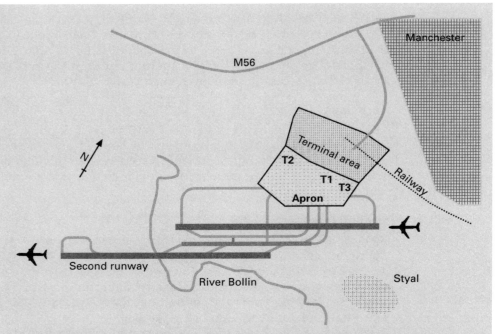

Figure 11.9 Manchester Airport showing runway use in the prevailing wind

to the west of the existing one and used in such a way that aircraft would not fly any closer to the village than previously. It would handle peak traffic and never be used at night. In the prevailing westerly winds, its purpose would be for take-off. On the 20% of days when easterlies blow, it would be for landing. Enforced preferred noise routes protect communities further from the airport.

Questions

1 Use a mind map or systems map to sketch the capacity issues in the development of the airport.

2 Sketch a flow diagram showing the processes a passenger passes through from a tram to a flight. From the capacity management point of view, where can problems arise?

3 What would be the role of aggregate planning in the airport context?

4 Identify the types of forecasting mentioned in the case. What are the implications of any errors?

5 What other systems, not mentioned here, restrict or influence the operating capacity of Manchester Airport?

Notes and references

1. National Grid (2000) *Seven Year Statement*, London: National Grid Group.
2. Hellier, D. (1994) 'Eurotunnel capacity challenged', *The Independent on Sunday Business News*, 1 May, p.1; http://www.eurotunnel.co.uk/corpuk/system.asp accessed 3 July 2001.
3. Burt, T. (2001) 'Drive to make investments sweat', *The Financial Times*, 24 May, p.8.
4. Faith, N. (1995) 'Third Heathrow runway to be ruled out in bid for terminal', *The Independent on Sunday Business News*, 29 January, p.1.
5. DuClous, P. (1993) 'Cream of the continent', *World Trade*, 6(8), September, pp.136–40.
6. Leaver, D. and Al-Zubaidi, H. (1996) 'Challenging conventional wisdom: A reappraisal of the UK DIY market', *International Journal of Retail and Distribution Management*, 24(11), pp.39–45.
7. National Grid Company plc (1994) *Highways of Power*.
8. Kleinwort Benson Limited (1990) *Mini Prospectus: The regional electricity companies share offers*, 21 November, pp.23–4.
9. Cannon, T. (1992) *Basic Marketing*, 3rd edition, London: Cassell, pp.156–71.
10. Render, R. and Heizer, J. (1994) *Principles of Operations Management*, Boston: Allyn and Bacon, p.216.
11. Dobson, S.M. and Goddard J.A. (1992) 'The demand for standing and seated viewing accommodation in the English football league', *Applied Economics*, 24(10), October, pp.1155–63.
12. Henderson, B. (1984) *The Logic of Business Strategy*, Cambridge, MA: Ballinger, p.49–50.
13. Search the website of a government department using the word 'forecast'. For instance, the DETR, http://www.detr.gov.uk, has Department of the Environment, Transport and the Regions (2000) *Air Traffic Forecasts for the United Kingdom* http://www.aviation.detr.gov.uk/atfuk2000/index.htm accessed 20 July 2001.
14. Case study is based on: Manchester Airport plc (1993) *Runway 2: Planning Application Supporting Statement*, July, mimeo; Cobham Resource Consultants and Consultants in Environmental Sciences Ltd (1993) *Runway 2: Environmental Statement – non-technical summary*, Manchester, Manchester Airport plc, July, mimeo; Manchester Airport plc (2000) *24R Runway Operations*, Manchester Airport plc Community Relations Office; Manchester Airport (2001) *Exciting New Public Transport Developments at Manchester Airport*, press release; www.manairport.co.uk accessed 20 July 2001.

CHAPTER 12

Scheduling

OBJECTIVES

When you have finished studying this chapter, you should be able to:

- Identify scheduling issues in intermittent and repetitive manufacture and service operations.

- Use Gantt charts to explain the complexity of task sequencing is a simple job shop; suggest how it may be managed.

- Apply Johnson's rule to illustrate the question of optimisation of intermittent processes.

- Explain the context and use of the MRP family of systems in batch scheduling; describe some difficulties that arise in implementation.

- Outline the theory of constraints and its contribution to resolving scheduling dilemmas.

- Show how just-in-time philosophy has been applied and how it can be used to gradually achieve a reduction in waste; illustrate how a basic kanban link works.

- Compare the use of techniques in intermittent and repetitive manufacture and discuss how they interact with the people who use them.

- Set service scheduling needs in a comparative framework.

- Explain some approaches to scheduling mass service.

OPENING CASE

Saxon fire appliances[1]

Customers for fire engines in the United Kingdom are mainly local fire authorities. The most common purchase is the pump/ladder appliance (PLA), costing between £120,000 and £180,000. Each is built upon a standard 10 to 15-tonne lorry chassis by extending the cab and fitting a powerful water pump, a 1,800-litre water tank and side storage racks. The latter, protected by the familiar aluminium roller shutters, hold securely a range of fire fighting and rescue equipment. They also support two portable ladders and other roof mountings. Fire brigades also purchase more specialised vehicles such as turntable ladder appliances, water carriers, command centres and so on. The market is very fragmented, with each brigade placing orders after a specification and tendering process; the brigades avoid switching costs by sticking to one brand of chassis from Renault, Volvo, Dodge and so on. They also specify layout, fittings, on-board equipment and many other details down to the fabric of the seats. Such minor variations can mean high design and manufacturing costs. Furthermore, customers often ask for changes during construction.

The market is changing in three ways. First, several brigades have been considering leasing contracts, rather than outright purchases. They, with the leasing company, will consider more carefully whole life operating costs and not just focus on the initial price. Eventually, a leasing company may own a fleet larger than any authority. This will raise interest in standardisation to lower both initial prices and maintenance costs. Second, public sector purchases are subject to EU competition rules, opening the largely domestic market to new competitors. The Austrian company Rosenbauer, among the top three in the world, is one that poses a threat. It is about ten times the size of Saxon Sandbec, the UK market leader. The third trend involves changes in the way equipment is used. The need for crew safety has led to many design improvements. For instance, new rules on crew numbers who must attend incidents imply larger cabs so the station need send only one vehicle.

Part of the Special Vehicles Division of the Johnston Group, Saxon Sandbec assembles appliances at its plant in Sandbach, Cheshire. Its output numbers some 100 PLAs per year from a staff of 120. Until 2000, the company followed the habit of the industry, accepting the variety of specifications and building each vehicle up from a chassis driven in from the supplier's plant. After arrival, each did not move within the workshop until ready for painting. The layout and atmosphere were typical of the jobbing shop, with a clutter of components, benches and hand tools among the vehicles. The process was difficult to schedule and control; deliveries were up to nine months late and labour input often over ran by 500 hours. This compounded the chaos of the workshop with even more stock waiting to be installed. The business was not profitable.

A new managing director saw that Saxon Sandbec must improve its planning, scheduling, materials flows and labour cost controls if it were to survive. He approached the problem on several fronts. First, the company should standardise design into a range of modules built away from the vehicle and fitted to the chassis when complete. Examples of modules are cabs, pumps, water tanks, 110-volt lighting systems, side storage boxes, equipment carried on the roof and sets of rescue and control equipment. While remaining prepared to meet any detailed specifications, Saxon Sandbec would point out to customers the savings from using standard modules. These would arise from simplification in estimating, designing and manufacture. Second, parallel to the first, the paper-based materials management procedures were replaced by a computer-based materials resources planning system. This greatly improved estimating, ordering and so on. The third change, dependent on the first two, was to outsource the supply of many components to specialist companies. Not only could they produce more cheaply, they could deliver alongside the flow line at the point where the items were needed. Early changes involved the stocks of fixings (nuts, bolts, rivets, washers) and sealants placed in racks next to the work stations. Going beyond these arrangements, the company replaced much of the work in its small and outdated machine shop with supply partnerships. In addition to product improvement, these agreements with specialists allowed simplification of the work flow enabling Saxon Sandbec to focus on its strengths. These were designing and assembling reliable fire appliances to match customers' specifications.

12.1   Introduction

Among the many changes introduced at Saxon Sandbec were those in its scheduling system. Dealing with increasingly demanding customers and facing strengthening competition, the company knew it had to speed its work flow to remain in business. Managed as a jobbing shop, with each appliance treated as a separate contract, managers found difficulty in meeting delivery promises. Delay was seen in the several almost finished vehicles waiting for the odd component or subassembly to be fabricated. Financing this work in progress contributed to the business losses. Entry of new competitors, coupled with a new awareness among customers of the benefits of standardisation, meant that things had to change. The key was scheduling.

The job shop is ideal for markets where small quantities and high variety are required. Yet such a company will fail when customers want, and rivals supply, a more reliable supply of standard items.

Scheduling deals with the timing of operations. To produce schedules, an organisation may start from capacity and aggregate plans, if it has them, and produce detailed instructions on the sequence and times for each operation it intends to carry out. This suggests that planning must be carried out in advance and in detail. Although this is true in principle, we shall see in practice that the problem can be eased by repetition, focus on key elements and the skills and experience of the people on the ground.

Schedulers not only plan jobs as they pass through the operations system. They also assign personnel, equipment, materials and other resources to each stage. The purpose is to optimise operational performance according to a combination of the following objectives:

- time the order spends within the system
- waiting time for the customer
- efficiency of use of resources
- inventory levels.

Having to optimise, or at least cope with, many factors simultaneously makes scheduling a complex job. Box 12.1 outlines four situations where resources must be combined for the activities to take place. Sometimes, the allocation of resources is automatic, established by practice over many repeats. In others, however, details of each element need to be worked out in advance.

BOX 12.1 **Some scheduling tasks**

Business	Some items for scheduling
Jobbing printer	Order sequencing; machine allocation; employee assignment; paper and ink supply; print setting
Parcel service	Collection and delivery routing; consolidation; vehicle allocation; crew assignment; sorting times
Brewery	Product sequencing; fermentation times; raw material flows; bottling, barrelling or despatch; employee assignment

Exercise 12.1   List the elements needing detailed scheduling at: a bus company; a secondary
school; a petrol retailer; and gas-fired power station.

To discuss the scheduling of manufacturing processes, we can return to our
classification of process technologies. Operations scheduling in jobbing and
batch production, that is *intermittent* systems, is different from that in mass
and process production, called *repetitive* production. The former systems are
characterised by separate processes that can produce a variety of items either
individually or in batches. Managers have to focus their attention both on these
processes, possibly in groups, and on the orders to be moved through them. The
job shop has the highest variety and the more ad hoc procedures. The batch
operation frequently runs batches of the same product and therefore finds it
worthwhile to make and keep plans that are more detailed. In repetitive manufacturing, attention is not so much given to the detail of individual orders but to
the steady flow of commodities through the whole production system.

The manufacturing process not included in the intermittent–repetitive typology is the project. Since project planning and scheduling usually focus on the
delivery of a single contract, the scheduling techniques differ from those used
elsewhere. Consequently, we discuss project management in a separate chapter.

Direct service operations are often designed to respond to demand as it arises.
Therefore, they cannot be scheduled in detail. Self-service systems need no
scheduling. Isolated services have, as we noted in Chapter 3, many characteristics in common with both intermittent and repetitive manufacturing systems.
Therefore, our examples will be drawn from both manufacture and isolated
service.

12.2 Intermittent manufacture

12.2.1 Job shop scheduling difficulties

Job shops are noted for their high variety of work and their low volume. Production is usually carried out to customers' orders, each differing in their requirements. Consequently, each order has to be planned and tracked all the way
through to its conclusion and despatch. Depending on the firm's previous experience and the variety of tasks to be undertaken, there can be considerable uncertainty about how much time each will take and planners have to allow enough
flexibility within the system to enable it to cope. We can understand this more
clearly when we recognise that new orders with yet further patterns of requirements are continually being received and inserted into the production sequence.

There are many scheduling techniques, each suiting a particular problem setting. They will focus on defined objectives, such as the minimisation of machine
idle time or the maximisation of throughput volume. Reliable and appropriate
techniques are vital in the jobbing shop. Ranging from the simple rule of 'first-
come-first-served' to full-scale manufacturing requirements planning, they move
scheduling from a hit-and-miss affair to a consistent and dependable management

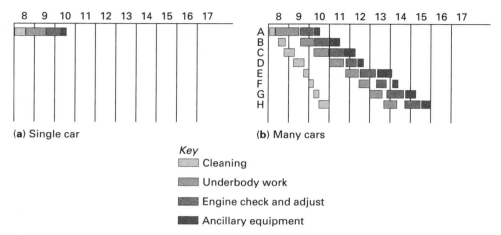

Figure 12.1 Servicing schedules for a single car and many cars

activity. What a job shop cannot achieve, however, is a pattern of constantly working machines, busy staff and no delays in orders passing through. Slack is needed somewhere.

To illustrate the difficulties let us look at scheduling in a car repair shop. Take the following example of basic servicing:

When I was last in Crane Bank Garage, I overheard a customer complaining that a two-hour job took all day. It looked as if the manager must have a scheduling problem. To simplify things, we shall consider all cars as requiring the same sort of service. In reality, the variety of tasks that customers ask for makes matters much worse! So let us say that there are four stages as follows:

C Cleaning. The garage does not carry out full service work without cleaning. This process takes place in a bay equipped with steam lances and ramps.

U Under body inspection and lubrication. Brake check and adjustment. This is done on a hoist fitted with oil changing equipment.

E Engine check and adjustment using the Krypton tuner to bring emissions into line with the regulations.

A Ancillary equipment check and repair.

Normal times for these jobs are well established for different makes of car. For our customer's model, the manager estimates them to be: C = 0.5; U = 0.75; E = 0.75; A = 0.5. Consequently, we might agree with the customer's assertion that they should take two hours all together. So why might it take all day?

To begin to investigate why the job takes longer, we could start by plotting the schedule for each task as shown in the left half of Figure 12.1. This is a Gantt chart, a widely used form of presentation for sequenced events. In its standard form, the times for each task are plotted as horizontal bars, on a time scale ranging from minutes to months as appropriate.

The first Gantt chart suggests that the job should be finished by 10:30. This would be the case if this were, as many clients believe, the only car in the shop. The difficulty is that our customer's is not the only one in. It has no particular priority over the others and the supervisor has used Crane Bank's usual scheduling rule: process cars in the order in which they are booked in. Cars waiting for each stage are taken, therefore, in the same sequence.

The second Gantt chart of Figure 12.1 shows the effect of the scheduling rule. Each row of the chart represents the progress of one vehicle. Each of the four tasks is indicated. On a Gantt chart, we code different tasks with a shading or colour scheme.

We could just as well use each row to plot the activity of each process and identify the cars by a shading code. This would be rather like a horizontal version of the multiple activity chart of Chapter 6. Which way the chart is drawn depends on the number of processes and jobs and on why we are producing it. Here our interest is on the progress, against the clock, of cars through the shop. Note that the irate customer's car is G and the workshop closes from 12:30 to 13:30.

Clearly, the irregular pattern of task times means that cars have to wait between stages. A two-hour job can indeed take all day. Of course, the garage could please its customer by servicing G more quickly. Yet, since not all customers can be given this priority, the manager has to decide whether to concede in this case and then explain the decision to the others. This is a typical function of the front office in isolating service operations.

Exercise 12.2

What other uses have you seen, or can you suggest, for a Gantt chart? Why would a manager use the bars to plot the work processes instead of the progress of cars?

Scheduling complexity

The repair shop example, although simplified, is typical of scheduling problems in jobbing and batch production. On the one hand, orders are being pushed through task sequences in as short a time as possible. On the other hand, these tasks have to be carried out efficiently. Harrison[2] quotes Shingo's description of the complexity of the system (see Figure 12.2). The production system is a multidimensional network of operations and processes. Workers and machines work on various processes. Provided there is always work waiting at each stage, these can appear to be very efficient. Yet jobs have to pass through these stages in many sequences. As Figures 12.1 and 12.2 both show, they may have to wait ahead of every process they come to, whether these are direct operations or inspection, transport and the like. A balance has to be achieved between the efficiency of the production system and the throughput of the jobs.

A moment's further inspection of the situation at Crane Bank Garage shows that, with a little planning, the time taken for most cars and the waiting time of each process could be reduced. For example, the day could start with car B because it requires the shortest period in the cleaning bay. The next process could then start earlier and so on. It looks as though the business could improve its performance by better scheduling. Is it possible to formalise the scheduling decision to make this possible?

Scheduling rules

Our repair shop example is, as we have already seen, typical of job shop scheduling problems. There are four principal elements:

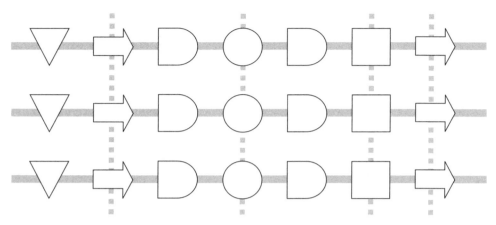

Figure 12.2 Conflict between production flow and efficiency of operational subsystems

- Several *work stations*: in our case these are the stages through which cars are processed.

- Several *jobs*: these are the cars themselves, the work on each being a complete job.

- A *sequence for each job*: for the purposes of our illustration there was one standard sequence but it easy to see that even these operations could be done in a different order provided the first was cleaning.

- A *time for each operation*: in a simple case, this is assumed to be known in advance and the uncertainty connected with it is ignored.

Sequencing rules, of which many exist, take the elements of the scheduling problem and, using a procedure, work out a plan. The rules include the following:

FCFS   First-come-first-served
LPT   Longest processing time first
SPT   Shortest processing time first
EDD   Earliest due date first

Exercise 12.3

Other rules have applications in different circumstances. Considering the wider business context, suggest three others that an owner–manager might have for sequencing.

12.2.2 Job shop loading: sequencing through one process

The simplest sequencing problem occurs when several jobs have to be passed through one process only. Take the following example of a job shop providing isolated service:

Bithell's Boats has a small dry dock that can take one canal cruiser at once for cleaning and repainting. At the time of our investigation, the dock had just become free and there were five boats waiting. They had been examined and Mr Bithell was

Table 12.1 Boat maintenance times

Boat	Servicing time (days)	Promised time ahead
Alexandra	12	16
Barbara	4	12
Caroline	16	36
Daphne	6	30
Ester	18	46

Table 12.2 Bithell's Boats with different decision rules

FCFS: First-come-first-served					LPT: Longest processing time first				
Boat	Time in dock	Total time	Promised days	Days late	Boat	Time in dock	Total time	Promised days	Days late
A	12	12	16	—	E	18	18	46	—
B	4	16	12	4	C	16	34	36	—
C	16	32	36	—	A	12	46	16	30
D	6	38	30	8	D	6	52	30	22
E	18	56	46	10	B	4	56	12	44
	56	154		22		56	206		96

confident about the work time required in each case. The trouble was that he had given estimated completion times to each customer. Table 12.1 shows the relevant data. In which sequence should the boats have been repaired?

Table 12.2 sets out the progress of the yard if it followed two of our decision rules.

Exercise 12.4 Extend the work in Table 12.2 to consider our other decision rules, SPT and EDD.

As with many scheduling techniques, selecting which outcome is the best depends on what Mr Bithell is trying to achieve. To help in this assessment we can propose three measures of performance: the mean time to complete; the mean number of boats in the system; and the mean number of days late.

$$Mean\ time\ to\ complete = \frac{Sum\ of\ all\ waiting\ and\ servicing\ times}{Number\ of\ boats}$$

$$Mean\ number\ in\ system = \frac{Sum\ of\ all\ waiting\ and\ servicing\ times}{Sum\ of\ servicing\ times}$$

$$Mean\ number\ of\ days\ late = \frac{Sum\ of\ days\ late}{Number\ of\ boats}$$

Table 12.3 compares the four decision rules against these measures of performance. It can be seen that no rule beats the others on every count. By the same token, LPT stands out as worst. For the rest, Mr Bithell could benefit from changing his work order from FCFS to either SPT or EDD. Yet, customers may object because they regard FCFS as the most equitable form of queuing. SPT may seem slightly better than EDD and it often helps employees' morale to see the quick jobs out of the way.

Table 12.3 Comparison of sequencing policies at Bithell's Boats

	Mean days to complete	Mean number in system	Mean days late
FCFS	30.8	2.8	4.4
LPT	41.2	3.7	19.2
SPT	26.0	2.3	3.6
EDD	27.2	2.4	2.4

SPT has an important disadvantage, however. Since the business is dynamic, it would be receiving a stream of new orders and enquiries. Any new work with estimated processing time less than boat E would be placed ahead of it in the queue. Consequently, E would be drift down the queue and may never be attended to! Using SPT, therefore, requires a regular review of the longest jobs.

12.2.3 Job shop loading: sequencing through more than one process

Sequencing becomes more complicated when work flows through more than one stage. There are very few theoretical solutions to the problem of scheduling several jobs on two or more work stations. We shall illustrate, however, Johnson's rule for two stations. It is designed to minimise both processing and idle time.

Johnson's rule has four steps:

1 List each job with the time it needs at each station, including set-up time.

2 Choose the job with the shortest processing time at either station. If this is the first station, put this job first. If it is the second, put the job last.

3 Take the selected job out of the list.

4 Repeat steps 2 and 3, filling in the intermediate positions in the sequence.

The data in Table 12.4 are processed as follows. #104 has the shortest time. It is on machine X so #104 goes first in line. #101 then has the shortest time, also on X, so it is put second in line. Then #102 is selected; but this time the shorter time is on Y so it goes at the end. We continue with #103. It goes next to the end and finally #105 is placed in the middle. The sequence is 104, 101, 105, 103, 102.

The outcome of Johnson's rule is depicted in the Gantt chart of Figure 12.3. The upper part of the diagram shows the preferred order while the lower illustrates what would happen if the processing took place in the arbitrary sequence of job numbers. The advantage of using Johnson's rule is evident.

Note the simplification in the analysis. No allowance is made for tasks that either precede or follow the five in question. It could be that the idle times for X

Table 12.4 Five jobs, two machines

Job no.	Machine X hrs	Machine Y hrs
101	5	8
102	11	6
103	13	7
104	4	11
105	9	10

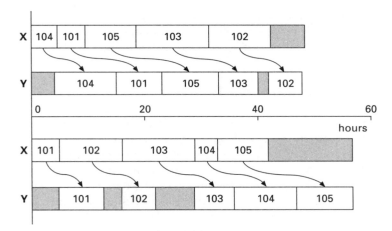

Figure 12.3 Illustrating Johnson's rule: five jobs and two machines

at the end and Y at the start could be absorbed by further jobs in the sequence. Consequently, Figure 12.3 may exaggerate differences in performance under the two rules.

More complex problems

Modelling longer sequences is beyond our scope. In any case, rarely can Johnson's rule be applied in practice. For the job shop supervisor, however, there is a suggestion of an applicable rule of thumb. This could be: *Ensure that the machines early in the sequence do sufficient jobs of short duration to keep the later machines busy.* With this approach, most of the machines would be filled with work and the efficiency figures would look satisfactory. Yet, we must not fall into the trap of stressing machine efficiency as the single goal. The result would be a pile-up of work in progress with its associated slow-down in flow through the business. Giving the downstream machines too much work is as bad as giving them too little.

Job shops with many work centres have to cope with complexity. They do so with a mixture of policies that can include:

- rough planning and sequencing in the office, together with some indication of priorities
- surplus capacity to cope with variety
- decentralisation of detailed sequencing to manufacturing cells or individual employees
- adaptable staff with a range of skills
- using progress chasers or expeditors to track orders and change local sequences
- intervention by supervisors and managers through progress meetings.

The job shop is characterised by limited planning resources in comparison to the number of orders it receives. Usually, the size and complexity of each job mean that any policy more sophisticated and expensive than these does not bring a return. Many businesses, however, can group jobs into batches of items that are the same or very similar. This reduces the variety of work going through the factory and makes more thorough initial planning more worthwhile.

12.2.4 Batch scheduling: MRPII

Batch production shops could work in similar ways to job shops by treating each order as a job and following more fully the policies set out in preceding paragraphs. By so doing, however, they would not be taking advantage of the relative scale of each order and associated reduction in variety. With the development of information systems that gather and combine data very efficiently, opportunities have opened to integrate the planning, scheduling and control of batch production more effectively than in the past. Among the best known applications is MRPII, manufacturing resources planning mark two.

There is not one MRPII method, rather a family of approaches with the same general principles. They use proprietary hardware and software from specialists in the field. MRPII grew from MRP, materials requirements planning, which applied information technology in leading companies in the 1960s. This was *dependent* materials control. Saxon Sandbec illustrates the change. Previously, the company ordered stocks of raw materials and components, from sheet metal and glass to lamp brackets, according to an estimated general usage. Items were drawn from the store as needed. The MRP system identifies the components needed for each order and schedules their supply only when needed.

MRPII goes beyond material ordering. In its various forms, it is a method for planning all manufacturing resources. It cascades down from the aggregate business plans, through the master production schedule (MPS) to provide detailed instructions to the purchasing department, suppliers, stores and the shop floor. Extensions can allow for tool supply, maintenance planning, personnel allocation and financial analysis. Figure 12.4 outlines the links among the core functions to be integrated within MRPII. This diagram shows an *open-loop* system because the feedback control links are not shown. The topic of control is covered in Chapter 15.

The core functions in MRPII are as follows.

Aggregate sales and operations plan

As explained in Chapter 11, aggregate plans cover the medium term. Without detailing individual orders, they identify the range of products expected to be ordered, with batch sizes, expected delivery schedules and so on. In making commitments at this stage, including estimated throughput times, advanced purchases of raw materials and short-range adjustments to capacity, the aggregate plan creates a framework for the MPS to be produced.

Master production schedule

The MPS is the linchpin of the MRPII system. It is a specification of what is to be made and when. Continually updated, the MPS fits in with the aggregate plan, financial plans and constraints, and known capacity. It has to consider not only

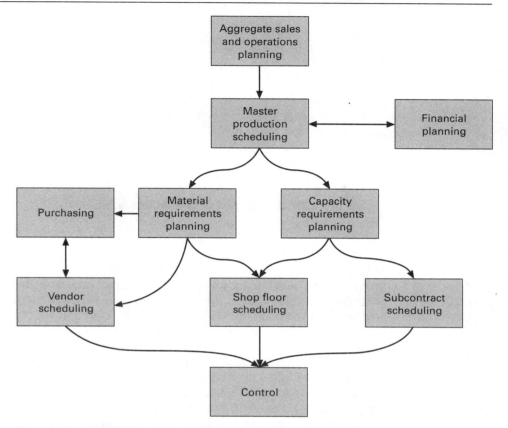

Figure 12.4 MRPII processes without the control loops

shop floor capacity but also leadtimes of vendors and subcontractors where these are used.

Material requirements plan

The master schedule can be itemised into the MRP through bringing together several modules. The bill of materials is an item-by-item list of the materials needs for each order. Stock records identify what material is already available *and uncommitted to any other order*. The MRP then sets out the further materials to be obtained for order completion. Under many supply chain agreements, requirements are sent to vendors automatically.

Capacity requirements plan

The CRP produces, in the first pass, daily or weekly estimates of the workload in each department, even analysing it down to key machines or processes. Its purpose is to anticipate difficulties in good time so that short-term adjustments can be made to capacity, if that is possible, or the MPS can be revised to bring forward or delay orders as appropriate.

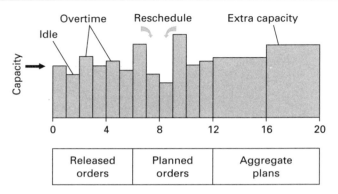

Figure 12.5 CRP at the level of one work station

Figure 12.5 suggests how to handle variations in capacity requirements. The MPS has six weeks of *released orders*, that is orders for which details have been prepared for the shop floor, suppliers and subcontractors. Resources have been committed to these orders. Variations in weekly load at a particular work station are shown in the diagram. They are relatively small and are coped with by allowing idle time in week 2 and overtime later in the period. After week 6, we have a further six weeks with orders planned but not released. Schedules must be confirmed as the picture becomes clear. For example, customers may wish to alter their own schedules. At this time, the load at the work station is not balanced and some of it must be rescheduled. For example, work from week 7 may be delayed and from week 10 brought forward. Beyond the twelfth week, we return to the field of aggregate planning in which rough capacity needs are identified monthly. Here, the MPS will show that the current aggregate plans will cause overload at the work station and arrangements must be made to provide extra capacity.

Detailed schedules for shop floor, vendors and subcontractors

The power of MRPII systems shows through when detailed schedules are produced. The information system brings together component-by-component vendor lead-times, shop floor manufacturing sequences and times and assembly sequences. For the first time any item is produced, the creation of this information requires substantial investment but, once in place, the files can be adapted and updated as changes in design and production processes are introduced.

MRPII is not an automatic scheduling system. While its software may contain algorithms for sequencing jobs at various stages as well as constraints and alarm functions to give warnings when leadtimes or capacity limits are likely to be violated, the basic decisions have to be made by managers. Factories will have a scheduling office manned by a few key persons whose role requires a blend of knowledge of the production processes with diplomatic skills to absorb the stress caused by changes in the plan.

MRPII can bring considerable benefits in terms of reduced costs and improved response to customer needs. Standards reported include figures of more than 95%

for both deliveries on time and manufacturing efficiency. While we have presented it here in the context of batch production MRPII has been used in other types of production technology, sometimes under other names. Spreadbury[3] described its success in continuous process scheduling at Dista, a pharmaceutical plant.

12.2.5 Problems with MRPII

Computing power

There is a danger that the technical power of MRPII can encourage excessive rescheduling. It is normal to review the whole MRPII weekly; this means moving the planning horizons forward and updating all changes occurring during the previous week. Changes could vary from the receipt of a rush order from a valued customer to a difficulty at a vendor's plant. Yet, this *regenerative* approach to the information system, encouraged by efficient computing, may be wasteful. It may create many small changes to the order sequences and hence revise instructions. *Net-change* MRPII, however, modifies only those areas that have changed significantly. It requires more sophisticated software but will reduce the dithering or *system nervousness* that can lead to stress among users. The operations system should respond to major changes but should absorb minor ones through its own flexibility.

Changing culture

The change of beliefs and behaviour throughout the operations functions of the business are significant parts of successful implementation. Luscombe describes two MRPII failure modes in this connection.[4] Both relate to the compromises needed in developing a workable MPS. First, the sales department finds that it is being asked to provide regular sales forecasts and that these forecasts are being used to decide the aggregate plan, the quantities and types of products that are to be available for sale. Often this requires sales to change their behaviour from taking what orders they can get, including 'slipping in' the odd urgent one where possible. The MPS now enables the scheduler to point out the knock-on effects of accepting an urgent order. Other orders, possibly already released with promised delivery dates, will have to be put back. In the past, such changes would not have been noticed amid the general chaos. The second problem follows on from the first. Even if the new relationship between sales and production can be established, it may not be supported by senior managers and by key customers. A valued customer may find that, suddenly, sales is unwilling to push a rush order through the system. The frustrated customer telephones a senior manager who decides that 'for once' the wishes of the customer must be satisfied. The order is accepted. The MPS credibility is weakened. Other orders become late. Fire fighting and progressing return and 'normal service' is resumed.

Production orientation

Is MRPII too dominated by production? Is it a return to a production orientation for the business in circumstances where greater efforts should be made in giving high levels of customer service? Luscombe answers these questions in this way:

BOX 12.2 **MRPII failure. Or was the problem deeper?**

There is widespread recognition among the members of the manufacturing management team that the factory is not performing effectively. High inventory levels, poor due date performance and manufacturing times all appear to be excessive. The general opinion is that major problems were encountered in achieving the manufacturing plan and the levels of expediting by management in trying to achieve the plan are excessive. The group gave the impression that individual responsibilities for scheduling the factory, inventory management and product delivery performance are not clearly established.

For example, the product-led expediting practice appears to set expediter against expediter in a battle to establish order priority within the manufacturing areas. One comment from the management team was that 'the right hand does not know what the left hand is doing here' and so one has to question the effectiveness of communicating shop floor data. As a result, a disproportionate number of manufacturing shop orders are on the highest priority, due dates are changed to effect queue jumping and real priorities, i.e. customer delivery dates, are masked.

The whole factory appears to be shortage and priority driven and, as a result, management appears to be reactive, jumping from one crisis to another . . . the real culprit is the [name] MRPII system as there are clear and obvious planning and control difficulties . . .

One possible explanation for this lies in the nature of the three product lines manufactured by [company name]. One application of [name] MRPII is used to control all of them yet factors in one may be different from the other two.

To give all customers the best possible service all the time, much better planning and control is required than has previously been possible. There was never any difficulty in rushing one urgent job through production to satisfy a particularly demanding customer. The price was in the poor delivery performance, inability to forecast despatch dates, high production inventory costs, and long lead time that were accepted as the norm for the bulk of customer orders.[5]

Managing complexity

Several surveys[6] point to frequent failure with MRPII implementation. It is not clear whether these amount to reductions in performance of the whole production system or a lack of achievement of high expectations which hade been set out at the start of projects. In any case, criticism has been levelled at MRPII schemes because of their attempt to manage the whole production system in detail. The more complex the system, the more difficult this task becomes.

Box 12.2 is drawn from notes made in interviews by a colleague at Liverpool John Moores University.[7] The first module of an MRP system at this factory had been installed in 1977 and had been added to over the following 17 years as MRPII became available. It appears that the factory managers had never been happy with the system except in as far as it gave them something, other than themselves, to blame! Our report invited the managers to return to the recognition that MRPII is merely a planning tool with known rules and logic. It will not optimise schedules itself and cannot cope with frequent changes imposed from above. The three product ranges were offered in different industrial markets and, although they shared some common components and processes, mixing them in the same plant did create problems of conflicting pressure. The factory had not given sufficient status to the role of the scheduling office so that decisions made by the small team that maintained the MRPII were not supported. The person responsible for the MPS had the same rank as first line supervisor.

The key to successful implementation lies in recognising that approaches such as MRPII is not a technical 'fix'. If treated in this way it becomes a rigid burden. Managers find they have to override it to regain the flexibility which successful batch systems require. Sillince and Sykes[8] point to the major *management* changes that are required if benefits other than inventory reduction are to be obtained. Brown[9] also stresses change on a grand scale. These are among others who identify continuing top management commitment among the keys to success. To this factor, Humphreys and colleagues[10] add the identification of a competent person to lead the change and benchmarking. Regarding the latter, the danger for a firm achieving some benefits from MRP is that it thinks it is doing well. External verification will confirm or challenge this view. We shall return to themes of implementation in Chapter 15.

12.2.6 Batch scheduling: OPT

If batch production is so complex, and it is so difficult to create a management system whose complexity is a match for it, where should management focus its attention to cut leadtimes and inventories as well as improve production performance? An alternative to MRP lies in the recognition that it not necessary to plan much of the plant at all. A plant does not consist of a set of machines that can and should be fully loaded. According to Goldratt and Cox,[11] plants are planned and organised incorrectly. They challenge three assumptions about the way production systems ought to be managed:

- capacity to be balanced with demand, followed by attempts to maximise the use of the capacity
- incentives to be based on the utilisation of workers in the tasks they have been set
- activation and utilisation of resources amount to the same thing.

These assumptions mean that the drive at the shop floor level is to keep as much as possible running for as much as possible of the time. Yet, much of this effort does not lead to progress. In a real manufacturing system, there are few *bottlenecks* and otherwise a great deal of slack. There are only a few key points on which managers should concentrate. Maximising the use of resources, including paying incentive bonuses to workers who are not working at bottlenecks, is not beneficial. All that happens is a build-up of partly finished items waiting for their turn at the bottlenecks.

It was from this simple realisation that Goldratt created the *Theory of Constraints* and developed the software system known as *Optimised Production Technology. The*

BOX 12.3 **Bottlenecks and constraints**

'We know that a very small number of constraints in a manufacturing system govern its overall level of performance.'

'Right. So you've got to identify what they are,' said Eric.

'Exactly,' said Alex.

Then he explained that, thanks to Jonah's experience, he knew that most companies are affected by a set of several constraints.

'For instance, you may find that the capacity of every resource in the organization exceeds the demand from the market,' he said. 'The resource with the lowest capacity in the system can handle 200 units, but the market can only handle 100.'

'So the market is the bottleneck,' said Eric.

'Well, no, a market is not a resource,' said Alex, 'so, by definition, it can't be a bottleneck. It can be, and often is, a constraint, but never a bottleneck.'

'Okay, gotcha,' said Eric.

'In other cases, you'll find that demand exceeds the capacity of at least one resource. And so this bottleneck resource is the constraint,' said Alex.

'Gotcha again,' said Eric.

'Most companies will be subject to several constraints. But, whatever they are, let's say you've found them,' said Alex. 'In a process of ongoing improvement, what do you think you would do next?'

Eric said, 'Run the entire system according to the constraints.'

'That's right,' said Alex. 'But how does everybody in the system know what to do?'

'Okay, you need awareness,' said Eric. 'You need to make sure everybody knows what the constraints are.'

Alex nodded. 'And every move they make is done with due consideration of the effect that their actions will have with respect to the constraints. It becomes the focus of attention for the entire organisation.'

Goal, in which Goldratt and Cox present the theory, is written as a novel, a 'thriller' according to the dust jacket. In telling the story of the turn round of a factory, the theory of constraints is both advanced and explained by the authors. Early in the novel,[12] they use a parable of a scouts' route march to point to the essence of the problem. Scouts walking in line need a small gap between each pair to allow for statistical fluctuations in their speeds. These gaps tend to increase, for while it is possible for each to slow momentarily, it is not so easy for them to catch up. In any case, each is limited by the speed of the one in front. The statistical fluctuations do not quite average out. They simply accumulate as the line gradually lengthens. Taking the broader picture, the whole group has to be constrained to move at the speed of the slowest member. These are the fundamental notions in the theory of constraints.

The theory is then worked out in a batch manufacturing setting. The extract in Box 12.3[13] shows how the notion of bottlenecks applies in a factory. The hero persuades an old friend of how he should improve things. Attention is on

BOX 12.4 **Some operations systems with bottlenecks and constraints**

Operation	Constraint (in environment)	Bottleneck (in operations system)
Brassware manufacturer	Supply of castings from foundry	Any process, e.g. turning, milling, plating
Retail shop	Access; parking; deliveries	Number of tills
Open-air pop festival	Roads near site	Food and water supplies; toilets; number of stage sets
Chocolate factory	Raw materials supplies	Any processing plant; distribution system
Hospital specialising in transplants	Donors	Theatre access; trained teams

constraints. In any operating system, there are only a few bottlenecks (constraints caused by internal resources) and constraints (outside the organisation). Apart from the obvious constraint of market demand, we can identify both in the examples of Box 12.4. Through concentrating on these elements, Goldratt's contribution lies in simplification and focus.

Exercise 12.5 List some constraints and bottlenecks in: a pizza delivery business; a television station; a bus company.

Bottlenecks, batches and inventories

Besides providing managers with a means of focusing their attention on those parts of the production system that really matter, Goldratt shows how his ideas can be extended to cut stocks of partly finished work. There are two aspects to inventory reduction, the first coming from recognition of bottlenecks and the second from batch size reduction.

First, it is clear that work done upstream of a bottleneck, if it is done ahead of when it is needed, does not contribute to delivery on time. While an hour lost at the bottleneck is an hour lost from the whole system, an hour saved at a non-bottleneck is worthless. All that happens is that stocks of partly finished goods are increased in value and the workshop looks more crowded. Commitment to the theory of constraints would encourage managers to allow resources at the non-bottleneck to remain idle rather than work unnecessarily. There are echoes here of the kanban system that we discuss later in the chapter.

Second, batch size reduction can reduce inventories and improve delivery performance. To illustrate, imagine 1,000 items scheduled to pass through two system bottlenecks A and B. If A can handle the job in four hours then it seems that B can be scheduled to start four hours later. But what if the batch size is cut to 250? B can start one hour after A provided that that there are four deliveries of items from A to B. This simple change may involve some slightly higher

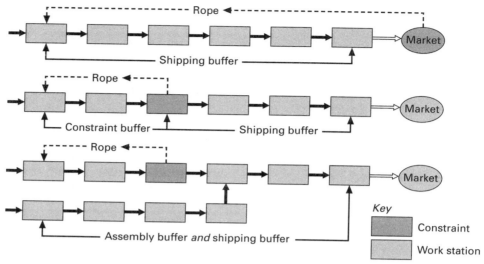

Figure 12.6 Examples of layouts with DBR scheduling

administration costs. Yet, it will take three hours out of the total time for the order. Furthermore, it will reduce the stocks within the system as the product goes through more quickly.

Drum, buffer and rope

Drum-buffer-rope, DBR, is a scheduling technique based on the theory of constraints. Its name comes from the story of the scouts' march. The drum is the schedule at the constraint; through following its beat, the rest of the system proceeds at the rate of this slowest stage. The rope represents the line behind the constraint; it stops it lengthening. In the factory, the rope 'pulls' work into the system at the right time to avoid the build-up of work in progress. A small buffer stock just ahead of the constraint allows for minor fluctuations and ensures that the constraint keeps going.

Figure 12.6 outlines three work sequences arising in batch production.[14] The first shows a product line with spare capacity and a market constraint. Material release into the system, either from stores or direct from a supplier, is scheduled ahead of delivery. This period is the *shipping buffer* acting as the rope to pull the material through.

The second layout is paced by an internal constraint. This bottleneck is the drum. A rope, now the *constraint buffer* pulls the material through to the constraint. Afterwards, the shipping buffer links the constraint schedule and the schedule for delivery. In the third example, we see two supply chains coming together into final assembly operations. One line has a constraint. The non-constrained parts are started according to a combination of the shipping buffer and the assembly buffer.

Control of this system is only required at key points. These are material release, where material enters the system, bottlenecks and junctions. At a junction where assembly occurs, for example, the schedule ensures that the constraint part is the last to arrive. This ensures no excessive stock and the system does not wait for non-constraint items.

Other resources do not need detailed schedules but can operate according to local conditions and simple rules. One could be, 'Work if you have materials, and do not if there are none.' There is no attempt to schedule each operation, thus setting DBR in sharp contrast with MRPII.

Impact of DBR

Gardiner and others[15] summarise the impact of the DBR approach as follows:

- Complexities become understandable.
- Number of resources to be scheduled is cut dramatically.
- Early warnings of potential disruption are given.
- Leadtime is reduced.
- Guidance on continuous improvement is given.
- Significant improvements over other systems are gained.
- Measures of performance at different organisational levels are aligned.

We shall return to some of these points in later chapters. The main one, however, is that DBR mounts a challenge to conventional planning philosophy in that it deliberately sets out to eliminate unnecessary controls. Scheduling complexity is reduced to the five simple steps of Goldratt and Cox:[16]

1 Identify the system's bottlenecks.
2 Decide how to exploit the bottlenecks (how to make them work as hard as possible).
3 Subordinate everything else to the decision in 2.
4 Elevate the system's bottlenecks. (Find ways of bypassing or duplicating them.)
5 If, in a previous step, a bottleneck has been broken go back to Step 1.

What then? OPT does not eliminate scheduling. Companies have used Goldratt's OPT or modified MRPII systems to match bottlenecks with external constraints. At the John Deere Engine Works an MRP system was simplified using the ideas expounded in *The Goal*.[17] Bottlenecks and upstream material release were scheduled in detail.

12.3 Repetitive manufacture

On the face of it, the scheduling of repetitive manufacturing processes, line or continuous technology, should be easier than for intermittent manufacture. This is, in some senses, true since variety is more limited. On the other hand, many firms are large and the nature of costs and competition in their industries means that there is a continuous pressure to reduce waste, improve throughput times and make the most of the resources that have been invested.

Scheduling has significant impact on stock levels and many improvements have generated much of their payback through elimination of the costs related to inventories.

We will concentrate on the just-in-time production system because it is widely used in industries such as automotive assembly. Further, it is spreading into many others. Seen by many as ideal for high-volume repetitive manufacture, it is also being developed in large batch production situations and some of its techniques are applicable in jobbing and small batch companies.[18]

12.3.1 Just-in-time production

The basic concept underpinning JIT is to keep all materials moving through the production system. This means minimising stocks of work in progress. It requires firms to:

- supply goods just in time for them to be used
- create subassemblies just as they are needed in the final assembly shop
- make components just in time for fitting to subassemblies
- receive bought in items at the time they are needed.

In its origins in Japan, JIT grew by linking many series of small factories each with hundreds, rather than thousands, of employees. Each plant made daily deliveries to its successor, the quantity being the exact amounts required for the following day's production. For this to be stable and efficient, all the suppliers knew the monthly production schedule set by the final assembler. This company became the driver that pulled the supplies through the system. *Kanban* is a widely quoted description of the way the information was recorded and process rates regulated. The name refers to the card attached to each component bin in the original system.

Development of the kanban system was helped by the close proximity of the factories. For example, until Toyota began overseas manufacture in the 1980s, all its plants were located in Aichi prefecture close to Tokyo. This has the area of a small British county.

Toyota, led by Taiichi Ohno as manufacturing director, was a pioneer of kanban. The company's performance after the sudden oil price rises of 1973–74 excited the interest of rivals in both Japan and elsewhere. Rivals Toyo-Kogyo, whose brand is Mazda, was almost bankrupted by the same oil shock. Its recovery had much to do with bringing in the Toyota production system, already regarded as good practice throughout the country. The involvement of Ford Motor Company with Toyo-Kogyo began when it bought a 25% stake in 1976. An intensive programme of training in Japanese techniques followed.

JIT *pulls* work through the system. It differs from conventional production planning with its *push* philosophy. In JIT, having deliveries at least once a day implies small batches and little stock. Yet, in many people's minds, the policy goes beyond stock minimisation to continuous improvement and incorporation into other business functions. For example, to operate flow systems with such little stock implies the following: each item must be of the correct quality, hence total quality management; that machines are highly reliable, hence total productive maintenance; and that all staff are well trained and motivated. In other words, JIT is as much a philosophy of the way the whole business should operate as a technical approach to the problem of scheduling.

12.3.2 **Waste elimination**

The advantages of JIT come from the elimination of waste at all stages. Waste arises in many ways in the production system:

- *In the process itself.* Some processes add no value. Fitting and other adjustments, or removing scale or burrs, are only required because of defects in upstream processes. If a machine cannot produce to defined tolerances, it should be replaced or the tolerances themselves reviewed and the design changed.
- *Running the process too fast or too early.* Overproduction leads to the build-up of inventory which not only wastes investment but wastes space and transport resources as the stock is moved several times to keep it out of the way.
- *Waiting.* Waiting time between processes is wasteful because the inability to deliver quickly loses sales.
- *Stock.* Just-in-time replaces the idea of 'just-in-case'. This meant that inventory was held only because there were problems in the production system. These made it impossible to supply within a period when customers wanted orders.
- *Material movement.* The effect of excessive distances between processes is often disguised in a production system. Such movements, and the associated stock that has to be in transit, add no value.
- *People movement.* Excessive movement of people may arise from poor job layouts but also from their having to go and look for materials for the next task. Shops crowded with inventory lengthen this search.
- *Defects.* An example of the interaction between the scheduling and quality systems, defects cost more than the value of the lost item. Habitual defects rates mean: schedulers set high batch sizes to allow for loss; correction delays waste time; customers become annoyed.

12.3.3 **JIT techniques**

Beyond the general statements of principle and the declaration of war on waste, JIT consists of a family of techniques that can be assembled and integrated. These fall into two groups: *JIT1* is preparatory, making the facility ready for high-flow, short leadtime production; *JIT2* techniques are the tactics used to cut waste. The following summarises key points.[19]

JIT1

- *Small machines.* Installing several small machines, each dedicated to one process, may appear less economical that having fewer, more powerful general-purpose machines. Yet, the gain in flexibility allows cuts in inventory and this in itself may fund the extra equipment and space. Fewer changeovers will save cost and batch sizes can be cut.
- *Set-up reduction.* Many firms have bad habits when it comes to set-ups. They may not have the next set of tools ready for installation; they may not allocate the optimal size of team; they may not train and practise enough. If set-ups

cannot be avoided, there are many ways of reducing the time needed for changeovers. Introduction these changes requires the cooperation of many members of staff.

JIT2

- *Scheduling.* The JIT factory has a master production schedule to create detailed instructions for the final assembly stage. From there, upstream processes are scheduled by signals from the next ones down the chain. Originally, kanban was a simple visible method of allowing routine material flow decisions to be made at shop floor level. It is still used but has also developed through information systems applications. Detailed operations of a link in the chain are explained in the next section.

- *Integration with other scheduling techniques.* While in some ways being presented as rival approaches to the question of shop floor scheduling, MRP, OPT and JIT can be combined. As Harrison points out,[20] possibilities for synergy include:
  - Preparation along JIT1 lines can be of use to all manufacturers.
  - JIT simplification can be carried out before the installation of an MRPII system, reducing the number of transactions and therefore the scale required.
  - All systems should avoid predefined batch sizes and lead times and they should not accept that scrap rates are fixed and to be planned for.
  - JIT is good at control but is only good at planning for regular repetitive manufacture. By the same token, MRPII plans in detail but is weaker at control because of the amount of detail required by the central MRP office.
  - JIT techniques can improve the capacity of OPT bottlenecks, for example design improvements can be made to avoid time in the bottleneck processes and set-up reduction can increase available machine capacity.

- *Vertical integration.* A JIT factory cannot work alone. JIT works best if the whole supply chain operates at the speed of the master production schedule. This means that there can be only one MPS. It is most likely to be decided by the final assembler who is in contact with details of customer demand. Assemblers beat the rhythm for the rest to follow.

The links between organisations require the development of a great deal of trust and cooperation. They must, for example, share plans and understand each other's capabilities and constraints. These relationships mean that JIT philosophy has entered the purchasing and supply arena with the ability to deliver to daily or even hourly schedules being an important element in vendor selection. One instance illustrates the impact of JIT ideas on supply channel planning:

In 1992, Sunderland Football Club announced a plan to build a new 40,000-seat stadium and leisure complex away from its cramped Roker Park base. Among the objectors to the application for planning permission was Nissan. The motor company's £900 million plant stood next to the 60-hectare greenbelt site. The company feared that congestion on roads leading to the 11,000-space car park would upset its JIT delivery schedules from seven local manufacturers. These flows, according to the engineering director, had a tolerance of minutes. In 1997, Sunderland opened its 48,300-seat stadium close to the city centre.[21]

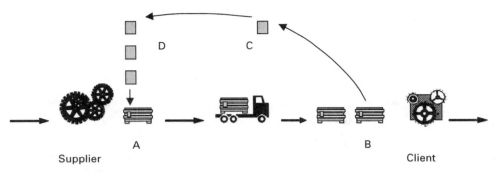

Figure 12.7 Circulation of kanbans

12.3.4 How a kanban link works

In contrast to documents in other planning and scheduling systems, the kanban (ticket) does not follow pieces of work all the way through the production chain. A set of kanbans circulates at every link in the production system. Each kanban travels down the stream with the material and returns from the next stage each time its bin is used. The number of tickets, and the information they carry, regulate production at the upstream stage. The kanban records:

■ details of the operation to be carried out on the piece

■ the origin and destination

■ the number of pieces per standard container

■ the number of pieces to be made in one batch

■ the number of kanbans in circulation within the link.

For the system to operate consistently, a set of rules must be followed:

1 Each bin (or trolley, rack, container etc.) has a kanban with details of the parts, their routing and quantity.

2 Parts are pulled by the next process.

3 Work is not started without a card.

4 Bins contain exactly their stated number of parts.

5 Defective parts must not be sent to succeeding processes.

6 When parts are taken by the next process, only enough to replace them can be made.

We can now look at how kanbans regulate the flow. The link between two production stages is akin to that between supplier and client. The kanban represents an open manufacturing order placed by the client on the supplier. When the supplier makes a consignment, each container in the batch carries a kanban, see step A in Figure 12.7. There the ticket remains while the container passes to the downstream, or client, stage and waits until used, B. When consumption starts, the kanban is removed from the container and sent back upstream, C. It becomes again an open order for manufacture.

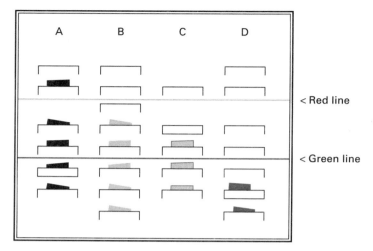

Figure 12.8 Kanban planning rack

There is usually a rack at the upstream stage to collect kanbans until process-ing starts, D. The quantity made is determined by the economic batch size for the process rounded to a multiple of containers to ensure that each is filled.

Kanbans take up different roles during their circulation. Flowing downstream, they are stock tickets indicating quantities and destinations. Moving upstream, they are job orders, communicating the requirements of the client stage. The number of kanbans circulating in the link is chosen to regulate the amount of work in progress. A pair of work stations linked in this way need not be close, but could be separated by workshop walls or even the distances between factories.

The kanban rack yields information. The supplier can see the stock ahead of the next stage and can decide work priorities. This will be important when the supplier is engaged in supplying more than one client with different compon-ents. For instance, it could be a multi-purpose miller in a machine shop or a press making book covers in a bindery. Simple rules are used. Figure 12.8 shows the planning rack for a stage with four customers. Kanbans in the rack show fewer than maximum full containers in circulation. Depending on batch sizes, a dif-ferent number of kanbans will trigger the production of new supplies. In a simple system, this will be shown by (say) a green line on the rack. Work may not start straight away so the kanbans continue to accumulate. A red line on the rack shows danger level, signalling that unless work is started immediately, the customer runs the risk of being out of supplies.

The stress in such presentation is clear communication and simple decision rules. The status of the system can be easily seen by all staff: the supplier knows the state of the client's work; the supervisor can tell if things are going wrong; the group can investigate areas for improvement.

12.3.5 The number of kanbans

The number of tickets in circulation is the sum of two components. First, there is the economic batch size, EBS, for the supply stage.[22] Second, there is buffer stock ahead of the client consumed during the link reaction time. When the planning rack reaches the green trigger, the stock of items at the client continues to fall while the supplier is making and delivering the next batch.

The reaction time, *RT*, is made up of several elements: time to produce a container full; transport of stock; machine setting; movement of the tickets up the chain etc. If the client's use rate is *UR*, then the client uses $RT \times UR$ items during the delay period. To allow for unforeseen variations and the possibility of delay if the supplier has more than one customer, a safety margin, *SM*, is added. *SM* may be 10 to 20%.

The maximum stock in circulation is given by:

$$Maximum\ stock = EBS + RT \times UR \times (1 + SM)$$

This yields the number of kanbans, *K*, required by the system. When each container holds *n* items:

$$K = \frac{EBS + RT \times UR \times (1 + SM)}{n}$$

To illustrate, suppose that the client stage consumes 1,200 pieces per day, that is 150 per hour. The supplier, serving more than one client, produces at the rate of 600 items per hour with a set-up time of 15 minutes. The economic batch size has been set at 400, or 5 containers of 80 items. The reaction time is $1^1/_2$ hours and the safety margin is 10%.

The consumption during the reaction time is $1.5 \times 150 \times (1 + 0.1) = 248$ pieces. Adding the EBS of 400 gives 648, which corresponds to eight kanbans of 80 items in circulation.

Setting the red line

Including setting up, the time taken by the supplier to produce the EBS is 0.25 + 400/600 = 0.92 hours or 55 minutes. During this period, the client consumes $0.92 \times 1.1 \times 150 = 151$ pieces. This means two containers of 80 each should be the minimum number ahead of the client when the supplier starts the next batch. The red line on the planning rack is set at 2 below the number of tickets in the system, that is at 6. With these six tickets on the rack, the supplier will know that the client has reached danger level.

The simplicity of the system is a strong part of its appeal. The formulae given here enable all to establish clear procedures and to make adjustments and improvements. For instance, the effect of cutting set-up times is plain. Not only will the EBS itself be reduced but the required safety margin will also fall. Alternatively, having a dedicated small machine in this example could reduce the ELS to one kanban, cutting the total in circulation to four.

The empty containers themselves are sometimes used instead of tickets. When each link has its own containers, their number determines the maximum stock in circulation. Where two work stations are within sight of each other, the height or length of stacks on the floor can act as signals for production to recommence.

Exercise 12.6   Demonstrate the effect of: using computers to halve link reaction times; cutting set-up times to reduce the economic batch size to 250.

12.3.6 Applications of kanban and the JIT philosophy

While the last worked example makes kanban operations look somewhat similar to the job shop processes, two features confine its application to repetitive manufacture. First, the volume of any individual item passing through the system must be large enough to make it worthwhile setting up continuously active loops. The range of items produced at any stage must be limited, otherwise simple rules will not enable operators to decide priorities and keep all clients satisfied. These points emphasise that JIT is applicable in high volume industries such as automotive and domestic equipment manufacture. Second, the daily production rate must be level. It can easily be shown that the kanban system would amplify oscillations in any demand placed upon the chain by the final assembler. In other words, the MPS of the final assembler must be level. The assembler copes with variations through holding a stock of finished goods. If the MPS is to change, then information is sent to the whole chain so that the planning boards and numbers of tickets in circulation can be adjusted.

JIT methods have been extended and adapted within high-volume repetitive production. For example, the need to focus and increase flows through chains has led automobile assemblers such as Peugeot Talbot to develop *partnership sourcing* with one supplier per component:

At Ryton, Coventry, the 8,300 components come from 380 suppliers, instead of the 600 before the programme was started. Hills Precision Components is a partly owned subsidiary company situated close to Ryton. Here, Peugeot orders for fascia assemblies arrive 12 times a day. Each specifies models, colours, left- or right-hand drive and so on. The fascias are assembled from a range of standard components and delivered within two hours. This speed of response means that fascia orders for any car do not have to be placed until after the build has started. HPC also makes components with fewer variations, such as seats, door casings and steering wheels. These are on continuous flow orders. Tickets are not used for any of these links because electronic data interchange is the favoured system. Kanbans are replaced by barcodes.[23]

The pressure in volume manufacturing is to improve speed of response through squeezing inventory out of the system. The philosophy of continuous improvement has led car assemblers to re-examine bottlenecks in their lines, especially the problems of switching from one model type to another. There is a tension between the need to standardise and the growing demand for individual cars, the process of customisation.

A typical car assembly line copes with a family of cars with related characteristics. Thus, the General Motors lines at Ellesmere Port cope with: cars and light vans; diesel and petrol engines from 1.2 to 1.8i; hatchbacks, saloons, estates and convertibles; two doors and four doors; trim from 'base' through L, LX, LA to GTE. The wide range means that it is normal to supply cars to customers' orders. This only works the market place if leadtimes can be minimised. Customers do not want to wait!

Colour is not easy to change frequently. This is because the paint booths and spray lines have to be cleaned out and primed at every switch. This costs time in terms of lost output and loses paint. Pauses between shifts are good times.

Some colours are more popular than others. White is at least five times more popular than blue, for example. The limit to the range of colours is the leadtime that can be offered. In the early 1990s, the least popular colour at the plant accounted for 5%

of sales. This means that if colours changed once per day, this colour would be applied once a fortnight. The average waiting time for customers wanting that colour was too long.

GM developed its paint equipment to cut changeover time and costs. This allowed more frequent spraying of the less common colours. Ironically, this encouraged the marketing department to argue for a wider colour range. Implementing this proposal meant that expected cost savings did not materialise but there was greater customisation.

12.3.7 People and scheduling systems

A comparison of scheduling systems from MRPII to JIT would not be complete without a note on the interaction between these systems and the people who work with them. Apart from different technical features, a major difference between MRPII and JIT is the degree of centralisation. OPT lies between the two. MRPII systems are centralised, the scheduling decisions becoming a set of instructions issued by the office for the shop floor to follow. In many respects in the western factory, this amounts to more of the same thing. The tradition of management control by taking over all aspects of decision making grew out of the tenets of Taylor's scientific management. MRPII is an extension of Taylorism, being a better way for the scheduling office to operate.

JIT, in its basic principles, encourages the involvement of shop floor staff in detailed scheduling and control. This is a move towards decentralisation, although constrained by the strict rules without which JIT would not work. Therefore, we see simultaneous moves towards autonomy and pressures for more discipline. Storey, in one listing, mentions the following as essential features of 'people preparation':[24]

- *discipline* – 'the critical essence of a manufacturing company'
- *flexibility* – growth in the long term through training
- *equality* – removal of divisions
- *autonomy* – having authority to stop the line, solve problems, control materials
- *quality of working life* – developing security and a sense of involvement and enjoyment
- *creativity* – harnessing the 'natural curiosity of company members to make improvements which affect the work they do'.

Whether these factors can exist in fruitful combination both defines, and depends on, the culture of the organisation. Whether they can be transferred from one national culture to another is a further question. There is no doubt that importing the best production management systems brings improved business performance. Some have argued, however, that the introduction of 'Japanese style' management practices happened in the context of a weak labour market. They say that forcing people to work as hard as possible merely builds up resentment. It might explode the next time workers feel they have enough power. Further, if an explosion does happen, those companies that have cut stocks and switched to single suppliers have compounded their strategic risk. They have made themselves more vulnerable to any discontinuity that may arise.[25]

Table 12.5 Nature of scheduling decisions in two manufacturing processes

	Level of detail	Decision-making latitude	Time horizon of decisions	Amount of uncertainty
Intermittent manufacturing	High	High	Short	High
	▲	▲	▼	▲
	▲	▲	▼	▲
Repetitive manufacturing	Low	Low	Long	Low

12.3.8 Comparison of scheduling in intermittent and repetitive systems

The job shop and the dedicated production line represent the two extremes of the scale of repetition – every unit different to every unit the same. Scheduling in the job shop consists of many ad hoc decisions over material, capacity, sequencing and delivery. In the dedicated production line, scheduling involves establishing a uniform daily rate for all operations and maintaining the flow continuously.

Table 12.5 summarises the characteristics of the two types of process.[26] Intermittent manufacturing is highly uncertain and requires concentration on detail in order to make it operate. Therefore, it is necessary to delegate much of the decision making to the shop floor. This policy recognises each decision is relatively small, having an impact within a short time horizon. At the other extreme, the dedicated, repetitive line needs planning well in advance to match market demands. The low level of detail and high certainty make central planning possible and necessary. Given the desire to integrate the whole system, there is little decision-making latitude at shop floor level.

The family of techniques we have discussed in this chapter fit between these extremes, each being adapted to local circumstances to aid shifts towards more uniformity or flexibility. Kanban, for example, is a means of allowing some flexibility into a high-volume manufacturing and assembly system. If there were to be a single product with no variation, kanban would be unnecessary because all stages could be designed to operate at the constant rate. Yet, the latitude for decision making within the kanban system is constrained by strict rules. Shop floor staff may decide priorities when tickets on the planning board rise above the green line, but they cannot decide for themselves the number of tickets within each loop.

12.4 Service scheduling

12.4.1 Service patterns

For a framework in which to discuss service scheduling, we can return to the model set out in Figure 3.1. Three patterns of service delivery were identified:

isolated service, self-service and personal service. In addition, Figure 3.1 shows the impact of scale. Increasing volumes correspond with standardisation while reductions imply customisation.

Isolated service

The challenge of scheduling varies by the type of service. Verma[27] found it related to both the isolation/integration and standardisation/customisation dimensions. Scheduling service delivery was a greater problem in the isolated and customised *service shop* than in the other patterns. Scheduling the work force, however, was most important in the isolated and standardised *service factory*. Remembering that isolated services are similar to manufacturing, we have covered these cases earlier in the chapter. The service shop is akin to jobbing and the service factory parallels batch and mass production.

Isolated service depends on a 'front office' to contact the customer. This is either personal or self-service. There can be a service outlet, such as a film depot or travel agency, or the contact can be by machine, as with the cash dispenser or Internet. The watch repairer, design service or bookkeeper use a combination to link with intermittent jobbing. The hospital laundry, film processor or credit card company do the same to join with repetitive processing.

Self-service

Unless the service capacity is limited, self-service needs no scheduling. The provider offers capacity that the customer will use when required. In the ideal case, there is no personal interaction; the user consumes any amount of the facility at any time. Payment systems, unless fees can be collected automatically, often need personal service as at the supermarket checkout. The supermarket is not, therefore, a pure form but mixed self/personal service. Examples of the ideal type range from free facilities such as municipal parks, through those where access requires a fixed payment, such as cable television or toll bridges, to cases such as telephones where billing is automatic.

Some telephone services with limited capacity have to be booked, as do keyboards in a busy learning centre or Internet cafés. In these cases, the self-service requires some personal service to regulate the flow.

Personal service

Personal or *direct* service is a recurrent problem in scheduling. Why is it so difficult?

- Demand for direct services is variable and cannot be levelled as with a master production schedule. Unless the operator can rapidly adjust service capacity, queues will form.

- Customisation is expected in many service activities. This ensures variety is high.

- The presence of the customer impedes adherence to any planned schedule. What if the customer needs, or asks for, a change of service halfway through?

We shall now examine some approaches to these problems.

12.4.2 **Scheduling direct service**

As noted already, the processes of *isolation* or *detachment* (see Figure 3.1) are important first steps in protecting most of the service facility from the effects of variability. Having laid out the facilities and designed the service process, however, there is little that the provider can do but fine-tune capacity and service levels in response to demand. Reservations or appointments systems work in some circumstances, from doctors' surgeries to theatres. Yet these are designed to manage demand to fit the chosen medium-term schedule rather than adjust the short-term schedule to fit demand.

When demand is variable and unregulated, how can a business adjust to maintain a high standard of customer service? It uses a combination of anticipation and changes in staff and service levels. Telephone home shopping is an example of mass personal service. In such bureaux, the capacity is established to cope with anticipated demand but local, short-term adjustments are always necessary.

Home shopping grew out of mail order. The leading companies, such as Great Universal and Littlewoods, now take over three-quarters of orders by telephone. Networks enable customers to call at local rates.

For the customer, order placement is easier, deliveries are faster, and, when stock-outs occur, alternatives are offered. Service quality is improved. Operators check customers' credit records on-line so that satisfactory orders are immediately placed in the despatch schedule and picking instructions sent to automated warehouses.

Better service raises expectations. Mail allows short-term queuing. Telephone users, however, find waiting frustrating and require quick responses. Typical targets are to answer within 20 seconds. Littlewoods needs a telephone bureau whose size balances the response target against the cost of having staff idle for much of the time. At peak times over 100 operators are working.

Callers join a single queue and are answered in sequence. The equipment connects desks in rotation. The call queue length is displayed prominently in the operating room to warn of excess demand.

Demand varies hourly and daily. Experience enables a forecast to be made for each half-hour interval. Enough staff are recruited and trained to cover the forecast pattern yet changes occur by the minute. To cope with short-term surges the supervisors can:

■ Reduce the time staff spend with each caller. When time permits, staff remind customers of special offers and pass on other information about the company. This activity is cut.

■ Ask staff to delay breaks or getting a cup of coffee from the machine.

■ Call to the manager to bring in more staff from other activities, although this usually takes several minutes to arrange.

12.4.3 **Scheduling mass service**

Many mass service operators have refined their process design to give it many of the characteristics of repetitive manufacture. Nowhere is this more apparent than in express parcels delivery which concentrate on establishing flows and schedules to meet customer needs. The hub and spoke system of Federal Express, which carries one half of all overnight packages in the United States, is a leading example of the way transport can be thought of in flow process terms. It is, in effect, a distributed service factory that communicates with the customer either through personal or, as we shall see, self-service.

Each evening, freight aircraft fly parcels along inward spokes to FedEx's sorting hub at Memphis, Tennessee. Here they are sorted and loaded for the outward trip to arrive by early morning. A late afternoon consignment from the main European capitals has a guaranteed delivery by 10.30 anywhere in North America. The system works by having clear fixed flight and sorting schedules and parcel-tracking software. Plane loads out of Memphis are thus defined well before the parcels arrive for sorting.

The Internet allows most customers to track their own parcels and time their consignments accurately.

For example, Laura Ashley clothes shops are restocked within two days, thus cutting out the risk and expense of local warehousing. Federal Express has more than 460 aircraft and delivers over two million packages a day. Excess demand is managed by delaying consignments on lower grade services.

Scheduling transport operations is an art in itself, especially for public services such as air and rail travel where terminals and track are shared with other services. Railway timetablers have used graphical methods since the 1840s. They were developed by the French engineer Charles Ibry. He hoped that both operators and the public would use them.[28] An Ibry diagram can show systems of great complexity, with hundreds of stations. Figure 12.9 is an example, showing a few hours of the weekday train service between Manchester and Chester.

The time scale is read across the top of the diagram and stations, positioned according to their distance along the track, appear down the side. Diagonals running from upper left to lower right show trains heading towards Chester. The other diagonals depict trains for Manchester. Some trains start from, or continue to, places beyond Manchester, hence the 'spikes' at the top of the chart. Chester is a terminus for all.

The advantage of the Ibry timetable is that it captures relevant dimensions of the service and enables problems to be visualised, anticipated and, therefore, managed. Steeper diagonals represent express trains (although there is none here). Xs mark where trains meet and minutes spent waiting result in horizontal lines (although the scale of this presentation prevents their being shown). Like the kanban planning board, the visualisation enables experienced operators to cope with the adjustments that are continually required.

Even our simple example repays study. Two short stretches of the route are single track. These are marked by tinted bands across the chart. Strict safety procedures prevent two trains entering these sections. However, it can be seen that careful management will be required if the late running of, say, the 17:20 out of Chester is not to delay the next incoming service by making it wait at Mouldsworth.

Beyond looking at features of the service, we can use the chart to follow the path of rolling stock and crews through their working days. For example, it is easy to visualise the trains turning round at the Chester terminus. During the middle-day off-peak period, trains run a little faster because six of the small

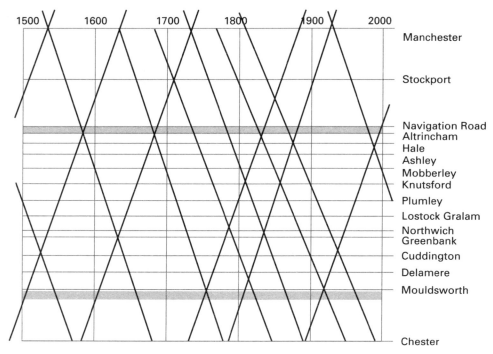

Figure 12.9 Ibry diagram of train service: Manchester to Chester

stations close. This saves rolling stock. For instance, the 15:41 arrival at Chester is in time to form the 15:50 departure.

Compared with Gantt charts, Ibry diagrams emphasise different aspects of the system being studied. Gantt was concerned with representing time spent at fixed positions, either in a queue or in process. Ibry focused on plotting locations in a space–time continuum. Gantt represents tasks and time in the factory; variations of Ibry can be used to picture, for example, the movement of products through a long process such as a series of glazing and firing stages in a kiln.

✔ Quick check-up

Can you:
- ☐ List four possible objectives for a scheduling system.
- ☐ Name the elements of a job shop scheduling problem.
- ☐ State four sequencing rules in such a shop.
- ☐ Summarise Johnson's rule and where it might be used.
- ☐ Define master production schedule; materials requirements plan; and capacity requirements plan.
- ☐ Distinguish constraints and bottlenecks; drums, buffers and ropes.
- ☐ Summarise the contents of a kanban.
- ☐ Sketch an Ibry diagram.

❓ Questions

Chapter review

12.1 Compare several objectives for a scheduling system for manufacture or isolated service. Is it possible to unite them into a single objective?

12.2 Discuss why scheduling is so difficult in intermittent manufacturing.

12.3 Explain the philosophy and purpose of JIT to someone in manufacturing yet unfamiliar with the idea.

12.4 Compare Gantt and Ibry charts, pointing out their relative advantages and where each might be useful.

Application

12.5 What changes in the Saxon Sandbec case contributed towards improvement in work flow? Where would any resistance to change arise and how might managers deal with it?

12.6 Outline how the drum-buffer-rope model may be used in a busy office. Examples are: a legal office pursuing injury claims through the county court; a daily newspaper; an Internet bookshop. Start with a mind map and process map of the stages of work.

Investigation

12.7 Use an Ibry diagram to plot vehicle movement in a public transport system. You could study an airline with Internet timetables, such as easyJet or Ryanair.[29] If studying a train service, choose a line that carries trains of different speeds, such as Birmingham to Oxford.

12.8 Several software companies publish case studies of successful implementation of their MRP and JIT systems. Analyse three of these for evidence of the benefits offered and the results obtained.[30]

CLOSING CASE

Engineering and Manufacturing-Oiso[31]

E&M-Oiso is a manufacturing plant of the NCR Corporation located some 65 km from Tokyo. It has 550 employees developing and assembling cash registers, point of sale terminals and financial terminals. The first two product groups are sold throughout the world.

In principle, the plant works by building to order. There is an aggregate production plan drawn up as 'a hedged version of marketing's sales forecast'. It considers factors such as capacity and leadtimes for subassemblies and suppliers' availability and delivery times. Risk is involved and has to be managed since sales never turn out to match the forecast. The monthly plan is based on firm orders. Variability in the flow of orders has to be matched with flexibility. Kanban systems are used to regulate the assembly of products to customers' orders. Certain processes, however, have long lead times that would not allow quick enough supplies.

Such leadtimes exist in the printed circuit board manufacture where the capacity of the surface mount technology is limited. The solution is to build

▶

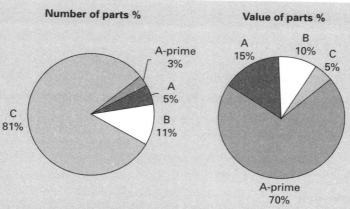

Figure 12.10 ABC analysis of supplies to E&M-Oiso

controlled lots of basic boards for stock. When firm orders set the kanban system in motion, these boards can be withdrawn for further components to be built on. Therefore there is a mixture of 'push' and 'pull' production scheduling. This achieves delivery requirements without the need to add SMT capacity.

E&M-Oiso uses computer-integrated manufacturing to manage the JIT programme. Its aim is to minimise leadtimes. Having set schedules that aim to have components arriving at assembly just when they are needed, the CIM system captures data on the status of all orders to ensure that they are progressing satisfactorily. All items carry barcodes.

The company works closely with its 192 suppliers to gain and share benefits from the JIT system. It sees relationships with these companies as sharing responsibilities for minimising the cost of ownership of bought-in components. Suppliers are involved in the process of design for manufacture.

Daily delivery is not required in the JIT system. Attention centres on those items that make up most of the value. Figure 12.10 shows how parts have been split into four categories from A-prime to C. The A-prime items are just 3.4% of the number but represent some 70% of the value. They are all in the JIT programme, which is to be extended to the whole A category. JIT will then cover 85% of parts by value. (See Chapter 15 for ABC analysis.)

Of the 192 suppliers, only three are offshore. The company wants to increase this number. The tight schedules make such sourcing difficult. Not only are shipping times longer but also risk is higher. Offshore supplies will have to be based more on the aggregate forecast than on actual orders and this will create inflexibility.

Visualisation is seen as important in the presentation of performance results. Data on weekly results, such as delivery performance, are prominently displayed in consistent graphical formats throughout the plant. Even the untrained eye can recognise the degree of goal attainment. While details are given of who is responsible for each element of the output, the intention is not to allocate blame but to contribute to team building and continual improvement. The company believes that cooperative performance depends on common knowledge.

Questions

1 What is E&M-Oiso doing when it says it uses a hedged version of the sales forecast? Why?

2 Identify the type of production systems likely to be found at E&M-Oiso. Suggest applications of MRPII and OPT in this situation.

3 What are the production and supply risks involved with offshore sourcing into Japan?

4 Why does the company set such store by presenting performance data?

Notes and references

1. I am indebted to the help given by managers at Saxon Sandbec; photographs of appliances are widely available on the Internet, http://www.jmccall.demon.co.uk/gallery.htm accessed 10 May 2001; see also http://www.rosenbauer.com/

2. Harrison, A. (1994) 'Just-in-time manufacturing' in Storey, J. (ed.) *New Wave Manufacturing Strategies*, London: Paul Chapman, p.188.

3. Spreadbury, A. (1994) 'Manufacturing resources planning' in Storey, J. (ed.) *New Wave Manufacturing Strategies*, London: Paul Chapman, p.154.

4. Luscombe, M. (1994) 'Of course I'm committed to MRPII but . . .' *Management Services*, March, pp.12–13.

5. ibid.

6. For example: Waterlow, G. and Monniot, J. (1986) *A Study of the State of the Art in CAPM in UK Industry*, London: SERC/ACME; Whiteside, D. and Ambrose, J. (1984) 'Unsnarling industrial production: Why top management is starting to care', *Industrial Management*, March, pp.20–6; Sum, C. and Yang, K. (1993) 'A study of MRPII practices in Singapore', *Omega*, 21(2), pp.187–97.

7. Turnover of this branch plant of a large combine was some £50 million. The interviews were conducted in 1994.

8. Sillince, J.A.A. and Sykes, G.M.H. (1993) 'Integrating MRPII and JIT: A management rather than a technical challenge', *International Journal of Production and Operations Management*, 13(4), pp.18–31.

9. Brown, A. (1994) 'Transformational leadership in tackling technical change', *Journal of General Management*, 19(4), pp.1–12.

10. Humphreys, P., McCurry, L. and McAleer, E. (2001) 'Achieving MRPII Class A status in an SME', *Benchmarking: An International Journal*, 8(1), pp.48–61.

11. Goldratt, E.M. and Cox, J. (1989) *The Goal*, Aldershot: Gower.

12. ibid. p.95.

13. ibid. p.270.

14. Gardiner, S.G., Blackstone, J.H.Jr and Gardiner, L.R. (1992) 'Drum-buffer-rope and buffer management', *International Journal of Production and Operations Management*, 13(6), pp.68–78.

15. op.cit.

16. op.cit. p.297.

17. Spencer, M.S. (1991) 'Using "*The Goal*" in an MRP system', *Production and Inventory Management Journal*, 32(4), pp.22–8.

18. Harrison, A., op.cit. p.181.

19. Harrison, A. (1992) *Just-in-Time Manufacturing in Perspective*, Hemel Hempstead: Prentice Hall.

20. Harrison (1994) op.cit. p.190.
21. Company News, *The Financial Times*, 23 January 1993, p.4; Tighe, C. (1993) 'Nissan and Sunderland FC cry foul in a local derby', ibid., 15 October, p.1; 'Sunderland gives stadium approval', ibid., 11 March 1994, p.7.
22. Economic batch size is found by balancing the savings in work in progress through smaller lots against the savings in set up time through larger lots. It is akin to economic order quantity (see Chapter 14).
23. Gooding, C. (1993) 'Technology: On the road to a slicker operation', *The Financial Times*, 22 July, p.16.
24. op.cit. pp.183–4.
25. Industrial Relations Services (1993) *The Impact of Japanese firms on Working and Employment Practices in British Manufacturing Industry*, London: IRS.
26. de Toni, A. and Panizzolo, R. (1993) 'Operations management techniques in intermittent and repetitive manufacturing: A conceptual framework', *International Journal of Operations and Production Management*, 13(5), pp.12–32.
27. Verma, R. (2000) 'An empirical analysis of management challenges in service factories, service shops, mass services and professional services', *International Journal of Service Industry Management*, 11(1), pp.8–25.
28. Tufte, E.R. (1990) *Envisioning Information*, Cheshire, CT: Graphics Press, p.108. The book includes several beautiful examples of this form of presentation.
29. http://www.easyjet.com; http://www.ryanair.com accessed 10 June 2001.
30. For instance, Geac Enterprise Solutions; http://www.geac.com/products/system21/ accessed 14 June 2001.
31. Based on: Tanabe, Masaru (1992) 'Making JIT work at NCR Japan', *Long Range Planning*, 25(5), pp.37–42.

CHAPTER 13

Supply chain management

OBJECTIVES

When you have finished studying this chapter, you should be able to:

- Define a supply chain and outline the wide range of types that are found in practice.
- Sketch a typical supply chain, showing its main features and distinguishing management functions within it.
- Summarise factors in the make or buy decision.
- Assess the benefits of few or many suppliers.
- Describe the process of vendor selection.
- Explain the context of customisation in supply chains and what constrains its introduction.
- Outline the *bullwhip* effect and how it can be overcome.
- Suggest ways in which electronic commerce changes operations management.
- Explain the emergence of B2B market places and the functions they perform.
- Review the models used by new Internet business services and their impact on supply chain operations.
- Assess the continuing problems in delivery to consumers and ways of responding to them.

OPENING CASE

Going bananas[1]

Cooperation among firms in the food industry has grown in recent years. In the United Kingdom, the 1990 Food Safety Act requires retailers to exercise due diligence with respect to food supplies. Sharing information with suppliers allows every product to be tracked from source to shelf and hence reduces risks such as contamination. Further, customers expect fresh supplies of a wide product range all year round; this requires all stages to work to rapid and regular schedules. Just-in-time deliveries promise lower wastage rates and more regular revenues compared with the traditional, unscheduled spot market system. Distributors and suppliers, therefore, are attracted by the security offered by membership of supply chains.

The buying power of large retailers has enabled them to reach backwards and replace traditional markets with contracts with growers. Bananas have long

▶

been transported to Europe in special 'banana boats'. Vertically integrated companies, such as Chiquita, Del Monte and Fyffes, are expert in growing, shipping, ripening and distributing the product. Over the past two decades, however, retailers have become more involved in managing the supply chain. They seek lower costs, more consistent quality and, of course, traceability.

This case describes a supply chain involving three companies. Noboa is the largest grower in Ecuador, which in turn accounts for one-third of the world's exports. In that country, Noboa is second only in sales to Ecuador Petroleum. Mack Multiples is the largest privately owned fresh fruit importer and distributor in the UK. It acts as an intermediary between many importers and retailers. The supermarket chain, J. Sainsbury sells about one-fifth of the fresh fruit and vegetables sold in the UK. The chain described here was developed by Sainsbury, which prefers to deal with well-established privately owned businesses. Noboa, recommended by Mack, had not previously traded in Europe in this way. The arrangement started with a trial at one Ecuadorian farm and built up after experience.

The banana market

The banana is a staple food in producer countries; they export about one-fifth of the annual 60 million tonne production. The European Union consumes about 35% of these exports. Traditional sources were countries with trade protected by duty-free agreements, such as the Lomé convention, or the contract between Britain and Geest (now part of Fyffes) to guarantee a market for Caribbean suppliers. However, market growth and trade liberalisation over the past two decades mean that so-called 'dollar' bananas from Latin America take an increasing share. They now account for two-thirds of the flow, although the UK market remains largely sourced from the Caribbean. Bananas are important in the UK market. The £650 million at retail price represents 28% of all fruit sales. Having doubled over the past ten years, per capita consumption reached 10kg per annum, that is 1 banana each week. By 2000, it had overtaken the apple as the nation's most popular fruit.

The leading importers into the EU are Chiquita, Dole, Del Monte and Fyffes. Together, they sell about 60% of the total. For the UK, the top four are Fyffes with 30% followed by Chiquita, Jamaica Producers and Del Monte at 15% each. At the retail stage in the UK, the multiples have about 75% of the market. Sales are steady throughout the year, with a slight decrease in the summer when local fruit is on sale.

Prices have been falling in real terms. Three factors hold them down. These are the dominance of the multiples, the fruit's presence in many 'shopping basket' comparisons and the limited opportunities for suppliers to differentiate the product. Although bananas from different regions and root stocks taste differently, retailers have concentrated on finding the one or two varieties that consumers want to buy rather than developing a range of named varieties as with apples or potatoes. Sainsbury, for example, combines the results of customer taste tests in its stores with opinions of its central appraisal panel. This information is sent back to the growers.

Banana supply

It takes about a year from planting to harvest a new crop. Quality management begins early with selection of sites and preparation of drainage. Growing fruit are wrapped in plastic to prevent scarring and insect damage. When harvesting, the wrappers are twisted into packaging to protect the fruit in transit. Bananas for the European market are cut when three-quarters mature, with the rest of the ripening controlled during transit.

The planned supply chain for bananas from Noboa plantation to Sainsbury supermarket is as follows:

- *From field to packing station.* Each packing station has some 50 staff serving about 200 hectares. Close communications allow cutting rates to be matched to packing capacity. Hands of bananas are hoisted on to a cableway protected from the sun until reaching the station where each is checked for quality. Flowers on the end of each banana are removed by hand. They then pass through a fungicidal dip that also drowns any insects before being packed into boxes for transit. It takes about three hours from picking to despatch. Traceability begins at this stage with box codes identifying both station and packer.

- *From packing station to loading in the ship.* Delivery to quayside takes five hours in a temperature-controlled lorry. Consignments wait at the wharf for up to a further six hours before ship departure.

- *Shipment to Zeebrugge.* Transit from Ecuador takes 13 days with boxes stacked on pallets or in containers according to customer needs.

- *Transport to Mack.* After inspection at the dockside by Mack personnel, the purchase is completed and the consignment moves overnight in a temperature-controlled lorry.

- *Storage at Mack.* The bananas are 'triggered' in ripening rooms at Paddock Wood, Kent, for 5–6 days until they match the specifications for colour and maturity set by Sainsbury.

- *Delivery to the Sainsbury depot.* Overnight delivery and holding in regional depots takes up to 12 hours. Transport is again in a temperature-controlled vehicle, this time bearing the Mack livery but contracted to a specialist produce carrier.

- *Delivery to retail store.* Time from depot to supermarket is less than two hours. Steady demand enables just-in-time delivery to achieve little wastage.

- *Display.* The 'sell-by' date allows two days on the shelf. Reordering at supermarket level is automatic using EPOS data generated at the checkouts. Central computers aggregate these data to make forecasts based on sales trends adjusted for the seasonal variations. They order from Mack and other suppliers.

In the future, Sainsbury plans to streamline the supply chain by further improving information flows among the three companies. This will make the chain more responsive to customer needs. As with many other product lines, the company sees competition in groceries as not simply between retailer and retailer but between supply chain and supply chain.

13.1 Introduction

The cooperation among Noboa, Mack and Sainsbury illustrates many features of supply chains. These chains have been developed to manage flows of products in many companies and industries. Sometimes, the chain is owned by a single, vertically integrated firm. For instance, both Jaeger, in Chapter 4, and IKEA, in Chapter 7, own many of the manufacturing and retailing stages. In other cases, work is outsourced to specialists. In contrast to Meubles Grange, which handles its own deliveries (see Chapter 3), Mack and Sainsbury have entered permanent contracts with specialist distributors. The advantage of 'doing-it-yourself' seems to lie in the certainty of complete control. Yet, in chains and networks involving several companies, managers have learnt the value of long-term relationships built on trust. Each party recognises the advantages that membership brings to the others and assists in achieving their goals.

Whether supply chains involve the sourcing of raw materials, the subcontracting of office services or the distribution of finished products, their common feature is planning and control. This means shared information and regular communication to integrate activities more closely than if merely markets linked them. For instance, in improving the jointly managed process of moving bananas from Ecuadorian farms to Sainsbury shelves, the retailer regularly shares data on issues such as sales, customer preferences and quality checks. This means the growers can select more preferred plant strains and the distributor can seek better ways of handling and ripening the fruit.

Establishing a formal supply chain is a strategic decision. An outline of some reasons for strategic cooperation appeared in Chapter 4. Managers recognise that success follows making effective links with other organisations in the environment. As shown in Chapter 4, these links can cover any feature of the value chain. For operations managers, this means integration of primary activities through thinking in terms of supply chains.

13.2 What is a supply chain?

Supply chains can vary from a single strand linking one firm at each stage of production to complex patterns or networks involving many firms. There is, therefore, no standard design; each firm and industry build them according to its needs. Among many definitions, APICS describes the supply chain as:

1 the process from the initial raw materials to the ultimate consumption of the finished product linking across supplier and user companies

2 the functions within and outside a company that enable the value chain to make products and provide services to the customer.[2]

We shall draw out the main features by reference to a model and then to some examples. First, however, we can outline how two important forms of supply chain developed.

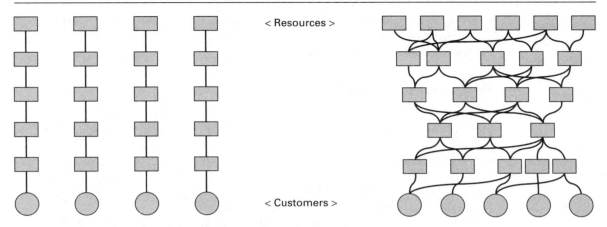

Figure 13.1 Vertical and horizontal industry supply chains

13.2.1 Vertical and horizontal

The terms vertical and horizontal refer to the form of the industry supply chain. Figure 13.1 presents two examples connecting basic resources to final customers.

Vertical supply chains

The types of supply chains we see today can be matched to two developments. First, for 100 years from about 1850, the economies of industrial nations were transformed by the emergence of vertically integrated corporations. Resource allocation, which had hitherto been left to markets, was transferred to the managers within these corporations. On the upstream side, spurred by developments in transport and communications, large companies took over all stages of the transformation from source to consumption. Among agricultural products, the antecedents of Unilever controlled ground nut plantations in West Africa producing the inputs to margarine plants in Britain and the Netherlands. Colonial links featured in many chains; the opening case mentioned how Geest was licensed by the British Government to run the banana trade with the Windward Islands. On the demand side, the newly powerful mass producers of consumer goods sought to control distribution to ensure their products reached all parts of the nation and the world. They set up transport companies, distribution centres and showrooms. Managers sought to control everything. Montague Burton was among several tailors with plant in West Yorkshire and shops in every UK high street. At a much larger scale, the oil industry became dominated by the majors. Firms such as Shell have interests extending from well to forecourt.

A vertical supply chain does not depend on the ownership of one company. The Marks & Spencer chain, with roots in the 1930s, was built on links with partner suppliers. Many extend over more than 50 years. Yet, inflexibility in the face of changing fashion, which brought down Burton in the 1960s to little more than a brand name, began to challenge Marks & Spencer at the end of the century. Innovation and change affect other industries too. Until the personal computer, IBM, DEC, ICL and others were vertically integrated. They offered every aspect of hardware, software and afterware (after-sales service, office supplies and so on), each provided from sites managed by the company. Designs and components were not interchangeable.

Horizontal supply chains

The personal computer is an example of the second development. In the early 1980s, IBM decided to outsource the supply of both software and the central processing unit to Microsoft and Intel. These small companies were 'let in'. Very quickly, product design shifted from integral, with one design for each application, to modular, where interchangeable components were connected through standard interfaces. Different vendors began to supply these components and much of the industry took on a horizontal structure.

Both vertical and horizontal structures persist, often mixed within the same industry. In computing, the Mac comes from Apple, while the PC is produced by anyone. In retailing, grocery markets in most nations are dominated by a few companies. Apart from a handful of leading manufacturers, the dominant brands are those of the supermarket. The horizontal structure is seen in the way Unilever, Nestlé and so on supply all retailers. Yet, the vertical model persists in other branches. Clarks makes and retails shoes, although it also sells them through other distributors.

Change

Stimulated by advances in communication and information systems, we see another wave of innovation in supply chains. New strategies include: the setting up of virtual markets, exchanges and nodes; balancing the whole chain to avoid wastage; closer matching of customers' needs to production capability, leading to various forms of mass customisation; and automatic creation and settlement of contracts. We will return to some of these ideas during the chapter.

13.2.2 Representing the supply chain

Figure 13.2 shows a consumer goods manufacturer with a supply network above and demand network below. This industry has a horizontal structure with different numbers of suppliers at each level, each supplying several companies at the next. The partners with whom the firm deals directly are called the first tier. In turn, first-tier partners are linked to the second tier, and so on. For a clothing company such as Jaeger, first-tier suppliers include weavers of cloth, the second tier makes thread for the weaver, while a third-tier company is involved in raw materials from wool to dyestuffs. On the demand side of a manufacturer, there may be further manufacturing or finishing processes followed by several stages of distribution. These last processes often occur in international trade.

Managers usually describe up to three tiers, although the number depends on the degree of specialisation in the industry. Differences between stages are not always clear cut; for example, some second-tier suppliers may deliver some items directly while others are inputs to the first tier. Such leapfrogging of stages is also seen in distribution, where a firm may offer goods through wholesalers and

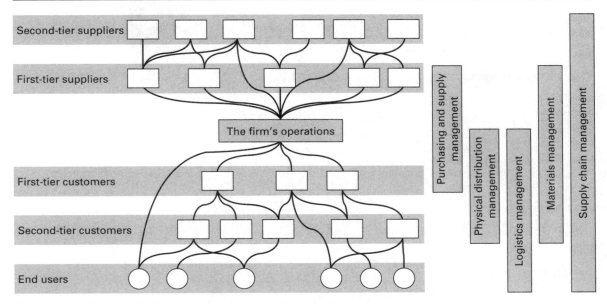

Figure 13.2 Supply chain for consumer goods manufacturer

retailers as well as directly to customers. Book publishers, for example, supply through all such channels.

To see the chain as simply describing the flow of supplies from source to consumer is to miss its purpose. As mentioned in the introduction, its advantage lies in the use of information for joint management. These information links, shown in principle in Figure 2.7, are best demonstrated by our opening case. An interpretation appears in Figure 13.3. Here we see the stages of the banana supply chain; these lie in three groups managed by Noboa, Mack and Sainsbury. Planning and control of the chain, however, depends on the exchange of information among the partners. Sainsbury gathers data both on current sales and on customers' responses to product quality. It shares these data with its partners both to manage current performance and to support development. For instance, analysis of damage in transit may lead to Mack and Noboa working together on improved carton design. In the other direction of information flow, Noboa can give its partners early warnings of any supply difficulties caused, for example, by bad weather or shipping delays. Therefore, both feedback and feedforward control can be identified.

13.2.3 Management functions within the supply chain

The right-hand part of Figure 13.2 locates some management functions often encountered when studying supplies. They refer to management of important aspects of the chain:

■ Purchasing and supply management is concerned with the links with first-tier suppliers. More than merely buying, these managers aim to obtain supplies according to the five 'rights':

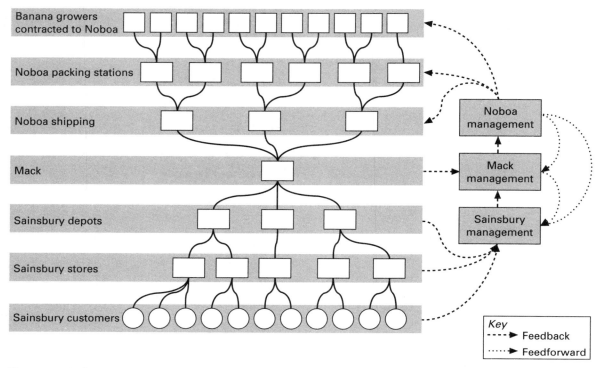

Figure 13.3 Supply chain for bananas

- the right price
- the right quantity
- the right schedule
- the right quality
- from the right source.

Leading companies have long recognised how these features contribute to the value offered in their own products. Establishing deep relationships with a few suppliers, so-called 'single sourcing', has allowed them to achieve improvements not available when buying is treated as a series of independent purchases. We shall return to this issue later in the chapter.

■ Physical distribution management, PDM, refers to managing the flows to first-tier customers. Organisations face questions such as number and location of depots, the type of transport and the schedules to which it operates. The skills and investment required in this activity mean that it is frequently outsourced to specialists.

■ Logistics is usually seen as an extension of PDM in considering the flow of products to consumers. While PDM considers the best way to deliver to the next tier, the logistician seeks to optimise the whole chain. For example, in the banana supply chain, a logistics specialist will study how packaging not only protects the fruit during transit but also carries information and serves as a unit for display on the retailer's shelves. A well-designed carton has features beyond those needed for transit from Ecuador to Zeebrugge.

- Materials management considers the flows of products both into and out of the business. This can be especially important for a manufacturer operating on many sites throughout different countries. Among questions to be considered are purchasing, location of plant and warehouses, stock control, and design of transport systems to offer high efficiency and flexibility.

- Supply chain management has emerged as a broad concept covering flows within and between companies. It incorporates all items in this list, although the contribution of each specialism remains important. As we have seen, its focus is integration.

13.3 Managing the supply chain

Many issues in supply chain management are common to operations within the organisation, for example planning, control, quality, location and inventory management. Since these are dealt with in other parts of the book, we shall consider here a selection of questions particular to the chain. These are: make or buy decisions; vendor selection; customisation; and the dynamics of the chain.

13.3.1 The make or buy decision

The make or buy decision refers to the choice of whether to provide a resource internally or obtain it from a supplier. A task of the purchasing manager is to investigate this choice. Table 13.1 presents some reasons for consideration.

The importance of each factor will differ in each case. For instance, managers have increasingly recognised the benefits of concentrating on their core businesses and outsourcing the rest to other organisations.

In the past five years, the Bradford and Bingley Building Society has considered subcontracting those activities not directly related to providing retail financial services.

Table 13.1 Factors in the make or buy decision

Reasons for making	Reasons for buying
■ Low production cost	■ Low total cost; convert fixed costs into variable costs
■ No suitable suppliers	■ Support suppliers on whom the organisation depends
■ Use spare internal capacity	■ Overcome capacity shortage
■ Obtain supply quickly, if capacity available	■ Support rapid sales increase
■ Maintain internal skills	■ Obtain fresh technical expertise
■ Protect intellectual property such as trade secrets, designs and so on	■ Access the benefits of a supplier's intellectual property and innovation
■ Maintain or increase organisational scope	■ Focus management attention on core business
■ Avoid risk of dependence on suppliers	■ Ensure alternative sources of supply
■ Manage quality	■ Access the best quality

In 1998, it appointed IBM to run its IT services. About 40 staff and their premises were transferred to the supplier company. In 2000, BBBS outsourced its printing function to Alistair McIntosh. The society found it had not been obtaining the best value. The expertise of McIntosh in printing gives access to the latest technologies as well as guaranteed costs and delivery standards. As with the IBM example, the company normally transfers operations and staff to new premises, centralising the processes if necessary. Its price agreement allows for both parties sharing savings that come from process improvements. Perceiving the management of print solutions as its core strength, McIntosh has similar contracts with other companies. In 2001, it opened a £10 million plant to supply the Bank of Scotland.[3]

| Exercise 13.1 | Drawing on Table 13.1, which factors seemed to be most important in the decision to outsource functions at BBBS? |

Many or few suppliers

The make or buy decision could apply to the purchase of each item. Indeed, the practice is common in project and jobbing manufacture where firms regularly use each other's spare capacity, often at short notice. Therefore, a building contractor may hire a crane from a local supplier, or a jobbing printer will pass on work beyond capacity or expertise.

The case of BBBS and McIntosh, however, goes beyond such casual relationships. The link is strategic, with both parties investing time and money at the outset and expecting the association to continue for many years. Furthermore, BBBS has opted to use just one supplier. In following a strategy of using few, or one, suppliers, a buyer is seeking benefits other than the lowest short-term cost resulting from competitive bidding for each contract. The advantages of using few suppliers are as follows:

- They understand the special needs of the organisation and its customers in terms of all aspects of the product–service mix.
- Suppliers can achieve economies of scale and can afford to invest in product and process improvements. Examples include design innovations and process development such as JIT.
- Transaction costs are reduced for both parties.
- Partners in long-term relationships develop multiple communication links and adopt a common approach to problem solving.

Research conducted from 1991 to 1995 among UK manufacturing companies in engineering and electronics showed a 35% fall in the number of suppliers. The main reason was the desire to manage relations with each supplier more effectively. Without this advantage, benefits such as those suggested already, could not be realised.[4] Quality was a critical factor for some companies. The need for assurance led them to limit links to partners achieving verifiable standards. The ISO 9000 series (see Chapter 16) was coming into widespread use at the time.

An example of rapid communication and problem solving between partners occurs in the relationship between Swindon Pressings (SP) and Honda in Swindon. Ease of assembly and quality of body finish are heavily dependent on the accuracy of manufacture of component body panels. If production staff at Honda discover a problem with a batch of panels, even a minor one, they can telephone their shop floor colleagues at SP. If necessary, they can arrange an immediate meeting without waiting for the management authorisation required in many organisations. These discussions are particularly valuable during the early production of new models. Solutions have involved immediate changes in the way panels are stacked and loaded for the two-mile trip between the plants.

Outsourcing arrangements have grown in the public sector under the policies of competitive tendering and best value. Local authorities have outsourced waste collection, street cleaning, gardening, information services and, more recently, housing management. The early practice of awarding contracts to the lowest bidder brought mixed results, with some contractors unable to deliver the service at the quoted price. The notion of value for money has replaced this low price policy.

13.3.2 Vendor selection

When an organisation considers long-term alliances with fewer suppliers it will recognise how it increases its dependence upon them and hence its risk. This means that extra care must be taken in the choice of vendors. Many companies engage in a process of *vendor selection*. It often incorporates weighted factor scoring similar to that introduced in Chapter 7. For a particular category of supplies, such as engineering components, the purchasing managers draw up a schedule of factors and weights. Then, each potential vendor is rated, following meetings, visits and assessment of performance on any previous business.

Leading companies practise open communication when conducting ratings, seeing the process as another step in establishing a long-term association. Rating is also used during review and extension of the relationship. Through sharing perceptions of the key factors, their weights and the performance of the supplier against them, partners can identify opportunities for improvement.

Some companies publish ratings summaries to all suppliers. Table 13.2 shows how the Tinplate Company of India uses four criteria in its regular review of materials suppliers – quality, cost, response and delivery.[5] For each criterion, performance is then either estimated or measured from records. These percentages are then weighted as shown in the table, so the maximum is 100. Tinplate Company regards a rating of 80 as excellent. It uses different criteria for each

Table 13.2 Vendor rating at Tinplate Company of India: April to June 2001

Supplier code	Supplier name	Quality (40)	Cost (30)	Response (15)	Delivery (15)	Total rating (%)
M025	Mahadev Engineering	40.00	24.00	15.00	9.38	88.38
A073	Arjunlal Banwarilal	40.00	27.24	14.40	2.14	83.78
A101	Anjana Minerals	40.00	30.00	15.00	5.00	90.00
A125	Advance Sales	40.00	30.00	15.00	12.05	97.05
A226	Apex Corporation	40.00	27.00	15.00	3.75	85.75
A307	Agro Engineering	40.00	30.00	15.00	8.57	93.57
A412	A.U. Enterprises	40.00	28.50	15.00	12.35	95.85
A424	Abhishek Industries	40.00	30.00	5.00	12.50	87.50

types of vendor. For example, hauliers are assessed on placement (40), delivery (30) and service quality (30).

Exercise 13.2 What comments can you make on the data in Table 13.2?

13.3.3 Customisation within the supply chain

The idea of customisation appeared in Chapter 3 as an alternative to the standardisation of service patterns. Nowadays, in both service and manufacture, companies look to overcome the dichotomy. They look to combine the benefits of mass production of standard products with the market advantages of meeting each customer's special needs. This is *mass customisation*. Some manufacturers delay finishing until customers place an order. Dell, for example, has made its reputation from being able to build personal computers to order from an array of standard modules. Many Italian manufacturers of domestic appliances, sanitary ware and furniture have found ways of incorporating fashion ideas into their product marketing through postponement. Yet, the process remains in the hands of the manufacturers, relying on quick delivery to the domestic market.[6]

For global business with long supply chains, *postponement* of product variation must wait until the last possible moment in the flow. This enables consumers to acquire products with personalised features without having to wait for them to be processed through the whole chain.

Feitzinger and Lee[7] set out three design principles for bringing mass customisation into the supply chain:

■ *Create products from independent modules that can be assembled in various ways at low cost.* HP manufactures DeskJet printers in Singapore before shipping them to its European distribution centre in Stuttgart. Since power supplies are market specific, it designed these as separate, external items to be plugged in by the customer. Further, the Stuttgart operation orders instruction manuals and packaging. Direct manufacturing costs rose under the new arrangement, but total costs, including inventory and transport, fell by a quarter.

■ *Design processes with independent modules to fit different distribution channels.* A problem for paint manufacturers seeking to offer a wide colour range was the huge stock implied by such a policy. They solved this by supplying large retailers with base paints, pigments and a mixer. Customers now have a limitless choice of colours made up in the shop. Again, postponing the final mixing increases direct manufacturing costs, including transferring some to the distribution tier. Yet, the total cost of offering a wide colour range is reduced. Rival companies continue with a narrow colour range displayed in the store.

■ *The supply chain design – covering the location and function of all the tiers in the chain – should combine low cost with flexibility and responsiveness.* Coca-Cola and other soft drinks manufacturers achieve both low cost, flexibility and responsiveness in their supply chains by delivering bulk syrup to local bottling plants. These add sugar, water and gas during the packaging process – bottling or canning. Fluctuations in local demand can be coped with rapidly. The syrup manufacturers now also deliver bulk syrup to major outlets, such as McDonald's, where blending occurs at the point of delivery. Stocks and packaging costs are reduced further by this postponement.

Exercise 13.3	Lands' End, the international home shopping clothing company, hems trousers and adds monograms to many products according to customers' orders. Clothes are sourced globally but the finishing occurs at the distribution centre in Oakham.
	Compare this example with those given earlier, adding any others that you are familiar with.

Limits to mass customisation of complex products

Commentators see mass customisation as becoming the predominant form of manufacturing in the 21st century. Agarwal, Kumaresh and Mercer, however, are more cautious, especially when they compare the relative simplicity of supplying soft drinks or personal computers with the complexity of manufacturing products such as automobiles.[8] Moving to mass customisation would require many changes throughout the car supply chain and incur extra costs. It is unclear whether customers would be prepared to pay them. Surveys show that up to 20% of car buyers would consider a build-to-order option, yet the extra they would pay has not been established.

Agarwal and colleagues identify another option, using the power of information systems to achieve *virtual customisation*. In this approach, manufacturers would fill the supply chain with a greater variety of models than at present; stocks held at distribution centres and dealers, or in transit, as well cars in the production schedule would be planned to offer this variety. Information systems would then focus on *enhancing the customer's ability to find the right vehicle* and arranging for delivery. From the buyer's point of view, it does not matter whether the car has been truly built to order or has been drawn from a 'virtual' build based on stock held in the region.

13.3.4 Supply chain dynamics

Another approach to understanding the benefits of supply chain management is to compare the effects of different decision-making policies within simulated networks. One of the simplest studies has a chain with a single manufacturer, distributor, wholesaler and retailer at each tier. Each experiences a short delay between ordering and supply and looks after its own interests by trying to keep its own stocks steady. Results show that the retailer places orders on the wholesaler that vary more than the demand it receives from consumers. The wholesaler's orders oscillate even more than the retailer's do and those in the last link, between distributor and manufacturer, show the wildest behaviour of all. This phenomenon, where variability is magnified as orders are passed up the supply chain, is called the *bullwhip effect*.

The effect can be demonstrated in the well-known group exercise, the beer game, in which participants simulate stock-ordering decisions.[9] Alternatively, a

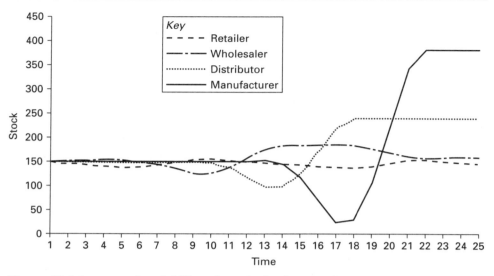

Figure 13.4 Increased variability of stocks in the supply chain

spreadsheet model reveals the effects of the independent stockholding decisions. Figure 13.4 uses a model with simple, independent decision rules for each actor. (For details, see the support materials for this book.) We see the stock levels of the four elements of the supply chain after a small perturbation in an otherwise steady demand. The bullwhip has two features: the amplification of the variation in consumer demand; and the delayed response of the tiers further up the chain. While this is an exaggerated example, the bullwhip effect leads to excess stock as each tier attempts to defend itself against stockouts.

Stabilising the chain

Dampening down the oscillations needs cooperative decision making and shared information flows. Frequently, a company at one end of the chain takes the lead. For the supply side, we can cite two examples. In retailing, Marks & Spencer pioneered the sharing of daily sales data to enable its suppliers to adjust the output of different lines. In car assembly, Toyota extended its just-in-time flow system to its suppliers. The JIT and kanban systems (see Chapters 4 and 12) work best when daily flow is steady, so Toyota accepts the responsibility for dampening down fluctuations in demand through its holding of finished vehicle inventories. For the demand side, we find major grocery manufacturers use *continuous replacement* policies, restocking their customers' distribution centres according to their EPOS data supplemented by forecasts.

In each case, the leaders seek to improve total chain performance, whether it be through more accurate matching of customer preferences, minimising cost through stabilising flows or guaranteeing reductions in inventories. Fisher shows that a supply chain design should match the type of product it carries.[10] For stable, undifferentiated products, such as many groceries and fuel, profit margins are low. The stress, therefore, should be on efficiency in the supply chain. Low stocks and regular distribution are important. In contrast stand *innovative* products;

these are new, change frequently and experience uncertain demand. The stress is on responsiveness, so managers concentrate less on cost minimisation and more on ensuring that the product is available to customers when and where they want it. Critics have argued that the difficulties at Marks & Spencer arose partly from designing the supply chain for all goods in the same way and emphasising efficiency in all cases.

13.4 Electronic commerce

Discussion of electronic commerce in any book poses difficulties since it is one of the fastest growing and uncertain areas of business. Witness the estimated £150 billion invested in B2B (business-to-business) infrastructure during 2000; this was followed by the collapse of many *dot.com* enterprises the following year. Clearly, there is little history to go on and the only certainty about predictions is that they will be wrong.

Another question concerns whether e-commerce is sufficiently different for it to be treated as a separate branch of operations management. We do not take this view, for e-commerce amounts to an array of developments that allow all aspects of business to be done better. Therefore, it should be integrated into them. The often quoted views of Andy Grove, founder and chairman of Intel, underscore this point:

> In some years' time, there will be no such thing as Internet companies because all companies that will be operating will be using the Internet in their business and in their internal operations. This belief is based on the conviction that the Internet provides a competitive advantage to companies that use it, that it is so compelling, and is going to grow even more compelling in time as to bring this thesis around.[11]

E-operations refers to the application of information and communication technologies (ICTs) to operations management. All aspects of the value chain are affected. Figure 13.5, based on the model of Figure 1.11, summarises how the support activities of the organisation are influenced by changed relationships among strategy, operations and ICT. While aspects of the value chain are changed by ICT, operations managers do not change their fundamental aims. Yet, they change the means for achieving these aims, using all the tools, including ICT, available to them. The rapidly developing resources offer two possibilities – how to conduct existing operations better and how to conduct operations in new ways. Clearly, these new ways could mean better internal processes, such as quicker design, improved scheduling or more thorough inventory management. Otherwise, managers could look outside to improving or changing the supply chain links we have been discussing in this chapter. In the next sections, we shall examine two aspects of these outside links, B2B and B2C.

13.4.1 Business-to-business (B2B) market places

Supply chain partners sometimes spend years developing links and honing their joint operations. Suddenly, the emergence of electronic market places, with more

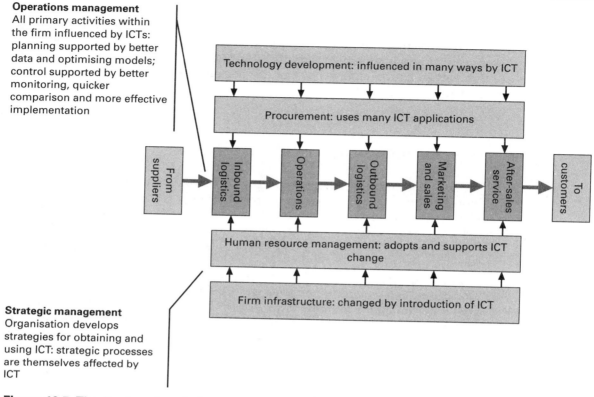

Operations management
All primary activities within
the firm influenced by ICTs:
planning supported by better
data and optimising models;
control supported by better
monitoring, quicker
comparison and more effective
implementation

Strategic management
Organisation develops
strategies for obtaining and
using ICT: strategic processes
are themselves affected by
ICT

Figure 13.5 The firm's value chain influence by ICTs

information available more quickly, suggests new arrangements to replace these
links. Yet, following a wide-ranging survey conducted in 2000, Hansen and colleagues found that changes had not been so dramatic.[12] Although markets for some
products had become more efficient for short-term relationships such as single
transactions, deriving long-term value from the new ICTs was no easy matter.

Market places perform either of two functions for the supply chain manager. First, they offer a service, especially in enabling a match between sellers and
buyers. Second, they enhance the purchasing capability of customers by, or provide them with, the information they need to carry out the purchase better. The
survey identified five models that differed in these functions:

- *Liquidity creators* (20%). Creating flexible markets for commodities reducing
  costs for buyers and sellers.

- *Transaction facilitators* (30%). Carrying out purchases and reducing the cost of
  administration.

- *Aggregators* (10%). Consolidating demand across several organisations, using
  this power to lower prices.

- *Supply consolidators* (15%). Identifying sources of supply and conducting purchases yielded easy access to many buyers and their product information.

- *Project/specification managers* (25%). Supporting the planning of complex purchases and improving the speed of new product development.

In the list, the first three market places focus on reducing transaction costs between parties. A more efficient market, however, does not encourage cooperation and, therefore, does little for the long-term development of supply chains. The last two models stress the value of information in seller–buyer relationships and hence can help in supporting effective supply chains. Hansen and colleagues conclude that B2B electronic market places will have most impact on supply chains when they perform these last roles, that is support the sharing of information. They were, however, in the minority in the survey and had yet to make a great impact.

13.4.2 Business web models

Beyond setting up markets, new Internet business services have emerged, either created from scratch (the *dot.com*) or extended from an existing operation (*bricks and clicks*). These new businesses replace existing components of supply chains whenever they offer enhanced value. Tapscott, Ticoll and Lowy identified five *business web models* to categorise the roles that these emerging organisations fulfil.[13] In different ways, they perform two basic functions. First, they *exercise hierarchical control* through being in command of prices, quantities or other product features such as quality. Second, they offer *integration* through improving the both vertical and horizontal links to support value chains and networks. Table 13.3 outlines the five models, indicating the impact that they have upon supply chain management. Examples quoted in the table are expanded in Box 13.1.

While the examples in Box 13.1 represent the five business models, matching the ideal types of the table is not exact. As with other businesses, they adapt to their customers' needs, frequently offering more than one type of service. Typical of this multiple approach to supply chain management is Future Electronics:[15]

Table 13.3 Roles for Internet businesses in supply chain management

	Market place	Aggregator	Alliance	Value chain	Distribution network
Explanation	Handles exchanges between buyer and seller	Adds value to the link between buyer and seller	Part of long-term cluster that designs or innovates	Partners adding value through integration to better match customers' needs	Provides transport links among all parties
Focus	Pricing	Delivery	Collaboration	Integration	Distribution
Critical processes	Comparing prices	Matching needs	Sharing information of all kinds	Shared design of products and processes	Optimising and integrating transport schedules
Involvement of operations management	Small	Requires integration of plans, schedules, inventories, etc.	Small – applies to design and development	Lead organisation manages whole process	Location, inventory and transport management
Examples	MetalSite	CheMatch	Ventro Corporation	Toyota, Dell, Marks & Spencer	Transport4

BOX 13.1 Examples of e-businesses within the supply chain[14]

- *MetalSite* is a good example of a market place, enabling buyers and sellers to meet directly. Its system reduces costs for the members: suppliers, producers, distributors and end users. It claims to be the largest of its kind, offering a high chance of finding a product, buyer or seller.

- *CheMatch* is more than a market place, offering both an exchange and information resource for bulk chemicals, polymers and fuels. It acts as a neutral third party, giving access to its list of products traded on the exchange. To some extent, it influences the prices. In other cases, aggregators exercise closer control over prices. Bulk sellers of airline tickets are an example.

- One of the functions of *Ventro* is to stimulate links among manufacturers, suppliers, customers and partners. Members use a global virtual workspace to collaborate on e-business processes such as complex purchasing, sourcing decisions, product development and program management.

- *Transport4* was designed by pipeline companies and their customers to improve sharing of information about petroleum product distribution. It aims to increase productivity, improve decisions and reduce costs. Members include schedulers, traders, terminal operators, accountants and pipeline companies.

FE carries the world's largest inventory of electronic components, which it distributes to customers. It is an aggregator, adding value from low prices and guaranteed high-delivery standards. Yet it is also involved in: alliances, advising customers on materials management strategies and electronic design; value chain links with regular customers, carrying bonded supplies; making up stocks through automated replenishment management; and distribution from its four main centres strategically located around the globe.

13.4.3 B2C operations

The widespread use of personal computers has boosted home shopping both for existing providers and for new entrants. For many products and services, the Internet represents another ordering channel, replacing the personal service of the telephone with the self-service of the keyboard. In other cases, products are offered for the first time or are put together in new ways to suit the special properties of the medium. Whatever the approach, the challenge for operations managers arises from the raised expectations that easy ordering brings. If the transaction takes just minutes, why wait seven days for delivery?

Delivery poses two problems. First, for bundles of products, such as groceries, how can the convenience of the service be offered at sufficiently low cost? Second, for any home shopping product, how can home delivery be achieved, again at sufficiently low cost?

Store-based picking versus warehousing

For home delivery of the household shopping, the choice between store-based picking and warehousing encapsulates many issues faced by operations managers.

Some retailers have chosen to supply orders from their existing stores while others are establishing special warehouses. Yet others have decided to outsource the whole of their home delivery services.

By 2001, the market leader Tesco had established its £250 million a year on-line business in which the goods were picked entirely from local stores. Asda, by way of contrast, had chosen a warehouse model, building two centres on the periphery of London. Costs estimated by Merrill Lynch were £24 for picking and £15 for the warehouse model, while each company was charging £5 for the service. While the picking approach involves little investment in new facilities, it incurs high variable cost. By the same token, the capital investment in warehouses is high and limits the rate of expansion of the service. In response, Sainsbury adopted a hybrid model, using picking for low volumes and building warehouses as demand increased.

Tesco's approach enabled it to expand rapidly and become recognised as the pace setter, albeit at a price. Coming later to the market and learning from its competitors' errors was Waitrose, a regional chain with a reputation for high quality and higher than average prices. Offering another variation, it combined picking for local deliveries with a warehouse to supply its special lines to those geographic areas where it had no stores. For the former, efficiency within the store was improved by using a special picking trolley with on board terminal. This allowed up to five orders to be picked at once from the aisles with the aim of cutting operating costs to £10.[16]

Although the retailers may make a loss on direct costs, they need to include other factors in their performance calculations. These include the increased order size of e-shoppers, the use of the Internet to acquire new customers and build loyalty and the possibly damage to trade in the store. About half of United Kingdom grocery shoppers are 'promiscuous'; this means they shop in more than one supermarket each week. Not having an effective web presence may lead to the loss of these customers.

The last mile

In discussion of e-commerce, 'the last mile' refers to two questions. One concerns the cost of providing broadband connections to homes; optical fibre trunks are cheap enough to lay, but the cost of the last link to connect each subscriber remains high. The other, which we shall focus on here, relates to the last part of the home delivery service. Multiple visits caused by customers being out of the house slow deliveries, choke the system and impose extra costs. The problem is made worse in countries like China, where the lack of a reliable credit system means that senders require cash on delivery and hence the presence both the customers and their money.[17]

Various models for the last mile are in use:

- *Delivery time windows.* Rivals offer different windows for customers to accept deliveries depending on products, leadtime and geographical area. Tesco offers two-hour slots booked a day or more in advance; Eurospar in Finland uses a one-hour range; in Sweden, Matomera has three evening windows for same-day delivery.

■ *Reception boxes.* Secure boxes installed at the customer's premises permit unattended delivery. The zBox is one of several home delivery bins tried in the United States. Costing $5 per month, it is opened from a keypad using a new code for each package, enabling both deliveries and returns.[18] Boxes could be refrigerated to permit chilled grocery delivery.

■ *Delivery boxes.* Delivery boxes are a variant of reception boxes. Instead of consignments being transferred from vehicle to a permanently installed reception box, the box itself is transported and secured to a special docking point. In this way, both the handling of goods and the number of boxes in circulation are reduced, but each consignment requires two trips. For regular customers, the empty box can be picked up the next time, but then the number of boxes in circulation has to be increased.

■ *Delivery points.* Drop-off points passed regularly by customers offer attractive potential to distribution companies. Proposals have included post offices, dry cleaning shops, supermarkets and filling stations. BP Australia service stations combined with on-line retailer Wishlist. The latter uses BP's network for pick-up, returns and payments. Further, stations display the Wishlist brand and the partners engage in joint marketing and customer acquisition. Typically, BP stations are open 24 hours a day.[19]

Using a simulation of the Helsinki area, Punakivi and Saranen compared various attended and unattended home delivery policies for regular deliveries.[20] They found that delivery boxes, collected on the next visit, offered the lowest total cost over the life of the assets.

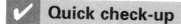

Exercise 13.4

Although costs are lower than for attended delivery, what problems do you foresee for a home delivery box system? How can they be overcome?

✔ Quick check-up

Can you:

☐ Define:
  - supply chain
  - second-tier supplier
  - horizontal and vertical chains
  - postponement
  - virtual customisation
  - bullwhip effect
  - e-operations.

☐ List five reasons for making and five for buying.

☐ Name four advantages in using few suppliers.

☐ Summarise the weighted assessment process in vendor selection.

☐ Name two functions for the operations manager fulfilled by a B2B market place.

☐ Compare the benefits of store and warehouse picking.

☐ Outline the last mile problem.

? Questions

Chapter review

13.1 Many firms are reducing the numbers of their suppliers. Why are they doing this and what are the limits to such a policy?

13.2 Using your own examples, explain the principles given by Feitzinger and Lee for enabling mass customisation in the supply chain.

13.3 Outline the functions performed by business web models.

Application

13.4 Use a Gantt chart to summarise the flow of bananas from plantation to retail store. Suggest points where problems may arise and how you might eliminate them.

13.5 Look up recruitment advertisements for staff involved in supplies. Compare the scope of roles such as logistics with those given in Figure 13.2.

13.6 Draw up a chart showing the costs of various forms of remote order fulfilment in groceries. Identify whether these costs are fixed or variable and sketch a break-even chart to compare them. How would you include opportunity costs in your evaluation?

Investigation

13.7 Use the idea of modular design to compare the offerings of tour operators offering mass or personal service in the travel industry.

CLOSING CASE

Schwan's service

With an estimated turnover of $3 billion, Schwan's Sales Enterprises is one of the leaders in the US frozen food industry. It supplies nationally to schools and colleges, hospitals, restaurant chains and retail outlets. Products include the industry's widest pizza range, ethnic foods and many other convenience items. There are six manufacturing plants in the United States and three in Europe. Al Schwan, company chairman, is optimistic about growth. 'Futurists say through the year 2025 there're three products that are going to be very big, and that's pizza, ice cream and hand-held food. . . . We're trying to get foods that can be prepared in less than 20 minutes. Most people don't know how to cook anymore.'

This family-controlled business started in 1952 in a struggling farm dairy. Marvin Schwan, younger brother of Al, recognised that ice cream was more profitable than milk. He began selling it from a 1946 Dodge van throughout rural Michigan. Sales reached $4.5 million by 1962. This activity has grown into the Home Service Division, whose yellow vans are a familiar sight in the Detroit area. They deliver a wide range of frozen food to customers who are now much more urban than rural. In 1998, the company launched its website, at first mainly to serve existing customers. This cautious, incremental approach means that the site has been profitable almost since its inception. Features are added only when the company is confident they will pay for themselves.

▶

The site carries the full list of some 350 frozen products, meals and side dishes. On the first visit, the customer finds that recent order history has been loaded and favourites highlighted. This record is continually updated. Schwan's finds that the convenience of the site means that customers order more compared with the telephone.

The delivery driver calls every two weeks. Buyers, choosing from the catalogue, may order in advance. If so, their consignments are ready. Otherwise, they can buy from unallocated stock, chancing that some items may be sold out. One customer reported how she valued ordering in advance as opposed to in a hurry when the driver calls. She uses the site as a shopping list, regularly updating her order online until the delivery day.

By 2001, fewer than 15% of Schwan's customers ordered by the Internet but the company had only just started to advertise its facility and seek new business. A recommendations feature enhanced the simple catalogue, suggesting food based on the customer's buying profile. The company was also testing a change in distribution from the biweekly schedule to delivery on demand.[21]

Questions

1 How has Schwan's used the Internet to develop its links with customers? Why do you think it has chosen this policy?

2 Compare the distribution method used by Schwan's with others in this chapter to assess how effective it is likely to be.

3 From a long-term perspective, what strategic problems may arise as Schwan's tries to expand its service using the Internet?

Notes and references

1. Wilson, N. (1996) 'Supply chain management: a case study of a dedicated supply chain for bananas in the UK grocery market', *Supply Chain Management*, 1(2), pp.28–35; Liddel, I. (2000) *Unpeeling the Banana Trade*, London: Fairtrade Foundation; http://www.fairtrade.org.uk/unpeeling.htm#UK

2. Cox, J.F., Blackstone, J.H. and Spencer, M.S. (eds) (1995) *APICS Dictionary*, 8th edition, Fall Church, VA: American Productivity and Inventory Control Society.

3. Hancock, J. and Oates, S. (2001) 'Minding other people's business: Perspectives on outsourcing at Bradford & Bingley', *Supply Chain Management*, 6(1), pp.58–9; www.alimac.co.uk accessed 6 August 2001.

4. Goffin, K., Szwejczewski, M. and New, C. (1997) 'Managing suppliers: When fewer can mean more', *International Journal of Physical Distribution and Logistics Management*, 27(7), pp.422–36.

5. The Tinplate Company of India (2001) *Vendor rating for suppliers from 01–Apr–2001 to 30–Jun–2001*, TCI, Kolkata; www.tinplateindia.com/buy1.asp accessed 10 August 2001.

6. Battezzati, L. and Magnani, R. (2000) 'Supply chains for FMCG and industrial products in Italy: Practices and the advantages of postponement', *International Journal of Physical Distribution and Logistics Management*, 30(5), pp.413–24.

7. Feitzinger, E. and Lee, H. (1997) 'Mass customization at Hewlett Packard: The power of postponement', *Harvard Business Review*, 75(1), January–February, pp.116–21.

8. Agarwal, M., Kumaresh, T.V. and Mercer, G.A. (2001) 'The false promise of mass customization', *The McKinsey Quarterly*, No.3.

9. Sterman, J. (1992) 'Teaching takes off, flight simulators for management education', *OR/MS Today*, October, pp.40–4; Sterman, J. (1988) 'Modeling managerial behavior: Misperceptions of feedback in a dynamic decision making experiment', *Management Science*, 35(3), pp.321–39.

10. Fisher, M.L. (1997) 'What is the right supply chain for your product?' *Harvard Business Review*, 75(2), March–April, pp.105–16.

11. Grove, A.S. (1999) *Speech to conference of Confederation of British Industry*, London, 21 September; Grove used to include 'in five years' time' in his assertion, but became more circumspect.

12. Hansen, M.A., Matthews, B.A., Mosconi, P.A. and Sankaran, V. (2001) 'A buyer's guide to B2B markets', *The McKinsey Quarterly*, No.2, pp.33–6.

13. Tapscott, D., Ticoll, D. and Lowy, A. (1999) 'Rise of the business web', *Business 2.0*, November, pp.198–208.

14. www.metalsite.com; www.chematch.com/home.jhtml; www.chemdex.com/about/index.html; www.teppco.com/transport4.htm accessed 14 August 2001.

15. Future Electronics (2000) *E-commerce solutions*, sales promotion material; www.futureelectronics.com/1033/about/default.asp#Overview

16. Ody, P. (2001) 'Shop or warehouse? That's the question', *Financial Times Survey: Supply Chain Management*, 20 June.

17. People's Daily Online (2001) 'Last-mile barriers cripple e-commerce'; www.peopledaily.com.cn/english/ accessed 18 August 2001.

18. www.zbox.com

19. Aldred, J. (2000) 'Wishlist to complete last mile with BP', *australia.internet.com*, 29 June; australia.internet.com/news/daily accessed 14 August 2001.

20. Punakivi, M. and Saranen, J. (2001) 'Identifying the success factors in e-grocery home delivery', *International Journal of Retail and Distribution Management*, 29(4), pp.156–63.

21. Newman, H. (2001) 'Marshall, Minn.–based Schwan's takes grocery service online by degrees', *Detroit Free Press*, 16 August; Clouston, D. (2000) '30 years after buying Tony's, Schwan's keeps enterprise growing', *The Salina Journal*, 9 April; www.schwans.com accessed 18 August 2001.

CHAPTER 14

Project management

OBJECTIVES

When you have finished studying this chapter, you should be able to:

- Explain the principles of project planning and how it is carried out in various types of organisation.
- Justify the activities of specialist project management companies.
- Compare the key features of project management with other management activities.
- Outline the growth of scheduling methods from Gantt charts and the early networking tools.
- Detail the procedure for setting out a project as a network and, from it, producing a schedule.
- Outline how to manage resource allocation within constraints, time–cost trade-offs and approaches to project restructuring.
- Show how risks of overrun are estimated and how these estimates can be incorporated into the plan.
- Give the main features of project control and relate them to the control model.

Rolling out Zuquala steel[1]

The Zuquala Steel Rolling Mill was an import substitution project by the Ethiopian government. Opened in 1997, it converts billets, $100 \times 100mm \times 3.5m$ long, into square bars, strips and angle iron. Continuing foreign exchange constraints meant that the Basic Metals and Engineering Industries Board (BMEIB) had looked for a second-hand mill. By chance, the Iron and Steel Company of South Africa (ISCOR) was closing its plant at Durban and agreed to sell. BMEIB and ISCOR created the project management team as a cooperative organisation. It included equal numbers from each group.

The broad plan identified major tasks, such as dismantling and packing the mill, transport to the port, shipment to Assab, Ethiopia, and delivery. The master schedule also included converting an existing building to take the mill, extending the stores and building a temporary residence for the ISCOR team. Conversion included installing a new roof and reinforcing the structure to take heavy overhead cranes. Meanwhile, main electrical equipment was to be refurbished in South Africa.

The broad plan had some 20 elements. Within these, each was broken down into sub-tasks worked out in detail. The links among these were established and set out in the master schedule. Alongside each were statements of resources needed and problems that might arise. For these, the team identified possible corrective action.

The critical path for the whole project was: civil works; refurbishing and assembling mechanical components; electrical engineering; and installation of other utilities such as the water cooling system. There were many links among the tasks. For example, electrical supplies were installed during the assembly of the mill so project management required the integration of the work of different contractors.

Within the civil works element, the following lay on the critical path: design; drawing up contracts; furnace foundations and flue with high-temperature lining; mill foundation; cooling bank foundation; and electrical cable trenches. The plan allowed three months for this group.

Project planning, and subsequent management, was supported by Microsoft Project software. This allowed all senior engineers to access information and report on progress. Weekly meetings among BMEIB, ISCOR and board members supplemented the daily $^3/_4$-hour review meetings. They measured progress and decided corrective action. The performance of all employees was appraised regularly.

A party for all employees marked the achievement of each milestone. Completion was both on time and with only minor variances from the original objectives. Import substitution of rolled steel bars was achieved and the transfer of knowledge by developing local technicians set in train. Product quality was high. Unfortunately, the mill remained dependent on the import of raw steel billets, accounting for 74% of production costs. Foreign exchange policies restricted their supply so the mill ran at first below full output. By 2000, however, annual output reached 105,000 tonnes, close to design capacity. The Zuquala plant employs some 200 workers at all levels.

14.1 Introduction

From time to time, an organisation takes on a substantial and complicated project. Examples include expansion of facilities, relocation, reorganisation or retrenchment. They look to specialists to supply expertise. Some are engineers, others financiers; we find also information systems people and consultants in international business. The most significant expertise, however, is project management. Many firms also hand over this task to specialists. The supermarket chain, electric company or shipping line are not specialists in the building of stores, stations or tankers and will normally sign *turnkey* contracts to specialists requiring them to deliver a fully functioning facility that they can use at the agreed date.

In contrast, many changes and developments are handled internally. Since they are often outside the mainstream of the organisation's operations, they present managers with difficult problems. For example, an organisation set up to manage a JIT production chain will not readily cope with a one-off reorganisation or installation of a new process. A special team usually handles project organisation, to be disbanded when the work is over.

The Zuquala mill project illustrates the process followed by project managers in the cycle from initial idea to commissioning the finished plant. First, there is *planning*. After the initial feasibility study and approval to go ahead, this comprises the setting of goals and the selection and organisation of the team. Second, there is *scheduling*. Here, there is the specific sequencing of tasks to be done and the allocation to them of resources of people, plant, materials, cash and so on. Project scheduling uses specially developed tools that differentiate it from other types of scheduling. Third, there is *implementation*, the carrying out of the plans right through to the end of the job. Inherent in all this activity is the need for *control*, which involves monitoring progress against both time and budgeted cost and steers the project along the planned route. Again, the project management tools are valuable for control.

The Zuquala mill is typical of modern projects in another way. It was built on time and close to budget. This majority of schemes, from constructing buildings to laying roads, are well tried and experts can predict their outcomes reliably. Only the large, risky and politicised ones gain attention. Failures flow from lack of experience, excessive optimism, change and poor management.

14.2 Planning and organising the project

The initial feasibility study for a project may result, for a specialist company, in a tender to carry out the work. Alternatively, an internal project follows an approved proposal. Whether under a contract or internal approval, a project starts with a definition of the following:

- The *scope* of the project. This defines the result and outlines how it is to be achieved. This includes the responsibilities of the various groups or firms associated with the project. Project managers call outputs *deliverables*.
- The *time* within which the project is to be finished.
- The *budget* for the work.

Within the total plan, the approved document will include a breakdown of the work to be done into broad categories with identified resources for each. This *work breakdown structure*, WBS, gives a framework for the detailed planning and scheduling which is to follow. It summarises the deliverables expected from each stage. In construction projects, such as Zuquala, the WBS is usually split by specialism such as civil, mechanical and electrical engineering. This enables contractors to be responsible for major elements.

An early decision concerns how project work is to be organised. The outcome depends on factors such as the firm's prior experience, how many projects are running at once, the significance of any project and the expertise and preference of decision makers. Approaches vary from making no special provision through to setting up either temporary or permanent units:

- *No special provision.* A project involving several departments of a small firm may be managed from the top with work tasks assigned through normal processes.

The policy is advantageous where the organisation is small and the project cuts across the whole hierarchy, making it worthwhile involving all departments in it.

- *Minimal provision: project co-ordinator.* Here, the project is carried out through the normal managerial hierarchy with an individual appointed as co-ordinator. If the scale is small, the work could become the responsibility of a senior manager as an extension of normal duties. Otherwise, the task could require a full-time secondment. Although the appointee can focus on progressing the work, setting up the role outside the normal hierarchy may restrict authority to make necessary changes. The backing of senior managers is essential.

- *Project matrix.* In the matrix arrangement, staff in addition to the co-ordinator are assigned to the project. Since this attachment is intermittent, there may be difficulties in balancing the demands of the special work with employees' normal duties.

- *Project team.* When the project has major significance, or is likely to last a long time, building a dedicated team will work best. The project group then has its own internal budget and controls and can co-ordinate its work as though it were a separate department. This arrangement is common in organisations whose business is project work. Examples range from defence contractors supplying external clients such as national governments to research departments working through a series of development tasks for other departments acting as clients. A permanent project team is difficult to arrange for a single task in a conventional organisation. The necessary flexibility may be lacking and there may be problems of return to the mainstream for staff who have been seconded for a long time.

- *Joint ventures.* In some industries, it is common to form consortia, frequently called joint ventures, to conduct project work. This arrangement stems from clients seeking the turnkey contracts mentioned earlier. The arrangement replaces previous systems where the client either managed and co-ordinated several separate contracts or appointed a main contractor with co-ordination responsibilities. For example, increased scale and complexity means that only the largest firms have the capacity to build new power stations, transport systems or telecommunications networks, or reorganise large administrative structures.

  The external co-ordination among two or more firms engaged in a joint venture can present operating problems. The extra dimension of difficulty involves the co-ordination of project teams who are jointly and equally responsible for making progress within budgets.

In most of the arrangements listed here there is a project manager. This person is responsible for achieving the defined aims. This sometimes has to be done without the usual line authority of the typical hierarchy. Then the person needs a combination of technical expertise and diplomatic skills. Technical expertise goes beyond knowledge of the disciplines required by the work breakdown schedule. It means applying project management techniques to scheduling and controlling of all tasks. Moreover, it means managing a mixed team of professionals, each of whom is in the team because of his or her expertise.

Very large projects will be broken down into a hierarchy of levels. The high-level work packets will themselves be seen as projects, each under the control of its own project manager.

14.2.1 Features of managing projects

Project management differs in significant ways from both the intermittent and repetitive operations we have discussed in previous chapters. In discussing the question of control, Anthony[2] identified a range of special features:

- *Single objective.* In contrast to facing multiple objectives in the operations function, the project manager's job is focused. The aim is to achieve a stated outcome within a stated time. Some performance measures are, therefore, more clear cut.

- *Superimposition.* As we noted earlier, a project is often superimposed on existing structures and operations processes. This makes it ambiguous. It requires new relationships among current departments and their managers. Usually, the budgetary control system is inappropriate.

- *Control.* Conventional control, whether of accounting budgets or other performance measures, usually follows a fixed cycle, say of weeks, months or quarters. The progress of a project is different. It moves between key moments, or *milestones*, when reviews are meaningful. A later example illustrates the use of such milestones. We should note that they do not occur at fixed intervals. Their irregularity calls for a special information system.

- *Trade-offs.* Within the single objective just mentioned, managers can make trade-offs between costs and time and even adjust the scope of the project if circumstances change.

- *Unique performance standards.* Since project work involves assembling tasks in a unique combination, the performance standards to be applied have to be less finely worked out than for routine operations. In the latter, long experience allows standards to be developed for all aspects of the work from quality and quantity to cost and productivity.

- *Frequent change.* Leading firms engaged in tasks such as road construction or mechanical engineering are well practised at project management. They can transfer learning from one project to another. In contrast, some projects break new ground and hence face higher risk. These are more prone to changes, with each affecting the progress of succeeding elements.

- *Project rhythm.* The tempo of activity in project work differs from that in conventional tasks. It builds from a slow beginning to a peak and then tapers towards the end. The types of work being done, and the corresponding skills needed, change continuously. During plant construction, for example, the work of civil engineers reaches a peak earlier than for other disciplines. After the two-thirds stage they have usually disappeared.

- *Environmental influence.* While all activities are shaped by the environment, its influence is more marked in project work. We have seen how manufacturing and isolated service functions are isolated from changes in the environment by boundary-spanning functions such as marketing. Their role in absorbing variations allows operations to work as efficiently as possible. In many projects, however, we see the influence of the natural environment, from weather to geology. Furthermore, the very size of many projects excites interest and response from individuals and groups. They include competitors, customers, lobbyists, protestors and so on.

- *Resources are brought to site*. In most project work where the output is a physical good, materials and components are brought to site. This is the stay-put layout. Not only does the movement often need special equipment but also the sequencing of materials, components, plant and staff requires special skills that differ from those needed in conventional factories.

In noting the distinctions set out in the list, we should recognise that they are not clear cut. Project work, for example, can involve the creation of readily movable goods or the delivery of a service. Further, what may be treated as a special item by one organisation may be seen as part of the routine of another.

14.3 Project scheduling

The scheduling task involves taking the elements of the WBS and arranging them in the optimal sequence. To this end, these *work packages* should be of fairly uniform duration, have clearly recognisable starting and finishing points, and be under the control of one manager.[3] Therefore, each manager runs a 'mini-project' with defined scope, time scale and budget. This will have its own WBS and be divided into smaller elements. Given the possibility of many hundreds of work packages within a large contract, firms need special tools to help them decide sequences and control progress. They create a *network schedule* that shows all the work packages and their sequential relationships.

14.3.1 Development

With few tasks, the Gantt chart allows sequences to be set out conveniently. After Gantt's development in 1917, the next great advances in project scheduling came in 1956 when two network planning techniques, CPM and PERT, emerged independently, see Box 14.1. The techniques had much in common, although there were detailed differences. Their importance has gradually declined as planning has moved from drawing board to keyboard.

Some 40 or more years on, the growth of software,[4] which even on a personal computer outperforms manual methods, has led to an integration of the techniques and the elimination of most minor differences of notation and layout. While some still recognise PERT as laying more emphasis on the probabilistic distribution of work package durations, both traditions now include the possibility of time–cost trade-offs and the generation of the full range of control reports. Furthermore, the limitations of the computer screen and printer have favoured the production of tabulated plans rather than large schematic diagrams whose setting out was part of the training of many planners and designers. The Gantt chart has made a comeback. We shall use it in this chapter as the basic means of presenting our discussion.

14.3.2 Scheduling procedure

The network scheduling procedure has three phases – planning, scheduling and controlling – that we can divide into seven steps.

BOX 14.1 **Background of CPM and PERT**

Critical path method

CPM grew out of the desire of the du Pont company to improve the planning and scheduling of work done during maintenance shutdowns. It was developed in 1957 by du Pont's M.R. Walker and J.E. Kelly of Remington Rand Corporation.

Since the method was intended to schedule work packages whose separate durations were already well known, CPM treated the duration of each element as if it were deterministic, that is it had a fixed value. The context is of limited total time available and CPM included routines for making a trade-off between time savings and extra costs.

Programme evaluation and review technique

PERT was a 1950s development among the United States Navy's Projects Office as customer, the contractor Lockheed and the consultants Booz, Allen and Hamilton. It was created to improve the management of special projects, including the Polaris undersea missile programme. There were more than 3,000 organisations involved in that project.

Since many of the Polaris work packages had not been carried out before, it was decided to include the uncertainty surrounding their duration as part of the scheduling technique. PERT, therefore, treats times as probabilistic distributions.

Network planning

Step 1 Define the project with its work breakdown structure of all significant elements.

Step 2 Identify all the direct links between pairs of elements. Decide the logical sequence linking each with its immediate predecessors and successors.

Step 3 Draw the network to represent this set of planned sequences. Drawing follows the conventions established within CPM and PERT, modified by computer software.

Network scheduling

Step 4 Estimate the duration of each work package. This may result in a single time value or a distribution, depending on policy.

(If time–cost trade-offs are to be investigated, assign costs to each work package. This information, as we shall see, may also cover the costs associated with shortening or extending their durations.)

Step 5 Work out the longest time path through the network from start to finish. This *critical path* decides the total time for the project. Ascertain the schedules for the rest of the activities within the network.

(Again, if time–cost trade-offs are to be investigated, use the network to test alternatives to create more economical or faster project delivery.)

Monitoring and controlling

Step 6 Use the results to calculate detailed work schedules ready to compare with progress.

Step 7 Review progress regularly, update the plan and reallocate resources to keep the project on track.

Conventions

The first step is to create the work breakdown structure of events and activities. An *event* is a moment marking the start or finish of a work package. An *activity* is the work package itself, having a finite duration between its starting and finishing events. The network is a graphical representation of the linking of activities and events in logical sequences. Although usually read from left to right, a network represents links; it is not scaled to depict the elapse of time.

Unfortunately, there are two conventions used to represent activities and events in networks. One, *activity on arrow* (AOA), depicts the activities as arrows joining the nodes as events. Arrows carry labels with durations and their directions represent the passage of time between nodes. The other notation, *activity on node* (AON), reverses the rule. Activities become the nodes in the network while the arrows represent not the events but the logical sequence of the activities. The arrows only represent precedence; they are not scaled.

Using one or other notation depends on personal preference and the practice of the planning office. To avoid confusion, we use only one, AON. There are two reasons. First, while AOA used to be more common, most software generates reports in AON format. Second, AON avoids some technical difficulties in setting out sequences. Preparing visual presentations in AOA is more complicated.

14.3.3 Worked example of scheduling procedure

We can show how a network is created through a simple example. Let us imagine a client has asked how long it would take to plan and carry out a survey of the condition of old houses in the inner city. The local authority wants us to interview a large sample of householders and note the state of key features of the dwellings.

In approaching this problem, experience tells us that preparation for the survey task itself requires work on two parallel, yet interconnected, tracks. These are creating the survey instrument and staff recruitment and training. The size of the project requires a substantial number of temporary staff who, because of the skills they need, will be recruited from among construction faculty students. They will need training in interview and survey techniques.

Network planning

Step 1 The first column of Table 14.1 lists the main activities that make up the WBS. A complete list of the top level tasks is the starting point for all further work.

Table 14.1 Activities and precedences: survey project

Activity	Predecessors	Successors
Agree detailed plan		Develop questionnaire Recruit survey staff
Develop questionnaire	Agree detailed plan	Select sample and locations Train and allocate staff
Select sample and locations	Develop questionnaire	Carry out survey
Recruit survey staff	Agree detailed plan	Train and allocate staff
Train and allocate staff	Develop questionnaire Recruit survey staff	Carry out survey
Carry out survey	Select sample and locations Train and allocate staff	Analyse data
Analyse data	Carry out survey	Write report
Write report	Analyse data	

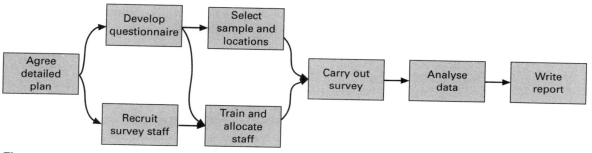

Figure 14.1 Basic network: survey project

Step 2 For each activity, the table shows those tasks that must directly precede or succeed them. In this case, we list all forward and backward links. Giving them twice is unnecessary but we shall show a full layout for this first example.

Step 3 Figure 14.1 depicts the network corresponding to the activities and precedences set out in Table 14.1. The AON notation has the activities in boxes with arrows showing logical sequences. The information in the table and diagram should match exactly so that either can be produced from the other.

Network scheduling

We can now return to the activity table to work out estimates for the times that each task will take. Then we can schedule all the activities in the network.

Step 4 For this example, let us imagine that we have carried out similar tasks before and, therefore, we can estimate their durations with confidence. This information is given in Table 14.2.

Step 5 Referring to Figure 14.2, we can see how the values in Table 14.2 are incorporated in the network diagram:

(a) Label the lower left-hand cell of each node with the activity duration, D.

Table 14.2 Activity durations: survey project

Activity	Duration in days, D
Agree detailed plan	3
Develop questionnaire	8
Select sample and locations	2
Recruit survey staff	6
Train and allocate staff	5
Carry out survey	10
Analyse data	5
Write report	5

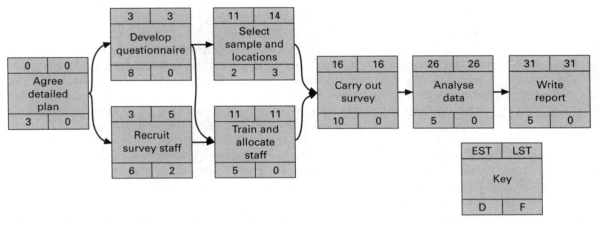

Figure 14.2 Scheduled network: survey project

(b) Work out the *earliest starting time*, EST, for each activity by passing through the network from start to finish. The EST for the first activity is set at zero. Then we can compute its *earliest finishing time* as:

$$EFT = EST + D$$

For each subsequent activity, its EST depends on when its predecessors finish. Since the start of any activity depends on all of the previous ones having been completed, the EST is the greatest value of their EFTs. That is:

$$EST = Max(EFT)_{previous} = Max(EST + D)_{previous}$$

Thus, in our case, the EST for the activity *train and allocate staff* is the greater of $(3 + 8)$ or $(3 + 6)$, that is 11. The remainder of the ESTs are computed in the same way.

At the end of the project, we find the EST for the last activity is 31. This means its EFT is 36, the total time for the whole project. The ESTs appear in the top left-hand corners of each node, as shown by the key.

(c) Work out the *latest starting times* for each activity. We do this by reversing the procedure for ESTs. Starting at the last activity, its *latest finishing time*, LFT, is set as the same as its EFT. (In the case of projects where a known finishing day has been stated, then this can be used as the LFT.) The process works backwards by computing *latest starting times*, LSTs, and LFTs in turn. For any activity, LST = LFT

– D. Therefore, the latest starting time for the last activity is $(36 - 5) = 31$ if the project is to be completed on time.

At junctions in the logical sequence, reasoning similar to the ESTs is applied. Yet, it is reversed. For any activity:

$$LFT = Min(LST)_{following} \text{ and so } LST = Min(LST)_{following} - D$$

Therefore, in the case of *develop questionnaire*, its LFT is the smaller of 11 and 14 and its LST is the smaller of $(11 - 8)$ and $(14 - 8)$.

It is conventional to enter the LSTs in the top right-hand corner of each node. We could also enter EFTs and LFTs in the diagram. Yet, they do clutter all but the simplest diagrams and, in any case, does not appear in many computer printouts. The key used here is taken from BS 4335: 1987.

(d) The longest path through the network is the critical path that decides the minimum total time for the project. We can spot activities on the critical path with equal ESTs and LSTs. In those cases, there is no room for manoeuvre. In the other activities, just two in our simple example, there is a difference between the EST and the LST. For example, *recruit and survey staff*, the task could begin any time from day 3 to day 5 without having an impact on the total project duration. This 2-day reserve is known as *float* or *slack*. It is easily found from *Float = LST – EST*.

Sometimes, as in our case, the activity can be delayed by the time of the float without having an effect on the start or finish of any other activity. This is *free float*. In other situations, the float is shared with other activities along a chain. Whatever the type of float, its value is placed in the lower right-hand cell of each node. This confirms the activities on the critical path. It is usually a single path through the network connecting all activities with zero float. Highlighting float identifies the manager's freedom for scheduling within the LST–EST window.

Monitoring and controlling

Monitoring refers to collecting relevant information about project progress. The process of controlling involves comparing this information with standards to detect deviations and then decide whether to act. Progress is compared with detailed work schedules.

Step 6 Rather than use the network diagram for detailed work schedules, it is usual to present the results as tables or a Gantt chart. The latter forms an excellent visualisation of the network with the added advantage of the time scale. Indeed, using appropriate codes, the Gantt chart contains much information and repays careful study.

Figure 14.3 shows the schedule for each activity in the network. Each is shown starting at its EST but some could be scheduled later. The vertical dotted lines are sketched to emphasise the links with the network diagram. They suggest the ways that activities come together at key moments. In joining up time paths through the Gantt chart, they have echoes of the Ibry chart of Chapter 12. Yet, in more complex project networks, Ibry lines clutter and confuse and they are usually not shown.

Step 7 The information generated during planning and scheduling forms the basis of control. Reports, such as in Table 14.3, allow actual progress compared with the plan. It identifies areas for action to be taken.

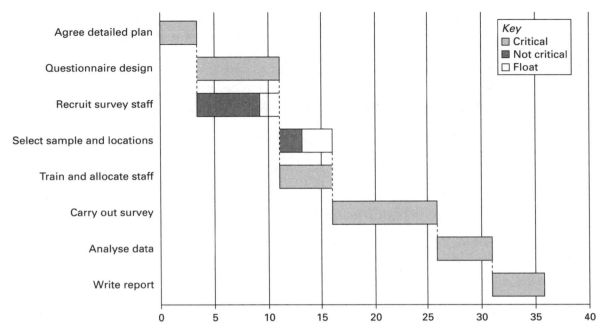

Figure 14.3 Progress report: survey project

Table 14.3 Progress report: survey project

Activity	D	EST	LST	F	AST	AFT	
Agree detailed plan	3	0	0	0	*0*	*3*	*OK*
Develop questionnaire	8	3	3	0	*3*	*10*	*—*
Select sample and locations	2	11	14	3	*12*		*—*
Recruit survey staff	6	3	5	2	*3*	*9*	*OK*
Train and allocate staff	5	11	11	0	*12*		*Late!*
Carry out survey	10	16	16	0			
Analyse data	5	26	26	0			
Write report	5	31	31	0			

The AST and AFT columns refer to actual starting and finishing times that are entered as the project progresses. In this report, made on Day 13, a critical activity is noted as running one day late. Managers will have to consider if some changes must be made to catch up.

Exercise 14.1 Explain what would happen to the project if any one of the following activities were delayed by three days: analyse data; recruit survey staff; select sample and locations. Sketch the effects on Figure 14.3.

If the project management tools went no further than to provide fixed schedules for monitoring and control they would remain valuable items in any manager's toolkit. They go beyond this basic analysis, however, to enable exploration of means of improving project performance through resource allocation and exchange and task restructuring. They also permit estimates to be made of risks of overrun and means of reducing this risk where it is unacceptable. To illustrate these points we need a more complex worked example.

14.4 Resource allocation

To illustrate resource allocation, we take the role of manager in a small firm that develops traction equipment for special underground railways. These are used in applications as diverse as silver and tin mining in South America and sewer sinking in Southampton. In preparation for the industry's biennial trade fair, the firm wants to create a new high-efficiency locomotive. The prototype, to be called ProtoLoco, will be shown at the fair to gain contracts for the supply of units or small batches to a wide range of potential customers.

The project manager has drawn up a work breakdown schedule and has estimated durations that the various work packages will take. These, with precedence relationships, appear in Table 14.4. This listing then enables the network to be drawn up (Figure 14.4). Compared with the conventions used in our introductory example, several have been changed or added. Changes come from the need to simplify the diagram to fit the page. Additions are the *milestones* at the start, finish and a key point during the project. The milestones are events (treated as activities with zero duration) marking out significant points in project development. They can be placed anywhere in the sequence to mark occasions of major review or moments when connections with events outside the detailed project schedule are possible. Examples of the latter are planting seasons, weather windows for oil rig installation, seasonal market opportunities or the juxtaposition of planets in space exploration.

The next diagram to be created is the Gantt chart (Figure 14.5) which shows all the activities and milestones. The time scale is marked in intervals of 20 days, that is periods of four working weeks. Critical activities have no float. Others mainly have free float. Exceptions are *model construction* and *mechanical design* which, in effect, share the 5 days' float. This means that a delay in the first affects the second although it will not necessarily change the total project time. *Equip working area* also shares this 5-day float and has two days of its own free float.

Table 14.4 Work breakdown schedule: ProtoLoco

Label	Activity	Duration (days)	Successor	Label	Activity	Duration (days)	Successor
A	Receive approval	—	B	J	Obtain materials and components	40	K
B	Agree project outline	5	C, D	K	Component manufacture	20	L
C	Equip working area	8	F	L	Subassembly manufacture	20	M
D	Schematic design	10	E, F	M	Final assembly	30	P
E	Power system specification	10	G, H	N	Produce promotional materials	15	R
F	Model construction	15	G	O	Programming	20	P
G	Mechanical design	40	I, N	P	Test	10	Q
H	Electronic design	50	I, O	Q	Deliver and install	5	R
I	Design stage complete	—	J	R	Open exhibition	—	—

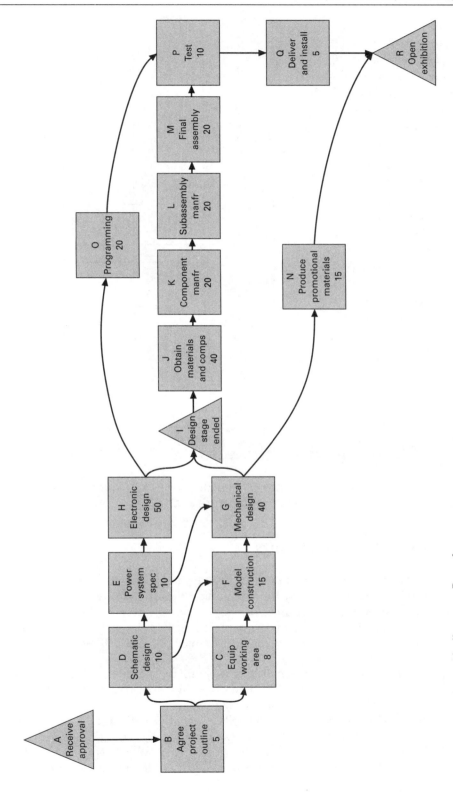

Figure 14.4 Network diagram: ProtoLoco

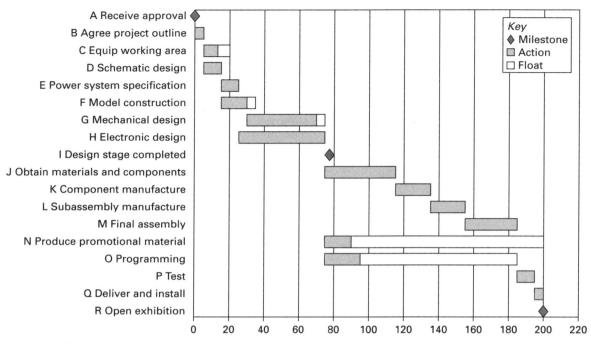

Figure 14.5 Basic Gantt chart: ProtoLoco

Starting from the basic project schedule, we can explore some further ways in which a project manager uses network analysis.

14.5.1 Resource constraints

So far, we have assumed that, except for the logical sequences, the work packages can be carried out at any time, including simultaneously. Yet, in reality, the tasks may use common resources of people and equipment. This limitation may prevent their being done at the same time. It is important, then, to check that sufficient resources are available to cover the tasks. If not, further constraints must be introduced.

For example, in our small firm we employ one mechanical engineer (ME) and one electronic engineer (EE). Their work includes trying out ideas in the laboratory as well as theoretical design. Let us see what happens when these engineers, along with the project manager (PM), are allocated to the tasks in the network.

Table 14.5 sets out the work packages again. This time it has an extra column showing the staff who are primarily involved with each task. With this information, we can pass across the Gantt chart to check whether the proposed

Table 14.5 WBS with staff allocation: ProtoLoco

Label	Activity	Duration (days)	Staff	Label	Activity	Duration (days)	Staff
A	Receive approval	—		J	Obtain materials and components	40	PM
B	Agree project outline	5	PM, EE, ME	K	Component manufacture	20	Wkshp
C	Equip working area	8	PM	L	Subassembly manufacture	20	Wkshp
D	Schematic design	10	EE, ME	M	Final assembly	30	Wkshp
E	Power system specification	10	PM	N	Produce promotional materials	15	PM
F	Model construction	15	ME, EE	O	Programming	20	EE
G	Mechanical design	40	ME	P	Test	10	ME, EE
H	Electronic design	50	EE	Q	Deliver and install	5	ME, EE
I	Design stage complete	—		R	Open exhibition	—	

sequence breaks any of our people constraints. Thus we find that, between days 25 and 30, the electronic engineer is required for two activities – *model construction* and *electronic design*. We are now faced with a problem. If there were no alternative personnel, we would have to schedule the tasks at non-overlapping times, for instance making the second job follow the first immediately. Since neither activity has float, any extra time required will push out the total project length.

Moving further to the right in Figure 14.5, we will find that the project manager is down for two tasks between days 75 and 85. These are *obtain materials* and *produce promotional material*. Here, however, the latter activity has ample float. One simple solution is to delay it until day 120, although some work could be done between 70 and 80.

The effect of these two changes is shown in Figure 14.6. It can be seen that the need to allocate the one electronic engineer has caused *model construction* to replace *power system specification* on the critical path and the total project time is increased by five days.

When project work involves the use of teams of people, it is normal to plot the numbers required during each period. It may be possible to even out peaks and troughs by adjusting the schedules of non-critical activities. Otherwise, where the peaks are the result of critical or near-critical work packages, extensions to the total time may be considered. This process, known as *resource smoothing*, is an important part of project management.

14.5.2 Trade-offs between time and cost

As an alternative to letting the finish date be put back by five days, the problem of the overload on the electronic engineer may be resolved by drafting in a colleague for the relevant period. The ability to do so will, of course, depend on the size of the firm, other work going on and the availability of a suitable candidate. Using the extra help from days 25 to 40 will bring two benefits. First, it will allow the two tasks already shown to be clashing to go on simultaneously. Second, it may allow the time for the work package *electronic design* to be cut from 50 to, say, 35 days. Again, we can examine the effect by rescheduling. The Gantt chart

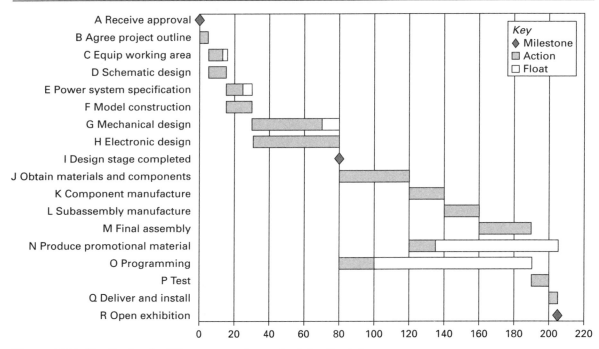

Figure 14.6 Gantt chart with personnel constraints: ProtoLoco

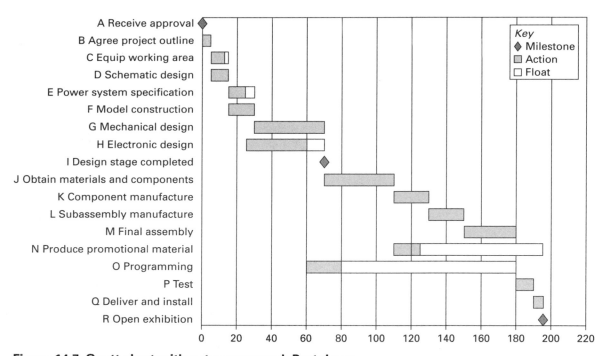

Figure 14.7 Gantt chart with extra personnel: ProtoLoco

Table 14.6 Selected activities with daily costs of duration reduction: ProtoLoco

Label	Activity	Duration (days)	Reduction	
			up to 3 days	4 to 10 days
G	Mechanical design	40	£140	£170
H	Electronic design	50	£150	£150
J	Obtain materials and components	40	£180	unavailable
M	Final assembly	30	£130	£170

lets us compare the effect of these changes with the original plan by relating Figure 14.7 back to 14.5.

The comparison shows a 5-day saving on project finish and the route for the critical path again changing, this time to include the *mechanical design* activity. Cutting the time for *electronic design* by 15 days does not show through into a corresponding effect on total time. Indeed, the 10 days' float created in that activity may be a waste of resources.

Spending more to save time

Project managers commonly experience the results shown here. Spending extra funds can bring delivery times forward. This is called crashing. The idea raises two questions, whether it is worth spending these funds and, if so, which activities will yield the best returns:

■ *Whether to spend extra.* Sometimes, such as with our ProtoLoco, it may not be advantageous to deliver early as the project is aimed at a fixed target date. In other cases, for example where the early introduction of new process technology would permit extra cost savings, early completion pays. If a new process were to save, say, £40,000 per month, then it would be worth spending an amount less than that for any month saved.

■ *Where to spend the extra.* Selection of which activities to reduce is not so straightforward. A basic study would start with those on the critical path. Of these, some items will be of fixed duration (such as waiting for suppliers or for concrete to dry) whereas other can be cut using known extra resources. The snag among the latter is the non-linear link between time saved and cost.

These points can be illustrated in the ProtoLoco project. Suppose that another opportunity arises to show the prototype earlier than the proposed trade fair. How can weeks best be saved? Table 14.6 shows four activities where duration reduction is feasible.

It is often cheaper, per day, to save a few days rather than many. For a few days, staff can be encouraged to work overtime or delay holidays. For more than that, it may be necessary to reorganise, bring in new members to the team or use different methods and equipment. This is shown in the data of Table 14.6, which gives daily costs of duration reduction up to three days and ten days. Days 4 to 10 have a higher marginal cost for activities G and L.

We can use Table 14.6 as follows. At first, it seems that, for any time saving up to three days, the extra resources should go into *final assembly*. Then follows *mechanical design*. But *mechanical design* is not on the critical path so spending on that activity would be wasted. Therefore, for the next five days of crashing, funds should be spent on *electronic design*. At this point, we know that *mechanical design* itself becomes critical but forms a duplicate path. Further spending on the design area would have to crash both activities to gain total time savings. This would cost £290 per day. Attention, therefore, switches back to *final assembly* for up to ten days in total. Lastly, it passes to *obtain materials*. We see the daily costs of crashing rise as we seek more and more time saving.

Exercise 14.2 Test out the effects of crashing the set of activities in Figure 14.7. Use the cost data from Table 14.6.

Resource exchange

We have seen how extra spending can be targeted on network items to reduce project time. We also noted those projects where time savings are not looked for. Even in these cases, time–cost trade-offs should be examined. Here, instead of shortening total time, resources are exchanged among work packages to save total cost. This approach involves both a shift of resources from non-critical to critical lines and a shift among the critical ones. In the latter case, the time savings in one activity may counterbalance the extra duration of another. Such switches can often be made without moving the completion date.

14.5.3 Restructuring the project

After the work packages have been laid out with their links, it is useful to re-examine them to see whether the links have been stated too conservatively. An area for investigation is the string of purchasing and manufacturing processes stretching from day 75 to 185 of the ProtoLoco project. We could ask whether the detailed elements of these packages could be organised to allow overlap between the end of one and the start of another. This idea has echoes in the policy of batch size reduction in the OPT system, explained in Chapter 12.

In Figure 14.8, the four activities from *obtain materials* to *final assembly* have been reorganised to allow each to start when its predecessor is half-completed. Adding a rule that each must finish 5 days after its predecessor spreads *component manufacture* from 20 to 25 days. Yet, the effect is to save 35 days.

Such changes are common practice and can be worth the extra planning and co-ordination required. For instance, when obtaining raw materials, the project manager must ensure that those required early in the manufacturing process come in first. It may be advantageous to issue special orders or arrange express deliveries if such actions would save time.

14.5.4 Managing time variations

We noted in Box 14.1 that, during early development, PERT was distinguished from CPM by the attention paid to the effects of errors in time estimates. This

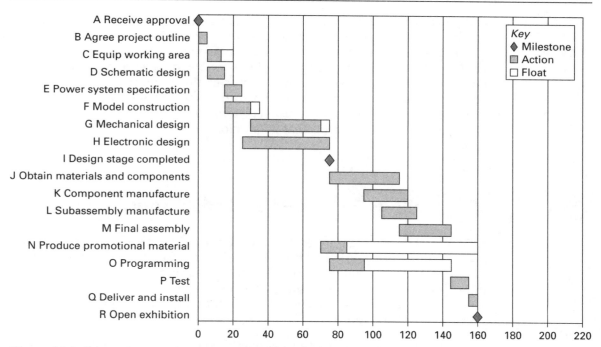

Figure 14.8 Gantt chart with critical activities restructured: ProtoLoco

difference has disappeared with the emergence of flexible software to allow quick analyses of alternatives. We shall note, however, the way in which time estimate variations were originally handled.

PERT used the Beta distribution to combine estimates and provide the manager with insights into the way errors may affect the project duration. The distribution allows for the possibility of very late work packages while recognising that their being very early is most unlikely. The method is to ask managers to make three estimates for task duration: the optimistic, OE; the pessimistic, PE; and the most likely estimate, MLE. From this information, the expected time, T, for the activity is given by the formula:

$$T = \frac{OE + 4MLE + PE}{6}$$

Its variance is found from the formula:

$$V_T = \left(\frac{PE - OE}{6}\right)^2$$

For example, the three estimates may be 30, 40 and 60 days. This gives an expected time of 42 days with a variance of 150 (corresponding to a standard deviation of 12 days).

The variance of the project completion time is the sum of the variances of all the activities on the critical path. Further, the fact that it is normally distributed allows for the probability of any completion time being achieved to be computed. This brings out the advantage of the approach. A manager can estimate the risk of a project exceeding a stated duration. This is essential, for instance, if a stadium is to be built or remodelled in time for a major public event, such as the Olympic Games. The contractor will not only estimate the construction time but also be anxious to avoid the risk of missing the deadline!

Now that projects can be readily scheduled and rescheduled on computers, the PERT approach to time estimations is less important. Managers conduct sensitivity analysis by asking direct 'What if' questions of work packages and simulating various possibilities.

14.6 Controlling time, cost and cash flow

CPM and PERT were developed in circumstances where organisations found difficulty in delivering projects on time. The early focus was, therefore, on scheduling and continually allocating resources to meet deadlines. While this task remains important, cost control and resource management now receive equal attention. This change reflects the changed grounds for letting many project contracts. There are two basic forms:

■ *Cost reimbursement.* Under this contract, frequently called *cost plus*, the client agrees to pay all the supplier's costs plus a reasonable margin for profit. It is suited to circumstances where many changes are expected during the work and many risks have to be coped with. There are problems. For the contractor, there is little incentive to control costs, except in as far as the firm will seek to protect its reputation of giving value for money. The client will need to control costs in detail and assign substantial resources to this task.

■ *Fixed price.* The fixed-price contract states total price and delivery date. There are usually penalties for late completion. On the face of it, the client is better off, with all problems of risk and control are taken on by the contractor. Given the latter's project management skills, the job may be in better hands. Yet, difficulties arise when unexpected circumstances are met or the client has a change of mind on some part of the specification. These lead to the issue of a *change order* to alter the contract terms. The scope, duration and price of the contract are renegotiated, in effect, with each change. In major projects, there are many hundreds of these orders. For instance, during the construction of the Channel Tunnel, the British and French governments changed regulations and the terms of the operating licence in response to new concerns over fire risks. Often it is said that the key expertise in the management of fixed-price contracts lies in the negotiation of profitable change orders.

Given the difficulties with both forms of contract, it is not surprising that many hybrids exist. For instance, under a fixed-price contract, a supplier may be protected from inflation or exchange rate risks by agreed adjustment methods. In another case, a cost-plus contract may include estimates for cost and time with incentives to beat certain targets. In exchange, the supplier must provide information on detailed internal costs and agree to auditing and arbitration in disputes.

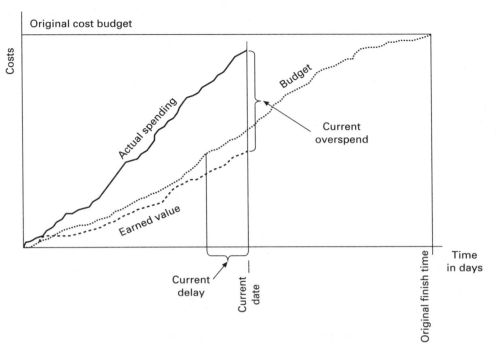

Figure 14.9 Project review

14.6.1 Reviewing time and cost progress

Monitoring and control are essential aspects of project management. Whatever the form of agreement, progress review is indispensable. At each review, the remaining work packages are examined, replanned and rescheduled as if they formed a new project.

Figure 14.9 shows one way to review both costs and time. The original budget set out the way costs were to be spent during the project. The graph also shows actual spending and the 'earned value' line.[5] This measures the work done using the original cost estimate for each element. The line shows variances from the budget in two ways:

- *Cost variances*. At the current date, a review shows that the actual costs exceed the budget. This may warrant investigation of causes or it may represent the fact that the work is ahead of schedule. Managers tend, therefore, to do variance comparisons according to milestones, or *deliverables*, rather than calendar dates.

- *Value variances*. This shows how far the current value achieved lags behind the planned delivery.

Using this information, the management team makes a new cost and time budget, shown in Figure 14.10. It creates a new plan beyond the current date. Both overspend and delay are anticipated in this new budget. The managers then have to investigate whether to accept the changes or allocate more resources to catch up.

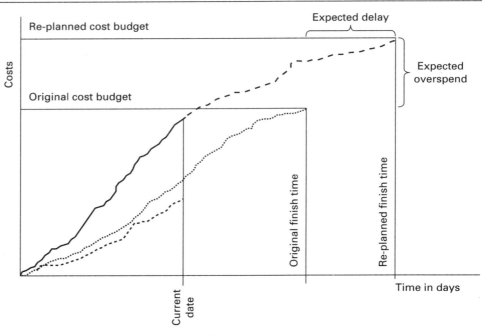

Figure 14.10 Project re-planning after review

14.6.2 **Reporting progress**

To support the decision-making process, project managers use special reports. Project management software readily generates forms such as time sheets, progress tracking charts and statements of the remaining work to be done. Among the more important reports are:

- *Delay statements.* Comparisons of the planned schedule for each work package with outcomes will identify whether and where action should be taken.

- *Costs so far and costs to complete.* At any review, many tasks will be partially complete. This analysis prepares an estimate of progress for each task to work out its expected total cost. From this statement, a revised budget can be presented as in Figure 14.10.

- *Cash flow analysis.* It can often be a mistake to complete operations too soon. This can create problems from the physical to the financial. For the former, it may be that assemblies ready for final installation arrive on site too early and stand around wasting space and deteriorating. Perhaps more important, completing a large work package too early means that cash will have been spent when it should have been conserved. Therefore, for jobs not on the critical path, managers should consider their sequence not only in terms of resource smoothing but also in their impact on cash flow. It may be practicable to delay work packages installing expensive purchased components. Naturally, working to latest starting and finishing times brings with it an increased risk of delay. Managers, therefore, must be cautious in planning tasks down to the last possible moment.

A variation occurs when cash comes in before project completion. The client may pay when a facility is partly opened, as in a new tramway or sports stadium, or if a client pays in instalments according to reaching agreed milestones.

- *Exceptional reports*. While routine reporting may form the basis of good control, managers should also be aware of unusual problems. These may have occurred or may be anticipated. Such difficulties include: unexpected geological conditions; changes in legislation; entry of new competitors in a market; delays in supplies and so on. Events like these should be reported to enable responses. Frequently, the client will agree a delay if the cause could not be anticipated. In any case, the schedule will be restated with new plans for resource allocation and cash flow.

14.6.3 Types of control

In the last examples of the ways that managers run projects, we can see examples of the classes of control introduced in Chapter 4. During the project, there is a stream of reports causing adjustments to schedules, new allocations of resources and so on. This is *concurrent control*, where the control action follows very closely upon the performance itself. To the extent that managers are also regularly updating their plans, they exercise *feedforward control*, anticipating the changes to outcomes following their control actions. Finally, at various stages throughout the project, and after completion, teams review progress and reflect on ways to change the way the work was managed. In this way, learning can be built into arrangements for next time. This is *feedback control*.

Concurrent control within the work packages dominates the scene during the process of the project. While modern computer systems allow new optimisation to be carried out in the light of each event, a surfeit of minor changes creates *system dithering*, a problem mentioned in connection with MRP systems. Changes made too frequently are stressful and demotivating.

14.7 Developments in project management

Project management is an art carried out in a dynamic setting. We began the chapter by asserting that the discipline gains from aiming at a single goal – project completion. We have found, however, an increasing interest in the trade-offs among time, cost, cash flow and risk. Despite the decision aids embodied in modern software, finding the optimal solution among these objectives remains a matter of judgement. Theoretical work in the years since the CPM and PERT developments of the 1950s has sought solutions to various aspects of project scheduling. While these exist for some aspects, however, there is no general rule that will enable a manager to optimise time, cost, cash flow and risk simultaneously.[6] The best outcomes must be judged by scheduling, rescheduling and careful attention to all budgets.

Such is the power of the network scheduling approach that it has been taken up by operations managers more widely. A firm, faced with some sort of task cycle, can usefully consider its operations as a series of projects. One isolated service factory performed major overhauls on some 30 railway carriages per week. On average, each spent four weeks on-site, meaning there were 120 vehicles out of service at any time. Through tracking each carriage as a project, it was found that many tasks could be removed from what had been assumed was the critical path. Rather than remove, repair and replace key components, for example, any items to be removed could be replaced immediately from a float of reconditioned items. This is standard practice in many types of routine maintenance.

Longer cycles can also be managed as if they were projects. A good example is in the fashion industry as shown in Jaeger, the closing case of Chapter 4. The firm has a sequence of interrelated tasks to be completed during the 11-month preparation for each season. Project management skills are ideally suited to keeping the activity on track.

Exercise 14.3   The repair time in the carriage works was cut to 2½ weeks. What effect did this have on the number of vehicles on site? Who would gain from this change?

✔ Quick check-up

Can you:
- ☐ Name three key components of a project definition.
- ☐ Name nine special features of project management proposed by Anthony.
- ☐ State what CPM and PERT stand for.
- ☐ List the three phases of project management.
- ☐ Identify WBS, EST, LST, EFT, LFT and float.
- ☐ Show how to calculate any EST and LST.
- ☐ Name four reports useful to project managers.

? Questions

Chapter review

14.1   Explain the interaction between project management choices and organisation structure.

14.2   Show how project management has developed from scheduling to resource optimisation.

14.3   Sketch a graphical approach to project control and replanning.

Application

14.4   What would be the effect on the project of Figure 14.1 if either *select sample and locations* or *recruit survey staff* were delayed by five days?

14.5   Review the effects on crashing choices if the costs in Table 14.6 were changed as follows: *mechanical design*, all days cost £170; *final assembly*, 3 days cost £160 per day, up to 10 cost £180.

14.6   Explain how a project can be broken down into work packages and milestones, using the Zuquala mill as illustration.

Investigation

14.7 Use the current press to select some projects that are exceeding their budgets or are seriously late. Using Anthony's list as a guide, identify and discuss themes they have in common. Recent examples are expansion of Heathrow airport, the Eurofighter and a new office for members of parliament.[7]

14.8 Show how managers can use networking ideas to control the activities described in the closing case of Chapter 4, Jaeger.

CLOSING CASE

Automating The British Library[8]

Among the main features of The British Library, which opened in 1997, is an automated system for item search and retrieval. The project was among the most important of its kind ever undertaken. Its implementation required a blend of skills in librarianship, information systems and project management.

Incorporated in the new £500 million building at St Pancras, London, was space for both a mechanical book-handling system and the cabling to feed desktop terminals. Notwithstanding these advantages, the library saw that implementing the automation was a large and difficult project. There were many risks and the cost of failure would be high. The library needed someone who combined experience in technology, the skills to handle a large project and the ability to influence people at the top of the organisation. Using consultants, it appointed an interim project manager, Eric Mason, a senior IT specialist, to begin in January 1997. His experience included installations with many companies and he had recently led a project installing a reference and archive system for a local authority.

Through this appointment, The British Library completed a team combining its own staff with external managers bringing in relevant experience.

There are some 150 million items to which about 3 million are added annually. Requests for books from remote users reached 4.15 million in 2000 while the reading rooms receive some ¹/₂ million visits. Books storage is in the basement, with each detailed on the new database. Readers access items from over 300 terminals which enable every item to be located. The automation project included the development of a special public access catalogue with more than 12 million records. Its digital alpha servers were designed to be flexible and offer fast response. The database is split into some 20 interlinked catalogues, for example humanities or printed music. The project required all to be searchable using keywords and wild cards in many combinations.

The book request system checks the availability of an item, prints the request in the book store and follows the delivery progress from the store to the reader. It was specified with high security, reliability and flexibility. The book conveyor system routes the request to the most convenient collection point. Although most material was expected to arrive within 30 minutes, performance in the year after completion was much slower.

The library opened to readers in November 1997 and the last books were brought from the 20 previous sites by the end of 1999. During 2000, 91% of requests were handled automatically. Eventually, the automated service will

▶

include rare books. The same processes will be used, with additional security features.

Questions

1 What features of the situation justified the use of formal project management?

2 With which other project schedules would the automated system project have interacted?

3 Suggest some milestones that Mason might have set out during 1997.

4 When and how would you evaluate the success of the project?

Notes and references

1. Degnitu, W. (2000) 'A case study of Zuquala Steel Rolling Mill', *Journal of the Ethiopian Society of Mechanical Engineers*, 3(1), pp.1–5; http://home.att.net/~africantech/ESME/ESME.htm; http://www.tradeport.org/ts/countries/ethiopia/mrr/mark0033.html

2. Anthony, R.N. (1988) *The Management Control Function*, Boston, MA: The Harvard Business School Press, pp.102–4.

3. ibid. p.107.

4. Well-known project management packages include Microsoft's *Project*, Hoskyns' *Project Management Workbench* and Mantix Systems' *Cascade*. The analysis in this chapter used the first of these, although the drawings were made separately.

5. Raby, M. (2000) 'Project management via earned value', *Work Study*, 49(1), pp.6–9.

6. Icmeli, O., Erenguc, S.S. and Zappe, C.J. (1993) 'Project scheduling problems: A survey', *International Journal of Production and Operations Management*, 13(11), pp.80–91.

7. Done, K. (2001) 'BAA pledge on fifth terminal viability', *The Financial Times*, 5 June; Hall, M. (2001) 'Eurofighter faces fresh dispute on bomber proposal', *Electronic Telegraph*, 5 November; Davies, C. (2001) 'Queen opens £235m office for 210 MPs', *Electronic Telegraph*, 28 February.

8. Thorncroft, A. (1999) 'Monument to literature: The British Library has finally been completed', *The Financial Times*, 31 July; Foot, R. (1998) 'Automating the British Library – a case study in project implementation', *New Library World*, 99(1140), pp.69–71; The British Library (2000) *Twenty-seventh Annual Report, 1999–2000*, London: The British Library Board.

PART FOUR

Quality and operations improvement

CHAPTER 15

Control of processes and inventories

OBJECTIVES

When you have finished studying this chapter, you should be able to:

- Differentiate between planning and control.
- Apply control ideas to operations and inventory management.
- Show where feedback, concurrent and feedforward control are used.
- Relate control to manufacturing and service systems.
- Show how effective monitoring is carried out.
- Demonstrate the benefits of different classes of inventory.
- Distinguish dependent from independent inventory and explain their implications for management.
- Summarise basic replenishment procedures.
- Apply ABC analysis to inventory management.
- Use EOQ inventory models.
- Justify the use of safety stock to maintain service levels.

OPENING CASE

Clockwork timekeeping on Swiss railways[1]

Swiss Federal Railways (SBB) presents the main purpose of its operations functions as producing train traffic. Its functional goals are: client orientation including quality guarantee; economical, safe and high-speed train running; delivering business results linked with different partners; and fostering a co-operative style of working, both within the organisation and with partners. To achieve these goals, operations transforms inputs of personnel, rolling stock and fixed installations into moving trains. These run according to standards set both in the timetable and by laws and operating rules.

Demand is rising. To run more trains through its network while maintaining standards, SBB seeks to improve all aspects of train scheduling and control. For example, to achieve convenient connections, the timetable at Zürich bunches the 1,500 daily train movements into a 30-minute period each hour. Already the country's busiest station, further growth by 2005 will come from compressing these train movements into a 20-minute slot to allow another on the half-hour. For many years a bottleneck in the European freight system, improvements to international goods train flow will come from the new Gotthard and Lötschberg tunnels, but trains will approach these new links on the busy

▶

existing lines. To support such improvements, SBB has introduced three inter-linked train management systems.

The first system, from 1993, was automatic vehicle identification (*Automatische Fahrzeug Identifikation*). Using microwave devices placed by the track, AFI inter-rogators read from and write to tags fixed to the frame of every vehicle. Local processors relate the vehicle identifiers to train numbers before transmitting the data to central control. This means that the centre can know the position and destination of each unit at all times. Not only does this cut down manual recording, but also it provides reliable reporting during periods when traffic is disrupted. Additional advantages cover cases such as special freight vehicles whose internal temperatures or liquid levels can be monitored.

Following the installation of AFI, SBB followed with SURF (*système unifié de régulation ferroviaire*). Based in three control centres, at Lausanne, Lucerne and Zürich, this train control system optimises flows. At its heart, SURF compares for each train the 'must' data, represented by the timetable, with the 'is' data gathered by AFI. It makes a forecast of the train's run and displays it graph-ically. Furthermore, it identifies emerging problems such as connections at risk, delays passed on to other trains and slow running caused by preceding slow trains. With this comprehensive forecast, staff can take preventive measures in good time. SURF also archives all data; this allows investigation and evaluation of many aspects of working.

The third service system is the Cargo Information System. It collects and uses real time data to manage consignments from order placement to delivery. When a client places an order, either online or by conventional means, all aspects of the transit are planned. These include destination, time, vehicle type and so on. Space is booked in vehicles or on trains. Wagons at marshalling yards are assembled into trains according to the bookings. In case of delay, the system informs the destination of the new arrival time. CIS is being extended to link with foreign railways, other hauliers, clients through the Internet and SBB's own evaluation processes.

Results are impressive. More than three-quarters of passenger trains arrive within one minute of schedule and 95% arrive within four minutes. Freight traffic is rising and becoming more efficient with fewer empty wagon movements.

15.1 Introduction

With the change to centralised control, railways can be seen as huge, widely dis-persed process plant. To maintain its impressive operating performance, SBB has invested heavily in control systems for trains and consignments. Backed by the AFI devices, staff at the centres can monitor and predict behaviour continuously. On a good day, the railway runs like clockwork. Nevertheless, a late TGV service from Paris to Lausanne or a fault on a wagon passing from Berlin to Milan, cause perturbations requiring process adaptation. Instructions on changes go to train crew, dispatchers, station staff and business partners. These people adjust their activities. The control loops surrounding the railway plant are then complete.

Exercise 15.1 Suggest reasons why SBB defines operations management as producing train traffic. What alternative definitions could you propose?

In this chapter, we use the control models to investigate the processes following the detailed operating plans. We are concerned with closing the feedback loop through monitoring and control action. The range of applications of these ideas is very wide. For example, budgetary control, dealt with in Chapter 4, relies on feedback of accounting data and quality management, in Chapters 16 and 17, relies heavily on control ideas. Here we investigate the application of control ideas to two areas within the operations function, namely operations and inventory. The operations discussion concentrates on the control of MRPII systems and process plant but also recognises the issue of control in service operations. Inventory management is itself a service operation. Its success in maintaining availability levels within realistic expenditure limits makes an important contribution to business performance.

15.2 The control concept

15.2.1 Planning and control

In this book, we separate *planning*, choosing and organising what to do, and *control*, checking and ensuring that the desired results are achieved. Some see this as an arbitrary distinction. For instance, Anthony argued: 'Although planning and control are definable abstractions and are easily understood as calling for different types of *mental* activity, they do not relate to major categories of activities actually carried on by an organisation, either at different times, or by different people, or for different situations.'[2] He continued by pointing out that most people in organisations engage in both planning and control. Furthermore, the definitions of the terms in the literature are inconsistent; the function referred to by some authors and in some companies as 'operations planning' is called 'operations control' by others. Few texts have separate sections on operations control, either treating the issue as an adjunct to scheduling or hardly mentioning it at all.

The view taken here is that it is worth making the distinction. We have argued that managers fill many roles including leader, decision maker, motivator, negotiator and communicator. Planning and controlling are another two ways of looking at what managers do. Despite the fact that they are carried out by the same person in different proportions at different times, they are no less worthy of analysis. At the strategic level, managers spend a greater proportion of their time planning whereas shop floor staff have functions that are much more specific and include a greater proportion of control.

On the shop floor, control is focused on what Anthony calls *task control*,[3] which means ensuring that defined tasks are carried out according to objectives. The context of control will have already been established as part of the management process. For instance, the tasks are clearly prescribed and, barring unforeseen events, control can be exercised with little human intervention. Those involved work routinely, from the stock clerk making out a purchase order to a coating machine operator adjusting application thickness. Questions of employee motivation and attention, covered in Chapter 6, are relevant.

15.2.2 Control models

In Chapter 4, we identified three types of control. Their key points were:

Feedback control

Feedback control, set out in Figure 4.12, depends on monitoring outputs, comparing them with goals and learning from discrepancies. When changes are made, they are to avoid the errors in the future. This leads to the criticism that corrections occur after the event when the errors have been made and waste created. The focus is on information about the past.

Feedback control has an advantage in that it provides a check on the objectives and standards in use. If standards are not achieved consistently, there may be a case for changing them to make their attainment easier. This is not an argument for lowering standards arbitrarily; there are many opportunities in product and process design to make such adjustments without affecting the satisfaction of customers.

Concurrent control

Otherwise known as real-time control, this works as closely as possible with the current system performance. The steps of data collection, comparison and adjustment are closely integrated. The controller is, in effect, part of the system (see Figure 4.13). A supervisor may receive daily time sheets recording the activities on which the department has been engaged. This is feedback control. Most supervisors, however, prefer to operate concurrently, maintaining regular checks on progress in the section.

Feedforward control

In feedforward control, the accent is on anticipation. As Figure 4.14 shows, not only is there a feedback loop but also the feedback data run through a forecasting stage that provides information on the *future* consequences of *current* performance. This enables managers to actively anticipate problems and, therefore, prevent them. We have seen examples of feedforward control in preventive maintenance and project rescheduling after review.

We also noted in Chapter 4 how concurrent control could be seen merely as a variant of feedback control. To understand the difference, we need to consider perspective. If we study a job shop employee using a lathe to turn a few components, we will see a series of machining, measurement and adjustment steps until the work piece diameter is just right. At this level of detail, we can identify stages of feedback control as shown in the upper part of Figure 15.1.

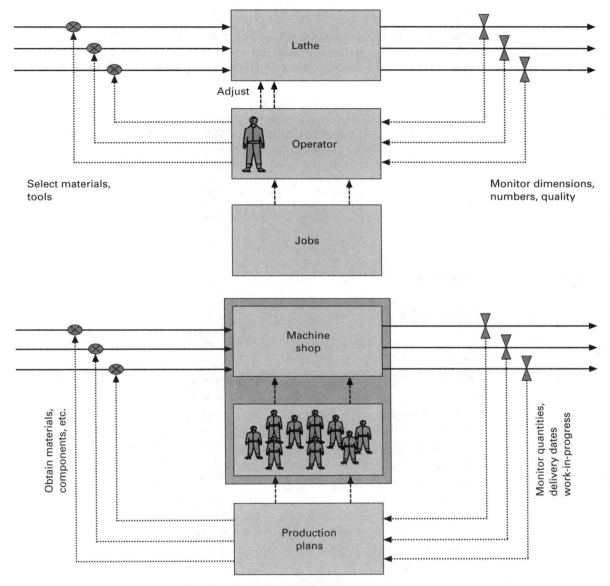

Figure 15.1 Perspectives on feedback and concurrent control

Labels in diagram:
Lathe
Adjust
Operator
Jobs
Select materials, tools
Monitor dimensions, numbers, quality
Machine shop
Obtain materials, components, etc.
Monitor quantities, delivery dates, work-in-progress
Production plans

If, however, we see the person–lathe system within the context of the whole production process, the perspective will be represented better by the lower part of the diagram. The staff and equipment within the machine shop are a manufacturing cell; they work as if using concurrent control. The people in the control office do not gather information about individual dimensions or pieces of work but about the general progress of orders through stages of production. The machine shop's detailed operations exist, as it were, in a *black box*. This is shown shaded in the diagram. From the point of view of the office, shop floor control is concurrent.

We can summarise the two reasons for the different perspective:

■ *Time*. Shop floor operators work on tasks measured in minutes, while work schedules may be planned in days or weeks. The feedback intervals perceived by the machine operator are too short to be noticed by the production controller.

■ *Detail*. Job planning and scheduling, especially in job shops, do not go down to the detail of the separate elements of each operation. It is neither feasible nor obligatory to issue such instructions. Within the broad production plan, staff use their skills to carry out tasks and control them concurrently.

Exercise 15.2 Can you relate the different perspectives on control to the discussion of systems at the start of Chapter 2?

15.3 Control of operations

15.3.1 Manufacturing

In a manufacturing environment, control fits into the sequence of activities from order receipt to despatch as follows:

■ *Rough-cut planning*. Broad resource allocation from sales forecasts, analysis, process planning, advance material ordering and capacity analysis.

■ *Detailed planning and scheduling*. Order receipt, documentation, allocation of resources of labour, materials, machine time etc. to each order. Establishment of priorities at each stage. Issue of manufacturing instructions.

■ *Monitoring*. Obtaining up-to-date and relevant data on order progress, resources used and available, completions, delays, stock levels and shortages and so on.

■ *Feedback and corrective action*. Evaluating the data in the light of plans and schedules. Short-term changes to the plan at shop floor level can be made. If these will not correct the variations, feedback into the planning system is required.

■ *Completion and despatch*. When the order is complete, instructions are removed from the operations system. Yet, this is not the end of the story for control. Records should be assembled of manufacturing cost, scrap levels and, later, defects that occur in service.

As de Toni and Panizzolo[4] point out, these five activities are carried out in very different ways in intermittent and repetitive production contexts. We noted the differences in planning and scheduling decisions in sections 12.1 to 12.6, so we will concentrate on control here. The issues are summarised in Table 15.1.

Intermittent manufacture

In the intermittent, job shop environment, the basic unit of control is the work order. The materials and components for this order are moved around the plant, grouped in batches if necessary. Records are linked under a single order number

Table 15.1 Control in intermittent and repetitive manufacture

		Control activity		
		Monitoring	*Corrective action*	*Post-despatch analysis*
Manufacturing system	*Intermittent manufacturing*	Order by order; stage by stage	Local expediting; rescheduling	Cost/profit; delivery dates per order
	Repetitive manufacturing	Emphasis on sufficient check points and rapid feedback to maintain the flow		Cost/profit per unit of output

BOX 15.1 Expediting: the example of Watmough

When I was a supervisor in the wagon works, one of my staff, Watmough, spent his days pushing a small handcart around the extensive, 48-hectare site. My section assembled bogie frames at about 40 per week. Although Watmough could not read, he knew every inch of the production process and every component that we needed. Work from the machine shops was often late. When this happened, he would pick up the first few items as they came off the machines and bring them over in his cart. He would also let me know how far behind things were running so I could slow the job down and put the crew on other work. When people from the 'top office' came across Watmough in the yard, they used to ask him where the problems were. They then went to their Monday scheduling meetings with grassroots information.

Watmough's rewards were recognition and an occasional cigarette from the works manager, a gift never offered to supervisors. He was a great expediter, using a mix of concurrent and feedforward control to run his personal MRP system.

used in transmitting instructions and monitoring progress through all the production stages. After each key stage, data on the order provide reports about its status. In the light of this information, corrective actions range from local expediting (see Box 15.1) to rescheduling. The latter means issuing new instructions about the pattern of orders going through the shop. When jobs are completed, data on costs, profits and delivery performance are collected. This forms a basis for future estimating and planning.

Repetitive manufacture

In repetitive manufacture, materials and components pass through stages in a continuous stream and not in predetermined batches. Each stage has limited scope, being capable of working on a narrow family of parts or assembling a known range of finished items. The purpose of the five activities is to instigate and maintain the flow of work without interruption. Since the plant is dedicated to the narrow product range, the first two stages, order review and release and detailed planning, are merged, the aim being to establish the speed at which the whole system must operate and ensure that corresponding resources are available. Much of the order-orientated activity of intermittent production, such as identifying different quantities of raw materials, is unnecessary, these tasks having been made routine within the plant design. Detailed plans are not needed. Jobs usually keep the same sequence throughout the line. Data collection for progress control occurs at the end, backed up by other checkpoints along the line. These points should be sufficiently frequent to allow rapid data feedback to support concurrent control.

In repetitive manufacture, concurrent control is orientated to maintaining the flow as opposed to tracking each order. Since orders are carried out in sequence, as on a car assembly line where basic models are customised to personal requirements, the issue of an order instruction into the line will inevitably lead to a product. With short leadtimes and interdependent sequences of machines, emphasis is placed on rapid feedback of data about the flow so that hold-ups can be detected and correction taken. At the level of each section of the line, supervisors use concurrent control to ensure that sufficient crews are available, machine defects are corrected and any difficulty with supplies overcome. Data on profit or performance are not collected for each order separately. The focus is on the performance through time, measured in terms of costs per week or per unit of output such as per tonne.

Exercise 15.3 Identify the control activities at SBB that parallel those in repetitive manufacturing.

15.3.2 Effective monitoring

The bridge from planning to control is monitoring. To be effective the collection system must provide data that are:

- *Relevant.* The data must be about the process and values being controlled. Sometimes, ignoring this simple point, people collect only easily observable data, expecting users to make the best interpretation.
- *Comprehensive.* Measuring performance using just a few parameters runs the risk of encouraging staff to ensure good performance in these areas at the expense of others.
- *Sufficient.* Sufficiency implies that there is adequate information to form the basis of control decisions. At the same time, the receiver can suffer from too much data that hides the key items required.
- *Timely.* The frequency of monitoring and reporting is an important issue in the design of effective control systems. For concurrent control, a continuous stream of data must be available to the staff. This is usually direct observation. Feedback, and feedforward, control systems will collect data intermittently. The choice of the intervals between observations has an impact on the effectiveness of the control system.
- *Reliable.* The temptation of fraud in some areas of business means that checks and audits are required, especially when handling funds. One problem, known as measurementship, occurs when individuals use controls to make themselves look good, possibly at the expense of others. All business control systems, therefore, should be transparent in their operation and subject to external checks and audits.

BOX 15.2 **Problems with feedback in financial dealing**

'When things go wrong at securities firms, they often go wrong in the back office.' The successes and failures of those who buy and sell securities, such as derivatives, are the material for newspaper headlines yet some of the greatest losses have come from a failure of the control system to identify a potential risk and take action. This problem may have caused the collapse of the 230-year-old Barings Bank in March 1995. Those responsible for control were unable to prevent a dealer taking a huge gamble on the Nikkei index of the Tokyo stock exchange.

Deals are recorded as they are made and traders make daily reports on the positions they take. In the Barings case, the roles of making the contracts and settling them were not separated and it was possible for these reports to be confused. Headquarters' monitoring was too slow. If the controls had been effective, the scale of trading could not have occurred.

The bank is not the only one to have failed in this way. Saloman Brothers lost well over £220 million from inaccurate recording of swap contracts. Another New York trader, Kidder Peabody, failed when one executive created false profits to boost his 1993 salary bonus to $9 million. The accounting system recorded each contract profit on the day it was formed, not on the day it was due to be settled. Deals could be rolled over to extend their life and thus delay settlement. It was only then that the false paper profits would be exposed. In 1982, Chase Manhattan Bank failed to detect that a $285 million loan was being made to a firm that was much too small to carry this size of debt.

Control cannot be left to the annual auditors. The difficulties can grow very quickly. Barings' 1994 audit had not been completed by the time of its 1995 collapse.

Questions of effective monitoring have been raised regularly in the operational control of financial trading (see Box 15.2).[5] The difficulty is compounded by the shortage of staff able to understand and evaluate newly devised financial instruments such as derivatives. Control is difficult in the culture of the city dealing room where cunning and risk taking seem to be encouraged and traditional values of honesty and caution are seen to demonstrate gullibility.[6]

Monitoring intervals

The choice of frequency of process monitoring must balance the cost against the benefits gained from the closer control. Figure 15.2 shows the effect of changing the frequency of monitoring. Suppose we are trying to control the value of a single variable to keep it as close as possible to a target value. The solid line shows what happens if the monitoring occurs every hour. Corrections steer the value back towards the target. The dotted line shows the effect of less frequent monitoring. The variable can change at the same rate as before but, given the greater time between adjustments, it can deviate further from the target. Clearly, if the intervals are too long, the variable being controlled can surpass sound or safe limits. For the tightrope walker, continuous monitoring is vital and practice leads to automatic responses to wobbles on the wire. In other cases, intervals are set

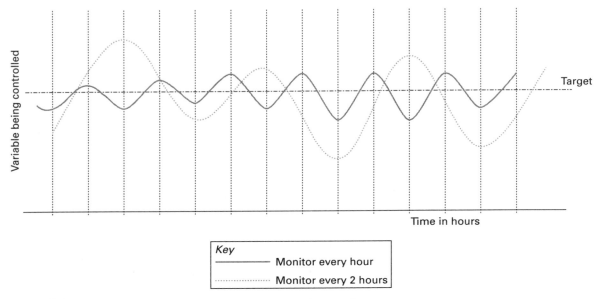

Figure 15.2 The effect of varying the monitoring intervals

according to statute, informed analysis or merely habit. They can be extended if the data stream shows stability and shortened if the risk of variability appears to rise. We return to this question in Chapter 17 when investigating quality control.

15.3.3 Control in the MRPII loop

Figure 12.4 presented MRPII as a series of stages within an open-loop model. Without feedback, however, this would be unsatisfactory. As Burcher proposed,[7] there are at least three levels of planning at which anticipatory resource checks could occur. Shown as the dashed lines in Figure 15.3, the feedback loops are:

1 Does the master production schedule meet the needs of the aggregate plan?

2 Are the 'rough-cut' capacity estimates for materials availability and production capacity adequate for the proposed MPS?

3 Are detailed schedules for the shop floor and subcontractors likely to meet the CRP?

Each of the checks should be part of the planning system with amendments made as circumstances change and new orders come in. Since the plan is modified ahead of production actually taking place, this is feedforward control and is one of the strengths of full MRP systems.

MRP also needs control after the event. Figure 15.3 shows how performance monitoring should gather data about the whole system performance. These are sent back to all stages (although the diagram shows only two feedback loops for clarity). It will be too late to use this loop to change current orders; so the information is used to adapt the way future decisions are made. The system, therefore, learns from its successes and mistakes.

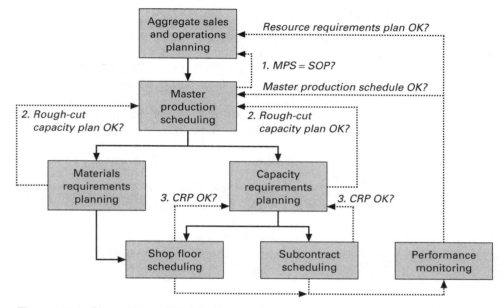

Figure 15.3 Closed-loop MRPII showing control loops

Experience in practice

The model in Figure 15.3 represents an ideal situation. Many companies find difficulty in its implementation and, consequently, are disappointed with the results. Burcher studied the extent to which MRPII was used in UK manufacturing in the early 1990s. He found that more than half of 349 companies responding to a questionnaire used capacity planning; rough-cut capacity planning (58%) occurred most frequently. Yet, about one-third of those using some sort of CRP felt it was unsuccessful. The most commonly cited difficulties were:

- absence of either job time standards or detailed routing paths through processes
- lack of efficiency or utilisation information that would allow machine or process effective capacity to be calculated realistically
- poor sales forecasts with resulting large volumes of unplanned orders.

Many companies did not use feedback from the CRP to the MPS. Reasons included a preference to change capacity using overtime or subcontracting, the lack of a MPS and a view that rough-cut planning was sufficient.

Closed-loop MRPII is, therefore, only partially implemented in many companies. The nature of the business and its environment strongly affect how easily it can be installed. Being able to predict task times is very important. The survey showed that companies engaged in repetitive manufacturing, or with products that changed infrequently, tended to have most output under standard times. Examples with a high proportion (95%) were brick, pottery, glass and cement industries. Textiles, leather, clothing and footwear, by way of contrast, averaged 68%, hardly a base for the establishment of detailed capacity plans.

Benefits of MRPII

The rewards available from full MRPII implementation are great. Spreadbury detailed the possibilities.[8] These included delivery more than 95% on time, better than 95% manufacturing schedule performance, improved inventory turnover, reduced waste and so on. Many European companies have reached these standards, including Kodak, ICI, Reckitt and Colman, Formica and Courtaulds Films. Implementation of full MRPII, however, involves major reorganisation and can seem to take a long time. Spreadbury argued that such changes ought to be treated like full-blown projects, divided into work packages with individual managers taking responsibility for each package. The key to success lies not merely in the first stage of application but in the continuous improvement that must follow.

The paradox of MRPII implementation is that its greatest successes have been reported from those plants whose production organisation is closest to repetitive manufacture. This is hardly surprising since these plants handle a narrow range of products and orders. So the plants that need MRPII systems the most – those with greatest complexity – find the most difficulty with its installation and, so far, have gained the least from it.

15.3.4 Control of process plant

Contrasting the complexity in many intermittent environments, dedicated process plants have control loops designed in. They often lend themselves to computer control because:

- There can be a large quantity of data.
- Many variables in the process can be continuously monitored using instruments. Examples are temperatures, flow rates and so on.
- Processes are well understood. This means that the computer can hold an internal decision model enabling it to operate automatically.
- Accurate control is required over long periods. Humans are notoriously poor at maintaining long-term vigilance when tasks are simple.
- Computers are cheap.

The simplest form of feedback control in a plant would be to monitor the quality of the finished product and, were it not to standard, make adjustments until it was so. This approach is unsatisfactory because of the waste that would be created. The lags between adjustments to the process and monitoring would result in large deviations from standards. In control of process plant, therefore, there is a need for monitoring of each stage of the system to ensure that the corresponding intermediate product is satisfactory. This shortens the feedback loop to the extent that the plant works under concurrent control.

This monitoring provides information on discrepancies earlier than before. In a fermentation process of a brewery, for instance, the reactions may not proceed at the normal rate and the whole plant is slowed down. Adjustments to the system are made almost as soon as the discrepancies occur. Is this the best that can be done?

In many cases it is possible to use feedforward control, provided the system is understood well enough. To use a motoring analogy, a good driver anticipates danger and is in a position to take avoiding action. A bad driver, of course, anticipates others' actions incorrectly.

Much of the monitoring of process plant is concerned with the variables that underlie the rates of production and its quality. Returning to the example of fermentation, monitoring of the temperature of the wort would enable one to anticipate a slow-down in alcohol production. Corrective action, through adding more hot water, could be carried out almost before the problem, low conversion rate, had arisen.

Concurrent process control requires, therefore,

- monitoring of many variables at many points
- rapid feedback of data
- computer systems to handle the high volume of data
- models permitting feedforward control.

Do computers run such plants? The answer depends on how well understood and predictable the processes are. It is normal to have automatic control of the system, provided it is operating between expected limits. Humans intervene only under unusual conditions. Yet, to design a system that can work safely under human control is extremely difficult. The following example comes from an incident on the Docklands Light Railway:

The DLR, in east London, uses computer-controlled trains without drivers. The first collision, in 1991, occurred at a junction. One train was running to schedule under computer control. The other, which should not have been there, was under human control because of an earlier computer failure.

15.3.5 Control of service delivery

Much of the activity in personal service involves concurrent control as the server continually decides what to do in the light of the customer's needs. The range of customers also means that it is difficult to set service standards that can be monitored other than through the eyes of each individual. We shall return to this theme when discussing quality in service provision in Chapter 17.

Many personal service organisations set internal standards that act as yardsticks against which performance is measured. They serve as indirect indicators of customer satisfaction. Marriott Hotels, for instance, supplements the comment cards handed to every customer with monitoring against formal performance targets. Having set a 15-minute standard for in-room breakfast service, otherwise it would be free, demand rose by 25%. Employees had to develop new ways of handling the orders, transmitting them to the kitchen and delivering the trays to the rooms.[9]

Box 15.3 outlines the control process used in the management of another personal service, Merseyside's emergency ambulances.[10] Collecting performance data in this way enables operations managers to spot discrepancies from standards and anticipate when and where problems may arise. Besides supporting day-to-day control, the data can be summarised and used in periodic reviews of targets and operating procedures.

> ### BOX 15.3 **Merseyside Ambulance Service targets**
>
> Each year, Mersey Regional Ambulance Service responds to 250,000 '999' calls and provides a million journeys for non-urgent patients. It serves a population of 2.4 million spread over 1,200 square miles. Despite including a large rural area, it works to the exacting standards for conurbations. These are set as follows:
>
> ■ *Category A emergencies (life threatening)*: 75% within 8 minutes, 95% within 14 minutes.
>
> ■ *Category B emergencies (serious but not immediately life threatening)*: 95% within 14 minutes.
>
> During each emergency, the qualified staff at the emergency medical despatch centre offer advice and support. They log the circumstances, location and the names of people and note the following times:
>
> − Call receipt
> − Information passed to vehicle
> − Arrival at incident
> − Departure to hospital
> − Arrival at hospital.
>
> Supervisors check these records every day to ensure achievement of targets.

We discussed in Chapter 12 how, except where capacity is limited, self-service needs no scheduling. Capacity is made available and the customer uses it when wanted. In the same sense, control action is not required in relation to each customer. A provider must ensure, however, that the service remains available at the appropriate level. To this end, monitoring of stocks, facilities, cash and so on is needed at appropriate intervals.

The other form of service, isolated service, takes place away from the customer and, like scheduling, has control characteristics related to its manufacturing counterparts.

A summary of control issues matched with different processes is set out in Table 15.2. The lists show how much control varies among process technologies.

15.4 Inventory control

15.4.1 Inventory

Our studies of the different operational processes have brought out many stages where inventories are found. One classification uses categories of raw materials, work-in-progress and finished goods. Although all appear as assets in financial accounts, it is the case that most companies would prefer to operate with very low stocks or even none if this were possible.

Inventory is often viewed as imposing dead weight on the business. Indeed, followers of the JIT philosophy see inventory in a negative light as it hides problems

Table 15.2 Summary of control in different manufacture and service processes

Process	Key control task	Focus	Information
Repetitive manufacture and isolated service	Rate of flow through all linked stages. In mass production, not all products need all components; in process plant each process modelled and managed	Maintaining full use of plant capacity to optimise the flow	Central control monitors and balances all stages continuously
Intermittent manufacture and isolated service	Progressing individual orders and batches through multiple stages; meet assembly schedules and promised delivery dates	Each order tracked through processes	Instructions to shop floor to establish sequences; monitoring progress and expediting
Project (manufacture or service)	Progress against milestones; obtaining and using all resources at the right time	Optimisation of single contract; close watch on critical path	Creating network; comparing time and costs against master schedule; rescheduling
Personal service	Matching service to changing customer needs	Satisfying each customer within constraints	Stream of information from customers; queue lengths; reservation systems
Self-service	Keeping to self-service 'offer' e.g. stocks of goods, money, equipment	Following customer flow	Inventory levels; customer demands

that should be brought to the surface. These are valid points. The cash tied up in stock could be used more profitably in other activities and so there is an *opportunity cost* associated with carrying any stock at all. Heaps of stock typify the inefficient job shop. We must recognise, however, that inventory does perform various functions contributing to the firm's need to add value through its processes. Functions of the three classes of inventory are as follows:

- *Raw materials*:
  - to protect the operating processes from shortages caused by uncertain supplies
  - to reduce materials costs by purchasing in optimal quantities at the most appropriate times
  - to hedge against inflation and unstable prices.

- *Work-in-progress*:
  - to enable each stage in the process to use optimal batch sizes
  - to decouple different stages working at different rates
  - to provide buffers along the whole process that allow for the variability of one or more stages.

- *Finished goods*:
  - to enable instant supply of goods
  - to smooth out production when demand is seasonal
  - to protect the operating processes from unexpected shifts in customer demand.

Some reasons are defensive in nature and are only required to cover weaknesses in the production system or uncertainties in the business environment. Others are the result of choices within the scheduling system, where work-in-progress levels are the result of decisions on questions such as batch sizes. Finally, some

BOX 15.4 **High stocks, high margins, high performance**

The Montreal-based FAI company distributes electronic components to customers throughout America. Starting from scratch in 1968, it reached an annual turnover of over $1,000 million in 2000. In the volatile semiconductor market, FAI emphasises service as its strong selling point. It aims to supply from stock a much wider range than its rivals and has, in consequence, a turnover ratio lower than the 2.5 industry norm. The volatility means that many distributors buy on 'price protection' contracts from the major manufacturers such as Motorola and Intel. If the distributors can show that goods have had to be sold on at lower than anticipated prices, the manufacturers will give rebates. Therefore, the latter take on the price risk in the market.

FAI is the only major distributor that does not participate in these contracts, seeing them as letting the manufacturers control the distributors' margins. FAI buys at fixed prices and uses its good service levels to 'get its price'. That is, it sells at margins comfortably above those of its rivals.

reasons can be more directly related to gaining competitive advantage. Raw material policies can be adjusted to optimise input costs and keeping a good stock of finished goods will affect sales rates in many cases. Box 15.4 shows how FAI makes a virtue of carrying large stocks.[11]

15.4.2 **Dependent and independent demand**

Different firms arrange their production systems partly with the intention of restricting stock levels. The job shop that supplies to order is not concerned with inventory of finished items and may carry little raw material because of space restrictions and uncertainty of the requirements in future orders. Such stocks are only carried if substantial quantity discounts are available or local suppliers cannot deliver within short leadtimes. The job shop's problem is work-in-progress!

At the other extreme, the process or dedicated mass production plant operates with the smallest possible level of work-in-progress, there being just enough of it to fill the relevant pipes and vessels or load the carriers on the assembly track. The steady, planned input flow means that these plant can limit raw materials stock by arranging long-term JIT supply contracts. At the other end of the production line, in contrast, problems arise. The assembler, in the JIT system, sets the rhythm of the steady daily production rate. As a result, it needs to hold finished stocks to decouple the manufacturing process from the variable market demand.

Process technologies between the job and the highly repetitive seek different mixes of the three types of stock.

Dependent demand

The most significant difference between operating processes and the way they affect stock management lies in whether the inventory is held to satisfy dependent or independent demand. In the former category are items that can be directly linked to demand for others. Demand is derived from that for the assembly of which it will form a part. These stocks are materials, components and subassemblies connected to each manufacturing order by a definitive bill of materials. An order placed by a customer automatically generates pro rata demand for the constituent parts. The materials requirements plan, MRP, will be the aggregation of these bills. It will form the basis for purchase orders and shop production whether the firm is using MRPII or other planning procedures. The quantity and timing of supplies can be figured out precisely.

There will be some non-dedicated stock held within a MRP system. It will cover advanced orders for components and materials whose leadtime is too great to fit in with customers' requirements. There are also casual items used around the plant for maintenance and related activities.

Independent demand

The independently demanded category of items includes, besides the non-dedicated stock just mentioned, goods and materials bought to underpin production as a whole. It is not bought for individual orders. For instance, many firms carry a stock of finished goods to match variable demand. This is the philosophy of *just-in-case*, as opposed to just-in-time. Stock levels are estimated from production and demand patterns using special techniques. Their management and control are thus very different to order-dependent stocks.

Having covered dependent MRP systems, we will now investigate independent inventory systems.

15.4.3 Independent inventory control systems

The inventory system consists of three main subsystems, shown at the centre of Figure 15.4. The *inventory holding system*, with receiving, holding and despatching components, consists of one or more stores, warehouses, stockyards or similar depots. This is controlled by the *inventory control system* that monitors the behaviour of the holding system to maintain stock levels according to policy and to monitor security. At a level higher than the control system is the *inventory management system* that monitors total performance and sets the goals and rules to be used.

The typical method of operation is for the control system to monitor levels of stock from the records of inputs and outputs, the so-called *perpetual inventory* method. Stock checking validates these calculations and identifies shortages caused by damage, deterioration or theft. Checks take place either at fixed intervals, say monthly, or continuously. The former is useful where the store can be closed for the count to take place but may require personnel to be drafted in at inconvenient times. The latter is better when the store operates without interruption and can take place during normal working hours.

The inventory control system uses the stock information and the control rules to generate orders, via the purchasing system, for suppliers to provide replenishment. General direction is provided by the inventory management system that gathers performance data, such as the frequency of stock shortages, and changes

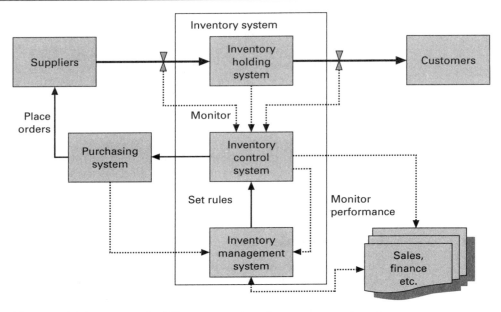

Figure 15.4 Inventory holding, control and management systems

the control rules if necessary. We see, therefore, two levels of control. First, concurrent control operates continuously to replenish stocks as they are depleted. Second, feedback control, after intermittent reviews, changes the way the control task is carried on. Feedforward control will also be seen if the inventory management system uses, say, information from the sales department on anticipated demand changes or from the purchasing department if input prices or suppliers' leadtimes are expected to shift adversely.

15.4.4 Replenishment procedures

Even small firms may stock thousands of different items. Consequently the inventory control system needs a set of rules to show when levels of each item are to be reviewed and refilled. We can look at four methods: fixed quantity, fixed interval, min–max and constrained budget. Of these, the first two are most common, the third is a variant of the first two combined and the fourth recognises the constraints imposed by cash budgets.

Fixed-quantity procedure

The pattern of inventory level under this procedure is set out in Figure 15.5. We can note the following features:

■ The inventory is replenished from time to time with a predetermined quantity of stock. This amount is chosen to be the most economical. It depends on a calculation set out later in this chapter. In this case, we assume that supplies arrive in a single batch, producing a vertical step in the inventory line. In other

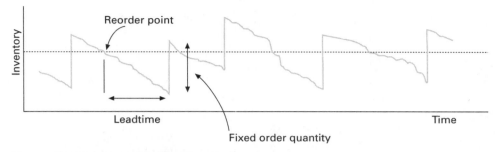

Figure 15.5 Inventory in fixed quantity system

cases, supplies are delivered as they are made and the line has a rising slope as shown in Figure 15.11.

■ Replenishment occurs at irregular intervals depending on consumption.

■ Orders for new supplies are triggered by the inventory falling to the *reorder level.* Delivery of these consignments follows the order by a delay called the *leadtime.* The reorder level is set high enough to limit the risk of there being a stockout before the next batch arrives. Risk arises from uncertainties in both consumption and the leadtime.

The fixed-order procedure is best suited to items whose demand is relatively constant, although with some variation, as shown by the irregular slope of the inventory line in Figure 15.5. Calculations of economic order quantities are based on usage estimates. Further, since the inventory level triggers fresh orders, the procedure requires a continuous record. Perpetual inventory, updating the record after each transaction, is clearly the most effective. Alternatively, the stock count needs checks that are frequent compared with the expected intervals between reordering. Keeping permanent track of stocks of many items can be expensive but its cost falls if recording is built into other processing such as the checkouts of self-service stores. The barcode system enables the organisation to keep detailed stock records at low cost.

In cases where item value does not justify detailed control, simple physical methods have been devised to check stock levels. A bin of screws in a workshop may have the lower half of its inside surfaces painted red. This will warn that an order for new supplies should be sent out. This is a cheap variant of the *two-bin* system that, conventionally, has a separate container for the stock consumed during the leadtime. Other interpretations include areas painted on the floor or lines around walls of storage bays. Small motorcycles have reserve tanks giving, say, a 60-kilometre range. In this way, they need no fuel gauge.

Fixed-interval procedure

The main features of this procedure are shown in Figure 15.6. They are:

■ Stock replenishment is triggered by the calendar. The timing is indicated along the horizontal axis of the figure.

■ The intervals between deliveries are usually constant, although there may be variations due to leadtime uncertainties.

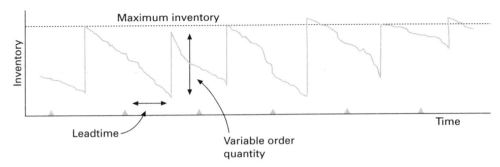

Figure 15.6 Inventory in fixed interval system

- Order quantities vary. They are aimed towards replenishment of the stock to a target level, making an allowance for the consumption that occurs during the leadtime. In effect, the order replenishes the most recent demand.

The fixed-interval procedure is most appropriate when:

- Several items are ordered from one supplier simultaneously. These *joint replenishment* items can, therefore, be bundled in regular consignments. The supplier may offer discounts based on order value and there may be transport savings. The firm's own ordering costs may also fall when orders are consolidated.

- Supplies are sent out at regular intervals. Many distributors have regular rounds whose intervals balance service quality with efficiency. Carpet wholesalers try to visit most areas in a region each week and many exporting companies make fortnightly or monthly runs to each target country throughout Europe. Meubles Grange, the closing case of Chapter 3, is a good example.

- The firm does not operate a perpetual inventory monitoring. Order placing work can be spaced out to smooth the load on the buying office. Clerks check each stock area on regular dates.

Difficulties with the procedure occur when these arguments clash. For example, different suppliers may have different delivery patterns and joint replenishment items may have different optimal order intervals. Furthermore, seasonal demand variations may mean that a fixed maximum stock level is too high much of the time. It can be adjusted for each season.

Minimum–maximum procedure

One disadvantage of the fixed-interval procedure is that it can mean many small orders. The min–max procedure avoids this by setting a minimum inventory above which orders are not placed. Min–max works as follows:

- Stock levels are reviewed at regular intervals.

- Replacements are ordered only if the stock has fallen below a minimum, as shown in Figure 15.7. After lower than average consumption, there are no new orders.

- Order size aims to return the inventory to the target maximum.

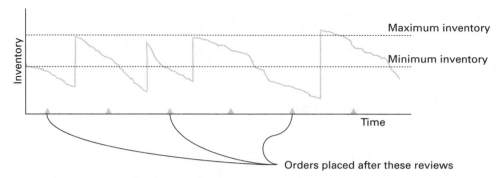

Figure 15.7 Inventory in minimum–maximum system

Min–max combines features of both previous systems. Stock review is regular but the decision whether to place an order is contingent on the stock level prevailing at the time. If the most recent demand is the best indication of the future pattern, then the curtailing of orders in response to slackness is advantageous. Yet, in other case the opposite will be true. Low drawings of an item from stock may simply mean that its main users are not engaged on their regular work. Demand during the next period may return to normal and there may even be an element of catching up.

A related disadvantage is that the average stock levels may be too high. If the minimum holding is sufficient for one period, then why not apply this to all periods and operate the inventory according to the fixed-interval procedure? As always, attention must be paid to achieving a balance between the cost of holding larger stocks and the administrative costs of placing more orders. This argument suggests that the min–max procedure is best suited to low-value items where the cost of administering small orders outweighs any savings that should flow from holding lower average stocks.

Constrained budget

The constrained budget policy is less of a procedure applicable to each item and more a general policy that limits the overall level of stock holding. It is especially applicable in retailing where sales are discretionary. To say that an off-the-peg fashion store sells what it stocks may be a truism yet it emphasises the basis of inventory policy in such establishments. Analysis may suggest the optimal range of sizes to be stocked but, when it comes to achieving a balance among, say, coats, suits, shirts, woollens and accessories, managers use discretion. To ensure a balanced offer in the shop, the budget allocates totals to each category.

Normally, the budget is financial, limits being set by the owner or head office or the insurers. Space also acts as a constraint. We can observe the varying allocation of shelf space in, for instance, supermarkets throughout the year. Many leading retailers limit their stocks to the amounts they can display plus a small backup behind the scenes. New brands, such as the Dubble fair trade chocolate bar, have to fight for display space with established lines such as Mars and Dairy Milk.

In manufacturing companies, the impact of budget constraints is felt indirectly. First, liquidity problems create pressure to reduce order quantities whatever the procedure. Second, there is often a desire to delay incoming supplies at the end of the financial year to massage the stock figures in the balance sheet.

15.4.5 ABC analysis

We have mentioned several times how inventory control policies need to be matched to the cost of the items being stocked. Their worth varies from many thousands to that of a paper clip. This is an example of the Pareto principle that contrasts the critical few and the trivial many. The ABC classification recognises this contrast and divides items into classes, usually three, to which different procedures are applied. It could be that there will be different review and order intervals or that some items will be managed under the fixed-interval regime and others with fixed order.

The ABC classification, sketched in Figure 15.8, creates an initial sort of stock items into groups according to the annual expenditure on each. The intention is to give greatest attention to those with the highest expenditure. These category A items may only number some 10% or 15% of the total yet may account for more that 60% of the annual spend. Among the trivial items in category C, numbering

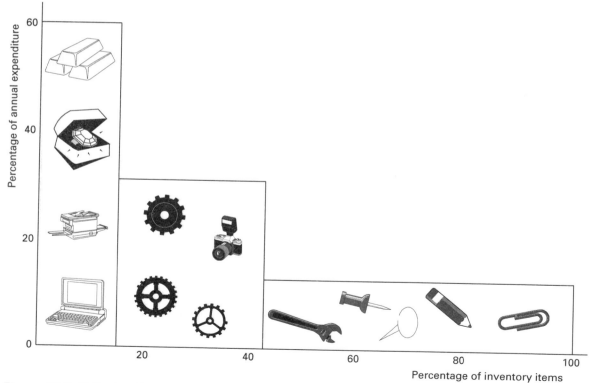

Figure 15.8 ABC classification

more than half the total, the expenditure may be lower than 10%. Between these two extremes lies category B, making up perhaps one-third of the number and a similar proportion of the outlay.

The procedure is as follows:

1 Estimate the annual amount spent on each line of inventory.

2 Rank all items in descending order of expenditure.

3 Divide the list into A, B and C categories at, say, the 15% and 45% points. This requires the exercise of judgement. It may be that there are 'break points' in the list to serve as a guide. Alternatively, certain products may be selected to serve as markers.

4 Adapt the list using other criteria if necessary. For instance, upgrading may result from the critical nature of a component, the need for special storage and limited shelf life, quality difficulties or scarcity.

The analysis is used to choose inventory control policies:

- Category A items are controlled more carefully than for C. Even a few months' extra inventory for A will be very expensive whereas for C it will not make much difference.

- Forecasts for A category demand require more attention, especially if there is a risk of obsolescence.

- Security for the A category should be more rigorous. C items are ideal for min–max, using an open two-bin system.

- Control records for the A category should be kept in more detail. In a repair shop, for instance, the costs of A items should be allocated to orders but the C parts can be regarded as general expenses.

Items in the B category fall between A and C. The group could have medium security and control rigour. Some firms, however, do not identify a third group, remaining content with two categories.

15.4.6 Independent inventory models

The basic EOQ model is perhaps the oldest and is certainly the best known inventory control policy. It is widely used as a basis for decisions. Yet, its renown could be because it has been so widely taught in business courses. Its value may be overrated because it is very difficult to estimate the data that the formula requires. We shall consider the method here, with some variants, before going on to summarise these limitations.

The policy for independent inventory control seeks a balance among a number of costs. Besides the cost of the goods, the significant items are those associated with placing, receiving and paying for orders with others associated with keeping the stock in good condition. In the first instance, let us assume a constant price for the incoming material and hence a given annual expenditure. This allows us to focus on the main variable, which is the amount ordered each time. Large batches mean higher average inventory and higher holding costs, as shown in Figure 15.9. Further, large batches mean placing fewer orders each year so the ordering cost goes down. Table 15.3 lists the costs sensitive to order quantity.

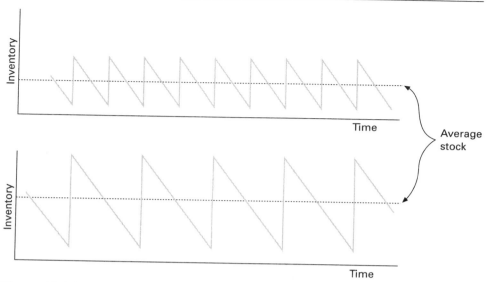

Figure 15.9 The impact of order size on inventory

Table 15.3 Costs affected by changes in order quantity

Costs increasing when order quantities increase and orders are placed less frequently	Costs falling when order quantities increase and orders are placed less frequently
■ Capital invested in inventory	■ Ordering
■ Storage, monitoring and handling of stock	■ Changeover costs between batches (if these can be avoided)
■ Storage space	
■ Insurance	■ Order tracking, receiving and, possibly, transport
■ Obsolescence due to design changes	
■ Damage and deterioration	■ Risk of supply interruption as low points are reached less often

One difficulty becomes apparent immediately. Many of the costs in the list have to be estimated and averaged across a large number of items. Furthermore, total order administration costs are usually fixed. Removing one order from a buyer's workload will have an imperceptible effect on administrative overhead. Although these are important problems, it is accepted that there is an optimal position between ordering large quantities infrequently and small quantities very often. The total comprises holding and administrative costs, as shown in Figure 15.10. The holding cost rises proportionally to the amount of inventory held while the ordering cost falls. Between the extremes, the total reaches a minimum at a point known as the *economic order quantity*, EOQ.

15.4.7 The basic EOQ model

In calculating the EOQ in a simple case, the following conditions and assumptions must apply:

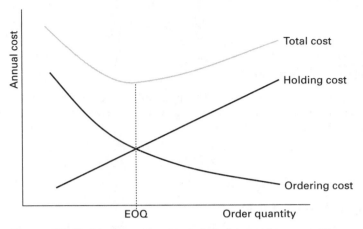

Figure 15.10 Inventory costs related to order quantity

- The demand rate is known and constant. This allows us to estimate the average inventory to be half the order quantity (see Figure 15.9).
- There are no quantity discounts.
- Orders arrive in one batch, so the upward steps in the inventory line are vertical.
- The leadtime is known so that orders arrive just as stock is exhausted.
- Order placement and receiving costs are known and are independent of order quantity.
- Inventory holding costs are a fixed proportion of inventory value. There are no economies or diseconomies of scale in this function.

These assumptions underpin the lines in Figure 15.10. It happens that, with smooth curves of the form shown in the figure, the minimum value of the total cost occurs at the point that the constituent cost lines intersect. This then suggests the following method of determining the EOQ:

1 Create an expression for the holding cost as a function of order quantity.
2 Create an expression for the ordering cost as a function of order quantity.
3 Set the two costs to equal each other.
4 Solve to establish the EOQ.

We shall use the following variables:

S = Cost per order
C = Cost of each item of inventory
i = Carrying cost per period (usually one year) as a fraction of inventory value
D = Demand during the period (again, say, one year) in numbers of items
Q = Order quantity

Step 1 Ordering cost

The annual ordering cost is found from the number of orders placed and the cost per order. Since the number placed is equal to D/Q, then:

$$Ordering\ cost = \left(\frac{D}{Q}\right) \times S$$

Step 2 Holding cost

The annual holding cost is found from the average inventory value and the annual holding cost per pound of inventory. The former is equal to $C \times Q/2$, see Figure 15.9, and the latter is i. Hence:

$$Holding\ cost = i \times C \times \left(\frac{Q}{2}\right)$$

Step 3 EOQ equation

The EOQ is found when the two costs are equal. That is:

$$\left(\frac{D}{Q}\right) \times S = i \times C \times \left(\frac{Q}{2}\right)$$

Whence the EOQ is given by:

$$Q = \sqrt{\frac{2DS}{iC}}$$

For example, in a company where: ordering cost is estimated at £5; holding cost is 20% of stock value; annual demand is 1,000 units at a supplier's price of £20; the EOQ is found from:

$$EOQ = \sqrt{\frac{2 \times 1000 \times 5}{0.2 \times 20}} = 50\ units$$

Fifty units should last about $2\frac{1}{2}$ weeks and reordering should take place to match.

Reorder point (ROP)

Having decided how much stock to order, the second question for inventory control is when to place the order. The time between placing the order and receiving delivery is the leadtime. This is based on suppliers' promises and the accumulation of experience. Given our assumption about steady, predictable demand, we can estimate the reorder point from the demand and leadtime:

$$ROP = Demand \times Leadtime$$

Weeks or days, or even hours, could serve as time units in this equation. Hence, if rolled steel sections are available on a 14-week leadtime, and we use a particular size at the rate of 200 linear metres per week, the ROP should be 14×200 or 2,800 metres.

Depending on the importance of the item to the firm, it may raise the ROP by an amount called the *safety stock*. When the delivery arrives, the safety stock will not usually have been used. It is there to allow for both demand and leadtime variations. More details on the ROP appear in a later section.

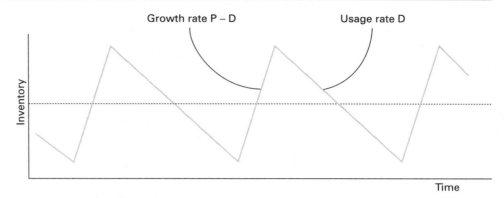

Figure 15.11 Inventory model with production flow

15.4.8 Variations on the EOQ model

We have just set out several assumptions to simplify the EOQ presentation. It is possible to modify these to make the model more representative of different circumstances. We shall look at two practical cases – simultaneous production and quantity discounts.

Simultaneous production

In this case, delivery of replacements does not come in one batch but 'trickles' in. This represents a common situation where goods are supplied from another department in the same organisation. Now, the saw tooth graphs of Figure 15.9 change to look like Figure 15.11.

For a given order quantity Q, the average inventory under the revised assumption will be lower. This is because of the time it takes for the product to come in. If the production rate is P, the time for that production will be Q/P. Further, we know that the usage rate is D and so, during the production period, $D \times Q/P$ will be consumed. Hence, the stock will rise by the order quantity *less* this consumption, that is $(Q - D \times Q/P)$.

Calculations of the EOQ under the new conditions follow the previous procedure. We shall only give the result here:

$$Q = \sqrt{\frac{2DS}{iC} \times \frac{P}{P - D}}$$

We can extend our previous numerical example. If the supplies arrive at 100 per week, which is 5,200 per year, then:

$$EOQ = \sqrt{\frac{2 \times 1000 \times 5}{0.2 \times 20} \times \frac{5200}{5200 - 1000}} = 56 \ units$$

Price discounts

Suppliers offer an endless assortment of price discounts. These range from reductions for large quantities of a single item to discounts for total order value,

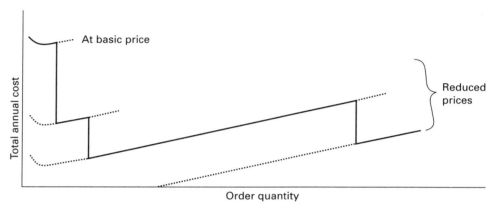

Figure 15.12 Costs related to order quantity: case with price breaks

accumulated annual sales or even for repeat orders for the same items. Clearly, each case must be assessed on its merits. We shall confine ourselves to one example here, the price discount for larger quantities of a single item.

Let us say that the vendor lists four prices, depending on order quantity. Now the total cost line is modified by steps as shown in Figure 15.12. Each step occurs at a price break. For each price, there is a total cost curve falling towards the notional minimum. As suggested by the dotted lines, most of these minima do not apply because they fall outside the quantity range for that price.

In the graphical representation of Figure 15.12, the EOQ lies at the second price break. This can be confirmed by sketching the complete relationship between cost and order size. This, however, is unnecessary since the best points are clearly just above price breaks and at any minima in the total cost curve. We must now use total annual costs, including the purchase prices. A full approach is as follows:

1 For each price, calculate a 'notional EOQ'. Check that this EOQ lies within the quantity range qualifying for the price. If not, reject it. Otherwise, accept it and calculate the corresponding annual total cost.

2 Work out total costs for quantities just above each price break, again including the purchase costs.

3 Select the lowest cost. This gives the EOQ.

Example

Mineral fibre ceiling panels have a basic price of £6. As is common in the distribution trade for building materials, quantity discounts apply. Here, there is a 10% discount for orders over 1,000, those over 2,000 are at list less 15% and over 10,000 it is list less 20%. A distributor estimates the ordering cost to be £25 per order and the cost of holding this type of stock to be 25% per annum. The current demand is 1,000 panels per month, which is 12,000 per year.

The first step is to compute the notional EOQs for each price. These are:

$$Q_{list} = \sqrt{\frac{2 \times 12000 \times 25}{0.25 \times 6}} = 632 \; units$$

Table 15.4 Annual purchase, ordering and holding costs

Quantity ordered on each occasion	Price each £	Annual payment to supplier £	Annual ordering cost £	Annual holding cost £	Total annual cost £
632	6.00	72,000	475	474	72,949
1000	5.40	64,800	300	675	65,775
2000	5.10	61,200	150	1275	62,625
10000	4.80	57,600	30	6000	63,630

$$Q_{>1000} = \sqrt{\frac{2 \times 12000 \times 25}{0.25 \times 5.4}} = 666 \; units$$

$$Q_{>2000} = \sqrt{\frac{2 \times 12000 \times 25}{0.25 \times 5.1}} = 685 \; units$$

$$Q_{>10000} = \sqrt{\frac{2 \times 12000 \times 25}{0.25 \times 4.8}} = 707 \; units$$

Clearly, only the first of these is feasible. The next step is to compute the total annual purchase, ordering and holding costs for Q_{list} and above the three price breaks. These are set out in Table 15.4.

We can see that the 15% discount for order quantities of 2,000 panels looks attractive. This means placing six orders each year.

Exercise 15.4   Why not search for other minimum cost points? Answer this question by sketching the curve for total costs for order quantities up to 12,000.

Would the recommended order quantity change if:

- the price for sales over 10,000 was cut to £4.70
- there was a new price of £5.00 for sales over 5,000 each year?

15.4.9 Uncertainty and the reorder point

A brief note on the ROP was given in an earlier section. There, as in the rest of our discussion, we assumed that the system behaviour was regular and the inventory could be forecast. In figuring out the ROP, the inventory manager forecasts likely demand during the leadtime. To allow for errors, a safety stock is added to the reorder level so that the inventory line looks like Figure 15.13. In normal conditions, the minimum stock does not fall below the safety level.

How is the safety stock decided? If experience and judgement of buyers and inventory managers are used as the basis, it will inevitably increase. This is because the purpose of the inventory system is to give service, either to customers or to other departments within the firm. Managers want to avoid a stockout, which is lack of service. Yet, the safety stock contributes to the average stock on hand. Safety is not cost free. As with the rest of the inventory, it has to be paid for, stored, checked and eventually discarded when obsolete.

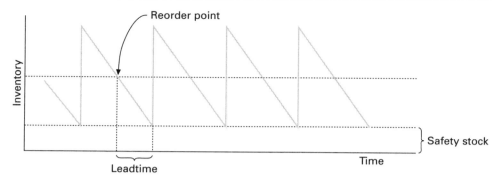

Figure 15.13 Inventory line with safety stock

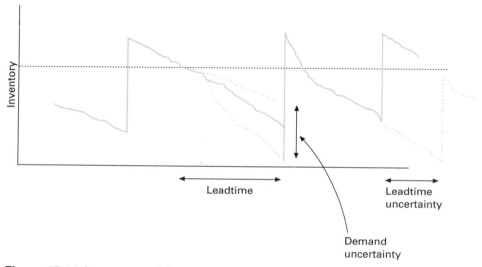

Figure 15.14 Inventory with uncertain demand or leadtime

Let us look a little more closely at the pattern of demand during the leadtime. Clearly, it is reasonable to expect the mean demand rate to remain the same as in the recent past. Furthermore, we could forecast a maximum demand during the period. If this can be done, the reorder point should be set to cover this maximum. The possible stock movements during the leadtime are then as shown in Figure 15.14. In practice, we will rarely be able to establish a maximum demand with certainty, we can only estimate probabilities. We must accept that there will be occasions when demand exceeds the maximum and a stockout occurs.

A second uncertainty surrounds the leadtime. Figure 15.14 shows what happens if this stretches unexpectedly. Again, the safety stock takes account of this possibility. Good purchasing managers keep an eye on trends in their supply industries, especially for inputs of some metals or computer chips whose leadtimes vary widely.

Recognising these problems, inventory managers establish service level targets. If a retail store is to maintain a reputation for keeping a wide range of goods, it will set a service level of, say, 98%. This means that 98% of the product lines are

Table 15.5 Factors affecting safety stock policy

Higher levels of safety stock are preferred when . . .	*Lower levels of safety stock are preferred when . . .*
■ The cost, including opportunity cost, of stockout is high	■ The cost of a stockout is low; alternatives are available or backup can be obtained
■ Ordering frequency is high so the risk is met repeatedly	■ Orders are placed infrequently so the stock rarely dips into the safety zone
■ The cost of carrying safety stock is low	■ Safety stock holding costs are high
■ Demand is variable and uncertain	■ Demand varies little and is expected to remain steady
■ Leadtimes are long	■ Leadtimes are short

on the shelves at any time. In setting the service level, a balance has to be struck between the cost of achieving a high service level and the cost of not having the item available. Table 15.5 summarises the issues.

It is possible to go beyond simple judgement to set safety stock levels if there are enough data to attach probabilities to demand and leadtimes. Computer stock control systems use estimates of the probability distributions from recent records of each stock item. They adjust the reorder point in the light of given service level targets.

ABC analysis of service levels

Leading companies adopt ABC analysis to discriminate among inventories that need different service levels. For example, ICI's engineering division purchases each year more than £1,000 million of materials, equipment components and other supplies. Items are categorised according to the effect of stockout and hence have different service level targets:

- *Category A items* are those whose absence would cause a plant shutdown. Examples in the limestone quarries include spare drive motors and their components, conveyor belting and so on. In the salt mines, there are many items of equipment critical to safety. These include lifting cables and other hoist components, many of which are on long leadtimes. A fault in any of these demands an immediate replacement.

- *Category B items* are close to those in A except that it is recognised that the consequences of a stockout are less severe and operating problems can be overcome at some cost. Service targets of 99% are set for these items.

- *Category C items* are covered by 95% service targets. The consequences of a stockout are not so serious. Sometimes, alternatives are available. Otherwise, the result can be extra administrative and transport cost as an urgent order is placed. As one buyer reported, 'In the end, we can always send out to B&Q!'

Many retailers and service companies rely on the support of regional stockists to cover the vast range of components and spares for which they cannot carry any level of stock. Halford's service centres carry spares for popular cars and endeavour to obtain any other within an hour. Within the same industry, leading car assemblers support their distributors with rapid delivery systems. Volkswagen has its own aircraft and Rolls Royce claims to be able to supply a spare for any car it has ever made to anywhere in the world. These policies need the support of excellent information and communication systems.

15.4.10 Comment on inventory models

We have studied a range of basic models in this chapter. Many extensions and adaptations are possible, suited to different circumstances. A common difficulty, however, is their reliance on data of doubtful quality. This is particularly true of estimates of ordering and stockholding costs. Weaknesses include the marginal effects of small changes and the assumption that holding cost relationships are linear. Clearly, the formulae can be modified to respond to the problems, but the advantages of doing so are limited.

The general principles, however, hold. These are:

- There is likely to be an economic order quantity and it is worthwhile trying to estimate it. Since the total cost curve tends to be flat around its minimum point, errors in estimates of the EOQ have only minor effect. Depending on their circumstances, firms are likely to use some variant of the EOQ formula and then modify it. In the light of pressure to reduce average inventory holdings, pushing levels down to slightly below the ideal EOQ will have minor operating cost effects. Yet it may release capital that could yield greater benefits elsewhere. In another approach, reducing the cost of placing orders, such as by setting up long-term contracts with automatic call-offs, feeds directly through to the EOQ formula and therefore reduces inventory.

- The fixed-quantity reorder procedure, which uses the EOQ formula, is attractive in that it directly addresses the question of the cost of holding stocks. It is not, however, applicable in all situations. The expense of operating the perpetual inventory system that underpins the process, the lack of past data and the uncertain effects of seasonal demand changes are just three reasons why some firms operate other procedures for at least some of their inventory.

- Safety stocks are required because companies do not know in advance what demand and leadtimes are likely to be. Again, procedures based on historical data will suggest safety stock levels corresponding to service targets. Companies will take these as a starting point and modify them in the light of experience. The models show that stock-reduction policies increase the frequency of stockout. Whether this is tolerable will depend on the items and how they are used. ABC analysis will help such decisions.

- Reorder points are, in the first instance, determined independently of the EOQ. Small order quantities, however, mean frequent orders and regular exposure to the risk of stockout. Therefore, safety stock levels may be increased, countering some of the benefit of the reduced EOQ.

- The optimisation of independent demand inventory is a difficult task. Many firms have to face it, especially at the interface with retail customers. Upstream from this point, however, there is a trend to share information between different stages of the supply chain. Each supplier is presented with derived or dependent demand from its immediate customer. This change enables JIT,

MRP and related systems. Safety stocks are supplanted by information and control replaces buffer stocks.

Fast response distribution systems yield competitive advantage. The stock–service relationship can be balanced more effectively. One trick learnt by leading companies is to delay customisation to as late as possible in the chain. This means that both the upstream-dependent systems and the independent demand inventory operate with less variety and hence lower cost.

The Italian domestic equipment, fashion and machine tool industries are examples. Battezzati and Magnani[12] explain how they are the core business of the Italian economy. Although there are many small and medium enterprises, postponement makes possible a huge variety of products. This means that manufacturers run their plants efficiently with low stocks to produce standard components. Only at the last stages of supply are they customised. This means assembling them in different ways for each order. Many kitchen furniture manufacturers achieve high variety despite having low market share.[13]

✔ Quick check-up

Can you:
- ☐ Define task control.
- ☐ Distinguish between control activities in intermittent and repetitive operations.
- ☐ List five criteria for effective monitoring.
- ☐ Outline control loops in MRPII.
- ☐ Summarise the functions of three classes of inventory.
- ☐ Sketch an independent inventory control system.
- ☐ Name four stock replenishment procedures.
- ☐ Demonstrate ABC analysis in stock control.
- ☐ Define: leadtime, EOQ, ROP, safety stock.
- ☐ Illustrate the effect of uncertainty on inventory management policies.

？ Questions

Chapter review

15.1 What is effective monitoring? Illustrate by reference to stock control and production control in a job shop.

15.2 Summarise the use of different types of control in the management of inventories.

15.3 What are the weaknesses of the EOQ inventory model? In the light of them, how would you advise a manager in its use?

Application

15.4 Referring back to Chapter 13, explain the advantages of switching to dependent inventory control for members of a supply chain.

15.5 From the opening case, identify the types of control used by SBB operators to achieve the operations objectives.

15.6 Discuss the application of the feedback control model to the SBB case through commenting on how controllers monitor system outputs and adapt inputs. What factors are beyond their control and what can they do to cope with them?

Investigation

15.7 Why is personal service so difficult to control? Investigate the use of service standards in the operations of a public service such as health, housing, transport and so on.

CLOSING CASE

The Home Shopping Bureau

We saw in 12.4.2 how supervisors in the telephone service bureau coped with sudden peaks in demand by reducing the time spent with each caller, delaying rest breaks and calling for reserve staff. Of particular value to the supervisors is the prominent display showing the length of the queue at any moment.

Outcomes are reviewed at three levels. First, each week, the supervisors receive information on operators' performance levels including the times that each individual takes to handle calls. They are expected to check on operators whose performance appears to be out of line. Difficulties are usually resolved by discussion. It is important not to over-stress the times, as the quality of customer service is vital. The trick, at peak times, is to give good quality while maintaining an efficient tempo.

At the second level, the departmental manager is responsible for achieving service standards within cost constraints. Enough staff must be allocated to the operation to enable more that 99% of calls to be answered within 30 seconds but this has to be done within operating cost budgets.

The manager plans the allocation of staff according to latest demand forecasts. Beyond taking into account hourly, daily and seasonal fluctuations, they are adjusted for growth trends in the business. These forecasts are updated weekly. In addition, the manager has available summarised information on costs, staff performance against standards, average time to answer calls, average length of call and the number of enquirers who hung up before their calls were answered. Using this information, the manager discusses the weekly programme with the supervisors.

The third level of control is with the divisional manager who receives summarised performance information each week on all departments including both telephone and mail order. Problems and possible changes are discussed with the departmental managers. Additionally, the divisional manager works with other departments on methods of improving the ordering activity in the longer term. These include: changes to the information system; new order-processing methods; improved query handling; and clarifying instructions and information given to customers. The divisional manager must also consider increasing use of the telephone, the possibilities of using fax or e-mail and new marketing policies. Some new products, such as insurance and other financial services, may require specialist advice at the point of contact.

Questions

1 Describe the different patterns of control used in the management of the order bureau.

2 To what extent does the control guarantee first-class service every time? List any other objectives that apply here.

3 What further areas of activity could be monitored? Explain how and why you would collect and use data in these areas.

Notes and references

1. Railway Gazette International (1998) 'Untangling the Zurich knot', December; (1999) 'Swiss support huge rail spend', January; SBB web pages http://www.sbb.ch/bf/betriebser_e.htm accessed June 2001.
2. Anthony, R.N. (1988) *The Management Control Function*, Boston, MA: Harvard Business School Press, p.27.
3. Anthony, op.cit. p.37.
4. De Toni, A. and Panizzolo, R. (1993) 'Operations management techniques in intermittent and repetitive manufacturing: A conceptual framework', *International Journal of Operations and Production Management*, 13(5), pp.12–32.
5. Cohen, N., Kelly, J. and Urry, M. (1995) 'The back office: When things go wrong, the first place to look', *The Financial Times*, 28 February, p.2.
6. Donkin, R. (1995) 'When preservation takes precedence over profit', *The Financial Times*, 1 March, p.13.
7. Burcher, P.G. (1992) 'Effective capacity planning', *Management Services*, October, pp.22–5.
8. Spreadbury, A. (1994) 'Manufacturing resource planning' in Storey, J. (ed.) *New Wave Manufacturing Strategies*, London: Paul Chapman.
9. Phillips, S. and Dunkin, A. (1990) 'King Customer', *Business Week*, 12 March, p.91.
10. Mersey Regional Ambulance Service Trust (2001) 'Emergency service performance', MRAST; www.mrast.nhs.uk/performance/performance.htm accessed 28 June 2001.
11. A private communication.
12. Battezzati, L. and Magnani, R. (2000) 'Supply chains for FMCG and industrial products in Italy: Practices and the advantages of postponement', *International Journal of Physical Distribution and Logistics Management*, 30(5), pp.413–24.
13. Naylor, J., Hawkins N. and Wilson, C. (2001) 'Benchmarking marketing in an SME: The case of an Italian kitchen furniture manufacturer', *Marketing Review*, 1(3), pp.325–39.

CHAPTER 16

Quality management

OBJECTIVES

When you have finished studying this chapter, you should be able to:

- Define quality and recognise the difficulties encountered with the variety of quality definitions.
- Show how definitions differ between goods and services.
- Explain the importance of quality both in terms of costs and in creating competitive advantage.
- Identify the costs of quality and outline how an organisation can change the balance among them.
- Apply control models to quality issues, relating them to process technologies.
- Recognise the contributions of leading advocates of the quality message; identify the important elements of the work of Deming and others.
- Evaluate the benefits of product and process standards, identifying why process standards have grown in importance.
- Define and explain the key features of total quality management; outline its limitations in practice.
- Show how quality concepts can be applied in the management of service functions and in relating design to operations.

OPENING CASE

Perfecting the Big Mac[1]

McDonald's mission includes delivering operational excellence. At the heart of its effort to increase sales and profits lie policies on food and service quality designed to make the firm stand out from its rivals. While the Big Mac is not to everyone's taste, the company was cited by *Fortune* as the world's most admired food service company. It aims for zero defects, that is to serve hot, fresh, tasty food of good value to customers on every occasion. About 45 million visit the 28,000 restaurants every day.

Achievement means high standards at every link in the supply chain, from dairy herds to lettuce seedlings and flour to chicken rearing. McDonald's sets exacting requirements for quality and safety. It will only use ingredients whose source can be traced and which satisfy all regulations. Quality assurance staff carry out audits and site visits to verify the supply chain. They also cooperate with suppliers to improve product quality. For instance, lard was replaced by vegetable oil in buns, fat levels in sauces were cut and saturated fats in the cooking oil were reduced.

▶

To disseminate its commitment to quality among its 4,000 suppliers, the company introduced the Sweeney Award in 1990. Judging takes place every two years. Criteria are based on those used for the Baldrige Award.[2] The 2000 winner, Sunny Foods (Thailand), supplies chicken products to more than 200 outlets in Hong Kong. Another company in the same group, Sunny Fresh Foods, gained the Sweeney in 1998 and the Baldrige in the following year.

Standardisation of the product range helps to assure quality. Staff training is simplified by the limited range and process development, including the provision of computer-controlled cooking facilities. Chicken McNuggets are shaped into uniform sizes from breast and thigh meat to ensure cooking consistency. Like all meat, the chickens are traceable, in this case to their grandparents. Their food and water, medication and litter are also traceable to source. Fish products use cod whose origins can be matched to the vessel and day of catch. Boning is a matter of great concern and 23 checks occur during fish product manufacture. McDonald's prefers to use free-range eggs in the United Kingdom.

Food quality and safety policies are closely linked to concerns for the environment. Pressed to improve its wasteful practices in food packaging and serving, the company works on reducing its use of materials and energy. Operations, purchasing and training policies all include a strong theme of waste reduction including distribution in reusable containers, using recyclable packaging and installing heating and lighting controls.

16.1   Introduction

The success of McDonald's is based partly on its record on food quality, the hygiene standards of its outlets and the speed and style of service. In the case study, we see many aspects of good-quality practice. Processes are designed to 'build in' quality and then standardised; company requirements complement and exceed legal minima; training concentrates on customer safety; inspections take place at critical points; traceability allows rapid response to problems; and all aspects are continually reviewed with an eye to improvement. These are the marks of excellence. Quality policies also link with others related to the environment and being a good corporate citizen.

During the last quarter of the 20th century, the critical significance of quality has been recognised as industry after industry has been challenged by innovation and international competition. While manufacturing and service organisations that could not keep up have suffered in the new climate, those who have absorbed the quality message have prospered. Success has bred success as customers respond to rising standards and have their demands satisfied like never before. In the transformation of the fast-food outlet of the 1970s into the quick-service restaurant of today, weaker establishments have been left behind.

Companies whose products fall below the new specifications and do not carry industry standard warranties have only themselves to blame. Quality, as we shall see, requires good management to mobilise the whole organisation in its achievement.

The discussion of quality is divided between two chapters. This one deals with policy issues, that is definitions, standards, organisation and mobilisation in manufacturing and service settings. The next chapter deals with tools and techniques of problem analysis, change and control. The two areas form a whole such that to discuss one without the other is somewhat artificial. There is, therefore, some overlap where necessary.

16.2 What is quality?

People use different definitions of quality in different contexts. Consider the following examples:

A European company ordered some semiconductor components from a Japanese supplier. The order stated something like, '10,000 items required, with a defect rate of 0.02%'. The consignment duly arrived in two containers. The larger carried 9,998 good components and the smaller held the two defects, clearly labelled. The supplier could not understand why the customer wanted the defects but they were sent all the same.[3]

A traditional, family-run clothes shop near my home closed down. Its place was taken by a 'factory seconds' chain store selling rejected textiles, mainly clothing. Prices are much lower and the new shop has a brasher and cheaper image compared with its predecessor. There were complaints. The local newspaper carried letters grumbling about the way such shops have lowered the tone of the town and the quality of the shops in the centre.[4]

Exercise 16.1

What do the examples just given say about quality? Are there such things as high quality and low quality? Is the bespoke tailor better than the factory seconds store?

In everyday use, we speak of high quality as being superior to low quality. In so doing, we imply that some characteristic, such as designed life, has a higher value to us. A pair of shoes is, in these terms, of high quality if it gives five years' wear instead of two. Yet, what of the people who do not want shoes to last five years? To these customers, fitting the fashion may rank more highly than fitting the foot! In short, they prefer a different combination of attributes. Clearly, in any product, there are many. Customers search for those that most closely fit what they want. We can summarise the overlapping ideas about quality as follows:

- *Quality defined by the customer.* This perspective, preferred by marketing managers, looks for quality definition through what has become known as *the voice of the customer.* It is particularly critical in the delivery of personal services, where each customer comes along with individual needs and evaluation criteria. Yet, the variety of interpretations that the definition implies poses a problem for mass producers. They must interpret varied needs into more formal standards when they design their products and delivery systems. We shall see later in this chapter how this perspective has been incorporated into ISO 9000. An example of monitoring customer satisfaction is shown in Box 16.1.[5]

BOX 16.1 J.D. Powers reveals the consumers' perspective

J.D. Powers conducts customer surveys in many markets and industries.
Its car hire customer satisfaction survey was begun in 1996. In a 2001 study
Powers reported that satisfaction among leisure travellers depends on: the
reservation, pick-up and return processes; price and value; and cleanliness and
features of the cars.

Table 16.1 Quality as safety

	Front and side impact rating	Pedestrian test rating
Audi A3	****	**
Citroën Xsara	***	**
Ford Focus	****	**
Ford Escort	**	**
Vauxhall/Opel Astra	****	*
Peugeot 306	***	*
Renault Megane: 1998	****	*
Volkswagen Beetle	****	**
Volkswagen Golf	****	**

- *Quality in use.* Many individually specified attributes relate to product application. These include *performance* (will it do the job?), *reliability* (under individually defined conditions), *serviceability* (again, after particular use) and *fit* (especially the aesthetic relation to other products to which it will be related). *Safety* is another feature that many would include, although it is not easy for individuals to make detailed appraisals.

    Government, industry and independent organisations provide some data for some products. For instance, looking at a car gives little guide to its safety. From 1997, the European New Car Assessment Programme has helped consumers compare safety. It tests for front and side impact to assess 'crashworthiness'. An extract, showing examples of small family cars appears in Table 16.1.[6]

- *Quality as grade or features.* In referring to quality, many customers are using the term to mean *grade*. For instance, Rhodes's *Carron Lodge* Cheshire Cheese (First Prize, Nantwich Show, 2001) is a higher grade (said to be better quality) and more expensive than a basic product. The range of *features*, such as the number of cycle options on a washing machine, is another aspect of this confusion.

- *Quality to guide processes.* Operations managers need standards, preferably defined by or agreed with the customer, to provide clear yardsticks. They can then decide whether they have achieved their target of *right first time*. In this view, if different bottling plants all produce their cola drinks to the specifications laid down by each syrup maker, then their quality is satisfactory. Customer brand preferences do not feature in this assessment.

- *Quality as product attribute.* For some, the notion of quality is an attribute of the product itself, independent of intended use. Legal standards for many products, such as marmalade, chocolate, sausages, petrol and electric cable are defined within such frameworks.

■ *Quality as service characteristics.* Despite many similarities between goods and services, many have noted special definitions in the latter. Zeithamal, Parasuraman and Berry[7] present five factors important in service quality assessment. Forming the basis of the *SERVQUAL* model, discussed in Chapter 17, they are:
  – *reliability* – giving the promised service precisely and dependably
  – *responsiveness* – helping customers promptly with their varying needs
  – *tangible factors* – the condition of facilities and the appearance of staff
  – *assurance* – the demeanour and knowledge of staff and the way they convey trust and confidence
  – *empathy* – caring and offering individual attention.

16.2.1 A working definition

These ideas are common and frequently mixed. We need, therefore, a more usable definition of quality combining attributes and standards with the purpose to which the product is to be put. Crosby has been influential in this argument. 'Quality has to be defined as conformance to requirements, not as goodness . . . The setting of requirements may simply involve only answers to questions. Requirements, like measurements, are communications.'[8]

In stressing *conformance to requirements*, Crosby is emphasising two features. First, quality is about matching, that is conforming to, some standards. Second, these standards, or requirements, have to be established and communicated in some way from their origin, be it customers or some other external source. If we are talking about individual service, it may be possible to adjust operations for each client. By the same token, mass production within competitive markets works because standards exist across whole industries.

Quality is, therefore, about using information to set standards and then conforming to them. These ideas are captured in the definitions within the international standard, ISO 9000, listed in Box 16.2.[9]

BOX 16.2 **Quality defined**

Definition:

Quality is the degree to which a set of inherent characteristics fulfils requirements.

A *characteristic* is a distinguishing feature. It can be: physical (such as the strength of a material); sensory (smell, taste etc.); behavioural (honesty, courtesy, truthfulness); temporal (reliability, punctuality, availability); ergonomic (physiological or safety related); or functional (such as maximum speed).

Requirements are needs or expectations that are stated, implicit or mandatory. They can have many sources, including those indirectly affected by a transaction. Therefore, an aircraft design should consider the interests of passengers and crew, users of other aircraft and all who may be affected by its flight. Implicit, or *generally implied*, requirements are based on common practice among the organisation, its customers and others.

Exercise 16.2 Before the establishment of the ISO series, both the British Standards Institute and the American Society for Quality Control had adopted the following definition of quality:

> **The totality of features and characteristics of a product or service that bear on its ability to satisfy stated or implied needs.**[10]

What differences do you notice between this and the later definition?

16.2.2 The importance of quality

The story of a supplier sorting defects from good items emphasises how Japanese companies gained competitive advantage from supplying quality goods. The remarkable progress of the Japanese consumer goods manufacturers is further, more solid evidence. Quality is a strategic factor that works through virtuous cycles to build market share and reduce costs. Figure 16.1 illustrates some key relationships. The *quality improvement* area of the diagram has two zones related to product improvement, making it more suited to customers' needs, and process improvements, ensuring better conformance to standards. Improved quality increases demand and enables the firm to charge higher prices for the value differentiation that it offers. An important second-order effect is the way customers learn about quality and continue to feed back their demands into product design. Achieving customer satisfaction is not, therefore, a one-off process; rising standards

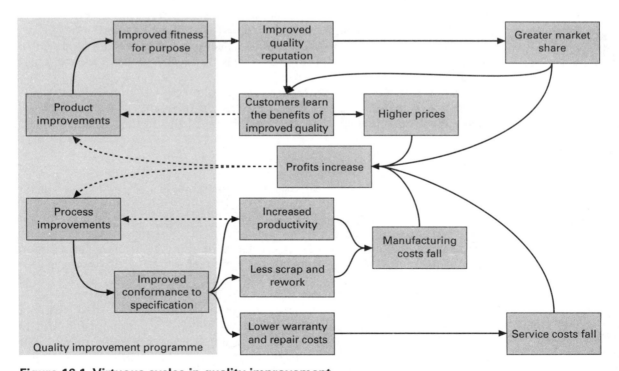

Figure 16.1 Virtuous cycles in quality improvement

Table 16.2 Quality up, costs down

Item	Defects before change 11%	Defects after change 5%
Total cost	100	100
Number of good items	89	95
Cost per item	1.12	1.05

create demand for even higher standards in the competitive market place. Within the organisation, process improvements have direct impact on costs and also show feedback as the habit of continual development is self-reinforcing. Lastly, the increased profits both provide the funds for, and justify policies devoted to, quality improvement.

Managers in Japanese firms have recognised these interactions since the 1950s.[11] It may be difficult, initially, to accept that improving quality will lead to improved productivity but the fewer delays, mistakes and rework more than pay for themselves in terms of rises in net output.

Deming used a simple example to make the point.[12] He referred to a production line running with 11% defective output, a level that the management was unaware of. The line was well controlled, showing consistent performance over time. The main cause of the defects was that both operators and inspectors did not understand sufficiently the kind of work that was acceptable or unacceptable. To them, 11% was normal. The manager and two supervisors made a special study and, in seven weeks, came up with a practical definition of work standards. They displayed this for everyone to see. Defects fell to 5%. The corresponding benefits, shown in Table 16.2, were achieved at very little cost. Productivity rose 6% and, as Deming noted, 'Customer happier. Everybody happier.'

Defects are not free. Someone is paid to make them, resources are used and, as Deming's example shows, opportunities of making saleable products are lost. There is a danger if this argument is overstressed. Problems are not always so serious that, in Crosby's words, *quality is free*.[13] We should recognise that there are many operational situations where some improvement in quality will bring reduced operating costs, so much so that there will be nett gains to the organisation.

Service quality

Service operations often echo the manufacturing line of Deming's case. Quality standards are ill defined and consequently difficult to implement. At the same time, their effect can be critical in winning and holding on to customers. As cost pressure reduces the firm's service-offering capacity, so competitive forces and the experience of good quality intensify demands, as in Figure 16.1. The solution is not to spend more and do more but to be more effective. Quality must be seen through the eyes of the customer who only recognises what he or she *gets out* of the service process, not what the firm *puts in*.

Why provide quality service? There are good reasons. The satisfied customer will not only do more business in the future but will recommend the firm to others. The *dissatisfied* customer will not only reduce profitability directly but also will deter new customers. In addition to the effects in customers, poor service is demoralising for staff. They spend time coping with complaints and are

Table 16.3 Reasons for quitting

Upset at treatment	68%
Become dissatisfied	14%
Move to competitors	9%
Find substitutes	5%
Move away	3%
Die	1%

frustrated when nothing seems to be done to relieve them. Lister referred to data on the effects of poor service.[14] Depending on the industry:

- For each complaint there may be 26 unresolved problems.
- Of those who do complain, between 50% and 70% will do business again if their complaints are handled effectively.
- Dissatisfied customers will tell between 10 and 20 people whereas satisfied customers tell between three and five.
- Customers stop doing business for the reasons shown in Table 16.3.

The importance of quality is to recognise that, although '. . . everyone is doing his best,' the 'best efforts are not sufficient.'[15] Without leadership focused on consistently improving quality, these best efforts cause a random walk; such a walk takes you from your starting point an unknown direction and distance.

16.2.3 Costs of quality

The *costs of quality* include those flowing from poor quality as well as the efforts taken to prevent defects. We can split them into three categories, failure, appraisal and prevention as set out in the following:

- *Failure.* This category includes failures that occur within the process and those that occur, or become apparent, after the product is supplied to the customer. In both cases, failure means that the product has not reached intended standards.
  Internal failure costs include:
  - costs of producing items scrapped or downgraded to be sold as second quality
  - costs of rectification of defects to raise items to the specified standard
  - waste of time and materials incurred at all stages including design and planning as well as manufacture and supply
  - re-inspection and investigation of causes.
  External failure costs include:
  - repair, extra servicing and replacement under warranty
  - extra handling of returned items
  - loss of goodwill through any of these and customers' complaints in general
  - consequential losses risking litigation and damages
  - financial compensation paid to customers outside litigation
  - further inspection, investigation and administration.
- *Appraisal.* This group of costs relates to the assessment of all incoming materials, components and services and all processes within the organisation's value chain to ensure achievement of standards:

- inspection of all materials whether bought in or produced by intermediate processes
- final inspection of products and services
- quality audits to assess whether the quality control system is operating satisfactorily
- vendor rating, part of which is involves a quality audit of suppliers' standards and procedures
- equipment and processes explicitly devoted to inspection
- the costs of quality appraisal, control systems and organisation.

■ *Prevention.* Prevention costs refer to the investments made in quality before production begins. They relate to the setting up and maintenance of processes aimed at preventing failures while also limiting appraisal costs. Frequently called quality assurance, the prevention costs cover:
- identification of customer requirements for quality and producing relevant specifications to cover all components, assemblies and services
- creating the system to optimise the balance between prevention, appraisal and failure costs
- time and effort required to build in quality to all products. The cost of quality research, good design and prototyping is included
- training of all staff to appreciate their own contribution to quality, especially failure prevention
- administration of quality programmes.

Exercise 16.3 Can you identify examples of these costs in the McDonald's case study?

As explained earlier, the failure to control quality results in extra costs. Put another way, the failure to plan and manage quality means too much expenditure on the quality costs listed above. Almost certainly, the excess will lie in the *failure* category. Gador quotes the experience of Tennant, the world's largest manufacturer of floor sweepers and scrubbers.[16]

A steering committee of six senior managers was set up to redirect corporate culture towards quality and productivity. As shown in Figure 16.2, the change resulted in a substantial reduction in quality costs and a shift in the balance of these costs towards prevention and away from correction.

This is an example of a more general relationship between the ability to match quality to customers' expectations and the direct quality costs. This is shown in Figure 16.3. Where the quality capability is low, failure costs are high and dominate the total. With improving capability, both failure and appraisal costs can be cut, resulting in better performance overall. The change takes time and the response is itself dynamic. Consequently, the organisation should not seek a stable optimum position. The costs of quality should continue to fall as it learns new approaches within an ever more exacting environment.

The two main thrusts of a quality plan are, therefore, prevention (quality assurance) and appraisal (inspection and control). Clearly, we should avoid the costs of failure. Such a policy is called the ZD or zero defects policy. However, the cost of avoiding *all failures* may be prohibitive and the technology to do so may not be available. Despite all efforts, if failures occur, the organisation should make an

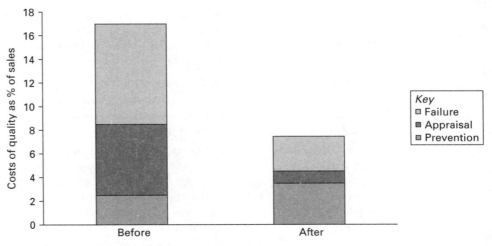

Figure 16.2 Improving quality costs at Tennant

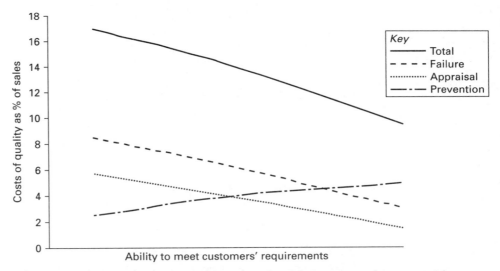

Figure 16.3 Quality costs fall as the organisation becomes more capable

effective response. This is especially true if the problem becomes known after supply to the customer.

16.2.4 Quality and the control model

Quality runs through the whole production process. The need for integration becomes more apparent as organisations learn to prevent failures and incorporate this learning into standard procedures. Shifting to prevention is a shift towards feedforward control as it implies that getting the inputs to each stage right will have a significant effect on their outcomes. Choosing the appropriate form of control is not only relevant to the timing of interventions but also has an effect on employee motivation. Finished product inspection has an important function, yet if it is separated from operators and staffed by a special group, the former will regard it as a burden restricting their ability to earn bonuses.

In the quality system, we see all three forms of control at work:

- *Feedforward quality control.* This covers all the inputs to the production process, from materials and components, whose standards are measured by agreed means, to design, specification and planning processes whose effectiveness has such a great impact on outcomes.

- *Concurrent quality control.* Covering the monitoring and continual adjustment of work as it takes place, concurrent control is needed to ensure that defective parts are never passed on to the next stage. Tools of quality management (see Chapter 17) and recognised standards come into use here.

  While being concerned with monitoring work 'as it happens', prudent managers will focus their efforts at points where defects and rework make a substantial difference. Adopting ideas from optimised production technology in Chapter 12, it is best to inspect as follows:

  - *Before*: costly operations; operations on expensive or sensitive machines; operations that temporarily disguise defects; irreversible assembly or installation; storage.
  - *After*: operations with high defect risk; process sequences where inspection can easily be included as the last step.

- *Feedback quality control.* Inspecting the quality of finished products is carried out by all prudent organisations. Feedback data should be drawn from more sources, however. These include orders for spares, investigation of all complaints and product returns, debriefing of the sales force, studies of products in use, and evidence of brand loyalty (or the lack of it).

16.2.5 Who controls quality?

The impact of production technology

It is unfortunate that effects of some production technologies run counter to the desire to mobilise all employees in quality improvement. The deskilling of work, a process that ran alongside the development of both mass production lines and mass service operations, changed the approach to quality. When managers focused on inspection as the most important means of ensuring quality output, they faced two adverse outcomes. First, the presence of the inspectors themselves made the production workers less interested in building quality into their own work and debating the issue with colleagues. The fact that the role of inspector was often a promoted grade only reinforced the alienation. Second, the inspection task began to be surrounded with its own mystique. Staff in the 'inspection department' wore white coats to emphasise the scientific nature of their roles. They used special equipment to assess quality and their analysis and reports used the technical language of statistical process control. The precision measuring equipment had, of course, to be housed in a separate room. In service operations, inspectors would require separate access to customers or other means of observing the service delivery activity. Arriving *incognito* became normal practice.

The coercive nature of inspection often reflected the lack of trust between managers and workers. Beynon quotes a senior shop steward at Ford's Merseyside plant shortly after production had started in the 1960s. Referring to supervisors who had been transferred from the main plant at Dagenham, the steward said, 'They thought they could treat us like dirt, them. We were just dirty scousers who'd crawled in off the docks out of the cold. We'd never even seen a car plant before and these sods had been inside one since they were knee high.'[17] Similarly, in France of the 1950s and 1960s, immigrants obtained the dirtiest jobs in industries such as car assembly. Etcherelli has a supervisor, indicating Algerian track workers, emphasise to an inspector, 'Listen, you are here to control *their* work.'[18]

Specialised, efficient and even necessary as these inspection methods may be, organisations have come to recognise the illogicality of separating the responsibilities of doing a task and taking care of its quality. Contrast the examples we have just seen with the long periods of training and team building that typified the start-up of the new United Kingdom car plants of Honda, Nissan and Toyota.

Other process technologies

The separation of quality responsibility from operating tasks has been less of a problem in job shops, process plants and professional service. Job shops and professional service maintain the intimate relationship between the individual provider and the output and it is natural that quality is built into the process. Continuous process plants have quality embedded in the work in a different way. It comes from the design of the plant itself and it could be said that all staff are, in effect, quality controllers. These points are drawn together in Table 16.4, which brings out the difficulties of delivering quality in key sections of business and industry, namely mass production and mass service.

Table 16.4 Process technology and responsibility for quality

	Technology	Relationship between task and person	Who is responsible for quality?
Intermittent manufacture	Unit and small batch (project and job shop)	Integrated in skills and experience of the worker	Mainly the person who carries out each step of the process
Repetitive manufacture	Large batch and mass	Deskilling and lack of training mean the individual avoids responsibility for most aspects of the job	The employee is responsible in theory, yet lack of involvement and inability to trace problems back to the individual mean reliance on inspectors and quality control systems
	Continuous	Integrated into process and plant design	The same person or group is responsible for all aspects of output which cannot be separated
Personal service	Professional service	Provider, customer and task closely linked	Professional ethos emphasises personal responsibility
	Mass service	Frequent deskilling, lack of training and low customer expectations	Inspectors and supervisors faced with external failures and customers 'voting with their feet'

16.3 Sources of quality ideas

16.3.1 Leaders in attitude change

Perhaps more than in other fields of management, the move of quality to the top of the operations agenda has been associated with the names of experts. The quality 'gurus' have moulded the attitudes of a generation of managers. Interest in quality as a competitive weapon took root in the West with the tide of imports of Japanese consumer products. The ideas then spread from the factory into all organisations from service businesses and non-profit organisations to government operations and administration. We shall pick out a few names of advocates of this slow process.

W. Edwards Deming

In the late 1930s, Deming was responsible for mathematics and sampling at the United States Bureau of Census. His methods of statistical control achieved great improvements in the productivity and quality of the 1940 census. This work led to invitations to train industrialists and military personnel and he worked with many thousands of US military engineers and technicians to improve quality. In 1947, he was in Japan with the government of occupation to prepare a census there. At that time, the Japanese business community became so impressed by the standards of American military equipment that it invited Deming, in 1950, to advise on industrial recovery. While Deming based his work on advanced statistical methods, his contribution lay in presenting the ideas in a simple way. The results were both impressive and influential, so much so that eventually the Deming prize was created. It remains Japan's leading quality prize.

Deming's main argument against traditional quality control was that it focused on the product rather than the process. Keeping down the number of delivered defective products typically meant high expenditure on inspection and rework and, in any case, many defects slipped through. Deming advocated the use of statistics to measure process variability, which was the chief culprit of poor quality. He then argued for continual investigation and fine-tuning to improve the production system incrementally. He proposed a framework for this continuous improvement, the PDCA cycle, which we shall return to in a later section. Participation of everyone in the process was, at the time, a revolutionary notion.

It was not until the early 1980s that Deming's work was recognised in his own country. He spent the last part of his life spreading his message to large audiences throughout the United States and setting up the Deming Institute, in 1993, to continue his work.[19] He died the same year, at the age of 93.

Kaoru Ishikawa

A professor at the University of Tokyo, Ishikawa advocated quality ideas before the Second World War. He founded the Union of Japanese Scientists and Engineers, which became the focus of Japan's quality developments as its economy recovered. The UJSE was responsible for Deming's 1950 invitation. Ishikawa advocated the notion of customers being both internal and external to the organisation and popularised the fishbone diagram as a problem investigation tool as well as other techniques.

Ishikawa saw that western management practices could not be grafted on to Japanese habits. He was a pioneer of quality circles, which emphasised the role of the group in working and learning. His first circles were at Nippon Telegraph and Cable in 1962; by 1978, there were more than one million quality circles in Japanese manufacturing industry.

Joseph M. Juran

Like Deming, Juran's background was in statistics. He also had strong influence on Japanese managers, being linked to Ishikawa's UJSE. Many Japanese workers were illiterate, this problem being a serious hindrance to the introduction of quality processes. Juran took advantage of this situation. Large businesses had already started 'reading circles' led by supervisors and others with the necessary skills. Juran had his ideas published in forms suitable for learning materials for these groups. The pamphlets were even sold through newspaper kiosks. For the reading circle using Juran's material, it was a short step to the quality circle.

In 1979, Juran founded a training consultancy, the Juran Institute,[20] and through this, spread his ideas about partnerships and teamwork, internal customers, problem-solving techniques and application of Pareto analysis to quality issues. He was concerned about fitting quality improvement programmes into a company's current strategies and plans to minimise the risk of rejection. For him, quality was *fitness for purpose*, a wider definition than conformance to specification, which he regarded as very limiting. In this approach, he differed from Deming's more conservative adherence to the idea of matching specifications. Like Deming, however, Juran continued to speak on quality into his nineties.

Genichi Taguchi

In 1989, Taguchi was honoured with the award of MITI's Purple Ribbon from the Emperor of Japan for his contribution to the development of industrial standards in that country. His strength has been in the application of statistical methods, not to quality control where they had already found wide application, but to improving products and processes. He applied methods in novel ways to: making products less sensitive to variations in their components and in the environment in which they are made; improving reliability; and improving testing procedures. A family of techniques, called 'Taguchi methods' has grown up. Yet Taguchi himself did not like the use of the term, especially when it was used to describe standard statistical methods. Moreover, while many acknowledge his contribution to the engineering design of experiments, they criticise his use of statistics as being inefficient and cumbersome.[21] We shall refer to Taguchi methods in Chapter 17.

Philip B. Crosby

Author of *Quality is Free*, Crosby's career as a quality advocate grew from his experience as a manger in ITT where he developed the total quality management programme. With credibility founded on his experience and well-documented examples of uncovering the costs of waste, scrap and rework, Crosby has become well known in the field. He argues that *getting it right first time* is an achievable goal. This zero defects strategy is important because the costs of poor quality are seriously underestimated.

ZD is part of the 'four essentials' of quality management:

- Quality is conformance to requirements. To Crosby, either a product conforms or it does not. There is no such concept as 'good' quality and quality has nothing to do with notions such as elegance.
- Prevention is the route to achieve conformance, not appraisal.
- Zero defects is the only acceptable performance standard.
- Quality is assessed by the cost of non-conformance.

Compared with the work of the other authorities just described, Crosby's change programme is more behavioural. It stresses management and organisational processes rather than the application of statistical methods. While this enables a fit with current cultures and hierarchies it gives little detail of the practical tools of analysis that are essential in quality improvement.

16.3.2 The emergence of standards

International trade has implications for quality standards. Standards, as Crosby argued, are communications. They pass between customers and suppliers to convey information about the clients' needs summarised in conventional form. The European Union made harmonisation of standards one of the main planks of its construction of the single market.

Product standards

Product standards have existed ever since the creation of assay offices to ensure that gold was not being alloyed with other metals by unscrupulous traders. Gradually, the British Standards Institute (BSI) along with parallel organisations, such as Deutsche Industrie-normen (DIN) and the American National Standards Institute (ANSI), have developed product standards covering items from reinforced concrete and rolled steel sections to cables and thread. Table 16.5 gives a small extract from one of the early British Standard specifications, for steel I-beams. In its many tables and multiple editions, BS 4 set out the dimensions of standard steel sections that could be used by engineers to select and specify beams to use in their designs. Standardisation in specification and manufacture reduced design time for engineers, stimulated a competitive market and enabled the more efficient producers to gain economies of scale.

Industry standards and norms have developed along other paths. These include: industry agreements, such as the emerging specifications for digital television; the success of a leading design or brand, such as the personal computer; or almost by chance, as evidenced by the dimensions of wallpaper, cloth, railway track and vinyl records. Nowadays, many product standards are backed by statute, often at the international level. There are many EU regulations covering product specifications from the strength of vehicle seat belts to the noise emitted by domestic lawn mowers.

Table 16.5 Extract from I-beams, BS 4 (1932)

Depth × breadth (in)	Weight per foot (lb)	Area (in²)	Modulus (in⁴)
3 × 3	8.5	2.52	3.81
4 × 1³/₄	5	1.47	3.66
4 × 3	10	2.94	7.79
5 × 3	11	3.26	13.68

Exercise 16.4

What products that you use carry BS, DIN or ANSI codes for some of their features? What benefit do these codes bring to the supplier and to you, the user?

The BSI kitemark and other quality labels are recognised as marks of product quality and safety. Not only must the product regularly pass tests within the standards, but also the supplier must undergo assessment of the process underpinning consistent quality. Despite these advantages, product standards have several drawbacks:

■ *Limited scope.* The time taken to agree standards, and the difficulty of reaching agreement, means that they relate to only to a limited range of the products in general circulation.

■ *Limited applicability to assemblies.* Product standards often apply only to components, or a few features, of assemblies. For instance, standards in domestic equipment usually refer to their electrical safety and not to their performance.

■ *Applied only to some properties of a product.* BS 476, for example, specifies testing methods for fire resistance of building materials. The attachment of this label to a batch of, say, decorative panels will say nothing about their acoustic or other properties.

■ *Complexity.* The multiplicity of standards almost takes away the point of having them. Lacking common standards, many companies and purchasing authorities have felt obliged to issue their own specifications. Government purchasing, especially of military equipment, became subject to standards and conventions such as the 05 standards of the Ministry of Defence and NATO's Allied Quality Assurance Publication.

Since many items of military hardware were very complex and had to have quality built into every component, defence procurement authorities required suppliers to have their manufacturing processes open to inspection. Indeed, when small companies manufactured supplies for the MoD, an external inspector had to observe every stage. From the frustration, confusion and costs of this system, and the burgeoning number of standards in the civil sector, grew a new approach, concentrating on the processes themselves.

Process standards

The first major process standard, BS 5750 was published in the United Kingdom in 1979. It responded to the need to externally validate those many situations

BOX 16.3 **Benefits of quality management registration**

Internal:

- Clearly defined responsibilities.
- Procedures form a point of reference for all staff.
- Reduced costs of failure.
- Strengthened morale and motivation.

External:

- Enhanced marketability to customers buying only from registered suppliers.
- Greater customer confidence.
- Enhanced image and reputation.

where product certification was not practicable. A national standard usable by organisations of all sizes, it was built around basic quality disciplines. It ensured that procedures could consistently meet the specifications set out by the company. Quality in every process had to be evidenced with relevant documentation. Compliance with the provisions of the standard, validated by an inspection organised by the British Standards Institute, led to certification and an inclusion in the *QA Register*.[22] Unannounced checks were made up to four times a year.

Recognising the benefits of BS 5750, the International Standards Organisation, ISO, adopted it as the core of the first version of ISO 9000 in 1987. Its formal title BS EN ISO 9000 identifies it as the national, European and international quality process standard.

At first, some companies found the registration effort very onerous. Yet, certification spread. By 1998, 127,000 organisations had joined, with 54,000 in the United Kingdom.[23] The need to assure the quality of process inputs meant that companies began to require registration as a condition of joining lists of approved suppliers. International sourcing was facilitated by the common approach. Nowadays, many recognise the range of benefits listed in Box 16.3.[24]

Experience of ISO 9000

Committees of the International Standards Organisation approve amendment to all standards and undertake major reviews at intervals of about five years. Experience with the 1987 and 1994 versions identified several deficiencies. These were:

- *Weak links between product and process standards*. Assessors focused on validating internal procedures according to standards set by the company. The source of these standards was not questioned. Moving products from the centre of the stage was intended to promote both widespread registration and innovation. In taking this approach, however, the ISO 9000 label did not guarantee any particular product. Makers of lead balloons could be certified as long as they make them consistently according to the procedures declared during the registration process.

- *Narrow definition*. By fastening its attention on the consistency of the supply process in achieving its own product standards, ISO 9000 ignored those other dimensions of customer satisfaction that many would include in a broader definition of quality. Possibilities are speed of response, customisation and continuous improvement. The service element of manufacture, that is the extra dimension that can be given along with the product, is very important in achieving customer satisfaction.

- *Universality meant average.* Through establishing norms achievable by a wide range of organisations, the excellent standards of leading companies were not affected. Apart from the formal recognition, ISO 9000 was valuable to neither them nor their customers. They simply registered and continued unchanged. Furthermore, small and medium companies were pressed into creating what they perceived as excessively complex procedures. Following a meeting of the European Foundation for Quality Management, Dickson reported on 'The fuss over European-wide certification – notably complaints by small and medium-sized suppliers about the time and money spent on acquiring the quality standard ISO 9000 to appease their demanding customers.'[25]

- *Improvement.* The universal approach looked for achievement of standards but said little about how these standards were to be raised. Lessons from the best companies, however, were that standards of themselves did not lead to good and improving quality and gave no guide as to where any changes should be made.

16.3.3 The ISO 9000: 2000 series

Responding to such comments, new versions of ISO 9000 were published in 2000. There are three main documents:

- ISO 9001 specifies a quality management system for use internally by an organisation, or for certification, or as the basis of contracts with customers.

- ISO 9004 offers guidance on the wider objectives of a quality management system, especially for continual improvement. It is not used for certification or contracts but is for those organisations that want to go beyond the requirements of ISO 9001.

- ISO 9000 provides an introduction and vocabulary.[26]

We can see that registration is achieved using ISO 9001. A summary of its main requirements appears in Box 16.4.

Convergence of approaches

In its stress on two themes, customer focus and continual improvement, the ISO 9000 series presents a model of total quality management. Figure 16.4[28] shows how the requirements of Box 16.4 are set out as a transformation process. The process converts customer requirements into both products and customer satisfaction. There are two control loops. First, we see the control *within* the quality management system, ensuring that defined quality standards are achieved all the time. Second, we see the wider loop, highlighting the importance of review and continual improvement. This second loop passes beyond the first system because it involves change; it interacts with all aspects of managing the organisation.

BOX 16.4 **Main provisions of ISO 9001: 2000**[27]

- *Quality management system.* Registered organisations are required to 'establish, document, implement and maintain a quality management system and continually improve its effectiveness'.

- *Management responsibility.* 'Top management shall provide evidence of its commitment to . . . the quality management system.' To achieve this they should establish a clear quality policy with focus on customer satisfaction, and plan, organise, communicate and review performance.

- *Resource management.* The competence of staff shall be maintained together with infrastructure and the work environment to assure quality in the products.

- *Product/service realisation.* Design and development of all products should centre on meeting customers' requirements along with standards set by regulations. Purchasing should ensure that inputs conform to specified requirements and their origins can be traced.

- *Measurement, analysis and improvement.* Management should 'plan and implement the monitoring, measurement, analysis and improvements processes' needed to establish conformity, ensure that the quality system is effective and continually improve the system.

The relationship among these elements is summarised in Figure 16.4.

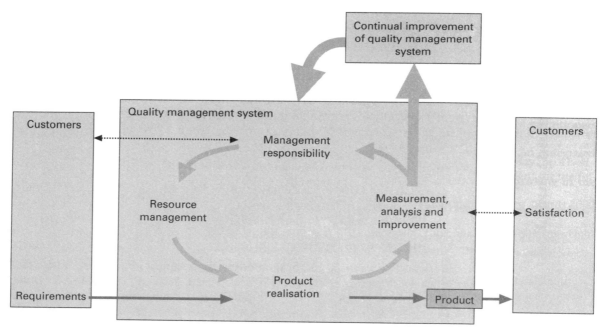

Figure 16.4 Process-based quality management system

BOX 16.5 **The 9 elements of the EFQM Excellence Model**

Enablers:

- Leadership
- People
- Policy and strategy
- Partnership and resources
- Processes

Results:

- People results
- Customer results
- Society results
- Key performance results

Each criterion has a detailed definition and a set of sub-criteria to enable detailed assessment.

Exercise 16.5   Match the stages of the ISO process model to the control models introduced in 4.21.

The broadening of quality ideas beyond process standardisation has led to convergence among sponsoring organisations. The European Foundation for Quality Management[29] was established in 1988 by 14 leading businesses. It adopted its 'excellence model' as a framework based on nine criteria. Five are 'enablers', representing what an organisation does, and four are 'results', what it achieves. They are listed in Box 16.5.

Promoting quality through awards

By including society results among its criteria, the EFQM model acknowledges how improved quality benefits more people than the parties to the immediate transaction. This perspective is also present in ISO 9004, where the broader 'interested parties' replace the 'customers' of Figure 16.4. Having recognised the benefits, governments and business organisations have made quality a plank of industrial policy and have sponsored awards both to promote interest and disseminate best practice.

Among the best known awards are the European Quality Award (based on the EFQM model) and, in the United States, the Baldrige Award. Both focus on customer satisfaction and quality improvement and results are disseminated widely. The Deming Prize is narrower, stressing problem prevention using statistical methods.[30] There are also many industry and company honours; the Sweeney award, offered among the suppliers of McDonald's, was noted in the opening case.

16.4 Total quality management

16.4.1 TQM defined

In an earlier section, we saw the many and varied definitions of quality that are in use. Total quality management also has a number of interpretations. This divergence is underpinned by the fact that many advocates are consultants anxious to advocate their own line or nuance. In essence, TQM brings together the ideas we have covered so far in this chapter and links them to detailed methods and techniques that we shall cover in Chapter 17. In that sense, TQM is a philosophy of quality that links policy and operational practice. The need for quality products in the competitive market place is clear. Sometimes lacking, however, is the setting of appropriate organisational goals and the mobilisation of all members to commit themselves to achieving them.

Of the three elements of TQM:

- *total* suggests wholehearted commitment of everyone in the organisation

- *quality* means, following Juran or Crosby, continuously meeting customers' requirements

- *management* implies an active process led from the top.

For our discussion, therefore, we shall use the following definition:

> **Total quality management is a process of involving everyone in an organisation in continuously improving products and processes to achieve, on every occasion, quality that satisfies customers' needs.**

Key implications of this definition are:

- involving everyone in the company through teamwork, trust and empowerment
- continuous improvement
- identification of customers and their needs, and then focusing on them
- using tools and techniques jointly to resolve quality problems.

In the next sections, we shall discuss these items in more detail.

16.4.2 Teamwork, trust and empowerment

The holistic approach of TQM distinguishes it from conventional approaches where the responsibility is assigned to a 'quality department'. For some, it even goes beyond the quality circle (see Box 16.6) which can be seen as a means of management delegating some quality responsibilities while retaining most of the control. Indeed, Japanese workers sometimes see QCs as coercive. The holistic goal is commitment and sharing of the quality issue among all employees so that the contribution of each is both recognised and influential.

Empowerment can only occur when people are well trained, given access to relevant information, know and use the best techniques, are involved in the decisions and receive appropriate rewards. Most quality problems relate to materials,

BOX 16.6 Quality circles

Quality circles have made major contributions to the success of Japanese companies. Conventionally, staff are organised into groups of, say, 6 to 12. Training and guidance in the concepts of quality and problem-solving techniques are given by middle managers. The group meets regularly to select problems to work on, and then analyse and solve them. It sets its own targets, not only for quality improvement but also for related issues such as production flow, planned maintenance, working conditions and safety.

Among many variants, QCs may:

- have people from one or several work groups
- have people from one or several levels in the organisation
- have a nominated leader or decide to rotate the leadership role
- be stimulated by a scheme that rewards suggestions through financial incentives.

From the first QC in Japan in 1962, the number has expanded to, perhaps, 100,000 registered with the Union of Japanese Scientists and Engineers. (There are an estimated 1,000,000 further circles not formally recorded.) In 1990 Yamaha had 700 circles, Toyota 6,700 and the medium-sized Toppan Printing 150 among a mere 2,000 workers. More than 13 million Japanese people participate, always voluntarily and usually outside working time. Each QC generates about 50 suggestions a year. The movement is seen as a driving force behind the continuous improvement of products and processes.

The QC fits well into the Japanese organisational culture with its emphasis on the group, as opposed to the individual, its lifetime loyalty (at least in major firms) and lack of serious demarcation of job roles. Although tried in the West with some success, the different context makes the idea difficult to transfer without removing or diluting some of the key principles that make QCs work.

designs, specifications and processes and have little to do with poor employee performance. Yet, these same employees are usually well aware of the shortcomings of the production system and can be invaluable in finding solutions.

16.4.3 Continuous improvement

Many programmes for operational change are based on the notion of restructuring the system and moving it from one state to another. This requires three stages: preparation for change, the change itself and the confirmation of the new arrangement. In contrast, advocates of improvement, or *kaizen*, see striving for quality as an endless journey rather than a trip to a known and fixed destination. Normal behaviour, in this view, is experimentation, adjustment and minor improvement to every detail. If kaizen is accepted, employees expect small developments and do not see them as challenges to existing working practices and relationships. No one is ever quite happy with the status quo.

According to Imai, every person's work comprises two parts, continuation and improvement.[31] The former, which Imai calls maintenance, refers to the current

BOX 16.7 The five principles of *gemba*

1 When an abnormality occurs, go to *gemba* first and right away!
2 Check with *gembutsu*. *Gembutsu*, in Japanese, means something you can touch, such as machine, material, failures, rejects, unsafe conditions etc.
3 Take temporary countermeasures on the spot.
4 Find and remove the root cause.
5 Standardise for recurrence prevention.

work. People must know what they are supposed to be doing and follow these standards and agreements. The second half of everybody's job is improvement. This means finding a better way of doing the job and raising the standard. It happens that people find new ways of doing jobs without raising the standard. Imai argues that this behaviour should be seen as deviation rather than improvement because the key factors of quality, cost and delivery have not been affected. For improvement to take place, the standard must be raised. Kaizen, then, implies continuous challenges to the standards we have in our daily jobs.

Imai noted that most work at shop floor level is directed towards continuation. The role of managers is to take on more responsibility for improvement, with those at the top almost fully engaged in it. Imai suggests a set of questions to act as guide when a problem occurs. Did it happen because:

- There was no standard?
- The present standard was inadequate?
- Staff did not follow the standard?
- Staff were not trained to follow the standard?

When problems arise, the manager's job is to find out what has happened, using these questions. A better standard or method can be worked out. This, in Imai's view, is most important, because standards guide both continuation and improvement. There can be no quality without them. With them, however, recurrence can be prevented and the variability within all processes can be controlled. The history of quality improvement in Japan is the history of standardisation.

Going to *gemba*

Closely associated with this commitment to involvement in the detail of standards and improvement is *gemba*. This means the place where the activity takes place. It can refer to: the shop floor; the customer's offices where a salesperson is calling; the customer's site where an installation is being made; the screen or drawing board where an engineer is working out a design; or the hotel reception area, bedroom, restaurant or sauna. Imai sets out the improvement process based on five *gemba* principles (Box 16.7).[32]

Many solutions can are found during the first two steps. Yet the real solutions are achieved only after the last ones are taken. Otherwise, managers not using the discipline remain fire fighters. The principles have implications for the roles of senior managers. They should be there to remove restraints on *gemba*; that is they must help people lower down the hierarchy to investigate and solve problems without excessive constraints. Since managers are ultimately responsible for everything that happens in *gemba*, they need to stay in touch and become involved when problems arise. Hence the opening maxim, 'Go to *gemba* first and right away!' For Imai, the problem with most managers is that they believe their workplace is their desk.

Exercise 16.6 If not the desk, where is the manager's workplace? Consider the answer using examples that you know.

16.4.4 Being customer centred

We have seen that both Ishikawa and Juran advocated the notion that, in the TQM organisation, everyone has customers. They may be internal or external. Internal customers are other members of the organisation who rely on the next person along the quality chain for inputs to get their work done. Sometimes, people's work can be so interconnected that they are *mutually dependent*, that is each is the other's customer. Whatever the relationship, they are all part of quality chains. When it comes to quality, the internal customer is very much like an external one. The difficulty of the customer's work, and the quality of the output, are strongly affected by the quality of the input.

As for external customers, it is obvious that the TQM company will require *all employees* who deal with them to be committed to satisfying their needs. Being customer focused entails:

- appreciating situations through customers' eyes so that needs are anticipated
- listening to customers, especially the detail of what they want
- understanding possible ways of satisfying customers' wishes
- providing the appropriate response.

Box 16.8 illustrates how leadership can become negative. The tale represents customer service failure.[33] The manager puts aside the question of who is responsible

BOX 16.8 The blaming trap

A senior railway manager once told me: 'The trouble for the railways is that the people in the organisation who deal with the public are the people at the bottom.' Without too much reflection, I noted his statement and we went on to another point. Later, I saw the serious implications of the assertion. The critical points of contact between travellers and railway staff are not at ticket sales or general enquiries but when a passenger has a problem or a complaint. Then, the manager is implying, 'the sort of people we employ' on the shop floor (porters, train crew and so on) are ill equipped to handle the problems. If only the complaints were immediately handled by intelligent and articulate staff (like the manager himself) passengers would be better satisfied.

for the problems. Then the argument ignores the impossibility, in a mass service organisation, of a small elite of managers dealing with all customers in the way suggested. The TQM business acknowledges that everyone contacts customers. Rather than criticise the inadequacy of recruits, it develops its people to achieve high standards. This means leadership, training, standards and rewards.

Retailing can teach a great deal about customer orientation for the whole organisation. Writing on excellence, Peters likened retail, in the classroom or the showroom, to a performance art. True, to locate, build and stock a store, or to organise a management seminar, require skills from purchasing to project management. Yet, when everything is in place, and the shop opens or the class begins, success is down to personal delivery. Just as there are good and bad actors and actresses, so there are good and bad shopkeepers, receptionists, ticket collectors and teachers. Being good means giving the customer the best of what they want every day. Peters wrote 'You are the absolute master, ruler, tsar. You alone bring that space, or those five restaurant tables, to life. Ninnies or saints, fearful or fearless, management can't hold you back.'[34]

16.4.5 Tools and techniques

We shall investigate in Chapter 17 the more important tools for solving quality problems. Imai warns, however, that too much stress can be laid on the need to learn the techniques.[35] He believes that most quality problems can be resolved by simple steps using common sense. Imai's procedures for putting common sense into practice are:

- *Go to gemba.* This is the most important rule.
- *Standardisation.* Standards are the basis of both continuing activity and improvement. If there are no standards, they should be introduced. If the standards are failing, they should be modified.
- *Don't get it, don't make it, and don't send it.* Based on the premise that quality is everyone's job, one should be determined not to receive rejects, create them or pass them on.
- *Speak with data.* Collecting data is the starting point of analysis. People should be prepared to measure before changing anything.
- *Ask why.* Problem solving means asking why as often as necessary to find the root cause. Only then can the problems be eradicated.

Others argue that quality cannot be sustained without quality measurement techniques. This is undoubtedly true, but the emphasis in the TQM organisation is less on the measurement and more on the use of appropriate measures to support continuous improvement. Rather than use detailed recording and trend analysis at the end of the production process, it may be much more effective to enable a process worker to take some simple measurements earlier on and make adjustments immediately if such action were necessary. Matching the complexity of quality tools with the training and experience of the users is a vital part of involving people at all levels. The tools are clearly a necessary but not sufficient basis for a TQM programme.

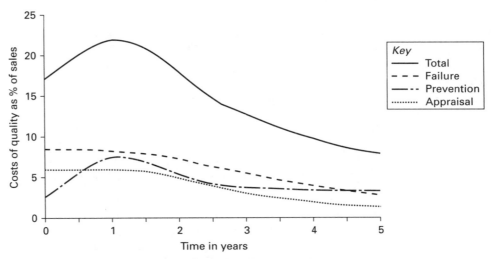

Figure 16.5 Cash flow associated with quality investment

16.4.6 **Limitations of TQM**

At its core, total quality management is a simple idea. The search for competitive advantage through quality is best sustained by applying basic ideas right across the organisation. Yet to the simplicity have been added a great deal of jargon and extra techniques that take the focus off quality. The large firms may register because to do so is easy; the small may feel forced to do so and grumble about the costs of consultants and the appraisal process itself. European firms may not have committed themselves to TQM as much as Japanese and, it appears, North American ones. We can examine this further by looking at costs and people.

Costs

When examining the costs of quality and changing the balance among them earlier in this chapter, we came across the idea that quality programmes would eventually pay for themselves. 'Quality is free' because the total costs of prevention are less than the costs of failure. This begs two questions. First, what happens in the firm once it has cut its costs of failure to a more moderate level? Usually, this will be the easy part of the improvement and, from then on, gains will become more difficult to come by. Further quality developments may be difficult to justify on financial terms, especially when there may be other problems on the managerial agenda. Second, quality programmes are an investment. As with other development programmes, there is an additional short-term cost before the benefits start to flow. Figure 16.5, which draws on Figure 16.3, shows how the quality spending may be changed during a 5-year development programme.

The graph tracks cash flow to cover all spending, whether treated as expenses or as investment. Note how, over the first two years, there will be a bulge in prevention spending before it settles to a new level higher than before. This is mainly related to reorganisation and training. The benefits come after the peak in investment in prevention. Failure costs reduce as the programme begins to take effect and, as confidence in the new system rises, the resources put into appraisal systems can be cut.

Human resources

Dawson sounds several warnings when discussing changes in technical and social processes during the introduction of a TQM programme.[36] He first points out that TQM is not a panacea. Many plants have problems that need to be resolved, either as a prerequisite of a quality programme or separately from it. Further points concern social issues:

- There may be problems within the work groups during the transition. To participate in TQM, through quality circles for example, is voluntary. Yet, to work under the restructured operating system is mandatory. Those employees who, because of pre-existing problems, find it impossible to join in will not support the change. The TQM development may, therefore, make current social tensions worse.

- Employee involvement may be difficult to mobilise at first and may have to be considered as an eventual objective. Cultural, language and structural constraints create barriers:
  - *Culture and language.* Dawson quotes a Pirelli plant in Adelaide, Australia, where there were language differences among shop floor workers, many of whom were recent immigrants. These hindered the deep levels of communication which cooperation requires, a problem that would not arise in the remarkable homogeneity of Japanese society.
  - *Structure.* The relevant structures at shop floor level include plant layout and the shift system. Both may hinder participation in TQM, either through physical or temporal separation of individuals and groups. In such circumstances, workers will have grown used to relying on supervisors for co-ordination and they are likely to see TQM in the same light. Night shift workers, fewer than day staff, often perceive themselves as being independent of management and are reluctant to commit themselves to personal involvement.

- Employee ability may be limited, not only by cultural and language diversity but by general levels of education. Dawson comments that the value of TQM techniques, especially statistics, had been exaggerated. Groups used brainstorming methods at first but relied on one or two members or co-ordinators to produce simple graphical material. A further problem for those left out of the discussions by such barriers was that they were expected to go along with the decisions that were made.

In a wider context, it may appear that the emphasis on personal and group development, backed up by training, would provide great opportunities for the development of personnel policies and practices generally. Yet, personnel functions are not heavily involved. TQM accomplishment is very much an operations activity, often established under a project leader who is a line manager. Therefore, the stress will be on business results rather than long-term development of employees.

16.4.7 Deming's contribution to the management of quality

Paramount among the developers of quality principles was Deming, whose brief biography appears in Section 16.3.1. Although he did not invent the term TQM, Deming's teachings covered the full range of issues from quality practice to commitment and top management support. In the context of the 1950s, where narrow scientific management was strongly adhered to in the best companies, the ideas were revolutionary. Some of them were so challenging to existing management attitudes that it is not surprising that Deming was ignored for so long. Nowadays, however, many have become incorporated in conventional management training and practice. To us they seem less revolutionary and rather quaint. In proposing his *14 points*, Deming emphasised that they are the permanent obligations of top management, none of which is ever completely fulfilled. The points are set out, with comments, in Box 16.9.[37]

Deming may have made more progress with a more subtle attack on the backward ways of western management. Yet, in spite of a rather curmudgeonly approach, Deming was eventually listened to because of his experience of Japan and the simple rigour of his problem-solving approach. He pressed for the adoption of informed decision making based on good-quality data. He advocated the plan-do-check-act (PDCA) cycle (Figure 16.6).[38] He called this the *Shewhart cycle* in recognition of the founder of statistical quality control but the Japanese, and others, call it the *Deming cycle*.

In using the PDCA cycle, managers are encouraged to start with small changes about things that are really important. The approach is set in the tradition of research and trial-and-error experimentation. Actions and reflections are grounded in observed data. In this belief in experimentation, Deming is close to Taguchi. The four stages of the continuous PDCA loop are:

- *Plan*. Work out changes based on observed data. Decide whether a pilot experiment is needed and how one is to be conducted.
- *Do*. Make the change or carry out the planned pilot experiment.
- *Check*. Observe the effects of the change or collect the results of the small experiment.
- *Act*. Study the outcomes of the work and establish the lessons to be learned. Confirm the change, or otherwise. Interpret the results of the experiment. Start to plan again.

The cycle is not original. As with many of his ideas, Deming's contribution was to draw them together and apply them both rigorously and vigorously to the quality question.

16.5 Applying quality ideas

The basic process improvement tools of TQM are just some of the techniques applicable in the quality context, either for continuation and control or for improvement. We shall study these in the next chapter. There remain, however, some wider issues concerning the application of 'quality thinking' in different

BOX 16.9 Deming's 14 points

1 *Create constancy of purpose*
Constancy means taking the long-term view; innovate with materials, methods, and services and in all aspects of the business. Fund research, education and equipment of all kinds.

2 *Learn the new philosophy*
Managers must become dissatisfied with current levels of defects, unsuited materials, poor training and management. They must learn to be smart.

3 *Ask for evidence of process control along with incoming parts*
Purchasing managers must learn control methods to include them in supply contracts. Inspection is futile.

4 *Be prepared to reduce the number of suppliers*
Managers should consider the costs of having more than one vendor. If they cut the number, they must trade off quality and price and not just buy based on the cheapest.

5 *Use statistical methods to find out, in any trouble spot, what are the sources of trouble*
Deming asserted that judgement always gives the wrong answer when it comes to finding out where a fault lies. (Here his background in statistics is revealed in the confidence he places in those methods. Note how this contrasts with Imai's reliance on common sense explained earlier.)

6 *Institute modern aids to training on the job*
Deming argued for major changes in training, using statistics to discover whether it would be beneficial. A person fully trained and in control of the task can do no better. If unsatisfactory, the person should be moved.

7 *Improve supervision*
Deming said many supervisors were deplorable. Calling attention to every defect or mistake may be wrong and counterproductive. They should lead and use statistics as aids to improving the production system.

8 *Drive out fear*
Employees may do jobs the wrong way because they are afraid to ask how and why. Security means no fear. Insecure people do not ask questions, report difficulties or discuss with colleagues how to do things better.

9 *Break down barriers between departments*
Bureaucratic barriers hinder achievement of the common goal: customer satisfaction. Deming quotes the case of two suppliers each meeting the specifications for certain components. Yet, the differences between the two sets of supplies imposed heavy costs on the production department. The specification was too loose, a problem not picked up by the bureaucracy because it was not included in the reporting system.

10 *Eliminate numerical goals, slogans, pictures, posters, urging people to increase productivity, sign their work as an autograph etc., so often plastered everywhere in the plant*
Posters such as 'ZERO DEFECTS' do not lead to people doing better jobs. Numerical targets lead to frustration, they simply show managers' lazy attempts to convert their budget promises into shop floor action.

11 *Look carefully at work standards*
Consider whether quotas and numerical targets bring the benefits so often claimed. They encourage people to forget quality. Deming rejected the practice of management by objectives.

12 *Institute a massive training programme for employees in simple but powerful statistical methods*
Deming's belief in statistics as a medium for investigation and communication made him see that it should be part of everyone's training. Further, there should be many experts who can guide the rest.

13 *Institute a vigorous programme for retraining people in new skills*
The programme should match developments in models, processes, materials, machinery, rules and so on.

14 *Create a structure in top management that will push every day on these 13 points*
Since development is everyone's job, leaders should recognise this and take full responsibility for the changes needed.

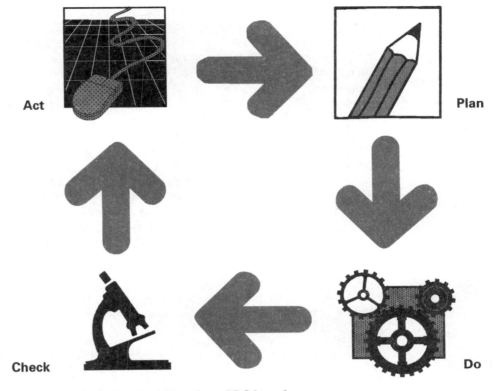

Figure 16.6 The Deming-Shewhart PDCA cycle

settings. These are the special problems associated with service delivery and the integration of the operations function with other business disciplines, especially design.

16.5.1 Quality in the service dimension

We have emphasised that almost all supplier–customer transactions include significant service. The quality of the whole transaction, therefore, is strongly affected by the way the service is provided. Although one could not support the railway manager's attitudes expressed in Box 16.8, one should, nevertheless, recognise that service is vulnerable at its weakest points, the moments of direct interaction with customers. These are the *moments of truth*. In the restaurant, good food can be spoiled by indifferent service, while in the supermarket passing through the checkout can be a positive or negative experience. The TQM service organisation pays attention to four interconnected factors that contribute to quality.

Organisation and staffing for service quality

The nature of the service will, largely, determine the way it is provided. Personal service is delivered in the presence of the customer and with the customer's participation. Otherwise, the isolated service is organised out of contact with the customer who is contacted through the 'front office'. Separation of backroom personnel from customer contact can be a retrograde step if the organisation, for the most part, loses its orientation towards service quality. Maintenance of this orientation can be helped by use of quality circles, training, job rotation and appropriate controls. Matching the needs of service organisations with selection and training of appropriate staff is the first step towards providing good service. It may even be possible to automate the customer contact aspects of the delivery, as in the case of simple banking transactions.

Much service delivery is prone to uncertainty. We tend to forget that even making a small purchase in a shop is an acquired skill. Usually, however, both parties to the transaction are familiar with its usual course and duration. In other service situations, uncertainty can be the result of genuine unpredictability of outcomes or unawareness on behalf of the customer as to what to do. Customers may not know many of the things that service personnel regard as normal. Does one help oneself or wait to be served? Can one sit anywhere? May one make a noise?

Exercise 16.7

I visited the snack bar of a ferry on a Holyhead to Dublin sailing. Having bought tea, I settled at a table in a quiet corner. After a moment, a staff member came over to tell me I should not be sitting there because the area had just been cleaned. I replied that that seemed to be an excellent reason for sitting there and refused to move. I suppose I went down in the log as an 'awkward customer'.

Who was wrong?

Difficulties caused by uninformed customers may result in perception of lower quality not just for them but also for other customers who are disturbed or displaced in some way. Customer 'training', through advertising, announcements, personal guidance and notices, can go a long way to overcoming these difficulties. In other words, not only should it be clear what is on offer, but also when and how it is offered and the best way for the customer to become involved. There is little worse than having a customer expect one quality of service and the firm deliver another. In the spring of 1995, Eurotunnel had launched its *turn-up-and-go* car transit service. Difficulties with train capacity and underestimation of demand, however, meant that, at weekends, long queues formed at the terminal and angry passengers blocked the roads. Eurotunnel was forced to introduce bookings for Saturdays.

The TQM organisation, then, recognises that customer satisfaction depends on matching perception and expectation as closely as possible. We saw in Chapter 9 how important this was in the design of processes where queuing may occur. Yet narrowing the perception–expectation gap is critical in all service situations and requires the commitment of all to achieving it.

The service process

Imai's arguments about standardisation apply equally to manufacture and service. Good management of the service process must include specification of standards

Table 16.6 Hard and soft thinking about service attributes

Hard thinking		Soft thinking	
Minimise variation	*Deviation avoided*	Maximise adaptation	*Be able to respond*
Get it right first time . . .	*. . . without fail!*	Ensure relevance over time	*Make it work for the customer*
Measure attributes	*Assess the facts of the service*	Measure customer experience	*How the service functions*
Zero defects	*No faults at any time*	No breaks	*Do not interrupt the flow of service*
Fitness for purpose	*Build value in*	Ease of application	*Getting value out*
Standards . . .	*. . . and adhere to rules*	Resilience	*Adaptation, renewal*
Uniformity	*Everything the same*	Consistency	*Can provide the customer's needs each time*
Durability	*Product lasts*	Reliability	*Things work*
Cause and effect	*Clear links*	Interactions	*Solutions in complex situations*

to be achieved at all operational stages. Standardisation is crucial in mass service but it is difficult to be so specific when it comes to personal service. In either case, the production thinking of manufacturing may be carried over with unfortunate consequences. Focus on standards and uniformity in the service organisations run the risk of too much attention being paid to delivering the 'hard' aspects of service at the expense of the 'soft'. 'Getting it right first time' is important in service quality but the slogan hardly helps if the business wrongly defines the *it*.

The specification of quality standards in service functions is difficult and tends to concentrate on quantifiable elements, especially the time taken for various stages of delivery or the frequency at which certain tasks are carried out. The non-quantifiable aspects, such as the overall impression of the helpfulness and politeness of the staff, are more difficult to assess although they can be observed by supervisors and monitored using sample surveys. Unfortunately, the latter do not give the detailed immediate feedback needed for concurrent control. Vandermerwe distinguishes between 'hard' and 'soft' capabilities, arguing that customers evaluate the service they receive on what they *get out*, while firms, using conventional quality measurement and control, concentrate on what they *put in*.[39] The contrast between the capabilities is shown in Table 16.6.

Facilities, equipment and materials

Facilities, equipment and materials have differing degrees of importance depending on customer expectations and the nature of the service. In food retailing for example, they are all very important whereas professional advisers make little use of materials and equipment.

Development of information systems has enabled more services to be provided through self-service. In these cases, ergonomics and the study of human–machine interaction should play a significant role in the design of equipment. The quality of such equipment will itself have an impact on the customer's perception of

BOX 16.10 **Customer survey card: P&O European Ferries**

The two-sided comment card uses a combination of yes/no, four-point and open-ended scales to solicit comments on accommodation, catering, bar, service and general points. For example:

Cabin accommodation
Was your cabin ready for you?   Yes   No   (Please circle)

	Excellent	Good	Average	Fair
How was your cabin in terms of cleanliness and maintenance?	☐	☐	☐	☐

Catering

	Excellent	Good	Average	Fair
Quality of the food	☐	☐	☐	☐
Taste of the food	☐	☐	☐	☐
Temperature of the food	☐	☐	☐	☐
Appearance of the food	☐	☐	☐	☐
Choice of the menu	☐	☐	☐	☐
Efficiency of the service	☐	☐	☐	☐
Level of courtesy	☐	☐	☐	☐
Appearance of the catering staff	☐	☐	☐	☐

Any other comment _____

the service package as a whole. Its reliability is critical, as witnessed by any customer who has been let down by a cash machine when trying to obtain £10 for a late-night taxi.

Quality monitoring in services

Effective quality control requires the establishment of clear standards and the ability to measure conformance to these standards. Only then can action be taken to ensure compliance and also decide where standards themselves can be improved. The example of P&O European Ferries, given in Box 16.10, is typical of leading companies. It shows how monitoring of both objective and subjective measures can be carried out. But note that the effectiveness of the audit will depend on its covering characteristics important and relevant to the customer. Furthermore, the way the information from the survey is used will have a strong influence on whether quality levels are maintained and improved. Used as a basis of cooperative problem solving it can do much to advance the cause, but if it is used punitively, or mainly for financial incentives, then the benefits will not be realised.

The question for service quality monitoring is how to combine hard data with the much more difficult soft data. The latter may say a great deal more about the customers' responses to the service. Vandermerwe[40] argues that it is the language of monitoring that has to change. Table 16.7 lists *hard* and *soft* factors to illustrate this point. The aim, for instance, is to evaluate the rapport achieved with each customer rather than measure average satisfactions.

Table 16.7 Assessing hard and soft factors: language contrasts

Hard	Soft
Calculate	Assess
Quantify	Observe
Average	Case specific
Figures	Language
Single level	Multilevel
Static	Directional
Inspect	Reflect
Change	Improve
Schedule	Prioritise
Replicate	Originate
Set routine	Improvise

16.5.2 Design and quality

Successful designers have always recognised customers' needs and devised means of satisfying them through the design and supply process. Many organisations today, however, are unwilling to rely on intuition as the dominant basis for decision making and prefer to apply one or more formal methods. We shall look briefly at formal ways of identifying customer needs and controlling the design process so that these are effectively incorporated into product specifications.

Incorporating customer needs

Customers' needs in relation to quality are difficult to establish. This stems partly from the many definitions in use but also from the inexperience of customers in separating quality from other factors involved in the purchase. In response to these problems, quality function deployment has been developed. It recognises the strategic role of design and integrates design activities which, hitherto, had been independent. These are:

- *Conceptual design.* Finding solutions to satisfy the market demand.

- *Preliminary design.* Giving priorities to design features in isolation from customers.

- *Detailed design.* Detailing the key characteristics that will enable manufacturing to create the product.

- *Process design.* Specifying how the product is to be made.

At the later stages of the sequence, design changes may be required to enable the product to be made and these will necessitate a review of the previous work. It has been estimated that the lack of integration of the stages means that 45% of design time is spent on adjusting to such changes. Further, when it comes to manufacture, 75% of all problems, and 40% of quality problems, are those that have been created during the detailed design phase.[41] When designs are changed early on, the costs can be small; if modifications happen after manufacturing starts, the costs can run into millions.

QFD has been adopted, in various forms, by companies which believe that the extra cost incurred at the 'finding out' stage, and integrating the design process around the results, is more than balanced by the savings by avoiding expensive mistakes later on. The challenge is to transform the attributes of a product that are recognised as important by the customer into characteristics that can be expressed in engineering terms and therefore can be made. The particular QFD factor association procedure uses a special matrix called *the House of Quality*. (See Chapter 17 for details.)

Controlling the design process

In many circumstances and industries, the design process is seen as quite separate to production. Nowhere is this more acutely seen than in building and construction where design is frequently let as a separate contract. Since the cost of design is usually a small proportion of the total project cost, its significance is often ignored. Yet, an increase in design expenditure can often reduce the total life costs, that is the combination of investment, operating and maintenance costs of the building. McGeorge quotes an example where the design costs of a hospital came to 5% of the total. He argued that if more resources had been put in at the design stage, increasing its expenditure to $7^{1}/_{2}$%, other costs could have fallen enough to cut the total outlay by 7%, even allowing for the extra spent on design.[42] The normal practice of awarding design contracts on criteria heavily weighted towards price reduces quality.

Designers have to be flexible as the process they are engaged in is one of learning and interaction with other designers, suppliers, manufacturers and so on. Poor process quality in the design office is one reason for poor eventual product quality. Unless the production of designs and specifications is well controlled, with adjustments recorded and checked, it is unlikely that those who follow can do a good job.

Table 16.8 shows what might happen throughout the engineering design process in three design departments.[43] In the first there is no control, in the second things are improving while the third has a good-quality set of procedures. It is fair to say that only the last would receive accreditation under ISO 9000. The importance of design in the whole quality process makes it inevitable that large sections of both of these standards should be devoted to the control of procedures in this area.

16.5.3 Design, process capability and manufacturability

Another area in which habit and tradition play leading parts is interaction between design and production. In many engineering companies, the designers have considerable shop floor experience and are very familiar with manufacturing capabilities. Yet, when faced with an engineering challenge, the unwise are likely to say, 'The works? They're good, they can make anything.' This enthusiasm needs to be tempered with an awareness of direct costs and the indirect effects of adding complex tasks into a production system that may already be overloaded. This caution is embedded in the notion of *manufacturability*:

> **Manufacturability is a measure of a design's ability to consistently satisfy product goals while being profitable.**[44]

Table 16.8 Changing the way the design process is controlled

Procedure	Department's control of design process		
	No quality	*Improving . . .*	*Good quality*
Requirements specification	Intuition based on experience	Occasional meetings with sales department	Regular interaction between sales and design
Drawing control	Engineer makes sketches and notes for craftsmen to interpret	Supervisor reviews sampled drawings	Regular reviews using multidisciplinary teams
Changes	Verbal instructions	Written notices	Changes to be assessed for impact before approval
Calculations	Handbooks and experience combined	Calculations reviewed by supervisor	CAD systems operated by specialists
Non-conformance control	None	Consultation by production over problems	Reviewed by specialists
Engineering records	Not prepared	Drawings and notes sent to filing	Integral part of organisation's record management procedures
Evaluation by management	Little evaluation from outside department	Management only involved when problems occur	Internal audits to look for improvements in all processes

The product goals referred to in the definition of manufacturability include performance, reliability, availability and quality. Taken together, they are a specification of the conformance to customers' specifications. To understand how designs can satisfy this definition, we need to examine the nature of defects and how they arise.

A defect is the variation of any specified parameter outside the customer specification. Defects occur because the manufacturing process cannot consistently make the product exactly to the design specification. To investigate this we will consider one parameter, a single dimension.

Component with one parameter

Here we refer to a parameter as some measured property of a product that needs to conform to a customer requirement. While we will consider length here, the parameter may have any value, for example, a weight, a colour, a strength, electrical resistance etc. Whatever the material, it is not possible to produce products to an exactly consistent dimension. Furthermore, many substances, such as wood and paper, change continuously after they have been made.

We can note that it is usually the case that items can be measured more accurately than they can be manufactured. Therefore, random variations that occur in all processes can be detected by inspection equipment. To allow for these variations, specifications are usually written in the form, for example, of 600 ± 2mm. Here the ± 2mm is called the *specification width* about the central value of 600mm. How is this value to be determined?

The random variations in parameters usually approximates closely to a normal distribution. The distribution can be described by its mean, μ, and standard

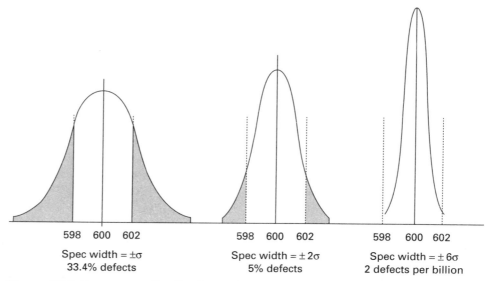

Figure 16.7 **Frequency distributions of dimensions with varying ratios of process capability and specification width**

deviation, σ. One of the properties of the normal distribution is that 16.6% of the values lie more than 1σ above the mean value and a further 16.6% are more than 1σ below the mean value. Therefore, if we produce our product, whose specification width is ±2mm, in a process which happens to create a standard deviation also of 2mm, more than 33% of the output will be defective. These defects are shown as the shaded areas under the first graph of Figure 16.7. This shows the frequencies with which different dimensions occur.

Clearly, two courses of action are available to cut the defect rate. The specification width can be increased or the process can be improved to reduce its variation. A third choice, to check all items and reject the one in three that lie outside the limit would be a last resort.

The normal distribution tails off quickly. For example, while 33.4% of measurements lie outside ±1σ, 5% lie outside ±2σ and only 0.3% lie beyond ±3σ. This effect is shown in Table 16.9, which compares defect rates with the ratio of specification width to process standard deviation. Two cases from the table form the second and third graphs of Figure 16.7 (the heights are not to scale). The second shows the 5% rejects if SW is set at ±2σ and the third shows the much tighter process capability of SW = ±6σ. This last case has often been mentioned as a quality target – the six sigma specification – where, at two items per billion, the zero defects standard has almost been achieved.

It is worth noting that the data in columns 2, 3 and 4 of the table are repetitive and only included to emphasise the effect. For instance, in the sixth data row, 99.99%, 100 defects per million and 10,000 parts per defect are merely different ways of saying the same thing.

Table 16.9 assumes that a defect is defined as any item lying outside the specified range on either side of the central value. That is why each range is expressed as ± SW/σ. In some processes however, defects will only lie to one side

Table 16.9 Effect on defect rates of changes in specification width

SW/σ ±	Yield %	Defects per million parts	Number of parts per defect
2	95.0	50,000	20
2.5	99.0	10,000	100
3	99.7	3,000	333
3.3	99.9	1,000	1,000
3.9	99.99	100	10,000
4.0	99.994	60	16,666
4.4	99.999	10	100,000
4.9	99.9999	1	1,000,000
6	99.9999998	0.002	500,000,000

Table 16.10 Defect rate per thousand: parameters with SW/σ equal to 3

		Parameters			
		1	10	20	40
Parts	1	3	30	59	114
	10	30	260	452	699
	20	59	452	699	910
	40	114	699	910	992

of the value. Then the defect rates will be half of those in the table. Drink dispensing illustrates this point. Serving a little too much is not illegal and customers will not complain. See, however, the consequences for the landlord illustrated in Exercise 16.8.

Exercise 16.8 An automatic beer pump dispenses pints (545ml) with a standard deviation of 2ml. To what volume should the machine be set so that only 1 in 2,000 customers misses a full pint? What are the consequences? What should the landlord do?

Components with many parameters

It is clear that, to achieve very low defect rates, careful attention should be paid to product design and the specification of key dimensions and other parameters. Why is it necessary to aim for such low defect rates? The answer to this question lies in the fact that most products have many parameters specified simultaneously. Such components can quickly show defects.

Suppose our design policy is to make all product specifications with SW equal to ±3σ. Table 16.9 shows that, for one parameter only, the number of good parts will be 99.7%. What if we consider two parameters together? This is a case of joint probability.[45] The overall proportion of good parts will be:

$$0.997 \times 0.997 = 0.994; \text{ that is } 99.4\%$$

In practice, products have many components, each of which has many parameters. Table 16.10 expands the joint probability calculation to show how the combination of components and parameters increases the defect rate of an assembly. For example, with 20 components each with 20 parameters, we are considering 400 measurements and the success rate will be given by:

$$0.997^{400} = 0.301; \text{ that is } 301 \text{ parts per thousand}$$

In a practical design, things are more complicated because parameters are not all independent and it is possible to easily arrange for some ratios of SW/σ to be much higher than others. This is where the parameter is much less critical from the user's point of view. The results demonstrate, however, that in order to achieve quality standards it is necessary to incorporate two factors into the design:

- *Specification width high.* The specifications should be wide compared with process capabilities

- *Number of parameters low.* There should be as few critical parameters as possible.

The purpose of this discussion is to bring out the way the design and manufacturing departments must cooperate closely in designing and specifying items to be made. The debate is by no means complete. For example:

- The definition of quality is based on conformance to specification – a manufacturing concept. Taguchi would point out a flaw in this approach. With a specification of 600 ±2mm, a panel of 601.9mm would be good quality and 602.1 would be rejected. Yet, the difference between the two, 0.2mm, is much less than the 1.9mm deviation of the former from the target size of 600!

- Uncontrolled irregularities about a target mean value are only one of the problems of process variability that the quality organisation must cope with. Other factors have to be monitored.

We shall discuss these and other issues of quality appraisal in Chapter 17.

✔ Quick check-up

Can you:

☐ List:
  - five definitions of quality, including the one used in ISO 9000:2000
  - five factors important in service quality assessment
  - three costs of quality.

☐ Name three leaders in the development of quality ideas and outline their contributions.

☐ Define:
  – TQM
  – *gemba*.

☐ Set out the steps of the PDCA cycle.

☐ Define manufacturability.

☐ Define six *sigma* operations.

❓ Questions

Chapter review

16.1 Discuss whether quality can be 'free'.

16.2 Compare the three forms of control and their effectiveness in achieving quality standards.

16.3 Who is responsible for quality?

16.4 Summarise the difficulties in implementing TQM and suggest ways of overcoming them.

16.5 Why are quality circles less common in the west than they are among Japanese companies?

Application

16.6 Explain how the idea of 'costs of quality' would apply in a quick service restaurant and how McDonald's takes steps to minimise them.

16.7 What benefits do product and process standards bring to McDonald's? Would you advise the company to gain ISO 9000 registration?

16.8 How does the organisation of Amtico (Chapter 3) contribute to achieving quality links between design and manufacture?

Investigation

16.9 Examine the bid of a recent winner of the European Quality Award.[46] Compare the bid to the ideas on quality management set out in the chapter to identify the key features that the case study teaches us.

CLOSING CASE

Shering weighs it up[47]

Founded in 1946, Shering Weighing Group is a family-owned business making weighbridges and related equipment. Bucking the 1980s industry trend towards outsourcing most components, the company retained design, manufacture and after-sales service in-house. It opened a new headquarters and plant at Dunfermline in 1991 and has invested heavily in a stream of new products designed to solve customers' problems. It led the introduction of electronic weighbridges with tamper-proof instrumentation and telemetry communication; it developed extra long models up to 45 metres and extra wide ones up to 5.5 metres and 180 tonnes; its patented *restraint post* system protects the precision load cells from shocks and damage; and detailed design and surface coatings promote safety and durability.

Quality of products and service has been at the core of these innovations. Shering has ISO 9001 accreditation and is approved under the stringent European Weights and Measures standard EN 45501. The rules require annual calibration using standard test weights. The cost of hiring these is included in the full maintenance service, which also has a two-hour response target if problems arise. The latest installations have modem links to enable condition monitoring from Scotland; software upgrades are also installed by this means.

Shering's products have many applications. In quarrying, weighing is a critical component of the process. Without accurate equipment the quarry cannot function and goodwill is lost. One of Shering's customers, RMC Western Aggregates, had had three problems with a previous supplier: excessive wear and tear under the heavy traffic of some 1,000 vehicles per day; reliability of maintenance service; and the wish to integrate data into its management information system.

Another customer, quarrying stone for distribution throughout Munster, added fraud prevention and safety to the list of solutions required of a quality weighing system. Now, as the driver enters a J.A. Wood quarry area, the entry driver terminal automatically recognises the vehicle through a secure link and matches it with the booking. The terminal prints a ticket and directions for the driver on where to collect the load and shows a green light. The EDT transmits corresponding instruction to the cabs of the loading vehicles. These shovels can measure the materials reasonably accurately. The driver then returns to the unmanned weighbridge, sometimes along a public road, where the load is checked and confirmed automatically. Detecting a full vehicle at the exit terminal, the system cancels the loading instructions, prints details of gross, net and tare weights for the driver and updates all records. Opportunities for fraud are reduced and, since the driver does not leave the vehicle, many accident risks are eliminated.

Questions

1 Select from the case study one example of each of the three costs of quality.

2 Shering is one of many companies that stress the benefits of a full after-sales service. What are these and who gains from them?

3 Using the evidence in the case study, outline how well Shering matches the latest ISO 9000 standard.

Notes and references

1. McDonald's (2000) *McDonald's Fact File 2000*, London: Corporate Affairs Department, July; McDonald's (2001) McDonald's Presents 'Sweeney Quality Award' to Asian Cargill Subsidiary, Sun Valley Ltd McDonald's Corporation, 13 February; www.mcdonalds.com accessed 20 July 2001.

2. National Institute for Standards and Technology (2001) *Baldrige National Quality Program*, Gaithersburg, MD: NIST; www.quality.nist.gov/ accessed 2 June 2000.

3. Besides illustrating a point about quality, I find this story interesting because it shows something about the development of organisational myth. I have heard it in presenta-

tions and conversations from buyers who were sure that the events, albeit with different numbers, happened to someone in their own organisation. I took to asking speakers to give more details and have learnt that they never know but could refer me to someone who might. My conclusion is that such incidents are common or that they do not happen at all. In either case, we have a simple story told to audiences who are ready to believe. Truth and myth are indistinguishable.

4. There is even another shop, in a cheaper part of town that sells 'thirds'.

5. J.D. Powers and Associates (2001) *Rental Car Companies Compete Fiercely to Satisfy Customers*, press release, 10 April; www.jdpa.com/studies/pressrelease.asp?StudyID=512&CatID=4 accessed 2 July 2001; Ulrich, L. (2001) 'Toyota, its Lexus division lead in car-quality study', *Detroit Free Press*, 18 May.

6. Automobile Association (2001) *European New Car Assessment Programme*; www.theaa.co.uk/motoringandtravel/safety/index.asp accessed 20 June 2001.

7. Zeithamal, V.A., Parasuraman, A. and Berry, L. (1990) *Delivering Service Quality: Balancing consumer perceptions and expectations*, New York: Free Press, p.26.

8. Crosby, P.B. (1984) *Quality without Tears*, New York: McGraw-Hill, p.60.

9. British Standards Institute (2000) *ISO 9000:2000 Quality management systems – fundamental and vocabulary*, London: BSI, pp.7–12.

10. British Standards Institute (1987) *BS 4778 Part 1 Section 3*; Johnson, R. and Winchell, W.O. (1989) *Production and Quality*, Milwaukee: American Society for Quality Control, p.2.

11. Ho, S. (1993) 'Transplanting Japanese management techniques', *Long Range Planning*, 26(4), pp.81–9.

12. Deming, W.E. (1981) 'Improvement of quality and productivity through action by management', *National Productivity Review*, 1(1), reprinted as 'Reading 7' in Latona, J.C. and Nathan, J. (eds) (1994) *Cases and Readings in Production and Operations Management*, Needham Heights, MA: Allyn and Bacon, pp.223–36.

13. A best-seller that did much to bring quality ideas to a wide audience: Crosby, P.B. (1980) *Quality is Free: The Art of Making Quality Certain*, New York: Mentor.

14. Lister, R. (1994) 'Beyond TQM . . .' *Management Services*, May, pp.8–13.

15. Deming, op.cit., p.223.

16. Gador, B. (1989) 'Quest for quality – Tennant Company, Minneapolis, MN', *Target*, Fall, pp.27–9.

17. Beynon, H. (1973) *Working for Ford*, Harmondsworth: Penguin, p.77; scousers are inhabitants of Liverpool.

18. Etcherelli, C. (1985) *Elise où la vraie vie*, London: Methuen, p.137.

19. www.deming.org accessed 24 January 2001; for further notes on Deming and the other quality gurus, see the site of the Department of Trade and Industry www.dti.gov.uk/mbp/bpgt/m9ja00001/m9ja000011.html accessed 7 July 2001.

20. www.juran.com accessed 24 January 2001.

21. In a special issue of *Quality and Reliability Engineering International*, 4(2) (1988) on Taguchi Methods, a number of articles show how the statistical methods can be improved. A general evaluative paper is: Box, G., Bisgaard, S. and Fung, C. (1988) 'An explanation and critique of Taguchi's contributions to quality engineering', ibid., pp.123–31.

22. HMSO (2001) *QA Register*, London, HMSO; www.quality-register.co.uk/about.htm accessed 16 May 2001.

23. British Standards Institution (2000) 'How much does registration to ISO 9001/2 cost?' www.bsieducation.org/higher/sect3d.html accessed 2 July 2001.

24. British Standards Institution (2000) 'How can an organization benefit from registration to ISO 9001/2?' www.bsieducation.org/higher/sect3c.html accessed 2 July 2001.

25. Dickson, T. (1993) 'Management quality street cred – TQM is struggling to make an impact in Europe', *The Financial Times*, 20 October, p.16.

26. British Standards Institution (2000) *BS EN ISO 9000:2000 Quality management systems – requirements*, London: BSI, pp.vi–vii.

27. ibid., pp.2–13.

28. Based on: *Figure 1 – Model of a process-based quality system*, ibid., p.3.

29. www.efqm.org accessed 1 July 2001.

30. Izadi, M., Kashef, A.E. and Stadt, R.W. (1996) 'Quality in higher education: Lessons learned from the Baldrige Award, Deming Prize and ISO 9000 registration', *Journal of Industrial Teacher Education*, 33(2), pp.60–76.

31. Imai, M. (1992) 'Solving quality problems using common sense', *International Journal of Quality and Reliability Management*, 9(5), pp.71–5.

32. ibid. pp.72–3.

33. It should be noted that BR, and its successors, have worked hard to improve in this area in recent years. The change from 'passengers' to 'customers' is a minor symbol of the development of a retailing philosophy.

34. Peters, T. (1994) 'Theatre on the retail stage', *The Independent on Sunday Business News*, 6 March, p.26.

35. op.cit., p.74.

36. Dawson, P. (1994) 'Total quality management' in Storey, J. (ed.) *New Wave Manufacturing Strategies*, London: Paul Chapman, pp.103–21.

37. Deming, op.cit., pp.229–35. Various versions and interpretations of the points can be found. For example: by Deming himself (1985) 'Transformation of western style management', *Interfaces*, 15(3), pp.6–11; (1986) *Out of the Crisis*, Cambridge, MA: MIT Press, pp.23–96; (1991) 'Philosophy continues to flourish', *APICS – The Performance Advantage*, 1(4), p.20; Aguayo, R. (1991) *Dr Deming: The man who taught the Japanese about quality*, London: Mercury, pp.121–2. Curiously, Aguayo has 16 points in his list of 14.

38. Deming (1986) op.cit., p.88.

39. Vandermerwe, S. (1994) 'Quality in services: The "softer" side is "Harder" (and smarter)', *Long Range Planning*, 27(2), pp.45–56.

40. ibid., p.53.

41. Ansari, A. and Modarress, B. (1994) 'Quality function deployment: The role of suppliers', *International Journal of Purchasing and Materials Management*, October, pp.28–35.

42. McGeorge, J.F. (1988) 'Design productivity: A quality problem', *Journal of Management in Engineering*, 4(4), pp.350–62.

43. Based on: Burgess, J.A. (1988) 'Assuring quality in design engineering', *Journal of Management in Engineering*, 4(1), pp.16–22.

44. Heidenreich, P. (1988) 'Design for manufacturability', *Quality Progres*, May, pp.41–4.

45. Strictly, we must assume that the different measurements are independent for the following analysis to be sound.

46. European Foundation for Quality Management (2001) European Quality Awards 2000 Brussels, EFQM; www.efqm.org accessed 15 June 2001.

47. Shering Weighing Group (2001) *Western Aggregates Case Study*; www.sheringweighing.demon.co.uk/pr2.htm accessed 11 July 2001.

CHAPTER 17

Investigating and controlling quality

OBJECTIVES

When you have finished studying this chapter, you should be able to:

- Demonstrate the use of charts in speaking with data to investigate and communicate quality issues.
- Show how control charts are designed and used for both quality variables and attributes.
- Summarise the key features of benchmarking for establishing quality standards.
- Illustrate the quality function deployment process using the House of Quality.
- Explain Taguchi's quality loss function and his notion of robust quality.
- Identify sources of dominance and summarise their implications for quality control.
- Evaluate the advantages and disadvantages of sampling in quality systems.
- Explain the nature and role of acceptance inspection and how sampling plans balance risk and cost.
- Explain and evaluate the SERVQUAL approach to service evaluation.

OPENING CASE

The best laid plans . . .[1]

In the first half of 2001 Sony had to recall mobile phones four times because of production faults. The worst case risked the future of the joint venture with Ericsson announced in April. This was heralded as combining the stable technical platform of the Swedish company with Sony's strengths in styling and marketing. Within three months, however, the project found that half a million handsets risked overheating because of a flaw in battery manufacture. This failure, confined to Japan, would cost more than £50 million and eliminate the 30% sales growth expected in that country.

Finding it difficult to establish a pattern in the technical problems, one Sony manager suggested that bad luck had played a part. Critics were not so generous. One criticised the push for market share based on packing as many new features into the products as possible. Design and production teams could not keep up as the many innovations increased the risks of bugs. Another noted Sony's history of bringing products to market as quickly as possible, although that meant many post-release repairs. The original Walkman was failure prone.

►

Growing quality problems at Mercedes-Benz, the luxury car subsidiary of DaimlerChrysler, led to warranty payments of some €1.7 billion in 2000. This was a threefold rise in three years and roughly equalled the division's development costs. Competitive pressure to shorten development cycles and save money on quality control had contributed to the problem; for example, long-distance test driving had been abandoned. Mercedes-Benz launched two new series between 1998 and 2000, the A-Class and the M-class. Output had risen by 14%.

Despite having 'perfect' components, building a trouble-free car is difficult. This is especially true when managers are bringing in new models and increasing output. DaimlerChrysler set up quality circles throughout all divisions to tackle the issue.

In April 2001 Mars was forced to destroy 3 million Twix bars at its Slough factory after beetles turned up in the flour supply. Twix is number five in the market, with annual sales of 500 million bars. Having noticed black flecks in the biscuit base, inspectors discovered flour beetles in a silo. The high cooking temperature meant there was no risk to health; in any case, no affected bars had left the plant. In 1998, Mars was prosecuted after a customer found a mouse's head and shoulders in a Topic bar. Negligence was not proved, however, as the magistrate accepted that the company had taken all reasonable steps to prevent contamination.

17.1 Introduction

Even the most famous companies have quality problems. In two examples in the opening case, we see companies striving to match the rising tide of customer expectations. They must innovate while knowing how far quality leadership has helped them build their businesses. Failure brings great risks, with the possibility of a brand becoming associated with problems. Consumers satisfied with quality are four times more likely to buy again than from rivals; with industrial products, they are seven times more likely.

Managers may congratulate themselves on progressively reducing defects and errors. Yet, this approach may not be good enough. Feigenbaum[2] points to the danger of 'backward creep' with companies focusing on internal standards rather than matching the changing customer expectations. Not only must there be effective internal systems, but also a continual check among customers and benchmarking against the best rivals. After its launch in the United States market, one well-known car model averaged eight warranty claims per vehicle within 12 months in service. Rectification cost about £2,000 on each one. Within two years, the claim rate had been cut to three, costing about £750, with the trend falling further. Yet managers could not be satisfied with this better than average performance; Toyota led the field with 0.7, twice as good as the next brand.[3]

Failures do occur. The responses of companies vary. Mars was able to contain the flour beetle problem within the plant. After release, effective crisis management is called for. Many follow Johnson & Johnson's experience with Tylenol.

Some bottles of the painkiller had been deliberately contaminated with cyanide. The company immediately withdrew every bottle on the market, changed the packs and advertised to explain what had happened. Sales increased. McDonald's quick response to the 1995 BSE crisis in the United Kingdom was followed by a 70% gain in market share.[4]

Having process to match quality to standards is important. Yet, it must go along with means of tracking rivals' developments and the changing expectations of customers. In this chapter, we shall examine some tools and techniques that help the investigation of these issues. Statistics retains a key role in the TQM context. Within the scope of the book, we shall study the two most common applications: statistical process control and acceptance inspection.

17.2 Investigation

Among the repertoire of skills of both analysts and quality circle members is the ability to use charts. They help in problem awareness and breakdown and act as valuable records of group discussion. As an aid to the communication of complex ideas, a well-designed chart is difficult to beat. In the following sections, we explain several graphical means of analysing quality issues and communicating ideas about them.

17.2.1 Cause and effect

The cause and effect diagram is a valuable way of starting an investigation into, and opening up discussion about, quality questions. It is also known as an *Ishikawa diagram*, after one of its advocates, or a *fishbone diagram*, after its form. While often drawn to suggest a fish, there is no conventional method of presentation. Stars or sprays will do equally well. The essence of the diagram is to record discussion and ideas and connect them by lines. In the version of Figure 17.1, the starting point, at the fish's head, was the problem of egg damage in a supermarket. The other boxes represent main limbs where causes may lie and the small bones suggest some detailed reasons for these areas. Therefore, the diagram can summarise ideas of cause and effect in an informal, hierarchical way. It can summarise, for example, a collection of sticky notes placed on the wall during a quality circle meeting.

Having established a visual agenda, the team, or quality circle, can use the fishbone diagram to plan further investigation. This can follow Imai's instructions for kaizen as explained in 16.12. We should: *use common sense, go to gemba and speak with data.*

17.2.2 Speaking with data

Before a study becomes too involved in the complexities of statistical analysis and control, it is remarkable how much understanding can follow collecting some simple data and presenting them in basic, visual ways. To illustrate, let us

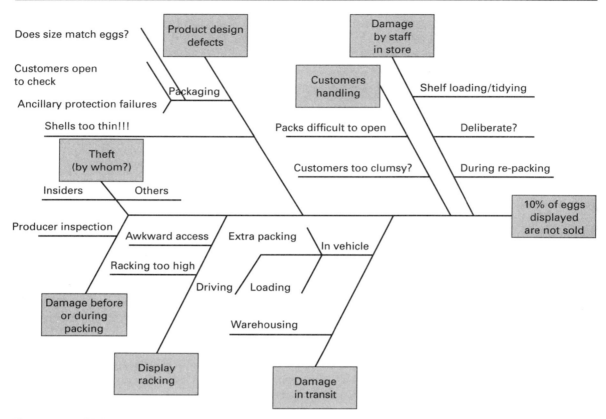

Figure 17.1 Fishbone diagram: egg wastage problem

imagine we are managers at Kobe Steel examining faults in output from a rolling mill. Suppose we were to discuss the question with staff throughout the plant. We would be given responses such as, 'We get a lot of surface markings because . . . ,' or, 'It's quite common to find . . . ,' or, 'Sometimes it's as though . . .' Staff will be very aware of at least some issues but are unlikely to agree on what the main causes are. Furthermore, their awareness would not be dependable as a source of frequency data for the various faults.

The next step is to collect data. Instead of gathering scrap material and sending it back for recycling without examination, we would assess the imperfections of each piece. In fact, one would expect this to be normal procedure in a steel rolling mill. The point of the exercise is to examine the data on reasons for failure in order to make some sense of them. Juran was one who pointed out that Pareto charts are useful for making the point. This form of presentation shows the frequency of events in ranked order. Figure 17.2 gives an example for the rolling mill during two study periods in consecutive years.

The data suggest that, between the two studies, great strides were made in the reduction of failures, especially those caused by roll marks in the steel. Yet, pock marks in the surface remained the most serious problem, dominating the others in terms of material spoiled. The Pareto presentation helps to focus the efforts at problem solving.

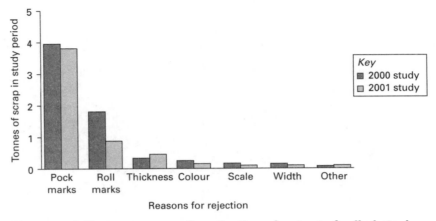

Figure 17.2 Data on reasons for rejection of output of rolled steel

The data compared in Figure 17.2 are a mixture of attribute quality (was the surface quality acceptable or not?) and dimensions. The latter can be further analysed because, as mentioned in Chapter 16, dimensions can usually be measured more accurately than they can be made. Carefully measuring thickness, rather than simply using a simple gauge to test whether a dimension meets a specification, enables us to dig more deeply into the causes of variations. This is a prerequisite to reducing them. In the TQM firm, it would be normal to keep records of critical parameters, not merely to appraise whether a product is acceptable, but also to aid understanding of the process. We shall return to this question of detailed process control later in this chapter, but first let us see what can be done with data and some simple charts.

Exercise 17.1 Outline how Sony may collect and use data better to understand the problem with product recalls.

17.2.3 Using simple charts

Imagine we are watching a rifle shooting competition. In the first series, competitors shoot ten rounds each. Figure 17.3 shows two of the targets. The left-hand competitor, LH, has scored four inners with the rest of the shots spread around the next ring. The right-hand competitor, RH, has all shots very closely clustered but none is in the centre. If hitting the inner is the sole criterion for success, then LH scores 4/10, RH scores zero and LH wins. We can say that LH is the better shot. Yet, whom would you back for the next round?

In the next round, RH can clearly improve by adjusting aim. This can be done either by pointing 'a little to the right and down a bit' or by adjusting the gun sight. In contrast, there is little that LH can do. It looks as if the aim is good but slight shakiness means that not all shots are true. The competitor suffers from random variations (nerves?), which cannot be overcome by simple adjustment. LH is already shooting at maximum performance.

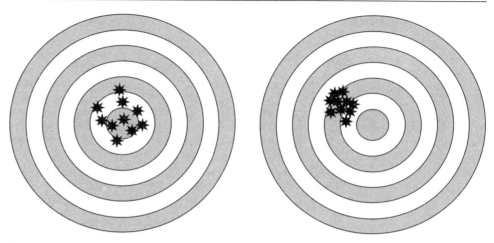

Figure 17.3 Whose is the quality shooting?

This illustrates an approach to manufacturing quality investigation. We have a sanding machine that finishes timber furniture components. Provided the sander produces a good surface finish, the key dimension is thickness. One way of tracking the process is to take samples every 15 minutes. Five panels each time will be sufficient. What story can we glean from the data? The answer to this question will clearly depend on the data.

Before going on to look at general cases, we can study one example, shown in Figure 17.4. The top half of the diagram shows the measurements taken for each of the five panels in each sampled set. Note that we have set out the raw data first. Working with means and measures of dispersion at this stage unnecessarily loses some of the data variety. The plots are rather like the rifle range results. From the raw data, we can see that, each quarter hour, the machine setting changes but it remains capable of performing close to that setting. To confirm our impression, we can calculate summary data. The line in the upper graph shows the mean values of the samples, emphasising how the product thickness falls by about 0.05mm during the time covered by the observations; the lower graph measures the dispersion of each sample by simply measuring its *spread* or *range*, the difference between the maximum and minimum.

Naturally, we do not know whether the machine is being adjusted to move it towards a target thickness or whether it is simply drifting out of control. Yet, we can conclude that the sanding process is capable of consistent quality output if the setting is under control. To this end, we would first recommend regular monitoring of sample thickness and machine adjustments if necessary. Second, we would note that quality would be improved if the cause, or causes, of setting changes were discovered and then eliminated.

The observations do not reveal whether the sanding machine is actually producing quality products during the trial. Investigation of this aspect requires targets and limits set in advance. These boundaries form the framework for control charts, proposed first by Shewhart in 1924. Shewhart aimed his statistical approach at separating common causes from special causes in process variation. Deming acknowledged that this formed the basis of much of his later work.

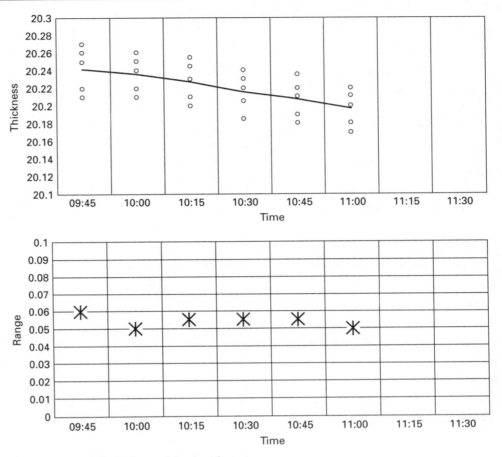

Figure 17.4 Sanding machine performance

17.2.4 Control charts

Control charts are used for setting out process variables in a standard form. The horizontal axis shows time and the vertical axis represents a variable. This could be a product property, such as length, weight, electrical resistance and so on, or it could be a process variable, for example the temperature of a fluid or its density or viscosity. The vertical axis shows the target value and two *control limits*, upper and lower. They may be the specification width but not necessarily so, usually being set more narrowly than this. Typical patterns are shown in Figure 17.5.

As with other charts, visual inspection can reveal a great deal:

A   *Normal behaviour.* The results are scattered around, and close to, the target.

B C   *One measurement outside the control limits.* The matter should be investigated and further samples taken to see if the results are freakish or part of an emerging pattern.

D E   *Two measurements close to the control limits.* These are danger signs. The result could be by chance or the process may need adjusting. Again, further samples should be taken before any action is taken.

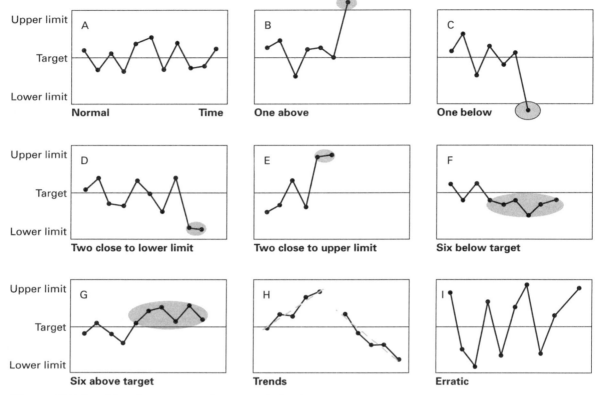

Figure 17.5 Looking for patterns in control charts

F G *Six to one side of target.* While being well within the control limits, the results are suggesting that the process needs adjustment. Again, the reason for the drift should be established. The number on one side that will trigger investigation will depend on experience with the process.

H *Trends.* Clear trends, which can be confirmed by collecting more data immediately, show that the output is likely to move out of range shortly. Immediate adjustment may be required. Again, the cause of the pattern should be sought.

I *Erratic behaviour.* This may be the expected pattern for the process and all is well. Yet, it does suggest that the machine is not good enough to operate within the chosen limits. It would be very difficult to control, for one could ask how to set this machine to the target and how one could pick out any of the behaviour patterns shown in D to H.

17.3 Setting standards

We noted earlier the need for setting targets and control limits. To look into this process, we must go back several stages from the operations scene to examine where the standards come from. Processes to be covered are *benchmarking, quality function deployment* and study of the *quality loss function*.

17.3.1 Benchmarking

As a source of ideas and standards of quality, service and other operational attributes, benchmarking has obvious attraction. After all, why not look to the best for our standards? We can define the term as follows:

> **Benchmarking is the practice of recognising and examining the best industrial and commercial practices in an industry or in the world and using this knowledge as the basis for improvement in all aspects of the business.**

More than imitation, this is a thorough analysis of success and a spreading of learning throughout the organisation. Most of the world's largest companies practise benchmarking, albeit using a diffuse range of approaches and seeking benefit in disparate aspects of business.

Exercise 17.2   Why not look to the best for our standards?

The method follows the ideas of Feigenbaum[5] who explained it as a continuous process of comparing business practices. The aim is to identify improvements and put them into effect. This implies uncovering critical performance measures to be used in the comparison with examples of what is now called 'best practice'. A systematic approach, based on exchange, benefits all participants.[6] Therefore, studies are best based on direct comparisons rather than stopping at analysis of anonymous in-firm or industry averages. Care is needed to avoid overreliance on the comparison and an uncritical aping of good (and bad) practices.[7]

Bhutta and Huq[8] identified seven overlapping types of benchmarking. Set out in Table 17.1, the list includes three categories based on *level* in the organisation; the last four represent what we may call benchmarking *direction*. The table shows how each may be used in the improvement of quality. Some authors suggest that firms should start with relatively easy internal comparisons (for example of parallel production units on different sites) through to more complex strategic appraisals. Yet others show there is little evidence for this in practice.[9]

Exercise 17.3   Given that engaging with competitors is not possible, suggest some opportunities for Sony, Daimler-Benz and Mars to benchmark their quality processes.

The benchmarking process

The many variants of the proposed process have themes related to the Deming-Shewhart PDCA cycle. Figure 17.6 follows a variant given by Cook.[10] The team

Table 17.1 Benchmarking types

	Type of benchmarking	Basis of comparison for quality
Bench-marking level	Process	Tools and processes to improve quality; comparison of product design and supply; good for detailed learning
	Performance	Performance measures to compare the organisation with others and with customers' expectations; counters backward creep
	Strategic	Quality strategy; infrastructure; management processes
Benchmarking direction	Generic	Organisations using similar processes or technologies, not necessarily in the same industry; sharing not difficult
	Functional	Organisations in same sector or industry at the detailed process or technology level; may be available through professional network
	Internal	Activities, functions or divisions of the same organisation; results may be unconvincing
	Competitor	Recognised 'best in class' competitors to establish standards; very convincing but may be inaccessible

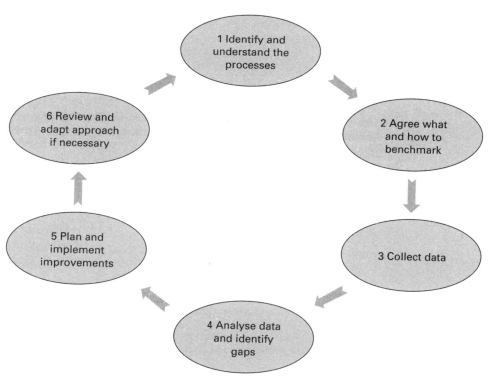

Figure 17.6 Benchmarking cycle

starts by building a good working knowledge of the processes carried out in the process chosen for the study (1). They then develop an understanding of the key success factors within the industry, and, from these, select a number of factors for benchmarking (2). This can be a difficult process as data, and the means of measuring them, may not be available. The third stage is data collection (3). How to do this depends on the benchmarking direction. Internal data should be readily available while those on competitors may come from industry reports and similar analyses. Data analysis, at the next step, begins to reveal the differences sought (4). Yet, these need checking to avoid reliance on errors. At the next stage (5), the action plan begins to emerge together with its implementation. Finally, the team reviews progress and appraises the success of their improvements (6). This last stage suggests modifications to the benchmarking criteria as well as to other elements of the loop. In this way, it echoes the PDCA cycle.

Outlined in this way, the process sounds straightforward. It can, however, run into problems with other companies, particularly fierce rivals. Yet much information is published already, products contain a wealth of data and can be readily bought or observed, and responses to different companies can be discussed with customers. Main gives some advice for use when approaching other companies:[11]

- *Don't go fishing.* This means that study should have a clear purpose and its scope should be limited to support areas that need improvement.

- *Send out the people who will have to make the changes.* This means letting people see for themselves. Raising awareness in this way is a great step along the path of change.

- *Exchange information.* The target company may well be involved in its own benchmarking exercise. Information exchange is a possibility and a firm should not be asking any question that it is not prepared to answer itself. Commonly, a study is welcomed by the target organisation.

- *Steer away from legal problems.* Sharing information on price, market share and related issues may suggest price and market fixing, which are illegal. Some companies forbid their managers even talking to people from rivals for this reason. The need to protect sensitive information about new products is also a factor.

- *Keep obtained information secure.* An organisation that shares information with a benchmarking partner may be alarmed if this is passed on to a competitor.

Benchmarking in action

Outside the industry, imaginative comparisons can be made between common or related functions. For instance: ICL has measured its training methods against those of the Royal Mail; a US regional airline compared its aircraft turnarounds with motor racing pit stops; other companies have looked worldwide to set best practice standards for research and development.[12]

Benchmarking can be both eye opening and a stimulus to action. When studying engine repair processes, British Airways found that technicians on Japanese Airlines took 40 minutes to turn round a 747 while BA's people took three hours. The process also has its limits, however. It works well for high-performance companies whose internal appraisal compares well with the best. Yet, for moderate performers, the exercise may only generate confusion and low morale. It is rather like my swimming, which I do to keep fit. I sometimes check my lengths against the clock to see whether I am improving at all. To compare my times with the Olympic champion is pointless. Low-performing companies should think in the same way. There are plenty of basic actions they can take, from team building to improving links with customers, before they start to worry about becoming world class.

Benchmarking is used best for evaluating existing products, processes and infrastructure among firms that are aiming for excellence. As mentioned, it does not help in the innovation area where firms jealously guard their proposals from competitors' eyes. Anyhow, innovation is neither about imitation nor about catching up. To develop standards for the future, one must go to the customers.

17.3.2 Quality function deployment (QFD)

Good companies incorporate customers' needs and expectations into their product planning processes. Market research takes the lead in finding out about these expectations. The design process converts them into specific products with specified performance. These should both satisfy the expectations and be capable of being supplied at reasonable cost. A major difficulty with this rational procedure is that customers' needs are expressed in different terms to those used by the suppliers.

Take, for example, the design of a popular camera. Customers may not know very much about camera design, especially as the average replacement rate spans several generations of technology. For the most part, they are likely to express their needs in terms such as convenient, flexible and simple to use. Of course, there are those with more knowledge who will talk in terms of centre field auto-focus, zoom ratio and red-eye reduction. We are talking, however, about a popular camera here and the firm is trying to reach the mass market. How does the company convert the customers' wishes into a viable product?

Quality function deployment is a methodology enabling firms to evaluate their current products and assess new proposals and the processes needed to supply them. It is both a philosophy, in that it implies a set of beliefs about the way products should be designed and supplied, and a communication tool, for it is used to underpin the links among marketers, designers and operations people. The goals are improved interpretation of what elements create customer satisfaction and dissatisfaction, quicker and more successful design, and more effective teamwork among all parties.

QFD is defined as:

> **A system for translating consumer requirements into appropriate company requirements at every stage, from research, through product design and development, to manufacture, distribution, installation and marketing, sales and service.**

Origins

The procedure was introduced at Mitsubishi Heavy Industries in 1972. By 1976, Toyota had taken it up, further developing the method and using it with its suppliers. This company had had, in the 1970s, a bad reputation for 'body durability' (that is to say, rust). It made rapid strides, both on that characteristic and in shortening and improving the design process. Through QFD, the start-up costs (those attributed to implementing the design in the production process by adjusting virtually every element) were reduced drastically. By the mid-1980s, the effect was such that 90% of design changes at Toyota were complete *before the manufacturing start-up*. The typical western company was still revamping its designs months after launch.

The matrices

QFD has been applied using seven steps whose results are laid out in a set of special matrices and tables linked as in Figure 17.7. The form of the figure gives the technique its name – *House of Quality*. The steps are as follows:

1 *Identify customer attributes, CAs.* At this stage, it is important to record these attributes in the customers' words. Using the *voice of the customer* avoids having their needs interpreted (that is, misinterpreted) by designers and engineers. Note that the customers need not be for consumer goods. The approach works equally well for services or for intermediate products sold to other organisations. Customers' requirements will, in some industries, be backed up by those of regulators. For instance, many standards covering motor car design are set by the government.

2 *Identify engineering characteristics, ECs.* Now the process uses the language of the engineer. Product features specify components, layouts, sequences, performance and so on. The features should be measurable so that they can be evaluated in comparison. The units of measurement are recorded in the diagram.

3 *Compare CAs and ECs.* This step uses the central matrix with the CAs listed to the left and the ECs across the top. Any cell with a relationship has an entry with a symbol indicating its strength. An EC can affect several CAs. For example, incorporating a high-quality, wide-range exposure meter in a camera addresses the CAs of ease of use and flexibility. It may be, however, that an engineering characteristic does not bear on any CA. In that case, the question is whether the EC contributes to product value or is unnecessary.

4 *Establish links between pairs of ECs.* Another matrix, forming the 'roof' of the house, summarises interrelationships between the EC pairs. Again, symbols represent strong or weak links. Recording them in a matrix enables the team to understand how changes in one element affect others. For instance, thickening the material in a vehicle frame will increase strength and safety but will add weight and therefore reduce acceleration.

5 *Evaluate competitors' products, CPs.* The method here is to rank or score rival products against the CAs. An extension is to establish weightings for the CAs to facilitate trade-offs among them. This evaluation process is done readily for existing products through standard market research procedures. The weightings or rankings appear as the 'chimney' of the house.

6 *Assess the ECs of the rival products as the basis for development targets.* Testing, inspecting and dismantling the rival products, if they are goods, form this step. Field observations assess competitors' services. Results appear as a set of

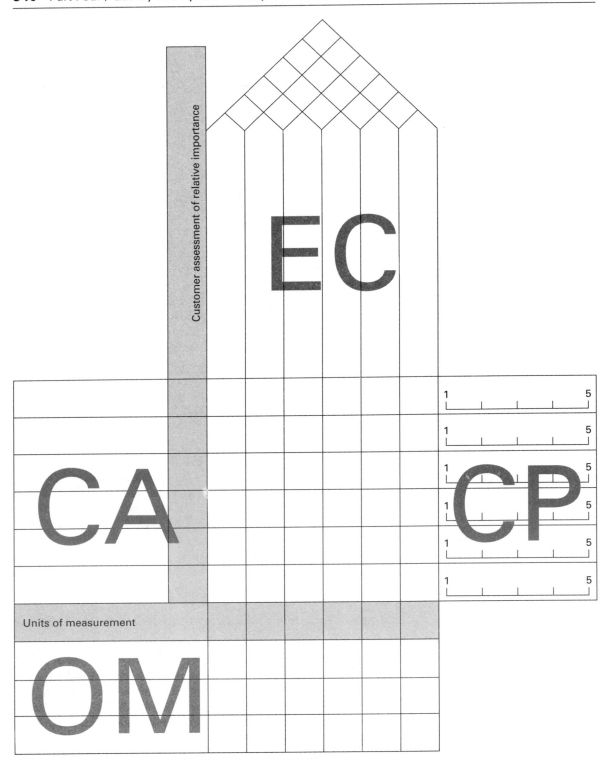

Figure 17.7 The House of Quality

objective measures, OMs, to form the house foundations. From a comparison of rival OMs of ECs, development priorities will be set out.

7 *Select ECs for development into detailed design, process design and operations*. This step not only confirms the main design specification but underscores the detailed attributes that need to be incorporated into he product to satisfy the CAs. The House of Quality, therefore, feeds the *voice of the customer* right through into the manufacturing or supply processes.

A practical illustration

To show how this works out in practice, let us return to the example of camera design. We will consider the sector for compact automatic cameras without zoom lens. This is a crowded sector with about a dozen leading suppliers and much 'feature' competition. Figure 17.8 shows how information would be set out. The CAs include notions such as 'easy to use', which ranks first, to 'easy to carry', which ranks fifth in the abbreviated list shown here. ECs list the main devices to be included in the EC specification. The roof matrix shows that the firm knows how to, say, design an automatic focus and exposure system with integrated flash and low power consumption. Yet, the flash itself consumes more battery power, particularly if it incorporates the red-eye reduction system. Further, electric film winding consumes power and adds weight. Hence, we have some negative symbols in the roof. The central matrix relates the ECs to the CAs. ECs of auto-focus and exposure strongly support 'easy to use', as does, to a lesser extent, electric film winding.

Units for the ECs are shown below the central matrix. They are metres, grams, milliwatts and f-numbers. OMs for the firm's current product and two leading rivals appear in the foundations. The three are compared with CAs in the CP area on the right. The array presents designers with a view of the problem they face and suggests where they may concentrate their efforts. At present, the firm's camera compares poorly with rivals on CAs, especially the most important, ease of use. Improvements to the controls for the focusing, exposure and, possibly, flash units seem to be a development priority. Naturally, studies would have to be conducted in much more detail and a practical House of Quality would contain many more rows and columns than the cut-down version shown here.

A flexible procedure

Hauser and Clausing[13] point out that the house is not a rigid procedure. It helps teams to set targets and summarise data in useable form. Like any good methodology, it acts as a guide, framework and agenda setter. The decisions still have to be made by the participants. The procedure is not rigid in another sense. Although one form of the process has been set out here, development teams would customise the House of Quality to suit their own needs. Details of how to select and evaluate rivals' products, for example, depend on the industrial setting. It is also clear that the process will differ if the firm intends to develop a new product, in which case the comparison procedure would be more open ended. Yet again, in the supply of services the terminology would change. The essence of the House of Quality, however, remains the same. It sustains the effort to convert the voice of the customer into real product characteristics.

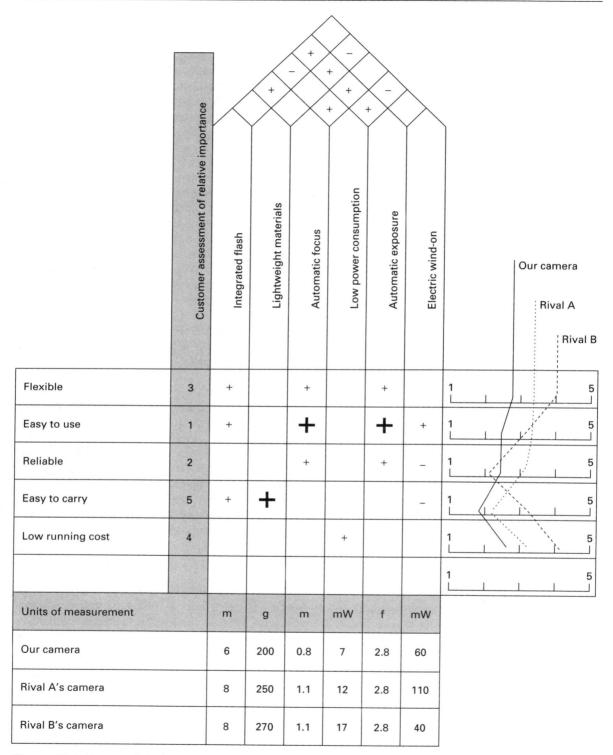

Figure 17.8 House of Quality: camera development

The house, or a 'row of houses', can be used through the whole development sequence. 'If our team is truly interfunctional, we can eventually take the "hows" [ECs] from our house of quality and make them the "whats" of another house, one mainly concerned with detailed product design.'[14] The ECs can become the equivalent of CAs in a 'parts deployment' house and so on. The four houses, shown in Figure 17.9, take the voice of the customer through to manufacturing. In another application, Ansari and Modaress show how QFD can be used as a vehicle to bring suppliers into the development activity.[15]

17.3.3 Quality loss function (QLF)

Taguchi argued that what has become the conventional way of looking at specifications is too naive. The conformance perspective, with its *specification width*, creates too sharp a distinction between acceptable items just inside the boundary and unacceptable ones just outside. The existence of the tolerance band, moreover, creates an attitude of mind that believes that all items falling inside the band are of equal value. Therefore, compared with real concentration on the target, this conformance-orientated quality leads to a greater proportion of products being further from it.[16]

The difference is illustrated in Figure 17.10. The upper graph shows the outputs of three conformance-orientated manufacturing processes. It does not matter whether the frequency distribution is centred on the target, or indeed whether there is any evidence of the process producing a peaked value, all of the output is acceptable. In the lower graph, by the same token, it is clear that the process has been set to achieve the target. Taguchi saw the latter as better practice.

Taguchi proposed a *quality loss function*, QLF, to underline the need to aim close to the target. It estimates the total cost in the long run of poor quality resulting from a product moving away from exactly matching the target value. The cost covers all losses from the time the product is delivered, including those incurred during use and the consequential effects of failure. It comprises service and warranty work, customer dissatisfaction, extra inspection and scrap as well as what Taguchi refers to as the general cost to society. There is practical support for this view in the manufacture of many goods. For instance, a high-speed drive shaft may be made within tolerance but very slightly out of true. The consequences of the error may never reveal themselves but if the assembly is used often enough, the defect will lead to extra bearing wear and premature failure compared with one that is 'spot on'.

The QLF has a simple squared formula, that is the loss increases by the square of the distance from the target:

$$L_x = C \times D_x^2; \quad TL = C \times \sum_{1}^{n} D_x^2$$

Here L_x is the loss for item x that deviates D_x from the target, and C is a constant. TL is the total loss from all n items of output.

Taguchi and Clausing[17] use the formula to estimate that, if a car manufacturer fails to spend \$20 on getting a gear exactly on the target, then it would eventually spend \$80 for two standard deviations, \$180 for three, \$320 for four and so

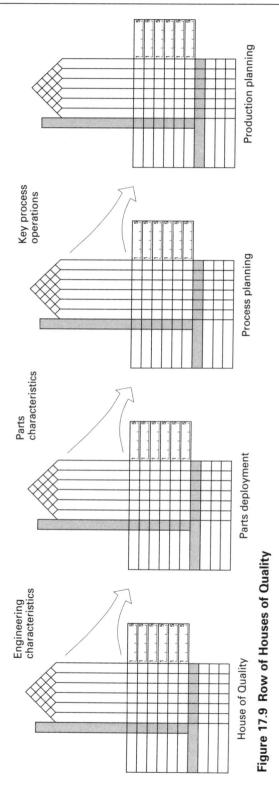

Engineering characteristics

Parts characteristics

Key process operations

House of Quality

Parts deployment

Process planning

Production planning

Figure 17.9 Row of Houses of Quality

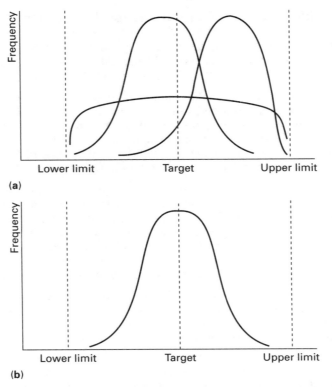

Figure 17.10 Conformance versus target-orientated quality

on. On this rather shaky estimate they comment, 'Actual field data cannot be expected to vindicate QLF precisely, and if your corporation has a more exacting way of tracking the costs of product failure, use it.'[18] More convincing is their use of the experience of Sony to contrast the two attitudes to quality specifications (see Box 17.1). Quigley and McNamara[19] looked at the question from the buyer's point of view. Purchasing can, in principle, be improved by recognising the quality differences between acceptable suppliers. If this is to be done, the buyer must be able to *decide the value of quality differentials* that exist within the specification. They proposed the use of QLF for this purpose.

17.3.4 Robust quality

Taguchi used the QLF in developing the idea of *robust quality*. Robustness refers to *quality in use*, that is the performance of a product when it has been used, misused, overloaded (a little), knocked about in service, not overhauled on schedule and so on. Customers assess products as much by how they perform outside the specification as how they conform to it in the first place. Naturally, designers attempt to overcome the effects of degradation by building in extra strength at key points. However, as Taguchi and Clausing emphasise,[20] many problems come not from weaknesses in individual items but from the interactions between slight variations in one item with others with which it forms systems.

BOX 17.1 Identical specification, identical televisions?

In the late 1970s, Sony had found that customers preferred a particular colour density in their television pictures. We can call this value 10. Dissatisfaction rose with deviation from 10, so Sony set limits at 7 and 13.

Sets were manufactured in San Diego and Tokyo. The ones produced in the American plant had colour values uniformly spread throughout the range 7 to 13. All output was inspected and no sets outside the limits were despatched. A customer was just as likely to be given a set with a 7.8 screen as one with 10.2. Meanwhile, the Tokyo products clustered near the target of 10, although about 3 per 1,000 fell outside the range. The output was not inspected.

Colour differences were not easy to perceive but they could be noticed. If a customer compared a new television, made to 13.1, with a neighbour's achieving 12.9, there would be no detectable difference and no dissatisfaction. Yet if it were compared with a demonstration model built to 10, the customer would see the difference and demand repair visits until the set had been put right. Sony San Diego produced 100% to company specification but received more complaints than Sony Tokyo, which could achieve only 99.7%.

If American workers were asked to produce to a specification of 10 ± 3, they would readily do so. The Japanese, in addition, would automatically strive to get as close to 10 as possible.

In one case, a very slight design deficiencies in the foundations of a power station hall allowed the alignment of an electric generator set to move a few thousandths of a millimetre out of true. The vibrations increased significantly the rate of bearing wear and damaged the generator windings.

Taguchi's argument may follow the following lines in this case. The generator hall should be built properly. Yet, unexpected conditions make it possible for building foundations to move. Therefore, good design of the electrical equipment should recognise this and be robust, that is operate successfully in spite of some slight variations.

Through the work of Taguchi and others, Japanese engineers became familiar with the design of experiments to test the robustness of their products. Taguchi's own contribution focused on: making products robust compared with environmental conditions; making products insensitive to variations in their own components; and minimising variation in manufacture.[21] We shall look at each in turn.

Robustness under environmental variations

To design for robustness, engineers have to understand the environments under which products are to be used. In the case of mechanical equipment, for instance, users will understand something of a product's limitations and look for good service within these limits. At the same time, they want to cope beyond this and will often look for the extra reliability, or at least ease of repair. The Land Rover, for example, built its reputation on both counts. Taguchi's contribution to the study of robustness was to propose a formal method for its investigation. Box 17.2 gives an example set in the field of home economics.

BOX 17.2 **Robust muffins**

Let us say we are considering the launch of a new muffin mix. We can, in the laboratory, develop mixes and test them under ideal conditions. Yet, the success of such a product depends largely on its quality in use, that is whether it will produce good outcomes in domestic environments. In the home, for example, oven temperatures are unreliable and, as anyone who cooks will know, baking time is approximate.

It may be that the mix that gives the best muffin under experimental conditions is not the best for sale. Alterations in the formulation may result in a product that is slightly less good. Yet, the design may be more robust in that it produces an acceptable output over a wider range of baking temperatures and times.

A Taguchi experiment would then vary the design factors – the amounts of plain flour, baking powder, salt, egg and milk powders and sugar – and assess the sensitivity of the outcome to the environmental factors already mentioned. The difficulty is that it is possible to conduct an endless number of trials. Taguchi proposed a means of designing the experiment in terms of which variables to change and by how much. These are set out in special arrays intended to allow the trials to home in on good results quickly. The search is not for the best muffin mix but for one that gives good results across a wide range of conditions.

Exercise 17.4   Use boiling an egg to illustrate the concept of robustness.

Making products insensitive to variations in their own components

Since many products have many components, it is clear that the performance of the product will vary if the component performances vary. Given the inevitability of some component variation, engineers seek ways of minimising these effects on the assembly. To illustrate the point, let us look at the choice of length of a clock pendulum.

The relationship between the period T and the length l of a pendulum is non-linear as in Figure 17.11. When a clock manufacturer makes pendulums with small length variations, these will become variations in period. As Figure 17.11 shows, however, the period variations depend on the length of the pendulum and are smaller when the pendulum is longer.

The effect can be seen from the formula for period and its differential:

$$T = 2\pi\sqrt{\frac{l}{g}}; \frac{dT}{dl} = \frac{\pi}{\sqrt{l \times g}}$$

Therefore, if the length variation depends only on the cutting machine and not on the total length of the pendulum, the designer should make the pendulum as long as possible.

This simple example demonstration is invalid if the manufacturing variation increases with the pendulum length. The basic notion is important, however. We can design products, such as electronic circuits, whose performance is insensitive

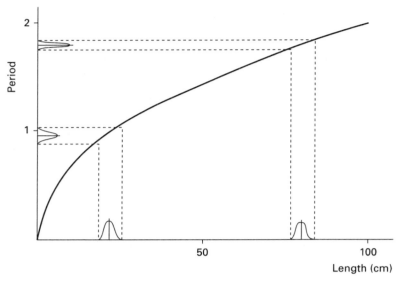

Figure 17.11 Pendulum errors

to their components. This is especially important when those components can be neither made nor adjusted precisely.

Minimising variations in manufacture

Variability is the enemy of mass production. Reducing it will reduce waste and scrap. As with the preceding examples, Taguchi argued that well-designed experiments would find ways of reducing variability caused by combinations of process factors. The approach can be illustrated by reference to a machine for filling detergent cartons (see Table 17.2).

It is commercially important for the weight of detergent entering each carton, and hence the fill rate, to be carefully controlled. Three factors affect the fill rate (kilograms per second) of the cartons: the chute diameter, the particle size of the detergent and the shape of the chute. Table 17.2 shows the experimental results

Table 17.2 Flow of detergent in experiment

Chute A		Particle size	
		Low	High
Diameter	Small	1.2 (0.011)	1.4 (0.031)
	Large	3.5 (0.008)	3.3 (0.045)

Chute B		Particle size	
		Low	High
Diameter	Small	1.0 (0.015)	1.3 (0.027)
	Large	2.8 (0.009)	3.2 (0.030)

using two values for particle size and chute diameter and with two chute shapes. The figures give average flow rates and standard deviations, both in kg/sec. It can be seen that only the chute diameter greatly affected average fill rate. The variation in the fill rate, however, was affected strongly by particle size, it being reduced if the particles were smaller.

If, then, the aim was to achieve a stated average fill rate with the smallest variation, this could be done by choosing small diameter particles and adjusting the chute diameter to hit the target rate.

17.3.5 Dominance

Related to the idea of robustness is dominance. Depending on which process is being considered, the production of quality frequently hinges on one specific element rather than others. Therefore, to attain optimal quality, that specific part of the process must be most closely controlled. Dominance, according to Juran, falls into four classes: set-up, machine, operator and component. We can compare them as in Table 17.3.

We can see from the fourth column of Table 17.3 that different methods of appraisal are to be applied under different assumptions about dominance. Clearly, if more than one factor arises, then more inspection is needed. This would be, however, a poor-quality process.

As the fourth column suggests, much inspection relies on some form of control chart. These use the basic ideas set out in Figure 17.5 but are more formal in

Table 17.3 Examples of dominance

Dominance	Explanation	Examples of processes	Control system required
Set-up	Setting up is the most important activity since the process is stable, equipment reliable and so on	Many operations in the machine or printing shop if equipment is in good condition; checkouts in supermarket	Inspect first piece to check setting; inspect last piece to confirm nothing went wrong
Machine	Tool wear, machines getting hotter, changes in environment or similar changes cause drift from target	Many processes require adjustment because of minor changes in conditions	Continuous control using charts to spot drift
Operator	Variations in operator skill and experience cause output differences	Judgement of bakers, painters and similar craft workers; cooks and waiters in restaurants	Comparative use of control charts; feedback control to evaluate operator performance
Component	Stable process has variations in material or component inputs that affect product quality	Many assembly plants; processes using natural products from grapes to grain	Inspection of incoming materials to accept or reject; measure key parameters

that chart boundaries and decision rules are worked out so that operators know what to look for in sample results. Their design depends on the application of statistical models to the field of quality. It is to this area that we now turn.

17.4 Statistical process control

We have looked at many examples of the application of statistical techniques, such as graphs and charts, experimental analysis and studies of variation. Going beyond these, there are two applications of great importance. These are statistical process control, SPC, whose objective is to eliminate variations in the process to achieve stability,[22] and acceptance sampling, which concentrates on screening out batches of items containing an unacceptable proportion of defects. Acceptance sampling is corrective control in that it covers items that have already been made and is concerned with picking out defects. SPC, if used at the very end of a process, will also have a corrective emphasis. Yet, if properly integrated at key stages of the production cycle, SPC can take on characteristics of concurrent and even feedforward control. Therefore, it is valuable in preventive control too.

17.4.1 Sampling

Before going on to examine the statistical techniques themselves, we need to consider the role of sampling. It is convenient but brings with it problems and risks. Why do organisations use it? The following reasons explain why samples are frequently taken instead of having full inspection:

- *Sampling is quicker.* A manufacturer may not need to know the exact value of a parameter, just whether it lies within the acceptable range. Sampling enables this to be done speedily and with enough accuracy to enable process adjustments to be made.

- *Sampling is cheaper.* Some tests are expensive in comparison with the value of the item being produced. Anyhow, the work done in inspecting a sample will be less than that required for all items. The manufacturer has to consider the cost advantage of sampling compared with the costs associated with making wrong decisions as a result.

    Customer satisfaction surveys are often based on samples for cost reasons and because continuous surveying of regular customers would eventually annoy them.

- *Some tests damage or destroy the product.* There are many good reasons for *destructive testing* of product samples, especially where the sample size can be small and the results valuable. Examples range from bolts to biscuits and fuses to flame-proof fabrics.

- *Sampling may be more accurate.* This curious notion can be explained by tests that show that inspection accuracy decreases as the number of tests made increases. The trade-off between well-conducted sample trials and 100% inspection done badly may favour the former on this ground alone.

■ *Sampling smoothes out random variations.* We need to be able to discriminate between random effects that arise in the process and events to which it is sensible to assign causes and, if necessary, make corrections. We do not want operators to adjust machines in response to every variation. (In fact, the central limit theorem tells us that, whatever the distribution of the parameters we are studying, the means of samples taken from it will be normally distributed. Therefore, since the normal distribution is well known, we can say much about risks and trends from sample data.)

The risk involved in sampling is that the wrong decision about the whole batch may results from the data about the sample. There are two types of error.

Type I errors

Type I errors are decisions that something is wrong when, in fact, the process is operating according to plan. The consequences of finding something wrong may be small, for example the rule may be to take further samples immediately. On the other hand, the rule could be to reinspect all products made since the previous inspection. In either case, extra costs are involved and these arise unnecessarily since there was nothing wrong in the first place.

How does a Type I error arise? In process control, the limits on the control chart are usually set more narrowly than the specification width. This is to ensure a safe, early warning of, say, process drift. Yet, it does mean that samples will come up which lie outside the control limit yet which still lie within specifications. The decision is to weigh the cost of a Type I error against the risk of its occurring.

Familiar Type I examples from life are: convictions of innocent defendants; unneeded tonsillectomies and dismantling your washing machine only to find nothing wrong.

Type II errors

The Type II error can be more serious than the Type I. It occurs when the process is not working as planned, yet the sampling procedure suggests that it is running satisfactorily. The consequences may be confined to the organisation, involving a great deal of rework at a later stage, or they may not be detected and result in problems in the market from complaints to legal action.

How does a Type II error arise? It may occur in what seems to be a highly reliable process where sampling frequency is low. Somehow, a fault arises and it does not show up in any of the samples. Alternatively, one fault is detected but is explained as a random event whereas it is actually a symptom of a process problem. Again, the costs of the errors must be balanced against the gain to be had from sampling.

Examples from life include: not convicting the guilty; failing to detect geological problems in a sample site survey; and a sample audit not picking up stock losses.

Table 17.4 summarises the issues. The sampling strategy should be chosen to match the hits in the 'right decision' cells.

Table 17.4 Errors of Types I and II

		Decision	
		Look for problem and take corrective action	Do nothing
Process condition	Process is satisfactory	Type I error	The right decision
	Process is faulty	The right decision	Type II error

17.4.2 Classes of control chart

Deming reported an example of an employee at the Nashua Corporation, a producer of carbon paper:

The carbon was sprayed onto the paper through an adjustable nozzle. The employee running the process would measure the amount on the paper and, in the light of whether there was too much or too little, would open or close the nozzle. Was there anything wrong with this? Even with a perfect process, random variations mean that half the product turns out below the mean and half above. And this is true whether or not the mean is fixed on the target value. Taking single sheets and adjusting the spray process in response to them meant that the operator was trying to adjust *randomness* out of the system. In fact it was found that this behaviour merely added variation.

It was better for the employee to collect and measure samples, take a mean value and, using a control chart, decide whether any adjustment was necessary.[23]

We can note the contrast of this response with one that Taguchi may have made. For him, the carbon variation would have been intolerable and the process should have been improved. Yet, we are focusing now on controlling a process whose random variations have been reduced as far as current knowledge permits. After all, while Taguchi methods place *reduction of variation* on the quality agenda, they do not claim to be able to eliminate it.

There are two classes of control chart – variable or attribute. The former records information about samples of specific measures, such as length, volume, diameter, temperature and pressure. Normally, plots are made of the sample average and its standard deviation or range. Sometimes, individual items are measured and plotted on an X-chart. Attribute charts do not deal in measurements but in the number of defects within the sample. All can be used in combination as they can support each other in diagnosing whether and why a process has a problem. They are summarised in Table 17.5.

17.4.3 Control charts for variables

To demonstrate how control charts for variables are set out, let us return to the example presented in Figure 17.4. Consider first the chart for $\bar{X}$. It requires a mean line, corresponding to the process target, and upper and lower control limits to warn when the process is straying too far from the mean. The mean line is decided by either:

Table 17.5 Common types of control chart

Type		Measure recorded	Explanation
Variable charts	$\bar{X}$	Averages of small samples of measurements	To pick out changes in process settings; very common
	R	Standard deviation (or range) of small samples of measurements	In combination with $\bar{X}$ to detect sudden changes in process variation
	X	Measurements of single items	Only one observation is practicable; more difficult to interpret than $\bar{X}$
Attribute charts	P	Proportion of defective items	Decisions are whether to accept or reject
	C	Number of defects	Samples are of same size; identifies different types of defect when decision is whether to accept or reject

- the standard specified at the design stage or
- a process capability study as in 16.5.3 or
- a study of at least 50 recent samples.

The choice is merely a starting point and such is the dynamic nature of control that the mean would be reviewed continually until the process was well settled.

The control limits are usually set at ±3 standard deviations (of sample means) from the mean line. Referring to Table 16.9, we can see that this corresponds to 99.7% of the normal distribution lying within the limits. Put another way, 0.3% of the sample means would fall outside the control limits due to random causes.

To establish the standard deviation of the process, two related approaches are possible:

- Take a series of, say 25, samples and measure their mean values. The number in each sample should equal the number intended in the future. Calculate the standard deviation directly. (The sample size should be consistent as the standard deviation of sample means depends on the chosen number, see the equation that follows.)

- Take a set of, say 100, individual measurements and calculate the standard deviation, σ. The standard deviation of the means of samples, sized n, is always smaller than this, the two being related by the equation:

$$\sigma_{\bar{X}} = \frac{\sigma}{\sqrt{n}}$$

A simpler approach replaces σ as a measure of dispersion with the *range* of the sample measurements, as in lower part of Figure 17.4. That is why this type is usually called an R chart. Using the range is easier to pick up when no calculator is available but the preferred method is the one shown here. Again, as with $\bar{X}$, data accumulate as the process is run and the boundaries can be checked in the light of recent information.

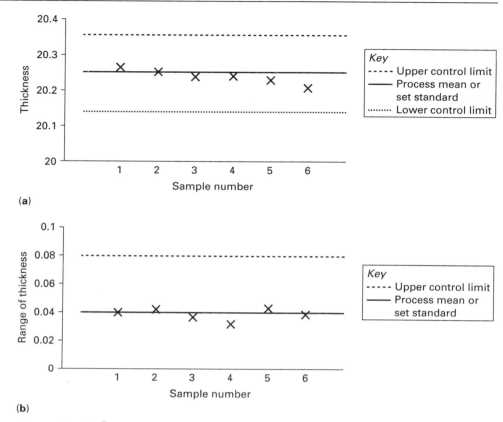

(a)

(b)

Figure 17.12 $\bar{X}$ and R control charts

Finally, the chart layouts should be checked against the product specifications. We are looking here at keeping processes under control by getting close to the target and staying there. The specification width should be much wider than the between-limits band we have established.

A completed chart is shown in Figure 17.12. The top half is the chart for sample means. Six samples have been plotted. We can see that, while the means lie well within the control limits, the process is drifting towards a lower dimension. This could be caused by machine or tool wear but other upstream factors may be relevant. The R chart suggests that the process is basically healthy. Investigation of the drift and adjustment are called for.

17.4.4 Control charts for attributes

The problem with attribute data is that values for means and standard deviations do not exist. The data often concern just two attributes, for example: does the light bulb work or not; did the bus run on time or not; is the loaf ready or not. Sometimes there may be more than two classes as in: is the steak rare, medium or well done; is the hat tight, the correct fit or loose; is the porridge too hot, too salty or just right. The data collected tell us how many elements of the sample fell into one or other category. This is usually summarised by the value p, which is the proportion of defective items in the sample. Hence, the P chart records the data and monitors the process to see if they are out of control.

As with control of variables, the P chart requires control limits. The target value can be set up initially and modified by experience. With a continuing process, it may be based on a long data run. The P chart assumes that the data for percentage defective follows a *binomial distribution* whose properties are used to set control limits.

For a mean value, $\bar{p}$, of the defect rate and a sample size of n, the standard deviation of the distribution of sample means is:

$$\sigma_{\bar{p}} = \sqrt{\frac{\bar{p}(1 - \bar{p})}{n}}$$

From this, the control limits of $\pm 3\sigma$ are set out in the usual way. It is usual to use sample sizes much larger than with charts. The idea is to ensure that samples contain on average at least one defective item. Full 100% inspection of batches is used where defect rates are very small.

The C chart is similar to the P chart except that it is usually used to count the number of defects per unit of product. We may be looking for more than one type of defect although the incidence of each is small. A good example concerns typing or data entry tasks. There are many possible errors, for example hitting the wrong key, transposition, spelling and so on. The work can be sampled to check error frequency per (say) 5,000 words or 5,000 data items entered. Under these conditions, the Poisson distribution makes a good approximation. Its standard deviation is given by $\sigma_c = \sqrt{c}$ and the 99.7% control limits will again be set at $\pm 3\sigma_c$.

17.4.5 Using control charts

Figure 17.5 illustrated some patterns of process data recorded on control charts. In a statistical process control system, managers must set up:

- means of monitoring
- means of recording the data so that they can be compared with standards – the control chart
- rules covering what action to take in the light of different emerging patterns.

These items correspond to the steps set out in the control model. The rules for action are worked out in the light of experience and analysis of costs of defects and their correction. For example, there may be one measurement outside the control limits, as in cases B or C of Figure 17.5. To adjust the process, or even stop it immediately, runs the risk of making a Type I error. The process may have been satisfactory and the sample mean may have that 1 in 333 that would have occurred by chance. By the same token, to do nothing risks a Type II error because the process really is defective. A sensible sampling policy under these circumstances is to immediately take another sample rather than wait until the next scheduled one is due.

Similar policies match out for other patterns. For instance, the variation may be increasing unexpectedly. This suggests failure of a machine component. If this can be spotted, then repair is required. However, the machine may appear to be working normally. Then the variation is acting as an early warning of possible trouble. In these circumstances, the intervals between sampling should be cut and a careful watch kept on the standard deviation.

17.4.6 Acceptance inspection

While its most common uses are at the two ends of the firm's production process, namely goods inward and outward, acceptance inspection prevents defective batches moving between any pair of stages. It involves taking random samples from batches to assess either attributes or variables. It assumes that there will be some level of errors, for 100% inspection is the only way of achieving none. The policy is to use the results of the sample to judge the condition of the whole batch and therefore whether to accept it, defects and all. If the decision is to reject, the batch can be returned or every item can be inspected at the supplier's expense.

We should stress that acceptance sampling will not make up for poor process control. In modern supply chains, acceptance sampling is replaced by validation of suppliers' quality procedures. ISO 9000 is important here. Acceptance sampling takes time and reduces the benefits of JIT supply systems.

The process reconciles the different interests of the supplier and receiver. They agree a sampling plan designed to judge quality fairly and avoid expensive mistakes. The *producer's risk* is having a good batch rejected. The *consumer's risk* is accepting a defective batch. The parties agree a *sampling plan* that identifies how samples are to be taken, their size and the decisions that follow the inspection. Each sampling plan has an *operating characteristic*. The OC is a curve showing, for a stated sample size and sample defect rate, the probability of accepting a batch compared with the real number of defective items in the batch.[24] The curve shown in Figure 17.13 is set up to satisfy the conditions agreed between producer and customer:

- *Acceptable quality level* = 2%. The AQL is the desired quality level for the whole batch. The sampling plan must be devised so that, if the batch reaches this level, it stands a very high chance of being accepted.

- *Producer's risk* = 5%. The producer's risk is a Type I error. It is the chance of a good batch being rejected under the plan. This will be caused by a sample, taken from a good batch, 'unluckily' containing more than the target number of defects.

- *Rejectable quality level* = 7%. The RQL, also called the lot tolerance percentage defective, LTPD, is the quality level for the whole batch that would stand little chance of being passed by the sampling procedure. In other words, batches worse than this must be highly likely to be recognised and rejected.

- *Consumer's risk* = 20%. The consumer's risk is a Type II error. It is the chance of a bad batch being accepted under the sampling plan.

Using both an AQL and RQL is a means of achieving low values for both producer's and consumer's risks. If just a *single sampling plan* were used, the AQL and RQL would be equal and the consumer's risk would be too high. Using the RQL set at a percentage higher than the AQL allows for three zones under the curve and the possibility of *double* or *multiple sampling plans*. With this approach, any

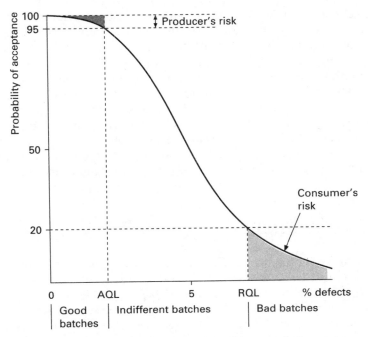

Figure 17.13 Example of operating characteristic curve

sample scoring fewer defects than AQL means its batch is accepted. Any worse than the RQL has the batch immediately rejected. For values between the two, further samples are taken and acceptance or rejection depends on the outcomes.

Sampling policy

What happens if either party finds that its risk is too high? The simplest solution is to increase the sample size. This reduces the risk of both parties, but also increases the cost.

To resolve the question of whether to sample, the firm should examine the cost savings resulting from sampling and compare these with the extra costs associated with the risks that they take. Essentially, 100% inspection is merited if:

- inspection costs are low
- costs associated with a defect are high
- the percentage defect rate is high.

This question broadens into one of whether to inspect at all. No inspection is a good policy where:

- inspection costs are high
- costs associated with a defect are low
- the percentage defect rate is known to be low.

Acceptance sampling, therefore, is somewhat of an intermediate policy to be carried out in circumstances where there is some concern about inspection costs, defect costs and the defect rate. A decision about whether to set up a procedure will depend on a study of all of these costs. There is, of course, the special case where testing is destructive and so sampling will always be used.

In many cases, acceptance inspection should be seen as a last resort, in the sense that it covers deficiencies in other aspects of the quality assurance process. It is also inefficient if both producer and customer feel bound to carry out the procedure. As a first step to building confidence between partners in a supply chain, the customer could agree to accept the results of the supplier's outward inspection. Moving on from there, the supplier's own quality systems should be improved to ensure that faulty items never reach the despatch stage. This argument takes us back to the ideas of total quality management.

17.5 Service quality

Shering Weighing, in the closing case of Chapter 16, is among the many manufacturing firms recognising that product quality is not enough. With the 'pure service' businesses, they share the problem of understanding customers' satisfaction. As we noted at the start of this chapter, customer expectations are dynamic, rising ever higher in response to improvements by companies or their rivals.

17.5.1 The SERVQUAL model

Parasuraman, Zeithaml and Berry[25] proposed measuring the gap between what customers expected and their perceptions of the service experience. The size of this gap would indicate areas for improvement. They developed the SERVQUAL questionnaire containing 22 pairs of questions derived from a larger survey. They are grouped in to five categories, called the dimensions of service quality, as follows:

- *reliability*: dependable and accurate performance as promised
- *responsiveness*: responding promptly to customers' needs
- *assurance*: competence and courtesy of staff, coupled with their ability to show trust
- *empathy*: caring attention to each individual
- *tangibles*: appearance of facilities, equipment, personnel; environmental factors such as noise and temperature.

Table 17.6 illustrates the questionnaire layout with two questions on tangible dimensions of a library service.[26] Taking each in turn, the scores on the Likert scales are subtracted to yield the satisfaction measure.

To allow for the varying importance of the dimensions in different settings, the questionnaire often asks subjects to weight the categories by sharing 100 points across them. The results of the weighted survey are then assembled in a report such as Table 17.7. We can see that, although the respondents reported the greatest gap in empathy, they found that dimension less important than assurance. The weighted score ranked the latter more highly.

Table 17.6 Part of SERVQUAL questionnaire applied to a library

When it comes to:	My expectation of the library service is Low————High	My perception of the library service is Low————High
1 Having physical facilities that are visually appealing	1 2 3 4 5 6 7	1 2 3 4 5 6 7
2 Having staff who give users individual attention	1 2 3 4 5 6 7	1 2 3 4 5 6 7

Table 17.7 SERVQUAL scores with weighting

	SERVQUAL score (P – E)	Weights %	Weighted SERVQUAL	Rank
Tangibles	−0.37	18.7	−0.31	5
Reliability	−0.41	23.8	−0.44	4
Responsiveness	−0.48	23.3	−0.51	3
Assurance	−0.67	19.8	−0.60	1
Empathy	−0.82	14.5	−0.54	2
Overall	−0.53	100	−0.48	

Criticism of SERVQUAL has been based on the importance of expectations and questions on the general application of the five-factor structure. In detail, interpreting the meaning of the (P – E) gap is difficult. In the wider, marketing context, others comment that the service dimension is only one element of the marketing mix. Notwithstanding these reactions, service organisations in many fields have taken up the model. For instance, the Accounts Commission for Scotland recommends it for the assessment of local government services.[27]

✔ Quick check-up

Can you:

- Define:
  - benchmarking
  - QFD
  - SPC
  - QLF
  - robust quality.
- Sketch:
  - Ishikawa diagram
  - Pareto chart
  - control chart.
- Outline how to build a House of Quality.
- Explain *dominance*.
- Identify Type I and Type II errors.
- Name five types of control chart.

- State the purpose of acceptance inspection.
- Summarise the SERVQUAL model.

? Questions

Chapter review

17.1 When would you use sampling in inspection?

17.2 Discuss Taguchi's argument that being inside the specification width is not good enough.

17.3 Explain how the practices of benchmarking and quality circles might be linked to improve quality.

17.4 Compare the advantages and disadvantages of using applying the SERVQUAL model in surveying customers' responses to a service.

Application

17.5 Managers at a chocolate biscuit plant are concerned over the prospect of contaminated flour being used in product despatched to customers. Use a fishbone diagram to set out possible causes.

17.6 Give details of how developers of a vacuum cleaner may use QFD to better satisfy customers' expectations (see Box 2.1).

Investigation

17.7 Investigate a product study such as one published in *What Camera?* or *Which?* To what extent is the idea of robust quality included in the evaluations? Can you suggest any improvements in how they are conducted?

CLOSING CASE

Madras cheque clearing system[28]

In the Madras area, there are about 800 branches of some 50 banks. Cheque clearing is the responsibility of the National Clearing Cell, a division of the Reserve Bank. Since 1987 the process has been automated around a high-speed reader-sorter system (HSRSS) for cheque data capture, linked to a mainframe computer. Cheques paid in at one bank and drawn on another are processed by the NCC. The system sorts the cheques by bank and branch code and prints reports, including the balances for each bank.

The HSRSS reads data from the magnetic ink character recognition band along the bottom of each cheque. As with UK cheques (which use optically read characters) basic data are pre-printed. This covers serial number, account number, branch code and so on. The payment is encoded after the customer has presented the cheque. Those that have incorrect codes, or are of poor quality, are rejected by the HSRSS and are sorted and have their data entered by hand. Two batches of cheques are returned to each branch. Those accepted by the machine are fully grouped while the other has to be separated by the branch. Therefore, a faulty cheque is sorted twice.

The efficiency of the system depends on the HSRSS acceptance rate. Following complaints from banks about the amount of labour-intensive work they were expected to do, it was found that the cheque reject rate was about 10%. The manual work was leading to high error rates in data processing, which in turn created reconciliation problems among the banks. The shift to computer processing had not resulted in the promised benefits.

In defence, the NCC manager pointed to the peculiarities of cheques presented in Madras and the high proportion that originated elsewhere in India.

After about a year of debate, steps were taken to improve NCC's internal processing. The tuning of the HSRSS equipment was adjusted and the whole operating area was cleaned to remove all traces of dust. This reduced the rejects by 1%. At the same time, NCC sent new instructions to the banks to improve the data encoding but this had little effect.

The next step was for NCC to inspect all incoming cheques and attempt to repair the bad ones. While this succeeded in cutting another 2% from the reject rate, it was only achieved at high labour expense. The intervention was abandoned.

Finally, the NCC decided to investigate the encoding procedures at the branches. Training of staff was carried out by five NCC staff across a sample of 50 offices. For two months little happened, but, as more branches were trained, the reject rate fell to 4.5%. The training programme was extended, new operators had to be taught and all branches had to designate one person with the responsibility of ensuring that only quality cheques were sent to NCC. People from the branches visited the HSRSS operation to learn of the impact of proper encoding on the whole operation. These steps led to great improvements but rejects refused to come down to the international norm of 3%.

Further studies analysed the errors in more detail. The banks were answerable for only one of the five fields encoded on each cheque. The others were the responsibility of the printers. At a meeting at NCC, these were asked to submit 100 cheques for proofing before producing an order. Print runs could run into millions. The NCC, in its turn, promised to return the test batch, with a report, in half an hour. Some printers agreed while others did not. Later, it was found that those who had cooperated produced rejects at fewer than 1%. Soon, the others fell into line and the overall reject rate fell to 2%.

The NCC manager then set about standardising the new procedures. It was found that the standards could be met by different personnel, rotated around jobs, thus proving that they were 'people proof'. A regular series of meetings with the banks was started. It shared feedback on operations and discussed suggestions for further improvement.

The project covered the work of thousands of employees. It had the backing of senior management. What had begun as a response to problems of poor service led to a transformation in the competence levels and empowerment of employees. There was a significant reduction in costs, although that was not the intention. The labour devoted to sorting was cut substantially, most cheques were sorted automatically and reconciliation errors fell to negligible levels.

▶

Questions

1 Use an Ishikawa diagram to express the causal links in NCC's service quality problem.

2 If you were investigating the causes of failure of the system, what sorts of data would you collect and how would you present them?

3 What would the relevance of a benchmarking study have been in this case?

4 For the more efficient operations after the change, explain how statistical techniques can be used to maintain control. How and where would you collect data and how would you use them?

Notes and references

1. Brown-Humes, C. and Harney, A. (2001) 'Sony's handset gremlins spell trouble for Ericsson alliance: A string of recalls has hit the Japanese giant's reputation and shares', *The Financial Times*, 11 July; Harnischfeger, A. and Reinking, G. (2001) 'Mercedes warranty costs hit $1.5 billion', *The Financial Times: Companies and Markets*, 8 May, p.1; Jones, A. (2001) 'Mars forced to destroy 3m Twix bars', *The Financial Times*, 24 April.
2. Feigenbaum, A.V. (2001) 'A challenge creeps up: It is not enough merely to maintain quality and safety control when customers' expectations are constantly changing', *The Financial Times*, 11 January.
3. A private communication.
4. Editorial (1996) 'Big Mac and little ministers', *Daily Mail*, 25 March; Oram, P. (1996) 'Consumers put the bite on burgers', *The Financial Times*, 26 March.
5. Feigenbaum, A.V. (1983) *Total Quality Control*, 3rd edition, New York: McGraw-Hill.
6. Elmuti, D., Kathawala, Y. and Lloyd, S. (1997) 'The benchmarking process: Assessing its value and limitations', *Industrial Management*, 39(4), July–August, pp.12–19; Holloway, J., Hinton, C.M., Francis, G. and Mayle, D. (1999) *Identifying Best Practice in Benchmarking*, London: CIMA.
7. Longbottom, D. (2000) 'Benchmarking in the UK: An empirical study of practitioners and academics', *Benchmarking: An International Journal*, 7(2), pp.98–117.
8. Bhutta, K.S. and Huq, F. (1999) 'Benchmarking – best practices: An integrated approach', *Benchmarking: An International Journal*, 6(3), pp.254–68.
9. Hinton, M., Francis, G. and Holloway, J. (2000) 'Best practice benchmarking in the UK', *Benchmarking: An International Journal*, 7(1), pp.52–61.
10. Cook, S. (1996) *Practical Benchmarking: A manager's guide to creating a competitive advantage*, London: Chapman & Hall.
11. Main, J. (1992) 'How to steal the best ideas around', *Fortune*, 126(8), 19 October, p.104.
12. Trapp, R. (1994) 'Benchmarking moves on to bench-testing', *The Independent on Sunday Business News*, 9 January, p.13.
13. Hauser, J.R. and Clausing, D. (1988) 'The house of quality', *Harvard Business Review*, 66(3), May–June, pp.63–73; *see also* Whitney, D.T. (1988) 'Manufacturing by design', *Harvard Business Review*, 66(4), July–August, pp.89–91.
14. ibid., p.71.
15. Ansari, A. and Modaress, B. (1994) 'Quality function deployment: The role of suppliers', *International Journal of Purchasing and Materials Management*, 30(4), pp.28–35.
16. Lofthouse, T. (1999) 'The Taguchi loss function', *Work Study*, 48(6), pp.218–22.
17. Taguchi, G. and Clausing, D. (1990) 'Robust quality', *Harvard Business Review*, 68(1), January–February, pp.65–75.

18. ibid., p.68.
19. Quigley, C. and McNamara, C. (1992) 'Evaluating product quality: An application of the Taguchi quality loss concept', *International Journal of Purchasing and Materials Management*, 28(3), pp.19–25.
20. op.cit., p.66.
21. The following examples are based on: Box, G., Bisgaard, S. and Fung, C. (1988) 'An explanation and critique of Taguchi's contributions to quality engineering', *Quality and Reliability Engineering Journal*, 4(2), pp.123–31.
22. Antony, J., Balbontin, A. and Taner, T. (2000) 'Key ingredients in the effective application of statistical process control', *Work Study*, 49(6), pp.242–7.
23. Quoted by Schmenner, R.W. (1993) *Production/Operations Management*, 5th edition, New York: Macmillan, pp.122–3.
24. British Standards Institute BS 6001 (1972, 1984, 1986) and BS 6002 (1979).
25. Parasuraman, A., Zeithaml, V.A. and Berry, L.L. (1985) 'A conceptual model of service quality and its implications for future research', *Journal of Marketing*, 49, pp.41–50; Parasuraman, A., Zeithaml, V.A. and Berry, L.L. (1988) 'SERVQUAL: A multiple item scale for measuring customer perceptions of service quality', *Journal of Retailing*, 64(1), pp.12–36.
26. Tan, P.L. and Foo, S. (1999) 'Service quality assessment: A case study of a Singapore statutory board library', *Singapore Journal of Library and Information Management*, 28, pp.1–23.
27. Accounts Commission for Scotland (2000) *Can't get no satisfaction? – Using a gap approach to measure service quality*, Edinburgh, May; available at wwww.audit-scotland.gov.uk accessed 8 July 2001.
28. Based on Sudhakar, K. (1994) 'Reject rate reduction at the Reserve Bank of India' in Dean, J.W. and Evans, J.R. *Total Quality: Management, organisation and strategy*, St. Paul: West Publishing Co., pp.167–8.

Index

Notes: Main entries are in **bold** type. The list uses abbreviated organisation names and does not include authors whose names appear only in the endnotes.